UNDERSTANDING

HUMAN

HISTORY

Other books by Michael H. Hart

The 100: A Ranking of the Most Influential Persons in History

A View from the Year 3000

UNDERSTANDING HUMAN HISTORY

An analysis including the effects of geography and differential evolution

by

MICHAEL H. HART

Washington Summit Publishers
Augusta, GA

A National Policy Institute Book
2007

© 2007 Michael H. Hart

All rights reserved. No part of this publication may be reproduced, distributed, or transmitted in any form or by any means, including photocopying, recording, or other electronic or mechanical methods, or by any information storage and retrieval system, without prior written permission from the publisher, except for brief quotations embedded in critical reviews and certain other noncommercial uses permitted by copyright law. For permission requests, write to the publisher at the address below.

Washington Summit Publishers
P.O. Box 3514
Augusta, GA 30914

Manufactured in the United States of America

Library of Congress Cataloging-in-Publication Data

Hart, Michael H.
  Understanding Human History : an analysis including the effects of geography and differential evolution / by Michael H. Hart.
      p. cm.
  Includes bibliographical references and an index.
  ISBN-13: 978-1-59368-027-5 (hardcover)
  ISBN-10: 1-59368-027-9 (hardcover)
  ISBN-13: 978-1-59368-026-8 (pbk.)
  ISBN-10: 1-59368-026-0 (pbk.)
1. Civilization--History.   2. Historical geography.   3. Evolution.
4. Social evolution.   5. Genetic algorithms.   I. Title
  CB69.H39 2007
  909--dc22

2006102193

This book was typeset using QuarkXpress 6.5. The body of the book is in 11-point Times New Roman, set 11-13, with six extra points between paragraphs. The index and footnotes are set 10/12. Chapter heads are in 18-point Arial Bold.

*To the memory of my father, Harold H. Hart,
in appreciation of the example he set of
intelligence, energy, and a passionate love of truth*

ACKNOWLEDGEMENTS

Like every serious scholar, I am deeply indebted to others whose ideas I have adopted and whose painstaking research I have made use of. Several of the central ideas presented in this book have already been presented by Richard Lynn, and his books and articles have been invaluable to me. I would also like to take this opportunity to express my gratitude to Dr. J. Philippe Rushton, partly because his own research has helped me so much in this project, and partly because of the encouragement he has given me. Most of all, I would like to thank Professor Arthur Jensen, in part for his extensive research concerning human intelligence, and even more because his example of careful scholarship and personal courage has been an inspiration to me.

I would be remiss, though, if I failed to acknowledge my debt to several scholars who have reached conclusions very different than my own. In particular, this book would scarcely have been possible had not Luigi Luca Cavalli-Sforza and his associates collected extensive information concerning DNA from all over the world. I am likewise indebted to Jared Diamond for information concerning the rise and spread of agriculture, as well as information concerning the origin and effects of epidemic diseases.

I am very grateful to Sally Barba for her careful drawing of the maps in this book, and for her careful typesetting. I am also grateful to Donald Archer, Tony Gahan, and the late Glayde Whitney for their useful suggestions concerning the text.

Most of all, I am indebted to my wife Merna for editing the book, for her help in clarifying my own thoughts on difficult topics, and for her endless patience and encouragement during the years I have spent in writing this book.

TABLE OF CONTENTS

List of maps and diagrams ... ix
List of abbreviations and symbols ... x

Introduction ... 1

PART 1 – Background material
1) The theory of evolution ... 4
2) Human races ... 10
3) Intelligence ... 17
4) The origin of *Homo sapiens* ... 28
5) Altruism ... 35
6) Bands, and the dual code of morality ... 40
7) Human sexual behavior and attitudes ... 43
8) The ice ages ... 46
9) Languages ... 51

PART 2 – Outline of major migrations during the Paleolithic
10) The expansion out of sub-Saharan Africa ... 60
11) Migrations and divisions of the σ-group ... 68
12) Migrations and divisions of the μ-group ... 72
13) Location of human groups 13,000 years ago ... 76

PART 3 – Racial differences
14) Physical differences between the races ... 79
15) Racial differences in intelligence ... 91
16) Nature or nurture? ... 103
17) How did racial differences in intelligence arise? ... 121
18) Behavioral differences between the races ... 126

PART 4 – The Neolithic Era
19) Advances in the Upper Paleolithic ... 133
20) The Neolithic Revolution: Description ... 139
21) Technological advances in the Neolithic ... 146
22) Some migrations driven by agriculture ... 149
23) The Neolithic Revolution: Explanations ... 160
24) An alternative explanation ... 173

PART 5 - Pre-modern history

- 25) The introduction of writing — 178
- 26) The Indo-Europeans — 183
- 27) The Ancient Middle East — 197
- 28) Ancient Egypt — 206
- 29) Ancient Greece — 213
- 30) The rise of ancient Rome — 221
- 31) The rise of Christianity — 228
- 32) The decline and fall of the Roman Empire — 230
- 33) The early Middle Ages in Europe — 237
- 34) The Islamic world — 246
- 35) China — 257
- 36) India — 268
- 37) Southeast Asia — 276
- 38) Australia, New Guinea, and the Pacific Islands — 281
- 39) Northern Asia — 289
- 40) The Western Hemisphere — 300
- 41) Sub-Saharan Africa — 310
- 42) The Late Middle Ages in Europe — 316

PART 6 – Modern history

- 43) The transition to modern times — 325
- 44) European exploration and colonization, 1500-1700 — 334
- 45) The rise of science — 346
- 46) Constitutional democracy — 358
- 47) The Industrial Revolution — 364
- 48) The Enlightenment and the French Revolution — 367
- 49) The nineteenth century — 374
- 50) The Jews — 389
- 51) The twentieth century — 398
- 52) Some broad trends in history — 412
- 53) Some final comments and predictions — 416

Appendices

- 1) Chronology — 418
- 2) Determining ancient dates — 430
- 3) Description of computer simulation — 435
- 4) Calculations concerning the Neolithic transition — 440

Bibliography — 443

Index — 457

LIST OF MAPS AND DIAGRAMS

Map	Title	Page
8-1	The Ice-Age World, 18,000 Years Ago	48
10-1	The Spread of HSS, from 60 kya to 13 kya	64
13-1	Location of Human Groups, 13,000 Years Ago	77
20-1	The Fertile Crescent and Nearby Regions	140
22-1	The Spread of Afro-Asiatic Languages	152
22-2	The Austronesian Expansion	154
24-1	Tilted Axes and E-W Expanses	175
26-1	Indo-Europeans, 4000-3000 BC	190
26-2	Indo-Europeans, about 2000 BC	191
26-3	Indo-Europeans, about 1400 BC	192
26-4	Indo-Europeans, about 600 BC	193
34-1	The Arab Conquests	248
37-1	Migrations into Southeast Asia	378
39-1	The Northern Mongolids	291
39-2	The Mongol Conquests	294
39-3	Altaic-Ruled Territories, 1700 AD	298

Diagram	Title	Page
10-1	Some human groups, 130-15 kya	66
14-1	Effect of off-center thrusts	85
26-1	Main branches of the Indo-European language family	188

LIST OF ABBREVIATIONS AND SYMBOLS

Abbreviation or symbol	Meaning	Chapter it first appears in
AHS	archaic *Homo sapiens*	4
^{14}C	isotope 14 of carbon (i.e., carbon-14)	Appendix 2
CRT	choice reaction time	3
EA	Eskimo-Aleut	39
f	The fraction of the gene pool of a population that comes from recent invaders or migrants, rather than from the people inhabiting the region prior to the recent invasion or migration.	Appendix 3
FDS	forward digit span	3
g factor	general intelligence	3
G	The fraction of δ_{1917} that was due to genetic differences between American blacks and whites	16
GDP	gross domestic product	51
HF	harshness factor	17
HGHG	*History and Geography of Human Genes*	10
HSS	*Homo sapiens sapiens*	4
IR	Industrial Revolution	47
kya	kiloyears ago (= thousands of years ago)	4
K	parameter affecting rate at which higher IQs evolve	Appendix 3
M-1, M-2	subgroups of the Mongoloids	12
ME	Middle East	147

N_0 group	The group of humans (living about 60,000 years ago in Africa) from whom the modern Negroids derive	10
NM	Northern Mongolids	39
PIE	Proto-Indo-European	9
r	correlation coefficient	3
r-K classification system	A method of describing species (or subspecies) based on comparisons of the extent to which they use their resources to produce large numbers of offspring (the r-strategy), or instead use their resources to produce hardy, well-adapted offspring (the K-strategy)	18
R	The "remnant factor," defined as the fraction that remains of the overall environmental disadvantage faced by American blacks in 1917 (relative to whites)	16
R_0 group	The "rest-of-the-world" group	10
SEA	Southeast Asia	37
SSA	sub-Saharan Africa	24
δ	The difference (in any given year) between the mean IQ scores of American whites and blacks	15
δ_{1917}	The value of δ in 1917	16
μ-group	The descendants of those members (the "main group") of the R_0 group who, some 60,000 years ago, migrated northward and gave rise to the Caucasoid and Mongoloid races	10
μ-1, μ-2, μ-3	subgroups of the μ-group	12
σ-group	The descendants of those members (the "southern group") of the R_0 group who, some 60,000 years ago, migrated eastward towards India	10
σ-1, σ-2, σ-3, σ-4	subgroups of the σ-group	11

There is no method of reasoning more common, and yet none more blameable, than in philosophical disputes to endeavor the refutation of any hypothesis by a pretense of its dangerous consequences to religion and morality. When any opinion leads to absurdities it is certainly false; but it is not certain that an opinion is false [merely] *because it is of dangerous consequence.*

      David Hume, 1748
      An Enquiry Concerning Human Understanding

Scholars of a future age,
    Reading this indignant page,
Know that in a former time,
    Truth, sweet truth, was thought a crime!

      (Inspired by a verse by William Blake, 1757-1827)

But unfortunately, however much we may deplore something, it does not stop it being true.

      Richard Dawkins, 1989
      The Selfish Gene

INTRODUCTION

Since there are already many books on world history, the reader may wonder why I have chosen to write another one. The answer is that most such books are unsatisfactory because they omit a crucial factor in human history.

At one time, most history books gave a great deal of space to kings, wars, and battles, and to the generals who won or lost them. Later on, many historians shifted their focus to economic and social developments. More recently, historians have come to appreciate the critical role that scientific and technological advances have on human affairs. However, although it is now common for world histories to mention such advances, they usually do not delve very deeply into their causes.

There are reasons why each particular technological or scientific development occurred when and where it did. However, it would be a mistake to consider only the special circumstances and not look for a common factor underlying those advances. In general, all such advances arise from human intelligence, and in particular from the application of the superior intelligence of one or more unusually talented individuals. This is obviously true for such inventions as television, computers, or holography; however, it is also true for earlier inventions such as the needle or the bow and arrow.

This, however, begs a further question: How did that high human intelligence arise? The answer comes from Darwin's theory of evolution. At some point in the distant past, the average intelligence of our ancestors was much lower than the average intelligence of humans living today. It is through the process of Darwinian evolution — and that alone — that the high intelligence needed to produce technological advances has arisen.

In general, Darwinian evolution results in a species (or some subgroup of it) gradually becoming better adapted to its environment. But throughout prehistory, and through much of historical times, human groups have been widely separated from each other geographically, with relatively little interbreeding between them. Hence, each group tended to adapt to its *own* environment, and in the course of time various differences arose between those separate human groups.

Some of the resulting group differences (such as the relatively dark skin of most Negroes, and the relatively light skin of most European whites) are easily visible; others are not visible to the eye, but are nonetheless of great importance. In particular, groups that resided for many millennia in regions with cold winters gradually — through the process of natural selection — evolved higher average intelligence than the groups living in milder climates.

As a result, the peoples living in Northern Asia and Europe now have mean IQs of about 100, while the peoples living in sub-Saharan Africa have average IQs of around 70, and those living in a broad intermediate zone (stretching from North Africa across southern Asia and into Indonesia) have average IQs in the 80-90 range. At least four different types of evidence confirm these differences in intelligence:

1) The results of numerous IQ tests taken over a period of more than 80 years, not just in the United States but in many other countries.

2) Measurements of the average brain size of the members of various racial groups.

3) The poor performance (on average) of blacks in Europe and America in economic matters, contributions to mathematics and science, and in games of intellectual skill, such as tournament chess and duplicate bridge.

4) The extreme backwardness of the countries in the secluded zone of sub-Saharan Africa before they had contact with either Islamic or European civilization.

The differences in average intelligence that evolved between the human races have been a major factor in the course of human history and prehistory. Any theory that ignores those differences, or denies their existence, will therefore be unable to explain various major aspects of history. Among the questions not adequately answered — indeed, often not even posed — by conventional history books are:

a) Although *Homo sapiens* went hundreds of thousands of years without developing agriculture, within a few thousand years of the appearance of agriculture in the ancient Middle East it appears to have been developed independently in at least two other distant regions (China and Mesoamerica). What is the explanation for this? (See chapter 23.)

b) In the second millennium BC, Indo-European tribes invaded India from the northwest and eventually conquered virtually all of northern India. How were they able to do this, despite being enormously outnumbered by the earlier inhabitants? (See chapter 26.)

c) The Western Hemisphere was not settled until long after sub-Saharan Africa, and prior to 1492 it had no contact with the civilizations of Eurasia. Why is it that, in pre-modern times, more advanced civilizations developed in Mesoamerica than in sub-Saharan Africa? (See chapter 41.)

d) The remarkable intellectual and cultural attainments of the ancient Greeks have long been noted. Why is it that the Greeks achieved so much more than the ancient Egyptians or Babylonians, or the Celtic and Germanic tribes? (See section 29-6 [i.e., section 6 of chapter 29].)

e) The Berber tribes that inhabited northwest Africa at the dawn of history — prior to the entrance of the Romans, Greeks, or Phoenicians — spoke a set of related languages. Why is it that those Berber languages are all related to ancient Arabic and ancient Hebrew, even though the ancient Arabs and Hebrews lived thousands of miles away from northwest Africa, and none had ever settled there? (See section 22-3.)

f) Why is it that China has usually been so much more politically unified and ethnically homogeneous than Europe? (See section 35-2.)

g) Why is it that in almost every European country today the dominant language is descended from a now-extinct language (Proto-Indo-European) that was spoken six thousand years ago by a relatively small number of people inhabiting a region much smaller than Europe? And why — even before the European expansion and conquests of modern times — were Indo-European speakers so widely distributed, and so much more numerous than the speakers of any other language group? (See chapter 26.)

h) Why is it that China has been repeatedly attacked (and on two occasions completely conquered) from the sparsely populated regions to its north, but has never been seriously attacked by the peoples living to its south? (See section 39-10.)

The realization that group differences in average intelligence have often affected human developments enables us to better understand each of those historical questions, and many others as well.

This book does not contain any suggestions as to what policies should be adopted — with the sole exception that we should attempt to ascertain the facts before deciding on questions of policy.

Obviously, this book is not "politically correct." I hope that the reader will nevertheless be open-minded enough to consider the evidence that it presents in favor of its thesis. If the quantity of data presented at times seems overwhelming, it is only because I fear that a lesser amount might not convince those who are skeptical of the thesis. It is my hope that those readers who do approach this book with an open mind will gain valuable insights into human history and the factors that have affected it.

CHAPTER 1

THE THEORY OF EVOLUTION

Section 1 – Natural selection

The theory of evolution is the central, unifying principle of modern biology. Although entire books have been devoted to explaining the theory in detail, its fundamental ideas can be summarized briefly.

1) The individual members of any given species vary considerably from each other, and some of that variation is due to genetic factors. Furthermore, new heritable traits are constantly arising because of random mutations.

2) Since, in each species, there are more offspring than the environment can support, many individuals die without reproducing.

3) Those members of the species who have inherited traits that make them less likely to survive will, on average, have fewer offspring. Hence, in the next generation, there will be fewer individuals with those traits.

4) The result is the selective elimination of less useful traits and, in comparison, the *natural selection* of more useful traits.

5) This leads to a series of small changes within a species; and the gradual accumulation of many such small changes eventually results in the formation of a new species, related to the original one.[1]

Note that two separate processes are involved: (a) random mutations (which occur entirely by chance); and (b) selection of the more useful traits (a process that is far from random). The notion that evolution is governed entirely by chance is therefore false.

At no stage in either process have the resulting organisms been deliberately designed. However, since natural selection results in organisms that are very well adapted to their environments, they usually give the *appearance* of having been designed.

Most frequently, selection is for traits that make it more likely that the individual organism will survive (such as greater size, speed, strength, intelligence, or resistance to disease). This might be called "survival selection." However, in sexually reproducing species, an individual cannot pass on its genes unless it mates with a member of the opposite sex. Consequently, traits that make an individual a more attractive mate will also be selected for, whether or not they aid in survival. This is called "sexual selection," and is an important evolutionary mechanism.[2]

Section 2 – Genes

Heritable traits are transmitted from parent to child by microscopically small particles called genes. All cells contain genes, but it is only the genes contained in the sperm and egg cells that are responsible for heredity. Normally, an individual receives two copies of each gene, one from each parent. However, he will pass only one copy of each gene on to his offspring.[3]

It is common for there to be two or more slightly different forms of a given gene. These variants are called *alleles*. If, for some gene, an individual receives identical alleles from his two parents he is said to be *homozygous* at that gene site. If instead he receives different alleles from his two parents at that gene site he is *heterozygous* for that gene. In the latter case, the individual often exhibits the trait corresponding to just one of those alleles (the "dominant" one), and the other allele (the "recessive" one) will have no effect. However, the recessive allele is not destroyed, and is just as likely as the dominant one to be passed on to the person's offspring.

A gene is a fragment of a large molecule called DNA. However, for most purposes, one can consider an individual gene to be an independent molecule, a molecule which consists of a long string of simpler units called *nucleotides*. There are four types of nucleotide; and the various genes (and alleles of the same gene) can differ from each other by containing either:

1) Different numbers of nucleotides; or

2) The same total number of nucleotides, but not the same number of each type; or

3) The same number of each type of nucleotide, but arranged in a different order.

Mutations occur when a gene in a sperm or egg cell is altered, most commonly by some random natural occurrence such as:

- cosmic rays
- gamma rays emitted from radioactive materials in the Earth's crust
- solar radiation (particularly ultraviolet radiation)
- certain chemicals ("mutagenic" chemicals)
- ordinary thermal agitation.

(Human activities can also produce gamma rays, ultraviolet rays, X-rays, and mutagenic chemicals; but so far these have had almost no impact on our gene pool.)

Initially, genes were thought of as simply the physical particles responsible for our inherited characteristics. Today, we know that the genes do far more than code for our original structure. A complete set of our genes is present in every one of our cells, and throughout our lives they direct the operation of those cells.

The genes in a person's body cells were produced by copying the genes present in the fertilized egg from which that individual started. Since an adult human being contains about a quadrillion (a thousand trillion, or 10^{15}) cells, each of the genes present in that egg must have been copied about a quadrillion times. To appreciate the magnitude of the task involved, we should take into account that the human genome — i.e., the complete set of genes present in a *single* cell — consists of tens of thousands of genes, totaling about one hundred million nucleotides!

The biological process by which genes are copied (or "replicated") is usually very accurate. However, it is not absolutely perfect, and many of our cells contain one or more incorrect nucleotides. Usually, the presence of a few incorrect nucleotides does not greatly affect the functioning of the cell, but sometimes it does. Indeed, there are instances in which a single incorrect nucleotide will cause a cell to malfunction and die. It is only because the copying process for genes is normally so marvelously precise that we are able to survive.

Section 3 – Genetic drift

Suppose that two alleles of a given gene are equally advantageous. Call the two alleles P and Q. One might think that the law of averages ensures that the percentage of the population holding allele P will not vary from generation to generation. However, chance variations from the law of averages occur quite frequently, and as a result the percentage of the population with allele P will vary. Indeed, such chance variations can even result in the complete elimination of an allele from the gene pool.

Changes in gene frequencies (strictly speaking, allele frequencies[4]) that result purely from chance are called "genetic drift," and are an additional cause of evolution.[5] If a species has a very large population, then genetic drift is usually a slow and relatively unimportant process. However, if the population size is small then genetic drift can be a significant factor. There are occasions when the population of a species is drastically reduced by a plague, famine, or other catastrophe, and genetic drift can be of great importance when such a "population bottleneck" occurs.

If different alleles of the same gene are not equally advantageous to an organism, the effects of natural selection will normally swamp the effects of genetic drift. Drift is therefore most likely to occur in those sections of the DNA that have no known genetic effect. (Such sections — which are surprisingly common — are often referred to as "junk DNA.")

Section 4 – Chickens and eggs

A wit once said, "A chicken is just an egg's way of making another egg." For a long time, that was considered to be just a clever quip; but we now realize that the alternative way it suggests of viewing reproduction provides valuable insights.

At first glance, these two statements appear to correspond perfectly:
- a) A person (or animal, or plant) uses genes to create another person (or animal, or plant).
- b) Genes use a person (or animal, or plant) to create more genes.

But although the statements are similar in form, there is an important substantive difference between them. When genes replicate, their "children" are identical to the original genes. But although human beings *reproduce*, they never *replicate*: human children are *not* copies of their parents. Genes make copies of themselves; human beings do not, nor do members of any other sexually reproducing species.

The biologist Richard Dawkins wrote a celebrated book, *The Selfish Gene*, in which he emphasized the "gene's-eye view" of reproduction. Of course, a gene is just a molecule, with no consciousness or purpose at all, selfish or otherwise. However, the result of natural selection is much the same as if the genes actually were selfish, and you will rarely reach a wrong conclusion by viewing them as such. (Of course, a conclusion reached in this fashion should be checked against the true test: differential replication rates.)

It is interesting to consider what the function of a human being is from the standpoint of his genes. Genes are just molecules, and they can easily be destroyed by heat, by radiation, or by dangerous chemicals in the outside world. To protect themselves, the genes construct a container around themselves to keep out harmful chemicals and radiation, a "house" with a thermostat that keeps the temperature nearly constant. If the "house" (i.e., the human being or animal produced by the genes) is well designed, then the genes can survive and replicate; if the house has serious defects, the genes inside it will die.[6] (Note the contrast: for a human being, the genes inside its sperm or egg cells are merely a means of reproduction; they do nothing to help the individual survive.)

Section 5 – Present status of the theory of evolution

The theory of evolution was introduced by Charles Darwin in 1859 in his great work, *The Origin of Species*. In the century and a half since then, there have been several important modifications of his original theory. For example, Darwin did not discuss genetic drift, rarely mentioned mutations, and knew nothing about genes. Furthermore, it seems likely that there will be additional refinements to Darwin's theory in the future. Still, virtually all modern scientists agree that Darwin's central insight — evolution by means of natural selection — was correct.

Nevertheless, lots of people have never really accepted the theory of evolution. The most obvious of these are religious fundamentalists, many of whom openly dispute the theory. A more important group, however, consists of the numerous persons who say (and think) that they accept the theory of evolution, but who in fact shrink from accepting the implications of that theory. Among those unwelcome implications are:

1) Human beings are animals: very unusual animals, to be sure, but nevertheless animals. In origin, we are not fallen angels, but apes arisen.

2) Evolution is a completely amoral process.

3) A person's physical capabilities and limitations are strongly influenced by his genes.

4) A person's mental attributes (i.e., his individual abilities and proclivities) are also influenced by his genes — not rigidly determined, but strongly influenced. The notion that we are entirely products of our environments is therefore false.[7]

5) The observed behavioral differences between the sexes are strongly influenced by our genes — again, not rigidly determined, but strongly influenced.

Even less welcome, perhaps, are these other implications of the theory:

6) Whenever two populations within a species are reproductively isolated, they will diverge from each other genetically. If they are in different environments, this will occur by natural selection; but it will occur by genetic drift even if the environments are the same.

7) The process of evolution did not stop with the emergence of *Homo sapiens*, nor with the emergence of *Homo sapiens sapiens* (the branch of that species to which all living humans belong). Rather, evolution has continued and has produced visible differences between human groups whose ancestors evolved in different regions.

8) There is no reason to suppose that the visible differences we see between the regional variations of human beings are the only differences that exist between them. On the contrary, it would be very surprising if that were the case.

These conclusions may be unpalatable, but they are amply confirmed by our knowledge of biology. Of course, the *extent* of the differences can only be determined by observation and experiment.

FOOTNOTES – CHAPTER 1

1) These ideas were first presented by Charles Darwin in *The Origin of Species by Means of Natural Selection, or the Preservation of Favoured Races in the Struggle for Life* (1859). Other restatements of his ideas can be found in most modern college textbooks on biology, for example: Wallace, R.A. (1992), chapters 1 and 10.

2) Sexual selection was discussed at length by Darwin in his second major book, *The Descent of Man, and Selection in Relation to Sex* (1871).

3) Most of the material in this section can be found in many introductory college textbooks, for example: Wallace, R.A. (1992), chapter 7.

4) Except in very technical writing, it is common to refer to alleles as "genes" when no confusion will result, and I shall often do so in this book.

5) Genetic drift is mentioned in standard college texts such as Wallace, R.A. (1992), chapter 10. More detailed discussions can be found in many places, including:

   (a) Kimura, M. (1983);
   (b) Cavalli-Sforza, et al. (1994), especially section 1.4, pp. 13-15; and
   (c) Wilson, Edward O. (2000), pp. 64-66.

6) Dawkins, Richard (1989), especially chapters 2 and 3.

7) See Pinker, Steven (2002), *The Blank Slate*, pp. 45-50 and 373-377.

CHAPTER 2

HUMAN RACES

Section 1 – Introduction

The entire topic of human races is a contentious issue, beset by ideological passions. Indeed, so intense are these passions that some people speak as if race is nothing but skin color, others assert that the notion of race is just a "social construct," and others claim that there is no such thing as race or races.[1]

Such a claim is ridiculous. Even a child can detect the obvious physical differences between members of different races. If the proverbial "man from Mars" were to visit Earth he would readily see that human beings come in different varieties. If he went to northern China, he would notice that most of the people living there have a yellowish tinge to their skins, straight black hair, very little body hair, and a configuration of their eyelids that give them a slightly "slant-eyed" appearance.

If he visited central or southern Africa, he would see that the great majority of the persons living there have very broad, flat noses (relative to Europeans and Chinese), with the nostrils flaring out. He would also see that most of them have brown skins, very curly hair, very little body hair, and thick, everted lips.

Finally, if he were to visit northwest Europe, he would notice that most people there have pale, "pinkish" skins, much more body hair than Chinese or black Africans, and relatively protruding noses. He would also notice that the number of people with blond or red hair is much greater than in China or Africa, as is the number with blue or green eyes.

In other words, he would readily detect the existence of the three large races (often called the Mongoloid, Negro, and Caucasoid races). Nor would he have any trouble in discovering that the above traits are inherited. Whenever two typical-looking north Chinese mate and produce a child, the child shares the attributes mentioned above, and the same is true for Europeans and Africans. Of course, he would also notice that there are many human beings who do not readily fit into any of the three categories just described.

The existence of races is not unique to the human species. Many animal species consist of more than one type, although in the case of animals these are usually called *subspecies* or *varieties* or *breeds*.[2]

A race (or subspecies, or variety, or breed) might be defined as a large group of individuals — all of them members of the same species — who have formed a partially or completely isolated breeding population for a significant period of time, and who consequently differ statistically from the rest of the species in various heritable traits by which they can be recognized.[3]

It is possible for one subspecies to be included in another, larger subspecies. (In other words, every member of the smaller group is also a member of the larger group.) In such cases, we call the smaller group a *sub-subspecies* (or *sub-variety*, or *sub-race*, or *sub-breed*). When this occurs, however, the differences between sub-subspecies may be quite small, so disputes as to classification often arise.

In most cases, it is geographic separation that has caused the group to be an isolated breeding population; however, there can be other causes. For example, social taboos against marrying someone of a different religion, social class, or ethnic group can be the cause; and the mating choices of domesticated animals are often restricted by their human owners, sometimes for the explicit purpose of creating a new breed.

If two breeding populations are separated from each other for a long time, the result will be an accumulation of genetic differences between them, either by natural selection or by genetic drift. If the separation continues long enough, they can diverge into separate species. However, as long as the two groups will usually mate (if given the opportunity) and produce fertile offspring, they are generally considered to be varieties of the same species.

Perhaps the best known example of a species that includes various breeds or subspecies is the domestic dog, *Canis familiaris*. If a zoologist who had never seen a dog before was shown a group of Irish setters, he would readily notice the large number of similar traits that they share. He would also observe that they freely mated with each other, and that their offspring shared the obvious physical traits of the prior generation. (In other words, they "breed true.") He would therefore classify them as a species, and — noticing their resemblance to wolves (*Canis lupus*) — might call them *Canis irishsetter*.

In like fashion, if the same zoologist was then shown a group of dachshunds, he would notice their resemblance to each other, and that they bred true, and he would probably decide that dachshunds constitute another species, which he might call *Canis dachshund*.

However, if he then permitted the Irish setters and the dachshunds to intermingle, he would soon find that they mated with each other freely and produced fertile offspring. He would conclude that rather than being two distinct species, Irish setters and dachshunds were merely different varieties or breeds of a single species. Despite their rather different appearance, he would realize that the two breeds must share many genes, including the ones responsible for mating and reproduction. He would reach the same conclusion, of course, for the dozens of other breeds of dogs.

The offspring of a dachshund and an Irish setter — or of any two dogs belonging to different breeds — is not a member of either breed. We call such dogs *mongrels*. (The term used for most other species is *hybrids*.) A mongrel, of course, is just as much a member of the species *Canis familiaris* as any purebred dog, and he possesses all the traits that are common to that species; he is just not a member of any of the special breeds.

The reader might ask whether we should consider mongrels to constitute a separate breed of dog. There are two reasons why we do not. In the first place, mongrels (unlike Irish setters) share no set of physical traits, except those common to all dogs. In the second place, mongrels (unlike Irish setters) do not "breed true."

Are mongrels better or worse than purebred dogs? That is a subjective question, since it depends upon what traits you value in dogs. If you value *speed*, for example, then greyhounds are better than mongrels. If you value the Irish setter's lovely reddish-brown coat, you are not likely to find a mongrel (or any other dog) that is quite that beautiful. But by most criteria, mongrels are neither better nor worse than purebred dogs.

However, in one important aspect, mongels tend to be slightly superior to purebred dogs. Like hybrids of most species, they often have fewer genetic defects than purebreds, and therefore (if equally well cared for) will on average be healthier. This effect — called *hybrid vigor* — is the exact complement of the tendency for offspring of incestuous matings to have a higher than average number of genetic defects, and it has the same cause.[4] The majority of deleterious alleles are recessive, so the more closely related two individuals are, the more likely it is that their offspring will be harmed by inheriting the same recessive allele from both of them.

Some people have objected to the entire concept of human races. One common objection is: "There are all degrees of gradations between the so-called 'races' of mankind, and many individuals do not fit into any single racial group. The concept of 'race' is therefore meaningless, or at least pointless."

Although that argument is often presented, it is fallacious, as can be seen by considering a few counterexamples: (a) It is useful and meaningful to employ the terms *blue* and *green* even though there are an infinite number of gradations between the two colors; (b) Similarly, although there are all gradations between rich and poor, it is nevertheless plain that John D. Rockefeller was rich, while at the same time large numbers of peasants in China and India were poor; (c) Likewise, the terms fat and skinny are widely used, as are the terms hard and soft. In all these examples, the extreme cases are obvious; and even though many intermediate cases are hard to classify, the terms are meaningful and widely used.[5]

Another common objection is that the word "race" is difficult to define, and dictionaries give varying definitions of it (most of which contain some ambiguities). That argument is also fallacious. Virtually all common terms are hard to define (except in mathematics and, to a lesser extent, in the hard sciences). Insistence on precise definitions for every term used would render *all* serious discussion (except in mathematics) virtually impossible.

The two objections just mentioned are typical forms of sophistry. People who make objections of this sort are ignoring the fact that similar objections would apply to their own reasoning on most other topics.

Despite the attempts of some writers to pretend that the word "race" is meaningless, I suspect that most readers of this book do not doubt that it refers to something real. (He may find it hard to give a precise definition of the word, but when he hears or reads it he know what is being talked about.[6]) As a well-known biologist put it, "It requires an almost superhuman feat of political zeal to overlook the conspicuous differences between our own local populations or races."[7]

Section 2 – The Australoids

Australian aborigines resemble Negroes in having brown skins and broad noses, but in many other respects they differ greatly from Negroes. For example:

- Their lips, although thick, are not everted.
- A significant number of them have blond hair.
- Their hair is typically wavy, unlike the very curly hair of Negroes.
- They have a substantial amount of body hair.
- Compared to most humans, they are prognathous (i.e., their jaws protrude forward).
- They have prominent brow ridges above their eyes (somewhat like the now-extinct Neanderthals), which are very rare among Negroes.[8]

It is therefore generally agreed that they should not be classified as Negroes, and DNA tests (see chapter 10) confirm that the two groups are not closely related.[9] Since they are so different from the three groups described at the beginning of this chapter, they are usually considered to belong to a fourth race, the *Australoids*.

Section 3 – Some sub-races

Although various other racial groups have been identified, most of them appear to be subgroups of the races already described. For example, because of their small stature, the Pygmies living in central Africa (the *Congoid Pygmies*) can easily be distinguished from the nearby Negro tribes. However, their resemblance to the Negroes — who constitute most of the population of sub-Saharan Africa — is obvious, so I think it reasonable to classify both groups as branches (or sub-races) of a larger racial group, which I shall call Negrids.

In southern Africa, there are two small groups — commonly called the Bushmen and the Hottentots[10] — which together comprise another distinctive racial group. Scientists call this group the Sanids, or Khoisan. Since the Sanids resemble the Negrids in many ways, it seems best to classify both of them as sub-races of a still larger group, the Negroids.[11] (See Table 2-1.)

TABLE 2-1

PRINCIPAL HUMAN RACES, AND SOME SUB-RACES

Races	Sub-races

Negroids	A) Negrids
	   1) Negroes
	   2) Congoid Pygmies
	B) Sanids (= Khoisan)

Caucasoids	
Mongoloids	A) Amerids (=American Indians) B) Mongolids (=Asian Mongoloids)
Australoids	

Similarly, since the American Indians have so many traits in common with the Mongoloids living in East Asia, I think it best to consider the two groups as comprising subgroups of a larger race. I shall call the Asian branch of this race the *Mongolids*, the American branch the *Amerids,* and the combined group the *Mongoloid* race.

(Note: A wide variety of nomenclatures have been used by various scholars when discussing human racial groups; the one used in Table 2-1 may be easier to use than most.)

Not all human beings are members of discrete racial groups. Many of us are of mixed parentage; such persons may be referred to as "hybrids." There are regions where hybrids are particularly common, and other regions (for example, the North China Plain) where they are comparatively rare. In some countries, there are important groups that contain a high percentage of hybrids. For example, most "blacks" living in the United States today are hybrids.[12] (The infamous *one drop rule* — "If you're one percent black, you're all black" — is a *social* rule that has no basis in biology.)

Among the important questions concerning human races which will be discussed in later chapters are:

1) Where and when were the various races formed?

2) Do the races differ in other ways, besides the physical traits mentioned?

3) Have the differences between the races had any significant historical consequences?

FOOTNOTES – CHAPTER 2

1) For example:
   (a) A statement drafted by several well-known scholars and issued by UNESCO in 1950 said: "For all practical social purposes 'race' is not so much a biological phenomenon as a social myth." See Montagu, Ashley (1972), p. 10.
   (b) According to James Schreeve, "Surveys of physical anthropologists have found that almost half no longer believe that biological races exist." (See the November, 1994 issue of *Discover*, p. 60.)
   (c) In the same issue of *Discover*, on p. 83, the well-known scholar Jared Diamond said, "The reality of human races is another commonsense 'truth' destined to follow the flat Earth into oblivion."
   (d) In Cavalli-Sforza, et al. (1994), the heading of section 1.6 (on p. 19) is "Scientific Failure of the Concept of Human Races."

2) (a) As a famous geneticist put it: "… members of the same species who inhabit different parts of the world are often visibly and genetically different. This, in the simplest terms possible, is what race is as a biological phenomenon." (Dobzhansky, T. [1970], p. 269.)
   (b) See also Whitney, Glayde (1999), and Wilson, Edward O. (2000), pp. 9-10.

3) (a) "A breed of dog is a construct zoologically and genetically equivalent to a race of man." (Freedman, Daniel G. [1979], p. 144.)
   (b) See also chapter 7 of *The Descent of Man* (1871), where Darwin discusses at length the question of whether the various races should be considered different species. He concludes that, although the human races are not separate species, "… it seems that the term 'sub-species' might here be used with propriety. But from long habit the term 'race' will perhaps always be employed."

4) (a) *Encyclopaedia Britannica*, 15th edition (1986). See article on "Heterosis" on p. 903 of volume 5.
   (b) Villee, Claude A. (1972), pp. 658-659.
   (c) Cavalli-Sforza, L.L. (2000), p. 47.

5) Here are two other counterexamples:
   (a) As there are at least 3 billion human beings with heights between 4'6" and 6'6", if one lined up everyone alive today in size place, the typical person would differ in height from the one adjacent to him by less than a hundred-millionth of an inch. Nevertheless, we have no trouble saying that those persons with heights greater than six feet are *tall* and that those with heights of less than five feet are *short*.
   (b) If you held hands with your mother, and she with her mother, and so on until the chain included 250,000 generations, those at the modern end of the chain would be obviously and indisputably human, while those at the early end of the chain (about five million years ago) would look like and be categorized as apes. Yet each individual on the chain would appear to be of the same species as her neighbor.

6) As Andrew Hacker put it: "In the United States, what people mean by 'race' is usually straightforward and clear, given the principal division into black and white." (Hacker, 1992, p. 5.) Indeed, the entire set of regulations involving racial preferences and/or "affirmative action" would be impossible to apply if the word "race" was meaningless.

7) Dawkins, Richard (2004), p. 399.

8) Descriptions of the physical appearance of Australian aborigines can be found in:
   (a) *Colliers Encyclopedia* (1963 edition). See article on "Australia, Primitive Tribes of" on page 275 of volume 3.

(b) *Encyclopaedia Brittanica* (15th edition, 1986). See article on "Human Evolution" (especially p. 975) in volume 18. Also see photograph on p. 971.
(c) Baker, John R. (1974), chapter 16, especially pp. 278-291. Also see photos on p. 274.

9) See Cavalli-Sforza, et al. (1994), Tables 2.3.1A and 2.3.1B on pp. 75-76.

10) The Bushmen and Hottentots refer to themselves as *San* and *Khoikhoi*, respectively.

11) See Cavalli-Sforza, et al. (1994), especially:
(a) Figure 2.3.2.B, on p. 78.
(b) Table 3.7.1, on p. 175, where he also says, "The San differ from other sub-Saharan Africans ... more than any other sub-Saharan group differs from any other."

12) For estimates of the average amount of Caucasoid parentage in the gene pool of American blacks see Reed, T. (1969); or Levin, M. (1997), p. 20.

CHAPTER 3
INTELLIGENCE

Section 1 – What is intelligence?

We all recognize that some persons are "smarter" than others. They reason more quickly and accurately (particularly about abstract questions), and usually learn more readily and retain information longer than other persons do. We say that such persons possess the attribute of "intelligence." Unfortunately, like many commonly used words, the word *intelligence* is hard to define precisely. In this book, I shall use as a working definition of intelligence: "general reasoning ability, and in particular the ability to carry out and understand abstract reasoning."

Not everyone, however, uses the word in that fashion. Howard Gardner, for example, in his theory of multiple intelligences, lists at least seven different types of intelligence,[1] including *musical intelligence* (as exemplified by the composer Igor Stravinsky) and *bodily-kinesthetic intelligence* (as exemplified by the dancer Martha Graham). While it is clear that Stravinsky and Graham possessed exceptional talents, referring to those talents as "intelligences" merely serves to obfuscate discussions of *intellectual* ability.[2]

The reader, of course, is free to use whatever terminology he or she prefers. In this book, however, the term "intelligence" will be used only in the sense of the word stated in the first paragraph. The advantages of this definition are:

- It accords fairly well with common usage.
- It is very close to such common dictionary definitions as "the ability to acquire and retain knowledge" and "use of the faculty of reason in solving problems." (It also resembles the dictionary definition of intellect as "the ability to think abstractly or profoundly.")
- It seems to describe the faculty that is actually measured in standard intelligence tests.

In any event, intelligence is not the same thing as *knowledge*. Memorizing a page from a telephone book increases your store of knowledge, but it does not make you any smarter. (Since a more intelligent person has a greater ability to acquire and retain knowledge, he will probably have accumulated a greater store of knowledge than a less intelligent person of the same age; the two concepts, however, are quite distinct.)

Section 2 – Correlations and the "*g* factor"

We all know individuals who have high verbal skills but who seem to have trouble with mathematics. Conversely, there are persons who are good at math, but whose verbal skills are weak. Nevertheless, if a large number of people are each given two tests, one measuring their verbal skills and the other measuring their mathematical abilities, we find that *on average* those persons who do well on one test also do well on the other one, and those who do poorly on one test also do poorly on the other. We can summarize this by saying that verbal abilities and mathematical abilities are *positively correlated* with each other.

The degree to which high values of one quantity are, on average, associated with high values of another quantity can be expressed precisely by a number that statisticians call the *correlation coefficient*. That coefficient, which is often designated by the letter r, is defined in such a way that it cannot be greater than 1.0 nor less than –1.0. A correlation of 1.0 would indicate that the connection between the two quantities is not merely statistical but is exact and invariable. A value of $r = 0.95$ would indicate that the two quantities are very closely correlated, whereas $r = 0.05$ would indicate only a very small statistical relation between the two quantities. A value of $r = 0$ would indicate that there is no statistical correlation between the two quantities. If, on average, those persons who did well on the math test did *poorly* on the verbal test (and vice versa) we would then say that mathematical and verbal abilities were *negatively correlated*, and such a result would be described by a value of r that was less than zero. (Although such a result is possible in theory, test results show that in fact mathematical and verbal abilities are positively correlated.)

Indeed, if we give a large group of people *any* two standard intelligence tests — even if the two tests seem to measure quite different aspects of intelligence — we almost always find a positive correlation between the results of the two tests,[3] and usually a rather high correlation. The simplest explanation of those results is that an individual's score on any well-designed intelligence test is strongly influenced by some underlying factor which we call his *general intelligence*, but is also affected (although to a lesser degree) by various special talents. The underlying factor is usually referred to as the "*g* factor."

The first person to define the *g* factor precisely was the British psychologist Charles Spearman,[4] although the general notion had been expressed many times before. Spearman also invented a mathematical technique ("factor analysis") by means of which an individual's *g* factor can be calculated from his scores on an assortment of standardized intelligence tests.

Some people have objected to the whole notion of the *g* factor, on the grounds that it is "just a mathematical construct." That objection, however, is without merit. After all, physicists seeking to give a precise meaning to the word *temperature* define it as "mean kinetic energy per molecule" — or sometimes, even more abstractly, as "the partial derivative of internal energy with respect to entropy." Should we dismiss the concept of temperature as "just a mathematical construct?" In some sense, it is; nevertheless, if you touch a hot stove, you will burn your finger!

The point is that although, in order to render the notion precise, we have defined temperature in abstract mathematical terminology, the term describes a phenomenon that exists in the real world. In like fashion, the "g factor" describes a phenomenon — an individual's general intelligence — that we had already noticed, and which has real, observable consequences.

We might still ask, of course, whether the g factor is a unitary talent or is instead a composite of several more basic abilities. At present, we are not sure; however, since the answer would not affect any of the other conclusions in this book, I will not dwell on that question.

One more point of terminology: Some intelligence tests correlate more strongly with an individual's g factor than others do. We say that such tests are "strongly g-loaded."

Section 3 – Variation of intelligence with age

A newborn child has very little reasoning ability, and his intelligence is therefore very low. However, a child's reasoning ability gradually increases as he matures. A rough approximation is that intelligence increases linearly with age, typically reaching a maximum at about age fourteen or fifteen. (Of course, at that age a person has much less knowledge and experience than he will have when he is older.)

The intelligence of an adult typically remains nearly constant for many years, and then gradually diminishes with age. None of us is as smart at age seventy as we were at twenty; however, in the absence of serious disease or injury, we are a lot smarter than we were at age seven.

Section 4 – IQ

As the average person's intelligence varies so little between ages twenty and fifty-five, we can almost regard his adult intelligence as a constant. However, we cannot do this for children, since a child's intelligence increases markedly as he matures. The notion of IQ — an abbreviation for "intelligence quotient" — was designed to estimate the (nearly constant) intelligence that a child is likely to have when he becomes an adult.

This is done by first determining a child's "mental age" (defined as the age of typical children who do as well as he does on a standard intelligence test) and then comparing it with his chronological age. His IQ is then defined as: IQ = (mental age/chronological age) × 100. A child of average intelligence for his age will therefore have an IQ of 100.

Empirically, we find that a child's IQ (as defined above) varies far less with age than do his raw scores on intelligence tests. IQ tests given after a child reaches the age of seven usually provide fairly good estimates of his adult intelligence.

The above definition of IQ applies only to children. It is usual to measure an adult's intelligence simply by his score on a normalized standard IQ test. ("Normalized" means that each person's raw score on the test is modified in a standard fashion so that the average score of the entire population is 100.)

Section 5 – Intelligence tests, and possible bias in testing

Throughout most of history, estimates of the intelligence of an individual were entirely subjective. The first attempts to construct objective tests of intelligence were made by Francis Galton in the last half of the 19th century. Although the tests he constructed did not turn out to be accurate measures of intelligence, Galton's writings stimulated work in the field. By 1905, Alfred Binet had developed a test that, although crude by modern standards, still did a fairly good job of measuring a person's intelligence.

Since Binets's day, intelligence tests have been steadily improved. Modern tests are statistically good predictors of both academic success and adult income. They correlate highly with each other, and with subjective assessments of an individual's intelligence. They also correlate with various physical attributes, such as brain size, and with the results of reaction time experiments (described in the next section).

It has often been asserted that intelligence tests are so culturally biased as to be worthless, or at least unreliable. As an example of such bias, proponents of this view often point to an analogy question that once appeared in an SAT (a test widely used in the United States for college admissions), to which the correct answer was:

RUNNER : MARATHON *as* OARSMAN : REGATTA.

Obviously this was a very poor question, heavily biased against persons whose upbringing and circumstances had not brought them into any contact with boating or regattas. However, it was only one question in an examination that consisted of more than one hundred, and therefore — while it may have detracted slightly from the accuracy of that test — it could not have drastically affected anyone's score.

Although this example is still widely quoted, it is taken from an examination given several decades ago, and such tests have been greatly improved in the intervening time. Test writers have become very sensitive to the question of test bias and now take great care to minimize it. Questions like the "regatta" item are unlikely to appear on an SAT test today.

It might seem that the extent of bias in an intelligence test is completely subjective. Actually, there are several established techniques for measuring it. For example, *internal* tests of bias begin by ranking the test's questions in order of difficulty (as measured by what fraction of all test takers answer them correctly), and then check whether the rank order of the questions varies greatly between different groups of test takers. If so, it implies that some questions are highly biased against a group. There are also *external* tests of test bias. Intelligence tests are often used for predictive purposes: for example, to predict the academic success of college students. If a particular test is biased against a group of persons, then their scores on that test will underestimate how well those persons do in college.

A large amount of data has been accumulated on such matters, and the subject of bias in intelligence tests has been analyzed in great detail, using both the internal and external evidence. These analyses show that the amount of bias in most modern intelligence tests is very small.[5]

Section 6 – Reaction time experiments

Two types of tests that almost everyone agrees are free of serious cultural bias are *reaction time tests* and *digit span tests*.

There are several types of reaction time experiments.[6] In the "choice reaction time" (CRT) experiment, the person being tested sits in front of a console on which there are eight translucent push buttons arranged in a semicircle, plus one more button — the "home button" — at the center. The subject starts with his finger holding down the home button. He is told that in a few seconds one of the translucent buttons will light up, and that he should then push that button down, as quickly as he can, using the finger that he had on the home button. Instruction is given in the subject's native language, and the task is so simple that everyone (with the exception of severely retarded or brain damaged persons) can do it with 100% accuracy. In fact, the task can be performed by chimpanzees, and they do about as well as normal eight-year-old children.[7]

The time it takes to push the button down after it lights up can be divided into two parts, which can be timed separately and automatically:

   a) The reaction time is defined as the interval between the instant the light goes on and the time the subject's finger leaves the home button.

   b) The movement time is defined as the time it then takes for the subject's finger to depress the target button.

Movement times are typically about a quarter of a second, and are not significantly correlated with intelligence. Reaction times *are* usually a bit longer and are significantly correlated with IQ.[8] The correlation is negative, which means that persons with higher IQs tend to have *shorter* reaction times.[9]

The "odd-man-out" experiments are quite similar to CRTs, except that:

   a) Three buttons light up instead of one, with two of the buttons being closer to each other than either is to the third button.

   b) The subject is instructed not to push either of the buttons that are close to each other, but to push only the lit button that is furthest from the other two.

These instructions, too, can be carried out accurately by virtually everyone. Movement times are typically about the same as in the CRT experiments; but reaction times are a good deal longer. The correlation between IQ and reaction times is much greater in the odd-man-out experiments than in the CRT experiments — about twice as large, in fact.[10] This is such a high correlation that the odd-man-out reaction time test can be thought of as almost an IQ test in itself. It is, of course, cruder and less comprehensive that ordinary IQ tests; but it has the advantage of being completely independent of any prior knowledge, and therefore free from any cultural bias.

In a digit span test, the subject is read a set of digits (at a standard rate of one per second) and asked to repeat them in the order given. The longest set of digits he can repeat without error is his *forward digit span* (FDS). In a variant of this test, the subject must repeat the digits, but in the reverse order. The longest set of digits he can repeat backwards is his *backward digit span* (BDS). Like reaction times, digit spans are independent of prior knowledge and free of cultural bias.

We might expect that an individual's FDS is greater than his BDS, and experimentally this is almost always the case. Both forward digit span and backward digit span increase during childhood. For adults of normal intelligence, FDS averages about seven while BDS averages about five. Both are correlated with general intelligence, but the correlation is about twice as high for BDS as it is for FDS.[11] Because of these correlations, digit span tests are often used as a component of more comprehensive intelligence tests.

Section 7 – How important is intelligence?
It is clear that high intelligence does not, by itself, ensure an individual's success. Indeed, persons of obviously high intelligence who have nevertheless failed to accomplish anything significant are so common that we have a special word for them: underachievers. Even a very smart person is unlikely to accomplish much if he lacks sufficient energy, dedication, and determination; and he might also be held back by a lack of social skills, or by poor health, or by lack of opportunity.

Nor is high intelligence — or even average intelligence — necessary for an individual to function capably in everyday life. Many people have the notion that a person with an IQ of 70 is an incompetent who needs to be institutionalized; but that notion is incorrect. Such persons can not only wash, dress, and feed themselves, but can also make and retain friends, marry, rear children, and support themselves economically. They can learn a wide range of skills by direct, hands-on instruction, or by simply watching more experienced persons. As long as their job or occupation does not require a high degree of abstract reasoning, such persons are able to perform their duties in an adequate manner.

Not only is this true today, but it was even more true in past ages, including the Paleolithic Era, during which most human evolution occurred. It did not require high intelligence for a parent to demonstrate to his child how to make a hand ax by chipping a piece of stone, or to show him which plants were edible and which should be avoided. The same is true for the typical skills needed by subsistence farmers.

However, although high intelligence is neither necessary for functioning in ordinary circumstances, nor sufficient by itself for marked success, it is not unimportant. In the first place, there are certain tasks for which high intelligence is an absolute requisite. For example, one can hardly imagine a person of average intelligence teaching a course in quantum mechanics.

In the second place, high intelligence enhances most other abilities. Even when a job or task can be performed adequately by someone of average intelligence, it can usually be performed better by a person of higher intelligence.[12] This holds for such varied tasks as planting crops, composing music, or waiting on tables. It is even true for many menial tasks.

Finally, high intelligence plays a crucial role in inventions. Every aspect of our modern world and its technology had to be invented, and virtually none of those innovations were obvious. It seems highly probable that throughout history (and prehistory) all the important inventions and innovations were made by persons who were far above average intelligence.

Section 8 – What causes differences in intelligence?

Since individuals differ greatly in intelligence, we may ask:

1) What are the direct biological factors responsible for those differences?

2) What are the underlying factors? In particular, are individual differences in intelligence caused primarily by genetic factors or by differences in upbringing and environment? (In technical language, what is the heritability[13] of intelligence?)

As for question (1), at least three biological factors affect the intelligence of a human being:

- The size of his brain.
- The microstructure of his brain. (For example, the surfaces of the cerebral cortex are extremely convoluted, and the extent of those convolutions — which is much greater in human beings than in any other animal — may be connected with intelligence.)
- The details of his brain chemistry, such as the abundance of various neurotransmitters.

It is plain that brain size is not the only factor. There are many persons whose high intelligence is undisputed but who have smaller than average brains, and vice versa. However, on average, persons with larger brains are more intelligent.

This is what we would intuitively expect. After all, larger hearts can pump more blood, and larger muscles can lift greater weights. We would therefore expect that larger brains can, on average, process more information. Furthermore, there is a high correlation between intelligence and brain size across animal species. Finally, since brains are very expensive organs metabolically, it seems unlikely that natural selection would have permitted the evolution of large brains unless they resulted in greater intelligence.

However, there is no need to rely upon intuition in this matter. There are several scientific studies that show a positive correlation between individual brain size and intelligence in human beings.[14] Estimates of the correlation vary, but cluster around $r = 0.35$.

Question (2) has aroused a great deal of controversy. Five possible hypotheses are:

(a) The differences are caused almost entirely by environmental factors.

(b) They are caused by a combination of factors, with the environmental factors normally being more important.

(c) Environmental and genetic factors are about equally important.

(d) They are caused by a combination of factors, with the genetic factors normally being more important.

(e) The differences are due almost entirely to genetic factors.

Offhand, (a) and (e) sound like extreme views, and the others therefore seem more likely. However, we need not rely on intuition alone, since there is a good deal of scientific data that bears on the question.

Perhaps the most straightforward way of measuring the heritability of IQ is by comparing the IQs of identical twins who were reared separately. Although such pairs (called "monozygotic apart" or "MZA" in the literature) are quite rare, because of their theoretical importance they have been sought out and carefully studied. Every study shows a high correlation between the IQs of MZAs, with the correlations ranging from 0.69 to 0.78.[15] These results strongly support hypothesis (d). (MZAs also show high correlations on a variety of personality traits and social attitudes.[16])

These results should be compared with the correlation between the IQs of ordinary siblings reared *together* which is only 0.49.[17] (Such pairs share half of their genes in addition to having been reared in very similar environments.) Even in the case of fraternal twins reared together, the correlation of the IQs is only about 0.60.[18] That is a high figure, but still a good deal lower than for identical twins reared apart, which suggests that genetic factors are more powerful than environmental ones in shaping a person's IQ.

Another approach is to compare the correlation between the adult IQs of ordinary siblings who have been reared apart (which is about 0.47) with the correlation between the IQs of unrelated adults who were reared together (which is nearly zero).[19]

A slightly different approach is to compare the IQs of adopted children who have never known their biological parents with: (i) the IQs of their biological parents; and (ii) the IQs of their adoptive parents. Careful studies show that the first correlation is greater than the second.[20] This strongly contradicts the predictions of hypotheses (a) and (b), but is consistent with hypothesis (d).

Although all studies show that the heritability of intelligence is non-zero — and indeed quite significant — its numerical value is still in dispute. The heritablility depends in part upon how old the subjects are (because the effect of the shared home environment is greatest during childhood and becomes less important as a person ages.) Plomin, after using several different approaches to the question, estimated the heritability of IQ to be about 50%.[21] Other scholars have concluded that, for adults, the heritability of IQ is about 60% or higher, rising to 70% or more in some age groups.[22]

I have spent so much time on this topic because in the past many persons have supported hypotheses (a) or (b) — which we can now see are plainly refuted by the scientific data — or have taken the position that we have no idea what the answer to question (2) is. The empirical data, however, makes it very clear that we do know the answer. *Both genetic and environmental factors affect a person's intelligence, with the influence of heredity being somewhat larger than that of his upbringing and environment, perhaps considerably larger.*

Section 9 – Summary

The essential points of this chapter can be summarized rather easily. Basically, many of the old common-sense views about intelligence that used to be widely accepted (and would probably be readily accepted today if racial concerns did not make us self-conscious) are compatible with recent scientific studies. Among these common-sense views are:

1) Some people are smarter than others, and all gradations of intelligence exist.

2) There are different aspects of intelligence, and typically an individual is not equally gifted in all those aspects. A person's overall mental ability is a combination of his or her general intelligence (which is usually the dominant factor) and various special intellectual strengths and weaknesses.

3) Those persons who are considered to be "very smart" typically have a high general intelligence, and their general intelligence can be applied to a wide variety of practical tasks.

4) There are many other important talents and character traits besides intelligence; and high intelligence, by itself, rarely results in success.

5) However, there are tasks that do require high intelligence, and high intelligence tends to enhance a person's other capabilities, sometimes quite markedly. Therefore, other factors being equal, a person of high intelligence will be able to perform a great variety of tasks better than someone of lower intelligence.

6) Modern intelligence tests, although certainly not perfect, are reasonably accurate; and a person's IQ provides a fair approximation to his general intelligence.

7) Individual differences in intelligence are caused in part by genetic factors, and in part by differences in upbringing and environment. However, in adult life the genetic factors are typically more important.

8) Although brain size does not rigidly determine a person's intelligence, there is a marked positive correlation between brain size and IQ.

FOOTNOTES – CHAPTER 3

1) Gardner, H. (1983). *Frames of Mind: The Theory of Multiple Intelligences.* New York: Basic Books.

2) Gardner's theory has also been criticized on other grounds, for example that he does not supply any quantitative evidence to support it. See pp. 18-19 of *The Bell Curve* (Herrnstein & Murray, 1994), or pp. 128-130 of *The g Factor* (Jensen, 1998) for a fuller discussion.

3) This is well established. See, for example:

   (a) Detterman, D.K. & M.H. Daniel (1989) who state on p. 349: "Positive manifold among mental tests is one of the most reliable, replicable, and important empirical discoveries about human ability yet found."
   (b) Herrnstein & Murray (1994), p.3.
   (c) Jencks, C. (1998). See pp. 59-60 in chapter 2 of *The Black-White Test Score Gap.*

4) Spearman, Charles (1904).

5) For a full discussion see *Bias in Mental Testing* (Jensen, 1980). For a briefer discussion see pp. 280-282 of Herrnstein & Murray (1994).

6) For a more detailed description of the reaction time experiments discussed here see Jensen, Arthur (1998), pp. 210-216.

7) Morris, R.D. & W.D. Hopkins (1995).

8) Jensen, Arthur (1998), pp. 212-214.

9) Jensen, Arthur (1987). Also see Deary, I.J. (2003), pp. 55, 61, and 62.

10) (a) Frearson, W.M. & H.J. Eysenck (1986).
    (b) Jensen, Arthur (1992).
    (c) Jensen, Arthur (1993).
    (d) Jensen, Arthur & P.A. Whang (1993).

11) Jensen, Arthur (1998), p. 221; see also note 22 on p. 263.

12) For a fuller discussion of this point, and some examples, see chapter 3 of Herrnstein & Murray (1994), particularly pp. 70-80.

13) The heritability of a trait is defined as the proportion of the total variance of that trait that is genetically explained. (The variance of a trait within a population is defined as the square of the standard deviation of that trait in the population.) Note that the standard deviation, and therefore the variance, is not a property of any individual, but is inherently a group property. It follows that the heritability of a trait is also a property of the group, and is not defined for individuals.

14) (a) Willerman, et al. (1991).
    (b) Andreasen, et al. (1993).
    (c) Egan, et al. (1994).
    (d) Wickett, Vernon, & Lee (1994).
    (e) Anderson, Britt (2003), especially pp. 30-35.
    (f) McDaniel, Michael A. (2005).

15) Levin, Michael (1997), pp. 97-98. Also see:

   (a) Newman, Freeman, & Holzinger (1937), see Table 96 on p. 347.
   (b) Bouchard, et al. (1990).
   (c) Pedersen, et al. (1992).

16) Bouchard, et al. (1990).

17) (a) Paul, S.M. (1980), whose study was based on over 27,000 sibling pairs.
   (b) Bouchard & McGue (1981). This review discusses the results for many other kinship relationships. It is based on over 100 studies which, together, include over 40,000 kinship pairs. For the 68 studies involving siblings reared together, they obtain a weighted average of 0.47, very similar to Paul's result.

18) Bouchard & McGue (1981), see figure 1, p. 1056.

19) Jensen, Arthur (1998), p. 178.

20) Scarr, Sandra & Richard A. Weinberg (1983), p. 262. Also see Jensen, Arthur (1998), p. 177.

21) Plomin, R. (1990). See also Chipuer, Rovine, & Plomin (1990).

22) (a) Bouchard, et al. (1990).
    (b) Pederson, et al. (1992).

CHAPTER 4

THE ORIGIN OF *HOMO SAPIENS*

Section 1 – Predecessors of *Homo sapiens*

Zoologists classify our species as part of the genus *Homo*, which in turn is part of the hominid family. The hominid family once included another genus (now extinct) called *Australopithecus*. One species within that genus was *Australopithecus afarensis*, which lived in East Africa about 3.5 million years ago, and from which the entire genus *Homo* is believed to be descended.

We are the only surviving species in genus *Homo* (indeed, in the entire hominid family), and our closest living relatives are the chimpanzees. Chimpanzees are not hominids, but belong to another family, the pongids (or great apes). The last common ancestor of chimpanzees and human beings probably lived about 5 million years ago.[1] (For information about how prehistoric dates are determined, see Appendix 2.)

Two major differences between hominids and pongids are: (1) We are fully adapted to bipedal locomotion; and (2) we have much larger brains. The purpose of our large brain size is clear enough: it enables us to have high intelligence. Otherwise, our large brains — which are metabolically very expensive[2] — would never have evolved.

Among the extinct species within our genus are *Homo habilis* and *Homo erectus*. (The official name of a species consists of two words, the first being the genus to which it belongs.) The exact evolutionary sequence leading to *Homo sapiens* is still disputed, but a common view is that we derive from *Homo erectus*, which derived from *Homo habilis*, which in turn derived from *Australopithecus afarensis*.

Adult members of *Australopithecus afarensis* were considerably smaller than we are. Their average height was about 3'6" (1.1 meters), and their average weight about 110 pounds (50 kg). They walked erect, but their brains were much smaller than ours, typically only about 450 cc (cubic centimeters). This is about the same size as that of an average chimpanzee, but only one-third that of a modern human. However, as they were considerably smaller than chimpanzees, their encephalization (i.e., the ratio of brain weight to body weight) was much higher, and they were probably a good deal smarter.

Our genus, *Homo*, originated about 2.5 million years ago, and its earliest known species was *Homo habilis*. As all species of *Australopithecus* lived in Africa, *Homo habilis* must have originated there; and indeed, fossil remains of *Homo habilis* have been found only in East Africa.

Although there were several anatomical differences between *Homo habilis* and *Australopithecus*, the most important one involved brain size. The brains of *Homo habilis* averaged about 650 cc in size — roughly fifty percent larger than those of *Australopithecus*, although only about half the size of ours. The increase in brain size was accompanied by a significant behavioral change: They developed techniques for making stone tools. Although the tools they produced were very crude, it was an important advance. (That early type of tools is called *Oldowan*, after Olduvai gorge in modern Tanzania, where many of the remains of *Homo habilis* have been found.)

About 1.8 million years ago a new species, *Homo erectus*, arose in East Africa. The brains of *Homo erectus* were much larger than those of *Homo habilis*, and for adults averaged about 1000 cc. Indeed, the largest *Homo erectus* brains lie within the range of our own species, although far below the human average.

Once again, the increased brain power of the new species was accompanied by behavioral changes, at least three of which are noteworthy. To begin with, *Homo erectus* was the first hominid to spread out of Africa into Asia and Europe. They reached Central Asia at least 1.5 million years ago, and must have entered the Middle East even earlier. Remains of *Homo erectus* have been found in northern China (in the cave at Zhoukoudian, near Beijing), and as far east as Java. Indeed, the first *Homo erectus* skull ever discovered was found in central Java in 1891; and for a while, the species was called "Java Man" or *Pithecanthropus erectus*. That skull might be about a million years old, and it therefore predates the earliest specimens of *Homo erectus* found in Europe.

In the second place, *Homo erectus* was the first of our ancestors to use and maintain fires. This advance was made at least 1.6 million years ago. Most primates lack the anatomical and physiological features necessary to survive cold winters, and — with the exception of those in genus *Homo* — they are only found in tropical regions. It seems likely, therefore, that it was only due to its mastery of fire that *Homo erectus* was able to move into such regions as Central Asia, northern China, and Europe.

Thirdly, *Homo erectus* created a new set of tools, better and more varied than any produced by *Homo habilis*. This improved toolkit is often called *Acheulian*, after the site in France where samples of it were first found. (For a list of some major prehistoric stone toolkits, see Table A2-1 in Appendix 2.)

Because of the higher intelligence of the new species, and the advances resulting from it, *Homo erectus* eventually supplanted all earlier hominid species, and by one million BC those earlier species had become extinct. A similar fate was to befall *Homo erectus* after *Homo sapiens* arose.[3]

Section 2 – Archaic *Homo sapiens*

The prevailing view among anthropologists is that *Homo sapiens* originated in Africa about 350 kya.[4] (Note: "kya" is an abbreviation for "kiloyears ago," and since 1 kiloyear = 1000 years, 350 kya means 350,000 years ago.) The new species spread widely and eventually replaced *Homo erectus* everywhere. *Homo sapiens* reached China at least as early as 210 kya, and possibly as early as 300 kya.[5] They probably reached Europe and Central Asia earlier than China, and the Middle East earlier still.

From their fossil remains, we can tell that those early humans looked somewhat different from us, so — even though their brains were roughly as large as ours — we often refer to them as "archaic *Homo sapiens*" (or *AHS*). Their possession of human-sized brains does not prove they had the same mental skills as we do, and it is doubtful that they did. However, their displacement of *Homo erectus* is consistent with the view that the larger brains of *AHS* gave them a clear advantage over the earlier species.

Since *AHS* was widely scattered throughout Asia, Africa, and Europe, and since inhabitants of each region had very little opportunity to mate with inhabitants of other regions, we would expect regional variations of *AHS* to arise. This indeed occurred. The variant that evolved in Western Europe was particularly distinctive and is often called "Neanderthal Man" or *Homo sapiens neanderthalensis*.

The Neanderthals were a successful subspecies, and specimens have been found in Eastern Europe, Southwest Asia, and as far east as Uzbekistan, in Central Asia.[6] They were a bit shorter than modern human beings, and more heavily built, which was an advantage in the cold climate they originated in. In addition, they probably evolved various physiological adaptations to protect them from the cold. Unfortunately, such adaptations are hard to detect from skeletal remains, so their exact nature is unknown.

The most obvious behavioral difference between *AHS* and *Homo erectus* lies in the markedly superior tools produced by *AHS*. In particular, the Neanderthals developed a set of tools — often called the Mousterian toolkit, after the French cave where the first samples were found — which were plainly more sophisticated than Acheulian tools.

For tens of thousands of years, the Neanderthals were the only hominids living in Europe. However, anatomically modern humans entered Eastern Europe about 46 kya,[7] and by 30 kya, only a few pockets of Neanderthals survived. They appear to have contributed very little to the gene pool of modern human beings.[8]

Section 3 – The advent of *Homo sapiens sapiens*

Besides the Neanderthals, there were several other regional variants of *Homo sapiens*. About 100 kya a new variant — *Homo sapiens sapiens* (or "*HSS*") — arose in sub-Saharan Africa.[9] This new variant is important because it eventually spread throughout the entire world, displacing all other variants (apparently with rather little interbreeding), and as a result all humans living today are members of that subspecies.

Some scholars dispute the claim that *HSS* originated only in Africa, and instead espouse the "multiregional model," according to which *HSS* evolved more or less simultaneously in several parts of the Old World.[10] However, the majority of anthropologists now reject that hypothesis[11] and accept the "out-of-Africa" model because:

(a) Early examples of *HSS* in Africa (at Border Cave and at Klasies River, both in southern Africa) are much older than the earliest examples of *HSS* in China, India, or Europe.

(b) Only in Africa do we find a convincing sequence of forms leading from archaic *Homo sapiens* (such as those at Broken Hill and at Eliye Springs), through transitional forms (such as those at Florisbad, Omo, and Laetoli) to early *HSS* (such as those at Border Cave and Klasies River).

(c) Studies of mitochondrial DNA from humans living in widely separated parts of the world show that they all have as one of their ancestors a particular woman (the so-called "African Eve"), and that she lived about 200 kya, not 1000 kya as the multiregional model suggests.[12]

The worldwide triumph of *HSS* over its rivals makes it plain that it was "superior" (in the Darwinian sense of the word) to those rivals. However, examination of the fossil remains reveals only small differences between the skeletal structure of *HSS* and the other subspecies, seemingly far too small to explain its rapid triumph over the others. The members of *HSS* did not have larger brains than their rivals; nor is there any sign that they were generally bigger, stronger, or faster than the other variants of *Homo sapiens*.

It has frequently been suggested that the superiority of *HSS* resided in their greater *linguistic* skills. Early humans certainly had some sort of primitive speech; but it has been suggested that *HSS* were the first humans capable of fully-developed language.[13]

Our brains appear to be "hard-wired" in such a way as to enable children to master language, and to do so long before they can master various other tasks that are far less complicated.[14] It is well established, for example, that there are sections of our brain — Broca's area, for example, and Wernicke's area — that are highly specialized for the production and understanding of human speech. If *HSS* (but not any other variant of *Homo sapiens*) possessed these built-in language capacities, its triumph over the other variants would be easily explicable — indeed, virtually inevitable.

Note that if, in earlier variants of *Homo sapiens*, Broca's area and Wernicke's area were less specialized for the production and understanding of language — or if they were smaller, or less developed, or even completely absent in those variants — we could not observe the difference just by examining the skeletal remains. The hypothesis that the superiority of *HSS* lay in their linguistic skills is therefore unproven, and may never be conclusively demonstrated. However, the hypothesis appears to be consistent with the available data; and since no better explanation for the triumph of *HSS* is known, I shall adopt it in this book.

Section 4 – Syntactic language and the human species

In the previous section, I mentioned that there was an important difference between "primitive speech" and "fully-developed language" without specifying the differences between the two categories. In primitive speech (such as many animals possess):

- The vocabulary is small.
- Each sentence consists of a single word.
- There are no grammatical rules.

On the other hand, in a fully-developed language (or "syntactic language"):

- There is a large vocabulary.
- Multi-word sentences (sometimes quite lengthy ones) are common.
- There are rules for expressing:
  a) Negatives.
  b) Conditional or hypothetical statements.
  c) The distinction between the subject and the object of a verb.
  d) A full range of tenses, including past, present, future, future perfect, pluperfect, and so forth.

In the period when the transition from more primitive language to fully syntactic language took place there must have been languages that did not fall clearly into either category. However, no such languages survive. All existing animal languages are primitive, and all existing human languages are syntactic. As the difference between primitive and syntactic languages is so enormous, I shall hereafter use the word *speech* to refer only to the latter.

In the course of human history and prehistory there have been many inventions of great importance, including agriculture, metalworking, printing, firearms, antibiotics, and computers. But none of those was nearly as important as the invention of speech. It is speech — syntactic language — that truly separates us from all other animals.

Taxonomists list *HSS* as a mere subspecies of *Homo sapiens*, and there is little doubt that matings between *HSS* and archaic *Homo sapiens* would have produced fertile offspring. But although the visible anatomical differences separating us from *AHS* are minor, behaviorally we are worlds apart. Behaviorally, any hominid without speech is closer to *Australopithecus* than it is to us.

It is sometimes said that two organisms or populations should be included in the same species if they produce fertile offspring. However, this method of classifying species is not always followed by biologists. Taxonomists consider lions (*Panthera leo*) and tigers (*Panthera tigris*) separate species, even though they have been crossbred in zoos and the offspring are fertile, because lions and tigers do not interbreed in the wild.[15] In like fashion, dogs and wolves are considered separate species. This is because — even though wolves are physically capable of mating with dogs and producing fertile offspring — in the wild they more commonly kill and eat them.

If we use "commonly interbreed in the wild" as our criterion, then *HSS* should be considered a separate species. Human beings who possessed syntactic language would surely have considered hominids without speech to be "subhuman," which explains why they rarely interbred with them. With rare exceptions, human females adamantly refuse to copulate with anything subhuman; and although young males will sometimes *copulate* with anything vaguely female, they will *marry* a female only if they consider her fully human.

Definitions, of course, are arbitrary and adopted merely for convenience. How we choose to define a word will not change any physical or biological facts. Therefore, you need not consider *HSS* to be a separate species if you don't want to. However, in the rest of this book I will use the terms "human," "human race," "human species," "human beings," and "humanity" to refer to *Homo sapiens sapiens*, and to them alone. When I wish to include other hominids, I shall use the terms, "*Homo*," "*Homo sapiens*," or "hominid."

FOOTNOTES – CHAPTER 4

1) Sarich, Vincent & Allan C. Wilson, (1967).

2) Typically, the brain of an adult human accounts for only about 2 percent of his weight, but it uses about 20 percent of his resting energy.

3) Most of the data in this section comes from either Fagan, Brian M. (2001), chapters 2 and 3; or Cavalli-Sforza, et al. (1994), chapter 2.

4) This date is very uncertain:

    (a) Clark, J. Desmond (1989) suggests more than 400 kya. (See figure 29.2 on p. 567.)
    (b) Bräuer, Günter (1989), suggests 450 kya. (See his figure 8.1 on p. 124.)
    (c) Caralli-Sforza, et al. (1994) says "at least 300 kya." (See p. 61.)
    (d) Fagan, Brian M. (2001) says 200-400 kya. (See p. 107.)

5) Brooks, Alison & Bernard Wood (1990).

6) See Cavalli-Sforza, et al. (1994), figure 2.1.2; or Fagan, Brian M. (2001), figure 3.16.

7) Mellars, P.A. (1993), pp. 202-203.

8) (a) Stringer, C.B. (1989), p. 241.
    (b) Klein, Richard G. (1989), pp. 334-343.
    (c) Diamond, Jared (1992), p. 53.
    (d) Diamond, Jared (1999), pp. 40-41.
    (e) Zubrow, Ezra (1989), p. 212.

9) The date is uncertain. My figure is based on:
    (a) Rightmire, G.P. (1989), p. 120.
    (b) Deacon, H.J. (1989), p. 561.
    (c) Bräuer, Günter (1989), p. 123.
    (d) Clark, J. Desmond (1993), p. 148.

10) A sophisticated presentation of this view is given by Wolpoff, M.H. (1989).

11) See Stringer & McKie (1996), pp. 117-119, 134-135, and 142-147; or Mellars, P.A. (1992), p. 198.

12) (a) Cann, Stoneking, & Wilson (1987).
    (b) Stoneking, et al. (1993).
    (c) Stringer & McKie (1996), chapter 5.
    (d) Horai, S., et al. (1995).

13) See Lieberman, P. (1968); Lieberman & Crelin (1971); and Lieberman, Crelin, & Klatt (1972). Also see Diamond, Jared (1992), pp. 55-56.

14) See Pinker, Steven (1994), *The Language Instinct*, and Chomsky, Noam (1975).

15) Wilson, Edward O. (2000), p. 9.

CHAPTER 5
ALTRUISM

Section 1 – The paradox of altruism

One might define *altruistic behavior* as any behavior by an individual organism that decreases its own chance of surviving and reproducing in order to help or protect some other individual. (No conscious motivation is required; even completely instinctive behavior could still be altruistic.) For many years, a major problem in the theory of evolution was to explain how any pattern of altruistic behavior could survive in a "dog-eat-dog" world. On the face of it, it seems as if genes that dispose an individual organism to be altruistic would necessarily render it less likely to survive and reproduce; consequently, even if genes for altruism were ever formed, they would quickly be eliminated from the gene pool by natural selection.

The argument appears to be very strong; nevertheless, many instances of apparently altruistic behavior by animals have been observed. Here are some examples:

1) In order to protect their young, certain ground nesting birds (such as wood ducks and pied stilts) often engage in "distraction displays" when a predator appears. A common form of such display is to feign injury, while moving away from the nest. In so doing, the adult is placing itself in danger that it could easily avoid.

2) Small birds (such as blackbirds, robins, and thrushes) often give an alarm call when they sight a predatory bird in the vicinity. This alerts the flock, which normally takes evasive action, but endangers the bird giving the call.

3) When a colony of ants or termites is threatened, the "soldier" ants of the colony will move towards the intruder, thereby putting themselves in maximum danger while protecting the colony. The dominant males in a band of baboons often do the same thing.

4) Worker bees will sting an animal that threatens their colony, even though stinging normally results in the death of the bee.

5) When a pack of wild dogs is sighted by a Thomson's gazelle, the gazelle often breaks into a stiff-legged bounding gait (called "stotting") that warns the other gazelles

in his band, but seems to increase his own danger.

6) Parent birds often spend much of their time and energy feeding their young.[1]

In the past, some biologists maintained that if instances of apparently altruistic animal behavior were examined closely, it would be found that in most — possibly all — cases the behavior was not actually altruistic. For example, although a gazelle that engages in stotting *appears* to be acting altruistically, it might in fact be acting selfishly. After all, the gazelle is clearly demonstrating to the predator that he is healthy and vigorous, and thereby sending this message to the predator: "You have little chance of catching me. If you are smart, you should therefore go after some other member of my group instead." (Of course, the gazelle need not have this thought *consciously* in order for the genes that dispose him to engage in stotting to be preserved.)

However, although this might be the explanation for stotting, several of the other examples presented above cannot reasonably be interpreted as selfish behavior. Clearly, a general explanation for the origin and continuation of altruism is required.

One theory proposed to explain altruistic behavior in animals was *group selection*. It is based on the observation that most animals find it difficult to survive in the wild alone, and can only survive as part of a group. The theory claims that genes which dispose an animal to protect its own group (even at some risk to itself) will — by making it more likely that the group survives — indirectly aid in the survival of the altruistic individual, and that such genes will therefore be favored by natural selection.

At first sight, this theory sounds convincing; and indeed, it is the one preferred by most laymen. The problem with the theory is that if an *individual* member of such a group possesses a gene that disposes him to ignore the interest of the group, and to selfishly look after himself, he will obtain the advantages of group cooperation, while avoiding the costs of altruistic behavior. He will therefore be more likely to survive than an altruistic member of his group; and in succeeding generations of the group his genes will occur with greater frequency. Even though a band whose members act altruistically will prosper, genes for altruistic behavior will inevitably be replaced by genes that dispose individuals to act selfishly.[2] It follows that group selection alone cannot explain altruism. (However, if some other effect made it disadvantageous for an individual to "cheat," then group selection would be an effective mechanism for increasing altruism.)

Another suggested explanation for altruistic behavior is *reciprocal altruism*.[3] ("You scratch my back now, in the expectation that at some later time I will scratch yours.") Although this may sound like a reasonable explanation of altruism, it does not explain example (4), as in that instance there is no hope of the bee's sacrifice being repaid. Nor does it explain examples (1) or (6), since most animals cannot reasonably expect their altruistic behavior to be repaid by their offspring. Nor does it explain example (2), since an individual bird that lacked the gene for giving warning would nevertheless benefit by the altruism of the other birds towards each other. In this instance, natural selection will favor the genes for "cheating" (i.e., being selfish, and sponging off the altruistic behavior of others).

The possibility of such cheating frequently undercuts any selective advantage reciprocal altruism would otherwise confer. Cheating is least likely to pay off when:

a) Individual animals are capable of recognizing each other and remembering which individuals did them favors; and
b) Encounters between two given individuals are frequent enough to make it likely that there will be opportunities for favors to be returned.

These conditions often hold within small groups of human beings, such as families and bands, and a considerable degree of reciprocal altruism is therefore likely to develop within such groups. However, a more general theory is needed to explain most instances of altruism in the animal world.

Section 2 – Kin selection

For about a century after Darwin proposed his theory of evolution, the origin of altruistic behavior in animals remained a puzzle. It was not until the 1960s, when William D. Hamilton proposed his theory of *kin selection*, that a satisfactory explanation was given.[4] That theory can perhaps best be explained by an example:

Suppose a man sees his identical twin drowning in a river, and estimates (correctly) that if he were to jump in and try to save his brother the probability of success would be 80%, while the probability that he would die in the attempt would be 20%. Consider these two alternatives:

a) Some of the man's genes strongly dispose him to rescue his brother, and he therefore jumps in and tries to save him ("altruistic behavior").
b) The man does not have genes that dispose him to rescue his brother, and he therefore stays on the shore and lets his brother drown ("selfish behavior").

In case (b), exactly *one* copy of the man's genes survives, and may later be replicated. However, in case (a), if the rescue attempt is successful, *two* copies of the man's genes survive (one in his own body, one in his brother's). As this will happen 80% of the time, on average 1.6 (= 0.80 × 2) copies of the man's genes will survive. In this situation, therefore, genes that dispose a person to altruistic behavior will — on average — have *more* surviving copies than genes that dispose a person to act selfishly and will be favored by natural selection.

Now consider a slightly different example. Suppose that the man on shore is a brother — but not a twin — of the person who is drowning. Case (b) will still result in one copy of his genes being preserved. However, since ordinary siblings share only 50% of their genes, if the man on shore succeeds in rescuing his brother then (on average) 1.5 copies of the man's genes will survive. Since 80% of the attempts will be successful, case (a) will on average result in 1.2 (= 0.80 × 1.5) copies of the altruistic genes surviving. Since 1.2 is greater than 1.0, the altruistic genes will be favored by natural selection in this case too.

Suppose, however, that the two men were not brothers, but merely first cousins. First cousins, on average, share only one-eighth of their genes. In this case, altruistic behavior results in only 0.9 (= 0.80 × 1.125) copies of the man's genes surviving, and natural selection will therefore favor the genes for *selfish* behavior.

The upshot is that a gene that disposes its bearer to behave altruistically toward a *close* relative can have a selective advantage over one that disposes its bearer to act completely selfishly. Furthermore, this can occur even though the relative never returns the favor, and even if the survival of the relative does not increase the group's chances of survival. It is not necessary that either reciprocal altruism or group selection operate for kin selection to result in the spread of genes that dispose their bearer to act altruistically toward close relatives.

Notice, though, that for kin selection to operate there are certain conditions that must be met. Among these conditions are:

1) The animal involved must be able to estimate, even if crudely, the magnitude of the risk or sacrifice that it is making in order to aid the other party.

2) The animal involved must be able to estimate, even if crudely, how closely a possible object of its benevolence is related to it. (It is unnecessary, of course, for either calculation to be conscious.)

The first condition is similar to the judgment needed for an animal to thrive in situations not involving altruism. For example, if a leopard detects some prey on the other side of a narrow, shallow, quiet stream, he will readily cross the stream in order to reach his prey; however, he will not normally attempt to cross a wide, raging torrent to reach similar prey. Indeed, an animal species would not survive if its members could not handle such problems reasonably well.

The second condition, though, involves additional skills, and skills not necessarily possessed by all species. It is useful to be able to recognize that another animal is a relative rather than a stranger; it is even better if one can distinguish individuals who are very closely related (children, parents, siblings) from less close relatives (such as half-siblings, uncles, aunts, nephews and nieces), and those from more distant relatives.

How do animals recognize relatives? Many animals rely heavily upon their sense of smell to do this. Human beings do not have as keen a sense of smell as most other mammals, and we rely more heavily upon sight and hearing. Because of our intelligence and memory, human beings are very good at distinguishing among relatives, and kin selection has been a very effective process within our species.

One other effect of kin selection should be noted. Bands whose members act cooperatively have an advantage over similar bands whose members do not. The only reason that group selection often fails to promote altruism is that it is undercut by the presence of "cheaters" within the band. Kin selection, however, by reducing the amount of cheating within a band, can enable group selection to operate.

FOOTNOTES – CHAPTER 5

1) Most of these examples come from chapter 1 of *The Selfish Gene*, by Richard Dawkins (1989 edition). For a discussion of stotting, see chapter 10 of that book.

2) See Pinker, Steven (1997), p. 397; Dawkins (1989), chapter 1; and Maynard Smith, J. (1976).

3) Dawkins (1989), chapter 10. Also see Trivers, R.L. (1971); and Axelrod & Hamilton (1981).

4) See Dawkins (1989), chapter 6; and Wilson, Edward O. (2000), chapter 5. The notion of kin selection was first analyzed by W. D. Hamilton in 1964.

CHAPTER 6

BANDS, AND THE DUAL CODE OF MORALITY

Section 1 – Types of societal organization

Cultural anthropologists often classify human societies into four main types: bands, tribes, chiefdoms, and states. These types differ from each other in their typical size and in their social, political, and economic structures.[1]

The smallest and most primitive societies — and the type in which virtually all human beings lived until the last several thousand years — are called *bands*. Most bands consist of just a few families, and have a population of between twenty and eighty persons. (If a band becomes much larger, it normally splits in two.) As bands are so small, every member is personally acquainted with every other member. Bands are almost invariably exogamous: That is, a band member seeking a mate is expected to select someone from outside the band.

Most bands consist of nomadic hunter-gatherers. Within a band, the males and females have different roles (for example, infants are cared for primarily by females, while hunting is done mostly by males), as do children and adults. Aside from that, there is almost no economic specialization, and all able-bodied persons forage for food.

Bands have no formal political organization or institutions: no kings or chiefs, no police, no formal laws, no treaties with other bands. Within a band, decisions are made by informal consensus. Some band members are more respected by their fellows, and therefore have more influence in band decisions; but they are not rulers, and cannot order the other members around.

Relations between members of nearby, related bands are not automatically hostile. Indeed, it is common for such bands to have periodic meetings in which they exchange brides. However, instances of violence between members of nearby bands are fairly common; and as there is no legal system to resolve the resulting grievances, the periodic meetings between bands can be very tense — indeed, quite dangerous — affairs.[2] Relations between unrelated bands are generally even worse. Indeed, if an individual strays into the territory of a strange band he might well be murdered.

Because of the frequently murderous hostility between unrelated bands, it is an obvious advantage for a given band to have as its neighbors other bands which have split off from it within living memory, or with which it has exchanged brides. Indeed, these nearby bands provide a vital cushion without which a band might be unable to survive.

Section 2 – The dual code of morality

It has often been noted that human beings living in civilized states appear to follow a dual code of morality. Within our own society, cooperation is highly valued, and killing another person is a grievous sin. However, when we are engaged in a war with another nation, not only are we permitted to kill members of that nation, but we are encouraged to do so. Indeed, those who are conspicuously successful in wreaking havoc and destruction upon that other nation are highly praised and considered to be heroes.

Nor is this dual code something that exists only in civilized states. It appears to be equally present in primitive tribes and bands.[3] Within a band, the standard of proper behavior involves helpfulness and cooperation. But that code holds only within the band. Members of unrelated bands can be attacked, plundered, or killed without incurring the disapproval of one's fellow band members.

Although I have been referring to this collection of attitudes as a "dual code of morality," upon consideration one can see that at heart these attitudes really comprise a single standard, which might be expressed as: "Do what is best for your *own* group."

Section 3 – Comparison with some other species

It is worth noting that the species that is most closely related to us — the chimpanzees — live in bands, and it is believed that all pre-human hominids also did. Bands are therefore the form of society that humans inherited from our predecessors.

Many other animals also follow the "dual code" described above. For example, the social insects are famous for the high degree of cooperation they exhibit within a colony. Yet ant colonies are notoriously aggressive toward one another, and warfare between such colonies has often been observed.[4] Chimpanzees also exhibit this dual code. They normally cooperate with members of their own band; but extensive observations of wild chimpanzees have revealed how murderously they act towards chimpanzees who are not members of their band. Indeed, aggressive behavior toward outsiders occurs within many vertebrate species. As an eminent biologist put it: "The strongest evoker of aggressive response in animals is the sight of a stranger, especially a territorial intruder. This xenophobic principle has been documented in virtually every group of animals displaying higher forms of social organization."[5]

From what was said earlier about kin selection and group selection, it is not hard to understand the origins of this dual code among social animals. Kin selection favors genes that foster cooperation within a group. Group selection then favors genes that dispose an individual to act in such a way as to promote the interests of his own group over the interests of other groups. Indeed, group selection can result in genes that dispose one to act with complete ruthlessness toward members of other groups or bands.

The behavior of human beings is not, and never was, completely determined by our genes. It is also strongly influenced by cultural factors. However, in most past ages — and throughout the Paleolithic Era — those cultural factors reinforced our inherited tendencies.

Since most human development occurred during the Paleolithic, we are (genetically) well adapted to the conditions prevailing then. The traits that we inherited from that era have operated throughout recorded history, and our history cannot be understood without taking those factors into account. Those traits might no longer be desirable in today's world; but it is unrealistic to think that they can be easily shrugged off or ignored.[6]

FOOTNOTES – CHAPTER 6

1) Much of this section comes from chapter 14 of Diamond, Jared (1999). See also Fagan, Brian M. (2001), pp. 19-20.

2) See, for example, pp. 265-266 of Diamond (1999).

3) See Pinker, Steven (1997), pp. 509-512 in chapter 7.

4) Wilson, Edward O. (2000), pp. 244-245.

5) Wilson, Edward O. (2000), p. 249.

6) See Dawkins, Richard (1989), chapter 1, pp. 2-3.

CHAPTER 7

HUMAN SEXUAL BEHAVIOR AND ATTITUDES

It has long been observed that men and women often have very different attitudes about sex, with resulting differences in their behavior. Women tend to be much more selective about whom they mate with; men are typically less choosy. Men are frequently eager to engage in casual sex; women are generally reluctant to do so, and often insist on a long-term commitment before engaging in sex. To the extent that men are selective, they tend to be especially attracted to women with youthful good looks. Women place relatively more importance on a man's wealth, income, and influence, and on his apparent sincerity.[1]

There are some extreme cultural determinists who claim that the male-female differences in attitude and behavior are due entirely to upbringing and social pressures; and they assert that if males and females were reared in the same environment those differences would not exist. This, however, seems implausible. Not only are those differences found in all known human societies, but similar behavioral patterns are commonplace among other mammals.[2] This suggests that the differences are genetic in origin, although they may be magnified by upbringing and social pressures.

There is a well-known theory ("parental investment theory") that explains in a straightforward fashion how these differences could arise through natural selection.[3] Parental investment theory begins with the hard facts of human reproduction: The female — who must carry the fetus in her body for nine months — of necessity has a large investment in each child. (A male might invest a lot of time in a child, but it is not a biological necessity.) In addition, a male's sperm cells are very tiny and extremely numerous. A man produces many billions of sperm cells during his lifetime, and they can be rapidly replaced after being expended. In contrast, egg cells are relatively large, and a female releases only a few hundred of them during her lifetime.

Because eggs are in relatively short supply, they are expensive compared to sperm. As a result, males compete with each other, sometimes violently, for reproductive access to the scarce, valuable eggs; and the losers in this competition, fail to pass on their genes. The most effective reproductive strategies for males and females are therefore quite different.[4] The "best" strategy for a male is to:

- Obtain *exclusive* access to one or more fertile females; and

- Copulate with other females whenever possible.

Notice that the word "best" in the preceding paragraph is not used in the moral sense of the word. The behavior outlined is best only in the Darwinian sense of reproductive success. Males who follow this strategy will pass down more copies of their genes to succeeding generations than males who follow alternative strategies.

For a female, a very different reproductive strategy is called for. A woman has a limited supply of eggs, and she cannot voluntary release more than one per month. In addition, once she is fertilized she is tied up reproductively for at least nine months (perhaps a few years, if she nurses the resulting child). Consequently, she is limited to a relatively small number of successful pregnancies, and to succeed reproductively she must make the most of those opportunities. Furthermore, she is vulnerable during the late stages of her pregnancy (as is the fetus), and for a considerable time after she gives birth her child is weak and helpless, and needs to be supported.

That being the case, the best reproductive strategy for a woman (i.e., the one which maximizes the number of her descendants) is to:

- Select a mate with good economic prospects, thus making it likely that he will be able to adequately support their children; and

- Obtain in advance a commitment from him to protect her during her pregnancy, and to protect and support their offspring.

Throughout the Paleolithic Era — and, indeed, all past ages — adopting a policy of promiscuous copulation was likely to harm a woman's prospects of propagating her genes. Such a policy might result in a higher number of pregnancies than if she confined her sexual activities to just one man, but only slightly higher. However, failing to obtain a commitment from a man to support her children — or choosing for a mate a man who is unable to support them — would probably result in fewer of her children surviving to maturity.

Note that there is no requirement that a female engage in careful, cold-blooded calculations before adopting the "best" strategy. Females of other species — who are not even aware of the connection between copulation and childbearing — follow similar strategies without engaging in any analysis; they merely follow their inherited inclinations. However, those females who inherited the "wrong" inclinations passed down fewer copies of their genes than those who inherited the "right" inclinations.

Similarly, in deciding whom to mate with, most males do not carefully calculate which female is likely to bear him the greatest number of children. But those of our male forebears who were attracted to females with full, firm breasts had (on average) more children than those men who were attracted to women with sagging breasts, or with flat chests. This is because full, firm breasts are most commonly possessed by young, fertile women near the beginning of their childbearing years.[5]

Human behavior, of course, is also strongly influenced by socialization. Male promiscuity (including the "hit and run" strategy often pursued by young males) is bad for the group as a whole, and is therefore disapproved of by most moral s. This has had some effect on male behavior; nevertheless, males who broke the moral code often passed on more genes than those males who followed it. On the other hand, the tendencies that females inherit with regard to mating strategies are generally good for society as a whole, and females are therefore more likely to conform to the moral code than men are.

It should be remembered that these behavioral tendencies evolved in the Paleolithic world, not the modern world of the West where there are social welfare programs and easily available birth control. But the Paleolithic world was not uniform; it included a variety of different environments. All of those environments favored the reproductive strategies for males and females described above, but not necessarily to the same degree. We should therefore expect differences in sexual attitudes and behaviors between those that evolved in strikingly different Paleolithic environments.

FOOTNOTES – CHAPTER 7

1) (a) Symons, Donald (1979), *The Evolution of Human Sexuality*.
   (b) Wilson, Glenn (1992), *The Great Sex Divide*, especially chapter 1.
   (c) Pinker, Steven (1997), *How the Mind Works*, especially pp. 469-476.

2) Wilson, Glenn (1992), chapter 3.

3) (a) Trivers, R.L. (1972).
   (b) Symons, Donald (1979).
   (c) Dawkins, Richard (1989), chapter 9.
   (d) Pinker, Steven (1997), chapter 7, especially pp. 463-471.

4) (a) Dawkins, Richard (1989), chapter 9.
   (b) Wilson, Glenn (1992), chapter 1, especially pp. 20-22.

5) Pinker, Steven (1997), chapter 7, especially pp. 483-487.

CHAPTER 8

THE ICE AGES

Section 1 – The Pleistocene Epoch and the Paleolithic Era

Although the earliest primates lived many millions of years ago, most hominid evolution occurred during the Pliocene and Pleistocene Epochs (see Table 8-1). Recorded human history falls entirely within the most recent geologic epoch, the Holocene.

Geologists define past eras and epochs by looking at rock strata and the fossils they contain. Archaeologists, on the other hand, define periods by means of human artifacts (most often stone implements, since wooden artifacts tend to decay relatively rapidly). Most of the period during which genus *Homo* has been on Earth is called the Paleolithic Era, or "Old Stone Age." It was followed by the Neolithic Era, or "New Stone Age," during which human beings practiced agriculture but still used stone implements rather than metal ones. Table 8-2 shows the approximate dates of the main archaeological periods.

Section 2 – The ice ages

Unlike most geological epochs, the Pleistocene was punctuated by a series of "ice ages," periods during which glaciation was far more extensive than it is now. The approximate dates of the last three major glacial periods are shown in Table 8-3. The last of these, the Würm, played a major role in human history (or rather, *prehistory*, since the Würm ended well before writing was invented). There were periods of less extreme cold during the Würm, one of which went from about 40 to 30 kya (the exact dates are disputed).

Not all parts of the Earth were equally affected by the ice ages. The glaciers were far more extensive in the northern hemisphere, and were less extensive in Siberia than in Europe and America. As can be seen from Map 8-1, at their greatest extent (about 18 kya) the glaciers covered much of northern Europe, including all of Scandinavia, most of Great Britain, and substantial parts of what is now Germany, Poland, and Russia. However, most parts of central and eastern Siberia (which at present are generally much colder than Western Europe) were ice-free.

TABLE 8-1
RECENT GEOLOGIC EPOCHS

Name	Approximate limits (in years before present)		
Pliocene Epoch	7,000,000	—	1,700,000
Pleistocene Epoch	1,700,000	—	10,000
Early (or Lower)	1,700,000	—	700,000
Middle	700,000	—	125,000
Late (or Upper)	125,000	—	10,000
Holocene Epoch	10,000	—	present

TABLE 8-2
SOME ARCHAEOLOGICAL PERIODS

Name	Approximate limits (in years before present)		
Paleolithic Era	2,500,000	—	10,000
Early (or Lower)	2,500,000	—	125,000
Middle	125,000	—	40,000
Late (or Upper)	40,000	—	10,000
Neolithic Era	10,000	—	5,000

TABLE 8-3
CHRONOLOGY OF ICE AGES

Name	Approximate limits (in years before present)		
Mindel	430,000	—	300,000
Riss	265,000	—	125,000
Würm	75,000	—	10,000

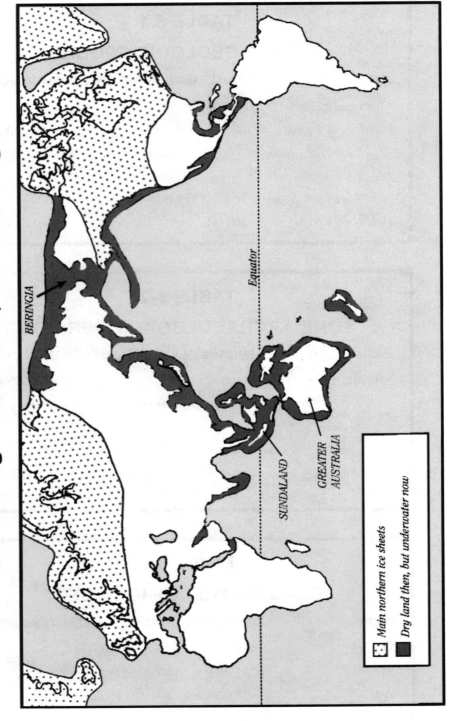

There were two main ice caps in North America. The principal one (the Laurentian ice sheet) covered all of eastern Canada, and the eastern half of the United States down to the latitude of New York City. In the west, there was a smaller ice cap (the Cordilleran ice sheet) centered on the great mountain ranges in Canada and the western United States. (Surprisingly, part of northern Alaska remained ice-free, even when southern Alaska and southern Canada were completely covered by ice.) During the coldest portions of the ice ages, the two large ice caps merged together to form an impenetrable wall of ice stretching from the Atlantic to the Pacific. However, when the glaciers receded a bit, an ice-free passageway — stretching from eastern Alaska into what is now the northern part of the Great Plains region of the United States — opened up between the two caps.[1]

Map 8-1 does not indicate the regions covered by low-latitude glaciers (such as those in and around the Himalayas); however, it does show the approximate extent of the regions covered by the large ice caps in high northern latitudes at the peak of the last ice age.

During the last ice age, so much of the Earth's water was tied up in glaciers that sea level was drastically lowered — indeed, by over 400 feet during the coldest periods. As a result, many regions now covered by shallow seas were dry land. In particular:

- What is now the Bering Sea was dry land. A broad, flat plain ("Beringia"), several hundred miles wide, connected Alaska to Siberia.

- Australia, New Guinea, and Tasmania were connected to each other to form a single landmass, which might be called "Greater Australia."

- Many of the Indonesian islands — including Sumatra, Java, and Borneo — were connected to each other and to Malaya to form the "Sundaland Peninsula" (or simply "Sundaland"), a large southeast extension of Asia.

- Japan was connected to the Asian mainland.

- The strait at the southern end of the Red Sea (the Bab el Mandeb) was dry land, making the Red Sea a long, narrow lake. As the Persian Gulf was also dry land, it was possible to walk along the coast of the Indian Ocean from Africa to India without having to cross any water.

- The Black Sea did not connect to the Mediterranean.

Note, however, that:

- Greater Australia and the Sundaland Peninsula were never connected to each other. There was always a stretch of open ocean between them, at no point less than 50 miles wide.

- The Strait of Gibraltar was always open; and at no point was there a land bridge across the Mediterranean.

- Madagascar was well-separated from any continent.

During the last ice age, large parts of the tropics were both drier and cooler than they are today. But the winters in the tropics were never *cold*: not in central and southern India, nor in Sundaland, nor in Brazil, nor anywhere in sub-Saharan Africa.

FOOTNOTES – CHAPTER 8

1) See Cavalli-Sforza, et al. (1994), pp. 304-305; and Fiedel, Stuart J. (1992), p. 47.

CHAPTER 9

LANGUAGES

Section 1 – The Italic languages

Linguistics — the study of human language — is a vast and complex field. For the purposes of this book, we are interested primarily in one branch of the subject, *comparative linguistics*, because it sheds light on the origins and migrations of various peoples, and on the historical connections between them.

The close relationship between Spanish and French, both in vocabulary and in grammar, is obvious to anyone with even a modest knowledge of them. Even closer is the resemblance between Spanish and Italian, and closer still is the similarity between Spanish and Portuguese. The reason for these similarities is well known. Each of those four languages is derived from ancient Latin — not the classical literary Latin, but rather the "vulgar Latin" of everyday discourse that was spoken during the heyday of the Roman Empire.

Languages are always changing; and it was common for some new word, usage, pronunciation, or idiom to originate in some part of the Roman Empire. As long as the Empire remained intact, with widespread trade between its provinces, any new word or usage that persisted would gradually spread throughout the Empire, so regional differences in Latin remained relatively small. However, after the fall of Rome trade between its former parts was greatly reduced, and the changes that occurred in the "Latin" spoken in one region did not readily spread to the others. Gradually, the dialects spoken in the various regions became unintelligible to the people living in other regions, eventually resulting in the separate but related languages we see today.

Similar processes have occurred in many other parts of the world. In general, whenever the regions in which a language is spoken lose contact with each other the language will fragment into separate dialects, and eventually into separate languages. The only unusual feature of Latin and its derivatives is that — because most of them were *written* languages — we are able to trace the whole process in far more detail than in most other cases.

The languages derived from vulgar Latin are called the *Romance* languages. (Among the other Romance languages are Rumanian, Sardinian, Catalan, and a few other tongues.) A slightly larger grouping, the *Italic* languages, includes the Romance languages, Latin itself, and some extinct relatives of ancient Latin.

Section 2 – The Indo-European family of languages

Another group of closely related languages includes Danish, Norwegian, Swedish, German, Dutch, English, and Icelandic. We call these *Germanic* languages. Presumably, they all derive from a common ancestor, usually referred to as "Proto-Germanic." Unlike Latin, however, Proto-Germanic was not a written language. As a result, we cannot trace the development of the Germanic languages in as much detail as we can the Romance languages.

Another well-known language group, the *Slavic* languages, includes Russian, Polish, Czech, Bulgarian, Serbo-Croatian, and a few others. In this case, the hypothetical ancestral language is called "Proto-Slavic."

A major breakthrough in comparative linguistics occurred in 1786 when the British scholar Sir William Jones gave a talk in which he stated that:

1) Most languages spoken in northern India — including Hindi, Bengali, Punjabi, and Gujarati — are related to each other. (Today, we call these the *Indic* group of languages.)

2) Just as the Romance languages are derived from Latin, the Indic languages are derived from ancient Sanskrit, the language in which the oldest and most sacred Hindu writings are written.

3) There are clear resemblances between the Indic languages and the Italic, Germanic, and Slavic languages.

4) It therefore appears that all of these are branches of a single large family of languages, usually called the *Indo-European* family. Some of the other members of that family are Greek, Armenian, and the Celtic languages.

The evidence in favor of Jones's hypotheses was overwhelming, and they soon became generally accepted. Today, no one disputes the existence of the Indo-European family, although there is some disagreement about how many branches we should divide it into. Table 9-1 shows the classification that will be used in this book.[1]

Jones's theory implies that there was once a language — generally called *Proto-Indo-European* (hereafter abbreviated *PIE*) that was ancestral to Greek, Latin, Sanskrit, Proto-Germanic, and the other Indo-European languages. Various attempts have been made to reconstruct *PIE*, and lists of Proto-Indo-European roots have been published. However, there is still a great deal of disagreement among scholars concerning just where and when *PIE* originated. (Those questions will be discussed in more detail in chapter 26.)

TABLE 9-1

BRANCHES OF THE INDO-EUROPEAN LANGUAGE FAMILY

Name	Number*	Principal languages in the branch
Italic	16	Latin(x); Italian; French; Spanish; Rumanian; Portuguese
Celtic	4	Gaelic; Welsh; Breton; Gaulish(x)
Germanic	12	English; German; Dutch; Danish; Swedish; Norwegian; Yiddish
Balto-Slavic	15	Russian; Ukrainian; Polish; Czech; Slovak; Bulgarian; Serbo-Croatian; Latvian; Lithuanian
Greek	2	Classical Greek(x); modern Greek
Albanian	1	Albanian
Armenian	1	Armenian
Anatolian	0	Hittite(x); Lydian(x); Lycian(x)
Tocharian	0	Tocharian A(x); Tocharian B(x)
Indo-Iranian	93	Hindi; Urdu; Bengali; Punjabi; Gujarati; Sanskrit(x); Nepali; Farsi (= Persian); Kurdish; Tajiki; Romany (= Gypsy); Scythian(x)

*   Number of languages in the branch that are still spoken today.
(x) Indicates that the language is extinct.

Note: Some scholars count Baltic and Slavic as two separate branches. Similarly, some divide Indo-Iranian into two branches.

Section 3 – The Afro-Asiatic language family

Although the Indo-European family is the largest family of languages known, it is not the only one. For example, the similarity between Hebrew and Arabic — neither of which is an Indo-European language — is obvious. Both of them are closely related to various extinct languages that were spoken in the Middle East in biblical times. These tongues are part of the *Semitic* group of languages.

In time, scholars realized that various other languages spoken in northern Africa are distantly related to the Semitic tongues. The large family that includes those languages and the Semitic ones is called the *Afro-Asiatic* family. Its main subgroups are:

1) The Semitic languages. One of these, Arabic, now accounts for more speakers than all the other Afro-Asiatic languages combined. Among the other members are Hebrew, Aramaic, Assyrian, Babylonian, Canaanite, Phoenician, and Syriac (most of which are now extinct). Amharic, the principal language of Ethiopia, is also a Semitic language.

2) The Berber languages. These are spoken in northwest Africa, and were the principal languages in that area before the Arab conquests of the seventh century AD. The group includes Riff and Kabyle (spoken in mountainous parts of Morocco and northern Algeria, respectively) and Tuareg (spoken by many tribesmen living in the Sahara Desert).

3) Ancient Egyptian. All these dialects are now extinct.

4) The Cushitic languages. These are spoken in Somalia, Ethiopia, and neighboring parts of East Africa.

5) The Omotic languages. These are spoken in parts of Ethiopia and Kenya.

6) The Chadic languages. There are over 120 of these, spoken by various Negro tribes living in the vicinity of Lake Chad.

Section 4 – The Sino-Tibetan language family

This family consists of two branches: Tibeto-Burman and Sinitic. Sinitic includes only twelve languages, but one of them is Mandarin Chinese, which has more native speakers (at least 800 million) than any other language in the world. Some of the other Sinitic (or Chinese) languages — such as Wu, Xiang, and Cantonese — each have tens of millions of speakers.

An interesting feature of the various Chinese tongues is that their *written* languages are identical to each other. Chinese writing does not employ an alphabet; rather, each Chinese character — there are thousands of them — represents an entire word. There have been many proposals made in China to adopt an alphabet, since this would make it much easier for children to learn to read and write. A major drawback of shifting to an alphabetic system of writing is that it would cause the written forms of the various Chinese languages to be mutually unintelligible, as the spoken forms already are.

All the Chinese languages involve tonality. That is, a given syllable can be spoken in any one of several different tones, and these tones differentiate between otherwise similar-sounding words. The result is not just a change in emphasis or mood: Words that otherwise sound the same, but have different tones, frequently have completely unrelated meanings and are represented by different written characters.

The Tibeto-Burman branch includes over 240 languages, most of which have only a small number of speakers. About a third of these are spoken in Tibet; the others are spoken in Burma or adjacent areas.

Section 5 – Other language families, and language isolates

There is still disagreement among experts as to just how many language families there are, and what names should be used for them. For purposes of this book, the list given in Table 9-2 (which is similar to that used by Ruhlen[2]) should suffice.

There are some languages that show no obvious resemblance to any other tongue. The most important of them are listed in Table 9-3. The two such *language isolates* with the largest number of speakers are Japanese and Korean. (Some scholars claim that those two languages are distantly related to each other; others go even further, and suggest that Japanese and Korean are both outlying members of the Altaic family. Neither hypothesis has won general acceptance.)

A celebrated language isolate is Basque, which is spoken by several hundred thousand persons living in southwest France and northern Spain. The Basque speakers are not recent intruders: Basque has been spoken in the region for at least two thousand years. It appears to be descended from a language spoken in the region before the Indo-Europeans arrived (see chapter 26). This makes it an oddity; all the other pre-Indo-European languages that were spoken in Spain, Portugal, France, England, and Germany have vanished without a trace. Many attempts have been made to prove a connection between Basque and other language families, but as yet none have been successful.

TABLE 9-2
LANGUAGE FAMILIES

Name used in this book	Other names used for the family	Number of languages	Millions of speakers	Main location of speakers	Some important member languages
Indo-European	Indo-Hittite	144	2,700	Europe & northern India	English; Hindi; Russian; Latin; Greek; Portuguese; Spanish; French; German
Sino-Tibetan		258	1,400	China	Mandarin Chinese; Cantonese; Wu
Niger-Congo	Niger-Khordofanian	1,064	500	sub-Saharan Africa	Zulu; Xhosa; Yoruba; Fulani; Swahili
Afro-Asiatic	Hamito-Semitic	241	350	North Africa; Southwest Asia	Arabic; Hebrew; Amharic; ancient Egyptian; Hausa
Austronesian		959	250	Indonesia; Pacific islands	Indonesian; Tagalog; Malagasy; Hawaiian
Dravidian	Elamo-Dravidian	28	250	southern India	Tamil; Telugu; Malayalam; Kannada
Altaic		63	140	Central Asia; Siberia	Turkish; Mongolian; Manchu
Austroasiatic		155	90	Vietnam; Cambodia	Vietnamese; Khmer (= Cambodian)
Daic		57	70	Thailand; Laos	Thai; Lao (= Laotian)

TABLE 9-2 (continued)
LANGUAGE FAMILIES

Name used in this book	Other names used for the family	Number of languages	Millions of speakers	Main location of speakers	Some important member languages
Uralic	Uralic-Yukaghir	24	23	northern Europe; northwest Asia	Hungarian; Finnish; Estonian; Lapp
Amerind		583	20	North & South America	Nahuatl (= Aztec); Quechua
Nilo-Saharan		138	20	Sahara; East Africa	Dinka; Songhai
Miao-Yao		4	7	Southeast Asia; southern China	Hmong
Caucasian		38	5	Caucasus	Georgian
Papuan	Indo-Pacific	731	3	New Guinea	
Na-Dene		34	0.2	western Canada; western USA	Navajo; Apache
Australian		170	0.1	Australia	
Khoisan		31	0.1	southwest Africa	
Eskimo-Aleut		9	0.08	northern Canada; Alaska	
Chukchi-Kamchatkan		5	0.02	extreme northeast Asia	

TABLE 9-3
LIST OF LANGUAGE ISOLATES

Name	Where Spoken	Number of Speakers
Japanese	Japan	126,000,000
Korean	Korea	78,000,000
Basque	Northern Spain and southwestern France	500,000
Burushaski	Kashmir (in northern India)	50,000
Gilyak	Mouth of Amur River (in Siberia); also, in the northern part of Sakhalin (a large island north of Japan)	4,000
Ket	Near the Yenisei River (in central Siberia)	1,000
Andamanese	Andaman Islands (in Indian Ocean)	1,000
Nahali	Central India	500
Ainu	Southern part of Sakhalin; also, on Hokkaido (the northernmost major island of Japan)	500
Tasmanian	Tasmania	(extinct)
Etruscan	Tuscany (in northern Italy)	(extinct)
Sumerian	Southern Mesopotamia (now in Iraq)	(extinct)

Notes:

Yukaghir (spoken in eastern Siberia) is sometimes listed as an isolate. However, the view that it is a distant branch of the Uralic family probably has majority support by now.

There are several unclassified languages in South America and in New Guinea, and some of them may turn out to be isolates.

Section 6 – Adoption of new languages

Most people are reluctant to abandon their native language. There are reasons why an individual might do so (for example: marriage, enslavement, or voluntary emigration), but under normal conditions an entire nation will not. We may take it as a general rule that *a nation living in its homeland will not abandon its language and adopt another unless it has been conquered.* Indeed, even conquered nations often retain their languages. For example:

(a) In the late 1700s, Poland was divided up between Austria, Russia, and Prussia. Although the Polish state ceased to exist, the Polish people refused to abandon their language, and they were still using it when Poland regained its independence at the end of World War I, more than a century later.

(b) The Spanish conquered the Incan Empire in the 1500s, and the Indians living there have never regained their political independence. Yet millions of them still speak native Indian languages.

Many other examples could be given. Indeed, it is hard to think of an instance in which a conquered people regained its independence fairly quickly, yet abandoned its language. We can conclude, therefore, that if a nation has abandoned its language it must have been conquered by some invader, and that its loss of independence either was permanent or continued for a lengthy period — at least a century, probably much longer.

FOOTNOTES – CHAPTER 9

1) The linguistic classification used in this chapter is similar (but not identical) to that suggested by Merritt Ruhlen in his book, *A Guide to the World's Languages, Volume 1: Classification* (1991). Another useful source is the article "Languages of the World" in Volume 22 of the *Encyclopaedia Britannica* (15th edition, 1986).

2) Ruhlen, Merritt (1991), op. cit.

CHAPTER 10

THE EXPANSION OUT OF SUB-SAHARAN AFRICA

Section 1 – Introduction

Homo sapiens sapiens — the human species — originated in sub-Saharan Africa sometime between 100 and 130 kya, and for many years thereafter almost all human beings lived in Africa. Eventually though, some of them migrated out of Africa, and by 13 kya humans had settled every continent except Antarctica. In this chapter, and the next three, I will present a general outline of that expansion.

Piecing the chronology together is like trying to solve a clever detective story. The evidence comes from linguistic studies, anthropometric information, archaeological finds, and genetic data. Because languages change so fast, the linguistic studies do not provide much information regarding the early stages of the expansion. Anthropometric data can be helpful, but can also be deceptive. The archaeological finds are very important; but they are scattered, and often have insecure dates. Consequently, the genetic data — deriving from DNA tests on various groups residing in different regions of the globe — is particularly useful in reconstructing this portion of human history.

Section 2 – Genetic data

Genetic data was in short supply until recently, but has become increasingly abundant and useful in the past three decades. A major source of such data is the monumental work by L.L. Cavalli-Sforza, Paolo Menozzi, and Alberto Piazza, *The History and Geography of Human Genes* (Princeton University Press, 1994), hereafter referred to as *HGHG*.

Not all genes are equally useful in determining the ancestry of a group, nor in deciding to which other groups it is closely related. Consider the genes responsible for light-colored skin. In high latitudes, these genes confer a selective advantage. Consequently, virtually all human groups whose ancestors lived in high latitudes for the past ten thousand years possess genes for light skin color, regardless of where their more distant ancestors came from. Such genes are therefore useless in determining the more remote ancestry of a group, or in deciding to which other groups it is closely related.

Consider, on the other hand, a mutation that consists of a slight change in the sequence of nucleotides within a gene, without creating any significant difference in the way the gene functions. Such a mutation, once introduced, can be transmitted from parent to child for tens of thousands of years. It can spread within an isolated group of humans, and it will be retained by that group (and its offshoots) regardless of where the group resides. Such a gene or allele, therefore, can provide information about the distant ancestry of a group and as to which other groups it is related.

In the first chapter of *HGHG*, the authors list 49 different genes whose distributions they have carefully studied and analyzed. (More precisely, they have studied the distributions of the various *alleles* of each of those genes in a wide variety of human groups.) Among the genes they list are those responsible for the production of various types of hemoglobin, immunoglobin, phosphoglucomutase, and peptidase, as well as the genes responsible for the various blood types in several well-studied blood group systems (including the ABO system, the MNS system, and the Duffy, Diego, Kell, and Kidd blood group systems).

The data presented in *HGHG* clearly shows substantial differences between the DNA of the inhabitants of different continents. These differences are only statistical. There are few, if any, alleles that are found on only one continent; nor are there many alleles that are completely absent on one continent although widespread on the others. However, the frequency of occurrence of various alleles varies markedly from one continent to another. By far the largest of these statistical differences in allele frequency are those between the inhabitants of sub-Saharan Africa and the inhabitants of the rest of the world (excluding recent migrants to or from Africa).

The investigations of Cavalli-Sforza and his associates also reveal considerable genetic variation within each continent. However, the magnitude of that variation is not the same on the different continents.[1] It is largest within Africa, smaller in Asia, even smaller in Australia, and smaller still within the Western Hemisphere. The reason for this is not difficult to see: Human beings have been residing in Africa for at least 100,000 years, during which time a large number of random mutations have occurred; humans have resided in the Western Hemisphere for less than 20,000 years, during which time many fewer mutations have occurred. The archaeological data leaves no doubt that Africa has been inhabited by humans far longer than South America has, but we could have reached the same conclusion merely by analyzing the genetic data from those two continents.

Section 3 – When did the expansion out of Africa occur?

Since *HSS* originated in sub-Saharan Africa, it is plain that the inhabitants of the other continents must be descended from people who migrated out of Africa, and it is plain that the early migrations occurred many thousands of years ago.

The earliest known human[2] settlements outside of Africa are those found in two caves in Israel (Skhul and Qafzeh). Scientific tests indicate that these caves were first settled around 92 kya,[3] and it is tempting to assume that it was those settlements which in time led to the peopling of Asia, Europe, and the other continents.

TABLE 10-1

OLDEST KNOWN HUMAN SITES IN VARIOUS REGIONS

Location	Date (kya)	Source	Comments
Bulgaria (Temnata)	46	Mellars[1]	TL dating[2]
Hungary	44	Mellars[1]	carbon-14 dating
Spain (northern)	40	Mellars[1]	carbon-14 dating
France (southwest)	36	Mellars[1]	carbon-14 dating
Indonesia (Borneo)	40	Fagan,[3] p. 114	Niah Cave
Southeast Asia (Thailand)	37	Fagan,[3] p. 115	Long Rongrien Cave
Australia (Jinmium)	75	Fullagar[4]	not generally accepted
Australia (southeast)	50	Bowler[5]	TL dating[2]
Australia (various places)	40	Jones,[6] p. 773	carbon-14 dating
New Guinea	40	Groube[7]	Huon Peninsula
China (Liujang)	67	*HGHG*,[8] p. 203	not generally accepted
China (northern)	29	Brown[9]	Zhoukoudian Cave
Siberia (northwest)	37	Pavlov[10]	northern Urals[11]
Siberia (southern)	32	Fagan,[3] p. 144	near Lake Baikal
Russia (north of Moscow)	28	Pavlov[10]	Sungir
Alaska (Bluefish Cave)	17	Kelly (1996)[12]	disputed
United States (Pennsylvania)	16	Adovasio[13]	Meadowcroft Rockshelter
Chile	14.5	Dillehay[14]	Monte Verde

1) Mellars, P.A. (1993), p. 203.
2) TL = thermoluminescence.
3) Fagan, Brian M. (2001).
4) Fullagar, Price, & Head (1996); they also give dates of 116 kya and 176 kya.
5) Bowler, J.A., et al. (2003).
6) Jones, Rhys (1989).
7) Groube, L., et al. (1986).
8) *The History and Geography of Human Genes*, by Cavalli-Sforza, et al. (1994).
9) Brown, Peter (1993).
10) Pavlov, P., et al. (2001).
11) Might be a Neanderthal site only.
12) The date given here is after calibration. Also see footnote 4 in chapter 12.
13) Adovasio, J.M., et al. (1999). I have calibrated their dates.
14) Dillehay, Thomas (2000). I have calibrated the date he gave.

However, there is no sign that the inhabitants of those caves ever spread out into other parts of the Middle East. On the contrary, no other human remains have been found in Southwest Asia — or anywhere else in the world outside of Africa — until much later.[4] Indeed, it seems possible that the human settlements at Skhul and Qafzeh died out around 74 kya when the climate became much colder.[5] On the other hand, it appears that Neanderthals — a group whom we know were strongly cold-adapted — were present in the Middle East subsequent to that date.[6]

From Table 10-1, it appears that no human sites outside of Africa can be clearly dated to the period between 80 and 50 kya. However, between 50 and 35 kya (and increasingly thereafter) there are clear signs of human habitation in widely separated parts of the Eastern Hemisphere. It therefore appears that the settlements at Skhul and Qafzeh were cul-de-sacs, leading nowhere, and that the main expansion of *HSS* out of Africa did not begin until long after those caves were settled. Since *HSS* reached Australia by about 50 kya, the migration out of Africa must have started several thousand years before that.

Section 4 – The R_0 and N_0 groups

The combination of the genetic and archaeological data mentioned above suggests that there was a period (perhaps about 62 kya) when several groups of humans living near the Red Sea migrated from Africa into Southwest Asia, and that their offspring eventually populated the rest of the world. I shall refer to those humans who migrated into Southwest Asia about then as the R_0 group, and to those who remained in Africa as the N_0 group. (N_0 = Negroid; R_0 = Rest-of-the-world.)

There have, of course, been other migrations from Africa to Asia since then. However, in those later migrations, the number of migrants was always very small compared to the number of persons already inhabiting Asia, and they therefore had only a slight effect on the Asian gene pool. The same was true of migrations back into Africa. Therefore, most of the Caucasoids, Mongoloids, and Australoids are descended primarily from the R_0 group, and most Negroids are descended primarily from the N_0 group.

Section 5 – The μ-group and the σ-group

The genetic data presented in *HGHG* shows clearly that within the R_0 group the greatest differences in DNA are found between two large subgroups:

a) A group that includes the Australian aborigines and related peoples; and

b) A considerably larger group that includes the Europeans, the residents of North Africa and the Middle East, the inhabitants of northern Asia, and the American Indians.[7]

This suggests that at some early stage, perhaps about 60 kya, the R_0 group divided into two subgroups. One migrated in the direction of Australia, while the other subgroup populated the Middle East, and from there spread out into Europe, Central Asia, northern Asia, and other regions.

64   *Understanding Human History*

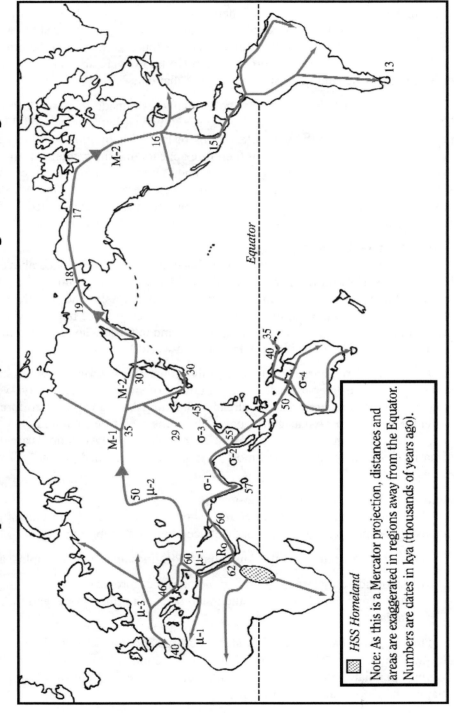

Map 10-1
The Spread of *HSS*, from 60 kya to 13 kya

Some authors refer to the first group as *Australoids*, because it includes the Australian aborigines. However, as relatively few members of that group reached Australia, or even got close to it, I shall instead refer to it as the *σ-group*. The other, larger subgroup will be referred to as the *μ-group*. (Note: The Greek letter σ ["sigma"] has been chosen as a mnemonic for the *Southern group*, while the letter μ ["mu"] has been chosen as a mnemonic for the *Main group*.)

In the course of time, descendants of the σ-group settled India, Southeast Asia, Indonesia, Australia, New Guinea, and parts of China. (They have since been partly displaced from some of those regions.) The descendants of the μ-group include the Caucasoids and the Mongoloids. (See Map 10-1 and Diagram 10-1.)

Section 6 – Replacement or hybridization?

The prevailing belief is that when *HSS* entered Europe, they displaced the Neanderthals who had been living there (perhaps by killing them off directly) with only a minor amount of hybridization between the two groups.[8] The question arises whether the same thing happened in other parts of the world when *HSS* entered.

Conquering peoples tend to look down on the groups they have conquered, often considering them to be vastly inferior, or even subhuman. Furthermore, because of the dual code of morality (see chapter 6) they are often quite willing to see the vanquished group die off. Because the earlier hominids that were displaced during the expansion of *HSS* did not have the full language skills that *HSS* possessed, the tendency to regard them as subhuman would have been even greater than usual.

Because many human males are willing to copulate with virtually any human female (indeed, anything that resembles a human female), a common result of conquest has been that the males of the defeated group are killed, but many females are kept alive for sexual purposes. The progeny of such matings ("half-breeds") are often not accepted as members of the conquering group. However, males of the dominant group will often copulate with female half-breeds; and after a few generations, hybrids whose ancestry is mostly from the dominant group are frequently accepted into it.

If that occurred during the expansion of *HSS* — as I suspect it did — the end result would have been that the earlier hominids were eliminated in each region, but with a small amount of hybridization occurring. In the process, the genes responsible for the conquerors' linguistic abilities would be strongly selected for and would be universally present in the final gene pool. But various genes that were possessed by the prior inhabitants — particularly those involving anatomical traits that were adaptive in the local environment — would also be selected for, and would be present in the resulting gene pool. Hence, we would expect that the *HSS* in each region will show some resemblances to the local hominids whom their ancestors had replaced.[9]

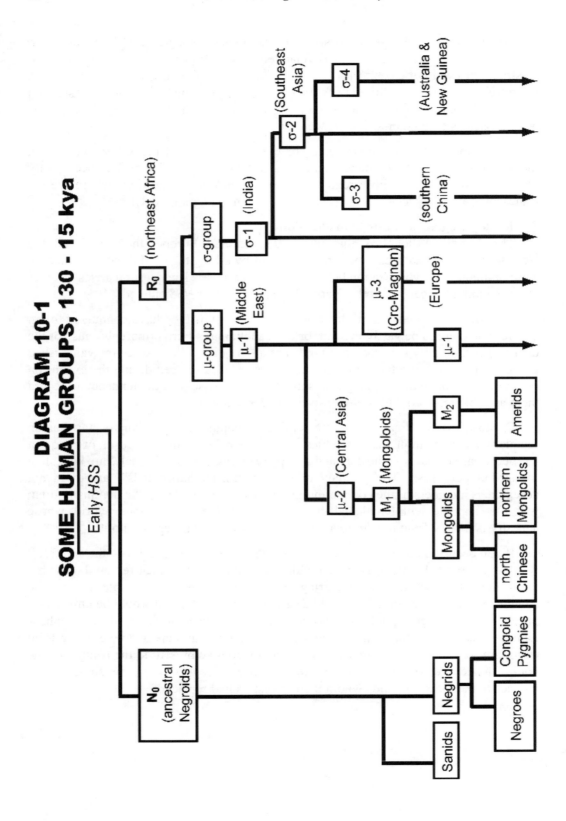

FOOTNOTES – CHAPTER 10

1) In table 2.3.1A, on p. 75 of Cavalli-Sforza, et al. (1994) the authors list the genetic distances between 42 different human populations. The largest difference within a single continent is found in Africa (2321 [in the units the authors used], between Berbers and Nilo-Saharans). In contrast, the largest genetic difference between groups within the Western Hemisphere is only 1072 (between Eskimos and South American Indians), and the largest listed within Europe is only 667 (between Lapps and Sardinians). The authors present similar data for Australia in table 7.6.1 (on p. 353), and the largest genetic difference they found between groups on that continent was 1154. See also Stringer & McKie (1996), pp. 129 and 183, and sources cited therein.

2) For the reasons given in section 4-4, the word "human" in this book refers only to *Homo sapiens sapiens*.

3) Valladas, H., et al. (1988). Also see Aitgen & Valladas (1993).

4) See Table 10-1 and the sources cited there. Also see Stringer & McKie (1996), p. 156.

5) Stringer & McKie (1996), p. 160.

6) For example, at Kebara, in Israel. See:
   (a) Bar-Yosef, O. (1989), p. 595.
   (b) Stringer & McKie (1996), p. 78.

7) Cavalli-Sforza, et al. (1994). See especially figures 2.3.2.A (p. 78) and 2.3.3 (p. 80).

8) (a) Zubrow, Ezra (1989), p. 212.
   (b) Stringer, Chris (1989), p. 241.
   (c) Diamond, Jared (1992), *The Third Chimpanzee*, p. 53.

9) Note that this shows that it is not necessary to invoke the discredited "multiregional" theory of the origin of *HSS* in order to explain morphological similarities between modern humans living in a given region and the archaic *Homo sapiens* that formerly inhabited that region.

CHAPTER 11

MIGRATIONS AND DIVISIONS OF THE σ-GROUP

Section 1 – The settling of Greater Australia

During the last ice age, when sea levels were lower, Australia, New Guinea, and Tasmania formed a single landmass (see Map 8-1), one which we might call *Greater Australia*. (It has also been called *Sahulland*.[1]) The archaeological evidence suggests that neither *Homo erectus* nor archaic *Homo sapiens* ever reached Greater Australia, and that it was uninhabited until *HSS* reached it about 50 kya.

How did humans reach Greater Australia? Certainly not by sailing directly across the Indian Ocean from Africa or the Middle East, since no boats remotely capable of such a voyage were built until much later. Nor could they have arrived from South America or New Zealand, as both of those were uninhabited at the time. The only plausible route is via Indonesia.

For much of the last ice age, most islands in western Indonesia were connected to each other and to the Asian mainland, forming a landmass which we might call the *Sundaland Peninsula*, or simply *Sundaland*. Sundaland and Greater Australia were several hundred miles apart and, although there were many islands in the sea between them, to get from Asia to Greater Australia required a trip across at least 50 miles of open ocean. A sea voyage of such length was a difficult feat; but those humans who succeeded in making the crossing found an untouched continent, one in which tropical or temperate climates prevailed.

How did members of the σ-group reach the Sundaland Peninsula? Obviously, from what is now mainland Southeast Asia, which is the land area closest to Indonesia, and which at the time would not have involved any overseas voyage.[2]

How had members of the σ-group reached Southeast Asia from the Middle East? Most probably, by a route going through India.[3] It is true that we have not uncovered any human remains in India that are older than the earliest Australian sites. However, the climate and soil in India are very humid and would have destroyed almost all human remains from those early times, so our failure to find such remains is not surprising. We conclude that the probable route of the σ-group (after it split off from the R_0-group) was eastward into India, thence to Southeast Asia, thence to Sundaland, and thence to Greater Australia. (Most others who have considered the question seem to have reached the same conclusion.[4])

Section 2 – The occupation of India (the σ-1 group)

A plausible chronology might go like this: At some early date, perhaps about 60 kya, some members of the R_0-group split off from the rest and migrated eastward. Eventually — either by moving along the northern coast of the Indian Ocean, or by going through the Middle East and Iran — some of them reached and settled India. I shall refer to the group which settled India as the σ-1 group.

Arabia and southern Iran were dry regions, and could not support a large population. However, when the σ-1 reached India they found a fertile land, with abundant game and edible plants. They settled there, and in time their population expanded. They had probably occupied much of India by about 57 kya, replacing any archaic *Homo sapiens* previously living there.

Section 3 – The effect of migrations on gene pools

In general, when a group migrates into a region that is already occupied, the number of immigrants is very small compared to the indigenous population, and the newcomers therefore have little effect on the resulting gene pool in the region. The immigrant group will have a large effect on that gene pool only if:

(a) the number of immigrants is large (i.e., not very much smaller than the number of natives); or

(b) the immigrants, although originally much less numerous than the natives, are (because of some special circumstance) able to expand much more rapidly than the natives, and eventually become comparable to or greater than the native population.

When the σ-1 first entered India, their numbers were probably much smaller than those of the hominids who were there before them. However — as in every case in which *HSS* expanded into regions previously occupied by archaic *Homo sapiens* or by *Homo erectus* — there was a special circumstance that enabled them to rapidly increase their numbers relative to the natives. That circumstance was the superior linguistic abilities of the *HSS*, which had a genetic basis and which gave them an overwhelming advantage over the earlier groups.

Aside from the original expansion of the *HSS*, there are many other instances in which an immigrant group became so numerous that it strongly affected the gene pool in the region they entered. In each such case, some special factor was present. For example, in many instances the immigrants possessed technology that gave them a great advantage over the natives. (This was an important factor in the formation of European colonies between 1500 and 1900.)

Section 4 – Southeast Asia, Sundaland, and southern China

Eventually, some of the σ-1 left India and migrated further eastward. By about 55 kya they had settled what is now mainland Southeast Asia, displacing any earlier hominids who had been living there. I shall refer to this group as the σ-2. By about 53 kya they had spread into the Sundaland Peninsula.

About 45 kya (or perhaps a bit earlier) some of the σ-2 migrated northward from Southeast Asia into southern China and settled there. I shall refer to their descendants as the σ-3. Although in recent millennia there have been substantial migrations of Mongoloids from northern China into the south, many of the people living in southern China today are of predominantly σ-3 parentage.

During the last ten thousand years there have been major migrations of the σ-3 back into Southeast Asia, and also into the Philippines, Indonesia, and other areas.[5] (Those migrations will be described in more detail in later chapters.) As a result, descendants of the σ-3 are today the most numerous branch of the σ-group.

Section 5 – The σ-4 group

About 50 kya, some of the σ-2 living on the east coast of the Sundaland Peninsula migrated to Greater Australia (or Sahulland).[6] I shall refer to these settlers and their descendants as the σ-4. Although there were probably several colonizing expeditions, the total number of migrants was quite small.

It seems likely that some of the σ-4 settled on the coast of northwest Australia. At first, they expanded by moving along the coast. They appear to have reached southwest Australia (near the modern city of Perth) by 38 kya, and Tasmania by 30 kya. However, much of the interior of Australia — a much drier and less hospitable region — was not occupied until about much later.[7]

The σ-4 who settled the northern part of Sahulland (i.e., what is now New Guinea) also appear to have first spread along the coast. They reached Bobongara (on the Huon Peninsula, near New Britain) by 40 kya; and by 26 kya some of them had settled in the interior highlands of New Guinea.[8]

New Britain and New Ireland – the two large islands in the Bismarck Archipelago, just north of New Guinea — were never connected to New Guinea by land, and additional ocean voyages were required for their settlement (about 60 miles to New Britain; and another 20 from there to New Ireland). Nevertheless, some σ-4 had settled New Britain by 35 kya, and New Ireland by 30 kya.

To reach the Solomon Islands, which are further east, required crossing at least 90 miles of open ocean. However, by 28 kya the σ-4 had managed to reach the nearest of the Solomon Islands,[9] and they eventually settled the entire chain.

Section 6 – Regions occupied by the σ-group today

In the last ten thousand years, there have been major incursions of Caucasoids into India. (Those incursions will be discussed in more detail in later chapters.) As a result, most of the present inhabitants of India are of mixed parentage, with the Caucasoid strain being predominant. Although virtually all living Indians have at least some σ-1 parentage, it is not clear that any individual is *primarily* of σ-1 descent.

Because of migrations of σ-3 from China back into Southeast Asia and Indonesia during the last ten thousand years, very few σ-2 remain. The Indonesians and Malays who now occupy most of the original σ-2 heartland are for the most part σ-2/σ-3 hybrids, with the σ-3 strain predominating, and with some admixture of north Chinese parentage as well. Although virtually all Indonesians and Malays have some σ-2 ancestry, most of them are descended primarily from σ-3. However, some of the Negrito groups living in the area — including the Semang (in Malaysia), the Andaman Islanders, and various small groups in the Philippines — are probably primarily of σ-2 descent.

When the Europeans first reached Australia, in early modern times, the aborigines they encountered there were nearly pure σ-4. In addition, the New Guinea highlanders are primarily σ-4, as are many residents of coastal New Guinea.

Today, by far the most numerous branch of the σ-group are the σ-3. Hundreds of millions of persons living in Indonesia, Southeast Asia, and southern China are primarily of σ-3 ancestry. In addition, many of the Pacific Islanders are primarily descended from the σ-3 group, with varying admixtures of σ-2, σ-4, and north Chinese ancestry. The original inhabitants of Madagascar were also σ-3, and their descendants still make up a large share of the population of that island.

FOOTNOTES – CHAPTER 11

1) Cavalli-Sforza, et al. (1994), p. 344.

2) See Diamond, Jared in *Guns, Germs, and Steel* (1999), p. 300.

3) See Map 10-1.

4) See, for example, Cavalli-Sforza & Cavalli-Sforza (1995), especially figure 5.5 on p. 122. Or also see Stringer & McKie (1996), figure 46 on p. 178.

5) See Diamond, Jared (1999), chapter 17 and p. 301.

6) For estimates of the date of human entrance into Australia see Table 10-1, and also
(a) Jones, Rhys (1989), and
(b) Bowler, J.M., et al. (2003).

7) See Jones, Rhys (1989), especially figure 35.1 on p. 757.

8) Jones, Rhys (1989), p. 757 and pp. 763-764. Also see Groube, L., et al. (1986).

9) Jones, Rhys (1989), p. 767. Also see Wickler & Spriggs (1988).

CHAPTER 12

MIGRATIONS AND DIVISIONS OF THE µ-GROUP

Section 1 – The origin of the Mongoloids

The genetic data indicates that the original µ-group was ancestral to the Caucasoids, the Asian Mongoloids, and the American Indians.[1] This chapter will attempt to outline that expansion, and present a rough chronology of it.

It is widely agreed that the American Indians (or Amerids) are much more closely related to the Asian Mongoloids (or Mongolids) than they are to any other group. The split between the Caucasoids and the Mongoloids must therefore have considerably preceded the division between the Mongolids and Amerids. The present geographical distribution of these groups suggests that the Caucasoids originated in the Middle East, and the Mongoloids originated in a much more easterly region. As the distinctive anatomical features of the Mongoloids are such as to adapt them to a very cold environment, it is usually conjectured that they evolved either in northern China or (more likely) in the region directly north of there — i.e., Mongolia and southern Siberia.

How did the Proto-Mongoloids reach that location from the Middle East? There seem to be four possible routes:

1) From the Middle East into southeastern Europe, thence into southern Russia, and thence across the Steppes to southern Siberia.

2) From the Middle East into Central Asia, and thence *north* of the Altai Mountains into southern Siberia and Mongolia.

3) From the Middle East into Central Asia, and from there *south* of the Altai Mountains into northern China.

4) From the Middle East into India and Southeast Asia, and from there into southern China, and then into northern China.

Route (1) is geographically plausible, but it is hard to make the dates fit. The objection to (3) is that typical Mongoloids are more cold-adapted than would be expected if the race had evolved in northern China. The same objection can be made to (4), with the additional problem that if it were correct we would expect there to be rather little genetic difference between the inhabitants of northern China and southern China, whereas in fact the observed differences are quite large.[2] Route (2) therefore seems the most probable one.

Section 2 – The expansions into Central Asia and Europe

It appears that by 55 kya the μ-group was firmly established in Egypt and the Middle East. From there, they gradually spread throughout North Africa and Iran, eliminating any remaining earlier hominids in the process. About 50 kya, a portion of the μ-group migrated into Central Asia (probably from Iran), replacing any earlier hominids that were there. I will refer to this group as the μ-2, and to those who remained in Southwest Asia and North Africa as the μ-1 group.

At about the same time, some of the μ-1 migrated from the Middle East into the Balkans. Although I will often refer to this group as the μ-3, they are more commonly referred to as the *Cro-Magnons*. The Cro-Magnons entered Bulgaria by 46 kya, and Hungary by 44 kya. They entered Western Europe by 40 kya, and had reached northern Russia by 30 kya.[3] The prior inhabitants of Europe (the Neanderthals) were not members of *HSS*, and they were replaced without much hybridization. Most Neanderthals were eliminated by 30 kya, although some small remnants lingered on for a few thousand years more.

Section 3 – The Caucasoid/Mongoloid split

By 40 kya, a group of the μ-2 in Central Asia had begun migrating north and northeast. I will refer to this group — the ancestors of the Mongoloids — as the *Proto-Mongoloids*. Eventually — probably about 35 kya — some of them reached southern Siberia (probably by moving along the northern flank of the Altai Mountains) and settled in a wide region around Lake Baikal. I shall refer to the people who settled in that area as the M-1 group.

Most of the μ-2 were not part of this migration. Of those who were not, some eventually migrated northwest, into southern Russia, where they mingled with the μ-3 that had entered Russia from the Balkans.

Section 4 – The pre-Amerindians, or M-2

Although it is generally agreed that the American Indians, or "Amerindians," are a branch of the Mongoloids, there are morphological differences between them and the Asian branch of the Mongoloids, the *Mongolids*. The Amerindians lack the "third eyelid" of the Mongolids; their faces appear less yellow (because they have less fat beneath the surface of their skins); and, in general, they are not as cold-adapted as the Mongolids. The simplest explanation for these differences is that the ancestors of the Amerindians split off from the Mongolids before becoming as markedly cold-adapted as the Mongolids are.

When did this split occur? I suggest that, although many of the early Mongoloids settled in Mongolia and southern Siberia, some of them continued migrating eastward.

About 30 kya, some of them reached and settled the coastal region bordering on the Pacific, a region that had a more moderate climate than the very cold continental climate of the area where the M-1 had originally settled. I shall refer to this group of Mongoloids — the ancestors of the *Amerids* (the racial group that includes most American Indians) — as the M-2 group. Since the M-1 and M-2 had been part of the same group for many thousands of years, the close resemblance between the two groups is not surprising.

The coastal region in which the M-2 settled included Japan, which in the last glacial era was directly connected to the Asian mainland. Since sea level was much lower then than it is now, significant parts of the region settled by the M-2 are now submerged beneath the Sea of Japan.

Subsequently, some of the M-2 migrated into northeast Siberia, including the territory that now makes up the Kamchatka and Chukchi peninsulas. By 18 kya, they had moved from there into *Beringia*, a broad landmass (now mostly under the Bering Strait) that connected Siberia and Alaska during the ice ages.

Section 5 – The settling of the New World

By 17 kya, some of the M-2 had settled in northern Alaska.[4] (They did not settle southern Alaska because it was entirely covered by glaciers at that time.) By 16 kya, some of the M-2 had made their way from Alaska to what is now the Great Plains region of the United States by traversing a narrow north-south passageway between the ice caps[5] (see section 8-2). From there, they spread rapidly eastward, westward, and southward. Their spread was particularly rapid because no other hominids had previously entered the Western Hemisphere. By 14.5 kya, the M-2 had spread as far south as Monte Verde, in central Chile,[6] and they reached the southernmost part of the Western Hemisphere, Tierra del Fuego, about 13 kya.[7]

Section 6 – Mongolid migrations into China, central Siberia, Korea, and Japan

About 29 kya, some of the M-1 migrated from Mongolia into northern China.[8] We may refer to those people — the ancestors of the north Chinese — as the *Southern Mongolids*, and the M-1 who stayed behind as the *Northern Mongolids*. As it is was difficult to travel directly across the Gobi Desert, the Southern Mongolids probably reached the North China Plain by way of Manchuria.

By 20 kya, some of the Northern Mongolids had migrated into central Siberia, and by 14 kya, some of them had even reached the shore of the Arctic Ocean at Berelekh.[9] Meanwhile, other Northern Mongolids were migrating eastward. By 13 kya, some of them had entered Korea and Japan, where they eventually displaced the M-2 who had previously been living there.

FOOTNOTES – CHAPTER 12

1) See Map 10-1. See also Cavalli-Sforza, et al. (1994), figure 2.3.2.A on p. 78.

2) On p. 225, of Cavalli-Sforza et al. (1994), the authors say: "North China and South China belong to different major clusters, thus confirming the suspicion that, despite millennia of common history and many migrations, a profound initial genetic difference between these two regions has been in part maintained." See also figures 2.3.2A (p. 78), 2.3.5 (p. 82), and 4.10.1 (p. 225) of that book.

3) See Table 10-1, and also page 203 of the article by Mellars, P.A. (1993).

4) So far, we have not unearthed any Alaskan sites that we can reliably say were occupied prior to 14.5 kya. (The date of 17 kya for Bluefish Cave is still disputed.) However, in view of dates of about 16 kya for Meadowcroft Rockshelter in Pennsylvania and for Cactus Hill in Virginia, it seems that the ancestors of the American Indians must have reached Alaska by 17 kya.

5) See Cavalli-Sforza, et al. (1994), figure 6.2.3 on p. 305. See also Fiedel, Stuart J. (1992), p. 47.

6) Dillehay, Thomas (2000), after calibrating his carbon-14 dates.

7) Fiedel, Stuart J. (1992), pp. xviii-xix.

8) Brown, Peter (1993), p. 217.

9) Cavalli-Sforza, et al. (1994), p. 305. According to a recent paper by Pitulko, et al. (2004), a settlement on the Yana River (only a few hundred miles west of Berelekh) was made as early as 27 kya.

CHAPTER 13

LOCATION OF HUMAN GROUPS 13,000 YEARS AGO

Section 1 – Introduction

By 13 kya, all the archaic forms of *Homo sapiens* (including the Neanderthals) were extinct, as were all forms of *Homo erectus*. Many parts of the Earth's surface were still uninhabited, including:

1) The desert and near-desert areas of the Earth.

2) The regions then covered by ice sheets. These included:
   (a) much of northern Europe, and adjacent parts of northwest Asia; and
   (b) most of Canada, and northerly parts of the United States.

3) High mountain areas, such as those in the center of Asia.

4) Madagascar, New Zealand, and Iceland.

5) Polynesia, Micronesia, and the eastern part of Melanesia.

6) Most of the small islands in the Atlantic and Indian Oceans, with the exception of those quite close to a continent.

Population densities were very low by modern standards. They were probably highest in tropical and semitropical regions such as India.

Section 2 – Africa

North Africa was occupied by μ-1, who had migrated there from Egypt and the Middle East, whereas sub-Saharan Africa was occupied by the Negroids, who were descended from the N_0-group. At some point — perhaps about 30 kya? — the Negroids had divided into two main subgroups: the N-1 (or Negrids) and the N-2 (or Sanids). Southern Africa was occupied by the Sanids; central and western Africa by the Negrids; and East Africa probably contained members of both groups.

Subsequently — perhaps about 20 kya? — the Negrids divided into two groups, the Negroes and the Congoid Pygmies (a small group confined to the rainforests of central Africa).

Map 13-1
Location of Human Groups 13,000 Years Ago

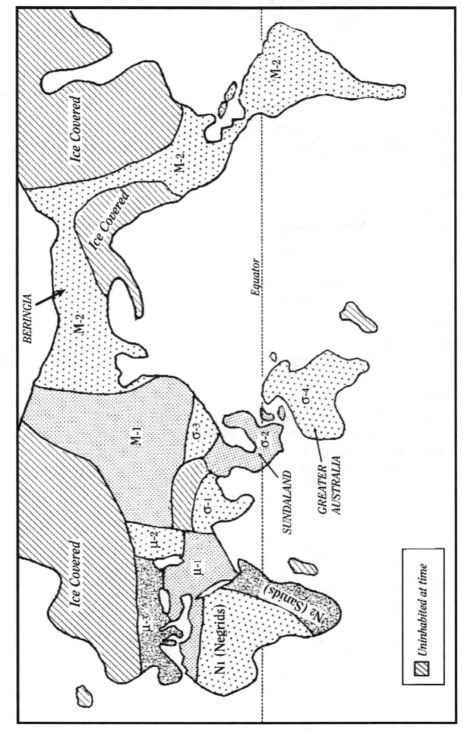

Section 3 – Europe, Asia, the Western Hemisphere, and Australia

With the exception of those areas covered by ice, most of Europe was already settled by 13 kya. The inhabitants of Europe were Caucasoids, descended from the Cro-Magnons, or μ-3.

Southwest Asia was occupied by the μ-1, who were also Caucasoids (although by then slightly different in appearance from the μ-3). Central Asia was inhabited by another Caucasoid group, the μ-2.

India was still inhabited by the σ-1. Southeast Asia, the Philippines, and the Sundaland Peninsula (which included most of what is now Indonesia) were inhabited by σ-2. Southern China was occupied by σ-3.

Much of Siberia was occupied by M-1, as were Japan, Korea, and northern China. Except for the very cold areas, most of the Western Hemisphere had been settled. The inhabitants, the Amerids, were part of the M-2 group.

Australia, New Guinea, and Tasmania were still part of a single landmass, and their inhabitants were all σ-4. Although the Bismarck Islands and the Solomon Islands (north and east of New Guinea, respectively) were not part of Greater Australia, they too were occupied by σ-4. The rest of Melanesia was uninhabited, as were Micronesia and Polynesia.

Section 4 – Location of racial groups compared with later ages

Map 13-1 shows the approximate locations of the main groups 13,000 years ago. Note that the Canadian ice sheets no longer extended all the way from the Atlantic to the Pacific, as they had 5000 years earlier (compare Map 8-1).

In general — with the important exceptions of India, Southeast Asia, and Indonesia — most regions of the Earth that were inhabited 13,000 years ago were still occupied by the same racial groups 11,000 years later. However, because of the events of the last two millennia, that is no longer the case.

CHAPTER 14

PHYSICAL DIFFERENCES BETWEEN THE RACES

Section 1 – How racial differences originated

Biologically speaking, human races are merely subspecies, formed by reproductive isolation of human groups, most commonly resulting from geographic separation. If two groups of the same species are separated geographically, and the two environments are different, then natural selection will cause the groups to diverge as each becomes better adapted to its own environment.

If the environments are very different, then group differences can evolve rapidly. However, even if the environments are similar, the two groups can still evolve differences through the process of genetic drift (see section 1-3).

In the interval from 60 kya to 13 kya, *HSS (Homo sapiens sapiens)* spread throughout most of the world. Because of the distances involved, humans living in different parts of the world were nearly isolated from each other during that period. Since the regions that *HSS* spread into had widely differing environments, all the conditions necessary for the evolution of group differences were present. Furthermore, the time intervals involved — tens of thousands of years — were quite adequate for the evolution of group differences, as we can see by simply looking at people living in different regions of the world today. In this portion of the book (chapters 14-18), I will mention some of the differences that arose between geographically isolated groups.

Some of the numerous ways in which racial groups differ physically are listed in Table 14-1. None of these differences hold for each and every individual; rather, they are statistical in nature. (For example, more Negroes than whites suffer from sickle-cell anemia; but not all Negroes do, and some whites do.)

Section 2 – Surface differences between racial groups

In general, these are the least important differences between the races, and I mention them first only because they are obvious, and they demonstrate incontestably that genetic differences exist.

TABLE 14-1

PHYSICAL DIFFERENCES BETWEEN RACES

- **A) Surface differences**
  - Skin color
  - Hair color
  - Shape of nose and lips
  - Shape of eyelids
  - Extent of body hair

- **B) Resistance and susceptibility to various diseases**
  - Sickle-cell anemia
  - Thalassemias
  - Malaria
  - Smallpox
  - Measles

- **C) Rate of physical maturation**
  - Age at which children can turn over
  - Age at which children can crawl
  - Age at which children can walk

- **D) Reproductive**
  - Frequency of dizygotic twins (fraternal twins)
  - Age at menarche
  - Gestation period

- **E) Body build**
  - Height
  - Stockiness
  - Density and weight
  - Fraction of quick-twitch muscle
  - Width of hips
  - Lung capacity

- **F) Miscellaneous**
  - Blood types
  - Lactose intolerance
  - Body odor
  - Brain size

The most frequently mentioned difference is skin color. (Note, however, that the other superficial differences are usually large enough so one can easily distinguish a European white from an African black from uncolored plaster busts.) The color of a person's skin is mainly due to the amount of melanin present. The standard explanation is that the typical skin color of a group is primarily an adaptation to climate. In the tropics, a dark skin helps to prevent damage from solar ultraviolet radiation, whereas in high latitudes, solar radiation is needed to help the body synthesize sufficient vitamin D.[1]

The correlation of skin color with latitude is indeed fairly high.[2] An apparent exception is provided by the Lapps who (despite living in the northernmost part of Europe) have darker skins than most other people living in northern Europe. The explanation is that the Lapps obtain adequate amounts of vitamin D from their diet, which includes a lot of seafood.[3]

Hair color is strongly correlated with skin color. This is not surprising, since dark hair is also caused by the presence of high levels of melanin. Most human beings have brown or black hair; the only groups in which blond hair is *common* are the fair-skinned peoples of northern Europe. Eye color is likewise correlated with skin and hair color. The only groups in which blue or green eyes are common are those in which blond hair is also common.[4]

Another feature that varies markedly between racial groups is the shape of the nose. Most Europeans have markedly protruding noses; in comparison, the noses of African Negroes often have a flattened appearance. The nostrils also differ between the two groups. Among European whites the orientation of the nostrils is usually more or less vertical, whereas among African blacks the orientation is comparatively horizontal.

Thick, everted lips are common among African Negroes. In comparison, most whites have thin lips. Thin lips might be an adaptation to climate, one that helps the body to retain heat.

Many Mongolids have a small fold of skin that covers the inner corner of the eye, and which gives them a "slant-eyed" appearance. It is obviously genetic in origin, and it may have evolved as a defense against cold.

Section 3 – Resistance to various diseases

The races differ markedly in life expectancy and in the incidence of various diseases. Some of those differences may well be due to poverty and other environmental factors. In some cases, however, it seems indisputable that genetic differences between the races are involved.

The best known example is sickle-cell anemia, a frequently fatal disease of genetic origin. The allele that causes sickle-cell anemia is recessive, so only those who inherit two copies of it are likely to get the disease. Curiously, persons who have one sickle-cell allele and one normal one frequently have greater resistance to malaria than those with two normal alleles. Because of this, in tropical regions where malaria is endemic the sickle-cell allele is preserved, and is indeed fairly common.[5] (Those regions include much of sub-Saharan Africa.) However, in groups that evolved in regions (such as northern Europe or America) where malaria is rare — because the mosquitoes that spread the disease do not thrive in cold climates — the sickle-cell allele is rare. American blacks live in a country where malaria is rare; however, many of them carry the sickle-cell allele, since their ancestors evolved in tropical Africa. The result is a large disparity between the number of American blacks and whites who suffer from this disease.

The incidence of certain hereditary anemias called *thalassemias* has a similar explanation. Each of these diseases is caused by a recessive allele. However, in many cases, possession of one copy of the "bad" allele and one copy of the normal one confers greater resistance to malaria. In regions where malaria is common, this permits the "bad" allele to remain in the gene pool, whereas in regions where malaria is uncommon, that allele is removed by natural selection.[6] The same thing occurs with various mutant forms of hemoglobin. As a result, the frequencies of all those alleles differ between the various races.

It is well known that smallpox, which had originated in the Old World, had a devastating effect on American Indians when they were first exposed to it. Most populations living in Europe, Asia, and Africa had gradually evolved some natural resistance to the disease, whereas the natives of the New World had not.[7] In similar fashion, measles — usually a minor disease in the Eastern Hemisphere, where significant natural resistance to it had gradually evolved — proved highly lethal in the Western Hemisphere.

Note that the genetic differences between the races in disease resistance frequently have lethal consequences. Hence, the claim that all racial differences are superficial and unimportant is clearly false.

Section 4 – Rate of physical maturation
In general, black children mature more rapidly than white children, and white children mature more rapidly than Mongoloids. Although black children in the USA are typically born about a week earlier than whites,[8] they are normally ahead of whites in bone development at birth. Differences in the rate of development of a variety of motor skills, beginning in infancy, have been observed and measured.[9] Black infants are able to hold their heads erect at an earlier age than whites, and when they are two months old they typically have better hand-eye coordination. On average, black infants turn over at an earlier age, crawl at an earlier age, and are able to remove their clothing at an earlier age than whites.

The physical superiority of black children over whites has also been measured and documented for five- and six-year-old children. Since black babies do not, on average, receive better prenatal care than whites, nor better medical care after birth, nor better diets, it seems clear that their physical precocity is due primarily to genetic factors.

Oriental infants are, on average, even slower to develop in these respects than whites are. The average age at which black babies first walk is about 11 months, whereas for whites it is about 12 months, and for Oriental babies about 13 months.[10]

Section 5 – Reproductive systems

The frequency of dizygotic (or "fraternal") twins differs greatly between racial groups,[11] as can be seen from Table 14-2. These differences are much greater than any plausible inaccuracies in the data, and are hard to explain by any differences in environment or upbringing. The frequencies of three-egg triplets and four-egg quadruplets show a similar progression, but with even more pronounced racial differences. (The frequency of identical twins is the same for all three groups.)

Studies show that the mean age at menarche of American whites has gone down substantially in the past two centuries, probably because of improvements in nutrition. Since whites have, on average, enjoyed better nutrition than blacks, we might expect that, on average, black girls would reach menarche at a later age than white girls. In fact, however, black females in America typically reach menarche at an *earlier* age than whites.[12] As it is not due to better nutrition or medical care, this racial difference is almost certainly due to genetic factors.

The significance of these racial differences will be discussed in chapter 18, where an evolutionary explanation of their origin will be offered.

Section 6 – Physique

Differences in the average height of various racial groups are sometimes very marked. Adult white males in Europe and the USA average over 69 inches in height, whereas among the African Pygmies adult males average only 60 inches, and only 57 inches for the shortest tribe, the Mbuti Pygmies.[13]

Groups who live in cold climates are, on average, stockier than those residing in warm climates. This is plainly an evolutionary adaptation that enables them to retain body heat. (The same phenomenon occurs among animal species.)

Studies show that American blacks typically have heavier bones than whites.[14] They also have slightly longer arms and legs.[15]

Human muscle fibers are not all the same. The two main classes are usually referred to as "fast-twitch" and "slow-twitch" fibers. Fast-twitch muscle fiber confers greater short-term speed and power; slow-twitch muscle is more useful for activities involving endurance. The fraction of a person's muscles that belongs to each class is affected by exercise and nutrition, but studies show that there is also a strong genetic component. Indeed, at least one of the specific genes involved has already been identified. Blacks typically have a higher fraction of fast-twitch muscle than whites.[16]

Section 7 – Width of hips

The laws of mechanics tell us that, in order to get the maximum benefit from a given thrust, the thrust should be precisely in the direction of the desired motion. Ideally, the thrust should be applied so that it goes directly through the center of mass

TABLE 14-2
FREQUENCY OF VARIOUS TYPES OF MULTIPLE BIRTHS*

	Two-egg twins*	Three-egg triplets*	Four-egg quadruplets*
Negroids	>16	0.7	0.06
Caucasoids	8	0.1	0.001
Mongoloids	< 4	0.01	negligible
Sources:	Bulmer (1970)	Allen (1987); Nylander (1975)	Allen (1987); Nylander (1975)

*Per thousand live births.

Note: The frequency of monozygotic twins (identical twins) is approximately the same for all groups, and is about 4 per thousand live births.

of the object or person being moved. If the thrust is applied off-center, then a portion of the thrust will be wasted. The wasted portion will create a torque that tends to turn the object, rather than propelling it forward (see Diagram 14-1). Note that the greater the angle θ is (in Diagram 14-1), the greater the fraction of the thrust that will be wasted.

When a person runs, some of the thrust of his legs is necessarily wasted, since each leg is offset slightly from his center of mass. This loss will be smaller if the person's hips are narrow — since that is equivalent to the points **E** and **G** in Diagram 14-1 being closer to each other (and to point **F**) — than if the person's hips are wide. This loss of thrust affects the speed at which a person can run. An important reason why men are typically faster runners than women is that, on average, men have narrower hips.

A well-documented difference between the races is that blacks, on average, have narrower hips than whites.[17] The probable origin of this difference between the races will be discussed in chapter 17.

Section 8 – Effect on athletic performance

In some fields, the superiority of black athletes is glaringly obvious. For example, although blacks comprise only 13% of the population of the United States, they account for 65% of the players in the National Football League and over 75% of professional basketball players.[18] American blacks are also markedly over-represented in boxing and in track. Blacks hold all the world records in sprinting; and every one of the 100 fastest times for the 100-meter dash was recorded by a black.[19]

The politically correct view is that all such racial differences in performance are due *entirely* to environmental factors. It is acknowledged that American blacks do not, on

DIAGRAM 14-1

ABCD is a solid object that you are trying to propel by applying a force. If the applied force is directed along the dashed line, directly through the object's center of mass, then the entire force will propel the object forward. If instead the force is exerted off center (at point **E**) it will create a torque that tends to rotate the object. In that case, the force can be divided into two components; one that creates the torque, and one that pushes on the center of mass, propelling the object forward (although not directly forward, but at an angle θ from the direction of the applied force.

The component creating the torque is proportional to the sine of angle θ. The other component (through the center of mass) is proportional to the cosine of angle θ. Note that if point **E** was further from **F**, the angle θ would be greater, and the fraction of the applied force used to propel the object forward would be smaller (since cosine θ decreases as θ increases).

Note also that if a *series* of thrusts are exerted, with the points of contact alternating between points **E** and **G** (equidistant from point **F**) the torques will cause the object to swivel back and forth while it moves forward. The larger the angle θ is, the larger will be the fraction of the applied force that causes swiveling, and is therefore wasted. To increase the efficiency, the distance between points **E** and **G** should be made smaller, thus making angle θ smaller.

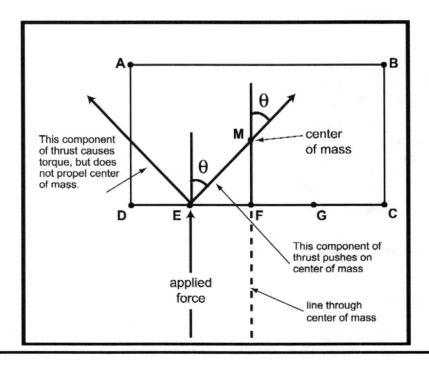

average, receive either better diets or better medical care than whites; so proponents of the official view usually claim that the difference is due to blacks being more motivated than whites to excel in sports. Two problems with this explanation are:

1) The pay received by successful athletes — not to mention the fame and adulation they receive — is quite sufficient to inspire enormous efforts by large numbers of young whites in the United States.

2) There is no direct evidence to support the assertion that aspiring white athletes do not train as hard as blacks, or try as hard in competition.

In any event, a simple counter-example shows conclusively that the politically correct view is wrong: African Pygmies are much shorter than American blacks or whites, and it is undisputed that this is due in large part to genetic factors. Does *anyone* believe that if Pygmies were given as much training and practice in playing basketball as American blacks (or whites) they would be as well represented in the National Basketball Association? Or that they could play volleyball as well? Or that Bushmen (whose average height is about four inches less than American blacks) could play basketball as well as American blacks if they were as well motivated? Clearly, then, the notion that racial differences in athletic performance are entirely due to environmental factors cannot be correct.

Among the specific physical advantages that blacks (on average) have over whites, and that lead to their superior performance are:

- Narrower hips.
- More fast-twitch muscle.
- Thicker, stronger bones.
- Relatively longer arms and legs.
- Less body fat.[20]

As a result of these (largely genetic) advantages, blacks hold all the world sprinting records, and many of the long distance records as well.[21] Blacks are also far superior in the vertical leap.[22] Only a few white athletes have been able to make vertical leaps of as much as 36 inches, but many blacks have surpassed that figure. Indeed, Darrell Griffith — a former NBA player, whose nickname was "Dr. Dunkenstein" — once leaped an astonishing 48 inches![23]

In professional football, sprinting speed and jumping ability are absolutely crucial for wide receivers and defensive backs, and those positions are almost entirely black. One can be a successful running back without great jumping ability, but leg thrust is crucial, so that position too is dominated by blacks. On the other hand those abilities are not very important for place kickers, punters, or offensive lineman, and there are many whites in those positions. Black quarterbacks are typically stronger and faster runners than most of their white counterparts; nevertheless, whites are better represented at quarterback than they are at most other positions, perhaps because intelligence plays a greater role in that position than in any other.

Foot speed and jumping ability are crucial in basketball, and black players dominate that sport. In baseball, speed is needed for outfielders (most of whom are black), but not for pitchers and catchers (most of whom are white). Sprinting speed and jumping ability are not needed in golf, bowling, billiards, and swimming, and there are few black champions in those fields.

In fact, the greater bone density of blacks is a decided *disadvantage* in swimming, and blacks are greatly under-represented there. Blacks hold virtually none of the world swimming records, and few American blacks have ever qualified even for the tryouts for the United States Olympic swimming team.[24] This is not because of any lack of motivation or effort; it is simply that the greater bone density of blacks keeps them lower in the water, which greatly increases the water resistance and thereby slows them down.

Section 9 – Miscellaneous differences

The incidence of the various blood types varies greatly between different human groups. For example, about 24% of the population of India has type B blood, but only 13% of sub-Saharan Africans, 8% of Europeans, 2% of Australian aborigines, and less than half a percent of South American Indians do. About 27% of Europeans have type A blood, as do 26% of East Asians, but only 1% of South American Indians.[25]

These differences may have arisen because the degree of resistance to certain serious diseases depends upon one's blood type. For example, people with type O blood seem to be more resistant to syphilis, but are considerably more susceptible to gastric and duodenal ulcers, whereas those with type AB blood are markedly more resistant to cholera.[26]

In addition to the ABO system, there are various other blood groupings (such as MNS, Duffy, Diego, and Rh factor). The blood types within each of those groupings are also unevenly distributed among the races. For example, type S blood is fairly common in Europe and Africa, and is possessed by 57% of the population of Central Asia, but is extremely rare among Australian aborigines.[27]

Although almost all human babies can digest lactose (a sugar common in milk), many adults cannot. The ability of adults to digest lactose — which depends upon a single gene — is more common among whites than among blacks. The gene involved was probably a mutation that proved advantageous among pastoral peoples.[28]

The characteristic body odor of African blacks appears to be primarily due to secretions by glands in the armpits. (Of course, individuals can also have odors that are due to their diet or habits, but the distinctive odor of blacks is plainly genetic.) European whites also have a characteristic odor (a different one than blacks) which some members of other races find strong and unpleasant. Mongoloids have relatively little body odor.[29]

The incidence of myopia (nearsightedness) differs significantly between racial groups. Chinese and Japanese have the highest rates (roughly twice the rate found among whites), whereas the incidence among blacks is much lower than among whites. Myopia is also far more common among Jews than it is among other European whites.[30]

Last, but not least, are the differences in average cranial capacity and brain size between various racial groups. In general, Mongoloids have slightly larger brains than Europeans do, and blacks have much smaller brains than either. Racial differences in cranial capacity were measured by Samuel Morton over 150 years ago.[31] However, in his influential book, *The Mismeasure of Man*, Stephen Gould insisted that because of Morton's unconscious bias his measurements were incorrect. As a result of Gould's assertions, many people think that there are no significant racial differences in brain size. However:

1) In 1988, John S. Michael remeasured the same skulls used by Morton and concluded that Morton's work had been well done.[32]

2) Gould's *own* measurements of Morton's skulls showed substantial racial differences in average cranial capacity (87 cubic inches for Mongoloids and modern Caucasoids versus only 83 cubic inches for Negroes).[33]

In any event, more recent data — obtained from large samples, involving many thousands of individuals — show substantial racial differences. The exact figures depend on whether one: (a) measures the endocranial volume of skulls, or (b) measures the weight of brains in autopsies, or (c) estimates brain size from external head measurements of living persons, or (d) estimates brain sizes from MRI studies. However, all methods show that, on average, blacks have substantially smaller brains than whites or Mongoloids. Averaging across the various methods (and the two sexes) gives these estimates for average adult brain size:[34]

Mongoloids	1364 cc
Caucasoids	1347 cc
Negroids	1267 cc

Section 10 – Summary and conclusions

Racial differences in physical traits are real, widespread, and often of great importance. Contrary to the claim of some ideologues, physical differences between the races are not confined to a few "superficial" traits. On the contrary, differences between racial groups include resistance to various diseases, and also appear in a wide variety of physical traits and systems, including the reproductive system, the bones, the eyes, the muscles, and the blood. Nor are the observed genetic differences without importance; on the contrary, some of the differences have large — even lethal — consequences.

FOOTNOTES – CHAPTER 14

1) Cavalli-Sforza et al. (1994), p. 145. Also see Loomis, W.F. (1967), and Stringer & McKie (1996), pp. 67-68.

2) Cavalli-Sforza, et al. (1994), figure 2.13.4 on p. 145.

3) Cavalli-Sforza, et al. (1994), pp. 266-267.

4) Cavalli-Sforza, et al. (1994), p. 266.

5) (a) Ridley, Matt (2000), p. 141.
   (b) Cavalli-Sforza, et al. (1994), p. 12.
   (c) Cavalli-Sforza (2000), pp. 48-49.

6) Cavalli-Sforza, et al. (1994), pp. 149-152.

7) McNeill, William H. (1976), chapter V, particularly pp. 215-217.

8) (a) Niswander & Gordon (1972).
   (b) Papiernik, et al. (1986).

9) (a) Geber, M. (1958).
   (b) Bayley, Nancy (1965).
   (c) Malina, Robert M. (1988).
   (d) Rushton, J.P. (1997), pp. 147-150.

10) Rushton, J.P. (1997), p. 149.

11) (a) Bulmer, M.G. (1970).
    (b) Rushton, J.P. (1997), p. 165.

12) Eveleth & Tanner (1976). Also see Rushton, J.P. (1997), p. 150.

13) Cavalli-Sforza, et al. (1994), pp. 167-168.

14) (a) Garn, S.M. (1963).
    (b) Jordan, J. (1969).
    (c) Heaney, R.P. (1995).
    (d) Wright, N.M., et al. (1995).

15) (a) Metheny, Eleanor (1939).
    (b) Jordan, J. (1969).
    (c) Himes, John H. (1988).

16) (a) Ama, et al. (1986).
    (b) Levesque, et al. (1994).
    (c) Entine, Jon (2000), pp. 253-256.

17) (a) Metheny, Eleanor (1939).
    (b) Jordan, J. (1969).
    (c) Himes, John H. (1988).

18) Entine, Jon (2000), p. 19.

19) Entine, Jon (2000), pp. 30-35.

20) (a) Metheny, Eleanor (1939).
    (b) Jordan, J. (1969).
    (c) Himes, John H. (1988).

21) Entine, Jon (2000), chapter 4, especially pp. 34-42.

22) A "vertical leap" is a jump taken from a standing start. In the common "Sargent test," the leap is measured by the highest point reached by the subject's outstretched fingers (with his arm raised over his head) less the corresponding height when the subject is standing.

23) Entine, Jon (2000), p. 252.

24) Entine, Jon (2000), pp. 282-283.

25) Cavalli-Sforza, et al. (1994), pp. 126-127 (see figure 2.10.2).

26) (a) Cavalli-Sforza, et al. (1994), pp. 126-129.
    (b) Ridley, Matt (2000), p. 140.

27) Cavalli-Sforza, et al. (1994), pp. 126-128 (see figure 2.10.2).

28) (a) Holden & Mace (1997).
    (b) Ridley, Matt (2000), pp. 192-194.

29) Baker, John P. (1981), pp. 172-177, and sources cited therein.

30) (a) Post, R.H. (1982).
    (b) Jensen, Arthur (1997), pp. 149-150 and 487-488.

31) Morton, Samuel G. (1849).

32) Michael, John S. (1988).

33) *The Mismeasure of Man* (revised edition, 1996), see Table 2.5. Note that the racial difference that Gould found amounts to over 4.5% of mean brain size, and leads to an average difference of several hundred million neurons between blacks and whites. (Gould was perhaps the best known, most prestigious, and most influential scientist advocating the view that there is *no* genetic difference in the average intelligence of whites and blacks.)

34) (a) Rushton, J.P. (1997), pp. 113-133 (especially p. 131) and sources cited therein.
    (b) Jensen, Arthur (1998), pp. 437-443 and sources cited therein.

CHAPTER 15

RACIAL DIFFERENCES IN INTELLIGENCE

Section 1 – Introduction

The general question of possible racial differences in intelligence has been the cause of much controversy. Two important aspects of this question are:

1) Are there differences in the average intelligence of various racial groups?

2) If so, what is the cause of those differences? In particular, are they entirely due to environmental influences such as diet, education, and child-rearing practices, or are they due in part to genetic factors?

However, before discussing those two questions, there is a preliminary point to address: Is it proper — or even acceptable — to discuss such matters?

Section 2 – Is the existence of racial differences in intelligence a moral question?

Many people seem to think so. They loudly proclaim that the belief that there are racial differences in intelligence is racist and profoundly immoral, and often denounce those who hold that belief as "Nazis."

I would suggest, however, that the existence of racial differences in intelligence is not a *moral* question at all, but merely a *factual* question. Such differences (if they exist) are merely facts of nature; as such, they may be unfortunate, but cannot be immoral. Plainly, if such differences actually exist it is not immoral to believe that they exist, nor to honestly state one's belief that they exist, nor to study the differences. And even if the differences do not exist, a belief that they do (if honestly held) is not immoral, nor is a serious inquiry into the question immoral.

The attempt to turn factual questions into moral questions is the essence of dogmatism, and has long been a hindrance to scientific progress. A well-known example involves the conviction of Galileo by the Inquisition in 1633. The members of the court that condemned him were turning a factual question ("Does the Earth revolve about the Sun?") into a moral question ("Is such a belief contrary to scripture, and therefore heretical?").

Section 3 – IQ data: Blacks and whites in the United States

The most direct evidence of racial differences in intelligence is provided by the results of intelligence tests given to Americans in the course of the 20th century. One factor that makes this evidence so convincing is the enormous size of the sample — hundreds of thousands of persons have been tested — which minimizes the likelihood of mistakes arising from random statistical errors.

Note that I am talking about statistical differences only. I am **NOT** suggesting that every black is less intelligent than every white. To emphasize this point, in referring to racial differences in this book I have repeatedly used terms such as "on average." Even where such terms are not explicitly used, they are omitted only for brevity, and not because I believe that *all* blacks — or all members of any other racial group — have low intelligence.

Some people have claimed that the difference in test scores is due to the tests being biased against blacks. However, the question of test bias has been analyzed carefully, and in the opinion of experts in the field the amount of bias in modern IQ tests is very small and cannot account for any substantial part of the difference between the test scores of whites and blacks.[1]

The first large data set that bears on the question of racial differences in intelligence came from the aptitude tests given to recruits by the US Army during World War I. Several different tests were used, but all revealed large differences in the average intelligence of American blacks and whites.[2]

Even more convincing evidence of large differences in mean intelligence between the two groups was compiled by Audrey Shuey in her book *The Testing of Negro Intelligence* (1958, 1966). In the latter edition, Professor Shuey described 380 separate studies that had been conducted, all based on actual test data. Some of the studies involved grade school children; others involved high school students, college students, the general adult population, prison inmates, and army recruits. All showed a sizable difference between the average intelligence of the two races, typically of the order of one standard deviation, which is about 15 points on standard IQ tests.

The well-known "Coleman Report," which was also issued in 1966, reached the same conclusion: "At the end of 12 years of school...Negroes' averages tend to be about one standard deviation below those of the whites."[3]

Many other studies have been made since then, utilizing a variety of intelligence tests. Although the studies differ, virtually all show a large difference between the average scores of American blacks and whites, with the differences clustering around one standard deviation. A few of those studies, including several of the largest ones, are listed in Table 15-1.[4] It is worth remarking, though, that those studies (like most others) probably underestimate the true value of δ (where δ is defined as the difference between the mean IQ of American whites of European descent and the mean IQ of American blacks). At least two factors contribute to this:

1) Many such studies include only students who are attending school, and omit high school dropouts. This factor causes us to overestimate average IQs. As proportionally more blacks than whites drop out of high school, the effect is to reduce the measured value of δ.[5]

2) Almost all such studies omit the prison population. Since prisoners, on average, have much lower IQs than the public at large, omitting them has the effect of overestimating the average IQ of every racial group in the United States. Since about 3% of American blacks are prisoners (but less than ½ of 1% of whites), omitting this factor leads to underestimating δ.

Even if we choose to ignore the effects just mentioned, the existence of a large gap between the IQ scores of American whites and blacks, and the approximate size of that gap, is clear. A report issued in 1982 by the prestigious National Academy of Science concluded that: "Many studies have shown that members of some minority groups tend to score lower on a variety of commonly used ability tests than do members of the white majority.... The roughly one-standard-deviation difference in average test scores between black and white students in this country found by Coleman ... is typical of results of other studies."[6] A subsequent NAS study came to the same conclusion.

The evidence is so overwhelming that even scholars who stoutly maintain that environmental factors can completely explain the difference in test scores between the two groups admit that the difference exists. For example:

a) In a major scholarly work, *The Black-White Test Score Gap*, the editors (Christopher Jencks & Meredith Phillips) insist that the gap can be explained by differences in upbringing and environment, but they agree that the gap actually exists.[7]

b) The highly respected Sandra Scarr stated explicitly that "Mean differences in IQ scores between racial, ethnic, and social-class groups are too well known to be restated at any length.... Briefly, there is often found an average difference of 10 to 20 points on IQ tests between black and white samples."[8]

Note again that this does **NOT** imply that no American blacks are highly intelligent and capable. On the contrary, from what I have said it follows that there are about 800,000 American blacks with IQs greater than 115, of whom about 50,000 have IQs in excess of 130.[9] These are large numbers, and they explain why — despite the low *average* IQ of blacks — we frequently encounter *individual* blacks who are performing very capably in intellectually challenging occupations.

Section 4 – Is the gap narrowing?

An interesting question is whether δ has been getting smaller, as suggested by Hedges & Nowell (1998).[10] They reached that conclusion by considering the studies listed on the first 6 lines of Table 15-1. As all those studies were confined to high school seniors (and omitted dropouts) the test sample is unrepresentative of American blacks, and probably underestimates δ.

If we instead consider *all* the entries in Table 15-1, the best fit to the data (using the standard linear regression method) is:

$$\delta = 16.9 - (\text{date} - 1917) / 30$$

which indicates that δ had decreased at an average rate of about one IQ point per 30 years. This suggests that δ was about 14½ points in 1992, and that if the trend had continued then δ would be about 14 points by 2007. However, subsequent data suggests that the black-white gap did not continue to fall after 1990, but instead has risen slightly.[11]

It should also be noted that in the pre-1946 studies, δ meant the difference between blacks and *European* whites (since, at the time, there were very few non-European whites in the country). Most of the later studies, though, include many non-European whites and mestizos in the white sample. Since these groups have average IQs about 10 points less than European whites (see section 7, below), in order to make the recent studies comparable to the early ones — which is necessary, if we want to accurately measure black improvement relative to European whites — we should probably add about a point to the recent white figures, and therefore to δ. We conclude that:

1) δ was probably about 17 points in 1917.

2) δ appears to have declined somewhat by 1992.

3) The exact value of δ in 1992 is uncertain. It was probably about 14 points, but may well have been a bit higher.

4) It is probably about 15 points today.

Section 5 – IQ data: African blacks

Many studies have been made of the intelligence of African blacks, using a wide variety of standard IQ tests. Results are available from at least 15 countries in sub-Saharan Africa (see Table 15-2).[12] It is prudent, of course, not to rely too heavily on the results of any one study, or of the studies conducted by any single investigator. However, the 28 studies listed in Table 15-2 were conducted independently by many different researchers, and therefore do not depend on the idiosyncrasies of any individual scholar. Furthermore, the tests span a period of several decades, and the samples include children of various ages as well as adults. Although some of the individual studies involved small samples, the combined sample size — more than 15,000 individuals were tested — is large enough to insure that the statistical probability of a serious sampling error is quite low.

The results are striking: From column 4 in Table 15-2 we can see that the average IQ of blacks in sub-Saharan Africa is about 70, or even less. (Taking the median of the studies instead of their average would produce an even lower result.) The last column in Table 15-2 shows the results of adjustments to the raw scores made by Lynn & Vanhanen (2002) in an attempt to compensate for the Flynn effect. As you can see, those adjustments have little effect on the overall average.

Section 6 – IQ data: Mongolids

Some studies of Japanese IQs are shown in Table 15-3. Unfortunately, none of those studies included any adults. Although Lynn & Vanhanen[13] estimated the average IQ of Japanese to be 105, I think that 102 would be a somewhat better estimate (see note [e] in Table 15-3).

The data regarding the IQs of Chinese is less clear, partly because of the paucity of studies, and partly because those we have are not representative of the Chinese population. (Most of the people tested came from big cities; and studies in Europe and America show substantial rural/urban differences.)

After a detailed analysis (that included corrections for standardization and the Flynn effect), Lynn and Vanhanen concluded that tests given within China indicate a mean IQ of 100 there.[14] The scores of Chinese in Taiwan, Singapore, and Hong Kong are much higher (105, 110, and 113 respectively according to Rushton; 104, 107.5, and 107 with Lynn & Vanhanen's adjustments). However, as the population of those territories is so much smaller than that of China itself, the high scores of Chinese living in those territories do not greatly affect the overall Chinese average. (The higher scores of the Chinese living in Singapore, Taiwan, and Hong Kong are probably a consequence of selective migration in the past.)

Two studies of IQs in South Korea indicate that the average is even higher there: 106, according to the analysis of Lynn & Vanhanen (2002).[15]

It is worth noting that although Mongolids typically do somewhat better on IQ tests than European and American whites, the difference is due entirely to the Mongolids' superior performance on those sections of the tests that deal with spatial relations.[16] On the sections measuring verbal skills, Mongolids score no higher — and perhaps even a bit lower — than European and American whites.

Section 7 – IQ data: Other groups

IQ averages from 22 European countries are given in Table 15-4. Most of them are fairly close to the US average, and to each other. (The standard deviation of the 22 numbers in the last column is only 3 points.) Nevertheless, inspection of the table makes it obvious that, on average, IQ scores are higher in northern than in southern Europe. Indeed, the correlation between the latitude of a nation's capital and the mean IQ of its inhabitants turns out to be significant ($r = 0.35$).

As can be seen from Table 15-5, the IQ scores of American Indians are, on average, lower than the scores of American or European whites, but well above those of American blacks. Like Asian Mongoloids (to whom they are related), American Indians generally do considerably better on tests of spatial relations than on tests of verbal abilities.

TABLE 15-1

BLACK-WHITE TEST-SCORE GAP IN USA

Year	Test used	δ	Source	Notes
1965	EEO survey	18	Hedges & Nowell (1998)	a, f
1972	NLS	17	Hedges & Nowell (1998)	b, f
1980	HSB, 1980	14	Hedges & Nowell (1998)	c, f
1980	NLSY	17	Hedges & Nowell (1998)	d, f
1982	HSB, 1982	14	Hedges & Nowell (1998)	c, f
1992	NELS	12	Hedges & Nowell (1998)	e, f
1922-44	various	13	Shuey (1966)	g
1945-66	various	16	Shuey (1966)	g
1917-18	AFAB	17	Loehlin (1975), Table 6.2	h
1944-45	AGCT	19	Jensen (1998), p. 376	i
1970	Wonderlic	14	Gottfredson (2004), Table 1	j
1983	Wonderlic	14	Gottfredson (2004), Table 1	j
1992	Wonderlic	13	Gottfredson (2004), Table 1	j
1974	WISC-R	16	Jensen & Reynolds (1982), p. 425	k
1981	WAIS-R	15	Reynolds, et al. (1987), pp. 327, 330	l
1991	WISC-III	15	Sattler (2001), p. 23	
1988	Stanford-Binet	14	Montie & Fagan (1988), pp. 321, 324	
Average (unweighted) =		**15.2**		

a) From the Coleman Report (*Equality of Educational Opportunity*), Coleman, et al. (1966).

b) *National Longitudinal Study of the High School Class of 1972.*

c) *High School and Beyond* survey.

d) *National Longitudinal Survey of Youth* (using the Armed Services Vocational Aptitude Battery).

e) *National Education Longitudinal Study.*

f) The data listed on these lines includes high school seniors only. They are the studies cited and described in chapter 5 ("Test score convergence since 1965") of *The Black-White Test Score Gap* (editors: C. Jencks & M. Phillips). See table 5-1, p. 154.

g) Average of many tests reported by Shuey (1966), summarized in Gottfredson (2004), Table 1. Shuey's book (*The Testing of Negro Intelligence*) lists about 380 studies.

h) Armed Forces Aptitude Battery (given to WW I recruits).

i) Army General Classification Test (given to WW II recruits).

j) Wonderlic Personnel Test (given to job applicants).

k) WISC = Wechsler Intelligence Scale for Children.

l) WAIS = Wechsler Adult Intelligence Scale. This was the WAIS standardization sample.

TABLE 15-2

RESULTS OF IQ TESTS GIVEN TO BLACKS IN AFRICA

Country	Dates of studies	Sample size	Average scores Raw	Adjusted
Congo Republic[1]	1952, 1994	408	66	73
Zaire[2]	several[3]	494	66	65
Equatorial Guinea	1997	48	63	59
Ethiopia	1991	250	65	63
Ghana	1981, 1992	1,864	66	71
Guinea	1935, 1962	1,194	64	66
Kenya	1985, 2000	1,427	78	72
Nigeria	1969, 1975	461	69	67
Sierra Leone	1966, 1984	82	64	64
South Africa[4]	several[5]	3,450	67	66
Sudan	1989	148	74	72
Tanzania	1967, 1985	3,138	74	72
Uganda	1980	2,019	72	73
Zambia	1964	759	74	77
Zimbabwe	1994	—	70	66
Mean of 15 countries (unweighted):			69	68
Median of 15 countries:			67	67

All data is taken from Appendix 1 in Lynn & Vanhanen (2002). The final column shows the scores after they adjusted the raw data to correct for the Flynn effect, and also to calibrate it against British norms.

1) Also known as Congo-Brazzaville.
2) Also known as Congo-Kinsasha.
3) 1959, 1993, 1995, 1996.
4) Blacks only.
5) 1929, 1950, 1990, 1992.

TABLE 15-3

IQ TEST SCORES OF JAPANESE

Dates	Age range	Sample size	Test	Average score	Source	Notes
1977-87	2-16	3,915	various	103	Lynn (1991), and sources cites there.	(a)
1977-87	2-16	4,194	various	106	Lynn (1991), and sources cited there.	(b)
1977-96	2-16	4,860	various	105	Lynn & Vanhanen (2002), p. 212 and sources cited there.	(c)
1986	2-8	110	McCarthy	98	Lynn & Hampson (1986a).	(d)
1986	6-16	1,100	WISC-R	102	Lynn & Hampson (1986b), table 4, p. 318.	(e)
1987	4-6	~200	WPPSI	101	Lynn & Hampson (1987).	(f)

(a) Average of overall IQ scores obtained from 9 separate studies by various researchers.

(b) Weighted average of non-verbal scores obtained from 8 separate studies (including many of those included in the first line).

(c) Average of overall scores obtained from 10 separate studies (including many of those included in the first line), but adjusted to compensate for the Flynn effect.

(d) *g* factor obtained by analysis of the scores (on the various test components) of the 7-year-old and 8-year-old students in the study. (This study, and the next two, were among the tests included in lines 1-3.)

(e) *g* factor obtained by analysis of the component scores. The adjusted overall IQ score was also 102. This appears to be the best single study made of Japanese intelligence.

(f) *g* factor obtained by analysis of the component scores of the 6-year-old students in the study (which also included 4- and 5-year-olds).

TABLE 15-4
AVERAGE IQs IN SOME EUROPEAN COUNTRIES

Country	Latitude of capital city	Average IQ
Austria	48	102
Belgium	51	100
Bulgaria	43	93
Czech Republic	50	97
Denmark	56	98
Finland	60	97
France	49	98
Germany	52½	102
Greece	38	92
Hungary	47½	99
Ireland	53	93
Italy	42	102
Netherlands	52	102
Norway	60	98
Poland	52	99
Portugal	39	95
Rumania	44½	94
Russia	56	96
Spain	40	97
Sweden	59	101
Switzerland	47	101
United Kingdom	51½	100
Average (unweighted)		**98**

The figures in the last column are from Appendix 1 of Lynn & Vanhanen (2002). They averaged the results of several sources (including Buj, V. [1981]), and also adjusted the test results to correct for the Flynn effect.

TABLE 15-5
IQ SCORES OF AMERICAN INDIANS

Country & Tribe	Sample size	Mean IQ	Source
Canada (Oneidas, Chippewas, Munceys)	103	91(a)	Turner & Penfold (1952)
Canada (Ojibwas & Crees)	67	90(b)	St. John, J., et al. (1976)
United States (various)	4,994	94	Coleman, et al. (1966)
United States (Navajo)	100	89	Howell, R.J., et al. (1958)
United States (Mexican immigrants)	1,435	88	Lynn & Vanhanen (2002), pp. 213-214
Mexico	520	87	Lynn & Vanhanen (2002), p. 213
Peru	4,382	89	Lynn & Vanhanen (2002), p. 216
Average (unweighted)		**90**	

(a) Grades 5-8 only.
(b) Under 9 years old excluded.

TABLE 15-6
IQs IN SOME OTHER COUNTRIES

Country	Dates of studies	Total sample size	Mean IQ
Morocco	1996, 1997	367	85
Egypt	1989	129	83
Turkey	1994	2,277	90
Iraq	1972	1,389	87
Iran	1959	627	84
India	1968, 1968, 1988, 1996	7,974	81
Thailand	1989	---	91
Phillipines	1972	203	86
Indonesia	1961	---	89
Australia (aborigines only)	1973	>1,000	85
Micronesia	1963	407	84

Note: The data for the Australian aborigines comes from the Appendix in McElwain & Kearney (1973). All the other figures come from Appendix 1 of Lynn & Vanhanen (2002), who adjusted all the raw figures from primary sources to correct for the Flynn effect, and also to make them comparable to the British norm of 100.

"Hispanics" in the United States are racially diverse: Some are whites, some are blacks, some are American Indians. Most of them, however, are *mestizos* (persons of mixed Indian and European descent). The largest Hispanic group in the United States consists of Mexican immigrants and their descendants, and the data indicates that their IQs are, on average, somewhat higher than blacks, but considerably lower than whites.

Results for some other groups are shown in Table 15-6. In general, these other groups also have mean IQs substantially lower than those of Mongolids or white Europeans, but considerably higher than those of African blacks.

Section 8 – Conclusions

The evidence that racial differences in intellectual abilities exist appears to be overwhelming, and the data indicates that the differences are substantial. However, we must still consider the question of whether those differences are caused by genetic factors or by environmental factors ("nature or nurture"). That question will be discussed in the next chapter.

FOOTNOTES – CHAPTER 15

1) See discussion in section 3-5. For a fuller discussion, see *Bias in Mental Testing*, by Jensen, Arthur (1980)

2) See chapter 5 of Shuey, Audrey (1966), especially pp. 308-318 and 320-329.

3) Coleman, et al. (1966), p. 219.

4) Also see Osborne & McGurk (1982); and Herrnstein & Murray (1994), pp. 276-278.

5) Because of this factor, studies that include only high school students typically show a black-white difference that is a few points less than those shown by studies (such as those made of enlisted men during WW I and WW II) that do not exclude high school dropouts. See Jensen, Arthur (1998), p. 376.

6) Garner & Wigdor (1982), pp. 71-72 of volume I. Also see p. 365 of volume II.

7) Jencks & Phillips (1998), p. 1.

8) Scarr, Sandra (1981), p. 37.

9) The distribution of IQ scores among blacks approximately follows the well-known "Bell Curve" (technically called a *Gaussian* or *normal distribution*), with a mean of 85 and a standard deviation, σ, of about 15. An IQ of 115 is therefore 2σ above the mean, and an IQ of 130 is 3σ above the mean. Tables that are readily available in statistics textbooks show that, for a normal distribution, 2.28 percent of the population is at least 2σ above the mean, and 0.13 percent is at least 3σ above the mean. There are now about 35,000,000 American blacks, and 2.28 % of 35 million = 798,000, while 0.13 % of 35 million is 45,500. (In the text, I rounded those results to 800,000 and 50,000.)

10) Hedges, Larry & Nowell, Amy (1998). Chapter 5 in *The Black-White Test Score Gap*.

11) (a) The *New York Times* (8/25/2000), p. A14.
    (b) The *Washington Times* (10/1/2000), p. C8.
    (c) See also the data presented in *No Excuses* by Thernstrom & Thernstrom (2003), pp. 17-20. The authors point out that the gap between the reading skills of 17-year-old whites and blacks has been *widening* since 1988, rather than narrowing. (So have the gaps in math skills and science knowledge.)

12) Taken from Appendix 1 of Lynn & Vanhanen (2002).

13) Lynn & Vanhanen (2002), pp. 210-212.

14) Lynn & Vanhanen (2002), pp. 200-201.

15) Lynn & Vanhanen (2002), p. 219.

16) Rushton, J.P. (1997), p. 134.

CHAPTER 16

NATURE OR NURTURE?

Section 1 – Introduction

The claim is often made that δ — the difference between the mean IQ scores of Americans of European descent and the mean IQ scores of American blacks — although real, is not due to any genetic differences between the two groups, but rather is due entirely to environmental factors such as differences in diet, medical care, schooling, social and cultural milieu, and the effects of poverty and racism. Here are five hypotheses we might consider:

[a] *Very strong environmentalism*: δ is caused almost entirely by environmental factors, and genetic factors are responsible for less than 10% of the difference in average IQ.

[b] *Strong environmentalism*: δ is caused primarily by environmental factors, but genetic differences between the races are responsible for a substantial portion (at least 10%, but less than 40%) of the difference in average IQ.

[c] *Weak environmentalism*: Genetic and environmental factors are of roughly equal importance in δ, with each responsible for somewhere between 40% and 60% of the difference in average IQ between the races.

[d] *Strong hereditarianism*: δ is caused primarily by genetic differences between the races, but environmental factors are responsible for a substantial portion (at least 10%, but less than 40%) of the difference in average IQ.

[e] *Very strong hereditarianism*: δ is caused almost entirely by genetic differences, and environmental factors are responsible for less than 10% of the difference in average IQ.

It should be mentioned that some persons take an even stronger view than [a]: They claim that δ is caused *entirely* by environmental factors, and that genetic differences play no part at all in the observed difference in IQ between the races. We might call that view *extreme environmentalism*, and denote it by [a+]. Although some of you may feel that [a+] is an extreme — even fanatic — view (and is badly contradicted by the facts), in many circles [a+] is the only politically correct view, and few persons are willing to publicly dispute it.

I want to make clear that I am *not* a proponent of hypothesis [e]; rather, I believe that the facts are most consistent with [c] or [d]. Indeed, none of the prominent scholars who are publicly disputing very strong or extreme environmentalism (these include such figures as Arthur Jensen, Michael Levin, Richard Lynn, Charles Murray, J. Philippe Rushton, and Vincent Sarich) espouse very strong hereditarianism, although their opponents often accuse them of doing so.

Within a given racial group, individuals vary greatly in intelligence. In section 3-8, it was shown that between 50% and 80% of the variance between individuals is due to genetic factors. It is tempting to assume that this implies that 50-80% of the difference in IQ between racial groups is likewise due to genetic differences. However, such an assumption is not warranted, as the following two examples illustrate.

a) It is clear that the height of an individual (and therefore the difference in height between two random individuals) is strongly affected by environmental factors such as diet. We might estimate that among individuals in the overall population the fraction of the variance in height that is due to environmental factors is about 40%, or quite possibly more. Nevertheless, the mean difference in height between human males and females is almost entirely due to genetic factors. (A more striking example is provided by the large difference in average height between Mbuti Pygmies in the Congo rainforest and nearby Negro tribes.)

b) On the other hand, consider a plant species in which (under normal conditions) 80% of the variance in height is due to genetic factors. Suppose we choose a group of identical seeds from the same individual plant, and plant half the seeds in fertile soil and the other half in arid ground. There will then be a large difference in average height between the two groups of adult plants, but that difference will be due entirely to environmental factors.

We see, therefore, that in order to determine the extent to which *group* differences in average IQs depend on genetic factors, we must examine evidence other than the heritability of intelligence on the *individual* level. In section 2, I will present arguments that indicate hypothesis [a] (very strong environmentalism) is incorrect, and that [d] (strong hereditarianism) is the most plausible alternative. In section 3, I will examine several common counter-arguments and reply to them.

Section 2 – Arguments that there is a strong genetic component in δ

A) *The magnitude of δ has changed very little in the eight decades since it was first observed.* Eight decades ago, when δ was first measured (from the tests given by the US Army in World War I), the average difference between the scores of American blacks and whites was about 17 points.

Of course, at that time (during the "Jim Crow" era) there was a vast difference between the environments in which most American blacks were born and raised (and continued to live in as adults) and the environment of most whites. The majority of American blacks lived in great poverty. Their job opportunities were severely limited — sometimes by company policies, sometimes by union rules, sometimes by custom, and sometimes by law. Most American colleges had miniscule numbers of black students, and many would not admit any blacks. In addition, the public schools that most blacks attended were severely underfunded. Because of their poverty, most blacks had poor housing, poor diets, and inferior medical care.

In the intervening decades, the situation of American blacks has improved enormously, both absolutely and in comparison to that of white Americans. Their average income is still considerably lower than that of whites, but there has been a very marked convergence between the environments of the two groups. It is difficult to measure the extent of this convergence precisely, but a reasonable estimate might be that the difference between the environments of typical American whites and blacks is only about one-third (or at most one-half) as great now as it was then. (We might call this fraction the *remnant factor*, or R.)

It follows that if δ was caused largely by environmental factors then it should have diminished enormously in the course of the last eight decades. Indeed, if hypothesis [a+] is correct, then δ should now be only about one-third to one-half of the original 17 points (i.e., 5.7 to 8.5 points). However, tests taken in recent decades indicate that δ is about 15 points today.[1] The discrepancy is so large as to clearly refute hypothesis [a+]. Indeed, since δ appears to have diminished by only 2 points during that long interval, hypotheses [a] and [b] are also implausible, and hypothesis [d] appears to be the one that best fits the facts.

Some readers may prefer to see a more detailed mathematical analysis of this point. Back in 1917, δ was approximately 17 points. Call that value δ_{1917}. Let us use G to designate the fraction of δ_{1917} that was due to genetic factors. (According to hypothesis [a+] that was zero; according to hypothesis [e] it was at least 90%; and according to the other hypotheses it had some intermediate value.) For any assumed values of G and the remnant factor R, we can calculate what δ_{now} (the current value of δ) should be.[2] The results of these calculations are shown in Table 16-1. Alternatively, for any assumed values of δ_{now} and of the remnant factor R we can calculate the value of G. The results of those calculations are shown in Table 16-2.[3]

From Table 16-2 we see that any value of δ today that is greater or equal to 12 IQ points implies (even with a high estimate of the remnant factor, R) that G is at least 0.412, or 41.2%. This result is strongly inconsistent with hypothesis [a]. If we assume that the most likely value of δ today is 15 points, and that a reasonable estimate of the remnant factor is 1/3, we find that G is about 82%. This line of reasoning therefore supports hypothesis [d], although it does not completely rule out hypothesis [c].

TABLE 16-1

EXPECTED PRESENT VALUES OF δ_{now} FOR VARIOUS VALUES OF G AND THE REMNANT FACTOR, R

	R = 1/4	R = 1/3	R = 1/2
G = 0 %	4.25	5.57	8.50
= 10 %	5.52	6.80	9.35
= 20 %	6.80	7.93	10.20
= 30 %	8.08	9.07	11.05
= 40 %	9.35	10.20	11.90
= 50 %	10.62	11.33	12.75
= 60 %	11.90	12.47	13.60
= 70 %	13.17	13.60	14.45
= 80 %	14.45	14.73	15.30
= 90 %	15.72	15.87	16.15
=100 %	17.00	17.00	17.00

G denotes the fraction of δ that was accounted for by genetic factors in 1917. Tests given then indicate that δ was about 17 IQ points at that time.

R (the "remnant fractor") denotes the fraction of the overall environmental handicap faced by blacks in 1917 that still exists.

The formula used to compute this table was:

$$\delta_{now} = \delta_{1917} \times [G + R \times (1 - G)].$$

One reason that I have spent so much time on this point is its historical importance. Most of the persons who in the middle of the 20th century urged reforms that would end the unjust treatment of blacks (or at least greatly diminish it) were aware that black scores on IQ tests were far below those of whites, and they believed that the reforms they were advocating would result in the test-score gap diminishing sharply.[4] Indeed, in 1969, when Arthur Jensen wrote an article[5] entitled "How much can we boost IQ and Scholastic Achievement?" in which he asserted that δ was due in significant part to genetic factors, and that the various civil rights reforms — no matter how justified on moral grounds — would probably not bring black IQs close to the white level, his conclusions were strongly denounced by those who believed in hypotheses [a] or [b]. Over three decades have gone by, and test scores show clearly that Jensen's predictions were right and the predictions of the extreme environmentalists were wrong.

TABLE 16-2

VALUES OF G IMPLIED BY VARIOUS VALUES OF δ_{now} AND R

	R = 1/4	R = 1/3	R = 1/2
δ_{now} = 12	0.608	0.559	0.412
= 13	0.686	0.648	0.529
= 14	0.765	0.736	0.647
= 15	0.843	0.824	0.765
= 16	0.922	0.912	0.882

R denotes the "remnant factor" (see text).
G is the fraction of δ in 1917 that was due to genetic factors.
Tests given in 1917-18 indicate that δ_{1917} was about 17 points.

The formula used to compute this table was:
$$G = ([\delta_{now} / \delta_{1917}] - R) / (1-R).$$

B) *The low average intelligence of blacks is a worldwide phenomenon.* Low black scores on IQ tests are not observed in just one school, one city, one state, or one country, but are a worldwide phenomenon. The phenomenon therefore requires an explanation that holds in all countries, not one that depends on the history of American blacks, and that therefore can explain only the low IQs of blacks in the US. In particular, explanations based on slavery are inadequate to explain the low IQs of African blacks (see Table 15-2), since very few blacks living in Africa were enslaved to whites. The simplest and most plausible explanation for the low IQ of blacks in so many different countries — in Africa, and in other regions as well — is the genetic one.

C) *None of the environmental theories that have been suggested adequately explains δ.* The most obvious such hypothesis is that δ is caused by the effects of poverty. On average, American blacks have lower incomes than American whites, receive inferior medical care, and inferior educations. (Other environmental hypotheses will be discussed in section 16-3; but none is as plausible as this one, and none is supported by the facts.)

The "effects of poverty" explanation sounds reasonable; however, it is badly contradicted by various observational data. In the first place, there is the data from the well-known SAT tests, which are taken by large numbers of American high school seniors who plan to enter college. Blacks, on average, do much worse on these examinations than whites. Studies have been made of the results by dividing the students into four groups depending on their parents' income. For both blacks and whites, average test scores rise sharply with increasing parental income. However, within each of the four income groups, the black average is at least 144 points lower than the whites. (Until very recently, the difference between a perfect test score and an absolute bottom was 1200 points.) Furthermore, blacks whose parental income exceeded $70,000 a year (the highest of the four categories) have on average obtained *lower* SAT scores than whites whose parental income is less than $20,000 a year (the lowest of the four categories). These results[6] appear to refute the notion that the low test scores of blacks are caused entirely — or even mostly — by their relative poverty.

In the second place, when we compare blacks and whites whose parents are from the same SES (socioeconomic status, as measured by a combination of affluence, occupation, and education) the difference in mean IQs between the races does not fall to nearly zero — as predicted by extreme environmentalism — but is still about 9 points, or more.[7] At first sight, this would suggest that genetic factors are responsible for only 9/15, or 60% of the difference in IQ scores. In fact, it indicates that genetic factors are responsible for *at least* 60% of the difference, since they might also be responsible for much of the difference in parental SES. (The first, incorrect inference is an example of the "sociologist's fallacy."[8])

D) *Even the best planned and most lavishly funded "early intervention" projects have failed to bring the average IQs of adult blacks up to, or close to, the white level.* Various attempts have been made to raise black performance by special programs that place black children in a highly enriched environment for a period of years, but all those attempts have failed. These programs include the Abecedarian Project, the Milwaukee Project, and various "Head Start" programs administered locally.[9] The data from these programs has been analyzed carefully. In general, they result in substantial short-term improvement, as measured by the results of IQ tests. However, the gain in test scores diminishes sharply after the program ends, and the long-term improvement is rather small.

In the Abecedarian Project, for example, infants entered the program at a very early age (typically, when they were about one month old), and received enriched nutrition and medical attention. They also received 30 or more hours a week of day care (with very high adult/child ratios) — including extensive cognitive enrichment activities — for a period of more than four years. This project seems to have been the most successful "early intervention" program, but even there the long-term gain was only 5 IQ points.[10]

A possible response to these disappointing results is that although the subjects spent 30 to 40 hours a week in the enriched environment, they spent *most* of their time in their culturally-deprived home environment. A way to avoid this problem would be to have black children adopted into middle-class white families at a very early age,[11] and such programs have sometimes been carried out.

TABLE 16-3

RESULTS OF MINNESOTA TRANSRACIAL ADOPTION STUDY

Group tested	Mean IQ at age 7	Mean IQ at age 17
Adopted white children	117.6	105.6
Adopted mixed race children	109.5	98.5
Adopted black children	95.4	89.4
Biological offspring of the adoptive parents	116.4	109.4

Note: The data includes only those children who were tested at both ages.
Source: Weinberg, Scarr, and Waldman (1992).

The largest and most carefully studied such program was the *Minnesota Transracial Adoption Study*, which was initiated and conducted by the highly respected researcher Sandra Scarr and several colleagues. The average age at adoption was less than two years, and the adoptees included white, black, and mixed-race children. The adoptive parents were upper-middle-class whites who were working in professional and managerial positions, were well-educated, and whose mean IQ was about 120.

The second column in Table 16-3 shows the results of IQ tests given to these children at age seven. Note that in each racial category the children in the study scored much higher than is usual for children of that racial group. Plainly, the enriched environment was highly beneficial. Nevertheless, when the children were tested again at age 17, most of the improvement in IQ scores had vanished,[12] as can be seen from the last column of Table 16-3. In particular, the average score of the black adoptees was 89.4, which is only 4.4 points higher than blacks in the general population, and more than ten points less than whites in the general population. Note that for the adoptees in the study, the gap between the mean IQ scores of 17-year-old whites and blacks was over 16 points — every bit as large a difference as found in the general population. Note also that, despite the similarity of the environments in which they were raised, the mixed-race adoptees scored much higher than the black adoptees, which is just what would be predicted on hereditarian grounds.

E) *The differences between the environments of American blacks and whites have not resulted in any black inferiority in physical skills.* In fact, as pointed out in chapter 14, American blacks appear to be athletically superior to whites. This suggests that the environmental difficulties that blacks face are not as large as is often claimed, and in any event are not nearly large enough to produce the great difference in average intelligence that has been observed.

F) *Since genes have caused so many physical differences between the races, it is implausible that they have not caused any mental differences.* We saw in chapter 14 that genes are responsible for numerous physical differences between the races, including differences in the skin, the hair, the eyes, the lungs, the reproductive system, the muscles, the bones, and the blood. It therefore seems unlikely that there are no genetic differences between the two groups that have any effect on their intelligence.

G) *Blacks, on average, have smaller brains than whites.* As mentioned in section 14-9, there is a substantial difference (about 6%) in the average brain size of blacks and whites. Since it is well established that IQ is positively correlated with brain size (see section 3-8), we would expect this to lead to a substantial difference in the average intelligence of the two groups.

Furthermore, as a substantial part of the brain is involved in activities other than reasoning (such as regulating temperature and heartbeat, receiving signals from sensory receptors, and coordinating muscle activity), and as the number of brain cells required for those activities is the same in blacks and whites, a difference of 6% in overall brain size would result in a somewhat larger difference in the number of neurons available for reasoning. Indeed, this factor might by itself explain a large part of the difference in the average intelligence of the two groups.

H) *Most of sub-Saharan Africa was extremely primitive before it came into contact with the West two centuries ago.* In the 19th century, when European explorers first entered the "secluded zone" of sub-Saharan Africa, they were struck by how extremely primitive the tribes in the region were.[13] This was not because Europeans were blinded by ethnic chauvinism. When European traders had reached China, they had brought back glowing accounts of Chinese civilization: The Chinese might be heathens, but there was no disputing their wealth, nor the quality of their engineering skills, nor the volume of their literature. In like fashion, Europeans who had seen Japan, India, Persia, and the Arab world did not dispute the quality of their architecture and their textiles, nor the elegance of their art, nor the ability of their leaders to capably administer a large kingdom.

Of course, it might be said that all those regions had had the benefit of at least indirect contact with the West. However, when European explorers reached the New World — which had been even more isolated from the rest of the world than sub-Saharan Africa had been — they were dazzled by the large, prosperous cities they found there. Nowhere in the secluded zone of sub-Saharan Africa have archaeologists found anything to compare with Machu Picchu in Peru, nor the ruins of Tikal in Yucatán, nor of Teotihuacán in Mexico, nor even with the statues found on tiny, remote Easter Island in the Pacific.

Furthermore, the countries in sub-Saharan Africa remain backward today, compared with third-world countries on other continents. Most of them have largely discarded the democratic institutions bequeathed them by the European countries that once ruled them, and on virtually every objective measure of social, cultural, or economic well-being they rank at the bottom. Countries such as Angola, Gabon, Zimbabwe, Guinea, and Uganda are separated from each other by thousands of miles; they differ in topography, climate, language, religion, and history. The only factors they have in common are race and the low average intelligence of their inhabitants.

I) *The low average intelligence of blacks is consistent with the paucity of blacks in occupations that demand high cognitive skills, such as mathematics and physics.* It is also consistent with the absence of black champions in intellectual games such as chess and duplicate bridge, and with the failure of blacks to make any of the major inventions or scientific discoveries of modern times.[14] The same can be said of the medieval era, and of the ancient world. Indeed, it appears that not a single major invention of the last 20,000 years was made in sub-Saharan Africa.

J) *The relative performance of blacks on different intelligence tests does not depend on the cultural content of the test, but rather it is closely correlated with the extent to which the test is "g-loaded."* It was pointed out in section 3-2 that not all types of intelligence tests are equally correlated with the *g* factor. Tests that measure short-term memory, for example, are only weakly "*g*-loaded," while tests of paragraph comprehension or of series completion are strongly *g*-loaded. If the low test scores of blacks were primarily caused by poor schooling, then we would expect them to do relatively worse on tests that depended on acquired knowledge (such as vocabulary tests), and relatively better on tests (such as backward digit span) in which acquired knowledge plays no part. In fact, however, this is not the case. Instead, the relative size of the black-white difference in various mental tests depends primarily upon the *g*-loading of the individual tests: Blacks do worst on those tests that are strongly correlated with general intelligence. This is true whether the tests are verbal or non-verbal, written or oral, timed or untimed, culture-loaded or culture-reduced.[15]

K) *While environmentalists often attack the evidence that δ is due to genetic factors, they rarely offer any **direct** evidence of the alleged equality of black and white native intelligence.* For several decades, a series of scholars have presented evidence that genetic factors are partly responsible for the observed difference in black and white IQs. Throughout that period, opponents have disputed that claim by arguing that the evidence presented is inconclusive. However, they rarely present any *direct* evidence to support their own claim that blacks and whites have, on average, equal native intelligence. If their claim was correct, it should have been easy to assemble large amounts of evidence directly supporting it. It is reasonable to infer that such evidence does not exist, and the reason it does not exist is that their assertion is incorrect. (Note that there is no *a priori* reason to assume that δ is entirely environmental in origin.)

Section 3 - Some opposing arguments

A) *"Scientists agree that δ is completely due to environmental factors."* The "argument from authority" is generally considered by logicians to be a weak argument, and it is clear that scientists who are studying a question should examine the evidence themselves rather than blindly accepting what other scientists have said. However, accepting the decision of "the experts" does seem to be a practical way for a lay person without expert knowledge (and without the time or inclination to consider in detail the arguments for and against some hypothesis) to make a decision. It is therefore worth asking what scientists working in this field really do say.

A survey conducted by Snyderman and Rothman (1988) showed that although hypothesis [a+] (extreme environmentalism) was the one normally presented in the media as the correct view, in actual fact only 17% of experts believed it to be correct. The majority of expert opinion supported the hypothesis that both genetic and environmental factors play a role in δ.[16]

B) *"Whites and blacks differ in only a small fraction of their genes."* This is one of the most common arguments presented, but it is invalid.[17] The error comes from assuming that small differences in the input to a system must yield small differences in the system's output. That assumption is false: On the contrary, it is often the case that small differences in the input result in large differences in the final outcome. Here are a few examples:

1) A batter in a baseball game hits a 400-foot home run. Had the batter swung his bat just one inch lower, it would instead have resulted in a high pop fly, and an easy out.

2) Those who have written computer programs are aware that typing a single word incorrectly can cause a lengthy computer program to malfunction completely. Indeed, the omission of a single letter — or a single comma, or even a single blank space! — can have that effect.

3) It has often been pointed out that human beings and chimpanzees differ in less than 2% of their DNA; nevertheless, the difference in intelligence between the two species is enormous.

4) Within the human species, a large part of the difference between males and females is due to a single chromosome, indeed to a single gene (the SRY gene). Furthermore, there are many genetic diseases that are caused by a single gene, and some of them (like Huntington's chorea) are lethal diseases.[18]

C) *"The difference in mean IQ between the races is much less than the spread of IQs within each race."* This is perfectly true, but irrelevant, since it does not imply that the difference in IQ is not genetic in origin. After all, the difference between the mean height of human males and human females is only a few inches — which is much less that the variation in height found within each sex — but the male-female difference in height is almost entirely genetic in origin.

D) *"There are large differences in wealth and income between whites and blacks, and these differences are responsible for the test-score gap."* This is by far the most common non-genetic explanation of δ, but it is badly contradicted by the data. For example:

1) Most of the racial difference in average IQ scores remains when we compare black and white children whose parents have similar incomes (see footnote 8).

2) Blacks whose parents have incomes over $70,000/year obtain (on average) lower scores on the SAT than whites or Asians whose parents have incomes under $20,000/year (see footnote 7).

3) The mean IQ gap between blacks and whites who were adopted into the same families when they were very young children and reared together — thereby eliminating differences in parental income — is as large as the black-white IQ gap in the general population. (See Table 16-3.)

4) Even in prosperous, racially-mixed suburbs the average grades of black students are much lower than those of whites, and their average SAT scores are typically much lower also.[19] A striking example is provided by Shaker Heights, Ohio (a prosperous suburb of Cleveland). Most of the blacks living there are well-educated and have middle-class jobs; the public schools are very well funded and racially integrated; and strenuous efforts have been made to improve the academic performance of blacks. Nevertheless, the scores of black high school students in Shaker Heights on statewide proficiency exams have been extremely disappointing.[20]

It has been said that "... determining why upper-income blacks score lower than others is the toughest question about the achievement gap."[21] However, that question is tough only for someone who dogmatically assumes that no genetic factor is involved in δ.

The failure of the "poverty argument" has provoked a search for alternative non-genetic explanations of δ, most of which lack data to support them. Here are a few examples:

E) *"American blacks perform poorly on IQ tests because they lack suitable (black) role models."* This is just a conjecture. There is no data that shows that lack of role models normally results in a lowering of 15 points in a person's IQ. Merely suggesting that this effect *could* occur is not the same as proving it *does* occur, and that it is large enough to explain δ. Note also that blacks *have* been presented with intellectual role models, including such figures as George Washington Carver, Charles Drew, Frederick Douglass, Thurgood Marshall, Colin Powell, and Martin Luther King, Jr.

F) *"Lack of self-esteem among blacks is responsible for their low scores on IQ tests."* This too is a purely conjectural notion, unsupported by data. Indeed, psychological tests show that on average black teenagers have *higher* self-esteem than whites, rather than lower.[22] It might also be pointed out that, despite the strong public feeling against Japanese-Americans in the years following the attack on Pearl Harbor (and the relocation of thousands of Japanese to internment camps), Japanese-Americans did not do poorly on IQ tests. Similarly, the widespread antagonism towards Jews has not prevented them from obtaining high scores on such examinations; and the popularity of "Polish jokes" — whose theme is the alleged stupidity of Poles — has not resulted in Poles doing poorly on IQ tests. Deaf children provide another counter-example to this hypothesis. Such children are often wrongly labeled stupid by those who mistake their physical disability for mental inferiority (in some cases, even close family members disparage them), but they do just as well on non-verbal tests as hearing children.

G) *"Peer pressure on black students not to 'act white' is responsible for the difference between black and white intellectual abilities."* Such peer pressure exists, but it is not ubiquitous, and there is no data to show that it can explain the magnitude of δ. It probably has little effect on blacks at prestigious universities (or in medical schools, law schools, or other graduate schools) since in these cases the "peers" of the black students are other blacks who are also trying to meet white intellectual standards. Note also that most middle-class black parents are well aware of the importance of education, and they strongly urge their children to study. In addition, virtually all black leaders encourage blacks to get a good education and to study hard.

H) *"Blacks are reared in a culture where intellectual attainment is not admired."* It may be true that intellectual attainments are not admired as much in the black community as they are in the white community, but no data exists to prove that this factor can explain the magnitude of δ. Furthermore, even if this succeeded in explaining the IQ difference in the United States, it would not explain why black IQ scores are low in virtually every country on Earth — unless the black culture in every other country also failed to value intellectual achievements. And even if that is the case, it would beg the question of *why* they fail to do so — an obvious answer to which would be a genetic difference in average intelligence.

I) *"Institutional racism is the cause of low black IQ scores."* This is perhaps the weakest of the hypothetical arguments, because it is so vague. What it seems to mean is that "black IQ scores and intellectual achievements are lower than those of whites, and we can't point to any testable environmental explanation."

J) *"Among American blacks, there is no correlation between IQ and skin color (or percentage of African ancestry).* Unlike the last five arguments, this one is testable and would be important if it was correct. Richard Nesbitt,[23] citing the data compiled by Audrey Shuey[24] claims that such studies show no significant positive correlation between lighter skin color and higher IQ. However, direct examination of Shuey's data shows the contrary. Shuey examined studies made between 1913 and 1964 by 13 different researchers, each of whom tested black-white hybrids and attempted to determine if light skin color (or other evidence of Caucasoid ancestry) correlated with the results of IQ tests. Twelve of those studies (with a combined sample size of 6,520) showed a significant positive correlation between Caucasoid ancestry and IQ scores — a large correlation in seven of the studies — whereas only four small studies (with a combined sample size of 460) failed to do so.

Because the studies that Shuey tabulated used different criteria, and did not reach uniform results, one cannot say that they provide conclusive proof that blacks with a higher fraction of white ancestry are more intelligent, but that is certainly the conclusion they suggest.[25]

The best recent data is that collected and presented by Sandra Scarr and her associates in their review of the Minnesota Transracial Adoption Study. That study found that — under conditions where environmental factors had been equalized to an unusual degree — black children and teenagers scored much lower than those of mixed-race, who in turn scored much lower than whites.[26] Furthermore, the results of that study show that the scores of mixed-race children and teenagers are roughly half-way between those of blacks and whites, which is consistent with the predictions of the strong hereditarian view.

K) *"The magnitude of δ has decreased in recent decades."* In the first place, a significant part of the apparent decrease seems to result from selection effects, rather than from an actual change in δ (see sections 15-3 and 15-4). In any event, the amount of the decrease is so small that it does not support hypothesis [a] (very strong environmentalism), but rather hypothesis [d] (strong hereditarianism). (See section 2A of this chapter for a fuller discussion of the data.)

It should be added that more recent data indicates that the gap between the test scores of whites and blacks is no longer decreasing, and may even be increasing. For example, a study released in 2000 by the US Department of Education found that, on average, 17-year-old blacks read only as well as 13-year-old whites; and among 17-year-old whites and blacks the gap in science scores in 1999 (52 points) had widened slightly in the past few years and was almost the same as the 54-point difference that was recorded in 1969.[27] According to data released by the College Board, the gap in SAT scores between blacks and whites actually *increased* slightly between 1990 and 2000. The gap in the verbal portion of the examination increased from 91 points to 94 in the course of the decade, and the gap in the mathematics portion increased from 96 points to 104 points.[28]

L) *"A study of the offspring of German women and American soldiers after World War II showed that those children with black fathers had the same mean IQ as those with white fathers."* That is true,[29] but there is no reason to assume that the black soldiers involved were a random sample of American blacks, or even of black soldiers in the US army. On the contrary, there is strong reason to believe that they were not a random sample.

We know that females are commonly selective as to whom they mate with, and intelligence is frequently an important factor in that selection. If, on average, the German females involved selected just as strongly for intelligence whether they were dealing with black or white servicemen, then we should not expect there to be any difference between the mean IQs of the white and mixed-race children. In any event, since the data presented in the study does not include any information about the IQ of the black fathers involved (nor about the white fathers, for that matter), no reliable conclusions can be drawn from the results.

M) *"The measured IQs of both whites and blacks have risen by about 15 points in the past 60 years (the 'Flynn effect'), which proves that environmental factors can affect IQs by amounts equivalent to δ."* Data compiled by James R. Flynn (and confirmed by other researchers) makes it plain that a secular rise in IQ scores has really occurred, and that the rise has occurred in many, perhaps most, countries.[30]

The exact cause of the rise is still in dispute. However, although scores on IQ tests have changed dramatically in the last six decades, the difference between white and black scores has changed only slightly in that interval (see section 15-4). It therefore seems unwarranted to infer from the Flynn effect that δ is caused entirely by environmental factors. Indeed, since the Flynn effect makes it plain that the various social, political, and economic changes that have occurred in the past 60 years have had a dramatic impact on test scores, the fact that δ has nevertheless remained nearly constant suggests that δ is only slightly affected by environmental factors, and is therefore largely caused by genetic differences between blacks and whites.[31]

N) *"The backwardness of sub-Saharan Africa was entirely due to deficiencies in the natural environment, such as a dearth of domesticable plants and animals, and the direction of the principal geographic axes in Africa."* This argument was presented at length by Jared Diamond in his best-selling book *Guns, Germs, and Steel* (1997). Professor Diamond's hypothesis is discussed in more detail in chapter 24 of this book, where it is shown that a comparison between the relative cultural and intellectual achievements of sub-Saharan Africa and Mesoamerica clearly refutes his theory.

In any event, the most that Dr. Diamond's argument could do is to counter *one* of the arguments supporting the notion that genetic differences are involved in δ (the one concerning the backwardness of sub-Saharan Africa). It would not affect the other arguments that have been made against very strong or extreme environmentalism.

O) *"Anyone who claims that δ is due (even in part) to genetic factors is a racist and should not be listened to."* This is by far the most common "argument" made in opposition to the hypothesis that IQ differences between the races are caused in part by genetic factors. Of course, it is not a logical argument at all, but mere invective. That it is resorted to so often is, if anything, an indication that those who advocate extreme environmentalism lack empirical data with which to defend their views.

Section 4 – Occam's razor

A satisfactory explanation of the cause or causes of δ must be consistent with a wide assortment of data. Those who assert that δ is entirely environmental in origin often ignore some of the inconvenient facts. However, there is an additional problem with the way environmentalists deal with hereditarian arguments: They usually offer a variety of unconnected explanations for the various facts to be explained.

For example, the poor academic performance of American blacks is explained by peer pressure, or by a lack of role models. The manifest backwardness of sub-Saharan Africa prior to the arrival of Europeans is explained by the lack of domesticable plants and animals. The low IQ scores of blacks are attributed to lack of self-esteem, or to bias in the tests. The smaller brain size of blacks is explained — when it is not simply ignored — by their poor diet, and inferior medical care (which, however, does not affect their athletic performance).

Such a set of *ad hoc* explanations — even if each one taken in isolation sounds reasonable — should be avoided if a simpler explanation of the facts is possible. In contrast, the single hypothesis that δ has a strong genetic component explains all of those facts.

The idea that a theory that succeeds in explaining the observations by means of a small number of general principles is to be preferred to one that involves a large number of *ad hoc* explanations is known as *Occam's razor* (after William of Occam, who enunciated it in the 14th century). The principle was later invoked by both Galileo and Newton in support of their theories, and is today accepted by all serious scientists as a criterion for the acceptability of a scientific theory.

Section 5 – Summary

Several of the individual arguments listed in section 2 of this chapter are strong and convincing even by themselves. In combination, they provide overwhelming evidence that genetic differences are an important factor — perhaps the main factor — in producing the gap between black and white IQs.

An excellent article that presents a detailed discussion of the evidence that δ includes a genetic component appeared recently in *Psychology, Public Policy, and Law*, a quarterly journal published by the American Psychological Association.[32]

Most of the arguments presented to oppose that view are demonstrably incorrect; the others are dubious and unconvincing. We conclude that there are substantial differences in the average intelligence of various racial groups, and that to a considerable extent they result from genetic differences between the races. Indeed, the overall evidence in favor of this conclusion is so great that no one would dispute the point if it was not an issue that aroused strong emotions on ideological grounds.

FOOTNOTES – CHAPTER 16

1) The most detailed and scholarly defense of hypothesis [a] is presented in *The Black-White Test Score Gap*, edited by Jencks & Phillips (1998). In chapter 5 of that book, Hedges & Nowell claim that δ has indeed declined in recent years. The lowest value they give for δ — based on a study made in 1992 (see their Table 5-1) — is 0.82 standard deviations, which is about 12.3 IQ points. In section 4 of chapter 15, I pointed out that the average of recent studies is somewhat higher than that, and the best estimate is that δ is about 15 points today.

2) A reasonable interpolation formula is: $\delta_{now} = \delta_{1917} \times (G + R \times [1 - G])$. The formula expresses the notion that: (a) The part of δ_{1917} that was due to genetic factors is unchanged, but (b) the part of δ_{1917} that was not due to genetic factors (i.e., $[1 - G]$) is reduced to a fraction R of its original value. If G = 100% (the most extreme hereditarian position), then the formula reduces to $\delta_{now} = \delta_{1917}$; whereas if G = 0% (the extreme environmentalist position) then the formula reduces to $\delta_{now} = R \times \delta_{1917}$.

3) Straightforward algebraic manipulations of the formula in the preceding footnote yield: $G = ([\delta_{now}/\delta_{1917}] - R) / (1 - R)$, which has been used to compute Table 16-2.

4) See, for example, Jencks & Phillips (1998), p. 9, where they say: "In the 1960s, racial egalitarians routinely blamed the test score gap on the combined effects of black poverty, racial segregation, and inadequate funding for black schools. That analysis implied obvious solutions: raise black children's family income, desegregate their schools, and equalize spending on schools that remain racially segregated. All these steps still look useful, but none has made as much difference as optimists expected in the early 1960s."

5) Jensen, Arthur (1969), in the *Harvard Educational Review*, volume 39, pp. 1-123.

6) Hacker, Andrew (1992), *Two Nations*, p. 143.

7) (a) Jensen, Arthur (1998), says (see p. 491) that when blacks and whites of the same SES are compared the difference in their mean IQ scores shrinks by about one-third (i.e., 5 or 6 points).

   (b) On page 286, Herrnstein & Murray (1994) cite the *National Longitudinal Survey of Youth* (1980) as showing that δ shrinks from 1.21 σ (= 18 points) to only 0.76 σ (= 11 points) if students are matched with others in the same SES; and on p. 719 (footnote 41) they cite three other studies as yielding similar reductions.

8) A more detailed discussion of the "sociologist's fallacy" can be found in Jensen (1998) on p. 491, and also in his footnote 7, p. 580.

9) See Thernstrom & Thernstrom (2003), pp. 221-225 and sources cited therein.

10) Jensen, Arthur (1998), pp. 342-344.

11) A strong supporter of the environmentalist position insisted that "Properly researched adoption is the only source able to establish whether a feature is, or is not, determined at least in part by biological heredity." (Cavalli-Sforza & Cavalli-Sforza, 1995, pp. 220-221.)

12) See Weinberg, Scarr, and Waldman (1992), or Table 12.5 on p. 474 of Jensen (1998).

13) (a) See section 8 of chapter 41.

(b) For a more detailed discussion see Baker, John R. (1974), chapters 19 and 20. The main sources that Baker takes his information from are the writings of these seven 19th-century explorers (each of whom traveled in parts of sub-Saharan Africa before European colonialists arrived in the area): David Livingston, John Speke, Francis Galton, Henry F. Fynn, B. P. du Chaillu, Samuel Baker, and G. Schweinfurth.

14) See for example:
(a) Asimov, Isaac (1982), *Asimov's Biographical Encyclopedia of Science and Technology* (2nd revised edition).
(b) Hart, Michael H. (1992), *The 100* (revised edition).
(c) Murray, Charles (2003), *Human Accomplishment*, especially chapter 11.

15) Jensen refers to this as "Spearman's hypothesis," and discusses it at length in Jensen (1998), pp. 369-399.

16) Snyderman, Mark & Stanley Rothman (1990), *The IQ Controversy* (paperback edition), p. 284 and Table E-1 on p. 285.

17) See the discussion in Pinker, Steven (2000), *The Language Instinct*, pp. 361-362.

18) Ridley, Matt (1999), *Genome*. See pp. 110-112 for a discussion of the SRY gene and pp. 55-56 for a description of the mutation responsible for Huntington's chorea.

19) (a) See the article by Pam Belluck in the *New York Times* (7/4/1999).
(b) See also Andrea Billups ("Blacks lag in academic scores") in the *Washington Times* (10/1/2000), Section C. She points out that: "In Prince George's County, one of the nation's richest predominantly black suburban areas, the combined SAT score for black students was a dismal 845 this year, 30 points below the average score for Hispanic students and 227 points lower than the average score posted by whites."
(c) See also William Raspberry in the *Washington Post* (6/30/2003).

20) (a) Thernstrom & Thernstrom (2003), pp. 121-124, and sources cited therein.
(b) Also see article by Michael A. Fletcher in the *Washington Post* (10/23/1998).

21) Craig Jerald, quoted by Andrea Billups in the *Washington Times* (10/1/2000), p. C8.

22) See Levin, Michael (1997), pp. 74-76, and sources cited therein.

23) See Nisbett, R.E. (1998), p. 89. Nisbett is a strong advocate of the extreme environmentalist position [a+].

24) Shuey, Audrey (1966). See especially her Chapter IX and Table Thirteen. Note that some of the researchers she cites published more than one study.

25) Even Nisbett admits that Shuey's data shows a positive correlation between lighter skin color and higher IQ. However, he claims that the low value (r about 0.15) of the correlation supports his position. See p. 89 of Nisbett (1998).

26) See Weinberg, Scarr, and Waldman (1992) or Table 16-3 in this chapter.

27) See article by Kate Zernike in The *New York Times* (8/25/2000), Section A, page 14.

28) See the *Washington Times* (10/1/2000), pp. C1 and C8.

29) See Nisbett, R.E. (1998), p. 91.

30) (a) Flynn, James R. (1984).
    (b) Flynn, James R. (1987).
    (c) Flynn, James R. (1994).

31) At present, the most promising explanation for the Flynn effect is that the extensive population movements which occurred in many regions during the past century (resulting, in part from improvements in transportation) have resulted in a marked increase in heterosis, or hybrid vigor. This was suggested by Jensen in 1998 (*The g Factor*, p. 327), and a more detailed analysis by Mingroni supports Jensen's conjecture. See Mingroni, Michael A. (2004).

32) Rushton & Jensen (2005). A strong point of the article is that it lists several predictions that have been made by the mixed genetic-environmentalist hypothesis and been confirmed by experiments or observations (the acid test of a successful scientific theory). Curiously, although the article was written to defend hypothesis [c], the data it presents actually favors hypothesis [d], strong hereditarianism (see their p. 279). The same issue of the journal also includes three articles by strong proponents of hypothesis [a] or [a+], and a rejoinder by Rushton & Jensen.

CHAPTER 17

HOW DID RACIAL DIFFERENCES IN INTELLIGENCE ARISE?

Section 1 – The effects of cold climates

The genetic differences that affect the average intelligence of the various races arose in the same fashion — natural selection — that physical differences between the races did.

In tropical regions, groups with an average IQ of 70 or less can survive. We know this because there are such groups living today in sub-Saharan Africa (see Table 15-2). However, surviving in a cold climate (such as Siberia) poses much greater difficulties. Human beings cannot survive in such climates without:

1) Warm clothing.

2) Sewing needles, to make that clothing with. (These were not invented until about 30 kya.)

3) Warm, sturdy housing capable of keeping out rain, wind, and cold.

4) Methods for accumulating food and storing it for the winter months.

Section 2 – Selection for high intelligence

Each of the items on that list — and many others needed to survive in a harsh, cold environment — required considerable intelligence. Since individuals with low IQs had poor prospects of surviving in Siberia, those genes which helped to create high intelligence were more likely to reach succeeding generations, while those which tended to result in lower intelligence were eliminated from the gene pool.

Furthermore, this selective process would also operate on groups. If the average intelligence of the members of a band was low, it was likely that the *entire* band would die out, including those individuals who were of high enough intelligence to have survived and reproduced if they had been members of a more capable group.

This selection process began as soon as *HSS* moved out of Africa into regions where there were cold winters, and it became increasingly powerful as human groups moved into colder and colder climates.[1] The process continued for tens of thousands of years, gradually resulting (in regions with very harsh climates) in groups evolving with average IQs of 100 or higher.

Section 3 – Why wasn't higher IQ an advantage in *all* regions?

Higher intelligence would be an advantage everywhere if there were no costs accompanying it. But what matters are not merely the positive benefits of a trait, but also the costs involved. The changes in human anatomy and physiology that lead to higher intelligence do not come cost free.

For example, one way for a subgroup of human beings to develop higher intelligence is for that group to evolve larger brains. However, larger brains impose at least three important costs:

1) *Larger brains require larger amounts of energy.* Since its neurons must be repeatedly recharged, the brain requires an amount of energy that is far out of proportion to its size. (A typical human brain contains only about 2% of the body's mass, but uses about 20% of a resting person's energy.) Larger brains, of course, require more energy than smaller ones.

2) *Larger brains require larger heads, which creates strains on the muscular and skeletal structure.* Standing on two legs is a complex problem in balancing, and weight situated near the top of our structure is particularly hard to balance. Larger brains and heads make this problem even greater.

3) *Larger brains (and heads) require wider female pelvises, and the wider pelvises result in less efficiency in walking and running.* The large size of the human head creates serious difficulties in childbirth (which is why human females typically have far more difficulty in delivering their young than do females of most other species). As brains and heads became larger, wider female pelvises were required to accommodate them. Since it was difficult for such a change to be confined to one sex only, the male members of those groups also wound up with wider pelvises. But wider pelvises and hips result in lower running speeds (see section 14-7) and less efficiency in both walking and running.

The combination of costs that are involved in having larger, more powerful brains explains why many human groups did not evolve brains as large as those typically found in north Asians and north Europeans. However, in cold climates, the advantages of higher intelligence outweighed the costs just described.

Section 4 – There is nothing unusual or surprising in such differences evolving

It is commonplace for geographically isolated portions of a species to evolve differently, and in such a way that each group is better adapted to its own environment. This has plainly occurred with regard to a large number of physical traits (see chapter 14). It is therefore not at all surprising that differences have also evolved with regard to mental traits. In fact, it would be surprising if such differences had *not* evolved between groups that developed in such different environments as Siberia and tropical Africa.

Section 5 – An estimate of the growth of human intelligence

Table 17-1 presents a possible chronology for the evolution of the intelligence of human groups living in various regions over the course of the last 60,000 years. The figures in that table — which are presented in the form of hypothetical IQ scores — were derived from a computer model.

In the model, the Earth was divided into 27 geographic regions, and each region was characterized by a number indicating the harshness of its environment, with the coldness of its winters being the main factor considered in choosing the "harshness factor." It was assumed that within each region the mean intelligence of its inhabitants would gradually increase, and that the rate of increase would be proportional to the harshness factor of that region. In order to take account, however roughly, of climate changes during the last sixty thousand years, some of the regions were given two different harshness factors, one applicable during the Ice Age and the other applicable during the last 10,000 years.

The starting point for the computer model was 60 kya, the approximate time when human beings began to migrate out of sub-Saharan Africa (see chapter 10). The model assumes that at 60 kya the average IQ of all human groups was about 70. This assumption was made because there are many human groups living in SSA today that have average IQs of about 70, and there is no strong reason to believe that human intelligence has declined in the past sixty thousand years.

At 1000-year intervals, the average IQ of the inhabitants of each of the 27 regions was computed, employing a simple algebraic formula. (The formula used was the simplest linear equation consistent with the assumptions mentioned.)

It was assumed that whenever *HSS* entered a region not previously occupied by humans any earlier hominids residing there were eliminated without significant interbreeding. However, if a human group migrated into a region that was already occupied by *HSS*, the average IQ of the resulting mixture would simply be the average of the IQs of the two groups, weighted in accordance with the relative numbers of the migrants and the earlier inhabitants. (The dates and weighting factors of the various migrations, the harshness factors of each region, and the other specifics of the computer model used are all listed in Appendix 3.)

The construction of this computer model required various approximations:

1) The real world consists of far more than 27 separate and distinctive geographic regions (each inhabited by a group that is largely endogamous).

2) A single parameter (and one with only a few possible values) cannot completely describe the full range of environments existing on the Earth.

TABLE 17-1

CHRONOLOGY OF GROWTH OF HUMAN INTELLIGENCE

Region (a)	60(b)	50	40	30	25	20	15	10	5	0(c)
SSA (d)	70	70	70	70	70	70	70	70	70	70
North Africa	70	71	73	74	75	76	77	77	84	85
Middle East	70	73	76	78	80	81	83	84	85	88
Southern Europe (e)	-	-	77	81	84	87	89	92	88	99
Northern Europe	-	-	-	81	85	89	93	96	91	101
Russia	-	-	-	81	85	89	93	96	99	102
Central Asia	-	73	76	79	80	82	83	85	93	98
Mong/Siber (f)	-	-	-	81	85	89	92	96	99	103
North China	-	-	-	-	85	89	92	96	99	100
South China	-	-	74	78	80	83	86	88	89	96
Japan/Korea	-	-	-	81	83	86	88	94	96	99
Arctic N.Amer (g)	-	-	-	-	-	-	89	92	96	100
Northern USA	-	-	-	-	-	-	89	92	95	98
Southern USA	-	-	-	-	-	-	89	91	93	94
Mesoamerica	-	-	-	-	-	-	89	89	89	89
South America	-	-	-	-	-	-	-	89	89	89
India	-	71	71	71	71	71	71	71	82	84
Southeast Asia	-	71	71	71	71	71	71	71	85	88
Indonesia	-	71	71	71	71	71	71	71	71	83
Australia	-	71	74	77	78	79	81	82	82	84
New Guinea	-	71	72	74	75	76	77	78	79	79
Melanesia	-	-	-	74	75	76	76	77	78	80
Micronesia	-	-	-	-	-	-	-	-	-	85
Polynesia	-	-	-	-	-	-	-	-	-	84

(a) The last footnote in chapter 17 explains why there are only 24 regions listed here.

(b) The dates in this row are expressed in kya.

(c) Migrations after 1500 AD have been ignored.

(d) Sub-Saharan Africa.

(e) This is the average of two regions: Southeast Europe and Southwest Europe.

(f) Mongolia and southern Siberia.

(g) Arctic North America (= Alaska, Canada, and Greenland).

Note: The numbers in this table were rounded to the nearest integer. When they were exactly midway between two integers they were rounded down.

3) Within each region, the climate changes that have occurred over the past 60,000 years were both smoother and more varied than those used in the model.

4) The weighting factors used to determine the results of migration and mixing were of necessity estimated rather crudely.

5) The model considers only the genetic factors affecting human intelligence, and omits the effects of culture.

Despite all these caveats and shortcomings, the results of this simple computer model are reasonably consistent with the average IQs of the various human groups today. In addition, you, the reader, are invited to judge for yourself as you read the later chapters of this book, how consistent the results listed in Table 17-1 are with the known facts of human history and prehistory.

Note that Table 17-1 is *not* a tabulation of measured IQs. Rather, it is simply a theoretical estimate of what the average IQs of various groups (at various points in time) might be expected to be if the basic assumptions of the model are decent approximations. Since many factors were omitted, or only crudely approximated, we should not expect exact agreement between the results of the model and measured IQs today. It is not claimed that the chronology given in Table 17-1 is the "true" chronology, or the only possible chronology, merely that it is one plausible approximation of what actually occurred.[2]

FOOTNOTES – CHAPTER 17

1) Both Richard Lynn and J. Philippe Rushton have presented this important notion. (See Lynn, 1992, pp. 373-374; and Rushton, 1997, pp. 228-231.) The earliest mention that I have located of this idea is in Chapter 6 of Part II of Grant (1921), on p. 170 of the 1999 reprinting. However, Grant lacked the data now available in support of his hypothesis.

2) The table in Appendix 3 lists the 27 regions that were used in the computer simulation. However, in order to make Table 17-1 more readable, only 24 regions are listed there.

   (a) The results for the *Northeast Siberia* region (not shown in Table 17-1) were very similar to those shown for the Arctic North American region.

   (b) The results for the *Taiwan/Philippines* region (not shown in Table 17-1) were very similar to those shown for Indonesia.

   (c) The results for the *Southeast Europe* and *Southwest Europe* regions were very similar to each other. The average of those two regions is shown in Table 17-1 on the line marked "South Europe."

CHAPTER 18

BEHAVIORAL DIFFERENCES BETWEEN THE RACES

Section 1 – Are there innate behavioral differences between species?

Obviously, yes. Animal instincts, such as the migratory habits of various birds and insects, have long been noted and studied, as has the remarkable behavior of the social insects (ants and bees). Pet owners are well aware that most dogs enjoy swimming and playing in the water, while almost all cats — although they can swim if necessary — hate being in the water. The natural timidity of rabbits is well known, and contrasts with the ferocity of many carnivorous species.

Section 2 – Are there innate behavioral differences between subspecies?

Yes, there are. If there were not, there would be no way for behavioral differences between species to arise, since new species arise by an accumulation of genetic differences within a species. Furthermore, such differences are commonly observed. Differences in temperament between the various subspecies, or *breeds*, of dogs are well known. (Compare, for example, pit bulls and cocker spaniels.)

Section 3 – Are the behavioral differences between individual human beings due *entirely* to upbringing and conditioning, or are they due (at least in part) to genetic factors?

Individuals differ widely in their behavior. Some writers have conjectured that all such differences are due entirely to differences in training, upbringing, and conditioning. Those of us who have reared more that one child usually think otherwise.

However, one need not rely on anecdotal evidence to refute that conjecture. Scientific studies confirm the common-sense notion that genetic factors play a significant role in human behavior. For example, careful comparisons regarding a variety of psychological traits (as measured by standard tests) have been made between identical twins reared separately, and the studies show high correlations between their traits. By comparing those results with studies of identical twins reared together, or with studies of fraternal twins, or with studies of biologically unrelated children adopted into the same family, we can obtain estimates of the heritability of various traits. For many important personality traits, the heritabilities lie in the range 0.4 – 0.5, completely refuting the "environment only" hypothesis.[1]

Section 4 – Are there any behavioral differences between human subspecies?

There are large statistical differences between the behavior of American blacks and whites. The politically correct view is that all such differences are due to poverty or other effects of white racism, but no one disputes that the differences exist.[2] Some well-known examples include:

1) Crime rates[3]

2) Personality and temperament traits, such as

- Aggressiveness[4]
- Excitability[4]
- Impulsivity[4]
- Self-esteem[5]

3) Differences in sexual behavior, such as

- Age at first intercourse[6]
- Number of sexual partners[6]
- Incidence of AIDS and other sexually transmitted diseases[6]
- Frequency of out-of-wedlock births[2]
- Divorce rates[2]

(Many of these differences in sexual behavior may be a consequence of the fact that blacks, on average, have higher levels of testosterone than whites.[7])

Time preferences are also correlated with race. An individual's time preference is a measure of his willingness to defer the use or receipt of some valuable item in order to obtain something more valuable in the future. To see how time preferences can be quantified, consider first a child who will not pass up an offer of one chocolate bar today unless given assurance that he will receive two chocolate bars tomorrow; we might say that such a child has a time preference equal to 2.0. On that scale, a child who will not give up one bar today unless he receives *three* chocolate bars tomorrow would have a time preference of 3.0.[8] A low time preference indicates a strong willingness to defer gratification in order to achieve a greater reward later, a trait which is normally important for success.

Studies have shown that blacks, on average, have considerably higher time preferences than whites.[9] Consequently, even if other factors were equal (which, of course, they are not), blacks would, on average, wind up with lower incomes and less wealth than whites.

Section 5 – Are any behavioral differences between human subspecies *innate*?

Since there are innate differences in intelligence between the human races there must be innate behavioral differences also — unless you believe that intelligence has no effect on behavior. But that seems unlikely, to say the least. (Do you really believe that a person with an IQ of 85 is just as likely to become a rocket scientist as a person with an IQ of 140?)

Even aside from intelligence, many of the other observed differences between racial groups appear to have a genetic component. For example, the well-attested fact that young black males are, on average, more active sexually than white males of the same age might be due in part to differences in environment and upbringing. It seems unlikely, though, that the higher testosterone level in blacks — which is largely genetic in origin — has no effect on their sexual behavior.

Striking evidence that at least some racial differences in behavior are due to genetic factors is provided by the studies that Daniel Freedman and his wife conducted with white and Chinese neonates. Among their findings:

- Caucasian infants cried more readily than Chinese, and were more difficult to console.
- When a cloth was placed over an infant's face, preventing him from breathing through his nose, a typical white (or black) infant would swipe at the cloth with his hands, or turn away, whereas a Chinese infant would simply lie still and breathe through its mouth.[10]

The early age of the infants involved seems to preclude the possibility that the differences in behavior were caused by differences in environment or upbringing.

More generally, we know that behavioral differences between species are affected by the genetic differences between them (see section 1 of this chapter), that behavioral differences between subspecies of the same species of animal are likewise affected by the genetic differences between them (see section 2), and that behavioral differences between individual members of the same subspecies are affected by genetic differences between them (see section 3). Those who claim that this general rule does not hold between *human* subspecies must therefore bear the burden of proof, and they need to clearly describe a mechanism by which behavioral differences are affected by genetic differences on both the species and individual levels, but not on the subspecies level. Since this has not been done, as a matter of common sense we should assume that the general rule holds, and that many of the observed behavioral differences between the races are due — at least in part — to genetic factors.

Section 6 – The *r-K* classification in zoology

How racial differences in natural intelligence arose was explained in the previous chapter. Can we also explain how genetically-caused racial differences in behavior arose? Yes, we can: The combination of the theory of "*r-K* strategies" and "paternal investment theory" provides the answer.

Zoologists, in discussing non-human species, have described two very different reproductive strategies that can be adopted by a species. One of these (the *r*-strategy) involves the production of large numbers of offspring while putting relatively little effort into child rearing. The success of this strategy depends on the high birthrate offsetting the low survival rate of the offspring. The other basic strategy (the *K*-strategy) involves the production of relatively few children, while putting relatively large effort into child rearing. In this strategy, the low birthrate is offset by the relatively high proportion of offspring who live long enough to reproduce.[11] Table 18-1 lists some characteristics typical of "*r*-strategists" and contrasts them with corresponding characteristics of "*K*-strategists."

The *r-K* classification is not an all-or-nothing choice, but rather a continuum. Rabbits are *r*-strategists compared to cattle or human beings, but are *K*-strategists compared to frogs or oysters (see Table 18-2).

TABLE 18-1
SOME TYPICAL DIFFERENCES BETWEEN *r*-STRATEGIST AND *K*-STRATEGIST SPECIES

r-strategists	*K*-strategists
1) Short interval between births	Long interval between births
2) Large litter size	Small litter size
3) Many offspring per female	Few offspring per female
4) High infant mortality	Low infant mortality
5) Little parental care	Much parental care
6) Children mature rapidly	Children mature slowly
7) Early onset of sexual activity	Late onset of sexual maturity
8) Low encephalization	High encephalization
9) Short life span	Long life span

Section 7 – Human races and the *r-K* scale

Compared with other animals, *all* human groups are extreme *K*-strategists. However, compared with each other, some human groups are more extreme *K*-strategists than others. In particular, there are a large number of biological and behavioral traits for which European whites are less extreme *K*-strategists than north Chinese, but are more extreme *K*-strategists than Negroes.[12]

The notion that Caucasoids, Mongoloids, and Negroids differ from each other on the *r-K* scale was first proposed by J. Philippe Rushton in his classic work *Race,*

> # TABLE 18-2
> ## THE r-K CONTINUUM
>
> | Type of animal | Typical number of offspring per year |
> |---|---|
> | Oysters | 500,000,000 |
> | Frogs | 200 |
> | Rabbits | 2 |
> | Hominoids (apes and humans) | < 1 |

Evolution, and Behavior. Among the numerous traits he mentions as examples of the *r-K* difference between the races are:[13]

- Age at menarche
- Length of menstrual cycle
- Length of gestation period
- Frequency of dizygotic twins (also, multizygotic triplets)
- Speed of physical maturation
- Age at first intercourse
- Frequency of intercourse.

Most of these traits are strongly affected by genetic factors, and all of them are part of the *r-K* pattern in animals.

Section 8 – Paternal investment theory

This set of differences between the races arose through natural selection, as geographically separated groups of human beings each adapted to local conditions. In particular, patterns of sexual behavior that were adaptive in the warm climates of sub-Saharan Africa were less adaptive in cold regions, such as Siberia, and had to be modified there.

The crucial difference was that Siberian winters were very harsh, making it far more difficult for infants to survive. In Siberia, a child that was reared only by its mother, with little or no assistance from the father, was quite unlikely to survive. Consequently, the "love 'em and leave 'em" strategy frequently adopted by males — which often worked very well in tropical and sub-tropical climates — was maladaptive in Siberia, since the progeny of such matings had very little chance of surviving and reproducing. In such cold climates, those males who invested more of their time and resources in rearing and providing for their offspring had a substantially greater probability of passing on their genes.[14]

For females in Siberia, the disadvantages of failing to find a man who would provide for her and her children during their childhood were much greater than they were in tropical climates, and females who were not careful to do so were much less likely to pass on their genes. Furthermore, because females in harsh climates were so demanding on this point, males who seemed unlikely to provide the needed assistance found it hard to find mates. In other words, there was a marked sexual selection against such males. Such selection could result, for example, in the peoples living in northerly climates gradually evolving lower levels of testosterone than the peoples living in sub-Saharan Africa.

The overall result was to push both males and females in Siberia (and, to a lesser but still significant extent, in climates milder than Siberia but harsher than sub-Saharan Africa) to become less promiscuous and more monogamous — in other words, more "Victorian" — in their sexual behavior.

The behavioral differences between those groups dwelling in tropical regions and those dwelling in colder northern regions arose during the Paleolithic Era as the various groups adapted to their own environments. However, at least statistically, those differences still endure. Note also that a difference in testosterone level frequently affects not only the sexual behavior of a young male, but also his aggressiveness.

(Despite the similarity in name, the "*paternal* investment theory" just described — a theory originated by Edward M. Miller[15] — is not the same as the "*parental* investment theory" described in chapter 7.)

Section 9 – Could these differences have been produced by social factors?
In principal, yes. It is not unlikely that the cultural norms that evolved in each region would be those that were adaptive there. However, that does not mean that genetic differences did not also arise. One would expect that cultural evolution and genetic evolution *both* occurred, and that they worked in tandem and reinforced each other in these matters.

Section 10 – Summary of Part III (chapters 14-18)
1) Blacks, whites, and Mongolids differ, on average, in a wide range of physical, intellectual, and behavioral traits. Many of these differences are large, easily observable, and significant.

2) These differences do not occur only within the United States, but are worldwide.

3) Some of the differences are primarily genetic in origin, and many others are at least partly genetic in origin.

4) Many of the differences can be explained in evolutionary terms as genetic adaptations to the climates in which different racial groups evolved.

FOOTNOTES – CHAPTER 18

1) (a) Rowe, David (1994), chapter 3, especially tables 3.2 and 3.5.
   (b) Pinker, Steven (2002), chapter 19, especially pp. 372-381.
   (c) Levin, Michael (1997), Table 4.3, pp. 100-101.

2) See, for example, *Two Nations* by Andrew Hacker (1992). Hacker (who is a whole-hearted environmentalist, and very sympathetic to the problems faced by black Americans) mentions sizable differences in divorce rates (p. 75), fertility rates (p. 71), illegitimate births (pp. 80, 83), and crime rates (pp. 180-183) between whites and blacks.

3) A clear presentation of the racial disparity in crime rates in the United States can be found in *The Color of Crime* (New Century Foundation, 1999), whose authors have carefully assembled data from government sources, including: (a) The Uniform Crime Reports (assembled annually by the FBI); and (b) the National Crime Victimization Survey (conducted annually by the Department of Justice). For racial disparities in crime rates in other parts of the world, see Rushton, J.P. (1997), table 7.3.

4) Rushton, J.P. (1997), table 7.2 and pp. 153-154, and sources cited therein.

5) (a) Crocker, J. & B. Major (1989).
   (b) Levin, Michael (1997), pp. 74-76.

6) See Rushton, J.P. (1997), chapter 8, (particularly pp. 166, 172, and 178-183), and sources cited therein.

7) Ross, R., et al. (1986).

8) Of course, the items in question need not be chocolate bars, but can be any items the subject finds valuable, including cash.

9) (a) Mischel, W. (1958).
   (b) Levin, Michael (1997), pp. 77-78.

10) Freedman, Daniel G. (1979), pp. 144-161.

11) (a) Wilson, E.O. (2000), pp. 99-103.
    (b) Rushton, J.P. (1997), chapter 10, especially pp. 199-207.

12) Rushton, J.P. (1997), chapter 10, especially pp. 213-216.

13) Rushton, J.P. (1997), table 1.1 (p. 5). See also his tables 7.1 (p. 148) and 8.1 (p. 166).

14) Miller, Edward M. (1994). See also Levin, Michael (1997), p. 176.

15) Miller, Edward M. (1994).

CHAPTER 19

ADVANCES IN THE UPPER PALEOLITHIC

Section 1 – Introduction

The main purpose of chapters 19-24 is to describe and discuss the Neolithic Era. However, before doing so it is worth considering the technological advances made in the last portion of the Paleolithic Era, the "Upper Paleolithic" (roughly, the period between 40 and 10 kya). Some of the most important of those advances are listed in Table 19-1. Perhaps the most striking feature of the list is how much longer it is than a similar list would be for any 30,000-year interval in the previous two million years.

Consider, for example, the development of stone tools. The earliest stone tools, some of which were made more than 2.5 million years ago, are called *Oldowan* tools (after Olduvai Gorge, in Africa, where they were first identified). Oldowan tools were made by primitive techniques, and were very crude — indeed, some can barely be recognized as man-made objects. Still, those tool-making techniques persisted for nearly a million years, and it was not until the advent of *Homo erectus* that new techniques for making stone tools were developed.

Tools made by the newer methods, which were introduced about a million and a half years ago, are called *Acheulian* tools. Most of them were hand axes, and they can usually be readily distinguished from Oldowan tools. Changes in the Acheulian toolkit were introduced only very slowly; indeed, there appear to be stretches of tens of thousands of years in which no improvements at all can be discerned. It was not until about 125 kya that a new toolkit, the *Mousterian*, was developed. The Mousterian toolkit (which was much more varied than the Acheulian) was still in use when the Upper Paleolithic began.

In striking contrast to that painfully slow rate of progress were the rapid changes that occurred during the Upper Paleolithic. Among the new tool industries developed during that period were the *Aurignacian*, the *Solutrean*, and the *Magdalenian*. However, it is not merely the variety of tool industries that is impressive; the newer tool industries were also clear improvements on the Mousterian.

TABLE 19-1

SOME IMPORTANT ADVANCES OF THE UPPER PALEOLITHIC

Advance	Date (a)	Where made
Aurignacian tool industry	34	Europe
Cave paintings	32 (b)	Europe
Sewing needles	30 (c)	Russia
Early ceramics	27	Europe
Solutrean tool industry	21	Europe
Bow and arrow	20 (d)	Europe (e)
Magdalenian tool industry	17	Europe
Harpoons	14	Europe
Fishhooks	14	Europe
Spear throwers	14	Europe
Pottery	13	Japan

(a) These dats are stated in kya. Most of them come from *The Human Career* by Richard Klein (1989), especially pp. 360-361 and 375-376.

(b) At Grotte Chauvet, in France. See Consilience, by Wilson, E. (1998), p. 226.

(c) This date is very uncertain. The earliest sewing needles recovered so far date to only about 20 kya.

(d) This is the date given by Klein (1989); much earlier estimates have been made. However, the earliest examples of bows and arrows that archaeologists have recovered so far date to no earlier than 12 kya.

(e) Or possibly North Africa.

By applying Oldowan tool-making techniques to a one-pound piece of flint, *Homo habilis* could produce only about 3 inches of cutting edge. Two million years later, by using Mousterian techniques, a similar piece of flint would yield 30 inches of cutting edge. However, using techniques devised in the Upper Paleolithic, the same piece of flint would yield 30 feet – 360 inches – of cutting edge.[1]

The new techniques were capable of producing much thinner, finer, more delicate tools. Using those finer tools enabled human beings to create such delicate objects as fishhooks and sewing needles. The latter were particularly important, since they enabled the production of clothing that could adequately protect the wearer even in very cold climates.

Many of the dates given in Table 19-1 are not well established. It is in general very risky to conclude that the earliest sample of some implement that we have uncovered so far is the same age as the first such implement ever made. For example: the oldest sewing needles unearthed so far only are only about 20 thousand years old; my estimate that sewing needles were made as early as 30 kya is an inference from the existence of human settlements that old in Siberia and northern Russia.

Section 2 – Why did the rate of progress increase?

Whatever the exact dates of the inventions listed may be, it is plain that the rate of technological advance was much, much higher in the Upper Paleolithic than in preceding eras. What was the cause of this great increase (the "Upper Paleolithic Revolution") in the rate of technological advance?

It is sometimes said that the rapid rate of intellectual and technological progress in recent eras results primarily from the fact that we are building on the foundations that earlier peoples laid. While this may be one factor, it is certainly not the whole story. After all, at most times in the distant past, human beings were *not* making advances over the achievements of earlier generations. The main reason why the rate of progress increased during the Upper Paleolithic was simply that humans living then were more intelligent than their distant ancestors had been. (One aspect of that greater intelligence, of course, was their greater linguistic ability.) Similarly, an important reason why the rate of progress has been even higher in recent millennia than in the Upper Paleolithic is that human intelligence has continued to grow, and is higher today than it was then. (See section 4, below.)

Section 3 – Which groups made the great inventions of the Upper Paleolithic?

From Table 19-1, it appears that almost all of the important inventions of that era were made by members of the μ-group. One of the inventions (pottery) was made by Mongolids; but it appears that most of the others were made by μ-3s dwelling in Europe. None were made by Negroids, nor by any other group living in tropical regions.

These facts are consistent with – and most easily explained by – the hypothesis that the groups that were living in cold climates had already evolved higher intelligence by 40 kya, and continued to evolve still higher intelligence during the next 30,000 years.

Table 19-2 includes, along with the estimated dates of several of those inventions, the estimated mean IQs of the human beings then living in the region where each invention was made. (The mean IQs are taken from the computer simulation described in chapter 17.)

Note that the inventions listed in table 19-2 fall naturally into two groups. The earlier set (which includes the Aurignacian toolkit, cave paintings, and sewing needles) seems to have been made by groups with mean IQs of around 80. The items in the later

TABLE 19-2

HUMAN INTELLIGENCE AND PALEOLITHIC INVENTIONS

Invention	Date (in kya)	Average human IQ in region in which invention was made
Aurignacian tool industry	34	79
Cave paintings	32	80
Sewing needles	30	81
Early ceramics	27	83
Solutrean tool industry	21	87
Bow and arrow	20	88
Magdalenian tool industry	17	90
Harpoons	14	92
Fishhooks	14	92
Spear throwers	14	92
Pottery	13	93

set (which include pottery, spear-throwers, fishhooks, and the bow and arrow) appear to have required greater intelligence for their invention; and, indeed, the human groups in which those inventions were made had considerably higher average IQs, typically about 90.

Of course, it is highly unlikely that any of these inventions were made by persons of average intelligence. The individuals who made these inventions (or improved them) probably exceeded the mean IQ of their group by three or four standard deviations, perhaps more. That has been the case for most of the important inventions of modern times (such as the steam engine, the phonograph, and the radio) and there is no reason to suppose it was not the case in earlier times. However, in a population with a mean IQ of about 70, even the "geniuses" would fall short of the level of intelligence needed to invent the bow and arrow. The level of human intelligence needed for that invention (and *a fortiori* for more sophisticated ones) evolved comparatively recently, and only in some regions.

Section 4 – The intellectual abilities of pre-human groups

Many people — perhaps influenced by movies such as *One Million B.C.* or by comic books or other fiction — assume that our ancestors hundreds of thousands of years ago had essentially the same intellectual ability as modern humans. A bit of reflection, though, will show that is highly unlikely.

TABLE 19-3

AVERAGE INTELLIGENCE OF VARIOUS SPECIES AND GROUPS

Species or group	Average brain size (cc)	Age of human children* with comparable reasoning ability
Chimpanzees	450	3 — 4 years old
Australopithecus	450	4½ — 5½ (?)
Homo habilis	650	6 — 7 (?)
Homo erectus	1000	8 — 9 (?)
HSS with IQs of 70	1270	10 — 11
HSS with IQs of 100 *	1350	14 — 15

* Modern Europeans

    The first column of Table 19-3 lists several groups in order of increasing reasoning ability. The last column shows the approximate age at which typical modern European children reach the same level of reasoning power.

    What is the source of the entries in the right-hand column? The entry in the bottom row comes from data showing that the performance of most individuals on intelligence tests does not rise appreciably after they reach fourteen or fifteen. (Of course, people continue to gain in knowledge and experience after their IQs level off.) The entry in the next-to-last row comes from test results which show that adults with IQs around 70 typically perform about as well as average 10- or 11-year-olds do. (Once again, in dealing with the problems of everyday life, the adults often make up in experience what they lack in raw intelligence.) The entry in the first row is based on observations of chimpanzees in captivity.

    The other three entries in the right-hand column are obviously highly speculative. We cannot directly observe or test the intelligence of any *Australopithicus*, *Homo habilis,* or *Homo erectus*. We do, however, know something about the average cranial capacities of those groups, and if we assume that in general, the species with larger brains had greater reasoning abilities, we can make some very rough estimates of the figures we should use in the right-hand column for those three species.

    Although it is plain that the figures in Table 19-3 are only rough estimates, it should be equally plain that any plausible estimates will indicate that the reasoning ability of the average adult *Homo erectus* must have been much lower than those of most modern adults. This factor alone suffices to explain the very low rate of technological progress in the Lower Paleolithic.

Some readers may object: "The ancient hominids were successful in coping with their environment, so they must have been more intelligent than Dr. Hart suggests." The answer to that objection is that it does not necessarily require a high level of intelligence for an organism to survive long enough to reproduce. Rabbits are highly successful (in the Darwinian sense) in coping with their environment, despite a very low level of intelligence. (For that matter, so are cockroaches, clams, and oak trees.) If — despite their obviously low capacity for abstract reasoning — monkeys can successfully cope with their environment, there is no reason to assume that *Australopithecus*, *Homo habilis*, or *Homo erectus* needed high IQs to cope with theirs.

FOOTNOTES — CHAPTER 19

1) Fagan, Brian M. (2001), Figure 3.19 (p. 102).

CHAPTER 20

THE NEOLITHIC REVOLUTION: DESCRIPTION

Section 1 – Introduction

The Neolithic Revolution has been defined as "the transition from food production by hunting and gathering to food production by raising plants and/or animals." It is generally considered to be one of the two or three most important developments in human history.

The Neolithic Revolution completely changed the whole manner of living of those peoples who adopted farming. It was also an indispensable prerequisite to the important developments that have followed. Since the Neolithic Revolution, every important invention or innovation has been made by peoples who had adopted farming. In addition, the growth of agriculture led to an enormous increase in population.

Section 2 – The origin of crop-raising

The Neolithic Revolution began about 11 kya in the Middle East, in and around the region now called the "Fertile Crescent." (See Map 20-1.) The first plants to be domesticated were emmer wheat, einkorn wheat, and barley. The wild ancestors of all three of those crops still grow in the Fertile Crescent today. At Abu Hureyra, in northern Syria, wild einkorn wheat was being harvested as early as 12 kya, and all three crops were being deliberately planted by 10.6 kya.[1] (The apparent dates of domestication are so close that it is hard to be sure which crop was planted first, and it seems possible that the success of the first crop led promptly to domestication of the other two.)

Within a few centuries, use of the three crops had spread to other parts of the Fertile Crescent and southern Turkey. From the Fertile Crescent, knowledge of agriculture spread in three main directions:

- Into Anatolia (quite early), and thence into Europe.
- Into Egypt and Ethiopia, and from there into the rest of Africa.
- Into Iran and India.

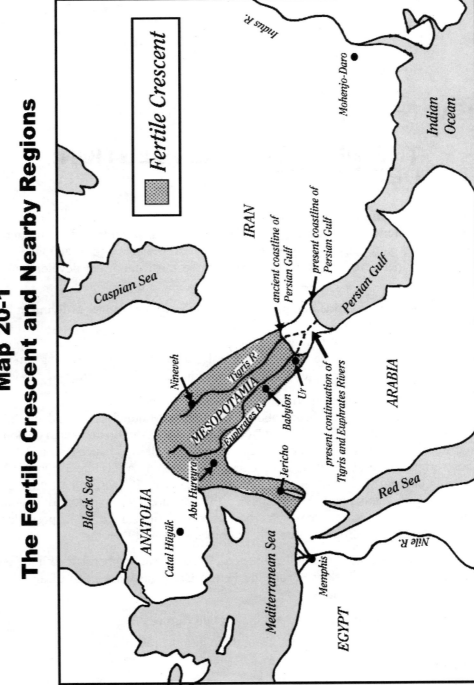

In neither Europe nor India was agriculture developed independently. It has been suggested that it was invented independently in tropical West Africa and/or the Sudan,[2] but the chronology makes this highly unlikely. We know that agriculture was being widely practiced in the Fertile Crescent by 9 kya, but it was not practiced in tropical West Africa until about 5 kya. In the intervening millennia, it had spread to Egypt (about 8 kya) and to Ethiopia, and from there across the Sudan, reaching the western Sudan about 7 kya.

Agriculture, using rice as the main crop, was invented independently about 9 or 9.5 kya in the Yangtze River basin in central China.[3] From there, rice farming spread into southern China, and thence into Southeast Asia, India, the Philippines, and Indonesia. Agriculture using millet as the main crop developed in northern China about 8.4 kya.[4]

Agriculture was also developed independently in the Western Hemisphere. It appears to have arisen independently in three parts of the New World: Mesoamerica, South America, and the eastern United States.[5] Neither wheat, barley, millet, rice, nor rye grew wild in the Western Hemisphere, and the main cereal crop developed there was maize.

It also appears that agriculture was invented independently in the New Guinea highlands. It was clearly being practiced there by 6 kya, but there is some evidence it may have started as early as 9 kya.[6]

Section 3 – Planting crops vs. plant breeding

In theory, people might decide to deliberately raise and harvest some naturally occurring plant, and do so without altering the plant genetically. In practice, this rarely happens. Farmers, when deciding what to sow, usually select the seeds of particularly good individual plants. As a result, the domesticated version of that plant evolves rapidly, a process that may be called *artificial selection*. (That is why strawberries sold in the supermarket are typically much larger than wild strawberries.) In similar fashion, domesticated animals soon become different from the wild animals they derive from. Evolution by means of artificial selection was mentioned by Darwin in the first chapter of *The Origin of Species*, and he provided many clear examples of it.

Even without any deliberate human attempt to improve the plant species, many plants evolve considerably when they are adopted as crops. For example, the seeds of wild wheat grow at the top of a stalk, and the stalk eventually shatters spontaneously, thus scattering the seeds on the ground, where some will produce offspring. However, there exists a mutant gene that prevents the stalk from shattering. In the wild, that gene is selected against, and is therefore rare. But ancient human beings who wished to bring food back to their families would, of course, pick a stalk that had not yet shattered. Seeds that fell off near the person's home (whether or not they were deliberately planted) were likely to possess the mutant gene. Hence, continued harvesting of wheat automatically tended to produce a variety whose stalks did not spontaneously shatter, and thus was more useful to early farmers.[7] Similar processes occurred with barley and with peas.

Section 4 – What crops were most useful for early farmers?

Although there are a large number of edible plants, not all of them are suitable as farm crops. From the point of view of early farmers, the most useful plants were cereal crops, as these were easy to plant, fast-growing, and had high yields per acre.[8]

Early farmers often grew wheat and/or barley because those crops were easy to domesticate. Furthermore, both of them (particularly wheat) are relatively rich in protein.[9] (Early farmers did not need to know anything about proteins in order for protein-rich crops to be preferred. Tribes with unhealthy diets either changed them or died out.)

Rice is a very desirable crop because of its high yield in calories per acre; however, it requires a lot of water, and the crop is therefore unsuited to many climates. Modern corn — which is the product of millennia of plant breeding — is an excellent crop, but the wild plant it derives from, *teosinte*, had much lower yields than early forms of wheat did and was therefore a much less desirable starting point than wild wheat.[10] Other useful cereals included millet, rye, oats, and sorghum.

Aside from cereals, the most useful crops were pulses (plants that yield peas or beans), since many of them are rich in proteins. Soybeans have a particularly high protein content.[11]

Among the edible roots and tubers are cassava (or manioc), potatoes, sweet potatoes, taro, and yams. Many of them are tasty, but their protein content is often low. The same could be said of most melons. Many fruits that grow on trees are very tasty; however, the interval between the time a tree is planted and the time it bears fruit is generally quite long, with the result that fruits played almost no part in the origin of agriculture.

Section 5 – The development of animal husbandry

The domestication of animals also started in the Middle East, although a bit later than the domestication of plants. The first farm animals were goats (about 10 kya), followed by sheep and pigs (9.5 kya).[12]

The wild ancestor of the domestic goat is the bezoar goat, which was native to Southwest Asia. The earliest evidence of its domestication is at Ganj Dareh, in western Iran. Domestic sheep are first found at Abu Hureyra, in Syria; they derive from a wild species, mouflon sheep, which is indigenous to Southwest and Central Asia.[13]

Domestic pigs are derived from the wild boar, which had a wide range in Eurasia and North Africa. The earliest sign of domestic pigs is at Çayönü, in Anatolia. In the Far East, the pig was the first farm animal to be domesticated.[14]

Cattle were not domesticated in the Middle East until about 8.7 kya.[15] All domestic cattle are derived from the *aurochs*, a species that became extinct in early modern times, but was once found in large parts of Asia, Africa, and Europe. Cattle are far more useful farm animals than either sheep or goats; but the aurochs was a less tractable animal than the mouflon sheep or bezoar goat, which is probably why it was not domesticated until long after they were.

Domestic horses are derived from a now-extinct species of wild horse that lived in southern Russia. They were even less tractable than the aurochs, and were not domesticated until about 6 kya.[16]

Only a few other large animals have been domesticated, and most of them are only important in limited regions. Among the most important are camels, donkeys, water buffalo, yaks, and reindeer.

Several potentially useful animal species — including horses and camels — had lived in the Western Hemisphere before it was settled by man, but it appears that they were quickly hunted to extinction by the Paleo-Indians. As a result, none of the those species were present in the New World when farming began there, and the only large animals domesticated in the Western Hemisphere were the llama and alpaca, and those only in parts of South America.

Dogs were probably domesticated in the late Paleolithic Era (by 12 kya in Western Asia, by 10.5 kya in North America), and one might therefore argue that they were not part of the Neolithic Revolution. However, both farmers and herdsmen found them to be very useful. The ancestor of the domestic dog was the wolf (*Canis lupus*), a species that had a large range in both hemispheres.[17] Since cats were not domesticated until much later (probably within the last 4000 years) they played no part in the Neolithic Revolution.

Section 6 – The formation of villages and towns

The Neolithic Revolution resulted in most humans dwelling in small farm villages. That pattern continued in most of the world until the 20th century. Although there was much variation, a typical village had a population of about 200. Among the earliest villages were Abu Hureyra in Syria, Ganj Dareh in Iran, Jericho in Palestine, and Çayönü in Turkey, all of which were in existence by 9.5 kya.[18]

Farmers could often produce considerably more food than they and their families required. This made possible the formation of towns (which, unlike farm villages, were not self-sufficient in food). The largest of the early towns was Çatal Hüyük in central Anatolia, which was flourishing by 8.2 kya and was conducting both copper smelting and textile manufacturing by then.[19]

Since much of the population of the larger towns were not engaged in the production of food, their time was freed for other pursuits. Towns often included many merchants, artisans, and craftsmen. Some of them also included an organized body of priests, government officials, and a leisure class. As result, there was a striking increase in the rate of inventions and innovations.

Section 7 – Formation of more complex societal structures

In the Paleolithic, almost all humans lived in small groups called *bands* (see chapter 6). With the onset of the Neolithic Revolution, larger and more complex societies began to arise. Many anthropologists divide these into three main categories of progressively more complex societies: tribes, chiefdoms, and states.[20]

For our purposes, the exact definitions of those three categories are not important. (The boundaries between them are imprecise, and other methods of classification have been proposed.) What does matter is the type of changes that occurred in a region as it gradually changed from a collection of bands to a collection of states. Among the principal changes were:

1) *Increased size of the units.* Primitive bands generally had populations of only 20-80 persons, all of whom knew each other personally, and many of whom were closely related by blood. States have populations of tens of thousands, often millions, and a given citizen is only personally acquainted with a small fraction of them.

2) *A change from nomadism to settled residences.* Bands were almost always nomadic; but larger, more complex societies usually include a fixed settlement such as a village, town, or city.

3) *Progressively greater division of labor.* Within bands, the only division of labor between adults was that between males and females. As societies grew larger and more complex, people adopted an ever wider variety of occupations.

4) *Increasing inequality between individuals.*

5) *Increasing centralization of decision-making and political power.* Bands had no political structures or hierarchies. As societies became larger and more complex, governing structures arose, and political power and decision-making became progressively more centralized. Also, formal procedures were instituted for the resolution of conflict between individuals.

6) *Formation of large organized religious establishments.* Although there is evidence that humans living in the late Paleolithic Era had religious beliefs, there were no organized religions, temples, or formal priesthoods during that period. These arose during the Neolithic Era, and were a prominent feature of all early states.

The progression from small bands to large states did not commence in a given region until agriculture was adopted there, and it normally took thousands of years to complete. It is therefore not surprising that it was in those regions in which agriculture took hold earliest — such as China, Egypt, and the Fertile Crescent — that the earliest states arose.

FOOTNOTES – CHAPTER 20

1) Smith, Bruce D. (1998), chapter 4, especially pp. 68-72. In that chapter, Smith presents the data in terms of uncalibrated radiocarbon dates; but I have used the chart he supplied in his preface to convert those dates to calendar years.

2) Diamond, Jared (1999), pp. 98-100. (However, he does not insist that agriculture did arise independently in West Africa, only that it might have.)

3) Smith, Bruce D. (1998), pp. 127-131. The heart of the agricultural homeland seems to have been the region directly north of Lake Tung-t'ing, near the boundary between Hunan and Hubei provinces.

4) Smith, Bruce D. (1998), pp. 133-137.

5) Diamond, Jared (1999), pp. 98-100.

6) (a) Smith, Bruce D. (1998), pp. 142-143.
   (b) Diamond, Jared (1999), pp. 100 and 303-304.
   (c) Fagan, Brian M. (2001), pp. 316-317.

7) Diamond, Jared (1999), p. 120.

8) Diamond, Jared (1999), p. 125.

9) Diamond, Jared (1999), p. 138.

10) Diamond, Jared (1999), p. 137.

11) Diamond, Jared (1999), p. 125.

12) Smith, Bruce D. (1998), pp. 56-65.

13) Smith, Bruce D. (1998), pp. 53-61. Also see Diamond, Jared (1999), Table 9.1 (p. 160).

14) Diamond, Jared (1999), Tables 9.1 (p. 160) and 9.3 (p. 167).

15) Smith, Bruce D. (1998), pp. 65-67.

16) Diamond, Jared (1999), Table 9.3 (p. 167).

17) Wilson, Edward O. (2000), p. 509.

18) Fagan, Brian M. (2001), Table 9.1 (p. 255).

19) *Historical Atlas of the Ancient World* (2000 edit.), p. 1.03.

20) Diamond, Jared (1999), chapter 14, especially pp. 267-281 and Table 14.1.

CHAPTER 21

TECHNOLOGICAL ADVANCES IN THE NEOLITHIC

Section 1 – Crops and beverages

The first crops planted in the Middle East were emmer wheat, einkorn wheat, and barley. The first ones planted in China were rice and millet. All of these are cereals. Among the additional cereals domesticated in the Neolithic were maize (in the Western Hemisphere), and sorghum (in Africa).

Among the roots and tubers domesticated in the Neolithic were yams (in sub-Saharan Africa), potatoes and manioc (in South America), and sweet potatoes (in Mesoamerica). Among the earliest fruits cultivated were olives, dates, figs, and grapes. These fruits were first cultivated in lands bordering the Mediterranean, although the ranges of the wild species were much larger.[1]

Among the other significant food crops grown in the Neolithic were peas, lentils, soybeans, lima beans, chickpeas, sugar cane, pumpkins, and peanuts. In addition, various fibers — including cotton, flax, and hemp — were cultivated. Beer and wine were being made by 6 kya (= 4000 BC), but distilled beverages were not made until much later.

Section 2 – Inventions related to agriculture

The Neolithic Revolution resulted in a great increase in the rate of inventions. Several of these are listed in Table 21-1.[2] Not surprisingly, several of the inventions were designed to increase the productivity of farmers. An important one was irrigation, which was being used in the Middle East by 7.5 kya. Crop rotation was employed by 6.5 kya in both Europe and the Middle East. Plows were being used in the Middle East by 6.5 kya, and in China by 5 kya.

Section 3 – Pottery

Strictly speaking, pottery is not a Neolithic invention, since it was invented *before* agriculture (in Japan, about 13 kya). Everywhere else, though, the manufacture of pottery came after the introduction of agriculture.

Pottery was invented independently in the Middle East, apparently about 9 kya. It

TABLE 21-1
SOME IMPORTANT NEOLITHIC INVENTIONS

Invention	Date (kya)	Where made
Pottery	13	Japan
Bricks (sun-dried)	10	ME (=Middle East)
Linen	8.5	ME
Copper smelting	8.2	ME
Irrigation	7.5	ME
Cotton	7	India
Plow	6.5	ME
Potter's wheel	6.5	ME
Wool	6	ME
Bronze	5.8	ME
Wheeled vehicles	5.6	Russia
Writing	5.4	ME (Sumeria)
Silk	4.7	China

appeared in southern China even earlier. However, pottery was not produced in the New World until about 6 kya.

Apart from its utility to the people who used it, ancient pottery is important to modern archaeologists and historians because: (a) It can often be precisely dated by modern scientific methods; and (b) The style of an item often indicates where it was produced.

Section 4 – Materials

Techniques for improving stone tools and weapons by grinding and polishing them were devised in this era, which is why it is called the *New Stone Age* or *Neolithic Era*.

Since metallic gold and silver often occur naturally, they were known in the Paleolithic. However, as they are not hard enough to make implements with, they were used for ornamental purposes only. The first metal to be used for implements was copper, which was being smelted in parts of the Middle East as early as 8.2 kya. Bronze — an alloy of copper and tin — is much harder and stronger than pure copper; and by 5 kya, in both Egypt and Babylonia, it was frequently being used to make tools and weapons. However, since tin ores are fairly rare, bronze was rather expensive, and this limited the use of bronze implements.

The earliest textile was linen, which was being made from flax by 8.5 kya in the Middle East. Cotton was produced in India by 7 kya, and in the Western Hemisphere by 5 kya. Wool was being produced in the Middle East by 6 kya (= 4000 BC). Silk production started in China about 4.7 kya (= 2700 BC).

Sun-dried bricks were being used for construction in Jericho by 10 kya; and by 8 kya, buildings were being constructed there using bricks and mortar. The earliest stone structures that we know of were constructed about 6.5 kya, in Western Europe.

Section 5 – Transportation

Draft animals were being used in both Europe and the Middle East by 6.5 kya. Sailboats, another Neolithic invention, were being used in both Egypt and the Middle East by about 6 kya. The horse was domesticated about 6 kya in southern Russia; and wheeled vehicles were being used there by 5.6 kya.

Section 6 – Writing

The introduction of bronze has traditionally been taken as marking the end of the Neolithic Era. However, as the invention of writing was far more important than the invention of bronze working, it seems to be more appropriate to choose the introduction of writing as marking the end of the Neolithic. If we do that, the era following the Neolithic might appropriately be called the "Historic Era."

Writing was first developed in the Middle East (more specifically, in Sumeria) in the fourth millennium BC. A discussion of the invention and spread of writing will be deferred until chapter 25.

Section 7 – Which groups made these technological advances?

From Table 21-1 it can be seen that virtually all of the important Neolithic advances were made by members of the μ-group (which includes both the Caucasoids and the Mongoloids). These, of course, were the groups whose natural intelligence had increased the most during the preceding epochs.

FOOTNOTES – CHAPTER 21

1) A more extensive list of plants (and animals) domesticated in the Neolithic Era is presented in *HarperCollins Atlas of World History* (1999 edit.), pp. 38-39. See also

   (a) *Historical Atlas of the Ancient World* (1998), p. 1.03.
   (b) *DK Atlas of World History* (2001 edit.), pp. 20-21.
   (c) Diamond, Jared (1999), tables 5.1, 7.1, and 9.1.

2) The data in Table 21-1 comes from various sources; however, most of the dates can be found in *Historical Atlas of the Ancient World* (1998).

CHAPTER 22

SOME MIGRATIONS DRIVEN BY AGRICULTURE

Section 1 – Introduction

The adoption of agriculture in a region normally resulted in a great increase in food production. Invariably, though, the human population in such a region increased until it pressed against the limit of the food supply. Often, at that point, some of the farmers in the region migrated to nearby lands occupied by hunter-gatherers.

This frequently led to conflict with the aboriginal inhabitants of those lands. However, the invading farmers usually had an enormous advantage in such conflicts, because the farming region had a far greater population than the hunter-gatherers in the contested region. Consequently, the result was normally that the contested region became occupied by farmers — either because the earlier population was displaced by the invaders (this is called a *demic expansion*), or because the hunter-gatherers adopted agriculture (this would be an instance of *cultural diffusion*), or by some combination of those two processes.[1]

In such cases, the languages of the aboriginal inhabitants were often replaced by the languages of the invading farmers. When this occurred, it often resulted in related languages being spoken over a very wide area. A few of the more important agriculture-driven expansions are described in this chapter.

Section 2 – The Dravidian invasion of India

The earliest signs of farming within the Indian subcontinent are found at Mehrgarh, a village in Baluchistan (the westernmost section of Pakistan), where agriculture was flourishing by 8 kya (= 6000 BC). There are, however, strong reasons for doubting that agriculture was invented independently in the Indian subcontinent.

- There are no signs of farming in Mehrgarh until about 2000 years after it was established in the Middle East.

- Baluchistan is the part of the Indian subcontinent that is closest to the Fertile Crescent.

- The earliest domestic crops and farm animals found at Mehrgarh (including a west Asian species of goat and a west Asian variety of wheat) had all been in use in the Middle East.[2]

These facts strongly suggest that agriculture was introduced into India from the Middle East. The linguistic evidence also supports this view. Today, Indo-European languages — which were brought in by the Aryan invasions of the second millennium BC — are spoken in most of northern India, while Dravidian languages are spoken in southern India. However, the presence in northern India and Pakistan of scattered regions where Dravidian languages are still spoken suggests that Dravidian languages were spoken throughout India prior to the Aryan invasions. Furthermore, Elamite — a now-extinct language that in ancient times was spoken in what is now southwest Iran — is an outlying member of the same language group, which suggests that Dravidian languages were once spoken in much of Iran as well.[3] The combined evidence suggests the following scenario.

About 9 kya — at a time when India was still inhabited by Paleolithic hunter-gatherers descended from the original σ-1 settlers — there were some Neolithic farming groups living on the eastern fringes of the Fertile Crescent who spoke a now-extinct language that we might call "Proto-Dravidian." Racially, these peoples were Caucasoids, descended from the μ-1 who had inhabited the Middle East for tens of thousands of years. In the course of the next millennium, some of those Neolithic farming groups migrated westward across Iran, replacing the hunter-gatherers who had previously lived there. By 8 kya, they had established some farming communities in what is now western Pakistan.

By 6 kya, descendants of those farmers had settled both the Indus Valley and the Ganges Valley; and by about 5 kya (= 3000 BC) agriculture had spread into central, eastern, and southern India as well. Since the invaders had the additional advantage of higher average intelligence, they largely pushed aside the aboriginal hunter-gatherers, although with some interbreeding.

By 2000 BC, these hybrids had formed a new racial group living in India, one which we might call the "Dravidian" race. The gene pool of this Dravidian race was mostly derived from the Caucasoid invaders, but included many alleles that had been prevalent in the aboriginal σ-1 and that were of adaptive advantage in the Indian climate.

Prior to entering India, the Proto-Dravidians had, on average, higher intelligence than the σ-1 living in India (see Table 17-1). The mean IQ of the resulting Dravidian race was between those of the two groups that it came from, but closer to that of the Caucasoid invaders.

Scattered throughout India there were still, in 2000 BC, some regions where the population was primarily of σ-1 parentage. Such regions were more common in eastern India than elsewhere. Indeed, in some of these regions, many of the inhabitants still exhibit more "Australoid" features than the bulk of the Indian population. However, it is not clear that any of the modern inhabitants of India are *primarily* of σ-1 descent.

Section 3 – The spread of the Afro-Asiatic speakers

Meanwhile, a somewhat similar set of events was occurring in northern Africa (see Map 22-1). There too, agriculture was not invented independently, but was brought in by migrants from the Fertile Crescent. As might be expected, therefore, the earliest Egyptian crops were wheat and barley (both of which had already been domesticated in the Middle East) and the earliest domesticated animals were sheep and goats.[4]

The linguistic evidence also supports this hypothesis. Ancient Egyptian is a member of the Afro-Asiatic language family, the same family that the Semitic languages spoken in Southwest Asia belong to. Likewise, the Berber languages spoken in North Africa belong to another branch of that family (see section 9-3). The combined evidence is consistent with the following scenario.

About 9 kya — at a time when Egypt (and, indeed, all of Africa) was still inhabited by Paleolithic hunter-gatherers — the western portion of the Fertile Crescent was inhabited by Neolithic farmers who spoke a now-extinct language that we might call "Proto-Afro-Asiatic." Racially, these people were Caucasoids descended from the original µ-1 stock who had settled the Middle East many thousands of years earlier.

In the course of the next millennium, some of those farmers migrated southwest into Egypt, and by 8 kya they had established farming communities there. By 6 kya (= 4000 BC), the Nile Valley was the home of many farming communities, and the earlier Paleolithic inhabitants had been displaced, albeit with some interbreeding. Among the languages spoken there — all descended from Proto-Afro-Asiatic — was an ancestral form of Ancient Egyptian.

Meanwhile, some of the farmers in Egypt had migrated further west, gradually spreading across North Africa. Some of them may have reached Algeria and Morocco as early as 7.5 kya, only 500 years after their ancestors had reached Egypt. In doing so, they displaced the earlier Paleolithic inhabitants, although with some interbreeding. These migrants spoke another offshoot of Proto-Afro-Asiatic, one that we might call "Proto-Berber," the language ancestral to all the Berber languages of North Africa and the Sahara.

Meanwhile, another group of farmers — coming either from Egypt, or directly from Southwest Asia — had migrated down the coast of the Red Sea, reaching and settling Ethiopia about 7.5 kya. The various Cushitic languages spoken in parts of East Africa today derive from the languages of those invaders.

From Ethiopia, farmers speaking Afro-Asiatic languages spread westward across the Sudan (the stretch of savannah situated between the Sahara Desert and the forests and jungles of tropical Africa). Some of them reached and conquered a region near Lake Chad that was inhabited by Negroes. In time, the Negro tribesmen adopted the language of their conquerors, and the tongues spoken by their modern descendants comprise the Chadic group of languages (see section 9-3). However, since the invaders were outnumbered by the earlier inhabitants, in the course of the intervening millennia (during which there has been a great deal of interbreeding) the genes of the invaders

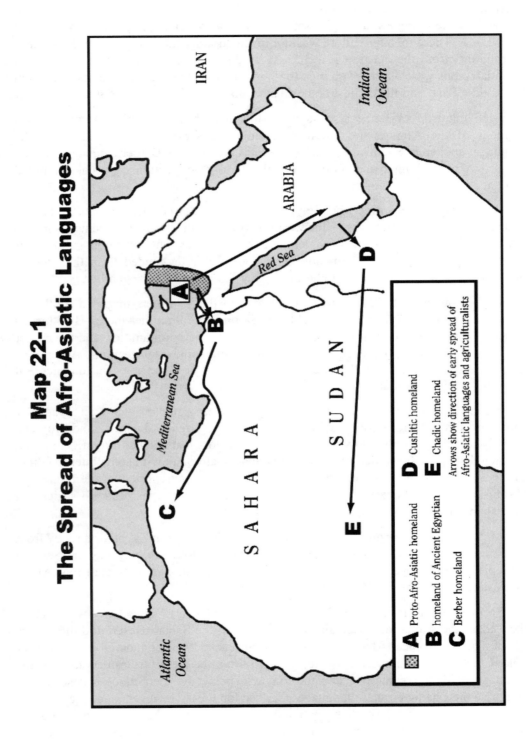

have been swamped by those of the earlier inhabitants, and the present population appears entirely Negroid. (Similar instances of elite-dominance followed by gene replacement have occurred in other parts of the world.)

While these events were occurring in Africa, the descendants of the speakers of Proto-Afro-Asiatic were also thriving in Southwest Asia. The languages spoken by them were in the Semitic branch of the Afro-Asiatic family. Some of those Semitic-speakers migrated southward into the Arabian peninsula, eventually taking over that region entirely. Competition was much fiercer in and near the Fertile Crescent, where other groups (including Sumerians, Elamites, Hittites, Hurrians, and others) also possessed agriculture. Nevertheless, by 1000 BC, most inhabitants of the Fertile Crescent spoke Semitic languages.

In the last millennium BC, Semites from southern Arabia crossed the Red Sea and conquered parts of Ethiopia. Their language (Amharic) is still the official language of that country. More recently, the Arab conquests (see chapter 34) spread Arabic throughout the Middle East and into much of North Africa, with the result that it now has more speakers than all the other Afro-Asiatic languages combined.

Section 4 – The Austronesian expansion

The Austronesian family, which includes nearly a thousand languages, has an immense range, extending from Easter Island (in a remote part of the Pacific), to Indonesia, to Madagascar (off the coast of Africa). Three of the four main branches of the family are spoken only on Taiwan. This suggests that the Austronesian languages on Taiwan have had more time to diverge from each other than they had elsewhere, and therefore that the early Austronesian-speakers spread out from Taiwan.[5] The archaeological evidence is consistent with that hypothesis. A scenario that seems consistent with the evidence goes as follows (see Map 22-2).[6]

The ancestors of the Austronesians were σ-3 farmers living in southern China, where they cultivated rice and millet. About 5.5 kya (= 3500 BC), some of those people — speaking "Proto-Austronesian" — migrated to Taiwan, which at the time was populated only by hunter-gatherers. Because of their command of agriculture, the migrants expanded rapidly, and within a few centuries they had taken over the whole island.

Population pressure resulted in further migrations. By 3000 BC, some of these people had migrated southward to the Philippines (which had previously been occupied only by σ-2 hunter-gatherers), and within a few centuries, the migrants had taken over virtually the entire archipelago. (The Negrito groups living in the Philippines today may represent remnants of the aboriginal σ-2.)

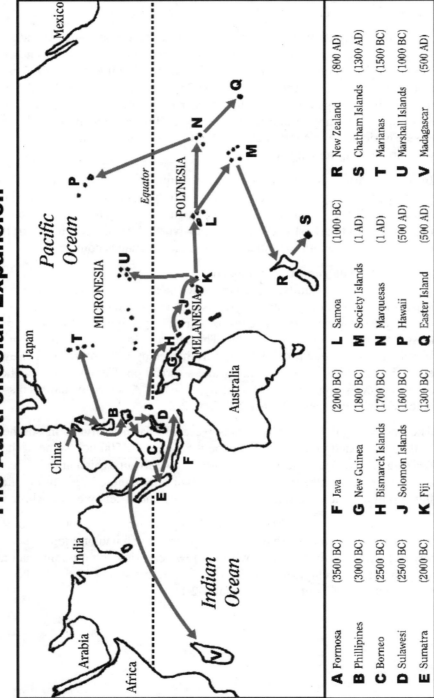

About 2500 BC, migrants from the Philippines entered Borneo and Sulawesi in Indonesia. Prior to that, Indonesia had been inhabited only by Paleolithic peoples belonging to the σ-2 group. Once again, the farmers increased rapidly in numbers and largely displaced the prior inhabitants. By 2000 BC, population pressure in Borneo motivated some of the Austronesian farmers to migrate into Java and Sumatra, which they soon took over. Perhaps a thousand years later, migrants from Borneo and/or Sumatra spread into the southern part of the Malay Peninsula.

Much later, migrants from western Indonesia traveled all the way to Madagascar — over 3000 miles away! — and colonized that previously-uninhabited island. (Although Madagascar lies only 250 miles off the coast of Africa, none of the Negroid peoples living in Africa had ever reached it.)

Meanwhile, when population pressure became a problem in Sulawesi, some of the Austronesian farmers migrated eastward to Halmahera, and from there to New Guinea. They soon took over the coastal lowlands of northern New Guinea, which had been populated only by hunter-gatherers; however, they did not take over the interior highlands, which were already populated by indigenous farmers. From northern New Guinea they spread to the Bismarck Islands (about 1700 BC), and the Solomon Islands (about a century later), again displacing Paleolithic peoples. In all those places, the Austronesian settlers crossbred to some extent with the prior σ-4 inhabitants.

From the Solomons, it took the Austronesian farmers only a few centuries to reach the rest of Melanesia (the Santa Cruz Islands, the New Hebrides, New Caledonia, and Fiji), which had previously been uninhabited. Fiji was settled about 1300 BC, and the westernmost islands in Polynesia (Tonga and Samoa) were settled by 1000 BC.

After reaching Samoa, the Austronesians paused awhile and honed their skills. East of Samoa, the island groups are further apart, and the islands are very small, making it more difficult to establish new colonies. The expansion was resumed late in the first millennium BC, and from then on was very rapid. By the first century AD they had settled all but the most remote of the other Polynesian islands.

To reach the remaining ones required very long voyages, in some cases, nearly 2000 miles. The Hawaiian Islands (which are far to the north of the rest of Polynesia) were reached about 500 AD, and Easter Island (far to the east) was probably reached about the same time. New Zealand (which is far to the south of the other Polynesian islands) was reached a few centuries later. The Chatham Islands, which are located about 500 miles east of New Zealand, seem to have been reached about 1300 AD.

Meanwhile, starting about 1000 BC, settlers from Fiji or Samoa had colonized eastern Micronesia. Western Micronesia was settled directly from the Philippines and Indonesia, starting a few centuries before that.

The people who carried out these remarkable sea voyages — often settling small islands that lacked any game or useful crops — had neither compasses nor astronomical instruments. Still, it is plain that the entire expansion was driven by agriculture, since most of the islands they colonized lacked the flora and fauna needed to support a Paleolithic population. (The original settlers, therefore, had to bring the necessary plants and animals with them.)

As a result of these migrations, the σ-2 group has been almost eliminated. Indonesia is now inhabited by a hybrid group, mostly of σ-3 parentage, but partly descended from σ-2. Melanesians, Micronesians, and Polynesians are also hybrids, partly descended from the Indonesian groups, but usually with some σ-4 parentage or Mongolid ancestry as well.

Prior to the Austronesian expansion, the σ-3 had evolved a higher average intelligence than the σ-2 or σ-4 groups. The various hybrids therefore have mean IQs intermediate between the σ-3 and the other groups.

Section 5 – The Bantu expansion

Today, most of sub-Saharan Africa is occupied by Negroes. That was not the case, however, three thousand years ago. At that time, a large part of eastern Africa, and most of southern Africa, were occupied by the Sanids, while the Pygmies occupied a much larger portion of central Africa than they do now. These two groups were still hunter-gatherers, but the Negroes practiced agriculture, which had spread to tropical West Africa by cultural diffusion from the Middle East.

Starting a few centuries BC, groups of West African Negroes — speaking a now-extinct language that we may call "Proto-Bantu" — started migrating eastward and southward from their homeland in or near Cameroon and Nigeria.[7] (Proto-Bantu was a member of the Niger-Congo language family.) In addition to their knowledge of agriculture, these migrants had another advantage over the peoples whose lands they were invading: they possessed iron weapons. Knowledge of ironworking had probably reached them by diffusion from the Middle East, where it had developed in the second millennium BC.

The expansion of these farmers was quite rapid, and by 1000 AD, most of Africa south of the Equator was occupied by Negro tribes speaking hundreds of closely related languages, all derived from Proto-Bantu.[8] Indeed, that expansion has continued, with the result that today the Pygmies are confined to isolated patches in the Congo rainforest, while the Sanids have been pushed into relatively barren lands in southern Africa.

Today, the combined population of Sanids (Bushmen and Hottentots) and Pygmies is only about three or four hundred thousand — less that one-tenth of one percent of the total population of sub-Saharan Africa. The Bantu expansion is therefore an extreme example of a *demic* expansion. As it is not clear that there was any significant difference between the average intelligence of the Negroes and the peoples they displaced, the success of the Negro invaders was probably due to their knowledge of agriculture and ironworking, although their greater physical size may also have been a factor.

The West African Negroes also expanded east and northeast into territory formerly inhabited by East African Negroes. (This is probably the reason why the regions where Nilo-Saharan languages are spoken are now rather scattered.)

Section 6 – The spread of agriculture into Europe

Agriculture was being practiced in the Fertile Crescent and southern Anatolia as early as 10 kya (= 8000 BC), and by 9.5 kya in western Anatolia as well. About 9 kya, the use of agriculture spread from Anatolia into Greece,[9] and from there it spread west and north into other parts of Europe.

By 8 kya, there were farm villages in parts of Italy, and by 7.5 kya agriculture had spread into southern France and southern Spain. By 7 kya, agriculture had spread throughout the Balkans, and up into southern Germany. By 6.5 kya, agriculture was being practiced in the Ukraine, and by 6 kya it had spread into northern France, northern Spain, and England. Finally, by 5.5 kya agriculture had spread into Scotland, northern Germany, and Scandinavia. (Most of these dates are obtained from carbon-14 dating of ancient European sites.[10])

Note that agriculture took only about 1500 years to spread all the way across southern Europe, from Greece to Spain; however, it took a good deal longer to spread northwards into Scandinavia and Scotland. The slower rate of spread into northern lands was probably due to the difficulty that people, farm animals, and crops had of adjusting to new (and harsher) climates.

As the farmers expanded into Europe, they tended to bring their own languages with them. However, since this was only partly a demic expansion (see the next section), language replacement was not nearly as complete as it was in the cases of the Dravidian, Austronesian, and Bantu expansions. Furthermore, even in those places where languages from the Middle East took hold, they were subsequently replaced by Indo-European languages (see chapter 26).

Section 7 – Resulting genetic and IQ changes in Europe

Maps of Europe based on the distribution of genes clearly show the effect of the migration of people from the Middle East into the Balkans, and thence north and west into other parts of Europe. In fact, those migrations account for about 28% of the total genetic variance found between different parts of Europe.[11]

Now if agriculture had spread entirely by cultural diffusion, we would not expect to observe this gradual cline from southwest to northeast Europe, but rather a relatively steep cline at the boundary between Europe and Asia Minor. However, it is also true that if the spread of agriculture was entirely a demic expansion (i.e., if the incoming farmers had *completely* displaced the Paleolithic aborigines) their migration would not have produced a large genetic variation between the regions of Europe. It appears, therefore, that the spread of agriculture within Europe occurred partly by cultural diffusion and partly by actual incursions of farming peoples from the Middle East, with both processes being important. That is what we might expect to happen if the outsiders possessed an advantage in technology but the aborigines had an advantage in average intelligence.

On the other hand, the archaeological evidence indicates that very little population replacement occurred in the Ukraine and Russia. In other words, in those regions, agriculture spread mostly by cultural diffusion.

In general, when an expansion or migration involves the mixing of two populations, the IQs of the resulting hybrids will be intermediate between those of the invaders and the aborigines. From Table 17-1 we can see that prior to the incursion of farmers from the Middle East the average intelligence within Europe had been greater than that in the Middle East. It follows that the agricultural expansion into Europe resulted in a *decrease* of average IQs in most sections of Europe. (One would expect this decrease to be greatest in southeast Europe, where there was the greatest influx of genes from the Middle East, with smaller decreases in southwest and central Europe, and the smallest decreases in northeast Europe and in Russia.)

In none of these regions was there a complete elimination of the various alleles that tend to produce higher intelligence. Therefore, natural selection subsequent to the spread of agriculture would tend to restore the *status quo ante* with regard to intelligence. Furthermore, there have been other important movements of people into and within Europe in the intervening millennia.

FOOTNOTES – CHAPTER 22

1) See Cavalli-Sforza, et al. (1994), pp. 108-109 for a more detailed discussion.

2) Fagan (2001), p. 453.

3) See Cavalli-Sforza, et al. (1994), p. 221.

4) (a) *Historical Atlas of the Ancient World* (1998), pp. 1.16.
   (b) Cavalli-Sforza, et al. (1994), section 3.2.b (p. 161).
   (c) Diamond, Jared (1999), pp. 100, Table 5.1.

5) Diamond, Jared (1999), pp. 338-339.

6) For a more detailed discussion see Diamond, Jared (1999), chapter 17.
   Additional information can be found in Cavalli-Sforza, et al. (1994), pp. 347-348.

7) (a) Diamond, Jared (1999), pp. 384-386.
   (b) *Historical Atlas of the Ancient World* (1998), p. 1.06.
   (c) Cavalli-Sforza, et al. (1994), section 3.2.e, pp. 162-163.
   (d) McEvedy, Colin (1980), pp. 32-35 (cf. pp. 20-21).

8) (a) McEvedy, Colin (1980), pp. 48-51.
   (b) Cavalli-Sforza, et al. (1994), section 3.2.e, pp. 162-163.

9) (a) Smith, Bruce D. (1998), pp. 96-98. (The dates he gives are uncalibrated. I have calibrated them in accordance with the table in his preface.)
   (b) Fagan, Brian M. (2001), p. 275.

10) (a) Cavalli-Sforza, et al. (1994), figure 2.7.2 on p. 108.
    (b) Smith, Bruce D. (1998), chapter 5.
    (c) *Historical Atlas of the Ancient World* (1998), p. 1.03.
    (d) Diamond, Jared (1999), p. 181.
    (e) Fagan, Brian M. (2001), chapter 10.
    (f) *DK Atlas of World History* (2001), pp. 20-21 and 174.

Some of these sources used uncalibrated C^{14} dates. However, even after calibrating, the sources often differ from each other by a thousand years or more.

11) Cavalli-Sforza, et al. (1994), pp. 291-292, particularly table 5.11.1 and figure 5.11.1.

CHAPTER 23

THE NEOLITHIC REVOLUTION: EXPLANATIONS

Section 1 – Introduction

Two puzzling questions about the Neolithic Revolution are:

1) Why did it not begin until about 11 kya; and

2) Why did it then occur in several widely separated places within a few thousand years?

Whenever some new invention or development appears in several different places, there are three types of explanations available:

a) Diffusion of the development itself.

b) Diffusion of one or more preliminary developments that makes the main development much more likely.

c) Chance.

Diffusion is a process in which a development that originated in one location is transmitted to other locations. An example of a technology that spread by diffusion is the use of radio waves for communication. This was never done prior to 1890, but was being done in many different countries in 1910. No coincidence was involved: The Italian inventor Guglielmo Marconi invented the radio in the 1890s, and the knowledge of his invention spread rapidly throughout the world. Other examples of diffusion (many more could easily be given) are the widespread use of automobiles using internal combustion engines; inoculation against diphtheria; and penicillin.

An example of the second process is provided by the nearly simultaneous discoveries of electromagnetic induction by Michael Faraday in England and by Joseph Henry in the United States. The preliminary development was the publication, just a few years earlier, of the discoveries of Oersted and Ampère concerning the magnetic effects of electric currents. Another example is the independent inventions of integral calculus by Newton and Leibniz within a few years of each other. In that case, the preliminary development was the invention of analytic geometry by René Descartes.

Chance, of course, is always a possibility, but it is an implausible explanation when a development appears independently in more than two places.

There appear to be at least three widely separated parts of the Earth in which agriculture arose independently (the Fertile Crescent in the Middle East; central China; and mainland Mesoamerica). It is unlikely that this "triple coincidence" occurred by mere chance. Furthermore, there are two or three other places where the rise of agriculture may have been an independent development (highland New Guinea; the eastern United States; and the Andean region in and near Peru).

The evidence also points against the diffusion of agriculture from a single source. If, for example, agriculture had reached central China by diffusion from the Middle East, then we would expect there to have been farming communities in intermediate regions before farming was practiced in China. But this is not what we observe. The earliest signs of agriculture in the regions between China and the Fertile Crescent (such as India, Central Asia, and Russia) are all much later than the rise of agriculture in China. Similarly, the earliest signs of agriculture in regions between mainland Mesoamerica and the Fertile Crescent (such as the West Indies, and the coasts of the United States and South America) are much later than early agriculture in either the Fertile Crescent or Mesoamerica.

We conclude that there were probably some necessary preliminary developments or preconditions to the development of agriculture that were satisfied in the late stages of the Paleolithic Era, and which had not been satisfied before.

Section 2 – Some suggested preconditions

Among the preliminary developments or preconditions that have been suggested[1] for the development of agriculture are:

1) Population increase.
2) Exhaustion of resources.
3) Social changes.
4) Climate changes.

Population increase. According to the first of these hypotheses, a rise in population in the late Paleolithic made it necessary for human beings to adopt methods of increasing the production of food. It is hard to see, however, how the human population could have remained far below the carrying capacity of Southwest Asia until the very late Paleolithic. Humans had entered Southwest Asia by 60 kya. Even if we assume an original population as small as 100 persons, and assume that the region was capable of supporting as many as 1,000,000 hunter-gatherers (a generous estimate), and assume that the excess of births over deaths was as little as 1% a year, the region would have reached the limit of its food supply in less than 1000 years (i.e., about 59 kya). Indeed, even if the rate of increase was only 0.1% per year, it would have taken less than 10,000 years.[2] It follows that by 50 kya Southwest Asia was already in Malthusian equilibrium, with the population pressing against the food supply. Furthermore, this hypothesis does not explain why Mesoamerica — which was settled about 45,000 years after Southwest Asia — became overpopulated only a few thousand years later than Southwest Asia.

Exhaustion of resources. Although there are historical instances of groups who exhausted the resources of their territory (for example, the inhabitants of Easter Island), the usual result has been a drastic population decline rather than the invention of a new technology. Furthermore, those who suggest resource depletion as the motive for the invention of agriculture give no reason why this should have occurred at nearly the same time in three widely-separated parts of the Earth.

Social changes. It has been suggested that social changes — such as the development of an elaborate hierarchical social organization, or an expansion of trade — might lead to the adoption of agriculture. Once again, it is unclear why these hypothesized changes occurred at roughly the same time in widely separated parts of the world. (Nor is it clear that those changes actually *did* occur in each region in the period preceding the development of agriculture.)

Climate changes. It is clear that agriculture first arose at about the same time that the last glacial era (the Würm) was ending. This suggests that the impact of severe climate changes on mankind was the basic cause of the Neolithic Revolution. One objection to this theory is that the regions where agriculture originated were not those where the glaciers were retreating. A more serious objection is that there had been several similar advances and retreats of the glaciers in the course of the Paleolithic Era, and that none of the earlier episodes resulted in the adoption of agriculture.

We see, then, that none of these four hypotheses are convincing; nor do they succeed in answering the questions posed at the beginning of this chapter. However, the problem can be solved by taking into account the combined effect of three requirements for the invention of agriculture within a region:

a) Sufficient human intelligence.

b) Suitable climate.

c) The availability of suitable crops (and domesticable animals).

Section 3 – One precondition for agriculture is sufficient human intelligence

The idea of planting crops, protecting them, and eventually harvesting them is not obvious or trivial, and it requires a considerable degree of intelligence to conceive of that notion. No apes ever conceived of that idea, nor did *Australopithecus, Homo habilis, Homo erectus,* nor even archaic *Homo sapiens.* It seems unlikely that such a notion could be originated by a group of humans with an average IQ of about 70.

The evolution of sufficiently high intelligence was therefore an essential preliminary for the invention of agriculture. The sequence of historical events suggests that an average IQ of about 79 was needed for the independent invention of agriculture, even in a region with a warm climate and abundant rainfall. This single factor explains why agriculture was not invented a million years ago — nor 100 kya, nor even 50 kya —

even though plants and animals suitable for domestication had been available throughout the Pleistocene Era. It also explains why agriculture did not originate spontaneously in tropical regions such as India, Indonesia, or SSA (sub-Saharan Africa).

Section 4 – Suitable climate

There are regions in which the climate is so harsh that agriculture cannot be practiced at all, or can be practiced only with modern equipment. It is obvious that agriculture could not have been invented in any of those regions (which include deserts, ice caps, tundra, and very rugged terrains).

We can, though, make an even stronger statement. Since domesticated plants are far superior for farming purposes to the wild plants from which they have descended (and which were the only ones available to early farmers), and since later agricultural techniques (including irrigation, and the use of plows) were superior to the techniques used by early farmers, it was much more difficult to be an effective farmer in the early Neolithic Era than in later periods. (In addition, it is always harder to *invent* a new process than merely to practice it.)

It follows that considerably better climatic conditions were needed for agriculture to be invented in a region than were needed to merely practice it after it was well developed. In particular, for an area to be suitable to the invention of agriculture, a long warm season was essential. This requirement ruled out Canada, Alaska, northern and central Europe, Siberia, and Mongolia as territories where agriculture could have independently arisen. The same was true for any other region with a "harshness factor" greater than 2.0 (see chapter 17). Among the regions that were for a long time ruled out by this requirement, but became suitable as the last ice age ended, were parts of Europe and the United States.

In addition, we would expect that the development of agriculture would be considerably more difficult in a region with a harshness factor of 2.0 than it would be in milder regions, and would require a population with a considerably higher average IQ than 79. Indeed, the historical record suggests that a population with a mean IQ of 88 was needed for agriculture to originate in such a region. Table 23-1 shows how the "threshold IQ" needed for agriculture to be invented in a region depends upon the harshness factor.

Section 5 – The combined effect of rising intelligence and climate

By combining the requirements of sufficient intelligence and suitable climate we can understand why the Neolithic Revolution did not commence until about 11 kya, and why farming then arose independently in more than one place within a few thousand years.

The absence of agriculture during the Lower and Middle Paleolithic Era is easily explained: Prior to 40 kya there was no region in which the average intelligence of the inhabitants was sufficiently high for them to invent agriculture.

In the interval between 40 kya and 15 kya, IQs rose gradually in many parts of the

TABLE 23-1

RELATION BETWEEN THE HARSHNESS FACTOR OF A REGION AND THE INTELLIGENCE NEEDED TO INVENT AGRICULTURE THERE

Harshness factor	Threshold IQ*
< 1.0	79
1.5	83.5
2.0	88

* Average IQ of the population of a region that is required in order for agriculture to be independently invented in that region.

world; and by 15 kya there was a large zone in high northern latitudes in which the mean IQ of the inhabitants was high enough for them to invent agriculture, had the climate been suitable. However, in no part of that zone was the climate sufficiently benign to enable agriculture to originate. At the same time, there was a large tropical zone that did enjoy the necessary combination of adequate rainfall and a long, warm growing season. However, there were no human groups within that tropical zone with a high enough intelligence for that development to take place. As can be seen from Table 23-2, there were as yet no regions in which the average IQ was as high as the threshold IQ.

Human intelligence continued to rise after 15 kya, which caused the first zone (the high IQ zone) to slowly expand into lower latitudes. At the same time, as the last ice age drew to a close, the zone of moderate climates expanded into higher latitudes. A little before 10 kya, the two zones (one with high intelligence, the other with a benign climate) started to overlap. Among the early areas of overlap (see Table 23-3) were:

1) The Middle East (in particular, the Fertile Crescent).
2) Southern China.
3) Mesoamerica (in particular, southern Mexico).
4) Southern Europe (Greece, Italy, and Spain).
5) The southern part of the United States.
6) South America (in particular, the Andean region).
7) The New Guinea highlands (not at 10 kya, but a few thousand years later).

To see why agriculture arose independently in some of those regions, but not all, we must take into account the third precondition mentioned at the end of section 2, the availability of suitable crops.

TABLE 23-2

CLIMATE AND INTELLIGENCE IN VARIOUS REGIONS ABOUT 15 kya

Region	Harshness factor	Average IQ	Threshold IQ
Sub-Saharan Africa	0	70	79
India	0	71	79
Southeast Asia	0	71	79
Indonesia	0	71	79
North Africa	1	77	79
New Guinea	1	77	79
Melanesia	1	76	79
Middle East	2	83	88
Central Asia	2	83	88
Australia	2	81	88

The harshness factors are taken from Table A3-1 in appendix 3.
The average IQs are from Table 17-1.
The threshold IQs are from Table 23-1.

Section 6 – Suitable crops and domesticable animals

The third prerequisite was the presence of suitable wild species for domestication, in particular, domesticable plants with a high yield of calories per acre. Although there are numerous edible plants, the only ones that meet that requirement are the wild ancestors of:

- Certain grains, including wheat, barley, rice, maize (= corn), millet, sorghum, and quinoa; and
- Certain tubers, including yams, sweet potatoes, manioc (= cassava), and potatoes.

There are other crops that were useful supplements to these — including various beans, peas, lentils, and squash[3] — but during the Neolithic Era no large group was able to convert to a primarily farming way of life without utilizing one of the "core crops" listed above (see Table 23-4).

TABLE 23-3

CLIMATE AND INTELLIGENCE IN VARIOUS REGIONS ABOUT 10 kya

Region	Harshness factor	Average IQ	Threshold IQ
Sub-Saharan Africa	0	70	79
India	0	71	79
Southeast Asia	0	71	79
Indonesia	0	71	79
Mesoamerica	0	90	79
South America	0	90	79
North Africa	1	77	79
New Guinea	1	78	79
Melanesia	1	77	79
Middle East	1	84	79
Central Asia	2	85	88
Australia	2	82	88
Southern China	2	88	88
Southern USA	2	91	88
Southern Europe	2	92	88

The harshness factors are taken from Table A3-1 in appendix 3.
The average IQs are from Table 17-1.
The threshold IQs are from Table 23-1.

Regions in which the average IQ had reached the threshold IQ are shown in bold face.

Many parts of the Earth had at least one of those crops, and several (including the Middle East, sub-Saharan Africa, and China) had two or more of them. However, some regions — including Australia and the USA — did not have *any* of the core crops, thus ruling out those regions as possible places for the initial switch to a fully agricultural mode of living.[4]

Also of importance was the presence of domesticable animals that would be useful to farmers. The most important of those were cattle, sheep, goats, and pigs.[5] The wild ancestors of all four of these were present in the Middle East, and wild pigs and cattle had a fairly wide distribution in the Eastern Hemisphere. But none of the four species was present in Australia, nor in North or South America, leaving the inhabitants of those three continents at a great disadvantage.[6]

Section 7 – The Neolithic transition in various regions

A) *The Middle East.* Because of the rise of global temperatures at the end of the last ice age, the transition to a farming way of life began in this region about 11 kya. (The theoretical calculations in appendix 4 suggest that the threshold IQ "should" have been reached about 12 kya — a surprisingly close approximation to the empirical data collected by archaeologists. Appendix 4 also shows the theoretical calculations for the other regions.)

With an excellent assortment of domesticable plants and animals (three core crops, plus several useful supplementary crops, plus all four of the most important farm animals) this region took only about one or two thousand years to pass through the Neolithic transition, and by 9 kya it harbored a large number of settled farmers. Since the Middle East was the first region in which agriculture was established, it is not surprising that farming soon spread out from there into nearby regions, including southern Europe, northern Africa, and India.

B) *China*. Ten thousand years ago, southern China had a harshness factor of 2.0, and a threshold IQ of 88. Since the average IQ of the inhabitants had recently risen to about 88, it is not surprising that the transition to farming commenced within a few centuries. There was an excellent core crop available (rice), as well as several useful supplementary crops (including soybeans), and a useful farm animal (the pig).[7]

This was not as good an assortment as the Middle East possessed, but it was quite sufficient. China went through the Neolithic transition fairly rapidly, and farming was flourishing in both central and southern China by 7.5 kya.

Was it a coincidence that the Neolithic revolutions in China and the Middle East were nearly simultaneous? Not at all. Both transitions occurred when the zone of high intelligence mentioned in section 5 began to overlap with the zone of moderate temperatures. In both eastern and western Asia, the expansion of those zones was driven by factors that were strongly latitude dependent; it is therefore not surprising that they occurred at similar times and latitudes in the two regions.

C) *Mesoamerica*. When the Spanish encountered the Aztec Empire in the early 16th century they found a society that was prosperous, but which was about 5000 years behind the Europeans in technology.[8] It seems clear that the reason the Mesoamericans were so far behind the Europeans in technology is that they had not adopted agriculture until a few thousand years after it was adopted in the Middle East and China.

TABLE 23-4

EARLY CORE CROPS IN VARIOUS PARTS OF THE NEOLITHIC WORLD

Region	Core crops	When domesticated or introduced (kya)	From Where
Middle East	Wheat, barley	11	indigenous
China (central)	Rice	9.5	indigenous
China (northern)	Millet	8.4	indigenous
Mesoamerica	Maize	6	indigenous
Andes	Quinoa, potatoes	5	indigenous
Europe	Wheat, barley	9	Middle East
India	Wheat, barley	8	Middle East
India	Rice	5.5	Southeast Asia
Egypt	Wheat, barley	8	Middle East
Ethiopia	Wheat, barley	7.5	Middle East
Ethiopia	Millet	7.5 (?)	indigenous
Sudan/Sahel	Sorghum, millet	7	indigenous
Tropical West Africa	Yams, African rice	5	indigenous
Southeast Asia	Rice	6	China
Indonesia	Rice	4.5	China *
New Guinea	Yams, taro	6	indigenous
Southwest USA	Maize	3.3	Mesoamerica
Eastern USA	Maize	2	Mesoamerica
Amazonia	Manioc	4.5 (?)	indigenous

* via Taiwan and the Philippines

It is tempting to assume that the late start of agriculture in the New World was because the Western Hemisphere was not settled until long after Europe and Asia. However, a careful analysis shows that that was not the reason. Indeed, we can see from Table 23-3 that the combination of benign climate and sufficient human intelligence to invent agriculture was reached as early in Mesoamerica as in the Middle East and China. However, the course of events in Mesoamerica was very different than in the other two regions.

The American Indians were already well above the threshold IQ when they first entered Mexico, about 15 kya. For a long time they were able to subsist comfortably on a combination of gathering edible plants and hunting large game (such as horses, antelope, and deer), and there was no incentive for the inhabitants to develop agriculture as long as the supply of large game remained abundant. However, about 11 kya, horses and antelopes became extinct in Mexico,[9] and we should probably consider that date as the equivalent of achieving the "threshold IQ" in China or the Middle East.

Why then, the reader may ask, did not the Neolithic transition begin in Mesoamerica within a thousand years of that date? The simple, if surprising, answer is that it did! The archaeological evidence shows that squash was domesticated in Mexico by 10 kya[10] — earlier than any plant was domesticated in China, and only a thousand years after wheat and barley had been domesticated in the Middle East. Nevertheless, it was not until about 5 kya that sedentary farming was firmly established in Mexico, roughly 5000 years after that stage had been reached in the Middle East.

Why did the Neolithic transition (which had taken only one or two thousand years in the Middle East and China) take 5000 years in Mesoamerica? The difference appears to be due to the paucity of domesticable farm animals and core crops in Mesoamerica. Not one of the major farm animals was present there. Nor were the major cereal crops of the Old World. The best cereal available in Mesoamerica was teosinte (the wild ancestor of corn); but as mentioned previously, teosinte was not a promising-looking crop. Indeed, when (about 5.5 kya) the Indians succeeded in domesticating it and producing an early form of corn, the resulting cobs were only about one inch long. However, by 5 kya they had produced cobs that were large enough to make corn a satisfactory core crop.

At that point, the combination of corn, squash, and beans permitted sedentary agriculture in Mesoamerica despite the absence of any large farm animals; and from then on, culture and technology progressed there at roughly the same rate it had in the Old World after the establishment of farming.

Should we consider it just a coincidence that agriculture in Mexico started within a few thousand years of its commencement in the Eastern Hemisphere? Not at all. The date that the Paleo-Indians reached Mexico (with its long warm season) was determined largely by the end of the last glacial period; while the high average IQ of the Mesoamericans was the result of their ancestors evolving in high latitudes. These were the same underlying factors that were responsible for the beginning of the Neolithic transition in the Old World.

D) *Southern Europe*. Because farming has flourished in Europe for so many centuries, it is easy to assume that conditions favored it originating there. However, none of the major core crops (wheat, barley, rice, corn, nor even millet) were indigenous to Europe. In addition, Europe lacked the wild ancestors of domestic sheep and goats[11] (although the aurochs, the ancestor of domestic cattle, was present there). Ten thousand years ago, therefore, Europe was in roughly the same situation as Mesoamerica: a decent climate and an intelligent population, but a scarcity of core crops and animals suitable for domestication.

Southern Europe, however, had one great advantage over Mexico: proximity to another region in which the needed domesticable plants and animals were available. By 9 kya, farming was well established in the Fertile Crescent and Anatolia, and farmers from the Middle East had begun moving into southeast Europe, bringing their crops and animals with them. Agriculture was soon thriving in southern Europe, and from there spread to northern Europe.

An important result of that history, though, was that civilization in the Middle East had a 2000-year head start on southern Europe, and an even larger one on northern Europe. Because of their higher intelligence, the Europeans were gradually able to reduce the gap, but it was not until the first millennium BC that the gap was eliminated.

E) *United States*. Like Mesoamerica and southern Europe, the United States had already passed the IQ threshold ten thousand years ago (see Table 23-3). But as far as the availability of useful crops and farm animals, the situation in the United States combined the worst features of Mesoamerica and Europe. Unlike Mexico, they did not even have teosinte; and unlike Europe they lacked cattle.

The archaeological record makes it plain that, starting about 4.5 kya, American Indian tribes cultivated various indigenous plants, including sumpweed, goosefoot, sunflower, and a species of squash (and, later on, knotweed, little barley, and maygrass).[12] Unfortunately, none of these could serve as a satisfactory core crop. As a result, the Indians living in what is now the eastern part of the United States continued to be primarily hunter-gatherers (although supplementing their diets with some domesticated plants) until the introduction of better crops from Mexico about 2 kya. At that point, the Mexican trio of squash, beans, and corn brought about rapid change. By the end of the first millennium AD, large parts of the United States had completed the Neolithic transition.[13] (Note that this parallels what had occurred in southern Europe about 7000 years earlier.)

F) *South America*. Table 23-3 shows that most of South America was above the threshold IQ by 10 kya, or even earlier. However, there is no sign of settled agriculture there until much later. For most of the continent, the explanation seems to be the same as for southern Europe and the United States: the absence of core crops.

The Mexican triad of corn, beans, and squash eventually spread through much of South America, leading to sedentary agriculture in many parts of the continent.[14]

However, two regions — Amazonia, and the Peruvian Andes — have been suggested as possible sites of an independent invention of agriculture.

It is clear that manioc (cassava) was being cultivated in Amazonia by 4 kya.[15] But (like the cultivation of certain local plants in the United States) this did not result in the full-fledged adoption of a farming way of life there. Manioc (which is a tuber, not a cereal) has lots of starch and calories, but very little protein. Only in combination with fishing (there is not much large game in the Amazon basin) was manioc cultivation able to support humans.[16] It seems, therefore, that the region was not one in which a fully agricultural mode of life independently developed.

The situation in the Peruvian Andes was different. There, cultivation of quinoa (a cereal), supplemented by potatoes, and combined with the domestication of the llama did result in settled agriculture about 5 kya. A reason for the late start is that the wild ancestor of quinoa was not indigenous to the region (it grows in Argentina), and the domesticated plant seems to have arisen in the south-central Andes sometime after 6 kya and spread into central Peru from there.[17]

G) *New Guinea*. The simulation described in chapter 17 indicates that the inhabitants of New Guinea were close to the threshold IQ by 15 kya (see Table 23-2); however, they did not reach it until about 5 kya. The archaeological data indicates that agriculture — based on yams and taro — arose independently in the New Guinea highlands about 6 kya,[18] in close agreement with the theoretical prediction. Pigs, chickens, and dogs were introduced into New Guinea somewhat later, probably from Indonesia.

Section 8 – Comparison of theory with empirical data

Summarizing, we see that agriculture was independently invented in five of the seven regions listed at the end of section 5, being frustrated in the other two by a lack of suitable domesticates (until they were brought in from the outside).

This does not, of course, prove that the theoretical calculations described in appendices 3 and 4, in chapter 17, and in this chapter are correct. The most it shows is that they are not inconsistent with the empirical data.

That these calculations — which ignore most cultural factors such as religion, art, and customs involving sex and marriage — can result in reasonably accurate estimates of when and where agriculture arose, is striking. It suggests that the factors which were considered (intelligence, climate, and the availability of suitable domesticates) were the dominant factors in the development of agriculture, and that cultural factors were of lesser importance.

FOOTNOTES – CHAPTER 23

1) See Fagan, Brian M. (2001), pp. 232-235.

2) As $(1.01)^{70} = 2.007$, a population increasing by 1% a year will take only 70 years to double. It follows that in 980 years (= 14 × 70 years) there will be time for 14 doublings. Now $2^{14} = 16,384$, so at a 1% annual growth rate an initial population of 100 will grow to about 16,384 × 100 (or 1,638,400) in 980 years. A more precise calculation, using logarithms, shows that only 926 years are needed for the 10,000-fold increase from 100 to 1,000,000. If the annual rate of increase is only 0.1%, then the time needed to increase from 100 to 1,000,000 would be: $\log(10^6/10^2) / \log(1.001) = 9,215$ years.

3) See Diamond, Jared (1999), Table 7.1 (pp. 126-127).

4) (a) For Australia, see Diamond, Jared (1999), pp. 308-309.
   (b) For the United States, see Diamond, Jared (1999), p. 365.

5) See Diamond, Jared (1999), Table 9.1 (p. 160). Note that the horse, although eventually a major farm animal, was domesticated much later than the others, and was not involved in the transition to farming.

6) Diamond, Jared (1999), pp. 160-163.

7) See Diamond, Jared (1999), tables 5.1 (p. 100) and 7.1 (pp. 126-127). Millet was domesticated in China about a thousand years after rice was domesticated there.

8) See chapter 40, especially Table 40-1.

9) See Fiedel, Stuart J. (1992), p. 173. I have recalibrated the date in accordance with his chronology. Note that the camel became extinct in the Western Hemisphere at about the same time as the horse (Adovasio & Page [2002], p. 119).

10) Smith, Bruce D. (1998), p. 168.

11) See Diamond, Jared (1999), p. 160, and Smith, Bruce D. (1998), pp. 53-62.

12) (a) Diamond, Jared (1999), pp. 150-151.
    (b) See also Smith, Bruce D. (1998), pp. 190-191.

13) (a) Smith, Bruce D. (1998), p. 200.
    (b) Fiedel, Stuart J. (1992), p. 261.
    (c) Diamond, Jared (1999), p. 188.

14) Smith, Bruce D. (1998), p. 147 mentions the use of the triad as far south as Argentina, and as far north as Ontario.

15) Fiedel, Stuart J. (1992), pp. 199-201. He gives a date of 4 kya (uncalibrated), which after calibration becomes 4.4 kya.

16) Fiedel, Stuart J. (1992), p. 199.

17) Smith, Bruce D. (1998), pp. 171-174.

18) Diamond, Jared (1999), pp. 100 and 147-148 suggests 9 kya; but that figure is based on a single, inconclusive observation (a trench that may be an old irrigation channel). All the other evidence points to a date of 6 kya. See, for example: (a) Smith, Bruce D. (1998), pp. 142-143; or (b) Fagan, Brian M. (2001), pp. 315-317.

CHAPTER 24

AN ALTERNATIVE EXPLANATION

Section 1 – Introduction

One thesis of this book is that the principal reason the inhabitants of Europe and China are more advanced in technology than the inhabitants of SSA (sub-Saharan Africa) is that, on average, they have higher intelligence than the Africans, and their higher intelligence is based — at least in part — on genetic factors. However, before accepting that thesis, it is sensible to consider alternative explanations for the superiority of European and Chinese culture and technology. Perhaps the most widely-accepted alternative explanation is the one given by Professor Jared Diamond in his well-known book *Guns, Germs, and Steel*.

Section 2 – Jared Diamond's hypothesis

Professor Diamond is eager to show there is no genetic component to the well-known gap in average IQ between whites and blacks, and in his book he attempts to explain how the Europeans became so much more advanced technologically than the inhabitants of SSA, the Western Hemisphere, Australia, and New Guinea despite the absence of any genetic superiority.

Near the beginning of his book, Dr. Diamond states that the notion that there are genetic factors which cause Europeans to be more intelligent (on average) than Australian aborigines is morally loathsome.[1] Surprisingly, though, within two pages of that statement, he himself expresses the view that as a result of natural selection the aborigines of the New Guinea highlands are probably genetically superior to Westerners in mental ability.[2]

However, in the remainder of his book, Dr. Diamond takes the position that all human groups are genetically equal in intelligence. He asserts that the comparative backwardness of the Western Hemisphere, SSA, and Australia in 1500 AD was entirely due to geographic factors. Those factors, he claims, had made it more difficult for those regions to develop agriculture, and their late start in agriculture then insured that they would also be behind in developing science and technology. Professor Diamond discusses three major geographic factors that greatly delayed the adoption of agriculture in those other regions:

1) *Flora*. Compared with Eurasia, the other regions had a dearth of edible plants that were suitable for domestication. For example, the wild ancestors of domestic wheat and barley grew in the Middle East, but they were not present in SSA, Australia, or the Western Hemisphere.

2) *Fauna*. Compared with Eurasia, the other regions had a dearth of large animals suitable for domestication. For example, the wild ancestors of domestic sheep, goats, and horses all lived in Eurasia 10,000 years ago, but they were not present in SSA, Australia, or the New World.

3) *Orientation of geographic axes*. Unlike Eurasia, which has an enormous geographic span in the east-west direction (much greater than its span from north to south), the geographic axes of the other regions are "tilted," with relatively short east-west spans and relatively long north-south spans (see Map 24-1).

This last factor is important because most domesticated plants cannot readily be grown in regions of different climate, nor in regions having markedly different growing seasons. Therefore, although the use of such plants in agriculture can spread rapidly in the east-west direction, it cannot spread readily in the north-south direction.[3] Dr. Diamond suggests that the same is true for livestock, and for the spread of inventions. As a result, the innovations made in different parts of Eurasia soon became used in other parts of the continent, whereas innovations made in different parts of the Western Hemisphere (or Africa, or Australia) did not easily spread to other parts of those regions.

In Map 24-1, lines A, B, and C represent the major axes of Eurasia, the Americas, and Africa according to Dr. Diamond's analysis. Line A, which represents the east-west span across Eurasia at latitude 50° N, is about 6200 miles long. (It appears longer, because a Mercator projection exaggerates E-W distances at high latitudes.) Lines D and E illustrate comparable E-W lines in Mesoamerica, and across Africa. (The longest possible E-W line in Africa — from Dakar in the West, to Cape Gwardafuy in Somalia — is only 4500 miles long.)

Section 3 – Critique: Comparison of data for SSA and Mesoamerica

There is certainly something to be said for Dr. Diamond's thesis. Eurasia, and particularly the Middle East, *did* have a far greater supply of useful and easily domesticable plants and animals than any other region. It is also true that both Australia and the United States were badly lacking in such species. However, the facts do not support his theory when it is applied to a comparison between sub-Saharan Africa and Mesoamerica.

1) *Flora*. Dr. Diamond rightly stresses the importance of cereal crops in the rise of agriculture. The only useful wild cereal that grew in Mesoamerica was teosinte, the ancestor of corn. However, teosinte is not nearly as nutritious as wild wheat, and it was far less amenable to domestication. In contrast, sub-Saharan Africa possessed *five* useful cereal crops: sorghum, bulrush millet, finger millet, teff, and African rice.[4] It seems, therefore, that SSA had an advantage in this regard. (SSA also had various

Map 24-1
Tilted Axes and E-W Expanses

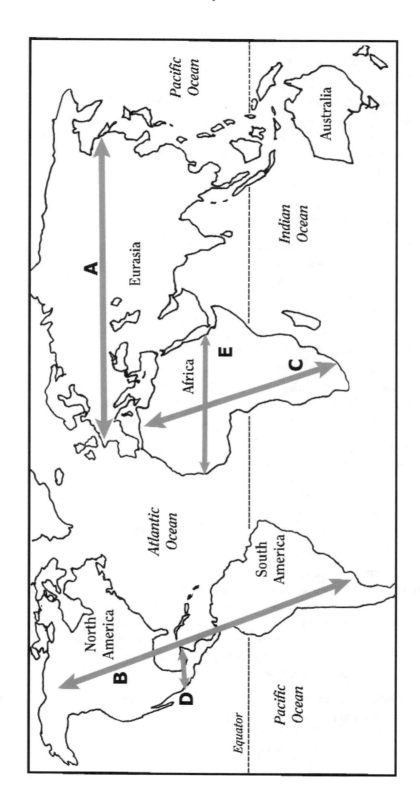

useful non-cereal crops, including yams, cowpeas, watermelon, oil palm, and groundnuts; but these were balanced by the availability in Mesoamerica of beans, squash, tomatoes, and sweet potatoes.)

2) *Fauna*. Few regions contain as many species of large animals as SSA, but Dr. Diamond insists that none of the wild species there are domesticable. For example, he states that zebras, although very similar to horses in anatomy, are hopelessly irascible, and points out that recent attempts to tame them have all failed. I find that example unconvincing. Wild horses were long considered to be untamable animals, as was the aurochs (the wild ancestor of domestic cattle), but both were domesticated in time. Until we have spent at least a few centuries trying to domesticate zebras, we should not rush to the conclusion that such attempts are hopeless.

However, even if it turns out that zebras are untamable, it still would not be true that Africa did not possess any potentially useful farm animals. The wild ancestor of domestic cattle — the most useful of all farm animals — was indigenous to North Africa,[5] and domestic cattle were being used in the Sahara by 5.5 kya, probably earlier,[6] and south of the Sahara by 5 kya.[7] (The Sahara was much wetter several thousand years ago than it is now.[8]) In addition, domestic sheep and goats were introduced into Africa by 7.5 kya,[9] and their use had spread south of the Sahara by 4 kya.

Mesoamerica, on the other hand, did not have a single large domesticable animal, since most of the megafauna in the Western Hemisphere had been killed off by the Paleo-Indians by 11 kya. As regards fauna, therefore, SSA had a great advantage over Mesoamerica.

3) *Orientation of geographic axes*. In Mesoamerica, the longest east-west span (from the eastern tip of Yucatán to Mazatlan, on the west coast of Mexico) is only 1300 miles. Contrast this with sub-Saharan Africa, where a vast stretch of savannah (the Sudan, situated between the Sahara and the tropical rainforest) stretches 3500 miles in an east-west direction, from the highlands of Ethiopia to Senegal. It is clear that transmission of technology and domesticates could — and repeatedly did — take place along the Sudan, and also across Ethiopia.

Furthermore, sub-Saharan Africa was not completely cut off from Eurasia, and some important aspects of Eurasian technology and culture did reach SSA. Techniques of pottery-making, bronze working, and ironworking reached SSA from the Middle East, as did the use of domesticated camels. (In addition, as already mentioned, domestic sheep and goats were introduced into SSA from the Middle East by 4 kya.) In contrast, prior to 1492, no Neolithic flora, fauna, or technology ever spread from the Old World to the Western Hemisphere.

We see, therefore, that the geographic factors mentioned by Jared Diamond strongly favored SSA over Mesoamerica. Using his criteria, civilization should have begun earlier in SSA than it did in Mesoamerica, and it should have progressed more there (prior to the European expansion of modern times) than it did in Mesoamerica.

In fact, though, by 1000 AD, Mesoamerica was *far* more advanced than SSA was, or ever had been. For example, Mesoamericans had originated writing on their own, had constructed many large stone structures, and had built large cities (rivaling any existing in Europe, and far larger than any in sub-Saharan Africa). Furthermore, the Mayan achievements in mathematics and astronomy dwarf any intellectual achievements in SSA.

We must therefore conclude that, although *Guns, Germs, and Steel* is an informative book, the obvious superiority of Mesoamerican technology to that of sub-Saharan Africa appears to be a fatal blow to the main arguments presented in it. In contrast, this book provides a simple explanation for that superiority.

Of course, even if Dr. Diamond had demonstrated that the backwardness of SSA could be completely explained by geographic factors, that would still not prove there is no genetic component to the observed difference in mean IQ between blacks and whites. Many other arguments were presented in chapter 16 for believing that that difference is due in part to genetic factors. At best, his argument would remove only one of the reasons for reaching that conclusion; the other arguments would remain, and are quite sufficient.

FOOTNOTES – CHAPTER 24

1) Diamond, Jared (1999), p. 19.

2) Diamond, Jared (1999), pp. 20-21. On p. 21 he says, "That is, in mental ability New Guineans are probably genetically superior to Westerners."

3) Diamond, Jared (1999), Chapter 10.

4) (a) *Historical Atlas of the Ancient World* (1998), p. 1.16.
   (b) *DK Atlas of World History* (2001 edition), pp. 21 and 158.
   (c) *Past Worlds: Atlas of Archaeology* (2003 edition), pp. 78 and 118-119.
   (d) Diamond, Jared (1999), pp. 126-127.

5) Diamond, Jared (1999), p. 160.

6) (a) Cavalli-Sforza, et al. (1994), p. 161.
   (b) *DK Atlas of World History* (2001 edition), p. 158.
   (c) *Historical Atlas of the Ancient World* (1998), p. 1.16.

7) (a) *Historical Atlas of the Ancient World* (1998), p. 1.16.
   (b) *DK Atlas of World History* (2001 edition), p. 158.

8) Cavalli-Sforza, et al. (1994), p. 161. The period of maximum wetness was about 9 kya.

9) (a) *DK Atlas of World History* (2001 edition), p. 158.
   (b) *Historical Atlas of the Ancient World* (1998), p. 1.16.

CHAPTER 25
THE INTRODUCTION OF WRITING

Section 1 – Writing systems

The invention of writing separates prehistory from recorded history. It is universally acknowledged to be one of the most important inventions ever made, and it is doubtful whether any subsequent one has influenced human life so profoundly.

We have no record of the earliest attempts to create writing. However, it is generally supposed that such attempts involved pictographic writing — that is, a system in which each word is represented by a single character, and each character is a simple, conventionalized picture or diagram that looks something like the idea it represents. All such attempts ran into the serious problem that there are many words whose meaning is difficult to convey by a single picture.

The problem was solved by making use of the symbols for various monosyllabic words to represent not just the word itself, but also the *sound* of that word. Those characters could then be combined to "spell out" many words for which no pictogram existed. A writing system that represents many words by single pictograms, while representing many other words by spelling them out syllable by syllable, is called a *logosyllabic* writing system. The earliest writing systems we know of were all of this type.

A major drawback of logosyllabic writing systems is that they involve a large number of distinct characters. As a result, in countries where the writing system was logosyllabic, learning to read was generally a lengthy and difficult task, and the rate of literacy in such countries was usually low.

In several places where logosyllabic writing systems were once used it was eventually realized that, if a character was available for each syllable that occurred in the language, then the pictograms that represented complete words would not be needed. If those other symbols are dropped, the result will be a *syllabic* writing system, a phonetic system of writing in which each character stands for a specific syllable. The "alphabet" of such a system is called a *syllabary*. A complete syllabary involves far fewer distinct characters than are used in logosyllabic writing, although many more than the number of letters in a true alphabet.

Fully alphabetic writing — where individual symbols typically represent either a vowel or a consonant sound, but not both — was a much later invention. The first alphabet was probably North Semitic, which was invented about 1600 BC. (The celebrated Phoenician alphabet was derived from it.) There does not appear to have been any other completely independent invention of an alphabet. (There are alphabets, such as Korean, that do not derive from the North Semitic, but they were composed by persons who had already seen alphabets derived from that one.[1])

Section 2 – Sumerian writing

Writing was first developed in ancient Sumeria, about 3400 BC. Sumeria, which consisted of a collection of independent city-states, was located in what is now southern Iraq.

The Sumerians seem to have been latecomers to the region, and their origin is shrouded in mystery. Their language is an isolate, unrelated to the Semitic languages spoken by most other peoples in the region, or to any other known language. Commerce played an important part in the economy of the Sumerian city-states, and many of the surviving samples of Sumerian writing are commercial records. The original Sumerian writing system was logosyllabic, but in time they developed a syllabic system.

One problem the Sumerians faced was the lack of any convenient material on which to write. For lack of anything better, they often wrote by making indentations on clay tablets. (Afterwards, such tablets could be hardened by baking.) Eventually, the practice arose of making the indentations by using a stylus with a wedge-shaped end. As a result, each character in Sumerian writing came to consist of a standardized pattern of wedge-shaped indentations. Hence it is often called *cuneiform writing*, after the Greek word for "wedge-shaped."

Section 3 – Early spread of writing from Sumeria

Within a few centuries, the idea of writing spread from Sumeria to neighboring peoples. One of the first of those to adopt writing (probably about 2900 BC) were the Elamites, a people who resided a bit east of ancient Sumeria, in what is now southwest Iran. Their writing began as logosyllabic, but in time the Elamites developed a syllabic system based on the Sumerian.

In the course of the third millennium BC, various Semitic peoples living in central and northern Mesopotamia also adopted cuneiform writing. Akkadian was being written (using a logosyllabic system) by 2300 BC, and both Babylonian and Assyrian were being written by 2000 BC. All of them eventually adopted a syllabic form of writing based on the Sumerian.

From Mesopotamia, the use of writing soon spread north into Anatolia. Hurrian (an isolated language) was being written by 2000 BC, and Urartian somewhat later. The first Indo-European language to be written was ancient Hittite, about 1600 BC.

Section 4 – Egyptian writing

Egyptian hieroglyphic writing originated about 3100 BC. Although it was a logosyllabic system, it differed greatly from ancient Sumerian writing, or from any of the cuneiform writing systems. It is therefore possible that Egyptian writing was a completely independent invention, not derived in any way from Sumerian writing. It seems more likely, though, that the Egyptians obtained the general *idea* of writing from their indirect contact with the Sumerians, but developed their own pictograms, without reference to the Sumerian symbols.[2]

The Egyptians did not use cuneiform, but they eventually developed their own syllabic writing system. They wrote on papyrus, which was a much more practical material than clay.

Section 5 – Writing in the Indus Valley and Minoan civilizations

In the middle of the third millennium BC, a writing system arose in the Indus Valley (or *Harrapan*) civilization, which was situated in what is now Pakistan. The writing has not yet been deciphered. The characters are quite unlike the Sumerian ones, and it seems likely that the Harrapans obtained the general idea of writing from the Middle East, but not the specific symbols.

Similarly, about 2000 BC, the Minoan civilization (centered on Crete) developed a logosyllabic system of writing. They later developed a syllabic system which is now referred to as "Linear A." Neither system has been deciphered yet. It is suspected that they, too, obtained the general idea of writing from their neighbors, but created their own set of characters.[3]

Section 6 – Chinese writing

The earliest surviving samples of Chinese writing are inscriptions on bones used for divination. These date to about 1500 BC; however, it seems very likely that the actual invention of Chinese writing predates those samples by several centuries. So far as we know, the Chinese development of writing was completely independent. Chinese writing has remained logosyllabic. (However, the Japanese — whose written language derived from Chinese — developed a syllabic form of writing in the first millennium AD.)

In early times, the Chinese often used bamboo as a writing material. Books made of bamboo were, of course, excessively bulky, and the lack of a good writing material may have held back Chinese civilization. However, after their invention of paper (about 100 AD), the Chinese possessed a writing material superior to any used in the West. Perhaps because of this, Chinese civilization soon caught up with the West, and for a while surpassed it.

Section 7 – Writing in the Western Hemisphere

Writing was also invented independently in Mesoamerica. The earliest writing in the Western Hemisphere was Zapotec hieroglyphic, which was developed in the Valley of Oaxaca about 700 BC. It was the basis for all the later writing systems in the New World, including Mayan and Aztec. All these systems were logosyllabic. Neither the

Incas nor any other South American Indians developed writing, nor did any American Indians living north of Mexico.

Section 8 – Rongorongo

It is sometimes claimed that the "Rongorongo" inscriptions found on Easter Island are the result of an independent invention of writing there, but that claim appears to be incorrect. In the first place, the earliest such inscriptions were not made until *after* contact with Europeans. Furthermore, Rongorongo is not a general system of writing, but has a limited vocabulary, and apparently was only used to record various prayers.[4]

Section 9 – Europe, India, and Southeast Asia

There was no independent invention of writing in Europe. All of the European writing systems are alphabetic, and all are derived from the North Semitic alphabet (via ancient Greek). In particular, the Latin alphabet — which today is the most widely used in the world — is indirectly derived from the Greek alphabet.

In India, too, the extant writing systems are alphabetic (although they do not all use the same alphabet), and they all derive from Middle Eastern writing. The same is true of the various written languages in Southeast Asia.

Section 10 – Africa, Australia, and New Guinea

With the exception of Egyptian hieroglyphics, there was no independent invention of writing in Africa. However, written forms of some Semitic languages spoken in Ethiopia have existed for a long time. They use the Ethiopic alphabet, which was invented about 400 AD, and derives from Semitic alphabets created in Asia.

The rest of sub-Saharan Africa did not have writing until modern times, when it was introduced from the outside. The first Bantu language to be written was Swahili, a language spoken mostly in East Africa. The earliest Swahili writings (which date from a bit after 1700 AD) use the Arabic alphabet. Many of the languages of sub-Saharan Africa have still not been reduced to writing.

None of the aborigines in Australia, or in the highlands of New Guinea, had a written language before the Europeans arrived.

FOOTNOTES – CHAPTER 25

1) A fuller discussion of logosyllabic, syllabic, and alphabetic writing systems can be found in the article "Writing" in the *Encyclopaedia Brittanica* (15th edition, 1986), Vol. 29, especially pp. 984-992.

2) A lengthier discussion of Egyptian hieroglyphics can found on pp. 999-1003 of the article on "Writing" in the *Encylopaedia Brittanica* (15th edition, 1986), Vol. 29.

3) The three most famous ancient writing systems that are still undeciphered are the Harrapan (or Indus Valley) system, Linear A, and ancient Etruscan.

4) For a fuller discussion of Rongorongo see the articles by Steven Roger Fischer at http://www.netaxs.com/~trance/rongo.html and by Jacques B.M. Guy at http://www.netaxs.com/~trance/rongo2.html. See also http://www.omniglot.com/writing/.

CHAPTER 26

THE INDO-EUROPEANS

Section 1 – The Proto-Indo-Europeans

The Indo-European language family was described in section 9-2 (also see Table 9-1). The existence of this group of related languages implies that there was once a parent language, usually called *Proto-Indo-European* (hereafter abbreviated *PIE*). That language was originally spoken by a single tribe, the "Proto-Indo-Europeans," which in the course of time repeatedly expanded and fragmented, giving rise to many tribes and nations speaking related languages.

The question of where and when the early speakers of *PIE* lived has aroused a great deal of controversy. The most common view among those scholars who have studied the question carefully (including Marija Gimbutas[1] and J.P. Mallory[2]) is that the homeland of the Proto-Indo-Europeans was the steppes of southern Russia, in the region north of the Black and Caspian Seas, and perhaps including some territory to the east of that region. Gimbutas identified the early *PIE*-speakers with the so-called Kurgan people who lived in that region about 6 kya. (These people get their name from the low mounds, or *kurgans*, in which they often buried their dead.) Gimbutas assembled impressive amounts of archaeological data concerning the Kurgan peoples and their expansion, and I find her arguments very strong.

However, not all scholars agree with Gimbutas and Mallory. An important alternative view, championed by Colin Renfrew[3] and others, is that the Proto-Indo-Europeans lived in Anatolia about 8.5 or 9 kya. Whichever view is correct, by 2 kya the Indo-Europeans could well have been described as "the tribe that conquered a continent," since by then their descendants occupied most of Europe.[4]

Actually, it was more than a continent, since Indo-Europeans also constituted most of the population of Iran, Afghanistan, Central Asia, and most of northern India. Furthermore, two large empires (the Roman and the Parthian) that had been established by Indo-Europeans controlled most of the Middle East and North Africa, although Indo-Europeans did not make up the bulk of the population of those regions.

By 200 AD, the expansion of the Indo-Europeans had ended, and during the next millennium the area they controlled shrank somewhat. Indo-Europeans lost control of

North Africa and the Middle East; and Europe itself was invaded by various non-Indo-European peoples such as the Huns, Arabs, Avars, and Magyars.

However, in the 15th century the expansion of the Indo-European peoples resumed. In the period between 1500 and 1900 AD, they conquered and occupied three other continents (North America, South America, and Australia), as well as much of northern Asia. They also gained temporary control of almost all of the Pacific Islands, most of Africa, and parts of southern Asia.

Aside from the question of where and when the speakers of *PIE* lived, there are at least three other important questions to be answered:

1) What underlying factor was primarily responsible for the remarkable territorial expansion of the Indo-Europeans in the last four millennia BC?

2) What underlying factor was responsible for their expansion since 1500 AD?

3) What explains the enormous intellectual accomplishments of Indo-Europeans, both in the ancient world (Greeks and Romans) and the modern world (Italians, French, British, Germans, Americans, and others)?

Section 2 – What caused the early expansion of the Indo-Europeans?

In principle, there are three ways in which a language — or rather, the territory in which it is spoken as a native language — can expand.[5]

Demic expansion. A substantial number of its speakers migrate into another region, where they become the bulk of the population.

Elite-dominance expansion. Some of its speakers invade and conquer another region. Subsequently, although the invaders constitute only a minority of the population, the conquered people adopt the language of the new rulers.

Expansion by diffusion. Without being conquered, large numbers of people adopt a new language voluntarily. Their reasons for doing so might be the usefulness of the new language for trade, the excellence of its literature, or any other factor that makes the new language desirable.

In practice, though, the third process almost never occurs. Within historic times, whenever we have observed a language being supplanted within some region, it has been due to one of the first two processes. It is reasonable to conclude, therefore, that prehistoric instances of a language expanding into already-inhabited territories were always a result of invasion and conquest.

Section 3 – Renfrew's hypothesis

An advantage of Renfrew's hypothesis — that *PIE* originated about 8.5 or 9 kya in Anatolia — is that it provides a relatively simple answer to the first question asked at the end of section 1. If his theory is correct, the expansion of the Indo-Europeans was enabled by their command of agriculture, and it was similar to the expansions of the Afro-Asiatic, Bantu, Austronesian, and Dravidian languages that were described in chapter 22. Nevertheless, although Renfrew's theory has gained considerable support in some quarters, most experts in Indo-European languages (and many archaeologists and anthropologists as well) do not accept it.[6] What are their objections?

One objection is based on the rapidity of language change. If *PIE* was spoken as early as 9 kya, then Latin and Sanskrit should differ much more than they actually do.

A second objection to Renfrew's hypothesis is that in several crucial regions — including Spain, Italy, Greece, Britain, and even Anatolia — when we first catch sight of the Indo-Europeans (between 2000 BC and 500 BC) they appear to be recently intrusive into the area, rather than having been there for millennia.

Spain: Indo-European tribes do not appear to have entered Spain until the first millennium BC, and as late as 500 BC there were still large parts of Spain that were occupied by non-Indo-European speakers. In addition to the Basques (who inhabited parts of northern Spain and southwest France), these groups include the Tartessians in the far south, and the Iberians in the east.[7]

Italy: The Romans, and other Italian tribes speaking similar languages, appear to have entered Italy from the north in the last half of the second millennium BC. As late as 500 BC there were still peoples in Italy (such as the Etruscans) who spoke non-Indo-European languages.[8]

Greece: It appears that Greek-speaking tribes first entered Greece sometime around 2000 BC. Among the indications of this are:[9]

1) The ancient Greeks made references to an earlier people (the *Pelasgians*) who had lived there before them.

2) The archaeological record indicates disruptive invasions into Greece from the north occurring around 2200 BC.

3) Several of the oldest place-names in Greece appear to be non-Indo-European.

4) The earliest samples of writing found anywhere in Greece are written in a syllabic system called *Linear A*. But the language recorded in Linear A — which was being used on Crete, about 1700 BC, by the Minoans (see section 29-3) — is not Greek, nor an Indo-European language at all. The earliest inscriptions in any Greek dialect date to about 1450 BC, and are written in *Linear B* (a different writing system, but one whose syllabary is derived from Linear A).

Britain: It is unclear when Indo-European speakers first entered Britain, although the most common view is that this occurred in the first millennium BC. (It has been conjectured that the Picts may have been a remnant of the earlier pre-Indo-European population.[10])

Anatolia: Even here — supposedly the Indo-European homeland — the first Indo-Europeans whom we know of (the Hittites) appear to have been recent intruders when we first catch sight of them, early in the second millennium BC. At that time, much of

Anatolia was occupied by speakers of non-Indo-European languages such as Hurrian, Hattic, and Assyrian. The Hittites appear to have entered Anatolia from the north, and they conquered the land of the Hatti in central Anatolia.[11] (Although we call these intruders "Hittites," after the land that they conquered, they called themselves *Nes*, and their language *Nesili*.)

The earliest writings in Hittite date to about 1650 BC. In contrast, the Hurrians and Assyrians had both developed writing systems (derived from Sumerian cuneiform) in the third millennium BC. If the Hittites had really been in Anatolia — so close to the region where cuneiform writing originated — for five millennia, it seems unlikely that they would not have had any writing system until 1650 BC.

Note that all these results are consistent with the Indo-Europeans first occupying the eastern and central part of Europe, and only later spreading into the southern and western fringes of the continent. Note also that classical Greek and Roman sources give no indication of encountering any pre-Indo-European tribes in Belgium, Holland, Germany, or Poland, or in southern or central Russia.

A third objection is based on the vocabulary of *PIE* as determined by linguistic analysis of known Indo-European languages. That vocabulary — which includes words for various fauna and flora — seems to be more consistent with an origin in southern Russia than one in Anatolia.[12] Furthermore, the *PIE* word for *horse* has cognates in widely separated branches of Indo-European, although horses were not domesticated until about 6 kya, and there were no domesticated horses in Anatolia until even later.

A fourth objection is that if *PIE* originated in Anatolia then we would expect it to include far more loan words from Semitic languages than it actually does. Instead, the language family that most resembles *PIE* is the Uralic family, not the Afro-Asiatic family.[13]

Another problem with Renfrew's theory is that it does not explain how the Indo-Europeans were able to subdue peoples (such as the Minoans and Etruscans) who already had agriculture, and who were originally more advanced than them. This problem is most serious with regard to northern India, where the Indo-European invaders (the Aryans) must have been greatly outnumbered by the earlier inhabitants of the Indus and Ganges valleys.[14]

In his original book, Renfrew dealt with this problem by conjecturing that it was the Indo-Europeans who, about 8 kya, were the people who introduced farming into India. He suggested that the Aryans who took over northern India around 1500 BC — and whose exploits are recorded in the *Rigveda* — were not foreign invaders, but just a branch of the Indo-Europeans living in India.[15] However, in a later article, he accepts the view that it was *Dravidian*-speaking peoples who originally brought farming to India[16] (see section 22-2). This concession, however, is very damaging to Renfrew's hypothesis, since it no longer provides a simple explanation of how the Indo-Europeans were able to conquer India.

Still another weakness of Renfrew's theory is that it at best explains the *original* expansion of the Indo-Europeans; their spread in modern times requires an additional explanation, as do their remarkable intellectual accomplishments.

Section 4 – Is there a better explanation for the spread of the Indo-Europeans?

What then does account for the remarkable conquests of the Indo-Europeans? Since these conquests occurred over a period of millennia, they cannot be due to the attributes of any single leader; nor are they due to some particular political system, or to some particular ideology.

Nor can they be explained as due to some particular terrain: The Indo-Europeans triumphed in the forests of Germany, the steppes of Central Asia, the mountains of Afghanistan, and the islands of the Aegean.

Nor can it be maintained that their remarkable early expansion was due to their possession of superior technology. Quite a few of the peoples they conquered — including the Minoans, the Etruscans, the Elamites, and the Dravidian-speakers of the Indus Valley — had more advanced civilizations than the Indo-European invaders did. It is likely that the some of the early conquests of the Indo-Europeans were due in part to their use of horses; but this could hardly account for their conquest of Crete, Britain, Switzerland, and Scandinavia. Nor would it account for their triumphs over the Egyptians and Babylonians, both of whom had been using horses in warfare for many centuries.

The simplest explanation is that the original speakers of *PIE* possessed, on average, considerably higher intelligence than most of the peoples they defeated (including the Egyptians, Babylonians, Assyrians, Carthaginians, Phoenicians, Pelasgians, Tartessians, Iberians, Etruscans, Berbers, and Dravidian-speaking peoples), all of whom had evolved in milder climates than had the ancestors of the Indo-Europeans. This hypothesis has the added advantage of also applying to the modern expansion of the Indo-Europeans, and it also explains their remarkable intellectual achievements. No other hypothesis comes close to explaining all of these phenomena.

Section 5 – The Proto-Indo-European homeland

From the vocabulary of *PIE*, it appears that the original speakers were an agricultural people who engaged in cattle-raising, and were well acquainted with horses and wagons. They knew how to spin and weave wool, and had a word for a metal (probably copper, although possibly bronze). All this is consistent with the hypothesis that the speakers of *PIE* were the Kurgan builders who lived on the Russian steppes, north of the Black and Caspian Seas, about 6 kya (= 4000 BC).

This hypothesis is also consistent with the genetic data. The regional variations of DNA within Europe strongly suggest that there was an important demic expansion westward from the Ukraine a few thousand years ago.[17]

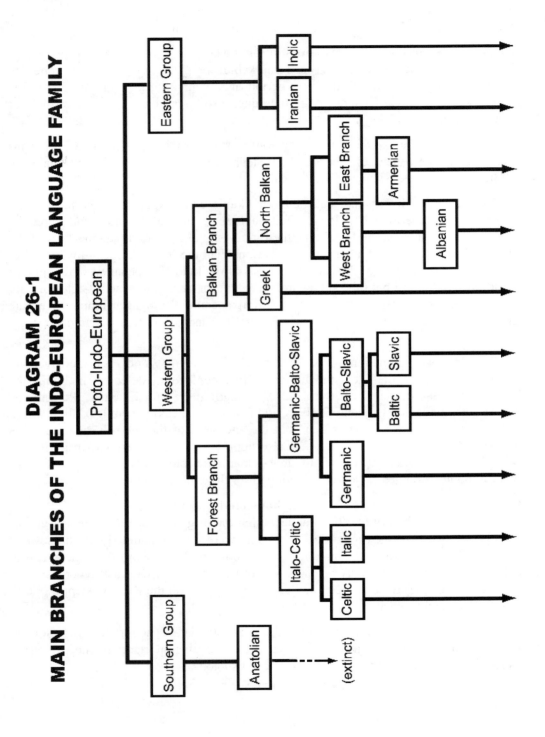

Section 6 – The expansion of the Indo-Europeans

Scholars do not agree on the chronology of the expansion of the Indo-Europeans. What follows in this section is merely a suggestion of what the sequence of expansions and fragmentations might have looked like.

The early Proto-Indo-Europeans were an agricultural and cattle-raising tribe who lived on the steppes north of the Caspian Sea about 4000 BC. They were among the first people — perhaps the very first — to domesticate horses, and their initial expansion was probably aided by that.

The Indo-Europeans soon expanded both to the west and to the east. By 3000 BC, they had divided into three main groups: a western one, an eastern one, and a southern one (see Map 26-1).

1) *The Western Group*. Within a few centuries, this divided into two main branches. The first of these migrated southwest, into the Balkans; the other migrated north and northwest, into the forested area north of the steppes (see Map 26-2).

 a) <u>The Balkan Branch</u>: Members of this branch had invaded and conquered part of the Balkans by 3000 BC. About 2000 BC, a group of them split off and entered northern Greece. As they moved south, they encountered the relatively advanced Minoan civilization and learned from it. By about 1450 BC, this first wave of Greeks had conquered the Minoans and occupied all of Greece. The Indo-Europeans who remained in the northern Balkans eventually divided into at least two subgroups, or branches (see Diagram 26-1):

> i) A western subgroup which included the Illyrians. Modern Albanian is probably descended from one of the languages they spoke.
>
> ii) An eastern subgroup which included tribes that migrated into Asia Minor in the first millennium BC. They were the ancestors of the Phrygians, and probably of the Armenians as well.

 b) <u>The Forest Branch</u>: The second large branch of the Western Group consisted of those who migrated north and northwest into the forests. By 2000 BC, they occupied a large region that included part of western Russia and most of Poland (see Map 26-2). Not long thereafter, they split into eastern and western sub-branches (see Map 26-3 and Diagram 26-1).

Both of those sub-branches continued to expand. As the eastern one (from which the Germanic, Slavic, and Baltic languages derive) expanded into Poland, and then Germany, the members of the western sub-branch (from which the Italic and Celtic languages derive) migrated into western and southern Europe.

By 1000 BC, the eastern one had divided into two groups: those speaking Proto-Germanic, and a more easterly group speaking Proto-Balto-Slavic (see Map 26-4). A few centuries later, the latter divided into Baltic and Slavic speakers.

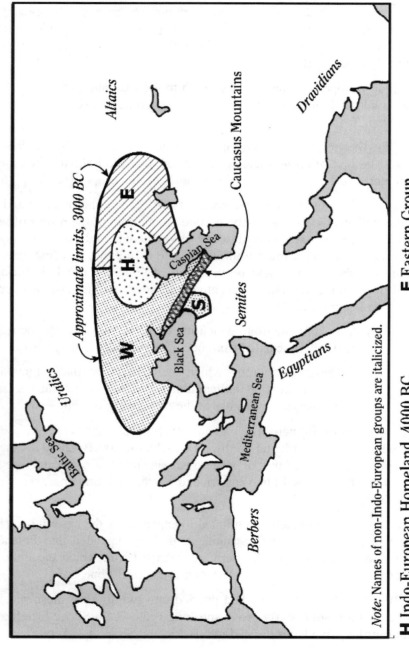

**Map 26-1
Indo-Europeans, 4000 - 3000 BC**

Note: Names of non-Indo-European groups are italicized.

H Indo-European Homeland, 4000 BC **E** Eastern Group
W Western Group **S** Southern Group (proto-Anatolian)

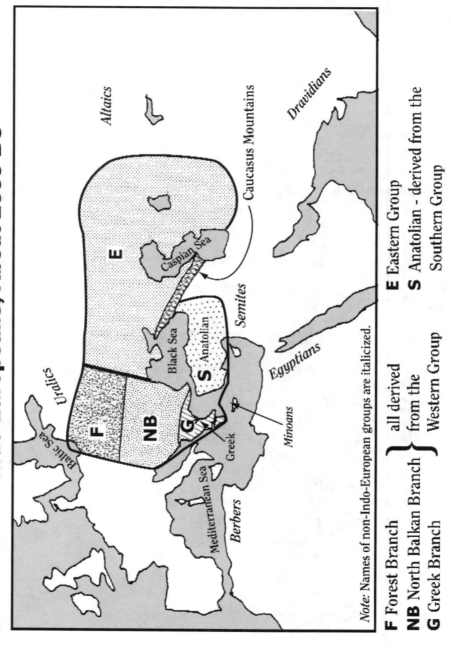

Map 26-2
Indo-Europeans, About 2000 BC

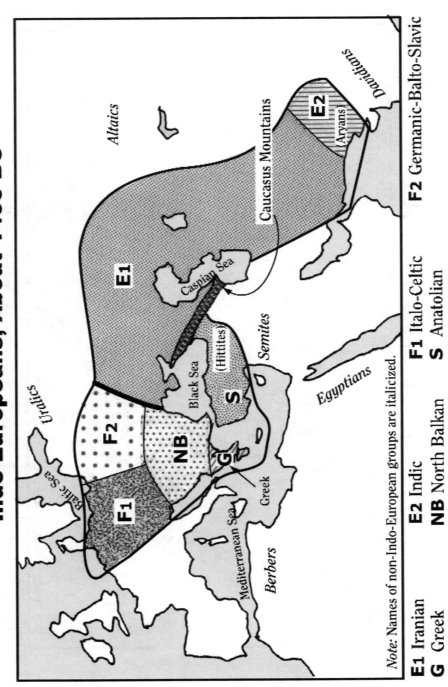

Map 26-3
Indo-Europeans, About 1400 BC

Note: Names of non-Indo-European groups are italicized.

E1 Iranian   **E2** Indic   **F1** Italo-Celtic   **F2** Germanic-Balto-Slavic
G Greek   **NB** North Balkan   **S** Anatolian

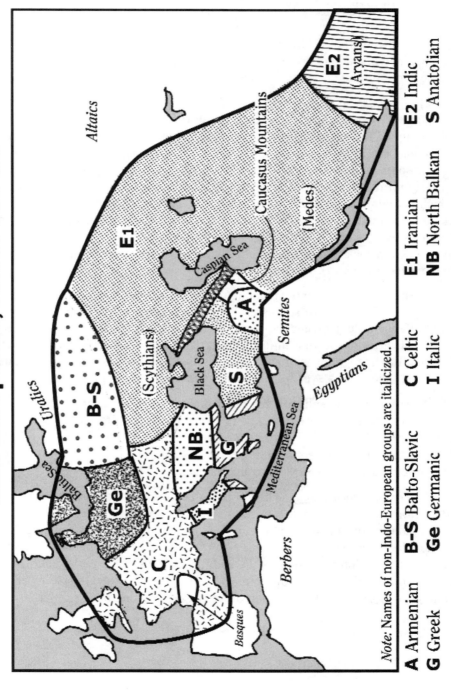

**Map 26-4
Indo-Europeans, About 600 BC**

Note: Names of non-Indo-European groups are italicized.

| **A** Armenian | **B-S** Balto-Slavic | **C** Celtic | **E1** Iranian | **E2** Indic |
| **G** Greek | **Ge** Germanic | **I** Italic | **NB** North Balkan | **S** Anatolian |

Meanwhile — probably about 1200 BC — a portion of the western sub-branch had split off, moved south, and migrated into Italy, where it gave rise to the various Italic-speaking tribes, including the ancient Romans.

The other members of the western sub-branch were the Celts. One of the Celtic groups (the Gauls) moved into France. Then, about 500 BC, some of the Celts pushed into Spain, while others invaded the British Isles. In the last few centuries BC, still other Celtic tribes migrated into the Balkans, with some moving from there into Asia Minor.

2) *The Eastern Group*. Meanwhile, the Indo-Europeans who had remained in the steppes were expanding eastward and southward into Central Asia. By 2000 BC, they had occupied the entire region between the Caspian Sea and the mountains to the east of China. By 1500 BC, one group of these (the *Aryans*) had split off from the others, moved south, and entered India from the northwest. These Aryan invaders, who spoke an early form of Sanskrit, soon destroyed the remnants of the Indus Valley civilization, which had already decayed badly before the Aryans entered. From there, the Aryans gradually spread out across northern India. (Note that it is ridiculous to refer the modern Germans as "Aryans." The two groups separated more than 100 generations ago, and modern Germans are much more closely related to the Poles and French than they are to the ancient Aryans.)

Eventually, almost all the inhabitants of northern India adopted the language of the conquerors. The modern successors of ancient Sanskrit (the *Indic* languages) include Hindi, Bengali, Punjabi, and various other tongues. Classical Sanskrit, with its complex grammar, arose in the first millennium BC out of one of the earlier Sanskrit dialects. Like the Latin taught in schools today, classical Sanskrit was a literary language, and it is unlikely that it was ever spoken by large numbers of people.

After the Aryans split off, the other members of the Eastern branch continued to thrive and expand. The languages they spoke gave rise to the Iranian branch of the Indo-European family. By 1000 BC, these tribes occupied Iran, Afghanistan, and Central Asia. Later on, some of these tribes (such as the Scythians) migrated back into southern Russia, and even parts of the Balkans.

3) *The Southern Group*. This group, which was smaller than the other two, moved south from the original Indo-European homeland and gave rise to the Anatolian branch of the Indo-European language family. Their most likely route was along the east coast of the Black Sea (perhaps first settling in the coastal region of what is now Georgia), then westward along the south coast, and from there south into the interior of Anatolia. In the 2nd millennium BC, one branch of them (the Hittites) established a powerful empire there. The Anatolian group of languages has long been extinct.

Although the sequence just given is only a conjecture, it is consistent with several ideas that most specialists in the Indo-European languages agree on,[18] including:

1) The Indic and Iranian language groups are closely related to each other, much closer than they are to any of the other branches of Indo-European.

2) The Baltic and Slavic language groups are also closely related to each other, much closer than they are to any other branches of Indo-European.

3) The language group that is most closely related to the Italic group of languages appears to be the Celtic group.

4) The Germanic and Balto-Slavic groups are closer to each other than either is to any other branch of Indo-European.

5) The Anatolian language group is an outlier, differing much more from the other branches of Indo-European than they do from each other.

FOOTNOTES – CHAPTER 26

1) Gimbutas, Marija (1970; 1973; 1977; 1980).

2) Mallory, J.P. (1989), *In Search of the Indo-Europeans*.

3) Renfrew, Colin (1987), *Archaeology and Language: The Puzzle of Indo-European Origins*.

4) The only parts of Europe that were not yet dominated by Indo-European speakers were the far north (which was occupied by Uralic-speaking peoples, such as the Finns), the Basque country (a region in northern Spain and southern France, straddling the Pyrenees), and the Caucasus.

5) Mallory, J.P. (1989), pp. 257-258.

6) See for example:
   (a) Trask, R.L. (1996), pp. 360-361 and 399-400.
   (b) Diamond, Jared (1992), chapter 15.

7) Mallory, J.P. (1989), pp. 105-106. See also Renfrew, Colin (1987), pp. 231-232.

8) Mallory, J.P. (1989), pp. 88-89.

9) Mallory, J.P. (1989), pp. 66-71.

10) Mallory, J.P. (1989), p. 106. See also Renfrew, Colin (1987), pp. 226-227.

11) Mallory, J.P. (1989), pp. 24-30.

12) Mallory, J.P. (1989), pp. 158-164 and 179.

13) Mallory, J.P. (1989), pp. 179-180.

14) The Aryan invaders of India came from Afghanistan or western Iran. Both these areas were far less fertile — and hence had far smaller populations — than the well-watered Ganges and Indus valleys.

15) Renfrew, Colin (1987), pp. 178-197 (especially pp. 189-197).

16) Renfrew, Colin (1989), pp. 113-114. Mallory, J.P. (1989), p. 45, presents several of the standard reasons for believing that the Aryans were intrusive in the Indus Valley.

17) Cavalli-Sforza, L.L. et al. (1994), section 5.11 (see especially pp. 292-293 and figure 5.11.3).

18) Mallory, J.P. has reprinted diagrams showing the supposed relationships between different branches of Indo-European that had been constructed by earlier scholars such as August Schleicher (1861), Johannes Schmidt (1872), Francesco Adrados (1982), Gamkrelidze & Ivanov (1985), and Raimo Anttila (1972). See Mallory, J.P. (1989), pp. 18-21 (figures 7 through 11).

CHAPTER 27

THE ANCIENT MIDDLE EAST

Section 1 – Introduction

Many writers include Egypt as part of the "Middle East." In this book, though, I shall use the term to designate only Southwest Asia (Turkey, Iran, and the countries in the Arabian Peninsula and the Fertile Crescent). Even with this restricted definition, the Middle East is a region of unique historical importance. It was there that agriculture was first developed, that writing was invented, that the first cities were built, and that civilization began.

Much of the Middle East is dry, but there is a large region, the Fertile Crescent, which was well-watered in ancient times (see Map 20-1). The eastern portion of the Fertile Crescent is dominated by two great rivers (the Tigris and the Euphrates) and Mesopotamia, "the land between the rivers."

Three important sections of the Fertile Crescent were:

1) *Sumeria*. This was the region in the extreme southeast part of the Fertile Crescent. It included the southern part of Mesopotamia, and it bordered on the Persian Gulf.

2) *Assyria*. This was situated in the northern part of Mesopotamia, and included the city of Nineveh.

3) *Babylonia*. This region was situated between Assyria and Sumeria, directly upstream from Sumeria. Its most important city was Babylon.

The Fertile Crescent is bordered on the south by deserts, and on the northeast by low hills that gradually rise into the Zagros range in Iran. But the region has no sharp natural boundaries, and it is exposed to outside attack from many directions. As a result, the region was one of frequent warfare.

The ancient Middle East had a complex chronology. Table 27-1 lists the approximate dates of some of the important events in the region. (Appendix 1 presents a more extensive chronology.)

TABLE 27-1	
ROUGH CHRONOLOGY OF ANCIENT MIDDLE EAST	
Agriculture invented in Fertile Crescent	8000 BC
Agriculture spreads to Egypt	6000 BC
Early Indo-Europeans; horses domesticated	4000 BC
Writing invented in Sumeria	3400 BC
Hieroglyphics developed in Egypt; first Egyptian dynasty begins	3100 BC
Sumeria conquered by Sargon of Akkad	2340 BC
Ancient Hebrews enter land of Canaan	1200 BC
King David rules in Jerusalem	1000 BC
Assyrians rule most of Middle East	700 BC
Babylonians defeat Assyria, rule Fertile Crescent	612 BC
Persians, under Cyrus the Great, conquer entire Middle East	539 BC

Section 2 – Sumeria

Recorded history began about 3400 BC, when writing was invented in ancient Sumeria, a country which was situated in the southeast corner of the Fertile Crescent, near the Persian Gulf.

The origin of the Sumerians is obscure. Their language is an isolate, unrelated to the Semitic languages that were spoken in most of the Fertile Crescent. The Sumerians may be descended from the Ubaid culture, which had occupied the same region during the preceding millennium, but the prevailing belief is that they were invaders who displaced the Ubaids. We do know that agriculture had flourished in the region for thousands of years before the advent of the Sumerian civilization, that domestic animals had long been used there, that pottery was being produced there, and that copper was being smelted.

Ancient Sumeria consisted of about two dozen small, independent city-states. The most famous of these — because it is mentioned in the Old Testament — is Ur, which was situated near the ancient coast of the Persian Gulf. (The coastline of the Gulf has changed markedly in the past 5000 years because of silt brought down by the two great rivers.) Among the other city-states were Eridu, Lagash, and Uruk. Uruk (= Erech) was for quite a while the world's largest city.[1]

Although the great majority of the population was engaged in agriculture, trade was an important factor in Sumerian civilization. Religion was also important, and every Sumerian city contained a sizable temple complex. No sign of any monotheistic religion or beliefs has been unearthed there.

Sumerian writing originated about 3400 BC, and for many centuries thereafter Sumeria had the wealthiest and most advanced civilization in the Middle East. In time, however, the peoples living upstream from Sumeria learnt from them, adopted writing, and became equally advanced.

About 2340 BC, Sumeria was conquered by Sargon the Great, the ruler of Akkad (later called Babylonia). Sargon's dynasty lasted for only about a century; however, about 2000 BC, Sumeria was again conquered, and this time it did not regain its independence. Thereafter, the Sumerian language gradually died out. By the time of Jesus, the very existence of ancient Sumeria had been forgotten, and it was not until the 19th century that archaeologists rediscovered Sumerian civilization.

Section 3 – Babylonia

The Babylonians were a Semitic people living directly upstream from Sumeria. Their first great ruler was Sargon of Akkad, who reigned from about 2371 to 2316 BC.[2] His original name is unknown; his adopted name, which means "the Rightful King," was probably chosen because he was, in fact, a usurper! His capital city, Agade, was probably close to Babylon, and perhaps 50 miles from the modern city of Baghdad. After obtaining the throne, Sargon invaded Sumeria, and then conquered the fertile regions of northern Mesopotamia and Syria, as well as Elam (in southwest Iran) and parts of southern Anatolia, thereby setting up the first "world empire."

Sargon's dynasty was eventually destroyed by invaders from the hills to the northeast. About 2000 BC, another Semitic people (the Amorites) established a new dynasty in Akkad, eventually choosing Babylon as their capital. The most notable king of this empire was Hammurabi (reigned 1792-1750 BC). Hammurabi assembled an empire about as large as Sargon's; but his lasting fame rests on the famous law code promulgated during his reign.[3]

The Babylonian Empire did not endure for long. Various tribes from the mountainous areas to the north and northeast conquered Mesopotamia in the middle of the 2nd millennium BC, and ruled most of it for several centuries.

Section 4 – Anatolia and the Hittites

Farming began at an early date in Anatolia (roughly, the region now occupied by Turkey), as did the smelting of copper, and the weaving of linen. By 8.2 kya, all three were being practiced at Çatal Hüyük, which was probably the largest town in the world at the time. The flooding of the Black Sea basin about 7.5 kya[4] may have sent many refugees into Anatolia, but the overall effect on the region is unclear. However, the invention of writing in Sumeria resulted in Mesopotamia pulling ahead of Anatolia culturally in early historic times.

The first Indo-European people to enter Anatolia were the Hittites, who appear to have invaded the region from the north about 2000 BC. By 1600 BC, the Hittites had established a considerable empire in Anatolia, and had invaded Babylonia. During the next few centuries, there were frequent wars between the Hittite Empire and Egypt, with the Hittites often getting the better of the fighting. However, about 1200 BC the Hittite Empire collapsed.

A language closely related to Hittite was Luwian, which was widely spoken in southern Anatolia after the fall of the Hittite Empire. (The "Hittites" mentioned in the Old Testament were probably Luwian speakers.) The Lycians and the Lydians also spoke languages related to Hittite. However, all of these peoples (together with Armenians, Phrygians, and other groups living in Anatolia) were conquered by Cyrus the Great of Persia in the sixth century BC, and thereafter most of them lost their separate identities.

Section 5 – The Assyrians and the Neo-Babylonians
The Assyrians had established a powerful state in northern Mesopotamia in the second millennium BC, but their greatest conquests came much later. Starting about 750 BC, a succession of very capable and aggressive rulers made Assyria the terror of the Middle East, conquering most of the Fertile Crescent and, for a few years, Egypt as well. The Assyrian capital, Nineveh, was beautified; and under Ashurbanipal (reigned 668-627 BC) an impressive royal library was built there, the largest the world had yet seen.

However, in 626 BC a widespread revolt, led by the Babylonians, broke out against the Assyrian tyranny. An invasion by the Medes (from Iran) helped the rebel cause. Nineveh was captured and burnt to the ground in 612 BC, and the last remnants of the once-mighty Assyrian Empire were destroyed three years later.

The victorious Babylonians (more precisely, the Neo-Babylonians, or Chaldeans) inherited virtually all the territory of the Assyrian Empire. By 550 BC, the Babylonian Empire had expanded, and had become even larger than the Assyrian Empire had been. But its day in the sun was short-lived. In 539 BC, Cyrus the Great of Persia overthrew it and took over most of the Middle East.

Section 6 – The Persian Empire
The Medes were an Indo-European people who developed a powerful state in Iran by 850 BC. They were part of the coalition that defeated the Assyrians in the late 7th century BC, but they did not control Mesopotamia afterwards. The Persians were a closely-related group, residing in southwest Iran, who for a while were ruled by the Medes.

Cyrus the Great (590-529 BC) started as a subchief within the Median kingdom. However, in 553 BC he led a revolt against the Median ruler, and after a three-year war succeeded in gaining the throne. He proceeded to attack the Lydian Empire in Anatolia (whose monarch was King Croesus, of legendary wealth). In 546 BC, Cyrus's iron prevailed over Croesus' gold, and Anatolia was added to the Persian domains. Cyrus then conducted a series of campaigns in which he gained control of eastern Iran. Cyrus's final conquest was the richest prize of all: the Neo-Babylonian Empire that ruled the Fertile Crescent. When this fell to him, in 539 BC, he ruled the largest empire the world had yet seen. However, ten years later Cyrus died in battle in an attempt to subdue the Massagetae, a semi-nomadic people living in Central Asia.

He was succeeded by his son, Cambyses, who conquered Egypt and thereby united most of the ancient world under a single empire. Following the death of Cambyses there was a struggle for succession, with the victory going to a man whose original claim to the throne was rather flimsy. Although a usurper, the new ruler (Darius I, often called "Darius the Great") proved to have outstanding ability, and he consolidated and reorganized the empire.

Darius made some additions to the territory of the empire; however, his attempt to add Greece to his dominions was unsuccessful. In 490 BC, an army he had assembled for that purpose was badly defeated by the Athenians at the Battle of Marathon. Darius died four years later; but his successor, Xerxes, organized another, larger invasion of Greece. In September of 480 BC, a Persian army entered Athens and pillaged it; however, later that month Xerxes' navy suffered a disastrous defeat at the Battle of Salamis.[5] Although the war dragged on for several more years, the Persians eventually abandoned their attempt to conquer Greece.

During the next century and a half the Persian Empire was large and wealthy, but its military strength gradually declined, which made it an inviting target. In 334 BC, Alexander the Great, the ruler of Macedonia (a large kingdom in northern Greece), invaded Persia, and within a few years he conquered it.

Section 7 – Greek and Roman rule

Alexander died a few years later, but his successors ruled the Fertile Crescent and surrounding areas for several centuries. During those centuries, Greek culture had an immense impact on the ancient Middle East.

In the first century BC, the Romans gained control of the western portion of the Middle East, including most of modern Turkey, Syria, Lebanon, and Israel. The Roman Empire (and its successor, the Byzantine Empire) ruled those lands for several hundred years, until the Arab conquests in the 7th century AD. Meanwhile, the eastern portion of the Fertile Crescent was ruled by Persians (either by the Parthian Empire, or by its successor, the Sassanid Empire). Note that all of these ruling groups — Persians, Macedonians, Greeks, Romans, Byzantines, Parthians, and Sassanids — were Indo-Europeans.

Section 8 – The Phoenicians

The Phoenicians were a small, Semitic-speaking people living on the Mediterranean coast, north of Israel (roughly, in modern Lebanon). Their origin is unclear. At times they were ruled by others; but about 1200 BC several Phoenician city-states became independent.

The Phoenicians were well known as traders, and for a long time were a major seafaring nation. They sailed widely throughout the Mediterranean, and even into the Atlantic. During their heyday, they established various colonies, the most important of which was Carthage, in modern Tunisia. Phoenicia was taken over by the Persians in 539 BC, and later became part of the empire of Alexander the Great.

The Phoenician alphabet was one of the first to be developed. It was probably the ancestor of the Greek alphabet, and (indirectly) of the Latin alphabet used today.

Section 9 – The Hebrews

The ancestors of today's Jews were a group usually referred to as the Hebrews, although they called themselves the "Children of Israel" after a legendary patriarch, also known as Jacob. The ancient Hebrews present a paradox: They were neither numerous, wealthy, nor powerful, and they contributed almost nothing to mathematics, science, or technology. Nonetheless, through their religious ideas and writings they had a major impact on civilization, and they were the forerunners of the world's two largest religions, Christianity and Islam.

When they first appeared in history, the Hebrews were semi-nomadic farmers and herdsmen. According to their oral traditions, their ancestors had been slaves in Egypt for many generations; then, about 1250 BC, a great leader named Moses led them into freedom. The story is very odd, and intertwined with various miracles, but probably has some basis in fact.

About 1200 BC, the Hebrew tribesmen invaded the land of Canaan (roughly the same territory as modern Israel) from the east. At about the same time, another people, the Philistines, invaded Canaan from the sea. The Philistines were difficult adversaries, and it was not until about 1000 BC that King David led the Hebrews to a convincing military victory over them. In the course of the next few centuries, the surviving Canaanites were gradually assimilated and lost their identity completely, as did the Philistines. (There is no evidence that the modern Palestinians are connected to the ancient Philistines.)

The most distinctive feature of the ancient Hebrews was their religion: In a world where virtually everybody was a polytheist, the Hebrew priests advocated an uncompromising monotheism, and eventually the entire nation came to accept that doctrine.

The source of Hebrew monotheism is unclear. They, themselves attributed it to a legendary patriarch, Abraham, the purported grandfather of Jacob. Others suggest that it was Moses who was the true founder of the religion. (A problem with that hypothesis is that Moses appears to be merely a legendary figure.) Some writers have suggested that Hebrew monotheism is derived from the religion of Ikhnaton (see section 28-6), which the Hebrews learned about during their stay in Egypt. It is a tempting hypothesis, but no proof has ever been presented.

For a long time, the fortified city of Jerusalem remained out of the grasp of the Hebrews; but, about 1000 BC, King David conquered the city and made it his capital.

His successor, King Solomon, built a magnificent temple in Jerusalem that became the center of Jewish worship.

Upon the death of Solomon, the Hebrew state split in two parts: a northern kingdom (Israel) and a southern one (Judea). The northern kingdom was destroyed by the Assyrians in 722 BC, and its inhabitants (the "Ten Lost Tribes") were scattered. In Judea — which was smaller, but included Jerusalem — the Davidic dynasty continued to rule until it was destroyed by the Babylonians in 586 BC. The Babylonian conquest ended with a successful siege of Jerusalem, after which the Babylonians burnt the city and destroyed the Temple. They also carted off 50,000 exiles to Babylon, including all the religious and political leaders of the Hebrew state.

It appeared as if this was the end of the Jewish people. However, the exiles prospered in Babylon and, rather than assimilating, they clung fiercely to their religion. Fifty years later, when Cyrus the Great conquered Babylonia, he granted the Jews permission to return to their old homeland. Most of them stayed in Babylon; but a sizable number did return, and in time they reestablished a thriving Jewish community in and around Jerusalem and built a new temple on the site of the old one.

It was not an independent community, of course, but simply a small colony within the powerful Persian Empire. Two centuries later, Alexander the Great overthrew that empire, and after his death Judea wound up as part of the empire of Seleucus, one of Alexander's generals. The Seleucid dynasty ruled Mesopotamia and Syria for two and a half centuries, and for much of that time controlled Judea as well. However, in 168 BC — more than 400 years after their seemingly final defeat by the Babylonians — the Jews revolted against Seleucid rule (the "Maccabean revolt"), and after a long struggle regained their independence.

The Maccabean kingdom lasted for about a century before it was swallowed up by the expanding Roman Empire. A revolt against Roman rule in 66 AD was put down with great loss of life, and another full-scale revolt in 135 AD was also suppressed bloodily. By then, the once-prosperous province was impoverished, with many of the inhabitants exiled and/or enslaved.

The importance of the ancient Hebrews does not, of course, lie in their buildings or their military feats (which were minor compared to that of other nations in the Middle East) but in their religious ideas and writings. The most celebrated of those writings are the "Five Books of Moses" (the *Torah*), which comprise the first five books of the Old Testament. These were composed during the Davidic dynasty, but were later edited and put into nearly their present form by Ezra (about 450 BC).

Many of the other books of the Old Testament record the teachings of various itinerant Hebrew preachers, collectively referred to as the Prophets. Together, these prophets transformed the Jewish religion. In the early books of the Old Testament, God was often depicted as a vain, powerful king who demanded obedience and the rigid performance of various rituals. The Prophets insisted that what God most demanded of a human being was not that he follow the prescribed rituals, but that he behave justly, fairly, and charitably towards his fellow humans. In brief, the message of the Prophets was: *Ethical behavior is more important than rituals.* (This idea, of course, was carried over into Christianity.)

The Old Testament also includes many historical books (most of which cover the period from 1200 BC to 586 BC), as well as collections of poetry and proverbs, and various legendary tales. The entire collection — composed by a few dozen writers from a small country — fits readily into a single volume. However, that one volume is the best known, most widely read, and most influential work of literature in all of human history.

Section 10 – Summary

The ancient Middle East was the cradle of civilization. Agriculture started there, as did irrigation, metalworking, cloth-weaving, and writing. As a result, 5000 years ago the Middle East was technologically and culturally the most advanced region on Earth. In the course of the next 4000 years, the Middle Eastern peoples made many other important contributions to human civilization including the alphabet, the arch, the arts of glass-making and ironworking, and two major world religions.

Nevertheless, by 300 BC the Middle East had plainly lost its dominating position in the world, and for most of the intervening time it has lagged behind Europe and China, often quite far behind.[6] Why did the Middle East fall so drastically from its position as the cultural leader of the world? Historians are not united on an answer to this question.

One suggestion is that there have been marked climate changes in the course of the past 5000 years, and that over that stretch of time the Middle East has suffered from increasing desiccation. A problem with this explanation is that the relative decline of the Middle East was already conspicuous by 300 BC, when the region was much wetter and more fertile than it is today.

Another suggestion — and, in my opinion, a better one — is that it was the higher average intelligence of the northern peoples (the Europeans and the Mongoloids) that enabled them to catch up with and surpass the Middle East. After discussing Egypt, we will describe the history and achievements of some of those northern peoples.

FOOTNOTES – CHAPTER 27

1) *Historical Atlas of the Ancient World* (1998), p. 1.10, where it is suggested that the population may have reached 50,000.

2) The dates in this section are taken from the *Encyclopedia of World History* (6th edition, 2001), pp. 25-28. Other sources give somewhat different figures.

3) The earliest known law code is the one promulgated about 2100 BC by Ur-Nammu, who was the ruler of Ur. See the article on "Iraq" in the *Encyclopaedia Britannica* (15th edition, 1986), Vol. 21, p. 917.

4) See Ryan, William & Walter Pitman (1998). In their book they present evidence that 8000 years ago the surface of the Black Sea was far below sea level, but that severe flooding occurred a few centuries later when a passageway opened near the Bosphorus that allowed waters from the Mediterranean to cascade down into the Black Sea. Many of the legends about the "Great Flood" (see *Genesis*, chapters 6-9) may derive from this event.

5) (a) A fascinating discussion of the Battle of Salamis can be found in chapter 2 of *Carnage and Culture* by Victor Davis Hanson (2001).
   (b) The best known ancient source concerning the battle is book VIII of Herodotus' *History* (5th century BC). This can be found in Volume VI of the *Great Books of the Western World* series (1952), pp. 266-276 and 323.

6) For a stretch during the Middle Ages, the Arab world surpassed the West in cultural matters and was about on a par with China, but that period only lasted for a few centuries (see section 7 of chapter 34).

CHAPTER 28

ANCIENT EGYPT

Section 1 – Introduction

It is a truism that a country's history is affected by its geography; but in few countries has the effect of geography been as great as in Egypt. On a map, Egypt appears to be a fairly large country, with an area (about 386,000 square miles) greater than France and Germany combined. However, most of Egypt is uninhabitable desert, and the country has less than 20,000 square miles of arable land. Rainfall is sparse, and a single river, the Nile, provides most of the country's fresh water. In the southern 5/6 of the country, the thin Nile Valley is sandwiched between two arid deserts. Except for the Nile Delta, and a narrow coastal strip, most of northern Egypt is also arid.

However, for a long time that same geography protected Egypt from external enemies. Because of the deserts, no foreign army could possibly attack the Nile Valley from either the east or the west. It was possible for tribes living upstream to invade the country from the south, but this was difficult, and rarely happened. The greatest danger was from the north. However, the African coast to the west of Egypt was sparsely inhabited, and the Sinai Desert provided protection from the northeast. It was probably because of this unusual degree of protection from foreign invaders that Egypt was the least militaristic of the ancient kingdoms.

With almost the entire population living close to the Nile, transportation within Egypt was very easy. As a result, there were fewer regional differences and disputes in Egypt than in other parts of the world.

Within the Nile Valley and the Nile Delta the soil was very fertile. However, the lack of rainfall made agriculture there entirely dependent on the waters of the Nile. Each spring, melting snows from the mountains in Ethiopia caused the river to swell greatly. When the extra water reached Egypt, the river overflowed its banks and automatically irrigated the entire Nile Valley. (Hence, Herodotus's description of Egypt as "the gift of the Nile.")

The best time for an Egyptian farmer to plant his crops was just before the flooding began. The early Egyptians did not have an accurate calendar; however, they noticed that the flooding usually started just a few days after the heliacal rising of the bright star Sirius (see section 6).

Section 2 – Review of Egyptian prehistory

Nine thousand years ago, Egypt was still a Paleolithic society. However, about 6000 BC, the country was entered by Caucasoid farmers from Southwest Asia, and in time those settlers took over the entire country.[1]

For a long time, Egypt consisted of many small independent regions. These were gradually combined into two larger states: Lower Egypt (the Nile Delta), and Upper Egypt (the Nile Valley). The two states were united about 3100 BC by Menes, the first king of the first Egyptian dynasty. The "dynastic era" lasted over 2700 years, until 343 BC, when the last native Egyptian ruler was supplanted by the Persians.

Section 3 – The dynastic era

The dynastic era is customarily divided into seven periods, in the course of which a total of thirty different dynasties rose and fell.[2] The seven periods are:

1) *The Early Dynastic Period* (~3100-2686 BC). This included the first two dynasties.

2) *The Old Kingdom* (2686-2160 BC). This included the next four dynasties. All the large pyramids were built during this period.

3) *The First Intermediate Period* (2160-2040 BC). This was an interval of political disorder that included five short-lived dynasties.

4) *The Middle Kingdom* (2040-1786 BC). A single dynasty, the 12th, ruled for this entire period.

5) *The Second Intermediate Period* (1786-1562 BC). The Middle Kingdom was followed by a long period of disorder in the course of which invaders from the north (the *Hyksos*, or *Sea Peoples*) conquered Egypt. This period included dynasties 13-17.

6) *The New Kingdom* (1562-1085 BC). In the 16th century BC, the Egyptians succeeded in expelling the Hyksos. The ensuing period is called the *New Kingdom*, and includes three dynasties. Many of the notable Egyptian monuments and temples were built in this era. Several of the New Kingdom pharaohs (including Thutmose III, Amenhotep III, and Rameses II) raised large armies, and attempted to conquer the lands to the northwest of Egypt (Israel, Lebanon, and Syria). These attempts had some temporary success; however, despite Egypt's wealth and large population, its empire did not endure long, and it never achieved the size that the Assyrian, Babylonian, and Persian empires did.

7) *The Period of the Decline* (1085-343 BC). After the 20th dynasty, Egypt went into a long period of political decline, an era that included dynasties 21-30. On several occasions, Egypt was conquered by outsiders (such as the Assyrians and the Persians), but eventually regained independence. However, in 343 BC the Persians conquered the entire country, and this time the Egyptians did not regain their freedom. The interval of

Persian rule was rather brief, though, since Alexander the Great conquered Egypt in 332 BC, and within a few years he completely destroyed the Persian Empire.

Note that from about 3100 to 1786 BC — an interval of over 13 centuries — Egypt had relatively little instability. However, by the end of that period improvements in transportation resulted in Egypt being less isolated from other countries, and after 1786 BC, it suffered more from foreign attacks than it had earlier.

Section 4 – The Graeco-Roman period

Alexander entered Egypt in 332 BC, and the country fell to him without a battle. While in Egypt, he founded a new city, Alexandria, on the Mediterranean coast, near the westernmost mouth of the Nile. Although the city was situated in Egypt, its ruling class and culture were Greek. It soon became a major port, and one of the great intellectual centers of the ancient world.

When Alexander died, in 323 BC, Egypt was seized by one of his generals, Ptolemy. The Ptolemaic dynasty lasted until the Roman conquest in 30 BC. Roman rule (including the Byzantine period) lasted until the Moslem conquest in 642 AD. Note that Indo-Europeans ruled Egypt for nearly a thousand years (343 BC – 642 AD) even though they made up only a small fraction of the population.

Section 5 – The pyramids

These royal tombs are by far the most celebrated achievement of the ancient Egyptians. Seven large pyramids were constructed, and dozens of smaller ones.

The first large one was the "Step Pyramid," built about 2650 BC at Saqqara, about 15 miles from modern Cairo. The Step Pyramid was the first massive stone building ever constructed. It was about 200 feet high — about five times the height (and more than 100 times the weight) of any earlier structure! Although much the worse for wear, it is still standing today.

The largest and most celebrated of the pyramids is the Great Pyramid, built about 2550 BC at Giza (now on the western edge of Cairo) as the tomb of Cheops. It was originally about 480 feet high, although only about 450 feet remain today. The Great Pyramid — still the heaviest building ever constructed — consists of about 2,300,000 blocks of stone, averaging about 2½ tons apiece. There are several sizable chambers inside it, connected by passages.

From an architectural point of view, pyramids are not very sophisticated structures. However, the degree of organization required to construct the large Egyptian pyramids is impressive. If we accept the statement of Herodotus that the Great Pyramid took 20 years to build, then an average of 300 massive blocks of limestone were added each day! Each of those stones had to be quarried, cut to size, transported, and lifted into place. (The limestone used was not local, but was quarried well upstream and transported down the Nile.) In addition, food, water, and other facilities had to be provided for the many thousands of workers involved in the project. Note also that Giza is on a cliff overlooking the Nile, and that before building the pyramid an immense ramp had to be constructed in order to bring the stone blocks to the construction site.

Section 6 – Other cultural achievements of the ancient Egyptians

Although the pyramids are the most famous structures built by the ancient Egyptians, they are certainly not the only noteworthy ones. The Valley of the Kings, the Sphinx, the temple complex at Karnak, and numerous other obelisks, temples, tombs, and monuments still enthrall modern visitors. In addition, the Egyptians produced many fine ornaments and works of jewelry.

The Egyptians invented a system of writing only about three centuries after the Sumerians did, and many samples of Egyptian hieroglyphics have survived. However, despite the long history of writing in Egypt, the Egyptian contribution to literature was meager. The best-known Egyptian work is *The Book of the Dead* (compiled from earlier writings about 1600 BC), which consists mostly of spells and magic formulas, but also includes some hymns. Few people look at it today, and its influence on world literature has been minimal.

The 18th-dynasty ruler, Ikhnaton (reigned 1379-1362 BC) was the first person we know of to assert that there is only one god. He was the son of Amenhotep III, one of the most famous pharaohs of the New Kingdom, and he ascended the throne as Amenhotep IV. Soon, though, he became convinced that the sun god, Aton, was the one true god; and thereafter the king built temples to Aton, composed hymns to Aton, and built a new capital city where the worship of other deities was forbidden. He also changed his name to Ikhnaton ("servant of Aton"), and did his best to convert the entire country to his monotheistic vision. After he died, though, his movement collapsed, and the priests of the older Egyptian religion regained their influence.

Historians are divided as to the long-term influence of Ikhnaton. It has often been conjectured that the Hebrews got the idea of monotheism from his movement, but that hypothesis is not generally accepted.

The Egyptians had a good working knowledge of practical geometry, although they never developed a theoretical structure. The earliest known text on algebra (the *Ahmes Papyrus*, written about 1650 BC) comes from Egypt. It describes how to solve simple linear equations, but goes no further.

The Egyptians observed that the bright star Sirius rose at a slightly different time each night. Once a year, there was a night when Sirius rose just before dawn. This event was called the *heliacal rising* of Sirius, and the Egyptians noticed that it came just a few days before the Nile overflowed its banks.

Section 7 – The importance of ancient Egypt is usually greatly overrated

Most of us, when we studied world history in high school or college, were told that the ancient Egyptians made enormous contributions to world civilization. A careful consideration of the facts, however, reveals that their contributions were actually quite meager.

For many centuries, European historians believed that ancient Egypt had been the first civilization on Earth. However, we now know that civilization originated in the

Fertile Crescent of Southwest Asia. The ancient Egyptians were *not* the first people to build cities, nor were they the inventors of agriculture. Nor were they the first to use plows, employ irrigation, rotate crops, or domesticate animals.

The ancient Egyptians were not the first people to invent writing: the Sumerians preceded them by two or three centuries. Nor did the Egyptians invent either the alphabet, paper, or printing. Nor did they originate pottery, glassmaking, or metalworking. (Copper and bronze were first used in Southwest Asia, and it appears that the Hittites were the first to smelt iron.) Nor did the Egyptians invent the wheel, or the use of wheeled vehicles.

The Egyptian contribution to mathematics was not great. Although, like many ancient peoples, they had a *practical* knowledge of elementary geometry, they had little interest in geometric theory. They may have been the first to use algebra (although it is possible that the Babylonians preceded them), but their knowledge was very limited, roughly to what is now studied in the first few weeks of an elementary algebra course.

The Egyptian contribution to astronomy was also minimal. Although the dry climate in Egypt made for near-ideal viewing conditions, they appear to have had less interest in the subject than any other ancient civilization. They had noted the heliacal rising of Sirius, but they made no significant contributions to astronomical theory, nor to physics, chemistry, biology, or geology.

Nor were the ancient Egyptians much interested in geography or exploration. From earliest times they had traded with the Nubians (a Negroid people who lived directly south of Egypt), and with the peoples living near the southern part of the Red Sea. However, they did not explore down the East African coast, and for many centuries they did not travel widely in the Mediterranean, and were unaware of the Strait of Gibraltar, or even of Italy.

According to Herodotus, about 600 BC an Egyptian king (Necho) commissioned an expedition to make a sea voyage from the Red Sea coast of Egypt to the Mediterranean coast (a trip which necessitated sailing around Africa), and the expedition was successful.[3] Herodotus himself was skeptical about the story, as are most modern historians. But even if the story is true, one should note that the project was not carried out by Egyptians (Necho hired Phoenicians to conduct the expedition). Furthermore, the Egyptians never followed up the voyage in any way.

If the ancient Egyptians' contribution to science and technology was small, their contribution to most other aspects of culture was even smaller:

1) Their language has been extinct for many centuries, and no major language derives from it.

2) They made no significant contribution to world literature.

3) Egyptian painting does not seem to have influenced Western art; and no Egyptian music has survived.

4) The Egyptian political structure (like that of most early states) was an absolute monarchy. It was neither an original idea, nor one that influences modern thinkers.

5) The ancient Egyptian religion was abandoned many centuries ago, and has no successors.

6) Nor did the Egyptians contribute to other branches of philosophy. Not a single major theme in modern philosophy derives from an ancient Egyptian source.

The Egyptian pyramids are, of course, very impressive. However, they had very little effect on the subsequent development of architecture. The pyramid is a very simple architectural structure, and for most purposes not a very useful one. The ancient Egyptians did not originate the arch, and they did not use it until fairly late in their history.

Section 8 – Why has ancient Egypt been overrated?
If the Egyptian contributions to language, literature, philosophy, art, science, exploration, and technology are so meager, why do so many history books talk about the "great contributions" of ancient Egypt? There appear to be two reasons which relate specifically to Egypt, plus another, more general reason. The first two reasons are:

1) Because the climate of Egypt is so dry, Egyptian architecture has been preserved far better than the architecture of other ancient civilizations. As a result, the Egyptian monuments are still so visible (and so impressive) that most people overestimate their importance to the growth of civilization.

2) The ancient Greeks — who were unaware of how many contributions to civilization had been made by the peoples living in or around Mesopotamia — mistakenly viewed the Egyptians as the originators of civilization.

The general reason is that, when historians and archaeologists evaluate ancient civilizations, they tend to greatly overestimate the importance of architecture relative to other aspects of human culture such as literature, painting, music, philosophy, law, medicine, mathematics, and science. They tend to do this because:

a) Stone buildings often endure for many centuries, or even millennia, whereas a painting or a work of calligraphy is far less likely to survive, and the work of a performing artist is ephemeral. A book, of course, may be copied; but since individual volumes are neither tough nor fireproof most ancient works have been lost.

b) Works of architecture do not need to be translated. The written language of the Indus Valley civilization has not been deciphered, and its literature is therefore inaccessible. The same is true for the Minoans, the Etruscans, and others. Furthermore, even in those instances when the surviving literature of a country *can* be translated, only a small fraction of it usually *has* been translated.

c) Many aspects of a nation's culture — law, for example — are very complex, and only professionals in the field can understand and evaluate them, whereas even a layman can view and appreciate an ancient stone temple or monument.

d) Many aspects of an ancient civilization — for example, the status of women — may be completely unknown to us.

Make no mistake: I am not suggesting that the ancient Egyptians were savages or uncivilized. The evidence of their construction skills is indisputable, and the Egyptian state seems to have been very well governed by the standards of the day. Like everyone else who has viewed them, I found the pyramids extremely impressive; and they provide clear evidence of the organizational skills of the ancient Egyptians. I am simply pointing out the Egyptian contributions to the progress of world civilization were not very great, and are vastly overstated by most history books.

FOOTNOTES – CHAPTER 28

1) See section 22-3. Also see *DK Atlas of World History* (2001 edition), p. 21; *Past Worlds: Atlas of Archaeology* (2003 edition), p. 118; and Diamond, Jared (1999), pp. 100-101.

2) Unfortunately, the original list of dynasties has been lost, and the present, reconstructed list is not completely reliable. I have followed the chronology presented in the article on "Egypt" in volume 18 of the *Encyclopaedia Brittanica* (15th edition, 1986). See especially pp. 149-166.

3) See book IV of Herodotus' *History* (5th century BC). This can be found in volume 6 of the *Great Books of the Western World* series (1952), p. 131.

CHAPTER 29

ANCIENT GREECE

Section 1 – Overview

Ancient Greece was a small country, and never very populous. Nevertheless, the ancient Greeks made enormous contributions to human civilization, dwarfing those of the Egyptians, Babylonians, or any other ancient people. The achievements of the Greeks revolutionized human thought and laid the groundwork for the accomplishments of the modern Europeans.

Section 2 – Geography

Ancient Greece consisted of three regions: the Aegean Islands; the mainland of modern Greece; and Ionia (the west coast of modern Turkey, which borders on the Aegean Sea). Since mainland Greece has numerous peninsulas and inlets, and most of the islands are quite small, most Greeks did not live very far from the sea. This proximity to the sea encouraged the mastery of maritime skills, which in turn encouraged trade and exploration.

Greece has a typical Mediterranean climate, with hot, dry summers and damp, mild-to-chilly winters. Most of the country is mountainous, a factor which led to the formation of many independent (and often warring) city-states. As a result, Greece was not unified politically until it was conquered by Macedonia in the 4th century BC.

Section 3 – Early history (before 500 BC)

Agriculture spread to Greece from the Middle East at a very early date, probably about 7000 BC. The first civilization to arise in Greece was the Minoan civilization, which was flourishing on Crete by 2000 BC. By then, the Minoans were using a logo-syllabic writing system; and by 1700 BC, they had developed a fully syllabic writing system which we call Linear A. Neither system has been deciphered, and we are ignorant of both the language and the origin of the Minoans. It does not appear, though, that their language was a form of Greek, or closely related to it.

The ancestors of the ancient Greeks were illiterate Indo-European tribesmen who entered the country from the north. The first wave of these invaders entered northern Greece about 2000 BC. (They sometimes referred to the previous inhabitants of the land as the *Pelasgians*, but we know nothing else about that group.) Originally, the early Greeks were less advanced than the Minoans; but the Greeks learned from them, and by 1450 BC had conquered them. The resulting culture is often called *Mycenaean*, after one of its largest cities.

The Mycenaeans altered the Linear A script, creating a new syllabic writing system, now called Linear B. (Inscriptions in Linear B were deciphered in the 20th century, and turned out to be an early form of Greek.) The Mycenaeans possessed considerable maritime skills. The legends about the Argonauts, the siege of Troy, and the wanderings of Ulysses probably date from the Mycenaean period.

In the 12th century BC, a fresh wave of Greek-speaking tribesmen (the *Dorians*) entered from the north. The early Dorians were relatively uncivilized, and they destroyed the Mycenaean civilization and plunged Greece into a "Dark Age" that lasted for over three centuries. In time, however, the descendants of the Dorians and the earlier Greeks intermarried and merged into a single people.

Classical Greece emerged from this "Dark Age" about 800 BC. Not long thereafter, the Greeks were heavily engaged in overseas trade, exploration, and colonization. Some of their colonies were situated along the coasts of the Black Sea; but the most successful ones were in Sicily and southern Italy, which became known as *Magna Graecia* ("Greater Greece"). Cumae (near the modern city of Naples) was founded about 750 BC; Syracuse, in Sicily, was founded in 734 BC; and Marseilles, in southern France, about 600 BC. Several of these colonies prospered, and for a while Syracuse became the largest "Greek" city in the world.

Homer probably lived in the middle or late 8th century BC.[1] However, the main intellectual flowering of Greece started about 600 BC with the philosopher Thales of Miletus.

Section 4 – Later history (from 500 BC to the Roman conquest)

By 500 BC, Greece was a very prosperous region, which naturally attracted the interest of the powerful Persian Empire to the east. Under Darius the Great, the Persians invaded Greece, and in 490 BC, they landed a large army on the Plain of Marathon, 26 miles from Athens. However, in the celebrated Battle of Marathon (September 12, 490), a greatly outnumbered Athenian army won a dramatic victory over the Persians. Ten years later, Darius' successor, Xerxes, invaded Greece again, and in September of 480 BC captured Athens. However, later that month the Persian fleet was badly defeated at the crucial Battle of Salamis,[2] and a few years later the Persians abandoned their attempt to conquer Greece.

The Greeks' successful defense of their homeland was followed by a tremendous flowering of Greek literature, philosophy, science, and mathematics; and the next two centuries are often called the *Golden Age of Greece*. Among the famous Greeks who lived during that period were Socrates, Plato, Aristotle, Pythagoras, Sophocles, Euripides, Herodotus, Euclid, and Hippocrates.

Unfortunately, their success in repelling the Persian invasions did not put an end to the conflicts between the Greek city-states. The Peloponnesian War — between Athens and Sparta (and their respective allies) — ended with the defeat of Athens in 404 BC.[3] Thirty-three years later, Sparta was defeated by Thebes, but Theban military superiority was soon contested by other Greek cities. By the middle of the fourth century BC, the strongest Greek state was not one of the old city-states, but rather the kingdom of Macedonia in the north, ruled by Philip II.

Philip believed that if the Greeks would unite under a single ruler, they would be strong enough to conquer the Persian Empire; and he naturally thought that the single ruler should be himself. To that end, he built up a large army, and at the Battle of Chaeronia (338 BC) he defeated the combined forces of his main Greek opponents. However, Philip was assassinated in 336 BC, before his plan to conquer Persia could be carried out.

Philip was succeeded by his second son, commonly called "Alexander the Great," who turned out to be an extraordinarily brilliant general, and one of the most dramatic figures in history. It was Alexander's goal to be the greatest warrior of all time; and, arguably, he succeeded. Alexander was only 20 years old when he ascended the throne, and several Greek states (including Athens and Thebes) soon revolted against Macedonian rule. Within two years, though, Alexander had quashed those revolts and had also defeated the Thracian tribes living north of Macedonia, thus safeguarding his northern border.

Leaving a sizable contingent in Greece, Alexander then led his main army into Asia where he won a series of crushing victories (Granicus [334 BC]; Issus [333]; Arbela [331]) against large Persian armies. Although Alexander died before reaching his 33rd birthday, he had by then made himself master of everything from Greece to western India — including Egypt, Anatolia, the entire Fertile Crescent, and Iran. He died of natural causes (from a fever, probably malaria) in Babylon, in 323 BC. In thirteen years of fighting, he had never lost a single battle.

Alexander had named no successor, and upon his death several of his generals vied for the throne. None was able to defeat all the others, and in the end Alexander's vast empire was divided into three large kingdoms — one consisting of Macedonia and most of Greece; another including Egypt; and the third consisting of most of his Asian conquests. The most profound result of Alexander's conquests, though was that all of western Asia was exposed to Greek culture, and absorbed many elements of it.

Starting in 215 BC, there were a series of wars between Macedonia and the rising power of Rome. These ended in 146 BC with the complete triumph of Rome, which by then ruled most of Greece. However, Greek cultural and intellectual achievements continued for several centuries under Roman rule, not ending until about 200 AD.

Section 5 – Some of the Greek contributions to civilization

I will divide their principal contributions into ten main categories.[4]

A) Mathematics

- *A theoretical framework for geometry*. Although various ancient peoples had a practical knowledge of elementary geometry, the Greeks were the first to construct a theoretical framework for it. Two centuries of work by a series of Greek mathematicians culminated in Euclid's great work on geometry, *Elements* (written about 300 BC). His book includes a complete deductive framework for geometry, starting with a few axioms and deducing all other geometric theorems from them. In modern times, mathematicians have applied Euclid's axiomatic approach to every other branch of mathematics, totally transforming the field. Today, this approach is the central feature of mathematics, and mathematics might rightly be called "the study of necessary consequences." Furthermore, this deductive geometric theory turned out to be an indispensable prelude to the advent of modern science.

- *Conic sections*. Euclid's successors carried his study of geometry even further. For example, Apollonius of Perga made a detailed study of the conic sections (ellipses, parabolas, and hyperbolas), a group of curves which have many applications in astronomy and physics.

- *Plane and spherical trigonometry*. The oldest surviving book employing these branches of mathematics is Ptolemy's great work on astronomy, the *Syntaxis* (also called the *Almagest*) which was written about 140 AD. However, Ptolemy made heavy use of the works of Hipparchus (190-120 BC), who is usually credited with founding this important field, even though his works have since been lost.

- *Irrational numbers*. The unexpected discovery that there are numbers that cannot be expressed as either whole numbers or fractions is usually credited to Pythagoras, who flourished about 500 BC. Nowadays, when it is accepted that most numbers are "irrational," such numbers are used freely by both mathematicians and physicists.

- *Prime numbers*. These were first recognized and studied by the Greeks. Euclid's book includes an ingenious proof that there are an infinite number of primes.

- *Integration*. Archimedes (287-212 BC) was able to obtain formulas for the area and volume of a sphere by using a technique (the "method of exhaustion") equivalent to any early form of integral calculus. (The technique had first been suggested by Eudoxus, about a century earlier.)

B) Geography

- *The shape of the Earth*. The central fact of geography is that the Earth is round. This discovery was made about 500 BC, and is usually attributed to Pythagoras.

- *The size of the Earth*. This was first calculated by Eratosthenes. His estimate (made in the 3rd century BC) was within a few percent of the correct value.

- *Latitude and longitude*. This useful system of coordinates was employed by Hipparchus, extending a suggestion made by Dicaearchus.

- *Map of the world*. An early one was constructed by Herodotus about 450 BC. Ptolemy's great work on geography (2nd century AD), included a much better one. (Neither map, though, included either the Western Hemisphere or Australia.)

C) Astronomy

- *The heliocentric theory*. Aristarchus of Samos (fl. 270 BC) was the first person to propose that the Earth revolves about the Sun. His contemporaries rejected his hypothesis; but it was later adopted by Copernicus and became one of the foundations of modern astronomy.

- *The precession of the equinoxes*. This was discovered by Hipparchus.

- *The motions of the planets*. Greek astronomers were the first to devise mathematical models to describe and predict the observed planetary motions. The most sophisticated such model was the one presented by Ptolemy in the *Almagest*. His book remained the standard text for fourteen centuries.

D) Biology and Medicine

- *A non-magical approach to disease*. In ancient times, most physicians assumed that diseases had supernatural causes. Hippocrates (460-370 BC), however, advocated the view that diseases had physical causes. He therefore instituted a program of carefully recording the symptoms of each disease, the treatment applied, and the results. He is often called "the father of medicine," as his approach lies at the heart of later medical advances.

- *Embryology*. Aristotle (384-322 BC) initiated the study of this subject.

E) Chemistry and Physics

- *Atomic nature of matter*. Various Greek philosophers — most notably Democritus — suggested that matter is comprised of extremely small, indivisible particles. (None of them, though, were able to provide convincing proof of their conjecture.)

- *Elementary substances*. Other Greek philosophers propounded what is now another pillar of chemical theory, the notion that there are only a few basic substances, and that every other substance is composed of some combination of those elementary ones. (The basic idea was correct, but their guesses as to which substances were elementary were far off the mark.)

- *Mechanics*. In addition to his mathematical works, Archimedes wrote the first treatise on hydrostatics. He also described methods for determining the center of gravity of various objects, and he formulated the principle of the lever.

F) Literature

- *Poetry*. Homer's two great works, the *Odyssey* and the *Iliad*, are the most celebrated works of epic poetry ever composed.

- *Drama*. The ancient Greeks were the first to elevate drama to a major art form. The greatest Greek tragic writers (Aeschylus, Sophocles, and Euripides) have rarely been equaled, and their works still move audiences today. Greek comic dramatists include Aristophanes and Menander.

- *Mythology*. By near-universal consent, Greek mythology is the most fascinating and charming composed by any nation.

- *Aesop's Fables*. It is unclear whether Aesop was a real person or a legendary figure, but in any event the fables attributed to him have charmed children — and adults — for many centuries, and are the best-known set of fables in all of literature.

G) Visual arts

- *Architecture*. The Greeks produced exceptionally elegant architecture (including such masterpieces as the Parthenon, in Athens), and their work has inspired architects in many other countries.

- *Sculpture*. Here, too, the best Greek artists set a standard of excellence that has rarely been equaled. Of their many great works, perhaps the most famous is the *Venus de Milo* (2nd century BC). The best-known Greek sculptors were Phidias (5th century BC) and Praxiteles (4th century BC).

H) History

- *Herodotus*. Although primarily a book about the Persian invasion of Greece, his *History* (written about 450 BC) includes a great deal of other material, and has been an invaluable source for subsequent historians.

- *Thucydides*. His book, *The History of the Peloponnesian War*, is more limited in scope, but far superior in accuracy to Herodotus.

- *Xenophon*. His book, the *Anabasis* (c. 400 BC), is the oldest surviving military memoir. It still reads well.

I) Philosophy

- *Socrates*. Although he left no writings, his ideas on ethics and politics have come down to us through the writings of his famous student, Plato.

- *Plato*. One of the best known of all philosophers, Plato (427-347 BC) wrote extensively about politics, ethics, metaphysics, and other branches of philosophy.

- *Aristotle*. A student of Plato, he wrote on virtually every branch of philosophy and science known at the time, and also carried out independent research. He was a leading exponent of a rational approach to philosophy, and shunned superstitious, magical, or religious explanations for phenomena. In addition, he was the first writer to discuss the field of formal logic. Like Plato, he has been an enduring influence on philosophic thought for over two millennia.

J) Politics

- *Democracy*. Although many of the Greek city-states were governed by hereditary monarchs, or by tyrants, Athens was for a long time an example of a functioning democracy. The Athenians were very proud of being free citizens of a republic, rather than subjects of a king.

- *Political theory*. Many of the Greek states had constitutions. Indeed, one of Aristotle's research projects was the collection of the constitutions of a large number of states, which he subjected to a comparative study. The works of Plato and Aristotle are among the oldest analytical writings on political theory.

Section 6 – Why were the Greeks able to achieve so much?

Although the above list is far from complete, it does show that the intellectual achievements of the Greeks completely dwarfed the achievements of any other ancient or medieval civilization. (For example, in 1600 AD the Chinese had still not progressed as far in mathematics as the Greeks had in 300 BC.) The intellectual achievements of the Greeks were so extraordinary that the phenomenon cries out for an explanation.

One suggestion is that the underlying factor was the geography of Greece. This caused the Greeks to become a seafaring nation and led them to engage — more than other nations — in exploration and trade. As a result, the Greeks gained access to a large number of ideas and technological skills; and it was the unusual size of this intellectual/technological base that enabled the Greeks to accomplish so much.

This is an interesting suggestion, and one that I believe is partly correct; but it is not, by itself, a sufficient explanation for the Greek accomplishments. After all, the Phoenicians — who for centuries were the leading seafaring/trading nation in the world — did not make many contributions to world culture. Furthermore, the Caribbean region, rather than being an intellectually advanced part of the New World, lagged far behind Mexico, Central America, and the Andean region of South America. Nor were either the Philippines or Indonesia a region of great intellectual achievements, although each consists of a large number of islands.

A simpler suggestion is that the extraordinary Greek achievements were due to the high native intelligence of the Greeks. This suggestion is also partly correct. It appears that the Indo-European tribes who were the immediate ancestors of the Greeks had, on average, substantially higher IQs than the Egyptians, Minoans, Sumerians, and the various Semitic peoples in the Middle East. (See section 26-4 and Table 17-1.)

However, that suggestion is also insufficient to explain what occurred. Table 17-1 shows that the various peoples living in the rest of Europe (Teutonic tribes, Slavs, etc.) during the period of Greek flowering had average IQs just as high as (or even higher than) the ancient Greeks; yet their intellectual achievements were negligible. High intelligence alone does not explain the Greek achievement.

The best explanation for the Greek phenomenon lies in a combination of genetic and geographic factors. The peoples living in the cold regions of Europe had, over a period of many millennia, evolved higher average intelligence than the peoples living in the Middle East. However, because of the mild climate in the Middle East, and the availability of a large assortment of useful domesticable plants and animals, the inhabitants of the Middle East developed agriculture long before the peoples of northern Europe. The early advent of agriculture and cities in the Middle East enabled them to make major progress during the Neolithic Era and the early historic era, and to get a big jump on the rest of the world in technology and in intellectual matters.

In time, the superior genetic endowment of the Europeans would enable them to overcome that head start. However, between European groups, the one most likely to advance *first* was the one which had the earliest opportunity of learning from the civilizations of the Middle East and Egypt. Because of their geographic location, the Greeks were the first European people to come into contact with those civilizations. It took the Greeks several centuries to absorb the cultural advances of those earlier civilizations; but once they had done so, the high intelligence of the Greeks resulted in the enormous intellectual advances for which they are famous.

The Celtic, Teutonic, and Slavic tribes were never in direct contact with the Egyptian and Middle Eastern civilizations. In 600 BC — when the Greeks had already been in contact with those ancient civilizations for many centuries, and through that contact had developed a fully alphabetic writing system — the Slavic, Teutonic, and Celtic tribes to the north of them had still had virtually no contact with those ancient civilizations, and were totally illiterate. The Greeks were the *first* group to possess the combination of opportunity and natural talent that is the prerequisite for great achievements.

The ancient Italians were approximately as intelligent as the Greeks. However, although they had some contact with the ancient civilizations, that contact was (because of the westerly location of Italy) both less than and later than the contact that the Greeks had.

What about the Hittites? Were they not a northern (and therefore high-IQ) group that came into contact with Middle Eastern civilization at an early date? A reasonable answer is that the Hittites who moved into Anatolia were a rather small group numerically, and their genes were soon swamped by those of the much larger indigenous population with whom they interbred. Hence, the Hittites soon lost most or all of their advantage in native intelligence. In Greece, there were several waves of invaders, and they entered a mountainous land where the indigenous population had been fairly small. Hence, the gene pool of the classical Greeks was derived mostly from that of the Indo-European invaders, and the average IQ of the resulting population was high.

FOOTNOTES – CHAPTER 29

1) See article on "The Homeric Epics" in *Encyclopaedia Brittanica* (15th edition, 1986), volume 20, especially pp. 695-696.

2) For a fascinating account of this crucial battle see chapter two of *Carnage and Culture* by Victor Davis Hanson.

3) The classic account of this struggle is *The History of the Peloponnesian War* by Thucydides.

4) Virtually every important ancient Greek work can be found in the *Loeb Classical Library*, with the Greek text and English translation on facing pages.

CHAPTER 30

THE RISE OF ANCIENT ROME

Section 1 – Introduction

The Roman Empire was the greatest empire of antiquity. Even the ruins of this great empire — the remains of its aqueducts, amphitheaters, and superb road system — fill us with awe today. At its peak, the empire extended from Morocco to Rumania, and from Scotland to Kuwait, and it contained one-quarter of the world's population. Although the Roman Empire was destroyed over fifteen centuries ago, its memory has never died, and the cultural legacy of Rome has influenced Europe ever since.

The rise of Rome from a small city-state into a gigantic empire is amazing. But more amazing still is the manner in which Rome ended. Most great empires have been brought down by large armies assembled by strong, rising nations. Rome decayed from within; and when Rome finally fell, she was defeated by small armies, far smaller than the ones she had prevailed against earlier. Furthermore, the nations who defeated Rome remained backward and barbaric for centuries thereafter.

The rise and fall of Rome is therefore both a great historical epic and an abiding mystery. It is also a fearful warning to us: If that great empire — so wealthy and well organized, and so superior militarily to its opponents — could not avert its internal decay and catastrophic fall, then perhaps the same fate awaits us, and perhaps in the not distant future?

Section 2 – Italy before the rise of Rome

Farmers from Greece (whose ancestors had come from the Middle East) reached Italy as early as 6000 BC, and they eventually settled the entire country, although there was some mixing with the earlier Paleolithic population.

In the period 1500-1000 BC, a group of Indo-European tribes, speaking languages related or ancestral to Latin, entered Italy from the north. These Italic tribes eventually became the dominant group in Italy, and the ancient Romans were among their descendants. However, in 500 BC, there were still many non-Italic tribes in Italy. These included the Greeks (in Sicily and southern Italy); the Carthaginians (primarily in Sicily and Sardinia); the Etruscans, Celts, Ligurians, Veneti, and Rhaetians (in northern Italy);

plus some smaller groups such as the Sicani and Siculi in Sicily and the Messapians in southeast Italy.[1] In addition to the Greeks, two of those non-Italic groups — the Carthaginians (see section 4, below) and the Etruscans — had a marked impact on Roman history.

The Etruscans occupied a sizable region (Etruria) on the northwest portion of the Italian peninsula. Their origin has been much debated, one view being that they were relatively recent migrants from the Eastern Mediterranean.[2] However, the evidence is inconclusive, and it may well be that the Etruscans were the descendants of one of the peoples who lived in Italy before the arrival of the Indo-Europeans. Whatever their origin, in 600 BC the Etruscans were a more advanced people than the Romans. At the height of their power, in the late 6th century BC, the Etruscans controlled much of the Po Valley and also ruled much of the west coast of Italy, including Rome itself.

Section 3 – Early Rome (up to 264 BC)

The earliest written records in Latin date from about 600 BC; however, according to Roman tradition, the city of Rome was founded in 753 BC. The old records make it clear that Rome was originally a small city-state governed by a king. In the 6th century BC, when Rome was still small and weak, some of the monarchs were Etruscan. In general, the Etruscans were a civilizing influence, and Rome prospered during this period. However, in 509 BC there was a revolt that expelled the king and installed a republican form of government that endured for almost five centuries.

Sporadic warfare between the Romans and the Etruscans continued for a long time thereafter. Meanwhile, a less civilized group, the Gauls (a Celtic people) invaded from the north; and in 390 BC they conquered Rome and sacked the city. In the long run, though, the invasion of the Gauls probably benefited Rome, since it severely weakened the Etruscans; and in the course of the next century and a half the Romans succeeded in gaining control of much of Etruria.

More importantly, in the interval 390-264 BC the Romans defeated the other Italic-speaking tribes in central Italy in a series of wars. The end result of those wars was that by 264 BC Rome had become the ruler of most of central and southern Italy.

Perhaps the most important feature of those victorious wars was that, rather than enslaving the population of the conquered cities, Rome would often annex the city and bestow Roman citizenship upon its inhabitants. As a result, instead of the Romans being a small ruling group in Italy, governing a large population of foreigners who hated them, Rome became the capital of a large, populous Italian nation. (Although they called themselves "Romans," that nation was really an amalgam of the original Romans and various other Italian tribes they had conquered.) It was that *Italian* nation — much more populous than the original Rome — that made the remarkable series of conquests described below.

Section 4 – The expansion of Rome

The city of Carthage was situated on the African coast, not far from the modern city of Tunis. It had been founded by Phoenicians sometime between 850 and 700 BC. By

300 BC, Carthage ruled a sizable empire in the western Mediterranean, an empire that included much of the African coast from Libya to Gibraltar, as well as the Balearic Islands, parts of the southern and eastern coasts of Spain, and parts of Corsica, Sardinia, and Sicily. The Carthaginians had a large navy and excellent maritime skills, and much of their wealth derived from trade. However, they had not absorbed the various peoples they ruled; consequently, their population was much smaller than that of the Romans.

War between the two rising powers, Carthage and Rome, was virtually inevitable. In the course of the First Punic War (264-241 BC), Rome achieved naval superiority over Carthage; and in the treaty ending the war, Carthage ceded control of Sicily to Rome. Not long thereafter, the Romans took control of Sardinia.

In the Second Punic War (218-201 BC), the Carthaginian general Hannibal invaded Italy, where he soon won several crushing victories against Roman armies.[3] But Hannibal could not capture the city of Rome, nor could he persuade most of the other Italian cities to switch their allegiance to him. In the end, the Roman advantage in manpower, and their control of the seas, proved decisive.

The military machine that had been assembled for the wars against Carthage was now turned against other countries, and the next 70 years saw a stunning series of Roman conquests.

The first important targets were Macedonia and Greece, situated just east of southern Italy. Even while the war with Carthage was still going on, Rome had already fought an inconclusive war with Macedonia (215-205 BC). In the five decades following the Second Punic War, Rome fought three more wars against Macedonia. By 148 BC Macedonia was a Roman province, and by 146 BC the rest of Greece was effectively subject to Roman rule.

During the decades in which Roman armies were subduing the Macedonians and Greeks, other Roman forces were busy elsewhere. Shortly after the Punic Wars ended, the Romans conquered the Po Valley, in northern Italy, from Celtic tribes. The Romans also won a war (the Syrian War, 192-189 BC) against the Seleucid Empire, which at the time was at its peak, with dominions stretching from Persia to Greece to Egypt. And, shortly before the conquest of Greece was completed, Rome forced another war on Carthage. This Third Punic War ended in 146 BC with the total destruction of Carthage.

While all this was going on, Roman armies were also busy in Spain. The Mediterranean coast of Spain had been part of the spoils of the victory over Carthage. However, subduing the interior tribes took many decades. Most of Spain was conquered by 133 BC; the rest by 19 BC.

This series of military successes brought in large amounts of plunder. However, most of the additional wealth went to a relatively small number of persons, while in the same interval (264-133 BC), large numbers of Roman peasants lost their lands, which resulted in great social unrest within Italy. In 133 BC, Tiberius Gracchus (an activist who had been promoting land reform and who had been elected tribune) was assassinated, and many of his followers were killed. This initiated a century of social turmoil and civil wars which lasted until 31 BC, when Octavian (later called Augustus Caesar) defeated Mark Antony, his last rival for power. Thereafter — even though he never claimed to be a king or emperor, and in theory, Rome remained a republic — Augustus was for all practical purposes an emperor.

Despite all the turmoil and civil wars, Rome's series of foreign conquests continued. The additions to Rome's domains during that century included Egypt, Gaul (consisting of what is today France and Belgium), the rest of Spain and North Africa, Illyria, Syria, Judea, and much of Asia Minor.

Section 5 – The Roman Empire at its peak

During the 40-year reign of Augustus, the Empire enjoyed internal peace, prosperity, and cultural flowering. Many of his successors in the period 14-96 AD were poor rulers.[4] Nevertheless, following the establishment of the Empire, the Romans made additional conquests in the Balkans, established the Rhine-Danube line as the Empire's northern boundary, and also conquered England.

The next period of the Roman Empire (96-180 AD) consisted of the reign of the "five good emperors" (Nerva, Trajan, Hadrian, Antoninus Pius, and Marcus Aurelius), and it might well be called the "Golden Age of Rome." Those five rulers are sometimes called the "adoptive emperors," because each of the first four adopted the next one as his son and successor.

During the interval 30 BC – 180 AD, although the Empire repeatedly fought wars on its northern and eastern borders, most parts of the Empire enjoyed internal peace (the *Pax Romana*) and prosperity.

Section 6 – The accomplishments of Rome

From the standpoints of area, population, and military strength Rome was the greatest civilization of antiquity. However, its cultural achievements fell far short of those of the ancient Greeks.

Literature. The literary output of Rome was immense and included epic and lyric poetry, comic and tragic drama, history and military memoirs, and theological and philosophical writings.[5] Among the famous Roman writers were Virgil, Horace, Plautus, Terence, Seneca, Plutarch, Tacitus, Julius Caesar, St. Augustine, Lucretius, Marcus Aurelius, Juvenal, Ovid, and Cicero.

Architecture and Engineering. Roman architecture was impressive, and the Roman engineers were the finest in the ancient world. In addition to a remarkable set of aqueducts, bridges, amphitheatres, and public buildings, they constructed an extensive network of excellent roads. The Romans also made greater use of the arch and the dome than any earlier people had.

Science and Mathematics. Although Vitruvius wrote an influential work on architecture and engineering, most of the leading scientists and mathematicians of Roman times were Greeks. The most famous of these are Ptolemy, Galen, Hero (who constructed a primitive steam engine), and Pappus.

Law. A field in which the Romans clearly excelled the Greeks was law. The sophisticated legal system they developed lasted for many centuries, and it became the basis of many later legal systems.

Section 7 – Historical determinism

The rise of Rome from a small city-state to the greatest empire in antiquity is a remarkable story. Is there any explanation for it? Was that rise inevitable?

The notion that historical events are inevitable can be called "historical determinism." It is clear that any extreme version of that doctrine must be false.[6] Because there are many chance events (such as plagues and earthquakes) there is no way to predict which individuals will live to maturity. And, since individual generals often affect the course of battles, and individual statesmen often determine the course of legislation, the detailed course of history cannot possibly be predicted.

However, the notion that history is just a collection of unconnected and unpredictable incidents is rejected by virtually all serious historians. It certainly seems that some of the larger-scale occurrences were *nearly* inevitable. For example, any knowledgeable person viewing the situation in Australia in 1800 could easily have predicted that some European country or countries would soon conquer that continent.

A reasonable middle ground, therefore, is that although we cannot expect any explanation to fully account for the details of Rome's rise (nor to demonstrate that the rise was inevitable), we might be able to show that — given the pre-existing circumstances — it was very likely that something *similar* to what actually occurred would happen.

Section 8 – Some suggested explanations for the rise of Rome

One explanation is that, by assimilating the Italian tribes they conquered, the Romans had created a nation which was more populous than most of the foes that they thereafter faced. That having occurred, the subsequent Roman victories over Carthage, Spain, and Macedonia, were — although not inevitable — highly probable.

A different explanation was offered by Polybius, a Greek historian writing in the middle of the 2nd century BC. Polybius suggested that Rome's unprecedented military successes and imperial expansion were due to the intense patriotism and religious devotion of the Roman citizens, which inspired them to act both bravely and honorably.[7]

Although there is considerable truth in both of those notions, I think that the rise of Rome can be better understood if we broaden the scope of our question, and also consider the rise of some other ancient empires.

Section 9 – A more general approach to the question

Let us consider the circumstances that existed earlier in the first millennium BC in such widely separated regions as Iran, Greece, Italy, France, and Spain. Each of these regions contained an assortment of tribes, some of which were Indo-European.

At first, the various tribes in each region were independent, and there were frequent conflicts between them. In none of those regions had the inhabitants yet devised the political and administrative skills that permitted a large regional state to function (as had already occurred in the older civilizations of Egypt and the Middle East). Gradually, though, as the peoples living in those five regions encountered the older civilizations, they acquired those skills. Naturally, this occurred first in the regions (Iran and Greece) that were closest to the older civilizations, somewhat later in Italy, and much later in the regions (France and Spain) that were furthest away. In fact, in the last two regions, the process was interrupted by foreign conquest before the indigenous tribes ever assembled into a single state.

Although it could not have been predicted at the outset which *particular* tribe or city-state would prevail; it could have been predicted that within each region *some* tribe or city-state would prevail; and it could also have been predicted — because of the higher average intelligence of the Indo-Europeans — that in each region it would probably be one of the Indo-European tribes that would prevail.

It could also have been predicted — again, with considerable probability, but not certainty — that the Indo-European tribe or city-state that prevailed in each region would then attack neighboring regions; and furthermore that they would likely prevail against any non-Indo-European peoples or states in those neighboring regions.

It is hardly a coincidence that this was exactly what occurred in three of the five regions: Iran, Greece, and Italy. (It did not occur in Spain and France, because in those regions the process was interrupted when the Romans conquered them.) In Iran, it was the Persians (under Cyrus the Great) who prevailed, and they soon attacked and conquered the major non-Indo-European states in the vicinity. These included the Babylonian Empire (which ruled the entire Fertile Crescent) and Egypt.

In Greece, the group that prevailed were the Macedonians; and under Alexander the Great they quickly defeated the Persians and occupied Anatolia, Egypt, Iran, and the entire Fertile Crescent. (Furthermore, it seems probable that had it not been for Alexander's early death the Macedonian empire would have become even larger.)

In Italy, it was the city-state of Rome that prevailed over its rivals. Like the Macedonians and the Persians, the Romans were Indo-Europeans; and like them, after consolidating their rule over their own region they attacked neighboring regions. And, like the Greeks and the Iranians, the Italian armies thoroughly defeated their non-Indo-European neighbors (such as the Carthaginians).

The Italians also attacked nearby regions (including Greece, Spain, France, and England) that were occupied by Indo-European peoples. In the latter three, the Italian invasion and conquest occurred before the region had attained political unity. In Greece, the Romans faced high-quality armies; however, the greater population of Italy, combined with political disunity in Greece, resulted in the eventual Roman (actually, Italian) conquest of the country.

We see, then, that the rise of the Roman Empire, although certainly not inevitable, was similar to other events of the first millennium BC, and appears to have arisen from similar causes.

FOOTNOTES – CHAPTER 30

1) See *Encyclopaedia Britannica* (15th edition, 1986), article on "Greco-Roman Civilization," volume 20, pp. 309-310. Also see Mallory, J.P. (1989), pp. 88-92.

2) *Encyclopaedia Britannica* (15th edition, 1986), article on "Greco-Roman Civilization," volume 20, pp. 303-308, especially pp. 303-304.

3) Three of Hannibal's notable victories were (a) at the Trebbia River (218 BC); (b) at Lake Trasimene (217 BC); and (c) his overwhelming victory at Cannae (216 BC), the worst defeat ever suffered by a Roman army.

4) The emperor Nero (54-68 AD) is perhaps the most notorious of these; however, Caligula (37-41 AD) was probably even worse, and may well have been the worst ruler in Roman history.

5) Reprints of virtually every important classic of ancient Rome can be found in the *Loeb Classical Library*, whose books contain the Latin text and its English translation on facing pages.

6) Modern scientists agree that determinism does not hold even in the inanimate world; *a fortiori*, it cannot hold in human societies. The notion that the laws of physics are not strictly deterministic is particularly associated with Werner Heisenberg (whose famous "uncertainty principle" was formulated in 1927); but by now, the notion is accepted by all serious physicists.

7) *Encyclopaedia Britannica* (15th edition, 1986), "Greco-Roman Civilization," volume 20, p. 324.

CHAPTER 31

THE RISE OF CHRISTIANITY

Section 1 – Introduction

Arguably, the most important legacy of the Roman Empire was Christianity. Christianity originated in one of the Roman provinces in the early days of the Roman Empire, and by the time Rome fell it had become the predominant religion within that empire.

Section 2 – Life of Jesus

Our knowledge of the life of Jesus is limited, and not too reliable. Our only source is the New Testament: in particular, the first three of its books, the "Synoptic Gospels." Those books (which were written about 30-60 years after he died, and by ardent followers) include various miraculous occurrences. Since an account of a miracle is inherently dubious — it is always more likely that the person recounting it is mistaken or fabricating than that there was a violation of the laws of nature[1] — it makes sense to be skeptical of the Gospel accounts.

According to those accounts, Jesus was born in Judea (probably in or about the year we now call 6 BC), and throughout his life was a devout Jew. As a young man he became an itinerant preacher, and he gradually attracted a following. About 30 AD, he was executed by the Roman authorities; however, according to the New Testament, on the third day he was resurrected. Jesus never married, and had no children, but he left behind a small group of devoted followers.

Section 3 – Christian doctrines

The teachings of Jesus, as recorded in the Synoptic Gospels, were extremely pacifist in nature. Among his most famous sayings is:[2] "...resist not evil, but whosoever shall smite thee on the right cheek, turn to him the other also." An even more striking statement is:

> *Ye have heard that it has been said, Thou shall love thy neighbor and hate thine enemy. But I say unto you, Love your enemies, bless them that curse you, do good to them that hate you, and pray for them which despitefully use you and persecute you.*[3]

His teachings particularly appealed to the poor and downtrodden. Indeed, part of the reason for the rise of Christianity during the first few centuries after his death was the increasing inequality of incomes within the Roman Empire.

Most of the basic theology of Christianity was developed by Paul of Tarsus (Saint Paul) in the first century AD. Among the doctrines he espoused were:

- Jesus was not merely an inspired human, but was actually divine.
- Christ died for our sins, and his suffering can redeem us. If any person sincerely accepts Jesus as his savior, his sins will be forgiven. ("Christians aren't perfect, just forgiven.")
- A human being cannot achieve salvation merely by attempting to follow the Biblical injunctions, but only by accepting Christ.
- A Christian need not conform to the ritual injunctions in the Old Testament such as circumcision, or the dietary restrictions.

Section 4 – The growth of Christianity

Paul's theology created an easy, appealing religion for the poor and the weak ("Believe, and ye shall be saved."), and in the course of the next few centuries the number of Christians in the Roman Empire grew steadily, despite repeated persecutions by the imperial government.

The great turning point came in the early 4th century, when Constantine I ("Constantine the Great") became the first Christian emperor of Rome. In 313 AD, he issued the Edict of Milan, which made Christianity a legal religion, rather than an officially persecuted one. Indeed, it soon became the preferred religion, and the number of Christians swelled rapidly during his reign.

Most of the succeeding Roman emperors were also Christian, and in 392 AD the emperor Theodosius I issued an edict prohibiting the worship of any pagan gods. By the time the Roman Empire fell (476 AD) most Roman citizens were Christians, and there had been significant Christian expansion beyond the confines of the Empire.

Christianity continued to grow after the Roman Empire fell, and within a few centuries had spread through most of Europe. In later centuries, it spread throughout the world, and for a long time it has had more adherents than any other religion on Earth.

FOOTNOTES – CHAPTER 31

1) See part I of section X of *An Enquiry Concerning Human Understanding* (by David Hume, 1748). Hume's essay can be found in volume 35 of the *Great Books of the Western World* collection (see p. 491).

2) Matthew 5:39. (The wording used is from the King James translation.)

3) Matthew 5:43-44.

CHAPTER 32

THE DECLINE AND FALL OF THE ROMAN EMPIRE

Section 1 – The decline of Rome

Starting in 180 AD, the Roman Empire entered a period of sharp decline. In that year Marcus Aurelius, the last of the "five good emperors," died and was succeeded by his son Commodus. Commodus turned out to be an extraordinarily bad emperor, and he was assassinated in 192 AD. The following year, Septimius Severus (a general with no legal claim to the throne) seized power with the aid of his troops. Severus (193-211 AD) was a capable ruler; but the overall effect was to convert Rome into a military dictatorship.

The decline of Rome continued in the third century AD, a period marked by repeated external invasions (mostly from the north), economic decline, increasing corruption, and loss of popular support for the government and the state. The period 235-284 AD, during which 22 persons (most of them military dictators) held or shared the imperial throne, was particularly chaotic, and on several occasions it seemed as if the Roman Empire would collapse.

The period of chaos ended with the accession of Diocletian in 285 AD. A career soldier, of lowly birth, Diocletian gained the throne with the aid of his troops. He turned out to be a strong and capable ruler who reestablished order, made major reforms, and tried to set up a regular procedure for choosing successors to the throne. Not long after gaining the throne, Diocletian decided that the Roman Empire was too large for one ruler to administer efficiently. He therefore divided it into two parts and named a loyal officer, Maximian, to rule the western one, while he continued to rule the eastern one. This practice was also adopted by some later emperors. Eventually the split became permanent, and the Roman Empire was divided into two independent states.

In 301 AD, in an attempt to deal with the Empire's economic problems, Diocletian instituted an extensive system of wage and price controls. These proved unenforceable, and he eventually repealed them. (This is perhaps the most famous example in history of the deleterious effect of such controls.) He also instituted the last major persecution of the Christians, but this too was unsuccessful. Diocletian retired in 305 AD — one of the rare examples of a dictator giving up his power voluntarily.

Diocletian's resignation was soon followed by a struggle for power between various Roman generals. The eventual successor was Constantine I ("Constantine the Great"), the first Christian emperor of Rome. Constantine created a new capital for the eastern half of the Empire at the site of the old Greek city of Byzantium, which he enlarged, beautified, and renamed *Constantinople*.[1] In time, its combination of being an administrative center and having a strategic location turned it into the leading city in Europe, perhaps in the world.

In an attempt to halt the economic deterioration of Rome, Constantine passed laws making certain occupations (for example, butchers and bakers) hereditary. He also issued a decree under which the *coloni* (a class of tenant farmers) were forbidden to leave their land; in effect, this converted them into serfs. These decrees can now be seen as the beginnings of the social and economic structure of Medieval Europe.

Section 2 – The fall of the Western Roman Empire

About 370 AD, Eastern Europe was invaded by the Huns, a central Asian people who were culturally backward but militarily ferocious. The Huns defeated various Germanic tribes (including the Visigoths and Ostrogoths) who had been living in Eastern Europe, and as a result, several of those Germanic tribes migrated west, and attacked the Roman Empire.

In the early fifth century, the western part of the Empire began to fall apart militarily. Starting about 406 AD, Gaul was overrun by various Germanic tribes. In 407, Roman troops evacuated England, which thereafter became the target of invaders from northern Europe (the Angles and Saxons). In 410 AD, the Visigoths, led by Alaric, sacked Rome — the first foreign conquest of the city in 800 years. Alaric died soon thereafter, and his successors left Italy and instead invaded southern France, and then Spain, where they set up a Visigothic kingdom. Meanwhile, another Germanic tribe, the Vandals, had invaded North Africa, and by 431 had established an independent kingdom there.

About 450 AD, the Huns (under their most famous leader, Attila) invaded Gaul and northern Italy. But in 451 Attila was defeated by a Roman-Visigothic coalition at the Battle of Châlons, and the following year, the Huns retreated from Italy. Attila died in 453, and his empire soon disintegrated.

This, however, did not save Rome. In 476 AD, the last Roman emperor, Romulus Augustus, was deposed by Odoacer, a Germanic chieftain. Seven years later, Odoacer was defeated and killed by the Ostrogothic king, Theodoric the Great, and the Ostrogoths became the rulers of Italy.

More striking than the political and military decline of Rome was the economic and social decay. During the three centuries before the fall of Rome, the Empire lost a large part of its population and wealth, many cities became depopulated, and some were completely abandoned. Trade declined drastically, as did literacy and learning.[2] These trends may have begun even before the accession of Commodus in 180, and they continued in Western Europe even after the fall of Rome.

The cause of this drastic social decay has been much discussed; but scholars have not reached a consensus. In any event, it was not that the emperors were unaware of, or indifferent to, the decay. On the contrary, many of the emperors were energetic administrators, and several of them instituted major reforms that they hoped would reverse the decay. None of them, however, was able to do more than to temporarily stem the downward trend.

Section 3 – The Eastern Roman Empire

Starting with Diocletian, various Roman emperors had divided the Empire into two parts. In general, the eastern part included Greece and the Balkans, Egypt, and all the Asian provinces. For a bit over a century, periods during which the Empire was united alternated with periods in which it was divided. The last person to rule a unified Roman Empire was Theodosius I. After his death, in 395, the two parts never reunited. The Eastern Roman Empire, often called the *Byzantine Empire*, lasted until 1453, nearly a thousand years after the Western Roman Empire was destroyed.

Section 4 – Why did the Roman Empire decline and fall?

No single explanation for the decline and fall of Rome has won the general acceptance of historians. We know that the armies that successfully invaded the Roman Empire in the 5th century AD were smaller and weaker than the armies that the Romans had defeated during the centuries of their expansion. A crucial difference was that in the 5th century AD the Roman state had little popular support, and by then there were very few Roman citizens who were willing to risk their lives to defend it. Many of the proposed explanations, therefore, approach the question by suggesting reasons for the social decay that had occurred in Rome in the preceding centuries. Among the reasons suggested are:

1) *Loss of faith in the traditional national religion*. A national religion can often be a powerful force motivating men to do what is best for their fellow citizens and their country, rather than pursuing solely the interests of themselves and their immediate families. In the centuries when Rome was expanding, virtually all Romans adhered to their traditional national religion. By 50 AD, though, most Roman subjects were conquered peoples who followed their own religions. In succeeding centuries, many Italians ceased to practice the traditional Roman religion; and by the 5th century AD, after the triumph of Christianity, only a few did.[3] (Christianity, although it encouraged unselfish behavior, was a *universal* religion, and did not promote loyalty to any particular state.)

2) *Loss of nationalist/patriotic feelings*. In 250 BC, the citizens of Rome were members of a single "Italian" nation. The Roman armies were comprised almost entirely of those citizens, and the soldiers therefore felt a strong loyalty to the Roman state.

By 50 AD, the situation had changed. Rome was now a multinational empire, and most of its inhabitants were conquered peoples who felt little or no loyalty to it. Only the Italians (most of whom were Roman citizens, and had a preferred status) had a strong loyalty to the Empire.

By 250 AD, the situation had changed even more. The Edict of Caracalla (212 AD) had granted citizenship to all free Roman subjects. From then on, Italians were no longer a preferred group; and those who were poor were merely subjects of a large multinational state that primarily benefited a small wealthy class. Under such conditions, one could hardly expect much patriotic fervor.

3) *Increased corruption*. In all societies, public officials are often tempted to accept or extort bribes. In the early centuries, when Rome was expanding, this tendency was held in check not merely by a fear of punishment, but also by patriotism and by belief in the traditional religion. As the latter two declined, corruption inevitably increased. Such an increase tends to feed on itself: "Since everybody else is doing it, I would be a fool not to." Widespread corruption, besides being very harmful to the economy, diminished the willingness of citizens to risk their lives for the regime.

4) *Impoverishment of the peasantry*. The backbone of Rome's strength in the Punic Wars had been the loyalty of the peasantry, since it was they who supplied the bulk of the Roman soldiers. However, in the course of those long wars, the farms that those men had left behind could not be maintained, and much of the land fell into the hands of a relatively small wealthy class. It was, indeed, this problem that was the root cause of the great social turmoil in the period 133-31 BC (see section 30-4). Although Augustus was able to reestablish civil order, the Italian peasantry never really recovered their original status, and ownership of land remained concentrated in a relatively small group. In subsequent centuries, this problem — which affected most parts of the Empire — gradually worsened, with the result that the lower classes had no stake in the survival of the regime.

Other theories have emphasized the interplay of military and economic factors in the decline of Rome. Among these hypotheses are:

5) *Lack of plunder*. As Rome stopped expanding, the plunder from foreign conquests that had financed the state in earlier centuries ceased. Attempts to make up the deficit by increasing taxes proved counter-productive.

6) *Foreign attacks*. Repeated attacks by Germanic tribes weakened Rome and strained the finances of the Empire.

Others have hypothesized that medical or biological factors were of major importance in the decline of Rome. Suggestions in this category include:

7) *Depopulation due to major epidemics*. Epidemics, of course, occurred frequently in the ancient and medieval worlds. However, an extraordinarily devastating epidemic commenced in 165 AD and continued for 15 years, and another equally virulent one raged from 251 to 266 AD.[4]

8) *Deterioration of the gene pool*. It has been suggested that the decline of Rome was due to the deterioration of the Roman gene pool, caused by interbreeding with conquered peoples and slaves who, on average, possessed lower native intelligence than the Romans.

9) *Lead poisoning*. Another suggestion is that the Roman practice of using lead in the construction of their municipal water pipes caused many Romans to suffer from chronic lead poisoning. In addition, lead vessels were sometimes used to distill grape juice, and lead would be ingested when someone drank the wine.[5]

10) *Climate change in Western Europe*. A possible explanation for the economic decline of Rome is that it was caused by a centuries-long period of reduced rainfall in Western Europe. A similar hypothesis is that average temperatures fell. A strong point of these hypotheses is that they explain why the economic decline was so much less in the eastern half of the Empire. Unfortunately, there is a dearth of hard data to support either hypothesis.

Section 5 – Evaluation of those suggestions

Although there is no unanimity, some form of the social-decay hypothesis seems to be the conventional explanation for the decline and fall of Rome. A major problem, though, is that those theories do not explain why the decline was so much more pronounced in the western portion of the Roman Empire than it was in the eastern portion. Furthermore, none of them adequately explain the magnitude of the economic collapse involved.

The military/financial explanations seem much less convincing. A problem with the lack-of-plunder hypothesis is that the period in which Rome enjoyed large amounts of foreign plunder ended in the 1st century AD, whereas Rome did not fall until 300 years later. As for the barbarian invasions, surely they were a *result* of the decline of Rome, rather than its basic cause.

The biological explanations are somewhat better, but still inadequate. It is true that the epidemics of the 2nd and 3nd centuries caused a great many deaths; however, it is typical for societies to recover from such disasters within a few decades. The worst epidemic in European history was the Black Death, an outbreak of bubonic plague that ravaged 14th-century Europe. The Black Death struck Europe in 1347, and by the end of 1350 roughly one-third of the population of the continent had perished: however, Europe recovered rather quickly from that frightful disaster. Indeed, although the loss of life from the plague was greatest in Italy, the Italian Renaissance continued, and the Italian accomplishments were even greater in the two centuries following the Black Death than in the two centuries preceding it.

The notion that the Roman gene pool declined due to interbreeding with conquered peoples would seem to fit in well with the ideas expressed elsewhere in this book. However, the evidence suggests that the Romans did not interbreed extensively with peoples of much lower intelligence. The majority of the Romans' slaves were Indo-Europeans (from Greece, Iberia, Gaul, Illyria, and Italy itself), and the average native intelligence of those peoples was about the same at that of the Romans themselves. Most of their other slaves were Caucasoids from North Africa and Asia. Although these peoples were, on average, less intelligent than the Romans, it would require an implausibly low estimate of their mean IQ, and an implausibly high estimate of the amount of interbreeding, for the gene pool of the Romans to have been seriously harmed from that interbreeding.

The lead-poisoning hypothesis is ingenious, but unconvincing. In the first place, although lead pipes were used to transport water in Rome itself, they were not used in the rural areas where most of the population lived. Furthermore, the ancient Romans were aware of the dangers of lead poisoning, but no contemporary sources indicate that many people were affected by it.[6]

The climate-change hypothesis is plausible, and very intriguing. It is clear that major changes in climate have occurred in the past 15,000 years, and that such changes have often had a major impact on human societies.[7] However, there is no hard data to confirm that there was in fact a major worsening of the climate of Western Europe in the early centuries AD.

Conclusion: The cause of the drastic decline and eventual collapse of Rome is still an undecided question. The most likely explanation is probably some combination of the social-decay hypotheses described above. However, the possibility that climate changes played a major role — perhaps even the central role — cannot be ruled out.

FOOTNOTES – CHAPTER 32

1) It is now called *Istanbul*.

2) Among the numerous books written on the topic, the best known is Edward Gibbon's 6-volume treatise (1776-1788), *The History of the Decline and Fall of the Roman Empire*.

3) Edward Gibbon, who was very unsympathetic to Christianity, emphasized the importance of the Christianization of Rome as a factor in the Empire's decline and fall.

4) On pp. 130-131 of *Peoples and Plagues* (1998 edition), William McNeill suggests that one of those two great epidemics involved the introduction of measles into Europe, while the other involved the introduction of smallpox. (Neither disease, he says, had been described by earlier European writers, including Hippocrates.) Today, we understand how dreadful the effect of those diseases can be in a population with no immunity to them.

5) The best-known presentation of this hypothesis is by Jerome Nriagu (1983).

6) An article marshalling the arguments against Nriagu's hypothesis is "The myth of lead poisoning among the Romans" by John Scarborough (1984).

7) Many examples are known of climate change that affected human societies.

   (a) Several are described by Lamb, H.H. (1995) in *Climate, History and the Modern World*. (See, for example, pp. 122-124, 130-131, 158-162, and 207-210.)

   (b) Another striking instance is provided by the ruins of Chan Chan in northern Peru. For many years, Chan Chan was the capital of the Chimú Empire, and at its peak (about 1400 AD) it had a population of many thousands and covered over 6 square miles. Today, only six centuries later, it is "utterly deserted and uninhabitable for lack of water." (*Encyclopaedia Britannica* [15th edition, 1986], volume 3, p. 217.)

   (c) Many parts of the Sahara Desert once had a wet climate. At Tassili-n-Ajjer (in southern Algeria, in what is now the middle of the Sahara Desert), a group of rock paintings have been discovered that leave no doubt that the region was once wet and fertile. These paintings (dating from roughly 8.5 to 5.5 kya) clearly portray herds of cattle, canoes, and even a hippopotamus (an animal that inhabits only rivers and swamps). See Cavalli-Sforza, L.L. et al. (1994), p. 161 and Lamb, H.H., (1995), pp. 122-124.

CHAPTER 33

THE EARLY MIDDLE AGES IN EUROPE

Section 1 – Description and origin

The Middle Ages (or "medieval era") is the period between the fall of Rome in 476 AD and the beginning of modern times, about 1500. The first half of that interval (until about 1000 AD) is called the "Early Middle Ages."

The eastern and western parts of Europe had very different histories during that period. The Eastern Roman Empire (which after 600 AD is usually referred to as the Byzantine Empire) continued to function throughout the Middle Ages. In contrast, the Western Roman Empire collapsed completely in the 5th century AD, and during the next few centuries the levels of poverty and illiteracy in Western Europe were very high, and the cultural achievements meager. As a result, the Early Middle Ages in Western Europe are often called the *Dark Ages*.

Most of the characteristic features of the Middle Ages originated during the late stages of the Roman Empire. These included the establishment of Christianity as the official religion, the importance of cavalry in warfare, the dominant role of a hereditary aristocracy, the establishment of serfdom, and much lower levels of trade and literacy than had prevailed during Graeco-Roman times.

Section 2 – The barbarian kingdoms

By 500 AD, Roman rule had ended in Western Europe, and various Germanic tribes had set up independent kingdoms in the formerly-Roman lands. England had been conquered by invaders from northern Germany (the Angles and Saxons) and was divided into several small kingdoms. Italy was ruled by the Ostrogoths; Spain by the Visigoths; and North Africa by the Vandals. The kingdom of the Franks included what is now Belgium, Holland, much of northern France, and parts of Germany. Burgundians, Lombards, Suevi, and others ruled smaller territories. However, most of those barbarian kingdoms — with the exception of the kingdom of Wessex (in southern England), and the kingdom of the Franks — did not survive for long.

In most cases, the barbarians who conquered Western Europe failed to impose their language on the conquered peoples. Instead, they eventually adopted the language spoken in the lands they had conquered, which was Latin — not classical Latin, but *vulgar Latin*, the language of ordinary speech. Hence, in many European countries the surviving languages are all modern forms of vulgar Latin, although the regional variations between them are so large that French, Italian, Spanish, Portuguese, and Rumanian are now separate languages.

Section 3 – Christianity and the Church

Virtually the only institution of the Roman Empire that survived and thrived in Western Europe during the Dark Ages was the Church. Most of the inhabitants of the Roman Empire had been converted to Christianity before Rome fell, and most of the Germanic tribes were converted in the course of the next three centuries. (The Scandinavians were converted somewhat later.)

In general, medieval Christianity was a very intolerant religion. The Jews — although subject to constant discrimination, frequent persecution, and occasional expulsions and massacres — were actually treated *better* than any other non-Christian group. Pagans were often given the stark choice of conversion or death; and eventually paganism was eliminated in every Christian country in Europe.

During the Dark Ages, when very few people in Western Europe could read or write, the largest literate group was the Christian clergy, all of whom were versed in Latin. To the extent that any learning survived there during the Dark Ages, it was mostly due to the clergy.

In many ways the medieval Church was a government, and in many fields (such as marriage and divorce) it exercised exclusive jurisdiction. The chief Church official in each region was the bishop, and he appointed the local priests. Understandably, each king wished to appoint the bishops in his kingdom; however, the Pope (who was the bishop of Rome) claimed the right to appoint the other bishops throughout Western Europe, which was a frequent cause of discord between medieval kings and the Papacy. Because so many of their subjects were devout Christians, the monarchs could not easily prevail in their disputes with the Church. In general, though, the secular governments cooperated with the Church. One benefit to the kings was that the Church validated the right of the monarchs to rule.

It has often been pointed out that, in many ways, the activities of the medieval Church diverged drastically from the teachings of Jesus, and that he would have been horrified to see what was being done in his name.

Section 4 – Infantry and cavalry

In very ancient times, armies consisted of infantry only; but by the second millennium BC, horses were also being employed. At first, horses were used to draw war chariots; only later were they used to carry mounted warriors. One would expect that mounted cavalry would naturally be superior to infantry. However, this was not always the case, because of the difficulty of staying on and controlling a horse while simultaneously wielding a weapon.

Around 700 BC, the Greeks began making use of *hoplites*, a type of heavily armed infantry. Typically, a hoplite wore a breastplate, greaves, a metal helmet, and a large shield. This defensive equipment slowed a hoplite down considerably, but the protection it gave him in combat more than compensated for that.

The Greeks eventually found that hoplites were most effective when used together to form a *phalanx*. A phalanx consisted of several straight rows of hoplites, with each soldier carrying a long thrusting spear. When a phalanx advanced in formation, it presented a row of spears. Since the soldiers all had tall rectangular shields, they created a defensive wall that gave considerable protection against incoming spears or arrows. In combat, an advancing phalanx would go through any disorganized group of soldiers, or through any phalanx that was less disciplined than they were.

By 500 BC, the Greeks had developed great skill in using the phalanx formation. At the Battle of Marathon, in 490 BC, a Greek army composed mostly of hoplites arranged in phalanx formation badly defeated a considerably larger Persian army, while suffering only minor casualties themselves. The victory clearly demonstrated the superiority of well-trained heavy infantry over cavalry. That superiority was maintained for nearly nine hundred years, during which time the successful Greek, Macedonian, and Roman armies all relied primarily on heavily armed infantry.

The Battle of Adrianople (378 AD) signaled the end of this period. In that battle, a Visigothic army that included a large cavalry contingent inflicted a devastating defeat on a Roman army that consisted mostly of infantry. The crucial factor was that the Visigothic cavalry made use of stirrups and improved saddles, thus enabling the horsemen to retain firm seating on their horses while wielding their weapons. Although this battle did not lead to the destruction of the Roman Empire (since the Romans quickly shifted to the use of cavalry themselves) it did establish the superiority of cavalry over infantry.[1] It was eventually demonstrated that *armored* cavalry, although slower, was superior to light cavalry. The result was that heavily armored knights became the decisive factor in warfare.

This was of central importance in the social structure of Western Europe during the Middle Ages. Since only the aristocracy could afford the armor, horses, and training needed to create armored knights, the hereditary aristocracy — although small in numbers — became militarily dominant. This military dominance was the key factor in their continued political dominance over a span of many centuries.

Although the view that cavalry dominated infantry during the 1000-year period after the Battle of Adrianople was once standard, there are some modern scholars who disagree. One of these is Victor Davis Hanson, who claims that well-trained and properly-equipped infantry could defeat cavalry throughout that period, and gives the Battle of Tours as an example.[2] (The importance of that battle between the Franks and an invading Moslem army is discussed in section 6, and also in chapter 34.) Contemporary reports of that battle are sparse; but, according to Hanson, the best sources indicate that the Franks, although possessing heavy cavalry, fought a defensive battle, and relied primarily on their heavily armed infantry to repel the Moslem cavalry.[3]

Hanson makes a convincing case as far as that particular battle is concerned; but it seems clear that Tours was a rare exception.[4] For the most part, cavalry dominated warfare during the Middle Ages. For example:

- After the Battle of Adrianople, the Byzantines augmented their cavalry, eventually building up large and very effective forces, which they used successfully for many centuries.[5]
- The Mongols — who were the most spectacularly successful conquerors of the entire medieval period — depended primarily on cavalry armies.[6]
- The Arab armies — second only to the Mongols in the magnitude of their conquests — were likewise composed mostly of cavalry.[7]
- Even within Western Europe, the Battle of Hastings (1066 AD) provides an important example of the superiority of heavy cavalry over infantry.[8]

European rulers during the Middle Ages were very hardheaded about military matters. They valued armored knights because experience proved that, under the conditions that then prevailed, those knights were far more effective than infantry.

Section 5 – The feudal system

In Roman times, governmental functions were carried out by a central authority which collected taxes and maintained a large professional army. When the Western Roman Empire collapsed, the need arose for a new system to carry out the functions of government. That new system — which was established gradually, over a period of centuries — is called *feudalism*.

Under a fully-developed feudal system, all land was in theory owned by the king. However, in order to maintain his control (against either foreign invaders or domestic rebels) the king needed armored knights. He obtained those knights by parceling out most of his lands to subordinates called *vassals*. Each vassal held his lands under a perpetual lease from the king, and when the vassal died, his leasehold passed to a relative (normally his eldest son). In return, the vassal pledged loyalty to the king, and promised to provide the king with a specified number of armed knights, for a specified number of days each year.

In general, the only way in which the vassal could supply those knights was to parcel out most of the land he had received from the king to subordinates under similar perpetual leases, and with promises by the sub-vassals to provide armored knights to their lord (the first vassal). This process of *subinfeudation* often involved several layers of vassals.

At the bottom of the heap were the serfs, the farmers who actually worked the land. The serfs were worse off than ordinary tenant farmers, since they were forbidden by law to leave the land and work elsewhere. However, the serfs were not quite slaves, since they could not be bought or sold, nor could their land be arbitrarily taken from them.

The chief advantage of the feudal system was that it enabled the monarch to assemble a powerful army without laying out a lot of money (and, therefore, without imposing the oppressive taxes which had characterized the later stages of the Roman Empire). The monarch also benefited by being a hereditary ruler, and therefore one who ruled by *right*, not merely as a military despot.

The large vassals benefited from the feudal system because it enabled them to possess sizable landholdings on which other persons (the serfs) were constrained to work. Although the lot of a serf was poor, he at least was assured of a parcel of land, and therefore a livelihood. In addition, his lord would — for reasons of self-interest, if not from a sense of duty — provide him with some protection from bandits and external invaders.

In general, feudal monarchs did not interfere much in everyday matters, but left most governmental functions in the hands of the local lords, custom, and the Church.

Section 6 – The Franks and the Holy Roman Empire

The Franks originally occupied Belgium and the lower Rhine Valley. Unlike most of the Germanic tribes, who migrated far from their homeland, the Franks simply expanded outwards from their base. Their first great king was Clovis, who reigned from 481 to 511 AD, and converted to Christianity in 496. Under his rule, the Franks conquered most of northern and western France. By 555, his successors ruled almost all of France, as well as much of southern Germany and Austria.

In 732 AD, a Moslem army invaded France from Spain and advanced northward. At the Battle of Tours (or Poitiers) the Moslem army was decisively defeated by a Frankish army led by Charles Martel. The Moslems withdrew, and did not threaten France again.

The grandson of Charles Martel is usually called Charles the Great, or Charlemagne. Charlemagne (reigned 768-814), conquered the Saxons, who lived in northern Germany, and forced Christianity upon them. He also conquered the Lombards in Italy, and decisively defeated the Avars, an Asian people who had invaded Europe from the East. Charlemagne set up border states on his eastern frontier in central Europe, stretching from eastern Germany to Croatia, and also in northern Spain.

In 800 AD, Charles went to Rome where, on Christmas day, Pope Leo III placed a crown on his head and declared him "Emperor of the Romans." This implied that the Roman Empire was being restored, although in reality Charles, his armies, and his successors were Germans rather than Romans. Nevertheless, the so-called "Holy Roman Empire" lasted over 1000 years.

Charles was also interested in promoting education, scholarship, and literature, and the period of his reign is sometimes called "the Carolingian Renaissance." He died in 814 AD, and by 843 his empire had been divided into three separate states. One of those states ultimately became France; another included much of modern Germany; the third was centered in northern Italy. (At times, the last two were united under German rule.)

Although the Franks had conquered Gaul (which is why that region is now called

France), they only comprised a small minority of the population there, and most of the inhabitants continued to speak a modified Latin, which eventually evolved into modern French. Although the French-German border has fluctuated since Charlemagne's day, most of the time it has roughly followed the linguistic border, which is approximately the same as the old boundary between the Roman Empire and the Germanic tribes.

Section 7 – External attacks on Europe during the Middle Ages

During the Dark Ages, Western Europe was militarily weak, and it was repeatedly attacked by outsiders. The attack of the Huns in the late stages of the Roman Empire has already been mentioned. Another Asian people, the Avars, invaded Europe about 560. By 650, they had conquered large parts of the Balkans and had entered Austria; however, by 700 their power was declining. Charlemagne defeated them badly in 796, and the remaining Avars were eventually assimilated.

Starting in the 6th century, various Slavic tribes pushed into Central Europe from the east. Another invading group, the Magyars (now called Hungarians), were not Slavs, although they originated in eastern Russia. The Magyars entered Hungary in the 9th century; like the Slavic tribes, they eventually converted to Christianity.

Meanwhile, Europe was also being attacked from the south. Arabs besieged Constantinople in 674-678, and again in 717-718, but the city did not fall. The Arabs conquered North Africa in the 7th century, and in 711 AD, a mixed Arab-Berber army invaded Spain. Within a few years they had defeated the Visigoths and gained control of most of the peninsula. However, their attempt to conquer France was thwarted by their defeat at Poitiers in 732, and they were forced to withdraw.

The Moslems also attacked Italy. They invaded Sicily in the 8th century, gained firm control of the island in the 9th century, and were not expelled until about 1050. They also conquered Sardinia, and launched frequent attacks on the Italian mainland.

Section 8 – The Vikings

During the Dark Ages, the Europeans were also attacked from the north, by the Vikings. The Vikings, or Norsemen, were seagoing raiders originally based in Scandinavia. They spoke Germanic languages, and were therefore Indo-Europeans. Their most frequent attacks were on coastal areas, or along rivers. Viking raids began in the 8th century, and became important in the 9th and 10th centuries. The early Viking raiders were pagans; however, by about 1000 AD most of the Norsemen had been converted to Christianity.

The Vikings did not confine their attacks to the northern and western coasts of Europe, but also penetrated the Mediterranean. For a while they ruled Sicily. In addition, Vikings from Sweden penetrated deeply into Russia, even reaching the Black Sea and the Caspian Sea.

Many of the Viking attacks were brief raids made for purposes of plunder. However, in time, Danes and Norwegians settled in the British Isles. For a while they ruled much of England, and parts of Ireland, but they were eventually assimilated.

Starting in the late 9th century, the Vikings colonized Iceland, which previously had been nearly uninhabited. They reached Greenland in the late 10th century, and founded two colonies there. In the early 11th century, the Vikings conducted expeditions from Greenland that reached parts of North America, including Labrador, Newfoundland, and New England. However, none of the Viking settlements in North America lasted for long, and their colonies in Greenland died out by 1500.

Perhaps the Vikings' most important conquest was a coastal province (now called Normandy) in northern France, which they gained control of in 911 AD. Their descendants, the Normans, were eventually assimilated. In 1066, when their ruler, Duke William of Normandy (now called William the Conqueror), invaded and conquered England, they were a French-speaking people.

When the Dark Ages began, Western Europe was militarily weak. However, the adoption of the feudal system gradually changed that. By the end of the Dark Ages, the tide had turned, and European armies were more than holding their own against Asian or Moslem armies, and against Viking forces too, whenever they could engage them in a pitched battle.

Section 9 – The Byzantine Empire

For eighty years after Theodosius, the Eastern and Western Roman Empires existed side by side. After the fall of the Western Roman Empire in 476 AD, the emperors ruling in the east considered their state to be "The Roman Empire," and themselves the rightful sovereigns of Italy and the lands once ruled by Rome.

Under Justinian I (ruled 527-565), a major effort was made to recover the lost lands of the west. Justinian succeeded in reconquering North Africa from the Vandals, and most of Italy from the Ostrogoths, as well as some coastal portions of France and Spain. He also ordered the construction of a comprehensive codification of Roman law. The resulting *Code of Justinian* is one of the most famous and influential legal codes ever composed, and Justinian's most lasting achievement. In contrast, not long after his death, much of the territory he had conquered in the west was lost, and was never recovered.

Throughout its history, the Byzantine Empire repeatedly had to deal with threats from two directions. In the Balkans, they were attacked from the north by a succession of Germanic, Slavic, and Central Asian tribes. On their eastern borders, in Asia, they faced a series of larger, more organized adversaries, including a revived Persian empire (under the Sassanid dynasty), the Arabs, and finally the Turks.

Shortly after 600 AD, a combination of attacks from the north and east came close to destroying the Byzantine Empire, and only the brilliant leadership of Heraclius (ruled 610-641) defeated the Sassanids. However, not long after that, the eruption of the Arabs under the early successors of Muhammad again brought the Byzantine Empire to the brink of destruction. The Byzantines lost Egypt and North Africa to the Arabs, plus Syria, Lebanon, Judea, and part of Anatolia. On two occasions (674-678 and 717-718) the Arabs reached the gates of Constantinople and besieged it; but on both occasions the defenses held and the Arabs were eventually repulsed.

For most of the next 350 years, the Byzantine monarchs ruled Greece, most of Anatolia, and much of the Balkans. But in 1071, the Byzantines were badly defeated by the Seljuk Turks at the Battle of Manzikert, which resulted in the loss of most of their territory in Asia Minor. From then on, the Byzantine Empire was a minor power. Nevertheless, it survived until 1453, when the Ottoman Turks, using artillery, successfully besieged and captured Constantinople.

Was the Byzantine Empire "Roman"? No, not really: Linguistically and culturally, it was more Greek than Italian. It is true that for a long time the Byzantines called themselves *Romanoi*, but most of the population was not of primarily Italian descent, nor did they speak Latin. The predominant language was Greek, and under Heraclius that became the language of the court.

During the entire Byzantine era, Constantinople was a great commercial metropolis, noted for its art, its artisans, and its wealth. Throughout the Middle Ages, the Byzantines preserved the writings of the Greeks, and their scholars read and admired the Greek classics. However, in most literary fields the Byzantines were conservative, rather than innovative. Their best fields tended to be those where the Romans had excelled: law, administration, military organization, architecture, and engineering. Hagia Sophia, constructed as a church during the reign of Justinian, has long been considered one of the masterpieces of world architecture.

Section 10 – Cultural activities

It is often said that Europe was a backward area of the world during the Early Middle Ages, far inferior culturally to China and the Moslem world. Obviously, though, this was not true of Europe as a whole: The Byzantine Empire was never a backward part of the world, but rather one of its most advanced regions. There were intervals when China and the Moslem world were more advanced than the Byzantine Empire; but they were never *much* more advanced than it.

In Western Europe, learning and cultural activities were much diminished during the Dark Ages, but they never disappeared completely. The literate class in Western Europe included the Christian clergy, most Jewish males, and various other people. An obvious indication of the continuation of literacy during the Dark Ages is the knowledge — incomplete, but not insignificant — that we have of historical events during those five centuries. For example, the first version of the *Anglo-Saxon Chronicle* was compiled in the 9th century.

No progress was made in science or mathematics during this period, but there were some men of letters. Among the best-remembered are Bede (an English historian, theologian, and philosopher) and Alcuin (an English scholar who was later active at the court of Charlemagne). The epic poem, *Beowulf*, written in Old English, was probably composed in the 8th century, but the author is unknown.

Around 600 AD, Pope Gregory I codified early Church music (hence: *Gregorian chants*). Our present musical notation has its roots in a notation (the *neumes*) used in such chants. Counterpoint arose gradually, starting as early as the 9th century.

Very little noteworthy architecture was produced in that era. However, the Palatine Chapel in Aachen (constructed about 800 AD) is of high quality, probably at least the equal of anything the Arabs were building at the time. Romanesque and Gothic architecture did not arise until after 1000 AD.

Obviously, these achievements were far less than those of the Romans or Greeks. However, they were miles above the cultural achievements in Australia, sub-Saharan Africa, and South America, or in most parts of Asia and North America. Even during the Dark Ages, European civilization and culture far surpassed that of most areas of the world.

FOOTNOTES – CHAPTER 33

1) (a) Eggenberger, D. (1967), *A Dictionary of Battles*. See especially pp. 4-5, where the author says that the Battle of Adrianople "...established the supremacy of cavalry over infantry for the next thousand years."
   (b) See also Dupuy & Dupuy (1993), *The Harper Encyclopedia of Military History* (4th edition), pp. 171 and 182-183.

2) Hanson, Victor Davis (2001), *Carnage and Culture*, chapter 5. See especially pp. 137-143 and pp. 157-166. Many writers, including Hanson, refer to this as the Battle of Poitiers. It was fought at some unknown location between the two towns.

3) See sources listed by Hanson (2001) on pp. 475-476 of *Carnage and Culture*.

4) See Eggenberger, D. (1967), pp. 441-442, where he states that the Battle of Tours "...was one of the rare times in the Middle Ages when infantry held its ground against mounted attack."

5) (a) Thompson, James W. & Edgar N. Johnson (1937), *An Introduction to Medieval Europe*, p. 119.
   (b) See pp. 671-672 of the article on "War, Theory and Conduct of" in *Encyclopaedia Britannica* (15th edition, 1986), volume 29.
   (c) Dupuy & Dupuy (1993), pp. 182-183 and 235.

6) See p. 672 of article on "War, Theory and Conduct of" in *Encyclopaedia Britannica* (15th edition, 1986), volume 29.

7) Hanson, Victor Davis (2001), p. 148.

8) The English and Norman armies were of roughly equal size; this factor favored the English, who held the higher ground and were defending. However, the English had no cavalry, while the victorious Normans had many mounted knights. See articles in *Encylopaedia Britannica* (15th edition, 1986) on "War, Theory and Conduct of" (volume 29, p. 672) and on "Hastings, Battle of" (volume 5, p. 742). See also Eggenberger, D. (1967), p. 188.

CHAPTER 34

THE ISLAMIC WORLD

Section 1 – The origin of Islam

Muhammad was born in 570 AD in Mecca, in southern Arabia, which at the time was a backward area of the world, far from the centers of trade and learning. He was reared in modest surroundings, and according to Islamic tradition he was illiterate. At the time, most Arabs believed in many gods; however, there were a small number of Christians and Jews in Mecca, and it was probably from them that Muhammad learned of a single, omnipotent god who ruled the entire universe.

In 610 AD, when he was forty years old, Muhammad became convinced that this one true god (*Allah*) was speaking to him and had chosen him as a prophet to spread the true faith. As he gained converts, the authorities in Mecca came to consider him a dangerous nuisance. In 622, he fled Mecca and went to Medina (about 200 miles north of Mecca) where he had been offered a position of considerable political power. This move, the *Hegira*, was the turning point of his life. Muhammad gained many followers in Medina, and within a few years he became virtually a dictator there.

At Medina, in order to raise money, Muhammad organized a series of raiding parties against passing trade caravans.[1] (By Western standards, of course, this was simply highway robbery; and doubtless it appeared that way to the victims.[2]) More importantly, he fought a war against Mecca, a war which ended in 630 AD with his triumphant return to his home city. In the course of the next two years, many of the Arabian tribes were converted to the new religion; and when Muhammad died in 632 AD he was the effective ruler of a large part of Arabia.

The central tenet of the religion that he founded, Islam, is an uncompromising monotheism. Islam is in some respects the most straightforward of the monotheistic religions. The required rituals are simple, and not onerous. Islam does not have the convoluted theology that some religions do; and unlike Judaism, it was from the outset a *universal* religion. Furthermore, Muhammad accepted several biblical figures — including both Moses and Jesus — as true prophets, which made it easier for Jews and Christians to convert to the new religion.

The holy book of Islam, the *Koran*, is a collection of the sayings of Muhammad. (Moslems believe that those sayings were the words of Allah himself, dictated to the Prophet by the archangel Gabriel.) Unlike the Bible, it has relatively few narrative portions, and consists primarily of affirmations of the glory of Allah and of exhortations for Moslems to behave morally. The *Koran* makes it plain that good and evil men will each receive their just desserts in the life to come.

Section 2 – The early caliphs, and the Shiite-Sunni split

When Muhammad died, a conclave of his followers promptly chose his close friend and associate Abu Bakr to be his successor, or *caliph*. Abu Bakr died two years later, and the next three caliphs were 'Umar ibn al-Khattab (634-644), Othman (644-656), and Ali (656-661). Ali (who was a first cousin of the Prophet, and also his son-in-law) was killed in the course of a civil war. The victor in that war was Mu'awiya, who became the founder of the Umayyad (or Omayyad) Caliphate. However, the supporters of Ali, the *Shiites*, continued to assert that his successors should rightfully be the caliphs. The split between the Shiites and the majority branch of Islam, the *Sunnis*, has never healed.

Section 3 – The Arab conquests

The century following the death of Muhammad witnessed a remarkable series of conquests — virtually unprecedented in their combination of scope and speed — by the Arabs, who were united for the first time in their history, and motivated by both religious fervor and a desire for plunder. (See Map 34-1).

During the brief caliphate of Abu Bakr, the Moslems completed their conquest of Arabia. The most important conquests were made under the second caliph ('Umar), who successfully attacked the two wealthy empires bordering Arabia: the restored Persian Empire (which, under the Sassanid dynasty, also controlled Mesopotamia) and the Byzantine Empire.

The Arabs routed the Persian armies at the battles of Qadisiya (637) and Nehavend (642). Mesopotamia was soon occupied, and by 651 the Sassanid Empire had been destroyed and the Arabs ruled Persia as well. Meanwhile, other Arab armies had invaded Syria and had defeated the Byzantine armies at the Battle of the Yarmuk (636). By 640, the Arabs had occupied both Syria and Judea. By then, the Arabs had already invaded Egypt (which had previously been controlled by the Byzantines), and by 642 they had conquered it. Under the next caliph (Othman) the Arabs built a fleet in the Mediterranean; and in 655, that fleet won a devastating victory over the Byzantine navy.

In 661 AD, in order to govern his vast dominions more efficiently, and because the center of the Arab world had shifted northward, Mu'awiya (the first Umayyad Caliph) moved the capital to Damascus, in Syria.

The Arab expansion continued under the Umayyads. Arab armies swept across North Africa, and by 705 AD, they had completed the conquest of what are now Libya, Tunisia, Algeria, and Morocco. In the east, Arab armies invaded Afghanistan and

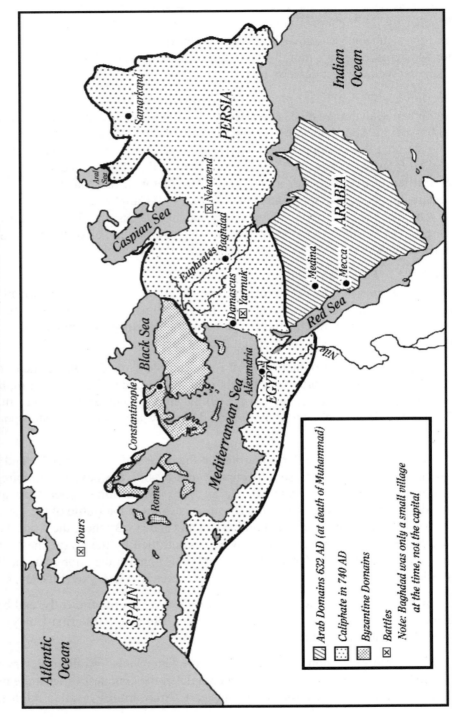

Map 34-1
THE ARAB CONQUESTS

Central Asia. In addition, the Umayyad caliphs made two major attempts to destroy the Byzantine Empire. An Arab fleet besieged Constantinople from 674 to 678 AD, but failed to conquer it, and a second siege (717-718) also failed.

The Moslems were more successful in their attack on Western Europe. Spain was invaded in 711 by a mixed force of Arabs and Berbers, and most of the peninsula was conquered by 715. In 732, a Moslem army invaded France from Spain; however, their army was badly defeated by the Franks at the Battle of Tours, and they withdrew from France. (However, the Moslems ruled much of Spain for several centuries thereafter.)

Section 4 –Developments in the countries the Arabs conquered
Originally, the Arab conquerors lived apart from the people they had conquered, dwelling in garrison camps outside the cities, and paying almost no taxes. Most people in the conquered lands converted to Islam within a century. Those who did not were called *dhimmis*. Dhimmis were not even second-class citizens, but rather non-citizens who lacked many ordinary civil rights (for example, they could not testify in court against a Moslem), and they were subjected to various humiliating rules. They also had to pay an onerous poll tax — the *jizya*, ordained in the Koran itself (Sura IX, verse 29) — that converts were exempt from.[3]

It has often been said that most of the conversions to Islam were voluntary, and that relatively few occurred at sword's point. However, when one considers the extra taxes that dhimmis had to pay, and their various civil disabilities, it is hard to tell how "voluntary" most of the conversions were.[4] Furthermore, conversion *from* Islam was a capital crime.

Gradually most of the conquered peoples in the Fertile Crescent, in Egypt, and in the coastal parts of North Africa abandoned their earlier languages (such as Syriac and Egyptian) and adopted Arabic. However, in some areas, such as Persia (Iran) this did not occur. By examining Table 34-1, we see that Arabization did not persist in any country where the bulk of the population had consisted of Indo-Europeans. The regions where it was most widespread, and has persisted, were those in which a relatively small number of Indo-Europeans had been ruling a population which spoke mostly Afro-Asiatic languages.

Note also that almost all the regions that the Arabs conquered permanently were regions that they had invaded and conquered within a few decades after Muhammad lived. Most of these victories had been won against the Sassanid and Byzantine Empires, two states that had recently exhausted each other in a series of long, expensive wars. With the exception of North Africa, the regions that the Arabs conquered after 650 were all eventually lost back. This suggests that the main factor involved in the Arab conquests was not the great strength of the Arabs, but rather the temporary weakness of their opponents.

Originally, the Arab conquerors were not as advanced culturally as the Byzantines and Persians. However, within 200 years, the works of the ancient Greeks had been

TABLE 34-1

THE ARAB CONQUESTS

REGION	WHEN CONQUERED	ORIGINAL LANGUAGE	ARABIZED	CONTROLLED BY MAIN CALIPHATE	STILL MOSLEM
Fertile Crescent	very early (by 650 AD)	Semitic	heavily	yes	yes
Egypt	very early (by 650 AD)	Ancient Egyptian	heavily	until about 1000 AD	yes
North Africa	by 705 AD	Berber	partly	until about 750 AD	yes
Iran	very early (about) 650 AD	Indo-European	no	until about 900 AD	yes
Central Asia	8th century	mixed: Turkic & Indo-Euro	no	until about 900 AD	yes
Anatolia	by Turks in 11th century (parts of it earlier, by Arabs)	mixed: Greek & Semitic	no	after 1000 AD	yes
Spain	711-715 AD	Indo-European	no	for about 30 years	no
parts of Italy	8th and 9th centuries AD	Indo-European	no	no	no

translated into Arabic, and thereafter Arab scholars made full use of the Greek achievements in mathematics and astronomy. In addition, various Hindu mathematical and technical works were translated into Arabic.

Section 5 – The Caliphate

Almost from the beginning there were a series of struggles for power within the Moslem world. Periods of internal peace were rare. Nevertheless, the Umayyad caliphs managed to rule a unified Arab state for nearly a century (661-750 AD). At its peak, their empire stretched from Central Asia to the Atlantic Ocean. However, the Umayyad dynasty was overthrown in 750 AD, and the Moslem world never regained its political unity.

The caliphs of the new Abbasid dynasty tried to secure their position by hunting down and killing every member of the Umayyad royal family; however, one of them escaped to Spain and established a separate Moslem kingdom there. The Abbasids never gained control of Morocco, either.

The Abbasid caliphs soon moved their capital to Baghdad, a new city (founded in 762) situated about 55 miles north of the ruins of Babylon. The Caliphate reached its peak a few decades later, during the reigns of Harun al-Rashid (786-809) and Mamun the Great (813-833).

It was not long, though, before the Caliphate began to disintegrate. By 900 AD, Persia was effectively independent, and in the tenth century Egypt became independent too. By 1000 AD, the Moslem world consisted of several independent states, with no central authority.

By then, the Abbasid caliphs in Iraq had lost most of their political power, although they retained their spiritual authority. Between 945 and 1258, Iraq had a series of rulers, including a Persian dynasty and the Seljuk Turks. (The Seljuks were a Turkish people who had invaded the Middle East in the 11th century, had been converted to Islam, and had conquered most of Anatolia.)

The Mongols invaded Iran in 1220, and by mid-century they had conquered most of Southwest Asia. In 1258, under Genghis Khan's grandson, Hulagu, they captured Baghdad and put an end to the Abbasid dynasty. However, by 1350 the Mongol invaders had been converted to Islam, and the state founded by Hulagu had disintegrated.

Another group of Turks, the Ottomans, conquered much of Anatolia during the 1300s. In 1453, they conquered Constantinople, thereby putting an end to the Byzantine Empire. By then, the Ottomans had also conquered a large part of the Balkans. Within a century, they had conquered Syria and Egypt as well; had secured control over the holy places in Arabia (including Mecca); and had conquered Baghdad. Thereafter, the Turkish sultans became, in effect, the successors of the caliphs. The Ottoman Empire lasted until World War II, making it the longest-lived of all Moslem dynasties.

Section 6 – Cultural achievements of the Arabs

The Arabs had possessed a written language even before Muhammad, and in the centuries following his death they produced an extensive literature. During much of what we call the Medieval Era, the Arab world was a flourishing commercial civilization, replete with skilled artisans. The Arabs were interested in the arts and sciences, and they valued education and learning. Culturally, they were far ahead of regions such as Australia, sub-Saharan Africa, and the Western Hemisphere. Indeed, for several centuries, the Arab world was more prosperous than Europe, and the arts and sciences were more advanced there. The cultural achievements of the Arabs during this interval included the following:

Exploration and Geography: Arab traders sailed down the East African coast as far as Mozambique and set up a series of trading posts along the way, several of which developed into cities. However, the Arabs made no attempt to sail around Africa, a feat that was achieved by the Portuguese about 1500.

Ibn Batuta (1304-1369) was the greatest traveler of pre-modern times. Although he did not attempt to construct a complete world map, his book *Rihlah* ("Travels") is a major source of information concerning the world of the 14th century.[5]

History: Ibn Khaldun (1332-1406) was one of the greatest of all pre-modern historians. His *Muqaddimah* ("Introduction to History") is an acknowledged masterpiece. In general, though, the Arabs' accomplishments in historical studies were held back by their contemptuous attitude towards most pre-Moslem civilizations. Although many of the remarkable ruins left by ancient civilizations — Sumeria, Egypt, Babylonia, Assyria, etc. — were situated in the Arab world, the Arabs largely ignored archaeology and ancient history.[6]

Philosophy: Although the Arabs wrote extensively about theology, most of their theological works are of little interest to non-Moslems. An important exception was the work of Averroës (1126-1198), who attempted to show that Moslem religious beliefs and Greek rationalism were compatible with each other. Many of his works were translated into Latin, and they influenced important Christian philosophers, such as Thomas Aquinas. Eventually, though, more conservative views triumphed in the Moslem world, and many of the ideas of Averroës became heretical.

Literature: The Arabs produced an extensive literature. However, since the bulk of it was lyric poetry — and poetry, notoriously, rarely translates well — the only item (other than the *Koran*) that is widely read by non-Arabs is the collection of tales known as the *Arabian Nights*. The Arabs produced very little drama, and very little in the way of novels and short stories; nor did they produce epic poetry.

Visual arts: Because of religious taboos against representation, the Arabs achieved rather little in the fields of painting and sculpture. However, their architecture was very graceful and of high quality, and they did excellent work in the decorative arts. Arab calligraphy is perhaps the finest the world has ever produced.

Mathematics and astronomy: Arab mathematicians were acquainted with the Greek works on mathematics and astronomy, which they translated, and eventually transmitted to Western Europe. They did the same for Hindu mathematical innovations, such as positional notation and "Arabic" numerals. Their own contributions, however, were relatively minor.

Chemistry: The Arabs were interested in alchemy (a primitive form of chemistry, strongly tinged with mysticism). One notable figure was Geber (721-815), who was perhaps the first person to prepare nitric acid.

Medicine: There were many fine physicians in the Arab world. Two noteworthy ones in the Hippocratic/Aristotelian tradition were Rhazes (845-930) and Avicenna (980-1037). Rhazes was the first physician to clearly describe smallpox and distinguish it from measles. He wrote extensively about medicine, and also did some work in chemistry. Avicenna wrote textbooks which (in translation) became widely used in Europe.

Physics: Alhazen (965-1039) was probably the greatest of all Arab scientists. His work on optics (in particular, on reflection, refraction, and lenses) was highly original. Although his work had no important consequences in the Arab world, it was eventually translated into Latin and probably influenced the great astronomer Johannes Kepler (1571-1630).

Engineering: The Arabs added nothing of importance to this field. Indeed, they do not appear to have equaled the achievements of the Romans, even though there were many Roman ruins in their territory.

Law: The Arabs constructed an elaborate legal system, the *Shari'a*, which embraces both religious and secular law. The *Shari'a* was created over a thousand years ago, and was widely applied for centuries. Saudi Arabia still applies it today. It has had very little effect, however, on the legal systems of non-Moslem countries.

Section 7 – Moslem cultural achievements: An evaluation

The set of achievements listed above clearly surpasses those of most other civilizations. Many recent writers, however, tend to exaggerate the importance of those accomplishments, and it has become fashionable to assert that Moslem civilization was *enormously* superior to European culture during the Middle Ages. It seems to me that that assertion is incorrect.

It is true that for several centuries the Moslem world was more advanced culturally than Europe, but there are two ways in which that superiority is commonly made to appear much greater than it really was:

1) Writers often compare the culture of the *entire* Arab world (sometimes, indeed, the entire Moslem world) with that of a *portion* of Europe, rather than with all of Europe, including the parts within the Byzantine Empire. Although at times the Moslem world was more advanced culturally than the Byzantines, it was never *much* more advanced.

2) Writers often compare Arab achievements in the entire Medieval Era with those of Western Europe during the Dark Ages alone. But the Dark Ages only comprise half of the Medieval Era.

Actually, the period during which the cultural level of the Moslem world was far superior to that of Western Europe lasted for only about six hundred years. Prior to 600 AD, the Arab world was still backward, and it was not until about 750 — halfway through the Dark Ages — that the Arab world had clearly drawn ahead. And, as we shall see in chapter 42, during the last portion of the Middle Ages (1300-1500) the cultural level of Western Europe was more advanced than that of the Moslem world.

In order to assess the overall contribution of the Arabs to world civilization, we should remember that until modern times the Arabs were not interested in drama, epic poetry, or the novel, and they produced virtually nothing in those fields. Nor did they produce any significant works of music, nor any great paintings. They made no *major* discoveries in mathematics or science, nor did they make any major advances in applied sciences such as medicine and engineering. In fact, there was not a single important invention that originated in the Arab world. (By way of contrast, in the interval 650-1300 AD, spectacles were invented in Italy, and the Chinese invented printing, gunpowder, and the compass.)

There is, of course, more to human culture than the arts and sciences. The growth of democracy, the abolition of slavery, the emancipation of women, the rise of religious tolerance, and the establishment of freedom of speech are advances that are more valuable than beautiful paintings, symphonies, or poems. Here too, however, the contribution of the Arabs was negligible.

It was not, of course, the fault of Islam that the world it emerged in was one in which extreme patriarchy was the rule, slavery was rampant, and most countries were governed by autocratic despots. But the Arabs certainly did nothing to improve the situation; indeed, in most of these matters, the Arabs have remained behind most other regions of the world.[7]

Section 8 – A possible explanation

The backwardness of the Arab world, relative to Europe, and the sparseness of its achievements, have been noticed before. That backwardness is particularly striking because the geographic location of the Arabs gave them the opportunity to learn from a wide variety of other cultures.

Few attempts have been made, however, to explain that backwardness. The most common explanation is that the natural talents of the Arabs have been thwarted by the triumph of a conservative fundamentalism in Moslem countries. (An analogy would be the way Spain fell behind the rest of Europe after the installation of the Spanish Inquisition.)

A simpler explanation is that the average intelligence in Arab countries was significantly less than it was in Europe. Table 17-1 suggests that we would expect the average IQ of the Arabs to be only about 88, or perhaps a bit lower. The few studies that have been made of test scores in Arab countries (see Table 15-6) are consistent with that theoretical prediction.

Both the computer simulation and the empirical data suggest that while the mean IQ in the Arab world was high enough to permit a commercial civilization to flourish, it was not high enough to generate a significant number of truly great geniuses (such as Aristotle, Galileo, Newton, and Shakespeare). This is consistent with the historical record.

During their heyday, the Arabs believed (correctly, in my opinion) that they were naturally more intelligent than the African blacks, and they attributed their cultural superiority in part to that. That same factor — higher average native intelligence —

seems to explain quite adequately why European culture has usually been so superior to that of the Arabs, and why the Arabs — even at the peak of their power and prosperity — produced so little in the way of major cultural achievements.

FOOTNOTES – CHAPTER 34

1) (a) Andrae, Tor (1936), *Mohammed: the Man and his Faith*, pp. 140-143.
   (b) *Encyclopaedia Britannica* (15th edition, 1986), article on "Islam," volume 22, p. 3.
   (c) Rodinson, Maxime (1971), *Mohammad*, pp. 162-164.

2) Some other examples — all from old Arab sources, not hostile to Muhammad — of how different his moral standards were from ours include:

   a) *His wholesale massacre of prisoners of war.* In 627 AD, after the entire Banu Qurayza tribe had surrendered to him, he had all the adult males (numbering about 700) beheaded in his presence. With one exception, the women and children were sold into slavery. See:
      (1) Andrae, Tor (1936), pp. 155-156.
      (2) Lings, Martin (1983), *Muhammad: his life based on the earliest sources*, pp. 231-232.
      (3) *Encyclopedia Britannica* (15th edition, 1986), article on "Islam," volume 22, p. 4.
      (4) Ibn Warraq (1995), pp. 95-97.

   b) *His marriage to Zainab, the wife of one of his sons.* Finding Zainab attractive, he had his son divorce Zainab so that Muhammad could marry her himself. This was morally repulsive even by the standards of the day; but Muhammad had a revelation from Allah (see the *Koran*, Sura XXXIII, paragraph 4) that such behavior was permitted because the first husband was merely an *adopted* son. (See Ibn Warraq [1995], pp. 99-100 for details.) Also see:
      (1) Lings, Martin (1983), pp. 212-213.
      (2) Andrae, Tor (1936), pp. 152-154.
      (3) Rodinson, Maxime (1971), pp. 205-207.

   c) *His assassination of critics, such as the poet Kab ibn al-Ashraf and the poetess Asma bint Marwan.* See:
      (1) Rodinson, Maxime (1971), pp. 171-172, 176, and 195-196.
      (2) Ibn Warraq (1995), pp. 93-95 and sources cited therein.
      (3) Andrae, Tor (1936), pp. 148-149.
      (4) Lings, Martin (1983), p. 171.

3) For more information on the status of *dhimmis* under Islam see
   (a) Bat Ye'or (1985), *The Dhimmi: Jews and Christians under Islam*.
   (b) Ibn Warraq (1995), pp. 225-231, and sources cited therein.

4) See Ibn Warraq (1995), pp. 233-236.

5) Ibn Batuta's travels took him across North Africa, and into Iraq, Turkey, Central Asia, Persia, India, Sri Lanka, China, and Indonesia, as well as Spain, southern Russia, West Africa, and the East African coast! An English translation of his book, the *Rihlah*, is available.

6) For example, the dramatic trilingual rock carving on the cliff at Behistun (which eventually enabled European scholars to decipher Babylonian cuneiform) was ignored by the Arabs, although it was only 25 miles from the important city of Kermanshah in western Iran, and less than 200 miles from Baghdad. (The inscription and relief sculpture at Behistun had been erected about 500 BC at the order of Darius the Great of Persia, who deliberately chose a site that could be easily seen by persons using a well-traveled trade route.)

7) A description of the status of women under Islamic law and custom can be found in chapter 14 of Ibn Warraq (1995).

CHAPTER 35
CHINA

Section 1 – Geography

China can be divided into three main regions: the northeast (commonly called northern China), the southeast (commonly called southern China), and the west (or western China).

The most important geographic feature of northern China is the North China Plain, a large flat region with fertile soil and high population density. The North China Plain is situated north of the Yangtze River and stretches from the Yellow Sea westward to the Loess Plateau, which consists of a thick layer of windblown dust. In general, northern China has cold, dry winters and hot, humid summers.

Southern China is more mountainous than the north, and somewhat wetter and warmer. In the far south the winters are warm, frosts are rare, and crops grow all year round.

Western China has little rainfall, and is sparsely settled. It consists largely of mountains, high plateaus, and arid and semi-arid regions. Parts of the west were usually independent of China, and many of the inhabitants are not ethnic Chinese.

Section 2 – The origin of the Chinese

Originally, the inhabitants of northern and southern China were very different racially.[1] Southern China was settled by σ-3 who entered from Southeast Asia, whereas northern China was settled by M-1 (Mongoloids), who entered from the north. (See Map 10-1 and sections 11-4 and 12-6.) The two groups differed in appearance and in average IQ. The M-1 had already evolved a high intelligence before their entrance into China, and the cold winters of northern China tended to continue that process.

After agriculture was introduced into northern China (about 6400 BC) the North China Plain became capable of supporting a high population. From then on, the people of the North China Plain enjoyed a combination of (a) high average intelligence, (b) a large region of very fertile soil and adequate rainfall, and (c) nearby regions into which they could expand.

It was this unusual combination that explains the rise, spread, and remarkable size of the Chinese population. As the population of the North China Plain increased, excess population kept overflowing into the rest of northern China, resulting in a large, relatively homogeneous population with a high average IQ. Because the geographic barriers within northern China are relatively minor, movement was easy, which resulted in relatively little linguistic variation within the region.

Eventually, the north Chinese spread into southern China, and gradually most of the southern Chinese have been assimilated into the dominant culture. However, there are still pockets in southern China (mostly in the hills) where aboriginal groups survive, speaking their own languages. Because the geographic barriers within southern China are considerable, the "Chinese" spoken there has diverged into several mutually unintelligible, though closely related, languages.

Because of substantial interbreeding between the two groups, the original differences in appearance and intelligence between the northern and southern Chinese have become muted in the course of the last two millennia.

Section 3 – Principal Chinese dynasties

Table 35-1 lists all the major Chinese dynasties.[2] According to later Chinese historians, the first sizable state in China was ruled by the *Hsia* dynasty (traditional dates: 2205-1766 BC). However, no written records survive from that period, and it is possible that the Hsia is only legendary.

The second Chinese dynasty was the *Shang* (1766-1122 BC), whose monarchs ruled a small kingdom of perhaps 40,000 square miles centered on the North China Plain.

The following dynasty, the *Chou* is the first for which substantial documentation survives. It endured for over 800 years, making it the longest-lasting Chinese dynasty. However, for the last half of that period the authority of the Chou kings was only nominal, and China really consisted of several independent warring states. Despite the weakness of the central government, the Chou period was one in which major technological and cultural advances were made. Like its predecessors, the Chou ruled northern China only.

A brief, but exceedingly important dynasty was the *Ch'in* (221-206 BC). Originally, the Ch'in kingdom was just one of the warring states that existed during the latter part of the Chou dynasty. In the third century BC, it became a powerful state (perhaps because the Ch'in monarchs adopted policies recommended by the famous philosophers of the *Legalist* school, Shang Yang and Han Fei Tzu).

The greatest of the Ch'in monarchs acceded to the throne in 238 BC, and by 221 he had defeated all the other Chinese states. He is best known by the title he then gave himself: *Shih Huang Ti* (PINYIN spelling: Shi Huangdi), which means "the First Emperor."

TABLE 35-1
PRINCIPAL CHINESE DYNASTIES

Name of dynasty		
Pinyin spelling	**Earlier Spelling**	**Approximate dates**
Xia	Hsia	2205 BC - 1766 BC
Shang	Shang	1766 BC - 1122 BC
Zhou	Chou	1122 BC - 256 BC
Qin	Ch'in	221 BC - 206 BC
Han	Han	202 BC - 220 AD
Sui	Sui	581 AD - 618 AD
Tang	T'ang	618 AD - 907 AD
Song	Sung	960 AD - 1279 AD
Yuan	Yüan (Mongol)	1279 AD - 1368 AD
Ming	Ming	1368 AD - 1644 AD
Qing	Ch'ing (Manchu)	1644 AD - 1912 AD

Shih Huang Ti — a man of great ability and energy, and limitless ambition — was determined to institute a "new order of the ages," and he perhaps succeeded in that goal more than any of the other megalomaniacs who have graced (or disgraced) human history. He led his armies into southern China, and for the first time large portions of that important region were incorporated into the Chinese state. He revised the structure of the Chinese government by scrapping the old feudal states, and replaced them with 36 provinces, each controlled by a governor appointed by the emperor and replaceable by him. He built an extensive system of roads leading out from his capital, so that the imperial armies could quickly suppress any revolts. In order to prevent incursions by the fierce barbarian tribes to the north of China, he combined earlier local walls into one enormous wall, the "Great Wall of China" (still the most massive structure ever built by human hands). In addition, Shih Huang Ti instituted a uniform set of laws throughout China, along with a uniform set of weights and measures, and a uniform currency.

The emperor's most famous decree was issued in 213 BC, when — in perhaps the most far-reaching act of censorship ever attempted — he ordered that all the books in China be burned, excepting only various technical works, and books expounding the official Legalist philosophy. (Among the books he ordered destroyed were the works of Confucius.) Fortunately, many books escaped this Draconian decree.

The emperor's construction projects and foreign wars inevitably led to high taxes. Revolt against his iron rule was impossible; but there were several attempts to assassinate him, all unsuccessful. Supreme over men, the emperor longed for immortality, and he consulted a series of magicians and alchemists to achieve it. But not even the all-powerful *Huang Ti* could defeat death, and he died of natural causes in 210 BC, at the age of forty-nine.

Shih Huang Ti was succeeded by his son, but revolts soon broke out, and within four years the Ch'in dynasty was overthrown and the entire line extinguished. The struggle for power that followed ended in the victory of Liu Pang (also known as Han Kao Tsu), the founder of the *Han* dynasty. This new dynasty lasted for roughly four centuries (from 202 BC to 220 AD, except for the interval from 9 to 23 AD).

The Han monarchs completed the conquest of southern China, and they also made conquests in western China, and even in Central Asia. Two of their internal policies are particularly noteworthy:

1) They originated the practice of selecting the government bureaucracy by means of civil service examinations, a system that became of very great importance in subsequent centuries.

2) They established Confucianism as the official state philosophy. (Since Shih Huang Ti had burned the works of Confucius, they denounced him as a villain; however, many of the policies he had instituted were continued.)

Following the collapse of the Han dynasty there was a long period of disunity in China, marked by the loss of western lands and a considerable decline in prosperity and culture. As the Han Empire in China roughly corresponded to the Roman Empire in Europe, this period of disunity (220-589 AD) corresponded to the Dark Ages in Europe; however, the economic decline was much less pronounced in China.

Chinese unity was restored by the short-lived *Sui* dynasty (581-618). The Sui was followed by the *T'ang* dynasty (618-907), which (if one considers both military strength and cultural flowering) was arguably the most glorious in the entire history of China. Under the T'ang, Chinese armies again pushed into Central Asia; and at the dynasty's peak during the 7th and 8th centuries, China was the largest, strongest, and most advanced country on Earth.

The T'ang was followed by a disorderly period in which there were several short-lived dynasties. Order was reestablished by the *Sung* dynasty (960-1279). China was generally prosperous under the Sung, and the arts flourished. However, during much of that period, China was militarily weak, and it was repeatedly attacked from the north. By 1126, the Sung had lost control of northern China to the Juchen, a group of Tungus or Manchu tribes who set up a rival dynasty (the *Chin*) in the north.

The Sung-Chin conflict was overshadowed in the 13th century by the rise of the Mongols under Genghis Khan. The Mongols conquered northern China by 1234 AD. By 1279 they had conquered all of China — the first foreigners ever to do so — and

Kubilai Khan (a grandson of Genghis) had established the *Yüan* (or Mongol) dynasty. However, Mongol rule lasted for less than 90 years. They were defeated and expelled from China in 1368, and a new dynasty, the *Ming,* gained power.

China was militarily strong during the Ming dynasty, but there was less creativity in the arts and philosophy than there had been in earlier periods. The Ming lasted until 1644, when another group of foreign invaders, the Manchus, conquered the country and established the last Chinese dynasty, the *Ch'ing*. Unlike the Mongols, the Manchus were not expelled from China, but instead were gradually assimilated. Very few ethnic Manchus exist today.

Section 4 – Confucius
Confucius was the most influential figure in Chinese history, comparable to Jesus in Europe, or to Muhammad in the Arab world. Unlike those two figures, however, Confucius was not a religious leader, but a secular philosopher.

Confucius (551-479 BC) was born in what is now Shantung province. Although he spent most of his life as a teacher, and served for a while as a government official, his importance rests entirely upon his philosophical writings, the most celebrated of which is the *Analects*.

According to Confucius, the two chief human virtues are *jen* (which might be defined as "benevolent concern for one's fellow man") and *li* (a combination of manners, custom, etiquette, propriety, and ritual). Confucius emphasized the importance of family loyalty and respect for one's parents. He also taught that respect and obedience were owed by wives to their husbands and by subjects to their rulers. However, Confucius did not approve of tyranny; rather, he insisted that government exists for the benefit of the people. Furthermore, although laws are necessary, a monarch should govern primarily by moral example rather than by force. Last, but not least, Confucius said, *"What you do not want done to yourself, do not do to others."*

Note that the ethical standards set forth by Confucius do not require his followers to be saints. He did not preach asceticism, nor did he urge his followers to save the world. Rather, he preached a rather straightforward, practical moral code for everyday life, one that can be followed by ordinary men and women. (The contrast with the injunction by Jesus to "Love your enemy" is striking.) Note also that Confucius never claimed to be presenting a *new* moral code; he always said that he was just restating the accepted wisdom of the past.

For many centuries, the civil service examinations utilized by the Chinese government were based primarily on knowledge of the Confucian classics. As a result, the attitudes of the entire Chinese bureaucracy were profoundly affected by the ideas of Confucius.

Section 5 – Some important social and political attitudes of the Chinese
In comparison to the West, the Chinese have generally accorded less weight to the importance of individual expression and welfare, and more importance to the good of

the group. They also place a higher priority than we do on a person's reverence for and obedience to his parents.

The Chinese were always convinced of their superiority to other nations, and they kept careful historical records. The most celebrated Chinese historian of antiquity was Ssu-ma Ch'ien (145-85 BC). His great work, the *Shih-chi* ("Historical Records") is generally considered to be superior to anything written by European historians before modern times.

In the past, Chinese monarchs tended to take a very hands-off approach to the personal and family matters of their subjects. Wife beating, child abuse, infanticide, mistreatment of animals or of slaves, and prostitution were — though not approved of — far less likely to be interfered with by the government in China than in western countries. (Some might describe this attitude as *Live and let live*; others might describe it as *Abuse and let abuse*.) Of course, custom and social pressures might restrain personal behavior in some of those matters.

Perhaps the most important difference between Chinese and Western attitudes was that, compared with the West, the Chinese were a conspicuously practical people, not much interested in theory. For example, they had relatively little interest in pure mathematics or in theology. (This may explain why religious persecution in China was rare and relatively mild, and why the Chinese had no religious wars.)

Section 6 – Inventions

One result of the practical outlook of the Chinese is that they made a large number of useful inventions. Among the most important of these were papermaking (by Ts'ai Lun, in 105 AD); block printing (8th century AD); gunpowder (10th century AD); printing using movable type (by Pi Sheng, in the 11th century AD); and the magnetic compass (12th century AD). Among their other inventions were cast iron, porcelain, wheelbarrows, canal lock gates, and the use of coal as fuel. This is an impressive list, and one that far surpasses the accomplishments of most other civilizations.

The invention of paper was especially consequential. Prior to that, no practical and inexpensive writing material was widely available in China, a circumstance that greatly hindered the growth of culture there. (Bamboo was often used, but books written on bamboo were necessarily cumbersome.) Ts'ai Lun's invention resulted in China possessing a better (and much cheaper) writing material than any available in the West. That may have been the main reason Chinese civilization advanced rapidly in the course of the next millennium, and in many ways surpassed that of the West.

Section 7 – Science and mathematics

In sharp contrast to the impressive list of practical inventions by the Chinese is the sparseness of their achievements in mathematics and science. The procedures that the Chinese developed for carrying out arithmetic calculations were somewhat better than those devised in the West, and they also developed both elementary algebra and simple, practical geometry. However, probably because of their general lack of interest in theory, they never developed an axiomatic treatment of geometry. As a result, Chinese mathematics bogged down at an early stage. When the Chinese were finally introduced to Western mathematics (by the Jesuit missionary Matteo Ricci, about 1600 AD) Chinese mathematics had still not achieved the level reached by Greek scholars 1900 years earlier.

Chinese contributions to astronomy were equally meager. The Chinese were quite diligent in keeping astronomical records, but they never created a theoretical structure. The ancient Chinese never deduced that the Earth was round, and their failure to do so made any significant progress in astronomy difficult. In 1600 AD, Chinese astronomy was at least 2000 years behind the West.

The Chinese made no contributions to either physics, chemistry, or geology. There is a record of a Chinese scholar who, upon noticing that there were seashells embedded in a sandstone cliff (hundreds of feet above sea level), correctly inferred that the sandstone must have derived from an ancient beach that had somehow been compressed and elevated. But this was an isolated observation, not part of any organized body of knowledge, and it was not followed up by other Chinese scholars.

Section 8 – Engineering, construction, and architecture

As far as practical projects are concerned, the Chinese record is impressive. The Great Wall of China has already been mentioned. The Grand Canal — connecting China's two largest rivers (the Yellow River and the Yangtze) — was completed about 605 AD, during the Sui dynasty. It was eventually extended at both ends, and it now runs from Hangzhou all the way to Beijing, a distance of over 1000 miles.

Chinese accomplishments in architecture are less impressive. The Chinese were relatively late in making use of the arch and the dome; and although they did build many attractive homes and other buildings, they did not construct anything that rivals the Parthenon in Athens, Hagia Sophia in Constantinople, or the magnificent cathedrals of medieval Europe.

Section 9 – Exploration and cartography

In general, whenever the Chinese were governed by strong leaders they tended to expand into neighboring territories, particularly into those on their western frontier, such as Xingjiang. Other than that, though, the Chinese showed relatively little interest in exploration.[3] (Indeed, they did not colonize Taiwan — less than 100 miles off the Chinese coast — until the late 17th century.) This may have been because their own country was so prosperous and appeared to be so complete in itself. Aside from Buddhism (which had originated in India), the Chinese were unaware of any foreign contributions to their culture.

Indeed, the Chinese were only dimly aware of India until the 5th century AD, when Fa-hsien (a Buddhist monk who made a pilgrimage to India about 402 AD) wrote a report of what he had seen on his trip. Even after that, for many years there was little contact between the two countries. In contrast, regular, large-scale trade between India and the Roman Empire had begun centuries earlier.

The Chinese never reached Australia or New Guinea; nor did they explore Siberia. In fact, for a long time they had little contact with the Philippines, Indonesia, or even Japan. As late as 1400 AD, the Chinese had not yet produced a map of the world that was as extensive as the one constructed by Ptolemy (about 150 AD), nor even as the one drawn by Herodotus (about 450 BC).

Section 10 — The Cheng Ho expeditions

Cheng Ho (PINYIN: Zheng He) was a Chinese admiral who lived during the Ming dynasty. Between 1405 and 1435 AD, he led seven large naval expeditions into the Indian Ocean, via the South China Sea. These expeditions sailed as far as the Persian Gulf, Arabia, and the east coast of Africa (stopping at India and Sri Lanka on the way). They were large expeditions, involving dozens of ships and at times more than 25,000 men. However, there was a change of policy when the emperor died (1424), and Cheng Ho made only one more expedition after that. The fleet was allowed to decay, and the whole project was abandoned.

The Cheng Ho expeditions have often been cited to prove that the Chinese were interested in foreign exploration. In fact, however, the whole project was a rare, and brief, exception to the usual Chinese policy of paying little attention to foreign exploration or to any countries not on their borders. Note also how late the expeditions took place, just a few decades before the beginning of modern times.

Section 11 – Arts and literature

The ancient Chinese did not write epic poetry,[4] nor (until the 13th century AD) did they regard the theater as an important art form.[5] Nevertheless, China produced a very extensive literature — including lyric poetry, fiction, history, and philosophy — in ancient and medieval times. Many of those old works are still widely read and admired within China. Only a few of them, though, have been read by Westerners. These include the *Tao Te Ching* ("The Classic of the Way and its Power") by Lao Tzu; some of the Confucian classics; and *The Art of War* by Sun-Tzu.

The Chinese produced high-quality works of sculpture and a large number of fine paintings. (Their landscapes are especially striking.) They considered calligraphy to be a major art form, and only the Arabs rivaled them in that field. The Chinese also excelled in the decorative arts.

Section 12 – Comparison with the Arab world

Although in many ways the achievements of the Arab world between 650 and 1400 AD were impressive, it seems plain that by Western standards Chinese civilization was superior.

- During that period, China enjoyed large stretches of internal peace, whereas the Arab world rarely did.
- China was in general considerably more prosperous than the Moslem world. (Marco Polo, who traveled in both, was clear on this point; and later European travelers agreed.)

- The Chinese produced inventions of the highest importance (paper, printing, gunpowder); the Arabs did not.

- And finally, virtually all of the admirable features of Chinese culture were created by the Chinese themselves; whereas much of the Arab world's knowledge was derived from outsiders (Byzantines, Persians, Hindus, and Chinese).

Section 13 – Comparison with the West

On an overall basis, Chinese civilization is the only one that rivals European civilization. The Chinese — virtually unaided by outsiders — created a complex and complete civilization, with a smoothly functioning government, and multitudinous achievements in technology, construction, literature, the arts, and philosophy. They had a wide variety of skilled craftsmen; they maintained large, powerful armies; and they created a school system, a network of roads, an elaborate (and delicious) cuisine, and all the other attributes of a sophisticated civilization.

In general, the Chinese enjoyed more internal unity than Europe. Europe has usually consisted of many independent states, often fighting one another. In contrast, China has usually been politically unified.

Between 600 and 1300 AD, China was clearly more prosperous than the West. Because of this, it has often been asserted that (until the rise of modern science in the last five centuries) China was *usually* more advanced than the West. However, that assertion is incorrect. In the first place, even during that period, China was far behind the West in mathematics and science. In the second place, the interval 600-1300 AD was atypical. For *most* of recorded history — and for most of the last ten thousand years — China has been well behind the Western world in both technology and the arts. The relative backwardness of China is apparent in such important fields as agriculture, writing, astronomy, mathematics, metalworking, and cloth making.

Agriculture: Both the planting of crops and the domestication of animals began in the Middle East well before they were developed in China. So did such important advances as irrigation and the use of the plow.

Writing: The earliest surviving examples of Chinese writing are no older than about 1500 BC. It is likely that Chinese writing actually developed several centuries before those samples (according to Chinese legends, around 2200 BC), but even that is more than a thousand years after writing was developed in the Middle East. Furthermore, the Chinese failed to invent (or even adopt) an alphabet, and the lack of one may have seriously retarded Chinese progress.

Astronomy: The Chinese kept extensive astronomical records, but their knowledge of astronomical theory never came close to the level reached by Ptolemy in the 2nd century AD, nor even that reached by Hipparchus three centuries earlier.

Mathematics: In 1600 AD, when China and the West first came into close contact, the Chinese still knew far less about mathematics than had been presented in Euclid's famous work, the *Elements*, which was written about 300 BC.

Metalworking: This, too, arose much later in China. Bronze was not known in China until the third millennium BC, which was far later than it was first used in the Middle East. Furthermore, since bronze never became really important in China, China hardly had a Bronze Age. Instead, when ironworking began in China — about 600 BC, which was roughly a thousand years after it had been developed in the West — China went directly from the Stone Age to the Iron Age. That was more than two thousand years after the Middle East had left the Stone Age.

Cloth making: The production of wool in Southwest Asia predates its use in China by two or three thousand years. The Chinese may have been producing silk by 3000 BC, but linen was being made in both Egypt and Europe by 3500 BC, and as early as 6500 BC in Anatolia.

It is easy to construct sets of parallels between China and Europe. For example:

Confucius	:	Jesus
Han Kao Tsu	:	Augustus Caesar
Ssu-ma Ch'ien	:	Herodotus
Pi Sheng	:	Johannes Gutenberg
Cheng Ho	:	Henry the Navigator

However, even more important are the instances where there was no parallel. Europeans created modern science; the Chinese did not. There were no Chinese equivalents to Copernicus or Newton. Nor were there any Chinese parallels to Bach, Mozart, or Beethoven; nor to Michelangelo or Leonardo da Vinci; nor to Columbus or Magellan.

It might be objected that those figures are all from modern times. However, there were no Chinese parallels to Aeschylus, Sophocles, or Euripides either. More importantly, there were no Chinese equivalents to Pythagoras, Aristotle, Euclid, or Ptolemy. It was this lack that later on, in the crucial period 1450-1750 AD, made it impossible for any Chinese man or woman — no matter how gifted personally — to match the accomplishments of Copernicus, Galileo, Kepler, or Newton.

FOOTNOTES – CHAPTER 35

1) "North and south China belong to different major clusters, thus confirming the suspicion that, despite millennia of common history and many migrations, a profound initial genetic difference between these two regions has been in part maintained." (Cavalli-Sforza, L.L., et al. (1994), p. 225; see also figure 4.10.1 on that page, and figures 4.9.3 and 4.10.2 on neighboring pages.)

2) In general, the dates in Table 35-1 follow those given in the article on "China" in volume 16 of the *Encyclopaedia Britannica* (15th edition, 1986); an exception is the date for the end of the Chou dynasty, which they list as 221 BC. Other sources — such as Latourette, K.S. (1950), p. 53; the *Columbia History of the World* (revised edition, 1981), p. 113; and

the *Encyclopedia of World History* (6th edition, 2001), p. 47 — say that the last Chou monarch was deposed in 256 BC.

3) See Latourette, K.S. (1950), pp. 28-29.

4) See article on "Chinese Literature" in volume 16 of *Encyclopaedia Brittanica* (15th edition, 1986), especially pp. 257-258.

5) Same article, p. 261.

CHAPTER 36
INDIA

Section 1 – Geography
In this chapter, the word "India" is used to denote the entire Indian subcontinent, embracing not merely the modern Republic of India, but also Pakistan, Bangladesh, Nepal, Bhutan, and Sri Lanka.

Despite its lengthy land frontiers, India is rather isolated. On the south, India is cut off from the rest of the world by the broad expanse of the Indian Ocean, while directly to the north of India is the highest mountain range on Earth, the Himalayas. The easiest approaches to the subcontinent are on the northeast and northwest borders; but both those regions are mountainous too. Until modern times, all invasions of India had come from the west and northwest.

Most of India lies in or close to the tropic zone, and as a result has a hot climate. The northwest part of the country is semi-arid to arid, but most of the country is humid. The hot, humid climate is very enervating, and this was probably an important factor in Indian history. However, the combination of warm climate and abundant rainfall has enabled India to support a very large population. Although the subcontinent includes less than 3% of the Earth's land area, it contains more than 20% of the world's population — more than Africa and South America combined.

Section 2 – The three waves of settlement
The climate and soil of India destroy human remains rather quickly, so very few remains of earlier hominids have survived. It is reasonable, though, to suppose that *Homo erectus* and *AHS* (archaic *Homo sapiens*) both reached India. From the linguistic and genetic data, it appears that there were three main migrations of *HSS* into India:

1) An early migration (before 50 kya) by σ-1 from the Middle East.

2) A second migration (about 8 kya), by Caucasoid, Dravidian-speaking farmers from the Middle East.

3) A third migration (about 3.5 kya), by Caucasoid, Indo-European-speaking tribes (the *Aryans*) coming from Afghanistan and/or Iran.

Section 3 – The σ-1 people

The first *HSS* to arrive in India (the σ-1) probably entered the region about 57 kya.[1] However, since no artifacts from this group have survived, the date that they entered India can only be estimated indirectly, from remains found elsewhere. In any event, the σ-1 displaced any pre-humans who had been dwelling in India (*AHS*, or possibly surviving *Homo erectus*), probably with only minor interbreeding.

Although the σ-1 were the distant ancestors of the Australian aborigines, the two groups separated so long ago (probably more than 50 kya) that we should not infer that the σ-1 looked much like modern Australian aborigines. It seems safe to say, however, that they were probably dark-skinned.

As the σ-1 had not passed through any cold regions during their migration from Africa, it seems likely that their average intelligence was not very different than the humans living in sub-Saharan Africa. Furthermore, because of the warm climate in India, there was very little tendency for the mean IQ of the σ-1 to rise while they remained in India, and it probably changed only slightly during the next 40,000 years.

Section 4 – The Dravidians and the Indus Valley civilization

Agriculture was not invented independently in India. However, as described in section 22-2, by 6000 BC various Neolithic tribes (speaking Dravidian languages, and descended from Caucasoids living in the Middle East) entered what is now Pakistan from the west, and from there they gradually spread throughout India. To a large extent, these invaders displaced the earlier σ-1. However, there was some interbreeding between the two groups, and in 3000 BC perhaps 25% of the gene pool of the Indian population was derived from the σ-1.

Since the average intelligence of the Caucasoid invaders was considerably higher than that of the σ-1 (see Table 17-1), the mean IQ in India increased considerably — perhaps by about 11 points — as a result of the Dravidian invasion.

In the course of the third millennium BC, a distinctive civilization arose in the Indus Valley, in what is now Pakistan. This *Indus Valley* or *Harappan* civilization made rapid progress after 2600 BC and reached its peak about 2000 BC. For reasons that are unclear, it declined rapidly after about 1700 BC. The Harappan civilization had a written language, but it has not yet been deciphered.

At its peak, the Indus Valley civilization covered a large territory (about 300,000 square miles), and was considerably more advanced than any then existing in China. The two leading cities were Harappa (in the north), with a population of over 20,000, and Mohenjo-Daro (in the south), with a population of 35-40,000. Both were carefully laid out, planned cities. They appear to have had some trade with the Middle East, but none with China.

Northwest India is not richer in resources than the rest of India. However, at least three factors favored the Indus Valley as the site of the first Indian civilization:

1) The climate there was less humid, and less enervating than in most parts of India.

2) It was closer than other parts of India to the older cultures of the Fertile Crescent, and it had more contact with them.

3) The population of northwest India had a higher percentage of Caucasoid parentage — and therefore a higher average IQ — than did the population of the rest of India.

Section 5 – The Aryan invasions

About 1500 BC, India was again invaded from the northwest. These new invaders, the *Aryans*, were Caucasoid tribesmen speaking Indo-European languages closely related to ancient Sanskrit. The invaders soon conquered the remnants of the Indus Valley civilization, and then gradually spread out over all of northern India. As a result, most of the modern inhabitants of northern India speak related languages, each derived from Sanskrit. (Most inhabitants of southern India continue to speak Dravidian languages.)

The Aryan invaders probably came from Afghanistan, or perhaps eastern Iran, and before that from Central Asia. Since the Aryans were rather light-skinned, the present inhabitants of northern India are, on average, considerably lighter than the inhabitants of southern India.

Since the regions that the Aryans came from are much drier than India, and could never have supported nearly as large a population as northern India, it is clear that the Aryan invaders must have been enormously outnumbered by the indigenous population. The most parsimonious explanation for their successful conquest of most of India is that they had, on average, greater intelligence than the earlier inhabitants. (This is consistent with the data presented in Table 17-1.) It follows that a side result of the Aryan conquest was to again raise the average IQ of the Indian population.

Section 6 – Political history

Unlike China, pre-modern India was never ruled by a single government, and only rarely was even most of the region ruled by a single state. Indian history, therefore, more closely resembles the political history of medieval Europe, a region in which there were many independent states, some of them quite small.

Very little is known of the political history of India prior to 327 BC. In that year, Alexander the Great invaded the Indus Valley, but his conquests there proved ephemeral. The first large Indian state that we have clear knowledge of was the Mauryan Empire, founded by Chandragupta Maurya (often called *Chandragupta* or *Candra Gupta*) about 321 BC. By the time of his death, about 297 BC, he ruled all of northern India. The empire reached its greatest extent under his grandson, Asoka, (reigned 273-232 BC) who conquered most of southern India as well. However, the Mauryan Empire declined rapidly after Asoka's death, and came to an end by 184 BC.

In the next few centuries, several foreign invaders (including the Sakas and the

Yüeh-chih, who were Indo-European peoples) entered from the northwest and ruled parts of northern India.

Perhaps the most glorious Indian empire was that ruled by the Gupta dynasty, which is renowned for its literary and artistic splendor. It was founded by Chandragupta I, who reigned from 320 to 330 AD. His son, Samudragupta (330-375), and grandson, Chandragupta II (375-415) completed the conquest of northern India. However, in the 5th century, India was invaded by a Central Asian people, variously called the *Ephthalites*, *Hephthalites*, *Hunas*, or *White Huns*; and by about 540 AD the Gupta state had collapsed.

The first Moslem people to enter India were Arabs who conquered Sind (the lower Indus Valley) about 712 AD. However, the Gurjara-Prathihara dynasty (740-1036) managed to unite most of northern India and thereby prevent further Moslem conquests until about 1000 AD.

After 1000 AD, Turkish Moslems began raiding northern India, and in time established states there. One of these, the Sultanate of Delhi, ruled much of northern India during the 13th and 14th centuries. That state's power was badly damaged when Tamerlane invaded in 1398-99; however, it endured until the 1500s, when it was conquered by the expanding Mughal Empire.

The Mughal dynasty was founded in 1526 by Babar (1483-1530), who was a descendant of both Tamerlane and Genghis Khan (see chapter 39). Under a series of strong rulers — which included Akbar (reigned 1556-1605), Jahangir (1605-1627), Shah Jehan (1628-1658) and Aurangzeb (1658-1707) — the Mughals conquered most of India. But the Mughal Empire declined severely in the 18th century, and its remaining territory was taken over by the British in the 19th.

Note that the only large empires ruled by native Indians were the Mauryan and Gupta empires, and that these endured for a combined total of less than 400 years. Note also that in its entire history India has never conquered, or even invaded, any sizable territory outside the Indian subcontinent.

Section 7 – Hinduism and caste

The dominant religion of India is Hinduism, which is a polytheistic religion. Since the *Rigveda* describes an early form of Hinduism, and the gods it mentions have Indo-European names, it appears that the religion was brought in by the Aryan conquerors, although elements from the religions of the prior inhabitants were probably added. Unlike Christianity and Islam, Hinduism had no specific individual founder.

Hinduism is an unusually eclectic and tolerant religion. It is a difficult religion to describe concisely, since its numerous sects vary greatly in their beliefs and practices. However, all Hindu sects accept the notion of reincarnatiion, and all subscribe to the notion of *karma*.

The institution of *caste* plays a major role in Hinduism. In Hindu society, each individual is born into a particular caste and cannot leave it. Although castes in India are something like social classes in Europe and America, the caste structure is much more rigid and restrictive. Castes are endogamous (that is, each person must marry within his or her caste), and a person's caste also restricts his choice of occupation. Consequently, there has been far less social mobility in India than in most other civilizations. There are four principal castes: *Brahmans*, or priests; *Ksatriyas*, or warriors; *Vaisyas*, or merchants; and *Sudras*, or workers, and they are divided into numerous sub-castes. Some people, however — including foreign minorities, Moslems, and the "tribals" (see section 9, below) — are outside the caste system.

The caste system in Hinduism originally had a racial basis. The Aryan invaders relegated the darker-skinned people whom they had conquered to the lowest of the four main castes (the Sudras, or workers), while reserving the three higher castes for themselves.[2]

Section 8 – Buddhism and Islam

Buddhism was founded about 528 BC by Gautama Buddha (563-483 BC). Unlike Hinduism, it recognizes no distinctions of caste. Although Buddhism obviously derives from Hinduism, the two religions are very different. The central Buddhist doctrines (*"The Four Noble Truths"*) are:

1) Human life is intrinsically unhappy.

2) The cause of this unhappiness is human selfishness and desire.

3) An individual's selfishness and desire can be brought to an end. (The resulting state, when all desires and cravings have been eliminated, is termed *nirvana*.)

4) The method of escape from selfishness and desire is the *Eightfold Path* — right views; right thought; right speech; right action; right livelihood; right effort; right mindfulness; right meditation.

One might wonder why, if Gautama believed that human life is inherently painful, he did not simply advocate suicide. The answer is that he (like most Indians of his day) believed in the doctrine of reincarnation. According to that doctrine, when the body of a human being (or other animal) dies, his soul does not perish, but rather is reborn in some other body or form.

Buddhism was a small, local religion until about 250 BC, when the emperor Asoka became a convert. Thereafter, he promoted the spread of Buddhism, both within India and into neighboring countries. Buddhism spread south into Ceylon (Sri Lanka) and eastward into Burma, Thailand, and the rest of Southeast Asia; and from there into China, Korea, and Japan. It also spread north into Tibet and Central Asia. After about 500 AD, Buddhism began to decline within India itself at the expense of a resurgent Hinduism, and by 1200 AD it had almost vanished in India. However, it has retained a large following in many other Asian countries.

Islam entered northwest India in the eighth century. However, it did not become a major force in India until the second millennium AD, when a series of Moslem invaders established states in northern India. Today, Moslems make up 30% of the population of the subcontinent, with the majority concentrated in the northwest and northeast. Over the centuries, there has been a great deal of conflict between Hindus and Moslems in India.

Section 9 – Tribal peoples

India includes a fair number of tribes who live in isolated areas and are not part of the caste system. In combination, these groups make up several percent of the total population of India, and therefore have a higher population than some fair-sized countries.[3] Some of the tribes involved consist mostly of persons engaged in plow-based farming; others consist of more primitive farmers using slash-and-burn techniques; some small tribes are still hunter-gatherers. The tribals are probably the descendants of aboriginal groups who were never conquered by the Aryans (and perhaps not by the Dravidian invaders either), although they were forced into less-desirable areas of the country.

Section 10 – Arts and literature

The earliest examples of Indian literature are the *Vedas*. The oldest of these is the *Rigveda*, a collection of hymns composed between 1500 and 1200 BC, although not reduced to writing until much later. The *Upanishads* (composed about 900-500 BC) are prose commentaries on the *Vedas*. Other ancient prose works include the *Brahmanas* and the *Aranyakas*. All of those works are in Sanskrit. The definitive work on Sanskrit grammar was written by Panini, about 400 BC.

The two most famous Indian works of epic poetry are the *Ramayana* (attributed to Valmiki, 3rd century BC) and the *Mahabharata* (begun about 400 BC, completed about 300 AD). Both have remained very popular, down to the present day. The celebrated *Bhagavadgita* is part of the *Mahabharata*. Another major epic poem is the *Bhagavata-Purana*, written about 950 AD. India has also produced a great deal of lyric poetry — some of very high quality — although none as celebrated as the epics mentioned above.

Theatre has been a major art form in India for many centuries. Among the most famous Indian playwrights are Bhasa (3rd century AD), Kalidasa (5th AD), and Bhavabhuti (8th AD). The Sanskrit literary tradition is also rich in narrative fiction.

Among India's famous non-fiction works is the *Arthasastra*, a manual on government written about 300 BC by Kautilya, who was a counselor to Chandragupta Maurya. Because of its ruthless, but practical, advice it has often been compared to Machiavelli's work, *The Prince*.

India has a long tradition of sophisticated music, and many works were written concerning musical theory. Painting was a serious art form in pre-modern India. More impressive though, both in quality and quantity, is Indian sculpture. India also has a long tradition of fine architecture. (The finest Indian architecture, though, was produced by Moslems, and mostly in modern times.[4])

Although this brief summary does not do justice to the Indian achievements in the arts, it should be enough to demonstrate that no other non-European civilization has produced nearly the variety of high-quality literature, music, and art that India has.

Section 11 – Mathematics, science, and invention

The mathematical knowledge of the ancient Greeks was eventually transmitted to India. However, the only important advance made by Hindu mathematicians was the invention of positional notation, which greatly simplifies arithmetic operations. Positional notation was probably invented about 700 AD; however, the first complete description is by Bhaskara, about 1150 AD.

Prior to the modern era, Indians do not appear to have made significant contributions to science; nor did any important inventions come from India.

Section 12 – Evaluation

The Indian subcontinent produced a thriving civilization, and in pre-modern times its culture was incomparably more sophisticated than that of backward regions such as Australia or sub-Saharan Africa.

A closer comparison is between Indian civilization and that of the Islamic world. Each region is characterized by a distinctive religion (Hinduism and Islam, respectively). Both had access to the mathematics and science of the ancient Greeks; however, neither was able to make many additional contributions to those fields, nor did either produce any important inventions. Both produced extensive literatures, and high-quality architecture.

If one compares the achievements of the two civilizations in exploration, law, or military conquests, then Islamic civilization seems superior. However, if one considers the arts — particularly drama, epic poetry, sculpture, and music — then Indian civilization seems more impressive. Overall, one might place the two civilizations on roughly the same level.

Every civilization, of course, is important to its own members; but some civilizations have also had an important impact on the rest of the world. It is fair to ask: How large has been the impact of Indian civilization on the rest of the world? Well, actually, not very large. India has made only one significant contribution to mathematics (positional notation), none to science, and none to technology. Virtually none of the great Indian literature is read in other parts of the world; nor has Indian music had much impact elsewhere. It would seem that the most important Indian contribution to the external world has been Buddhism, a religion that has spread to many other countries and currently is practiced by about 6% of the world's population — a substantial figure, but far less than Islam (~20%) or Christianity (~32%). This is a rather short list of contributions, considering the size of India's population and the number of centuries involved.

Section 13 – Explanation

How can we explain the paucity of India's contribution to world civilization? Three possible explanations are:

1) *The rigid caste system in India resulted in far less social mobility than existed in Europe or China. India thereby wasted a much higher proportion of its human talents than those two regions did.* This explanation seems to be at least partly correct. However, it fails to explain the gap between the Indians' achievements in the arts, and their much lesser achievements in mathematics, science, and technology.

2) *The hot, humid climate prevailing in most of India is very enervating, and greatly reduces the possibility of major achievements.* This idea, too, seems like a reasonable partial explanation, though it does not account for the gap just mentioned.

3) *The average IQ in India is considerably lower than in China or Europe.* If we assume that a very high level of the talents measured by intelligence tests is essential for major breakthroughs in mathematics, science, and invention, but not as crucial for artistic achievements, it would explain why Indian civilization was able to produce so much of the latter, but so little of the former. It seems likely, therefore, that this is the best of the three explanations.

FOOTNOTES – CHAPTER 36

1) This date is very uncertain. I have used the estimate made in section 11-2, which seems consistent with the archaeological data from Southeast Asia, Indonesia, and Australia. See also Map 10-1.

2) *Columbia History of the World* (1981 edition), pp. 99-100.

3) In the 1971 census of the Republic of India, the total tribal population was about 38 million persons. See Cavalli-Sforza, et al. (1994), p. 212.

4) The best known single structure is the Taj Mahal, built in the 17th century at the order of the Mughal emperor Shah Jahan as a memorial to his dead wife, Mumtaz Mahal. Many persons (including this author) consider it to be the most beautiful building ever constructed.

CHAPTER 37

SOUTHEAST ASIA

Section 1 – Introduction

Southeast Asia (SEA) includes both Indonesia and mainland Southeast Asia. Mainland SEA includes Myanmar (formerly called Burma), Thailand, the Malay Peninsula, Laos, Cambodia, and Vietnam.

The inhabitants of Indonesia are descended from farmers who entered from the Philippines about 2500 BC. Those migrants, who belonged to the σ-3 group, displaced the σ-2 who had previously inhabited the archipelago. (See section 22-4 and Map 22-2.)

Mainland SEA is inhabited by a complex mixture of ethnic groups, speaking over 300 separate languages. Among those groups are the:

- _Burmese_. The Burmese are the main ethnic group living in Myanmar. There are over 140 Burmic languages, all related to Tibetan.[1]

- _Karens_. Most Karens live in eastern Burma, near the border with Thailand, or on the Thai side of the border. The 14 Karen languages are related to each other, and more distantly to Burmic and Tibetan.

- _Thai and Laotians_. These two peoples are the dominant groups in Thailand and Laos. Their languages are very closely related.

- _Vietnamese_. Most inhabitants of Vietnam speak Vietnamese or related languages in the Austroasiatic family.

- _Khmers_. The Khmer are the main ethnic group in Cambodia. The Khmer languages are also part of the Austroasiatic language family.

- _Malays_. This is the largest ethnic group in the southern part of the Malay Peninsula. Their language is closely related to the principal language of Indonesia.

- _Miao-Yao speakers_. Scattered through mountainous areas in Vietnam, Laos, and Thailand are tribes speaking languages in the Miao-Yao language family. Other Miao (or Hmong) tribesman live in southern China.

- *Semang*. These are a group of Negrito tribes — strikingly different in appearance from all other inhabitants of mainland SEA — who live in the Malay Peninsula. They speak a group of closely-related languages that belong to the Austroasiatic family.[2] Although they resemble the African Pygmies in appearance, the Semang are not closely related to them; the similarity of appearance is the result of convergent evolution. Many Semang are still hunter-gatherers, although by now most of them also practice some agriculture.
- *Ethnic Chinese and Indians*. These derive from immigrants who entered the region within the past 2500 years.

Can we explain the origin of the other ethnic groups just described, and their relative locations? I think we can, and a suggested explanation will be presented in the next few sections. The explanation is consistent with the *Austric* hypothesis which holds that the Daic, Austroasiatic, Miao-Yao, and Austronesian language families are all branches of a single linguistic super-family called *Austric*.[3] The parent language, *Proto-Austric*, arose in southern China and was probably spoken there about 5000 BC.

Section 2 – Early migrations into mainland SEA

The earliest *HSS* to enter the region (the σ-2) came from India, probably about 55 kya. Somewhat later, perhaps about 45 kya, some of the σ-2 migrated north into southern China. In time, these evolved into the σ-3. (See section 11-4.)

Since neither the σ-2 people nor their ancestors ever lived in a region with cold winters, we would expect that their average intelligence was not much different than that of their African forebears. However, the σ-3 evolved in southern China; and although the coastal areas of southern China have no cold season, parts of the interior do (and, of course, winters there were colder during the Ice Age). The result was that the σ-3 gradually evolved a higher average intelligence than the σ-2 (see Table 17-1). By 5000 BC, many of the σ-3 were farmers (some of them speaking Proto-Austric), while the σ-2 were still hunter-gatherers. Within the last 7000 years there have been several migrations of Austric-speaking σ-3s back into SEA (see Map 37-1), and the σ-3 now provide the bulk of the SEA gene pool.

Section 3 – The Miao-Yao speakers

The first group to branch off from the Proto-Austric speakers were the speakers of Proto-Miao-Yao. About 4500 BC, some of them entered northern SEA.[4] In time, however, they were pushed aside by more aggressive (or larger, or more capable) groups, and today they are confined primarily to scattered areas of hill country in China and northern SEA.

Section 4 – The Austroasiatic speakers

The next to branch off from the Proto-Austric speakers were groups speaking Proto-Austroasiatic. A reasonable guess is that they began entering mainland SEA about 4000 BC. Because of their command of agriculture, they were able to spread rapidly throughout most of mainland SEA, displacing the Paleolithic tribes previously inhabiting the region. The only remaining σ-2 are the Semang, who have managed to survive

Map 37-1
Migrations into Southeast Asia

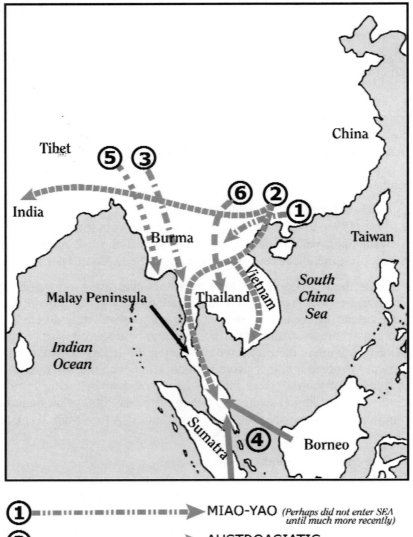

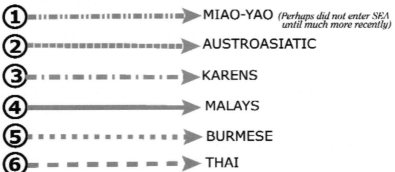

in the jungles of Malaya. (Over time, however, the Semang adopted the language of the intrusive σ-3s.)

By 3000 BC, agricultural peoples speaking Austroasiatic languages were occupying most of SEA, from Vietnam to Burma, and were spilling over into parts of Bengal (in eastern India), as well as the Nicobar Islands in the Indian Ocean.

Section 5 – The Malays

The next to branch off from the Proto-Austric speakers were the Austronesians. The Proto-Austronesians were σ-3 farmers who migrated from southern China to Taiwan about 3500 BC. From there, the Austronesians entered the Philippines, and then Indonesia, in time taking over both archipelagos. About 1000 BC, Austronesians from Sumatra and Borneo migrated into the Malay Peninsula. The modern Malays are their descendants.

Section 6 – The Karens and Burmese

The ancestors of the Karens and the Burmese were both Mongoloid groups who came from Tibet. A reasonable guess is that the Burmese entered Myanmar about 500 BC.[5] Since the Karen languages differ from Tibetan more than the Burmic languages do, it seems probable that the ancestors of the Karens left Tibet considerably before the Burmese did, perhaps about 1500 BC.

Although the Burmese invaders were numerically inferior to the prior inhabitants, by 100 AD they had established a state there. That kingdom (the *Pyu*) was destroyed about 830 AD. However, another Burmese kingdom, *Pagan*, was established by 850, and it lasted until it was destroyed by the Mongols in 1287.

Of course, today's Burmese and Karens are both hybrid groups, descended in part from the Austroasiatic-speaking peoples who had occupied the region before the Karens and Burmese entered.

Section 7 – The Thai and Laotians

The ancestors of today's Thai and Laotians came from southwest China, and entered SEA fairly recently, probably between 600 and 900 AD. The earliest Thai kingdom, Sukhotai, was founded about 1220 AD.

A result of the invasions of the Karens, Burmese, and Thai was to split the Austroasiatic-speaking peoples into two main groups. The first of these is a relatively compact eastern group that includes the Vietnamese and the Cambodians. The second consists of various peoples who are separated from the first group by Thailand and Burma. Some of these (the Munda) live in eastern India; some live in Malaya; and some live in the Nicobar Islands. There are also scattered tribes living in Thailand and Burma who still speak Austroasiatic languages.

Section 8 – Indians and Chinese

Indians have been trading with SEA for over 2000 years, and the cultural impact of India during that time has been immense. One result is that today a large fraction of the population of mainland SEA is Buddhist. In addition, Islam entered the region via India, and is today the dominant religion in Indonesia.

Immigrants from China have also had an important impact on SEA. The Chinese have been very successful commercially, which has often resulted in hostile feelings towards them.

Section 9 – Technological and cultural achievements

Architecture and sculpture of high quality were produced in many parts of SEA. In addition, the region produced fine works in various other arts, including literature, music, dance, and painting. However, neither mainland SEA nor Indonesia made any major contributions to mathematics, science, or technology, nor to secular philosophy, history, or the other social sciences.

Section 10 – Discussion

From the computer simulation described in chapter 17, we would expect the average IQ in the region to be in the high 80s. The limited observational data available is consistent with that expectation (see Table 15-6).

Unlike Southwest Asia and India, the region was never in direct contact with Europe, and in pre-modern times was unaware of the Greek works in mathematics and science. In view of this, the region's lack of achievements in science, mathematics, and technology is what might have been anticipated.

It obviously requires considerable intelligence to produce high-quality works in architecture; however, the level of intelligence needed to do so is not as high as that needed to produce progress in mathematics or science. The achievements that we observe in SEA, India, and the Arab world are all illustrations of this.

FOOTNOTES – CHAPTER 37

1) Ruhlen, Merritt (1991), pp. 331-333.

2) *Encyclopaedia Brittanica* (15th edition, 1986), article on "Semang," volume 10, p. 623. Also see Ruhlen, Merritt (1991), p. 337.

3) The Austric hypothesis has been championed by various prominent linguistic scholars. See Ruhlen (1991), pp. 148-153, plus sources he cites on pp. 156-157.

4) Some scholars believe that the Miao-Yiao did not enter SEA until quite recently. My estimate of an early date of entrance is based on the fact that they now inhabit small, widely-scattered areas that are not contiguous to each other. See Map 4.5 on p. 149 of Ruhlen (1991).

5) *Encyclopaedia Britannica* (15th edition, 1986), p. 372 of article on "Burma" in volume 15.

CHAPTER 38

AUSTRALIA, NEW GUINEA, and the PACIFIC ISLANDS

Section 1 – Introduction

Aside from Australia and New Guinea, the islands which are covered in this chapter fall into three distinct groups (see Map 22-2).

1) *Melanesia* includes the Bismarck archipelago, the Solomon Islands, the Santa Cruz Islands, the New Hebrides (=Vanuatu), New Caledonia, and Fiji. These islands lie in an arc about 2000 miles in length situated north and east of New Guinea. Many of the islands are fair-sized. New Guinea is often considered part of Melanesia, but I shall treat it separately.

2) *Micronesia* consists of several island chains situated north of New Guinea and Melanesia, and east of the Philippines. They include the Caroline Islands, the Marianas, the Gilbert Islands, and the Marshall Islands. Most of the islands are very small, and none are large.

3) *Polynesia* consists of a large number of island groups situated east of Melanesia, including the Society Islands, the Marquesas, and the Tonga, Samoa, and Tuamotu groups. Although New Zealand and the Chatham Islands lie far south of the groups just named, and the Hawaiian Islands are well north of them, it is customary to consider those outliers as part of Polynesia. Aside from the two principal islands of New Zealand, none of the Polynesian islands are large, and many of them are very small. The Fiji group, which is situated near the border of Polynesia and Melanesia, is usually considered to be part of Melanesia, even though it is closer to Tonga (in western Polynesia) than to any islands in Melanesia.

This chapter does not include Japan, the Philippines, or Indonesia; nor does it include the various small islands near the coasts of Asia, North America, or South America. A few small island groups in the eastern Pacific, such as the Galapagos and the Juan Fernandez Islands, are also omitted, as they were not inhabited in pre-modern times.

TABLE 38-1
THE PACIFIC ISLANDS IN 1500 AD

Region	Area (a)	Population (b)	Density (c)	Number of languages
New Guinea	315	1,000	3	800
Melanesia	50	500	5	(d) 500
New Zealand	100	200	2	1
Hawaii	10	250	25	1
Other Polynesia	3	60	25	(e)
Micronesia	2	40	20	(e)
Australia	3,000	250	0.1	500
Tasmania	26	3	0.1	1
Total	**3,500**	**2,300**	**0.66**	**1,800**

(a) in 1000s of square miles
(b) in 1000s
(c) persons/square mile
(d) including Polynesia and Micronesia
(e) included in the total for Melanesia

Section 2 – Population and population density

In early modern times, just before the Europeans entered the region, its overall population density was less than one person per square mile (see Table 38-1), but the population of the region was distributed very unevenly. Although Australia comprises about 85% of the land area of the region, most of the continent is very arid, and it had a population of only about 250,000. In sharp contrast, New Guinea (with less than 11% the area of Australia, but abundant rainfall) had a population of about 1,000,000. Although New Zealand has less than 4% the area of Australia, it had nearly as large a population; and the Hawaiian Islands — despite their comparatively minute area — may also have had a population of about 250,000.

The inhabitants of the region in 1500 AD derived mostly from two strains:

1) σ-4s, who had entered Greater Australia about 50 kya, and

2) Austronesian-speaking σ-3s, who had entered the region from Indonesia about 3.8 kya (= 1800 BC).

Section 3 – Australia

Australia was connected to New Guinea during the Ice Age. However, for the last ten thousand years they have been separated by the Torres Strait, which is about 80 miles wide.

There is considerable uncertainty as to when Australia was first settled. Most estimates fall in the range 40-60 kya, with 50 kya being the most common guess.[1] There may have been more than one wave of settlement during the Ice Age; but prior to the arrival of the Europeans in early modern times, the continent had been nearly isolated from other human groups for thousands of years. All the aboriginal peoples of Australia that were extant in 1500 AD were closely related to each other racially.

It is estimated that there were about 500 languages spoken in Australia at the time the Europeans arrived, of which about 170 are still spoken. While it is generally believed that all the aboriginal languages of Australia fall into a single family, this is not completely certain. At least one linguistic scholar believes that two of the languages, Tiwi and Djingili, may be isolates, unrelated to the other languages or to each other.[2]

The Australian language family has about 15 branches. However, one of those branches, *Pama-Nyungan*, includes about 2/3 of the extant languages; furthermore, all the other branches are confined to a relatively small region in northern Australia. If "Proto-Australian" (the last common ancestor of the existing members of the Australian language family) had been spoken 50,000 years ago, then by now its descendants would have diverged so much that they would not be recognizable as part of a single language family. Considering the rate at which languages change, it seems reasonable to estimate that all extant Australian languages derive from an ancestor that was spoken only about 8 or 10 kya. Wurm (1972) gives reasons for believing that *Proto-Pama-Nyungan* was spoken about 5 kya.[3]

None of the major farm animals was present in pre-modern Australia; and few of the significant crops used elsewhere grow there in the wild.[4] When the Europeans first visited the continent, the Australian aborigines were still hunter-gatherers, practicing neither agriculture nor herding. They did not use metals, nor the bow and arrow, nor did they make pottery. In fact, in 1500 AD the entire continent was still in the Old Stone Age.

Bows and arrows, crop-raising, domesticated pigs, and pottery had all been known in New Guinea for thousands of years. However, none of those useful innovations had spread to Australia, even though there are several inhabited islands in the Torres Strait, and the island-to-island trade routes left no gap between New Guinea and Australia.

On the eve of their discovery by Europeans, the Australian aborigines had not yet been organized into states or chiefdoms, but were still living in small bands.[5] They had no settled villages, nor any substantial buildings; nor had they developed writing. The only thing that they had invented (probably about 10 kya) was the boomerang, which they employed as a weapon.

Section 4 – Tasmania

Tasmania, which has an area of about 26,000 square miles, is an island located about a hundred miles south of Australia. The Bass Strait, which separates Tasmania from Australia, is fairly shallow; and prior to 10 kya, the two regions were connected by land. The climate of Tasmania is similar to that of northern California.

There were about 4000 aborigines living in Tasmania when the Europeans arrived. Racially, they were similar to the Australian aborigines. The prevailing opinion is that their languages were unrelated to the Australian languages.[6]

When the Europeans encountered them, the Tasmanians were even more primitive than the Australian aborigines. Indeed, some books describe them as the most technologically backward group of humans discovered anywhere on the planet. It appears that in the course of the ten millennia that they were separated from the mainland they had not developed any new technologies. Furthermore, they had lost various skills (such as the techniques for making needles and fishhooks) that their ancestors had possessed. That loss of skills was probably a result of the small size of the Tasmanian population.[7]

Section 5 – New Guinea

New Guinea is the second largest island in the world. It is located just south of the equator, and most of the island has a hot, humid climate. Much of the interior is mountainous, with some peaks more than 15,000 feet high.

New Guinea was probably settled at about the same time as Australia, and the aboriginal inhabitants of the two regions were probably closely related racially. However, there is no obvious resemblance between the languages spoken in New Guinea and those spoken in Australia.

Agriculture has been practiced in the New Guinea highlands for many centuries, probably starting as early as 4000 BC. It appears to have arisen independently there, rather than being brought in from the outside. However, the highlanders remained primitive Neolithic farmers, without either writing or metal tools, throughout premodern times, and were still so in the early 20th century. No sizable political structures ever developed in New Guinea.

In 1971, the noted scholar Joseph Greenberg asserted that (aside from some Austronesian languages spoken in the coastal regions) virtually all the languages spoken in New Guinea were members of a single language family which he called *Indo-Pacific*. The family (sometimes called *Papuan*) also includes some languages spoken in Melanesia and some spoken in eastern Indonesia. Although many linguists do not agree completely with Greenberg,[8] it is generally agreed that the great majority of the languages spoken on New Guinea fall into a single language group. Eight languages spoken there have so far defied classification, and may be isolates.[9]

Because of New Guinea's size, terrain, and climate, travel between the different sections has always been quite difficult. If the last common ancestor of the Papuan languages was spoken by the first settlers (40 or 50 kya), then by now the languages would have diverged so greatly that they would no longer be recognizable as part of a single linguistic family. It has therefore been suggested that the Papuan-speakers are descended primarily from more recent immigrants who arrived from Indonesia in several waves between 15 and 5 kya.[10] Austronesian-speaking peoples arrived from Indonesia about 3.8 kya and made settlements along the coast of New Guinea (particularly the north coast), but did not penetrate far inland.

Section 6 – Polynesia

The Polynesians are very different from the natives of Australia and New Guinea in both appearance and language. In both ways, the Polynesians (who derive primarily from σ-3s) more nearly resemble the Indonesians.

The Polynesians were always an agricultural people. In fact (see section 22-4), they originated as part of the Austronesian expansion, which was driven by agriculture. It appears that the ancestors of today's Polynesians migrated eastward from Indonesia, reaching the north coast of New Guinea about 1800 BC. From there, they spread into eastern Melanesia, finally reaching Fiji (which was probably uninhabited before then) about 1300 BC. Tonga and Samoa were reached by 1000 BC. These settlers brought with them a distinctive type of pottery ("Lapita") which originated about 1600 BC and has been found from the Bismarck Islands to Samoa.

The distinctive Polynesian culture developed in the Fiji-Tonga-Samoa area. By the first century AD, the Polynesians, traveling in outrigger canoes, had populated all of Polynesia except for the most distant, isolated islands (Pitcairn's Island, Easter Island, Hawaii, New Zealand, and the Chatham Islands). Easter Island and Hawaii were each colonized about 500 AD, apparently from the Marquesas. (Both of those settlements involved voyages of well over 2000 miles.) New Zealand was reached about 800 AD, probably from the Society Islands or the Cook Islands. The Polynesian feat of settling the widely-separated Pacific islands is the most remarkable maritime achievement of pre-modern times, surpassing the achievements of the ancient Phoenicians, the ancient Greeks, or the Vikings.

Thor Heyerdahl suggested that some of the pre-modern settlers of Polynesia came from South America, and in support of his conjecture he described (a) similarities in the artifacts found in the two regions, (b) striking physical resemblances between some of their inhabitants, and (c) various legends concerning ancient migrations.[11] (Heyerdahl did not assert that the settlers from South America were the only settlers of Polynesia, or the first ones, or that they were the main contributors to the Polynesian gene pool.) According to his hypothesis, the settlers from South America were fair-skinned, and many of them had blond or reddish hair, which certainly sounds as if they were European Caucasoids. It is unclear how such people could have been present in pre-Columbian Peru (but see the discussion in chapter 40).

Heyerdahl's celebrated "Kon-Tiki" expedition in 1947 — in which he and five comrades sailed on a raft from Peru to an island in the Tuamotu Archipelago — demonstrated that such voyages could indeed be made using only the technology existing in coastal Peru fifteen centuries ago. Despite the evidence he presented, his hypothesis has not yet gained general acceptance; but it has not been refuted either.[12]

Prior to the arrival of humans, the Polynesian islands had neither animals nor crops that would be useful for agriculture, making it necessary for the settlers to bring domesticated plants and animals with them. The Polynesians did not develop either writing or the use of metal tools, and they remained a Neolithic people throughout pre-modern times. They did, however, create sizable chiefdoms — some of which included many thousands of people — which were more sophisticated social-political units than any found in Australia or New Guinea.

Section 7 – Easter Island

Although this is one of the smaller Polynesian islands, it is one of the most interesting. This is partly because of the unique writing system which was developed there (see section 25-8), and partly because of the enormous stone statues — some of which are over 30 feet high and weigh 50 tons! — that were present on the island when the first Europeans arrived, in 1722.

How the Easter Islanders had constructed the colossal monolithic statues was a mystery for a long time. However, in his book *Aku-Aku* (1958), Heyerdahl appears to have given a satisfactory explanation of their mode of construction. Regardless of just how the Polynesians erected the statues, it is clear that a few thousand Polynesians living on a small, remote Pacific island managed to erect more noteworthy structures than any built in New Guinea, or in the "secluded zone" of sub-Saharan Africa (see chapter 41), or than any found on the continent of Australia.

Section 8 – Melanesia

Although many of the Melanesian islanders speak languages related to the Polynesian tongues, they do not look like Polynesians, but more closely resemble the New Guinea aborigines. How can this combination be explained?

We know that various islands in western Melanesia were settled prior to 20 kya by σ-4 from New Guinea. Later, between 3 and 4 kya, various Austronesian-speaking σ-3s reached those islands. The language of the intruders might be called *Proto-Oceanic*, since it was ancestral to the languages in the "Oceanic" branch of the Austronesian languages. It seems likely that the intruders set up small settlements on the coasts of those islands, but did not eliminate the aborigines, who were more numerous than they were. However, as the Austronesians were culturally superior, and dominated trade and commerce, languages derived from Proto-Oceanic gradually became spoken by many of the native inhabitants.

Some of the Melanesian islands were uninhabited when the Austronesian-speakers arrived, about 3-4 kya. Since those islands were fairly near ones where σ-4 were already living, after a while σ-4s began migrating to those islands. In most such cases, the σ-4 emigrants eventually learned the Austronesian language spoken in their new homeland; however, as those of σ-4 descent gradually came to outnumber the Austronesians, their genes eventually predominated on most of those islands.

Section 9 – Micronesia

Western Micronesia was settled from Indonesia and the Philippines, starting about 1500 BC. Eastern Micronesia was settled partly from Polynesia and partly from Melanesia, starting about 1000 BC. The population of Micronesia is therefore more heterogeneous than that of Polynesia. The languages spoken in Micronesia are, like those in Polynesia, part of the "Remote Oceanic" branch of Austronesian. DNA tests show that the Melanesians have contributed more to the Micronesian gene pool than they did to the Polynesian gene pool.[13]

Section 10 – Intelligence and accomplishments

Most σ-4 never lived in a cold climate, and therefore the population never developed the high average intelligence typical of those peoples who have. However, since most of Australia has a temperate climate, rather than a tropical one, average IQs there slowly increased.

In contrast, the early σ-3 had spent many thousands of years in southern China. While the coastal areas there have no cold season, in the hilly areas away from the coast the winters were cold. We would therefore expect their modern descendants to have significantly higher average IQs than the σ-4 do. Modern IQ data is consistent with these predictions. The data from Indonesia, SEA, and the Philippines indicate that the mean IQs of those peoples is about 89, whereas the data concerning Australian aborigines indicates mean IQs of about 85 (see Table 15-6).

Other factors being equal, we might therefore expect that the achievements of the predominantly σ-3 groups in the Pacific region would be greater than the achievements of the predominantly σ-4 groups. In fact though, the other factors were not at all equal. The widely-scattered islands of Polynesia contained much fewer resources than the lands inhabited by the σ-4 peoples (Australia, New Guinea, and even Melanesia). Also, the difficulties that the Polynesians faced in transport and communication were enormously greater than those faced by the σ-4. Despite these handicaps, it is clear that the achievements of the Polynesians were more impressive. For example:

1) No political structure in the σ-4 world came close to the sophistication and complexity of the large chiefdoms in Hawaii.

2) No sculpture, architecture, or construction in the σ-4 world came close to that produced on tiny, isolated Easter Island.

3) No technological achievement in the σ-4 world came close to the mastery of navigation demonstrated by the Polynesian mariners.

It seems likely that the extraordinary problems faced by the Polynesians produced a selection pressure for higher intelligence similar to (although probably not as great as) the selection pressure produced in North Asia and Europe by the necessity of coping with cold winters. Of course, the Polynesians lived in their difficult environment for a comparatively short time, so the opportunity for significant changes to evolve was much less.

FOOTNOTES – CHAPTER 38

1) See Table 10-1 and sources cited there. Other important articles discussing the question include:
   (a) Roberts, R. et al. (1990).
   (b) Chappell, J. et al. (1996).
   (c) Roberts, R. et al. (1998).

2) Dixon, R.M.W. (1980), p. 225.

3) Wurm, S.A. (1972), *Languages of Australia and Tasmania*, pp. 160-167.

4) However, species of yams and taro grow wild in northern Australia, and a wild millet grows in eastern Australia. See Diamond, Jared (1999), pp. 309-311.

5) Diamond, Jared (1999), p. 297.

6) However, Wurm (1972), pp. 173-174 lists 11 words (each included in Swadesh's well-known list of 100 basic words for purposes of comparative linguistics) which have cognates in Australian and Tasmanian languages. (The words are: *man, head, mouth, hand, tooth, tongue, foot, smoke, fire, stone,* and *two.*) This suggests that the possibility that the Tasmanian languages are part of the Australian language family should not be ruled out completely.

7) See Diamond, Jared (1999), pp. 312-313.

8) Joseph Greenberg's suggestion that the Tasmanian languages are part of the Indo-Pacific language family has met with a lot of opposition. See:
   (a) Crowley, T. & Robert M.W. Dixon (1981).
   (b) Trask, R.L. (1996), p. 386.

9) Ruhlen, Merritt (1987), p. 377.

10) See Tryon, Darrell T. (1985), pp. 150-151.

11) A brief summary of his reasons can be found on pp. 17-25 of *Kon-Tiki* (Heyerdahl, 1950). A much more detailed and persuasive presentation can be found in *American Indians in the Pacific* (Heyerdahl, 1953).

12) Cavalli-Sforza, L.L. et al. (1994), pp. 366 and 371.

13) Cavalli-Sforza, L.L. et al. (1994). See the tables on pp. 75, 76, and 363.

CHAPTER 39
NORTHERN ASIA

Section 1 – Introduction

By about 30 kya the M-1 or *Mongolids* (the Asian branch of the Mongoloid race) and the M-2 (or *pre-Amerindians*) had separated from each other (see section 12-4). The Mongolids are the most cold-selected branch of the human race and, with the possible exception of the European Caucasoids, the group with the highest average intelligence. The Mongolids eventually split into two main groups, which are genetically very similar to each other.

1) The *Southern Mongolids*. At an early stage, this group migrated southward into northern China. The North Chinese and some closely related peoples are descended from them.

2) The *Northern Mongolids* (hereafter abbreviated *NM*). This group remained in Mongolia and Siberia, although some of them later migrated into other areas.

The *NM* have never been very numerous; however, because of their military prowess they have had a great impact on the peoples dwelling south and west of them. It is probable that an important element in that military prowess was the high average intelligence that the *NM* evolved during their long stay in a region where the winters were so brutally cold.

Section 2 – Hybridization

On various occasions, relatively small groups of *NM* invaded and conquered a region that had a much greater population. Sometimes this resulted in the invaders being absorbed by the natives. An example would be the Huns, a nomadic group who invaded Europe in the 4th century AD, but were eventually absorbed completely.

Sometimes, though, the *NM* succeeded in preserving their cultural identity and imposing their language on the conquered peoples. Even then, however, the resulting hybrid population often more closely resembled the conquered people than the conquerors, who had been far less numerous. An example of this is provided by the inhabitants of Turkey. Genetically, the ethnic Turks are predominantly Caucasoid,[1] although the Altaic language that they speak derives from those of Mongoloid peoples who spread westward within historical times.

Section 3 – The Early Siberians

Archaeological finds show that modern humans began moving into central Siberia as early as 20 kya. By 14 kya, some of them had reached the shore of the Arctic Ocean and had created a settlement there, at Berelekh.[2] (See Map 39-1.)

Because of population pressures, there were repeated migrations of Northern Mongolids into Siberia. As a result of those repeated waves of northward colonization, most of the Siberian aborigines encountered by Europeans in modern times were derived from relatively recent migrations from the *NM* heartland, and they spoke related languages belonging to the Altaic family. However, a few of the Siberian tribes spoke non-Altaic languages; those tribes were probably the descendants of peoples who had migrated from the *NM* heartland much earlier, perhaps more than 9000 years ago.

Section 4 – Japanese and Koreans

It seems likely that at 20 kya both Korea and Japan were inhabited primarily by Southern Mongolids, genetically almost the same as the North Chinese. About 13 kya, though, some Northern Mongolids migrated southeastward from the *NM* heartland into Korea; and from there some migrated into Japan. Although outnumbered by the aborigines, the migrants were able to conquer the two regions and impose their languages on the population. Genetically, however, the populations have remained primarily Southern Mongolid. In the intervening time, their languages have diverged greatly from those spoken in the heartland (and from each other), so much so that modern linguists disagree as to whether there is now any discernible connection.[3] By 12.7 kya, the Japanese had invented pottery, although they had not yet adopted agriculture.

Section 5 – The Eskimo-Aleuts and the Chukchi-Kamchatkans

About 10 or 11 kya, a group whom I will call the *EA* (for Eskimo-Aleut) split off from the *NM* and migrated northeast. By 9 kya, or perhaps somewhat earlier, they had crossed over the Bering Strait and reached western Alaska. By about 6.5 kya, they had divided into two groups: the ancestors of the Eskimos (who then resided on or near the west coast of Alaska), and the ancestors of the Aleuts (who by then had entered the Aleutian Islands).

Starting about 6 kya (4000 BC), there was an eastward expansion of the Eskimos along the Arctic coast of Alaska and Canada, and also along the coasts of some of the islands north of Canada. By 2000 BC, some of them had reached Labrador (on the Atlantic coast of North America), while others had settled some of the coastal regions of Baffin Island and Ellesmere Island, and others had reached and settled in western, eastern, and northern Greenland.[4] The achievement of the Eskimos in mastering this exceedingly harsh environment — the harshest ever mastered by human beings until modern times — is truly remarkable.

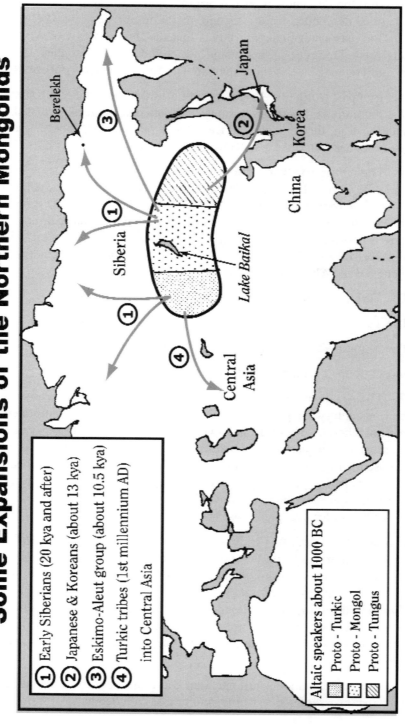

The Eskimos that the Europeans encountered in Greenland and Canada (the *Inuit*) are probably not the descendants of the original wave of Eskimo settlement. Rather, they appear to be descended from a second, much more recent, wave of migration out of Alaska. One reason for believing this is that the Eskimos east of Alaska all speak very closely related tongues. This would not be the case unless they separated from each other quite recently — no more than about 1500 years ago, probably less.[5]

Another group of Northern Mongolids split off from the main group somewhat later than the *EA* did and also migrated northeast. It has been suggested that they reached their present location (the Chukchi and Kamchatka peninsulas), about 2 kya.[6] The five languages they speak comprise a separate language family.

Section 6 – The Altaics: Introduction

The *NM* who were still living in the heartland in 2000 BC might be called the "Early Altaics," since it is probable that one of the languages they spoke was Proto-Altaic, the parent language of all the modern members of the Altaic language family. The Early Altaics were a pastoral people; and many of the Altaics achieved great skill at horseback riding. By 1000 BC, they had divided into three groups, corresponding to the three main branches of the Altaic language family (see Map 39-1):

1) The Turkics, occupying the western portion of the homeland.

2) The Tungus (or Manchu/Tungus), occupying the eastern portion.

3) The Mongols, occupying the central portion.

Each of those groups eventually made major conquests.

Section 7 – The Altaic expansions before the advent of Genghis Khan

By the first century AD, groups speaking Tungus languages had migrated north and northwest into Siberia. These groups eventually conquered most of central Siberia, displacing most of the earlier inhabitants. Their modern descendants include the Evenki. Subsequently, groups speaking Turkic languages migrated northeastward into Siberia, often displacing Tungus speakers. The largest of these Turkic groups were the Yakuts (who, for the most part, are now situated *east* of the Evenki). By 1000 AD, Altaic-speaking peoples occupied most of Siberia.

In the first millennium AD, Turkic peoples also expanded rapidly into Central Asia, displacing or intermarrying with the Indo-European tribes that had previously occupied the region. Some of these Turkic peoples — which may have included the Huns, the Bulgars, the Avars, and the Khazars (the origin of some of these groups is unclear) — invaded Europe during the first millennium AD. However, their numbers were small, and in every case their empires broke up and the invaders were absorbed by the European groups they had conquered. The modern Bulgarians, for example, are a Slavic people.

Other Turkic tribes raided south into Iran and India. For example, about 1000 AD, Mahmud of Ghazni assembled a sizable empire that included parts of Iran, Afghanistan, and India. Thereafter, Turkic tribes were a major force in northern India; and starting about 1200, the Sultanate of Delhi ruled much of that region.

The Seljuks were a Turkic tribe that settled in Central Asia. About 1000 AD, they invaded Southwest Asia. The Seljuks captured Baghdad in 1055, gained control of the Caliphate, and eventually conquered most of Iran and the Fertile Crescent. They invaded Anatolia in the late 11th century; and at the Battle of Manzikert, they crushed a large Byzantine army and gained control of most of Anatolia. However, their empire declined in the 12th century; and in 1243, they were defeated by the Mongols at Kose Dagh, and their empire disintegrated.

Section 8 – The Mongols

The Mongol tribes, with their cavalry skills and ample supply of mounts, had long been considered dangerous warriors, but before the 13th century most of their energies had been spent fighting each other. However, Temujin (1162?-1227) succeeded in uniting those tribes under his leadership; and in 1206 a convocation of tribal chieftains acclaimed him as their leader and gave him the title *Genghis Khan* ("Universal Emperor"). Under his leadership, the Mongol armies invaded northern and western China, conquered all of Central Asia, and raided India, Iran, and Russia.

Genghis was succeeded by his son Ogadai. During his reign (1227-1241) Mongol armies completed the conquest of western and northern China, conquered Russia, and successfully invaded Poland and Hungary. Following the death of Ogadai, the throne was held successively by three of Genghis's grandsons. The third and most important of these was Kubilai Khan (1215-1294).

Kubilai completed the conquest of China in 1279. By then, he had shifted his capital from Karakorum, in Mongolia, to Khanbaligh (modern Beijing) in northern China. Various relatives of his (all, at least nominally, acknowledging his primacy) ruled in Central Asia, in Southwest Asia, and in Russia. Other rulers in Tibet, Korea, and parts of Southeast Asia also recognized his suzerainty. It was the greatest empire the world had ever seen (see Map 39-2).

Given the technology of the time, it was impossible to hold an empire of that size together for long. After Kubilai's death, the various Mongol khanates outside of China stopped paying even nominal fealty to his successors in Khanbaligh. In 1368, the Mongol dynasty in China was overthrown, and the Mongols were expelled from China. Most of the other khanates were destroyed by 1400, but a few lingered on. The last one to fall was the Khanate of the Crimea, in 1783.

Section 9 – Altaic expansions after the Mongols
A) The Ottoman Turks.

Like the Seljuks, the Ottomans began as a Turkic tribe that settled in Central Asia, and then migrated westward. Although the early Turks were a Mongoloid people, the Ottomans probably became a Mongoloid-Caucasoid hybrid while they were still in Central Asia. In the late 13th century, following the dissolution of the Seljuk Empire, the Ottomans were a small tribe residing in northwest Asia Minor. However, under a

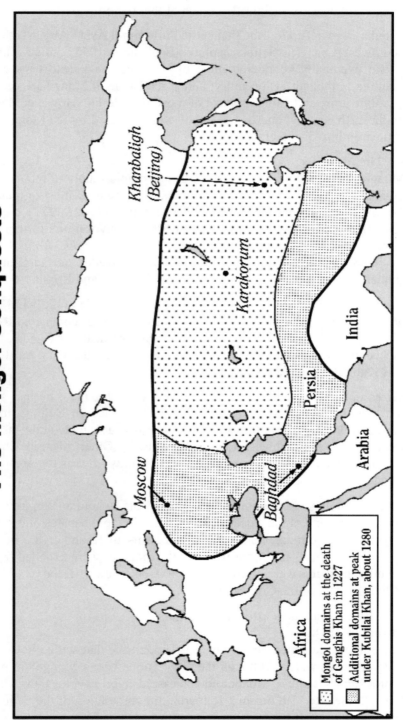

Map 39-2
The Mongol Conquests

Mongol domains at the death of Genghis Khan in 1227
Additional domains at peak under Kubilai Khan, about 1280

Genghis Khan had his capital at Karakorum

Kubilai Khan had his capital at Khanbaligh

succession of very able rulers they expanded rapidly. By 1400, they were the leading power in both Anatolia and the Balkans, and it appeared that they would soon conquer Constantinople. In 1402, though, they were badly defeated by Tamerlane (see next section) at the Battle of Ankara, and for a while it seemed as if the Ottoman state was on the verge of collapse.

However, under Mehmed I and Murad II the Ottomans recovered and resumed their advance. In 1453, using siege artillery, Mehmed II conquered Constantinople and put an end to the Byzantine Empire. Thereafter, the Ottoman Empire grew rapidly, particularly during the reigns of Selim II (1512-1520) and Suleiman I (1520-1566). At its greatest extent, the Ottoman Empire ruled significant parts of three continents:

1) In Europe, the Ottomans ruled almost the entire Balkan Peninsula, from Greece through Hungary and Rumania. They also ruled the Crimea, and nearby parts of southern Russia, including the entire coast of the Black Sea.

2) In North Africa, they ruled Egypt, and the whole Mediterranean coast up to and including Algeria.

3) In Asia, they ruled all of modern Turkey, plus all of the Fertile Crescent, plus Mecca and the entire Red Sea coast of Arabia.

An interesting feature of the Ottoman state was the *devsirme* system (originated in the 1300s), in which the Turks seized young Christian boys in the Balkans, removed them permanently from their families, reared them as Moslems, and raised them as the personal slaves of the Sultan. Gradually, as the system developed, a large number of important government positions were manned by these slaves! Some of these slaves comprised the *Janissary* corps, an army controlled directly by the sultan (and therefore independent of the Turkish nobility). In the hands of a capable sultan, the Janissaries were a most useful tool; however, when there was a weak sultan — and many sultans after Suleiman were weak — the Janissaries became the controlling force, and used the government for their own ends. (The Janissary corps was destroyed in 1826.)

The Ottomans reached their peak under Suleiman I ("Suleiman the Magnificent") who built numerous aqueducts and fortresses; adorned his cities with mosques, bridges, and other public works; and revised and improved the legal system. After 1700, the Ottoman Empire was a declining state; however it lasted until Turkey's defeat in World War I.

B) Tamerlane, and the Mughals.
Tamerlane (1336-1405) was born near Samarkand, in what is now Uzbekistan. He was a commoner of Turkic descent, who started as the leader of a small band of raiders. Through a combination of guile and his extraordinary military skills he rose to power and overthrew the Mongol kingdom (the Khanate of Chagatai) that had been ruling Central Asia. Thereafter, he led his armies in raids against all the nearby countries. These included Iran, India, Turkey, and southern Russia. In the process, he inflicted crushing defeats on the powerful armies of Toktamish (leader of the Khanate of the

Golden Horde) and of Bayazid (leader of the Ottoman Turks), both of whom had recently defeated European armies. Shortly before his death, Tamerlane assembled a large army to attempt the conquest of China; however, he died en route, and his armies turned back.

Tamerlane is notorious for the desolation that his armies left behind. For example, after conquering the city of Isfahan in Persia — a city which had rebelled after surrendering — his soldiers massacred the entire population, and then constructed a pyramid of 70,000 human skulls! Nevertheless, he was an admirer of learning, and greatly beautified his capital, Samarkand.

Although the Mughal dynasty was not founded until early modern times, it is perhaps best to discuss it here. It was founded in 1526 by Babar (1483-1530), who was a descendant of both Tamerlane (on his father's side) and Genghis Khan (on his mother's side). Babar was born in what is now Uzbekistan, and spent many years attempting to conquer Samarkand and establish himself as Tamerlane's successor. Eventually, though, he was decisively defeated by another Uzbek leader, and he turned his attention to Afghanistan and India.

Babar conquered Kabul in 1504 and Kandahar in 1522. Using Afghanistan as a base, he then made several raids into northern India. In 1526, his greatly outnumbered forces routed those of the Sultanate of Delhi at the Battle of Panipat. Three days later, he entered Delhi as a conqueror and the founder of a new dynasty. In the course of his remaining four years, Babar won two more major battles against heavy odds.

Babar's grandson, Akbar, was the greatest of the Mughal emperors. He expanded the Mughal Empire until it included all of northern India, and parts of southern India as well. His successors, Jahangir and Shah Jehan, were also capable rulers.

The last great Mughal ruler was Aurangzeb (1658-1707), an excellent military leader, but a fanatic and intolerant Moslem who persecuted Hindus. By the time he died, the Mughal Empire included all of India except for a small region near the southern tip.

Most of the great Mughal monarchs were cultured men who were admirers of learning and patrons of the arts. The famous *Taj Mahal* — considered by many the most beautiful building ever constructed — was built by Shah Jehan as a mausoleum for his beloved wife.

India was generally prosperous under the rule of the Mughals. However, the Mughal Empire declined rapidly after the death of Aurangzeb. Little was left of it by 1760, but the final end did not come until 1857.

C) The Manchus.
The Manchus were a Tungusic people, living in what is now Manchuria. Tungusic tribes had attacked China on many occasions; and in 1115 AD one of them (the Juchen, or Jurchen) managed to conquer much of northeastern China. Their dynasty lasted until 1234, when it was destroyed by the Mongols.

The founder of the Manchu dynasty was Nurhachi (1559-1626), who started as a chief of one of the Juchen tribes. Nurhachi succeeded in uniting all the Juchen under his rule and in establishing a powerful kingdom with its capital in Mukden. In 1618, noting the weakness of the Ming dynasty, he attacked China.

Nurhachi died in 1626, before the conquest of China was complete. However, his successors continued the attack on China; and in 1644 his grandson, Fu-Lin, conquered Beijing and proclaimed himself emperor of China. However, it was not until 1681 that the Manchus, under Fu-Lin's son K'ang-hsi (PINYIN: Kangxi), secured control of all of China.

K'ang-hsi (reigned 1661-1722) was an exceptionally able ruler — brilliant, energetic, and concerned for the welfare of his kingdom and its people. In addition, he gained control of Taiwan, which no prior Chinese dynasty had done, and he also ruled most of Mongolia and parts of Siberia, as well as dominating Korea and Tibet.

K'ang-hsi was succeeded by his son, and then by his grandson, Ch'ien-lung (reigned 1735-1796). Ch'ien-lung was another outstanding ruler, and during his reign the Chinese Empire — which included Manchuria, Mongolia, Tibet, and parts of Siberia and Central Asia — reached its greatest extent ever.

From Nurhachi to Ch'ien-lung, the Manchu leaders provided 200 consecutive years of high-quality rule. However, the monarchs who came after Ch'ien-lung were not nearly as capable; and faced with the impact of the West, the Chinese Empire declined. The last Manchu ruler was forced to abdicate in 1912.

Long before then, though, most of the Manchus had been assimilated into Chinese culture. This occurred even though the Manchu rulers had been aware of the danger, and had passed various laws designed to prevent assimilation. Today, ethnic Chinese make up most of the population of Manchuria, and the Manchu language is almost extinct.

Section 10 – An assessment of the Altaics

Three thousand years ago, less than 1 percent of the world's population spoke Altaic languages; and even today, less than 1½ percent do. It is therefore not surprising that the Altaics have not made a large contribution to the arts and sciences.

What is surprising is the extent of their military conquests. Most history books agree that the Mongol conquests of the 13th century were astonishing in their magnitude, and that by 1280 Kubilai Khan ruled the largest empire in history. What is rarely mentioned, though, is that the territory ruled or occupied by Altaics in the late 17th century was even larger, and far more populous than Kubilai's realm had ever been (see Map 39-3).

In 1700, the Ottoman, Mughal, and Manchu dynasties were all flourishing, and most of Central Asia and Siberia was also occupied by Altaic-speaking peoples. It is only, perhaps, because China, India, and Turkey are so widely separated from each other that most historians have treated the rise of the Manchu, Mughal, and Ottoman empires

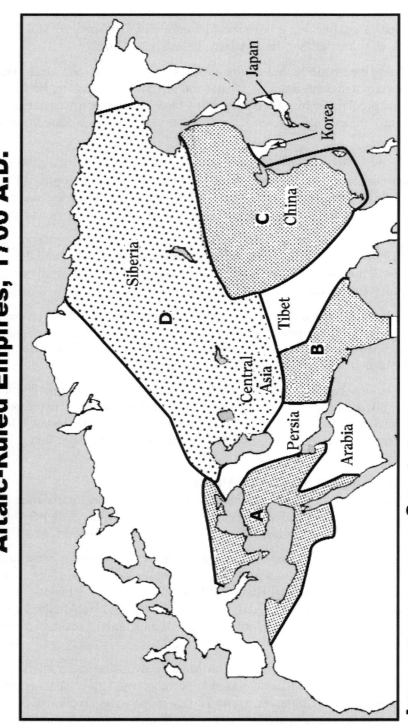

Map 39-3
Altaic-Ruled Empires, 1700 A.D.

A Ottoman Empire
B Mughal Empire
C Manchu Empire
D Regions inhabited primarily by Altaic speakers, but not part of the 3 main empires

as unrelated phenomena, and have not stressed (often, indeed, not even noticed) their common origin.

In 1000 BC, the Altaic-speaking people were illiterate herdsmen inhabiting a sparsely-populated region north of China (see Map 39-1). By 1700 AD, their descendants ruled or occupied territories stretching from Algeria in the west to the shores of the Pacific Ocean in the Far East; and the three large Altaic-ruled empires contained a majority of the world's population!

How can we explain the Altaics astonishing expansion? The Chinese, Indians, Arabs, and Europeans whose lands they had conquered were at least as advanced technologically as the Altaics, and outnumbered them enormously. The simplest explanation is that the average intelligence of the Altaics was very high (which is consistent with the theoretical calculations summarized in Table 17-1) and that this high intelligence manifested itself as a combination of very capable soldiers and extraordinarily able leadership.

FOOTNOTES – CHAPTER 39

1) Cavalli-Sforza, et al. (1994), pp. 242-245 and pp. 224-226.

2) Cavalli-Sforza, et al. (1994), p. 305.

3) Ruhlen, Merritt (1991), pp. 130-131 and (especially) p. 379.

4) Fagan, Brian M. (2001), p. 181. Also see Fiedel, Stuart J. (1992), pp. 148-151.

5) Fiedel, Stuart J. (1992), pp. 147-148, suggests only about 1000 years ago.

6) *Encyclopaedia Britannica* (15th edition, 1986), volume 14, article on "Arctic," p. 20.

CHAPTER 40

THE WESTERN HEMISPHERE

Section 1 – Introduction

The history of the Western Hemisphere has been strongly influenced by its isolation from the rest of the world. Because of that isolation, North and South America were settled much later than the other continents, probably not until well after 20 kya; and even after they were settled, for many millennia the people living there had almost no contact with the rest of the world.

Section 2 – Original settlement

There is widespread agreement that the main route of settlement of the Americas was from northeast Siberia to Alaska (via Beringia); and from Alaska to the rest of North America, and thence to Mesoamerica and South America. (See Map 10-1 and section 12-5.) The main route from northern Alaska to the United States probably involved a narrow opening between the ice caps covering eastern and western Canada. However, it is possible that some settlers migrated southward along the Pacific coast.

In the past, it was often conjectured that the Americas were first settled 30, or 40, or even 50 kya. Such early dates now seem highly unlikely. Not a single site has been found that was clearly inhabited by human beings as much as 20 kya.[1]

Constructing a precise chronology is difficult. A reasonable guess is that the ancestors of the Amerindians entered Beringia about 18 kya. Among the Alaskan sites with the earliest accepted settlement dates are those in the Nenana River Valley (at Walker Road and at the nearby Dry Creek site), both of which were probably inhabited by about 14 kya.[2] However, there is no reason to believe that evidence of the earliest settlements in Alaska has been preserved, and it seems likely that humans reached Alaska two or three thousand years earlier, perhaps about 17 kya.

It is agreed that there are sites in the United States (that is, the "lower 48") that were occupied by 14 kya, but all earlier dates have been hotly contested. Nevertheless, I find the evidence that Meadowcroft Rockshelter in Pennsylvania was settled by 16 kya reasonably convincing,[3] and the site at Cactus Hill, Virginia also seems to be that old.

It seems generally agreed that Fell's Cave (near the southern tip of South America) was settled by humans no later than 12.7 kya. This is consistent with a date of 14.5 kya at Monte Verde, in central Chile.[4] Much earlier dates have been proposed for some South American sites (for example: 20 kya for Pikimachay Cave in Peru, and over 32 kya for Pedra Furada in Brazil), but these are not accepted by most archaeologists. Note that the Paleo-Indians, advancing into uninhabited territory, took only 1000-2000 years to go from the Rio Grande to central Chile.

Various lines of evidence suggest that there were three major waves of migration from Siberia into the New World. According to one theory:[5]

1) Descendants of the first wave (the one just described) occupied most of the New World when the Europeans arrived in 1492, and the languages they spoke all belonged to the Amerind family.

2) The second wave of migrants entered the New World several thousand years after the first, and their descendants spoke languages belonging to the Na-Dene family. Aside from the Navajo and Apache in the western United States, the descendants of this wave were found only in western Canada.

3) The third wave, the ancestors of the Eskimos and Aleuts, probably did not enter Alaska until about 9 kya.

Section 3 – Did all of the early settlers come from Siberia?
There are various indications — none, as yet, conclusive — that some of the early settlers of the New World came from places other than Siberia.

a) In 1996, a skeleton ("Kennewick Man") of what appeared to be a Caucasian male was found along the banks of the Columbia River in the state of Washington. In itself, that would not be surprising; however, when carbon-14 dating indicated that the skeleton was over 9000 years old, it created an uproar. The possibility that whites were present in the Pacific Northwest at such an early date was astonishing, and scientists wished to examine both the site and skeleton more carefully. However, representatives of Indian tribes now living in the region asserted that the skeleton must be one of their ancestors, and should be promptly reburied.[6] The claim appears to be absurd, since there is no evidence that any of the tribes involved inhabited the area 9000 years ago; and in any event, from his appearance Kennewick Man was not an Indian at all. (Some scientists claim that Kennewick Man does not look like a Caucasian either, but more closely resembles a Polynesian or an Ainu.) Nevertheless, the whole matter has been tied up in the courts, thus stymieing any further research.

b) Carbon-14 dating has shown that a woman's skull found near Mexico City is about 13,000 years old, making it the oldest human skull found anywhere in the Western Hemisphere. The skull has an elongated, narrow shape, quite different from those of most American Indians. It appears to be that of a Caucasoid, but the matter is still disputed.[7]

c) Over fifty years ago, Thor Heyerdahl reported that on some Polynesian islands there are old stories of red-haired migrants arriving from the east, and that there are also stories in South America of a red-haired tribe that was defeated in battle and chose to emigrate by sea from the west coast of that continent. The dates involved in the stories seem consistent, and there are various corroborative details as well. To prove that such a voyage was possible, Heyerdahl and five comrades went to South America, constructed a primitive raft (the *Kon-Tiki*) made only of materials available at the supposed time of the emigration, and succeeded in making the 4000-mile voyage involved without using any modern implements. Although few anthropologists accept Heyerdahl's hypothesis, it has never been refuted. If correct, it strongly suggests the presence of a Caucasoid tribe in pre-Columbian Peru. (See section 38-6, and sources cited there.)

d) It has been noticed that the distinctive Clovis spearpoints (see section 5 below) do not resemble any others found in the New World, but that they do resemble Solutrean spearpoints made in parts of Western Europe between 21 and 17 kya. This has led to conjectures that Europeans crossed the Atlantic Ocean during the last ice age by sailing along the southern fringe of the ice shelf that then covered the northern part of the Atlantic Ocean.[8]

e) Many large stone heads built by the Olmec people of Mesoamerica about 1000 BC (see section 7 below) have Negroid features — in particular, they have thick, everted lips — which suggests that some Africans had succeeded in traveling across the Atlantic by then.

It is hard to know what to make of all this. However, whether or not there were ancient migrants from Europe, Japan, Polynesia, or Africa, it is plain that *most* of the ancestors of the American Indians were Mongoloids who had reached the New World via northeast Siberia and Beringia.

Section 4 – Destruction of megafauna

Prior to its settlement by human beings, the Western Hemisphere had been the home of many species of large mammals. However, within a few thousand years of the arrival of humans many of these species (indeed, 32 entire genera) became extinct. Among the animals wiped out were the mammoths, mastodons, giant sloths, lions, saber-toothed tigers, and (most importantly) horses and camels.[9] It seems likely that these animals, which had no previous experience of human beings, were all hunted to extinction in a relatively brief interval after the Paleo-Indians entered their territory. As a result, when farming arose in the Western Hemisphere (a few thousand years later), none of those animals was available for domestication.

Section 5 – The Clovis hypothesis

The Clovis culture is named after a distinctive type of stone spearpoints (the first of which was found in Clovis, New Mexico) that have been found in many ancient sites in the United States and northern Mexico. The earliest Clovis points date to about 13.5 kya.[10] A few decades ago, it was hypothesized that the Clovis points were developed at an early stage in the original settlement of the United States, at a time when much of the continent (and all of Central and South America) was uninhabited, and the New World was a hunter's paradise. According to that hypothesis,[11] the Clovis people spread out rapidly over the United States, and down into Mexico, in the process hunting most of the existing megafauna to extinction. Their descendants on the southern frontier of human settlement rapidly expanded into Central and South America, wiping out the megafauna there too.

At first, it appeared that the Clovis theory fit the data nicely, and it became widely accepted by anthropologists. It now appears, though, that the Clovis theory is probably incorrect, at least in its original form.[12] In order to reach Monte Verde (in central Chile) by 14.5 kya, the first wave of settlers must have entered northern Mexico no later than 15 kya, which is about 1500 years before the earliest Clovis points. It follows that the Clovis points were not developed or used by the settlers on the southern frontier, but rather by people who had remained behind in the United States while the first wave of Paleo-Indians were settling Central and South America.

Section 6 – Development of agriculture in the New World
The rise of agriculture in the New World was held back by a shortage of wild cereals suitable for domestication. Neither wheat, rye, barley, millet, nor rice was present there. The best cereal crop available in the Western Hemisphere was *teosinte*, which required thousands of years of domestication before it evolved into maize (corn). Fortunately, various beans were present in Mesoamerica and South America, as were some useful root crops such as manioc, potatoes, and sweet potatoes.

The lack of large mammals suitable for domestication was also a problem. During the period when agriculture was developing, the Western Hemisphere lacked cattle, horses, pigs, sheep, goats, and camels. Llama and alpaca were present in the Andes, but these are far less useful farm animals than the ones just mentioned.

Signs of incipient agriculture in Mesoamerica can be seen as early as 8000 BC, and in time a few crops were being cultivated there as a supplement to hunting and gathering. However, it was not until about 3000 BC that sedentary agriculture became firmly established there (see section 23-7C).

By 1000 AD, most of Mesoamerica, and large sections of the United States and South America, were practicing sedentary agriculture. However, the American Indians did not use plows before the Europeans arrived, nor had nomadic pastoralism developed in the New World.

Section 7 – Some civilizations of pre-Columbian America
A) *Mesoamerica*. The most populous and advanced kingdoms of the New World arose in Mesoamerica. The earliest civilization in the region was the Olmec (1200-600 BC). Its heartland was on the gulf coast of Mexico, in the vicinity of modern Vera Cruz.

From there, civilization spread southward. The leading city was in the hills, at what is now called Monte Alban, close to the present city of Oaxaca, in Mexico. Monte Alban was founded about 750 BC, and at its peak had a population of 25,000-30,000. It was probably near there, during the first millennium BC, that the first writing in the New World was developed.[13]

About 200 miles west of Vera Cruz is the Valley of Mexico (in which Mexico City is now situated). Starting about 100 BC, the city of Teotihuacán arose there. At its peak, between 450 and 650 AD, it had a population of at least 125,000 (perhaps as high as 200,000), which was far larger than any city in Western Europe. However, some time between 750 and 900 AD, it was sacked by invaders, burned, and abandoned. Its ruins lie about 30 miles northeast of Mexico City.

The Mayan civilization, which included several notable cities, developed in the Yucatán Peninsula and in the lowlands south of it, in Guatamala. It is generally regarded as the most sophisticated of the pre-Columbian civilizations. Its rise to greatness started about 300 AD, and it reached its peak about 750. Classical Mayan civilization collapsed rather quickly about 900 AD; the reason for the collapse is not clear. Although the Mayan people and language still survive, the civilization never regained its former glory.

The Toltecs had their capital at Tula (peak population: 30,000-60,000), in the northern part of the Valley of Mexico. In the 10th century they gained control of most of the Valley, as well as parts of the Mayan domains. However, about 1168 their empire was destroyed by northern invaders.

Among those northern invaders were the Aztecs. The Aztecs built up a large empire with its capital at Tenochtitlán (modern Mexico City), which they founded in 1325. Two centuries later, when the Spaniards arrived, Tenochtitlán was one of the largest cities in the world, with a population of about 200,000. The Aztec Empire was exceptionally militaristic, perhaps because the Aztec religion required large numbers of human sacrifices, most of whom were obtained from conquered peoples.

B) *South America*. In general, the South American civilizations were less advanced than the Mesoamerican ones. One early culture was centered on Tiahuanaco, a city located on the shores of Lake Titicaca (on the boundary of Peru and Bolivia). At its peak, the city had a population of 20,000-40,000. The Tiahuanaco culture arose about 500 BC and lasted to about 1000 AD.

Two cultures that were strongly influenced by the Tiahuanaco were the *Nazca* (on the coastal plain of southern Peru) and the *Mochica* (in northern Peru). Both civilizations flourished between 200 and 700 AD. The Nazca are celebrated for the giant designs — as much as a few hundred feet in size — which they made on the ground. The designs (most commonly of living things, but sometimes of geometric objects) can be readily seen from the air, but are usually too large to be discerned by an observer on the ground.

Starting about 1200 AD, the Chimú built up a sizable empire in Peru, but in 1465 they were conquered by the Incas. The Incan Empire was founded about 1410 AD. It expanded rapidly, and when the Spanish arrived it was the largest state that had ever existed in South America. It extended from northern Ecuador to central Chile, a distance of well over 2000 miles, and had a population of about 5 million. Despite the lack of a written language, the Incan state was well organized and prosperous.

C) <u>North America</u>. No large native state ever developed in the region north of Mexico. However, a series of cultures arose in the midwestern and southeastern regions of the United States. One of these was the Mississippian culture, whose largest city was Cahokia. At its height, around 1200 AD, Cahokia had a population of about 30,000. For reasons that are not known, Cahokia began to decline about 1250, and it was abandoned about 1450. Its ruins include "Monk's Mound" (near East St. Louis), which has a height of about 100 feet and a base of roughly 800 × 1000 feet.

The most celebrated of the southwestern cultures was that of the Anasazi, situated in the "Four Corners" region (near the point where Arizona, New Mexico, Utah, and Colorado meet). Their culture arose about 2000 years ago, and reached its peak between 900 and 1150 AD. At that time, they were building great cliff houses, the largest of which included hundreds of rooms. The largest Anasazi community was at Chaco Canyon in New Mexico, which included a large cliff dwelling (Pueblo Bonito) and over 200 small villages. Colonists from Chaco Canyon set up about seventy smaller colonies, some of them as much as 100 miles away, and linked by a system of roads. The Anasazi culture collapsed about 1150, and the cliff houses were abandoned. However, the Anasazi did not die out; their descendants are the Pueblo Indians, which include the Hopi and Zuni tribes.

The Mesa Verde people were intruders who entered the region about 700 AD and reached their peak about 1250. Mesa Verde is located in Colorado, about 75 miles north of Chaco Canyon. The cliff dwellings there are similar to those constructed by the Anasazi. The site was abandoned about 1300 AD.

The Navajo (who now make up much of the population of the region) are relative newcomers. They came from much further north, and did not enter the Southwest until after 1000 AD.

Section 8 – Collapse of civilizations
Several cultures of the New World underwent a rapid, severe decline, and in some cases we cannot trace this to external conquest. For example, Chaco Canyon, Mesa Verde, and Cahokia were all abandoned; and in none of those cases is the reason known. The decline of the classical Mayan civilization is also striking.

It has been conjectured that in some of these cases, the cities may have exhausted the resources of the region they were in. This suggests that the American Indians did not, in fact, understand that they needed to preserve their environment. The myth of the "noble savage" living in perfect harmony with his environment has its origin in wishful thinking, not history.

Section 9 – Development of writing in the New World
Indians living in Mesoamerica had independently invented writing long before the Europeans arrived. However, none of the South American Indians had done so, nor had any Indians north of Mexico.

Zapotec pictographic writing was invented about 700 BC by Indians living near where the city of Oaxaca now stands. By about 400 AD, the Maya had made improvements, and had created a fully logosyllabic writing system. The Aztecs also had a logosyllabic system, probably derived from the Mayan. Unfortunately, when the Spanish conquered Mesoamerica in the 16th century they destroyed almost all of the Aztec and Mayan writings, and there seems little hope of our now discovering the contents of their literature, or even its extent.

Section 10 – Technological achievements in pre-Columbian America

Metallurgy. North America and Mesoamerica were still in the Stone Age when the Europeans arrived. Although bronze had been made in South America for some time, before the rise of the Incan Empire it was used sparsely. During the expansion of that empire, the use of bronze for tools such as chisels and crowbars had increased rapidly. We can therefore say that the Andean region was making the transition from the Stone Age to the Bronze Age when the Europeans arrived.

Crop raising. Agriculture was widely practiced. The main crop was maize; but potatoes, beans, squash, sweet potatoes, and other crops were also grown. Irrigation was practiced in some regions; however, the use of the plow was unknown.

Animal husbandry. Turkeys and guinea pigs were raised. However, the largest farm animals (and the only ones used as beasts of burden) were the llamas and alpacas, and these were raised only in the Andean region of South America. Neither cattle, horses, donkeys, pigs, sheep, nor goats were known.

Pottery, glass, and fabrics. Pottery was made in various parts of the New World before the Europeans arrived, but glass had not been invented. Cotton had been woven for many centuries, but wool was unknown.

Transportation. Wheeled vehicles were unknown; and since there were no horses, almost all travel was on foot.

Weapons. The bow and arrow had been introduced from Asia about 1500 BC, and their use had become widespread before the Europeans arrived. Swords were unknown, but spears were widely used.

Mathematics and astronomy. Only the Mayas had any achievements in these fields. They independently invented positional notation and a sign for "zero" at about the same time as the Asian Indians did (and therefore well before these were known in Europe or China). The Mayas learned how to predict solar eclipses by following historical cycles, but they had no knowledge of astronomical theory.

Cities. Several of the cities in Mesoamerica had attained populations of 40,000 or more. Two of them, Teotihuacán and Tenochtitlán, had exceeded 100,000 at their peak (probably 200,000 or more). A few cities had been built in North and South America as well, although none were larger than about 40,000.

Construction. Neither the dome nor the arch were known in the Western Hemisphere. However, a few of the New World civilizations had built pyramids, often very large ones. Even more spectacular is Machu Picchu ("The Lost City of the Incas"), which was built at a remote site high in the Andes.

Section 11 – How far behind the Old World was the New World?

Table 40-1 compares developments in the Western Hemisphere with those in the ancient Middle East (defined, for this purpose, as the Fertile Crescent, Anatolia, and Egypt). As the reader can see, most important developments occurred at least 3000 years later in the New World, some of them as much as 7000 years later. The median of the time intervals presented in that table is 5000 years.

Section 12 – Evaluation and explanations

There were several geographic factors that caused the achievements of the Western Hemisphere to be less than those of the Eastern Hemisphere:

1) The Americas were cut off from the Old World by broad oceans, and therefore could not learn from technological developments there. Of course, that worked both ways; however, the peoples of the Western Hemisphere lost more from that isolation, since the Eastern Hemisphere (with its much larger population) had several large civilizations which were making and sharing technological innovations.

2) It is harder for plants, animals, and humans to adapt to a change in latitude (which generally involves a marked change in climate and growing season) than to adapt to a difference in longitude. The geographic separations between the civilizations of the Western Hemisphere were mostly in the north-south direction, whereas the separations between the major Old World civilizations were commonly in the east-west direction. Consequently, it was generally easier for new crops, techniques, and information to spread between the various Old World civilizations than it was for that to occur in the New World.[14]

3) There were fewer useful domesticable plants in the New World than in the Old, and there were *many* fewer domesticable animals.

This trio of handicaps explains why, in 1500, the Western Hemisphere was less advanced than India or the Middle East. The same line of reasoning implies that sub-Saharan Africa should also have been well ahead of the Western Hemisphere. However, the reverse was in fact the case. (See chapter 41 for more details.) This suggests that some additional factor was involved. That factor was the greater average intelligence of the inhabitants of the New World, which resulted from the many millennia that their ancestors had resided in cold regions of northern Asia.

TABLE 40-1

TIME LAGS BETWEEN DEVELOPMENTS IN THE EASTERN AND WESTERN HEMISPHERES

Item	When started in Middle East (a)	When started in Western Hemisphere	Time lag (b)
Sendentary agriculture	10	5	5000
Plowing	6.5	(never)	6500 +
Bronze-working	5.8	(never)	5800 +
Writing	5.4	2.7	2700
Wheeled vehicles	5.6	(never)	5600 +
Cloth	8.5	6.5	2000
Pottery	9	5	4000

(a) Dates in this column and the next are in kya.

(b) In years. The average of the figures in this column is more than 4500 years, but how much more is unclear. The median is 5000 years.

FOOTNOTES – CHAPTER 40

1) (a) Fagan, Brian M. (2001), pp. 152-162.
   (b) Cavalli-Sforza, et al. (1994), pp. 305-306.
   (c) Kelly, Robert L. (1996).
   (d) Fiedel, Stuart J. (1992).

2) Fagan, Brian M. (2001), p. 157.

3) (a) Adovasio, et al. (1990). I have calibrated the radiocarbon dates in that paper, and in the three other papers written by Adovasio that are cited in this chapter.
   (b) Adovasio, et al. (1999).

4) (a) Meltzer, D., et al. (1997).
   (b) Dillehay, Thomas (2000), p. 283. I have calibrated his radiocarbon dates.

5) Cavalli-Sforza, et al. (1994), pp. 307 and 320. Also see Greenberg, Turner & Zegura (1986).

6) A good source for news concerning the dispute has been the Kennewick Man Virtual Interpretive Center at http://www.kennewick-man.com/index.html.

7) The chief scientist involved was geologist Silvia Gonzalez. An account can be found on the internet at http://www.cnn.com/2002/TECH/science/12/03/oldest.skull/index.html.

8) The principal proponent of the theory is Dr. Dennis Stanford of the Smithsonian's Museum of Natural History in Washington, D.C. The arguments against it are summarized in Straus, Lawrence G. (2000).

9) (a) Fiedel, Stuart J. (1992), p. 61.
   (b) Cavalli-Sforza, et al. (1994), p. 306.
   (c) Diamond, Jared (1999), pp. 46-47.
   (d) Adovasio & Page (2002), p. 119.

10) Fiedel, Stuart J. (1999), p. 49 and the chronology on pp. xvi-xvii.

11) Martin, Paul S. (1973).

12) (a) Bonnichsen & Turnmire (1999).
    (b) Dillehay, Thomas (2000).
    (c) Adovasio & Pedler (1997).

13) (a) *Encyclopaedia Britannica*, article on "Pre-Columbian Civilizations," volume 26, p. 5.
    (b) *Historical Atlas of the Ancient World* (1998), p. 1.07.

14) See chapter 10 of *Guns, Germs, & Steel* (1999), by Jared Diamond, for a fuller discussion of this point.

CHAPTER 41
SUB-SAHARAN AFRICA

Section 1 – Peoples of sub-Saharan Africa

Prior to 1500, most of sub-Saharan Africa (or SSA) was inhabited almost exclusively by Negroid peoples. The Negroids include two main sub-races:

1) The *Sanids* (or *Khoisan*), a group which includes the San (often called Bushmen) and the Khoikhoi (often called Hottentots).

2) The *Negrids*, a large group that has two main branches, the Pygmies and the Negroes.

DNA tests show that the Sanids, although Negroids, resemble Caucasoids more than the other Negroids do. The origin of the San is unclear. One suggestion is that they originated in the Red Sea region as an early hybrid between Negroids living there and some Caucasoids who had migrated back into Africa,[1] and that from there the San gradually spread throughout East Africa, and then down into South Africa. The Khoikhoi appear to be a comparatively recent hybrid between the San and Bantu-speaking Negroes. The most striking physical characteristics of the Sanids — the unusually large buttocks of the females, and the extraordinary-looking "Hottentot apron"[2] — probably arose by sexual selection.

Despite the great difference in average height between the Pygmies and the Negroes, DNA tests show that the two groups are closely related. The distinctive physical characteristics of the Pygmies appear to be adaptations to living in the tropical rainforest, which is a hot and extremely humid environment.[3]

Aside from the Sanids and the Pygmies, the Negroids who inhabit sub-Saharan Africa fall into two different, but closely related, groups.[4]

- The larger group, which we might call the *West African Negroes*, includes most Negroes living in West Africa, central Africa, and southern Africa.

- The other group, the *East African Negroes*, also includes a few tribes living in other parts of Africa. They are typically thinner and slightly taller than the West African Negroes. The evidence suggests that this group once had a considerably wider geographic distribution than it does now.

The inhabitants of Ethiopia and Somalia are a special case. DNA tests show that despite their dark skins they are actually Caucasoid-Negroid hybrids, with the Caucasoid contribution to the gene pool being slightly smaller.[5] The mixture is probably a result of the expansion of Neolithic peoples from the Fertile Crescent which started about 6000 BC. (See section 22-3.)

Section 2 – Mean IQs

A major factor in the history of SSA has been the very low average intelligence of its inhabitants. Average IQ scores, as measured by conventional tests, vary from country to country, but are typically around 70 (see Table 15-2). As there is no reason to believe that they have fallen significantly in historical times, it seems likely that average IQs in SSA have been that low for many millennia.

Section 3 – SSA before the Neolithic

During the last ice age, the rainforests in the Congo basin were much less extensive than they are today. Furthermore, for a long stretch after that ice age ended, the Sahara was not nearly as dry as it is today. During the period of maximum wetness, about 7000 BC,[6] much of what is now the Sahara Desert consisted of grasslands, and there were cattle living there. (We know this because cattle are frequently depicted in the rock art drawn by the humans living there at the time.) Progressive desertification of the Sahara took place starting about 3500 BC.

Section 4 – The rise of agriculture in SSA

Cattle herding was being practiced in the Sahara by 6000 BC, and may have been an indigenous development. But farming was unknown in Africa until it was introduced into Egypt from Southwest Asia, about 6000 BC. Agriculture entered Ethiopia a bit later, and from there spread westward across the Sudan, reaching the central portion about 5000 BC. By 3000 BC, yams were being raised in tropical West Africa.

The first crops raised in Egypt were wheat and barley. Wheat was not present in the Sudan, and the main cereal crops there were sorghum and millet.

Agriculture did not spread to central and southern Africa until much later. As late as 1000 BC, those regions were still in the Old Stone Age.[7] Starting about then agriculture was introduced to these regions by Bantu-speaking tribes.

Section 5 – The introduction of metalworking

Copper was being used in parts of the Sahara by 1500 BC. By 600 BC, iron was being smelted by Negro tribes living in Nigeria.[8] It seems probable that knowledge of ironworking had been introduced from the north or brought in from the eastern Sudan. Neither bronze nor iron were known in central or southern Africa at that time.

Section 6 – The expansion of the Negroes

Starting a few thousand years ago, West African Negoes who spoke languages in the Niger-Congo family began migrating eastward and southward out of Nigeria into central and southern Africa.[9] Their main tongue might be called "Proto-Bantu," since all the Bantu languages derive from it (see section 22-5).

As the Negro tribes expanded, they pushed aside the San hunter-gatherers who had previously occupied much of southern and central Africa, and parts of East Africa. By the beginning of modern times, the remaining San were confined to what is now South Africa and Namibia, and their territory was still shrinking. Meanwhile, the Pygmy tribes (who were also hunter-gatherers) were being pushed into smaller and smaller parts of the Congo rainforest. The expanding West African Negroes also pushed into some of the territory previously occupied by East African Negroes.

Section 7 – The West African kingdoms

Camels were not indigenous to Africa. The wild ancestors of the domestic camels used there lived in Arabia. They were introduced into northwest Africa in the first century BC, and their use had become common there by the 4th century AD.[10]

The introduction of the camel revolutionized trade across the western portion of the Sahara. Starting about 500 AD, various aspects of Mediterranean civilization were transmitted to the western portion of the Sudan by Berber peoples such as the Sanhaja and the Tuareg.

The earliest known kingdom in that area was Ghana (which was not located where the modern country of Ghana is, but more nearly where Mali is). Ghana was probably founded in the early 7th century AD, and it lasted until the 11th century, when it was destroyed by the Almoravids.

The Almoravids were a group of Berbers from what is now Mauretania who adopted a very puritanical and militant form of Islam in the early part of the 11th century. By the end of the century, they had swept aside the kingdom of Ghana, and established their rule from the western Sudan to the Mediterranean. They also gained control over the Moslem part of Spain. The empire of the Almoravids collapsed in the 12th century, permitting the expansion of two large states in the western Sudan, Mali and Songhai. Both had been founded about 1000 AD, and both were Islamic states.

Mali reached its apex about 1330, at which time it extended from the Atlantic Ocean to the cities of Timbuktu and Gao on the Niger River. Because of its control of gold fields in West Africa, Mali became very wealthy. One of its kings (Mansu Musa) made a celebrated pilgrimage to Mecca in 1324, impressing the countries he passed through with his enormous wealth. He patronized learning, and by importing Moslem scholars made Timbuktu and Gao centers of Moslem scholarship. Later, Mali declined, and it collapsed about 1550.

Songhai, which was situated a bit east of Mali, was roughly contemporaneous with it, and for a long time the two empires struggled for ascendancy. Indeed, Timbuktu and Gao were often controlled by the Songhai Empire. Songhai collapsed in the 16th century.

Mali and Songhai were empires of considerable size and wealth, and possessed writing. However, it is plain that their writing did not arise from indigenous Negro sources, but was brought in by the Berber tribes to their north.

Section 8 – Cultural and technological achievements in SSA prior to 1500

In late pre-modern times, sub-Saharan Africa consisted of two very different portions, the *exposed zone* and the *secluded zone*. The exposed zone consisted of those regions which were in contact with the Moslem world or the European world. These included:

- West Africa
- Ethiopia and Somalia
- Small, isolated parts of the Indian Ocean coast where Arab traders had set up trading posts or colonies
- Those parts of the Atlantic coast where the Portuguese traders had set up small outposts.

The secluded zone consisted of the rest of SSA — i.e., most of East Africa, and virtually all of central and southern Africa. This was a vast region, roughly twice the size of Europe.

Parts of the exposed zone were reasonably prosperous, but it is hard to think of a single significant contribution to world civilization that was produced by the Negro tribes of that region. (Although there were a few written languages, the writing systems had been brought in from the outside by Moslem tribes or traders.)

The entire secluded zone was a primitive and backward region. This was true not just in 1500, but even in the early 19th century when European explorers first penetrated it. Here are some aspects of that backwardness:

1) Although there were some towns, there were no sizable cities.

2) There were no wheeled vehicles, nor did they use the potter's wheel. In fact, there were no mechanical contrivances with moving parts, such as scissors or hinges.

3) They had not devised means of joining together pieces of wood.

4) There were no coins or money.

5) Although cattle were raised, they were not used as beasts of burden, and there were no draft animals.

6) There was not a single written language in the entire region.

7) As a result, there were no law codes, no philosophical works, and no literature. Nor was there any orally-composed epic poetry, such as the *Iliad*.

8) There was no mathematics other than simple arithmetic.

9) Only primitive methods of construction were known. There were no domes or arches. Little use was made of stone, and there were no temples or large monuments. Nor were there any schools, hospitals, libraries, or paved roads. The most noteworthy example of construction in the secluded zone are the ruins of Great Zimbabwe, which cover over 60 acres (about a tenth of a square mile). However, in comparison with what

we find in other regions — such as Machu Picchu in South America, or the remarkable complex at Angkor Wat in Cambodia, or the large cities and religious buildings found in Mesoamerica — these are third rate, both in size and in quality. Indeed, the giant statues found on Easter Island (a tiny, isolated island in Polynesia) are more impressive than anything found in the entire secluded zone of SSA.

10) The maritime skills of the inhabitants were very limited. They never reached the Cape Verde Islands, just a few hundred miles off the West African coast. More surprisingly, the Africans failed to reach Madagascar (an enormous island, about 1000 miles long, that lies only 250 miles off the East African coast). Madagascar remained uninhabited until it was settled by people coming from Indonesia — more than 3000 miles away, on the other side of the Indian Ocean — about 500 AD.

In addition, the secluded zone was backward in social and political matters. Absolute rule, with no semblance of civil liberties or democracy, was the usual case. Cannibalism was rare, but was practiced by some tribes. Slavery was commonplace everywhere, and masters were free to put their slaves to death.

The paucity of cultural, technological, and political achievements in the secluded zone of SSA is not surprising; rather, it is about what one would expect of a population with a mean IQ of around 70.

Section 9 – Was the paucity of achievements due to geographic handicaps?

In *Guns, Germs, and Steel*, Jared Diamond asserts that the technological backwardness of the peoples of SSA is not due to any deficiencies in their intelligence, but is entirely due to accidental geographic factors. His arguments are ingenious; however (as was shown in section 24-3) the same geographic factors which Dr. Diamond claims favored Eurasia over SSA also favored SSA over Mesoamerica. Hence, if his theory were correct, civilization should have developed earlier, and progressed further, in SSA than in Mesoamerica. (That Mesoamerica was completely isolated from Eurasia in pre-modern times, whereas SSA was only partly isolated, should have made the advantage of SSA even greater.)

However, as we have seen, culture and technology progressed much further in Mesoamerica in pre-modern times than they did in SSA. Some examples of this superiority are:

1) Large cities had developed in Mesoamerica (such as Teotihuacán and Tenochtitlán), but not in SSA. Even the Mayan cities, although not as large as those in Mexico, far surpassed any contemporaneous towns in SSA.

2) There was impressive stone architecture constructed in Mesoamerica, whereas nothing comparable was built in SSA.

3) The Mayan achievements in mathematics and astronomy, and the calendar they constructed, dwarf any intellectual achievements in SSA.

4) A complete system of writing was invented independently in Mesoamerica long

before the region had any contact with the West or the Middle East. Most parts of SSA had no writing system in pre-modern times; and where writing was known it was a technique brought in from the outside, rather than an indigenous invention.

Professor Diamond's hypothesis is therefore convincingly refuted by the empirical data. The greater achievements of Mesoamerican culture (relative to SSA) can be readily explained by the higher average intelligence of the people living there, and are completely consistent with the theories presented in this book.

FOOTNOTES – CHAPTER 41

1) Cavalli-Sforza, L.L., et al. (1994), p. 175.

2) Baker, John (1974), pp. 313-318. (Note figure 56 on p. 315.)

3) Cavalli-Sforza & Cavalli-Sforza (1995), pp. 11-14.

4) See Cavalli-Sforza, L.L., et al. (1994), pp. 167-168. (Note: I have combined the groups described in the last two rows of his table 3.4.1 into the category "West African Negroes" and am using the term "East African Negroes" to designate the groups mentioned in the third row of that table.)

5) Cavalli-Sforza, L.L., et al. (1994), p. 174.

6) Cavalli-Sforza, L.L., et al. (1994), p. 161.

7) *Historical Atlas of the Ancient World* (Barnes & Noble edition, 2000), p. 1.05.

8) (a) *Historical Atlas of the Ancient World* (Barnes & Noble edition, 2000), p. 1.06.
   (b) *DK Atlas of World History* (2001 edition), p. 160.

9) The date that the Bantu expansion began is very uncertain, with some sources saying 2 kya and others as much as 5 kya. From Cavalli-Sforza, L.L., et al. (1994), pp. 162-163 and 165-166, it appears that 3 kya (=1000 BC) is a reasonable guess.

10) McEvedy, Colin (1980), p. 44.

CHAPTER 42

THE LATE MIDDLE AGES IN EUROPE

Section 1 – Recovery from the Dark Ages

By 1000 AD, Western Europe had made a partial recovery from the Dark Ages. There had been an increase in general prosperity and in commerce; an increase in artistic and intellectual achievements; and an improvement in military capabilities compared with neighboring regions. All these trends accelerated during the next five centuries. The *Late Middle Ages* in Europe (i.e., the period from 1000 to 1500 AD) was therefore quite different than the preceding five centuries.

The increase in artistic and intellectual activity was particularly striking after 1300 AD (see section 4). Even before 1300, though, there were several notable philosophers, such as: Peter Abelard, Albertus Magnus, St. Anselm, Thomas Aquinas, and Roger Bacon.

Among the most visible developments of the era were new modes of architecture. Romanesque architecture (a fusion of Roman, Byzantine, and Germanic forms) flourished in the 11th and 12th centuries. In the middle and late 12th century, Gothic architecture (featuring pointed arches, ribbed vaults, flying buttresses, and stained glass) began to replace Romanesque. Most of the great cathedrals of Europe — among which are those at Amiens, Chartres, Cologne, Lincoln, Ulm, and Wells — were begun in the 12th-14th centuries, and most are in the Gothic style, as are Westminster Abbey in London, and Notre Dame de Paris. These magnificent cathedrals are far more impressive than any architectural works of the Arabs or the Chinese from the same period.

By 1100 AD, Western Europe had recovered much of its military strength, and was pushing the Moslems back on several fronts. A well-known example of this was the Crusades (see section 3, below). Another example was the reconquest of the Iberian Peninsula. Christian kingdoms had reconquered more than half of the peninsula from the Moslems by 1150; and all but the small kingdom of Granada by 1275. Furthermore, by that time Sicily, Sardinia, Corsica, and the Balearic Islands were all ruled by Christian Europeans.

The Late Middle Ages also saw several notable voyages of exploration. Perhaps the best known of these are the travels of Marco Polo. Marco, who was a member of an Italian family of merchants, traveled to China in the late 13th century, spent many years there, and became acquainted with Kubilai Khan himself. After he returned to Italy, Marco wrote a celebrated book, *Il milione*, describing his travels and the wealth and splendor of China. The book was an instant success, and stimulated European interest in reaching the Orient. Although his travels were not as extensive as those of Ibn Batuta (see section 34-6) his book had more influence than Batuta's writings.

The Viking voyages of exploration — most of which occurred either before or not long after 1000 AD — were interesting achievements, but had little effect on history. However, the Portuguese exploration of the west coast of Africa, which commenced in 1415, turned out to be very important indeed. (See section 43-4.)

An important impetus to the progress made in Europe during the Late Middle Ages was provided by knowledge and technology brought in from outside (mostly by contact with the Arabs). For example:

1) Much of Greek science, mathematics, and philosophy was unknown in Western Europe during the Dark Ages, but was known to the Arabs. That knowledge was brought to Europe in the Late Middle Ages, partly by Crusaders returning from the Middle East, and partly by contacts in Spain.

2) Positional notation (using "Arabic" numerals) had been invented in India, but was transmitted to Europe by the Arabs. Arab discoveries in alchemy, mathematics, and medicine were also transmitted to Europe during the Late Middle Ages.

3) Both gunpowder and paper had originated in China, but reached Europe in the Late Middle Ages.

4) According to Marco Polo, the Chinese used a "black rock" for fuel, a technology then unknown in Italy. (However, coal may already have been in use in England by then.)

5) Many textbooks say that the Europeans learned of the magnetic compass from China. (However, it seems very possible that the Europeans invented it independently in the 12th century.)

6) Spectacles were invented in Italy about 1280 AD. Once introduced, the use of spectacles spread throughout Europe, and thence into other lands. (However, the Chinese may have invented spectacles independently.)

Section 2 – New weapons

The field in which late medieval advances in technology were most spectacular was weaponry. During the Dark Ages, it had been shown that heavy cavalry (armored knights using lances and swords) could defeat either infantry or light cavalry (see section 33-4). As a result, the group that those armored knights came from, the landed aristocracy, was politically dominant throughout that era.

The first weapon that undercut the dominance of the armored knights was the crossbow. A crossbow, using a hand crank, is almost like a gun. Even someone who lacks great strength can wind it up slowly, aim it, and fire it by releasing the firing lever (the equivalent of pulling a trigger). A good crossbow had a range of over 300 yards, and the metal bolt it fired could pierce chain mail. The only shortcoming of the weapon was that it took a long time to reload.

Effective crossbows seem to have been first developed in Italy about 1000 AD.[1] Naturally, the aristocrats were horrified at the introduction of this new weapon, which so seriously challenged their power. Rules were passed banning the use of crossbows,[2] but they were repeatedly violated. The first recorded use of crossbows in a major battle was by the victorious Normans at the Battle of Hastings (1066 AD), although the decisive factor in that battle was the Norman cavalry. Thereafter, the use of crossbows spread rapidly.

An even more effective weapon was the *longbow*. A longbow is merely a very large bow, about six feet high, made of a single piece of strong wood. The main advantage that the longbow has over the crossbow is its high rate of fire; a skilled longbowman can fire as many as seven arrows a minute.[3] However, to handle a longbow effectively requires both considerable strength and years of practice.

Most European armies never made extensive use of the longbow. An important exception was the English army, which adopted the weapon after observing how effectively the Welsh used it against them. Archery, using longbows, became a favorite sport of English peasants in the 13th century. This paid off for the English at the Battle of Crécy, in 1346. In that battle, the French armored knights were far more numerous than the English ones. However, the English army also included a contingent of 10,000 longbowmen, and those archers mowed down the French knights before they were able to get close to the English army.

A thousand years earlier, the Battle of Adrianople had established the superiority of cavalry over infantry, and thereby set the stage for the Middle Ages. The Battle of Crécy, by demonstrating that cavalry was no longer supreme, undercut the military position of the landed aristocracy, and therefore their political position. It was the beginning of the end of the Middle Ages.

Although the obvious lesson of Crécy (at least in retrospect) was that the era of armored knights was coming to a close, the French failed to learn from their defeat. Ten years later, at the Battle of Poitiers, French knights were again routed by English longbowmen. Amazingly, the French leaders did not learn from that second defeat either. As a result, in 1415, at the Battle of Agincourt, a third French army was cut to ribbons by English longbowmen. ("Those who do not learn from the past are destined to repeat it.") The French lost 6000 soldiers at Agincourt, including 1500 armored knights, while English casualties were negligible.

Today, of course, armies do not use either crossbows or longbows. Both have become completely outmoded by the invention of gunpowder and its use in firearms. Gunpowder — which consists of a mixture of potassium nitrate (often called *saltpeter*), sulfur, and charcoal — was invented in China, perhaps in the 10th century AD. It does not seem to have been used in warfare, though, until considerably later.

Artillery was being used in Europe in the 1320s.[4] Early cannons were rather crude weapons, and sometimes burst when they were fired. To prevent that from occurring, there was a tendency to make the barrels of the guns very thick. As a result, the early artillery pieces were extremely heavy, and had far too little mobility to be used in a battle on an open field.

However, those heavy pieces could be dragged into place and used against an immobile target, such as a medieval castle. Previously, many such castles — if reasonably manned, and well-stocked with provisions — had been almost immune from capture: Armored knights could not get through the castle walls, and usually a siege could not be maintained long enough to starve out the defenders. Large cannons, though, even if firing only one shot an hour, could blast holes in the strongest castle walls within a few days. In the first half of the 14th century, European kings employed artillery to destroy the castles of rebellious feudal vassals. In most European countries, therefore, the introduction of artillery had the effect of strengthening royal power.

Artillery could also be employed against cities protected by city walls. The formidable walls around Constantinople had enabled it to withstand many sieges over the centuries. But in 1453, the Turkish emperor Mehmet II had a set of 68 large cannons constructed and hauled into place around the city. In less than eight weeks, the mighty walls were smashed, and the Ottoman troops stormed in and conquered the city, thereby putting an end to the Byzantine Empire.

By the end of the 15th century, the Europeans had learned how to make cannons with thinner barrels that were still strong enough to withstand the force of the exploding gunpowder. Such cannons were light enough, and therefore mobile enough, to be used on battlefields. From then on, mobile field artillery was a major weapon in European armies.

Eventually, gunsmiths learned how to make a firearm light enough to be carried by a single soldier. Although some primitive handguns were built in the early 15th century, handguns did not become practical battlefield weapons in pre-modern times. Indeed, until about 1800, a handgun was not as effective a weapon (taking into account range, accuracy, and rate of fire) as a longbow in the hands of a skilled archer! Nevertheless, from 1500 on, European military leaders — convinced that the handgun was the weapon of the future, and not realizing how far away that future was — kept equipping their troops with the best available handguns, rather than utilizing the still-superior longbows.

Section 3 – The Crusades

The Crusades were a series of military expeditions launched by Western Europe in the Late Middle Ages with the goal of restoring Christian control of the Holy Land. Its direct cause was a speech that Pope Urban II gave in 1095 at the Council of Clermont. In that speech he denounced the desecration of Christian holy places by Moslems and the mistreatment of Christian pilgrims, and he asked the Christian world to liberate the Holy Land from Moslem rule.

The speech was remarkably effective, and within a year the First Crusade was underway. The largest number of crusaders came from France, but many other Western countries were represented. In 1099 AD, the Crusaders succeeded in conquering Jerusalem and establishing a Christian state in Palestine. However, that was not the end of the matter. Moslem armies counter-attacked, and a long series of Crusades (and Moslem counter-attacks) followed, lasting for about two centuries. In the end, the Moslems reestablished their control of the Holy Land.

Although religious motives were an important factor in the Crusades, they were certainly not the only ones involved. Many crusaders were motivated by a desire for glory, or for power, or for plunder, or simply by boredom and a desire for adventure.

Although the various small kingdoms that the crusaders set up in western Asia were all destroyed within two centuries, the Crusades had an enduring effect (although not the one that Urban II had intended). Those kingdoms were in close contact with Moslems for a period of nearly 200 years, and during that interval they learnt many things from their neighbors.

Among these were positional notation, and the art of papermaking. In the long run, though, the most important of the treasures the crusaders brought back were translations of the ancient Greek classics, including the works of Aristotle, Ptolemy, and Euclid.

Section 4 – The Renaissance

The term *Italian Renaissance* denotes the remarkable flourishing of artistic and intellectual activities that commenced in Italy about 1300 AD and continued for the remainder of the medieval era. The most conspicuous of those activities were:

1) Impressive achievements in the visual arts, generally characterized by much greater realism than had previously been the fashion.

2) A literature characterized by humanism ("a philosophy or attitude that is concerned with human beings, rather than with the abstract problems of theology").

3) A great revival of interest in the literature, philosophy, and art of ancient Greece and Rome (particularly Greece).

These attitudes and activities eventually spread from Italy into other parts of Europe in which the Roman Catholic Church had been dominant in 1300; we often use the term "the Renaissance" to describe the more general movement.

The Renaissance was sparked by the reintroduction of the ancient Greek writings into Italy that had occurred as an unintended consequence of the Crusades. It is plain, though, that another prerequisite for the Renaissance was the growth of cities, trade, and commerce that had commenced before the Crusades started and continued during them.

Although the Renaissance was a continuous process, it can be roughly divided into two portions: an early period (from about 1300 to 1450), and the late Renaissance (from 1450 to about 1550). Among the best known figures in the early Renaissance were:

a) In the visual arts: Giotto, Brunelleschi, Donatello, Fra Angelico, and Masacchio.

b) In literature: Dante, Petrarch, and Boccachio.

Even more impressive is the list of important figures from the late Renaissance. These include:

a) In the visual arts: Botticelli, Bramante, Leonardo da Vinci, Michelangelo, Dürer, Titian, Raphael, and Tintoretto.

b) In literature: Erasmus and Rabelais.

c) In philosophy: Niccolò Machiavelli.

In addition to its artistic and literary accomplishments, the period 1450-1550 also involved important technological advances. However, consideration of those advances will be deferred to the next chapter.

Section 5 – The Roman Catholic/Eastern Orthodox split

After the fall of the Western Roman Empire in 476 AD, Eastern and Western Europe slowly drifted apart, culturally as well as politically. An important aspect of this was that Greek was the dominant language in the Byzantine Empire, whereas Latin was the language of learned discourse in Western Europe.

Prior to the fall of Rome, the Bishop of Rome (the Pope) was acknowledged by most Christians as the leading church official in Europe. However, during the Dark Ages — when Rome was a small city, while Constantinople was the largest and richest city in Europe — Christians living in Eastern Europe tended to pay more attention to the leading church figure there, the Patriarch of Constantinople.

In 1054 AD, a disagreement between the Patriarch and the Pope led to a permanent split in the governing structure of the Christian church in Europe. After the split, most Christians in the Balkans and in Russia became Eastern Orthodox, whereas most Christians in the rest of Europe were Roman Catholic. Although the immediate cause of the break was a minor issue of doctrine, the main differences between the two churches were political, cultural, and linguistic.

Section 6 – International politics in Western Europe

By 1500, national boundaries in Western Europe had begun to resemble modern boundaries.

A) *Spain and Portugal*. In a long series of wars (collectively called the *Reconquista*), Christians had regained control of the Iberian Peninsula from the Moslems. Portugal had attained pretty much its present boundaries by 1275. Spain, though, was still divided in 1468. However, in 1469 Ferdinand and Isabella (the heirs to the thrones of Aragon and Castile, respectively) married, and thereafter — although legally each ruled only his own kingdom — they were in effect joint rulers of a united Spain. In 1492, Spain conquered Granada, the only part of Spain that had still been ruled by Moslems, and Spain assumed almost its present boundaries.

B) *France and Great Britain*. In 1066 AD, William of Normandy ("William the Conqueror") successfully invaded England, thus becoming King of England as well as Duke of Normandy. His immediate successors ruled both territories. In 1152, William's great-grandson, Henry II, married the heir to the throne of Aquitaine (in southwest France), with the result that the King of England also ruled half the territory of France. Naturally, the King of France felt that all that territory rightfully belonged to him, and a long series of wars followed. These continued sporadically for over 300 years, until the English kings lost all their French possessions. By 1500, France had roughly the same boundaries it has today.

In Great Britain, the English gained control of Wales by 1300, and have retained it ever since. However, the Scots (formerly controlled by England) gained their independence at the Battle of Bannockburn (1314), and Scotland remained a separate kingdom for most of the next four centuries.

C) *Scandinavia*. Although Sweden, Norway, and Denmark had roughly their present boundaries by 1300, between 1397 and 1523 they were bound together in the "Union of Kalmar." Iceland, which had been controlled first by Norway, and then by Denmark, was also a part of that union.

D) *Germany and Italy*. Both Italy and Germany were completely fragmented politically in the Late Middle Ages. Nevertheless, the region in which Italian was spoken was much the same as it is now. Most of the small principalities in Germany were included in the "Holy Roman Empire" (the continuation of Charlemagne's empire); however, in many cases the sovereignty of the Emperor was only nominal. The Holy Roman Empire also included most of Austria, and parts of neighboring lands, such as Hungary. Starting in 1452, most of the rulers of the Holy Roman Empire belonged to the House of Habsburg, who by then had made Vienna their capital.

E) *Switzerland*. The Swiss confederation, which had its origins in 1291 AD, had reached nearly its modern size by 1500. Unlike the other countries, it was not a monarchy, but remained a loose confederation.

Section 7 – International politics in Eastern Europe

In 1530, most of Eastern Europe was controlled by three large states: Russia, Poland-Lithuania, and the Ottoman Empire. The political map of Eastern Europe was therefore completely different at the end of the Late Middle Ages than it is today; nor did it bear any resemblance to the situation in Roman times.

One reason for this was that various Slavic tribes had expanded into much of Eastern and Central Europe during the first millennium AD. Another reason was that Mongol armies (led by a grandson of Genghis Khan) overran southern and central

Russia in 1240 AD, and for the next two centuries a Mongol state, the Khanate of the Golden Horde, directly ruled southern Russia.

In central Russia, though, the local states were generally left alone as long as they paid tribute to the Mongols and recognized their sovereignty. In the course of the 15th century one of those states, the Grand Duchy of Moscow, gradually won its independence from Mongol rule. One reason they succeeded was that the Golden Horde had suffered a devastating defeat when Tamerlane invaded southern Russia in 1395. Under Ivan the Great (Ivan III), who ruled from 1462 to 1505, Moscow achieved full independence from the Mongols, and also gained control of northern Russia. Mongol states continued to rule most of southeastern Russia, and the Grand Duchy of Lithuania controlled the Ukraine and western Russia.

Poland had emerged as a state in the 10th century, and the Poles were converted to Christianity in the 10th and 11th centuries. In 1241, the Mongols invaded Poland, crushing all opposing armies and ravaging the country. However, they soon withdrew and did not return.

In the 14th century, the Grand Duchy of Lithuania expanded and became the leading country in Eastern Europe. Late in that century, Lithuania and Poland were joined under a single ruler, and the Lithuanians were converted to Christianity. In 1500, the joint kingdom of Poland and Lithuania controlled most of the Ukraine and western Russia.

The Magyars (a Uralic-speaking people from eastern Russia) invaded the Hungarian plain about 900 AD, and under the Arpad dynasty they soon carved out a large empire in the northern Balkans. Like the Poles, the Magyars were converted to Christianity about 1000 AD. The Mongols invaded Hungary in 1241, at the same time as they invaded Poland, and with similar results: The Hungarian armies were crushed and the country devastated. However, as in Poland, the Mongols withdrew within a few months and did not return.

The Ottoman Turks conquered a large part of the Balkans during the 14th and 15th centuries, and they continued to expand during the 16th. Turkish armies conquered Belgrade in 1521, and five years later they annihilated the Hungarian army at the Battle of Mohacs. Within a few years, most of Hungary was ruled by the Ottomans, with the remaining portion ruled by the Habsburgs.

The invasions of Eastern Europe by Mongols and Turks had a profound effect on the region. Because most of the Balkans were under Turkish rule during that period, the Renaissance had much less effect there than it did in Western Europe; and because Russia was isolated and under Mongol rule for much of the period it missed out on the Renaissance almost entirely. However, Poland, although on the fringes of Western Christendom, remained a part of it, and the Renaissance did affect Poland.

Section 8 – Comparison with China and other civilized regions
In general, the Late Middle Ages was a period of increasing European wealth and

power. By 1450, Europe had regained its former position as the site of the world's leading civilization.

Europe's closest rival was China, which was prosperous and politically united. However, the Europeans had already received most of the crucial technological inventions made by the Chinese and were improving them more rapidly than the Chinese were. Even during the period when China was, on the whole, more advanced than Europe, the Chinese had never come close to the Greek achievements in mathematics and science.

Furthermore, Chinese civilization (perhaps because its prosperity had never depended on foreign trade) was inward-looking. China's one important episode of overseas exploration (the Cheng Ho expeditions described in section 35-10) was brief, and had ended in 1435. In contrast, by 1450 tiny little Portugal was conducting more exploration than the entire Chinese Empire.

In 1500, the Arab world was still almost equal to Europe in science and mathematics. However, the Arabs had never produced much in the way of inventions, and were about to fall far behind the more innovative West. The Arabs were also weak militarily, considerably inferior to both the Europeans and the Altaic-speaking peoples.

India had produced impressive works in art and literature. But it had produced little in the way of inventions and improved technology, and it was weak militarily.

The Altaic peoples were strong militarily, and were still increasing in strength. However, perhaps because of their small population, their artistic and technological achievements were much fewer than those of the West.

Despite Europe's political disunity, and despite the encroachments of the Ottoman Turks, by 1450 Europe's civilization was strong. Its economic and military strength were increasing, it was making rapid progress in intellectual and artistic fields, and it was poised for expansion.

FOOTNOTES – CHAPTER 42

1) *Encyclopaedia Britannica* (15th edition, 1986), article on "Crossbows," volume 3, p. 756.

2) For example, at the Lateran Council of 1139.

3) *Collier's Encyclopedia* (1963), article on "Archery," volume 2, p. 473.

4) *Encyclopaedia Britannica* (15th edition, 1986), article on "Technology of War," volume 29, pp. 546-547.

CHAPTER 43

THE TRANSITION TO MODERN TIMES

Section 1 – Introduction

The last 500 years have seen a series of drastic changes in the human condition, so much so that this period is rightly called "the modern era" as opposed to "pre-modern times." Among the distinctive features of the modern era are:

1) An enormous growth in scientific knowledge.

2) A large number of important inventions, including techniques for mass production and for rapid transportation and communication.

3) A resulting enormous increase in human wealth.

4) A great increase in human life expectancy.

5) A great increase in world population.

6) Extensive migrations of peoples.

7) Large political and social changes.

The transition to modern times occurred first within Europe, although it has since spread to most parts of the globe. The entire set of changes occurred with unprecedented speed. The only other transformation of the human condition that was at all comparable in importance was the transition from the Paleolithic to the Neolithic Era. However, that transition took thousands of years, whereas the transition from pre-modern to modern times in Europe took less than a century. Despite the Renaissance, Europe was still in pre-modern times in 1450, whereas most historians rightly consider 1550 to be part of "early modern times."

There were many changes in Europe during that century, but five of them were particularly important:

a) The development of printing by means of movable type.

b) The development of handguns.

c) The discovery of the Western Hemisphere, and of sea routes to the East.

d) The Protestant Reformation.

e) The rise of science.

Section 2 – The invention of printing

The basic idea behind printing is fairly simple and had been employed for thousands of years in the form of seals and signet rings. However, in ancient times the idea had never been applied to the production of pages of writing. Block printing (i.e., printing a page of writing by first making a woodcut of the entire page) originated centuries earlier in the Far East; indeed, an entire book (the *Diamond Sutra*) was printed in this fashion in China in 868 AD. However, creating the woodcuts needed for block printing involved so much labor that the process never became really important.

In the 11th century, a Chinese inventor named Pi Sheng developed printing by means of movable type. In this process, dies are made of the individual characters; these can then be arranged to form a plate from which an entire page can be printed. One advantage of this system is that, after a page has been printed, the individual dies need not be discarded; instead, they can be rearranged, and used to make plates for other pages. Pi Sheng's idea was very clever; however, the complexity of the Chinese writing system (which lacks an alphabet, but instead employs thousands of different characters) discouraged widespread use of his system in China.

The art of printing did not spread from China to Europe. However, in the 15th century, a German inventor, Johannes Gutenberg, independently invented a method of printing by means of movable type. As all written languages in Europe employed alphabets, the technique caught on very rapidly there.

Since the basic idea of printing is simple, the magnitude of the problems that Gutenberg had to overcome is easy to underestimate. To turn that basic idea into an effective and inexpensive process of mass production Gutenberg needed all of the following:

1) A cheap and reliable method of producing the large numbers of metal dies that were needed.

2) A suitable metal alloy from which the dies could be made.

3) A frame in which to arrange the characters for a page and hold them firmly in place.

4) An oil-based ink suitable for printing.

5) A mechanism — the printing press itself — for repeatedly pressing the plate against successive pieces of paper.

What Gutenberg invented, therefore, was not just a printing press, or the idea of movable type, but rather an entire process of mass production. As the first instance of mass production, this would be noteworthy in itself. What made it so revolutionary, though, was the item that was being mass-produced: *Books*! All that mankind has done, thought, or been is lying as if in magic preservation in the pages of books. They are the permanent repository of all our knowledge. Without books the past is silent, progress hobbled, science impossible.

Gutenberg printed his first edition (the celebrated *Gutenberg Bible*) in 1454. Although Gutenberg never made any money from his invention (and, indeed, wound up losing both his money and his equipment) the world has been enriched beyond measure. Other people were soon building printing presses, and the technique of printing spread rapidly throughout Europe, resulting in a dramatic decrease in the cost of books, and therefore an enormous increase in the number of books produced and sold. Before Gutenberg, it would have taken an army of scribes an entire decade to make 10,000 copies of a book. Consequently, no book had a wide circulation. After Gutenberg, a skilled printer could make 10,000 copies of a book in a single month! The impact on the growth of learning was overwhelming.

Historians often talk about the Stone Age, the Bronze Age, and the Iron Age. In my opinion, it would be appropriate to refer to everything after Gutenberg as the *Knowledge Age*.

Section 3 – Handguns

Gunpowder was invented in China, probably in the 10th century AD, but it was not used in warfare until considerably later. Siege artillery was being used in Western Europe in the early 14th century (for example: at Metz in 1324, and at Cividale [in Italy] in 1331).[1] It became important in the early 1400s, and in 1453 it was the decisive factor in the Turkish conquest of Constantinople. Field artillery (lighter and more mobile than siege artillery) was more difficult to construct. It was being used in the late 1400s, and by about 1550 was an important weapon in European armies, although still used in relatively small numbers.

The advantage of a cannon small enough to be carried by a single soldier was obvious from an early date, and some "hand cannons" were constructed in the late 14th century; however, those early handguns were ineffective. The first handguns that were at all practical were matchlock guns (invented about 1425). The harquebus, introduced about 1450, was an improvement, but it was still not a very effective weapon.

The first effective handgun was the musket, introduced about 1550. Although muskets were heavy, and slow to reload, the bullets they fired could pierce any armor that an opposing soldier might be wearing, and muskets quickly became the dominant infantry weapon. Later, it was realized that providing a musket with a rifled barrel would greatly improve its accuracy; so eventually the rifle replaced the musket as the handgun of choice.

Section 4 – The discovery of the New World and routes to the East

Although Viking expeditions had reached the Western Hemisphere about 1000 AD, that fact was not widely known in Europe, and had no great effect. As a practical matter, Europe's great age of exploration had its starting point in the career of a Portuguese nobleman known to history as "Henry the Navigator" (1394-1460). Henry was governor of Algarve, the southernmost province of Portugal; and he established a base there to promote exploration — in particular, exploration down the west coast of Africa.

Henry did not himself embark on voyages of exploration; but he sponsored and financed many such expeditions. In 1434, a ship sponsored by Henry succeeded in rounding Cape Bojador, the most southerly point reached by the ancient Romans. Seven years later, in 1441, one of Henry's caravels returned with some gold dust and slaves, thereby turning Henry's project into a profitable enterprise.

A Portuguese expedition reached the mouth of the Senegal River in 1445, and another of Henry's ships rounded Cape Verde (the westernmost point in Africa) the following year. By the time Henry died, in 1460, Portuguese expeditions had reached what is now Sierra Leone. In the process, the Portuguese had set up a series of trading posts/naval bases along the coast of West Africa. By then — although the trade in gold and slaves was highly profitable — the Portuguese had formulated a new goal: to find a sea route to India and the Indies by sailing around the southern tip of Africa. (It is not clear what Henry's original motive was; most likely it was simply to reach and form an alliance with the peoples dwelling directly south of the Moroccans with whom Portugal had been fighting.)

It had taken the Portuguese forty years to reach Sierra Leone. It took them only 28 more years to go the rest of the way to the southern tip of the continent. In 1488, Bartolomeu Dias rounded both the Cape of Good Hope and Cape Agulhas (the southernmost point of Africa), and proceeded eastward several hundred miles more. At that point, the crew wished to go no further, and Dias gave the order to return home.

The stage was now set for the voyage to India. However, before that trip was taken, an even more momentous voyage was made by Christopher Columbus (1451-1506), an Italian navigator sailing for Spain. Columbus's expedition left the Canary Islands on September 6, 1492 (it had left Spain on August 3) and reached an island in the Bahamas on October 12th. Columbus arrived back in Spain the following March, and the triumphant explorer was accorded the highest honors.

Most educated Europeans had already known that the Earth was round, and that therefore (at least in principle) one could reach the East by sailing westward from Europe. But Columbus's voyage *proved* that one could sail across the Atlantic, and that the voyage was not unreasonably long. By doing so, he stimulated a wave of travel, exploration, conquest, and colonization that eventually resulted in Europeans taking over the entire Western Hemisphere.

Columbus always believed that he had found a direct sea route to China and the "Spice Islands" (which are part of modern Indonesia). In this, he was mistaken, and his voyage did not enable the Spanish to obtain a share of the trade to those regions.

A practical sea route to the East was established a few years later when Vasco da Gama (1460-1524) led an expedition from Portugal to India (and back again) by sailing around Africa. Da Gama's expedition (1497-1499) first sailed deep into the South Atlantic — remaining out of sight of land for an astonishing 93 days! — then turned east and rounded the Cape of Good Hope, then sailed up the east coast of Africa, and then sailed across the Arabian Sea to Calicut, an important port in southern India. The round-trip voyage took two full years, and only 55 of the 170 men who embarked on the trip returned alive. (It was therefore a far longer and more difficult expedition than Columbus's.)

It took a while for Columbus's contemporaries to realize that Columbus had not reached China and the Indies by sailing west, and that he had therefore not proven that the Earth was round. However, conclusive proof that the Earth was round, and that one could reach the East by sailing westward from Europe, was provided three decades later when an expedition organized by Ferdinand Magellan succeeded in sailing completely around the world.

Magellan's expedition is rightly considered to be the most remarkable achievement in the entire history of seafaring.[2] The expedition started out with five small, leaky ships which left Spain on September 20, 1519. Three years later, on September 8, 1522, the one surviving vessel made it back to Spain. In order to succeed, the expedition had: crossed the Atlantic Ocean; weathered a sub-arctic winter; discovered and navigated the stormy, dangerous Straits of Magellan; sailed all the way across the Pacific Ocean (the main leg of the Pacific trip lasted 98 days, during which time most of the crew died of scurvy); then sailed the whole length of the Indian Ocean; and finally sailed around Africa and back to Europe. Of the 265 men who had set forth, only 18 survived the epic voyage! (Magellan himself was one of those who died on route; the captain who led the last ship back to Spain was Sebastian del Cano.)

Despite the theoretical importance of Magellan's expedition, the route to the East that he discovered was of no practical importance for trade. However, the route that Vasco da Gama discovered turned out to be very practical, and it made Portugal wealthy.

Section 5 – The Protestant Reformation

The Protestant Reformation was a religious movement in Christian Europe, originating as a protest against certain practices and doctrines of the Catholic Church, and resulting in the establishment of various independent Christian sects (the *Protestant* churches). Among the underlying causes of the Reformation were:

• Outside of Italy, many Europeans resented the fact that an institution that had so much power within their own country was controlled primarily by foreigners. (The Papacy was located in Rome, and most Popes were Italians.)

• Lots of Christians resented the worldliness exhibited by many members of the Catholic clergy. (The extraordinary success of the Roman Catholic Church had vested a great deal of power in the clergy; and, notoriously, power corrupts.)

- Differences in religious doctrine. Despite the name, the Reformation was not a reform movement, but a *revolutionary* movement. A reformer believes that the institution he wants to improve is fundamentally good. However, many of the Protestant leaders believed that the doctrines of the Roman Catholic Church did not follow the Holy Scriptures, and some even believed that the Pope was the Antichrist. They therefore did not wish to remove a few corrupt Church officials, but rather to destroy the Catholic Church.[3]

There had been earlier rumblings against the Church, including the movements led by Peter Waldo (late 12th century) in France, by John Wycliffe (1330-1384) in England, and by Jan Hus (1372-1415) in Bohemia. However, the outbreak of the Reformation is usually dated from 1517, when a German monk named Martin Luther posted on the door of a church his celebrated *Ninety-five Theses* denouncing Church venality in general, and the sale of indulgences in particular.

Three years later, Luther broadened his attack by publishing three longer tracts attacking various important doctrines of the Church. Not surprisingly, his writings were proscribed, and at the Diet of Worms, in 1521, he was declared a heretic and an outlaw by the Church. However, by then he had so much support among the German people (including various German princes) that he was able to avoid punishment.

Within a few years, Huldreich Zwingli was presenting similar ideas in Switzerland. Even more important was John Calvin, whose *Institutes of the Christian Religion* — perhaps the most influential of all Protestant works — was published in 1536. By 1541, Calvin had established himself in Geneva ("The Protestant Rome"), where he dominated the city government.

Prior to the Protestant Reformation, there had for centuries been a single religious orthodoxy in Western and Central Europe that dominated the philosophical climate of the entire region. After 1517, the doctrinal disputes between the Protestants and the Catholics (and between the various Protestant sects) encouraged individual Europeans to think for themselves rather than blindly following authority. The doctrinal disputes resulted in a long series of religious wars. In the long run, though, the intellectual ferment caused by the Reformation turned out to be of much greater importance than the wars.

Section 6 – The beginnings of modern science

It seems plain that the rise of science in Europe was set off by the rediscovery of the ancient Greek works. Two of those works — the *Elements* of Euclid, and the *Almagest* of Ptolemy — were particularly important.

Ptolemy's *Almagest,* in addition to summarizing classical Greek knowledge of astronomy, presented a mathematical model of the solar system from which, in principle, the position of any planet — at any date and time of day in the future — could be predicted. Some of the basic assumptions of Ptolemy's model were incorrect (in particular, his assumption that the Sun and the planets revolved about the Earth); but by including a great number of complexities, Ptolemy had been able to obtain a reasonably good fit between his theory and the observations. As the centuries went by, however, the discrepancy between his theory and the observational data steadily increased.

In 1543, Nicolaus Copernicus presented a very different model of the Solar System, the "heliocentric theory," which assumed that the Earth and the planets all revolved about the Sun. This hypothesis, he claimed, resulted in a better fit between theory and observation, and in addition was mathematically simpler than Ptolemy's model. The heliocentric theory, though, was very counter-intuitive, and Copernicus's book, *De Revolutionibus Orbium Coelestium*, set off a strident debate between his supporters and those who adhered to the older, Ptolemaic theory. The debate produced many polemical works, but it also engendered additional astronomical observations and mathematical analysis. By the time the debate was concluded — with the complete triumph of the heliocentric theory — it had led to the discovery of the basic laws of mechanics, and the activities which have led to subsequent scientific progress had been set in motion.

The first major book of modern times in the biological sciences was published in the same year as *De Revolutionibus*. That book was *De Humani Corporis Fabrica* ("On the Structure of the Human Body"), a book on anatomy written (and superbly illustrated) by the Flemish physician, Andreas Vesalius. By providing a far more accurate knowledge of human anatomy than any earlier text, that book was instrumental in the advances in biology that followed.

Section 7 – Why was Europe the site of the earliest transition to modern times?
Although the changes that are characteristic of modern times have by now spread throughout most of the world, it is clear that they began in Europe. It is reasonable to ask why the distinctive features of the modern world first arose in Europe, rather than in China, India, the Arab world, or some other region.

For most regions (the chief exception is China) the answer is obvious: The people living there were not, on average, as intelligent as the inhabitants of Europe; consequently, those regions lacked the supply of exceptionally talented persons necessary to produce the important discoveries and inventions that characterize the modern age and the transition into it.

That, however, does not explain why the transition did not occur first in China, where the mean IQ was just as high as (perhaps even slightly higher than) it was in Europe. Indeed, if in 1350 AD it had been divinely revealed to some intelligent human traveler that the advent of "modern times" was less than two centuries away, and if the general nature of that transition was described to him, he might well have predicted that China would be the site of the coming transition. After all, China was unified, and more prosperous than Europe, and the Chinese had already invented gunpowder, printing, and the compass needle. (Indeed, Marco Polo, who had seen both China and Italy, considered the Chinese to be wealthier, more intelligent, and more advanced than the Europeans.)

However, had a sophisticated *extraterrestrial* voyager visited the Earth in 1350, he might well have made a different prediction. Such an individual might instead have reasoned:

a) The Chinese system of writing (which uses thousands of different characters, rather than an alphabet) is poorly suited for printing. As a result, printing by means of movable type has not had a revolutionary effect in China. Sooner or later, though, the technique of printing with movable type will be introduced to Europe, either by transmission from China or by independent invention. Since every European language uses an alphabet, the introduction of printing with movable type will make books much, *much* cheaper there, and will have a revolutionary effect.

b) The entryway to the development of science lies in the application of mathematical analysis (in particular, geometric theory) to astronomical observations. However, the Chinese have never developed geometric theory (there has been no "Chinese Euclid") and consequently they are far behind Europe — at least 1600 years behind — in scientific matters. Unlike the Chinese, European scholars already know that the Earth is round (the crucial insight that is the starting point of astronomy), and they are rediscovering the ancient Greek works on mathematics and astronomy. Science is therefore much more likely to arise in Europe than in China.

c) China has a small coastline in proportion to its area, and most of the Chinese population lives far inland. The development of seafaring is therefore a minor concern in China. Because China is unified, and self-sufficient economically, the Chinese are relatively uninterested in maritime skills and overseas exploration. Consequently, even if some person comes along in China who is greatly interested in the development of seafaring, and even if that person manages to gain a position of prominence and to get a program of exploration started (which are big "ifs"), the program is unlikely to be followed up. Europe — with it numerous peninsulas and much larger coastline — is inherently far more interested in the development of maritime skills than China is; and overseas exploration is therefore far more likely to arise and flourish in Europe than in China.

d) Europe and China each now have gunpowder and primitive artillery. Because Europe is divided into many small countries, there is a perpetual arms race in progress there. China, however, because of its relative ethnic homogeneity, is frequently under the control of a single government, and is only rarely threatened by outside attackers. The race for improved weaponry is therefore sporadic in China. Consequently, Europe is more likely than China to invent improved firearms, such as handguns and better artillery.

e) These factors greatly outweigh the rather slight Chinese advantage in average intelligence, and the transition to modern times is therefore much more likely to begin in Europe.

Those arguments might not have been totally convincing at the time. But in retrospect, they seem to explain quite adequately why "modern times" originated in Europe, rather than in China.

FOOTNOTES – CHAPTER 43

1) *Encyclopaedia Britannica* (15th edition, 1986), article on "Technology of War," volume 29, p. 547.

2) An excellent book that tells about Magellan's epic voyage is *Conqueror of the Seas: The Story of Magellan*, by Stefan Zweig (1938).

3) See *Columbia History of the World* (1981), chapter 42, especially pp. 518-519.

CHAPTER 44

EUROPEAN EXPLORATION AND COLONIZATION, 1500-1700

Section 1 – The Western Hemisphere: Spanish conquests

Columbus made four voyages to the Western Hemisphere. On the first one (1492-1493) he discovered both Cuba and Hispaniola.[1] On his second voyage (1493-1496) he discovered Puerto Rico and Jamaica. On his third voyage (1498-1500) he reached the north coast of South America; and on his fourth (1502-1504) he reached the coast of Central America.

The first permanent European settlement in the New World was Santo Domingo, on Hispaniola, which was founded in 1496 by Bartolomeo Columbus, Christopher's brother. It soon became the focal point of the Spanish expansion in the New World. By 1515, all four large Caribbean islands had been conquered by the Spanish, and settlements founded on each of them.

The first Spanish settlement on the mainland was made about 1510, in Panama. In 1513, the governor of that province, Vasco Núñez de Balboa, led an expedition across the isthmus and reached the Pacific Ocean. The first permanent Spanish settlement in South America was Santa Marta, in Colombia, in 1525. Cartagena was founded ten years later, and Caracas — now the capital of Venezuela — in 1567.

The Spanish reached North America as early as 1513, when Juan Ponce de Leon landed in Florida; but the first permanent settlement in the United States (St. Augustine, Florida) was not founded until 1565.

Far more important was the conquest of Mexico. The first Spaniard to land there was Francisco Fernández de Cordoba, who reached Yucatán in 1517. In 1518, Juan de Grijalva led another expedition to Yucatán. While there, Grijalva heard of a large and very wealthy empire (the Aztec Empire) to the west, and he therefore explored the coast westward and contacted representatives of the Aztecs before returning to Cuba.

The following year, Hernando Cortés (1485-1547) led a larger expedition, including about 600 men and 17 horses, from Cuba to Mexico. Although the Aztec Empire had a population of about 30,000,000 (which was much larger than that of

Spain) it took Cortés less than a year to reach the Aztec capital, Tenochtitlán, and make the emperor Montezuma his prisoner and puppet. In June 1520 (while Cortés was away) there was a revolt, and the Spanish forces were driven out of Tenochtitlán. But Cortés returned the next year with more troops, and by August he had conquered the city permanently, and overthrown the Aztec Empire, although he still had to spend some time securing his control of outlying areas. In 1535, the Spanish crown consolidated their holdings in Mexico, Central America, and the Caribbean into the *Viceroyalty of New Spain*.

In 1540-1542, another Spanish explorer (Coronado) explored northern Mexico and the southwestern United States. It was not until the 17th and 18th centuries, though, that those territories were actually incorporated into New Spain, and even then, Spanish settlement of those regions was sparse.

The other large native state in the Western Hemisphere was the Incan Empire, centered in Peru. The Aztecs had not known of the Incan Empire; but in 1522 a Spanish explorer, Pascual de Andagoya, sailed down the Pacific coast from Panama, learned of the existence of a large, wealthy empire to the south, and reached its outskirts.

Not long thereafter, another Spanish adventurer, Francisco Pizarro (who had heard of Andagoya's voyage, and was inspired by Cortés' recent conquest of Mexico) decided to conquer the Incan Empire. Pizarro's first two expeditions (1524-25 and 1526-28) were not successful, so he returned to Spain and obtained funding for a larger one. That expedition left Panama in 1531, when Pizarro was 56 years old and far past his physical prime.

Pizarro's band included fewer than two hundred men; but in 1532 he led his small force up into the Andes in an attempt to conquer an empire with a population of about 6,000,000. On November 16, 1532, at Cajamarca, Pizarro's small band attacked an Incan army of about 80,000 and completely routed it, without the loss of a single Spanish soldier! In addition, Pizarro succeeded in capturing the Incan ruler, the Emperor Atahualpa. That one battle decided the war, and the following year, Pizarro's forces entered the Incan capital at Cuzco without a fight.

In 1537, serious fighting began between various Spanish factions in Peru. In the course of that fighting Pizarro was assassinated. Nevertheless, the Spaniards were able to suppress an Indian revolt and retain control of the region. In addition, Spanish forces from Peru were able to conquer much of Chile. Eventually, the Spanish kings organized Peru and Chile into a direct colony of the Spanish crown, the *Viceroyalty of Peru*, and organized Venezuela, Colombia, and Ecuador into the *Viceroyalty of New Grenada*.

Spanish colonization of the Rio de la Plata region began in 1535. Buenos Aires was founded in 1536,[2] and Asunción (now the capital of Paraguay) in 1537. The exceptionally rich silver mines at Potosí, in what is now Bolivia, were opened in 1545. In time, most of what is now Argentina, Uruguay, Paraguay, and Bolivia were combined by the Spanish crown into the *Viceroyalty of la Plata*.

In time, most of the natives in all of these areas were converted to Catholicism, and many of them learned Spanish. With the exception of some small portions that were taken from them by other European powers, the Spanish crown continued to rule these regions until the early 19th century.

Section 2 – Technological factors that aided in those conquests
The conquests described in the previous section are among the most remarkable in human history, both for their extent (the territories conquered had an area of over five million square miles) and for their speed (the most important conquests were completed in a period of less than 60 years). For the Spanish to achieve such far-ranging conquests so quickly, and despite a numerical disadvantage, cries out for an explanation. Part of that explanation is obvious: the Spanish (and other Europeans) had enormous technological advantages over the American Indians. The most obvious of these advantages involved weaponry; but the Europeans' maritime skills and their use of writing were also significant factors.

The Indians did have boats, but nothing like the ocean-going vessels that the Spanish possessed. The Spanish could move their troops and supplies relatively quickly, and were able to attack any target near a coast at a time of their choosing. The Indians could not attack Spanish settlements on islands (except with local forces), and they could not possibly attack Spain itself.

Furthermore, except for some groups in Mesoamerica (such as the Aztecs and the Mayas), the American Indians did not have writing; and even those who did have writing seem to have made little use of written communications for military purposes. Nor did they have the experience in mapmaking that the Spanish had.

The Spanish had been using cannons and handguns prior to their discovery of the New World, whereas the American Indians had no knowledge of explosives. Still, the use of firearms was not the major factor in the Spanish conquests. Most of the Indian casualties on the battlefield were caused by simpler weapons such as swords and spears. The crucial differences in weaponry arose from the fact that the Indians were still in the Stone Age. They had no swords, and their best spears were tipped with natural glass, which was useless against the Spanish armor. In contrast, Spanish swords easily cut through any cloth or leather armor that the Indians had.

Also important was the Spanish use of cavalry. There were no horses in the New World in 1492, nor any comparable animals that could be used in warfare. As a result, the Indians had no cavalry, nor did they know how to fight against it.

Section 3 – The role that diseases played in those conquests
In addition to the advantages in technology that the Spanish (and other Europeans) possessed, there was another factor that was important in the European conquest of the Western Hemisphere — contagious diseases. Historians agree that diseases brought in by the Europeans (which included smallpox, measles, malaria, yellow fever, influenza, and typhus fever) killed far more Indians than European weapons. These diseases did

not exist in the New World before 1492, and the American aborigines had no natural immunity to them.[3]

Smallpox. This was by far the greatest killer. Smallpox had been a major killer in the Old World for many centuries. Even among Europeans (who had evolved some natural resistance to it) the disease had a high death rate, perhaps about 20%. In the Western Hemisphere — where the disease had been unknown — the fatality rate was much higher: probably 50% originally, maybe more.

Measles. In 20th-century America, this was widely considered to be a minor disease of childhood. However, among populations who have not evolved any natural resistance to it, measles has a high fatality rate.

Influenza. Here too, the American aborigines had no natural immunity to the disease. Promptly after Columbus's second voyage reached the West Indies, a virulent epidemic (most likely a form of swine flu) broke out. Many Spaniards died in the epidemic; but the loss of life was far greater among the Indians.

Malaria. Malaria was one of the first diseases introduced by the Spanish; an epidemic was recorded as early as 1493. The microorganism that causes malaria is transmitted only by certain types of mosquitoes, which thrive in hot, humid climates. This disease had long been widespread in tropical parts of the Old World, and various genes that conferred partial resistance to the disease were present in the populations of those regions.

The impact of malaria on the Amerindians is not as well documented as that of smallpox. However, it is suggestive that the importation of African slaves was greatest in those parts of the New World (such as the West Indies) that had hot, humid climates. In such regions, the Europeans could not use native Americans as plantation slaves since they had no resistance to malaria. Instead, they imported slaves from Africa, where the inhabitants had evolved some natural resistance to the disease. (It seems possible, therefore, that if it had not been for malaria the transatlantic slave trade might never have developed.)

Yellow fever. This viral disease (which, like malaria, is spread by mosquitoes) probably originated in West Africa. It reached the New World in the early 1500s, and became a major health threat in hot, humid regions.

Although there are instances of European colonizers making deliberate efforts to spread smallpox among Indian groups, for the most part, the diseases were introduced unintentionally. Sometimes, indeed, smallpox was introduced into a region even before any European colonists or explorers entered the territory. (This could occur either by casual contact with traders or by contact with neighboring Indian tribes.)

Although no accurate figures are available, it seems likely that in many parts of the New World the introduction of European diseases reduced the population to less than 25% of its previous level, and in some cases to less than 10%.

Section 4 – Why didn't Europeans die from diseases indigenous to America?

In the interval 1500-1700, enormous numbers of American Indians died from diseases that had been common in the Old World prior to Columbus. In striking contrast, relatively few Europeans died from diseases that had previously been prevalent only in the New World. How can this difference be explained?

The primary reason seems to be that there were very few epidemic diseases in the New World before 1492. (Tuberculosis and syphilis are possible exceptions.) However, that begs the question: Why did such diseases occur only in the Old World prior to 1492?

It is easy to see why insect-borne diseases such as malaria and yellow fever did not accompany the original settlers of the New World. In order to reach the Western Hemisphere, the ancestors of those settlers had traversed Siberia, Beringia, and Alaska — all of which were cold, dry regions in which the mosquitoes that transmitted the disease could not live.

For diseases such as smallpox, measles, and swine flu, a likely explanation is that those diseases had originated as mutations from diseases that had previously afflicted farm animals, such as cattle and pigs. For example, it appears that smallpox originated as a mutation from cowpox, a disease of cattle that is not very dangerous to humans.[4] However, none of those farm animals were present in the New World; nor did the American Indians have any other large farm animals that could be a source of such diseases.

Note that, prior to 1492, the Western Hemisphere was probably a much healthier region to live in than the Old World. Paradoxically, however, their former healthiness was a cause of the disasters that befell the American Indians when they encountered the Europeans.

Section 5 – The Western Hemisphere: conquests by other European countries

A) **Portugal**. Other than Spain, the only European country that gained sizable holdings in South America was Portugal. In 1494, Spain and Portugal signed the Treaty of Tordesillas, which provided that a line 370 leagues (about 1100 miles) west of the Cape Verde Islands would mark the boundary between their overseas empires. Portugal thereby retained the right to settle Africa, and points east; while Spain thereby obtained exclusive rights to the West Indies and to all other parts of the New World that the Spanish knew of at the time. However, when Brazil was discovered in 1500 (by Pedro Cabral, a Portuguese), it turned out that the eastern portion of it was on the Portuguese side of the line.[5]

Brazil lacked the precious metals that made the Spanish conquests in the New World so profitable. Furthermore, much of the country was hot and humid, and the Portuguese made no significant attempt to settle it until 1530. Unlike the Spanish in Mexico and Peru, the Portuguese did not have to defeat any large native armies in order to gain possession of Brazil. There were no sizable native states there, and the aborigines were technologically backward, and relatively few in number.

At first, the Portuguese colonists remained in the western portion of Brazil (on their side of the treaty line). Gradually, though, they pushed inland, eventually taking over a great deal of territory on the Spanish side of the line.

In time, a sizable sugar industry arose in Brazil, with the large plantation owners controlling much of the colony's wealth. Many of the Brazilian aborigines died from European diseases; others fled westward to avoid the attempts of the white settlers to enslave them. Although there were some slave-raiding expeditions into the interior, for the most part, the colonists' desire for cheap labor (particularly for the large sugar plantations) was satisfied by the importation of Negro slaves from Africa. Overall, far more Negro slaves were imported into Brazil than into North America.[6]

B) France. Although various French expeditions explored parts of the New World in the 1500s, it was not until the 1600s that they established colonies.

Canada. The first French colony in the Western Hemisphere was Port Royal, in Nova Scotia, founded in 1605. Quebec was founded in 1608; Montreal in 1642. As a result of the French and Indian War (1755-1763), France lost its Canadian colonies to England.

Fewer than 10,000 Frenchmen immigrated to Canada during the long period of French rule, and for most of that time fur trapping was the major industry of the colony. The native population was sparse, and conflict between Europeans and Indians was less than in the Spanish, Portuguese, or English colonies.

The Mississippi Valley. Starting in 1673, various Frenchmen (including Jacques Marquette, Louis Joliet, and Robert de la Salle) explored the region. In 1699, colonies were founded at Biloxi and in Louisiana. Mobile was founded in 1710, and New Orleans in 1718; but French settlement in most of the Mississippi Valley was sparse.

The West Indies. The earliest French colony was St. Christopher, founded in 1625. Colonies were founded in Guadeloupe and Martinique in 1635, and by 1664 the French had settled several other Caribbean islands.

Although Spain claimed title to all of Hispaniola, Frenchmen settled on the eastern portion of the island during the 1600s. In 1697, Spain recognized French sovereignty over the eastern third of the island (now Haiti), and in the course of the next century, it became an exceptionally profitable French colony.

The aborigines who inhabited the West Indies generally fared even worse than those on the North and South American continents. Because the aborigines had been decimated, the French colonists imported large numbers of Negro slaves in order to satisfy their desire for cheap labor. The descendants of those slaves now comprise much of the population of those islands.

C) England. The first permanent English settlement in the New World was at Jamestown, in Virginia, which was founded in 1607. Their first settlement in New England was Plymouth, founded in 1620 by the Pilgrims arriving on the *Mayflower*. By

1636, English colonies had also been established in Maine, New Hampshire, Connecticut, and Rhode Island; and by 1685, there were English settlements in Maryland, New York, the Carolinas, and Pennsylvania as well.

There were no precious metals in New England, and the English colonists who settled there were primarily Protestant dissidents who sought religious freedom. From the beginning, therefore, they tended to resist royal attempts to set policy in their colonies.

Although the English settlers in the United States were not interested in enslaving the Indians, or in plundering their gold, they were encroaching on land that had formerly belonged to the Indians. This repeatedly led to conflicts, and the English, being better armed, normally got the best of the fighting.[7]

Starting in 1619, Negro slaves were introduced, particularly in the Southern colonies, but their numbers were much smaller than in the West Indies. Although there were some localities where blacks outnumbered whites, at no time did the slaves form a majority of the total population of the North American colonies.

Starting in 1625, the English also established various colonies in the West Indies. These colonies imported many more black slaves; and as a consequence, many of them have majority black populations today.

Section 6 – Sub-Saharan Africa
The Europeans made various coastal settlements in this region in early modern times, but — in strong contrast to their activities in the Western Hemisphere — rarely penetrated inland. The primary reason for the difference was probably the factor of disease. The major epidemic diseases of Europe had been known in SSA for a long time, so contact between Europeans and Africans did not result in epidemics destroying African societies. Indeed, the factor of disease often worked against the Europeans. When they tried to move inland, they frequently encountered diseases that were unknown in Europe (usually because the insects or other vectors that transmitted the disease lived only in Africa).

A second reason for the difference was that European maritime skills, although a great advantage along the coast, were of little use inland. No region in SSA compared with the West Indies, where most of the territory is near the coast.

Prior to 1800, the largest incursion into the interior of Africa occurred in 1591, when a Moroccan ruler employed a group of Portuguese and Spanish soldiers in his attack on the Songhai Empire in West Africa. Only half of the 5000-man force made it across the desert, but since they possessed firearms they were able to defeat the Songhai forces. As a result, the Moroccans gained control of the territory, and the largest native state in SSA was destroyed.

During the 1400s, the Portuguese had set up a series of bases along the Atlantic coast of Africa, and for a while, this made it difficult for other Europeans to compete with them. They were, though, unable to maintain their monopoly indefinitely. The Dutch established a base on the Guinea coast in 1595, and they founded Cape Town in 1652. The French set up a colony at the mouth of the Senegal River in 1626, and in 1637 they explored upstream and established a few posts there.

For a long time, the slave trade provided a large part of the European profits from the region. In general, the slave trade did not involve European raids into the interior. Rather, slaves were captured inland by Africans who brought them to the coast and sold them to the European traders.

Section 7 – India, Indonesia, and Southeast Asia

The vision of finding a sea route to the East — and thereby gaining control of the valuable trade in spices — had been a major motive for the long series of Portuguese expeditions down the African coast in the 1400s. In 1499, when Vasco da Gama returned from his historic voyage around Africa to India, the Portuguese rulers understood that the program had succeeded, and they eagerly seized the opportunity to cash in on their success.

Prior to da Gama's trip, the trade in spices from Indonesia had been dominated by the rulers of Egypt, the Mamelukes, who controlled the Red Sea route. (From Egypt, the spices were transported to Italy, and thence throughout Europe.) Starting with da Gama's second trip to India, in 1502, the Portuguese acted with great vigor (and complete ruthlessness) to establish their control of the trade with India and Indonesia.

The first Portuguese viceroy in the region, Francisco de Almeida, defeated a sizable Indian fleet in 1508, and won a crushing victory over a combined Egyptian/Indian fleet at the Battle of Diu in 1509. This victory firmly established Portuguese naval dominance in the Indian Ocean.

The next viceroy, Afonso de Albuquerque (1509-1515), secured Portuguese control of the principal maritime trade routes in the region by establishing permanent, fortified settlements at key points. Albuquerque built a fortress on the island of Socotra, from which entrance to the Red Sea could be blocked. In 1510, he captured Goa, on the southwest coast of India, and converted it into a strong naval base and the Portuguese headquarters in the East. He encouraged Portuguese to settle there, and Goa became a wealthy city, noted for its capable and enterprising population.

In 1511, Albuquerque captured Malacca, near the southern end of the Malay Peninsula, from which Portuguese ships could control the straits that led to Indonesia. Malacca became the main distribution point for spices from the East Indies. Because of their naval dominance, the Portuguese were also able to acquire trading privileges at Martaban, in Burma, in 1519, and to establish trading stations in Thailand in the middle of the century.

The principal goal of the Portuguese was trade, not conquest. Although they controlled the seas around India, the Portuguese never attempted to conquer the interior of the country. (Of course, in the interior, their naval superiority would have been useless, and their numerical inferiority would have been fatal.) Nor did they attempt to control the interior of the other eastern lands such as Burma, Thailand, and Indonesia.

About 1600, other European powers began to contest Portuguese dominance of the Indian Ocean. The Dutch built a factory at Palembang (in Sumatra) in 1596, and in 1619, they captured Batavia (now Jakarta) and made it their headquarters in the region. Within a few years they had become the main European power in the East Indies. The English entered the region a bit later, but by 1650 they had supplanted the Portuguese as the main European power in India.

Before being displaced by other European powers, the Portuguese had maintained their dominant position in the Indian Ocean and its coastal regions for over a century. Their remarkable success against both the Indians and the Arabs requires an explanation. Note that many factors that aided the Spanish and Portuguese in the New World did not apply to the Indian Ocean region:

a) Unlike the American aborigines, the Asian Indians and the Arabs had known of cavalry for many centuries, and had used metal weapons for millennia, so the Europeans' use of those weapons gave them no advantage in the East.

b) The Arabs and Indians were familiar with the magnetic compass, which they had learnt of from the Chinese.

c) The diseases (such as smallpox and malaria) that had decimated the inhabitants of the Western Hemisphere had long been prevalent in India and the surrounding regions, and European diseases played no part in the dominance of the Portuguese.

The factor of firearms is more complicated. Arabs and Turks had learnt of gunpowder from the Chinese, and had been using cannons since the 13th century. But firearms had not been widely used in India when the Portuguese arrived in 1498, and the initial Portuguese victories there can be explained by their possession of artillery.

That, however, that does not explain the *continuing* dominance of the Portuguese. Cannons were used in fighting between Indian forces at the Battle of Panipat in 1526, and increasingly thereafter in India. In the late 1500s, therefore, India — which was a much larger region — could have built far more artillery than Portugal. (Indian society was intact, and indeed prosperous, at the time.) However, the Indians — despite their enormous advantage in numbers, and despite the fact that Portugal had to conduct the struggle from thousands of miles away — were never able to gain local naval superiority over the Portuguese. Note also that, throughout this period, Portuguese manpower was spread very thin by the country's attempt to control widely scattered colonies in Indonesia, India, Africa, and South America.

How then was little Portugal (which prior to that time had been a small, poor country on the fringe of Europe) able to dominate the Indian Ocean region for so long against the far more numerous Indians and Arabs? The simplest explanation — and one which is consistent with the numbers presented in Table 17-1 and with the modern IQ results — is that the Portuguese were, on average, considerably more intelligent than either the Arabs or the Indians. Indeed, the dominance of the Portuguese during that period provides a striking demonstration of the intellectual superiority of the Europeans.

Section 8 – The dilution effect

The contrast between the accomplishments of the Portuguese in the 15th and 16th centuries and their achievements in more recent centuries is striking. Is this just one of those seemingly random changes that abound in history, or is there some explanation for it?

We know that the Portuguese who went overseas in those centuries often mated with women in the lands that they conquered. The offspring of such matings were sometimes brought back to Portugal, and the tendency there was to accept them as Portuguese. However, since the aboriginal populations of the overseas regions that the Portuguese were colonizing had, on average, substantially lower intelligence than the Portuguese themselves, the effect of this process was to lower the average intelligence of succeeding generations of Portuguese. Furthermore, since Portugal had started with a small population, and their overseas empire was extensive, and the process continued for centuries, the overall effect was substantial.

The effect is quite noticeable today, both in the physical appearance of the Portuguese (who are, on average, substantially darker than English or Germans)[8] and, more importantly, in their intelligence. IQs are, on average, somewhat lower in Portugal than they are in England, Germany, Poland, or Scandinavia, although still much higher than in most tropical countries.[9]

In the Spanish colonies, too, the tendency was to accept and assimilate mestizos (white-Indian hybrids) rather than categorize them as Indians for social purposes. Therefore, the same process that affected the Portuguese gene pool also affected the Spanish, although to a lesser extent since Spain had started with a much larger population than Portugal.

Why did not the same process result in a lowering of average IQs in England? Part of the reason is that Englishmen were more likely than Portuguese to bring their families with them when they went overseas. Another reason is that the English usually derided the hybrids as "half-breeds," and refused to accept them socially as a part of the English nation. (In like fashion, in English-speaking countries mulattos are socially categorized as blacks, although from a biological viewpoint it would be just as accurate to categorize them as whites.)

Section 9 – The Philippines, China, and Japan

The Spanish made a few attempts to conquer the Philippines during the first half of the 16th century, but they all failed. However, a successful settlement was made in San Miguel in 1565. Manila was founded in 1571, and by 1600, most of the lowland areas were ruled by the Spanish.

Meanwhile, Portuguese trading ships had reached China, and in 1557 the Portuguese established a permanent settlement at Macao. Thereafter there was continual direct trade between Europe and China. However, no European power tried to conquer China.

Portuguese ships visited Japan about 1543 and commenced trade relations. Spanish and Dutch traders followed. No attempts were made to conquer or colonize Japan, but Christian missionaries soon entered Japan, and for a while met with considerable success. The growth of Christianity worried the Japanese government, and in 1587 a decree was issued banning Christian missionaries from the country. For a while, the decree was not enforced; but starting about 1612 the Japanese government made a strong attempt to stamp out Christianity entirely. In addition, they threw all the Europeans out of Japan, permitting only a small Dutch trading post on an island near Nagasaki. This policy remained in force for over two centuries.

Section 10 – Russian expansion into Asia

Under Ivan the Great (reigned 1462-1505) the kingdom of Muscovy had freed itself from Mongol rule and had gained control of all of northern Russia. By 1580, the Russian state extended to the Ural Mountains.

East of the Urals, stretching thousands of miles to the Pacific Ocean, was Siberia. Most of Siberia was covered by boreal forests, which were very sparsely occupied by bands of hunter-gatherers. The Mongols had ignored those forest regions, which were lacking in both grazing land and in plunder. However, the abundant game in those forests provided a rich source of furs.

Russian expansion into Siberia began around 1581, and thereafter proceeded with great speed. Tyumen was founded in 1586, and Tobolsk in 1587. By 1619, Russian settlers had reached the Yenisei River, and a mere twenty years later they reached the Pacific Ocean. In 1649, they founded small ports on the Sea of Okhotsk and on the Bering Sea. Three years later, they founded Irkutsk, near Lake Baikal.

The Russian settlers in Siberia were few in number, but because of their possession of firearms they easily dominated the Siberian aborigines. However, since the Russians were primarily interested in fur trapping, they (like the French colonists in North America) had much less conflict with the aborigines than the Spanish had in Mexico and Peru.

The various Turkish tribes in Central Asia provided more serious resistance to the Russians, and that region was not conquered until much later. The Russians have recently relinquished their control of Central Asia; however, they still retain Siberia, and today comprise the great majority of the population there.

FOOTNOTES – CHAPTER 44

1) Hispaniola is the large island just east of Cuba. Two countries, Haiti and the Dominican Republic, are now situated on it.

2) Buenos Aires was soon abandoned, and it was not until 1580 that a permanent settlement was established there.

3) See Diamond, Jared (1999), *Guns, Germs, and Steel*, chapter 11. Also see McNeill, William (1988 edition), *Plagues and Peoples*, chapter V.

4) Diamond, Jared (1999), chapter 11. See particularly pp. 206-207 and table 11.1.

5) However, some historians believe that the Portuguese had discovered Brazil earlier (see Langer [1972], pp. 388-389). Most of the literature on the topic is in Portuguese and has not been translated. See http://www.uc.pt/bd.apm/bdee0378.htm for a list of some of the recent sources.

6) See *The Slave Trade*, by Thomas, Hugh (1999), and note table II in his appendix 3. Information concerning the approximate numbers of slaves that were imported into various regions can also be found at http://africanhistory.about.com/library/weekly/aa080601a.htm.

7) The most important of those early wars between the English settlers in North America and the Indian tribes was King Philip's War (1675-1676), which was fought mostly in New England. About 600 American whites died in that war, making it — from the standpoint of the whites — the bloodiest war, in proportion to population, in American history. Indian losses were very much greater, and the Indian tribes involved were devastated. See *Encyclopaedia Britannica* (1986 edition), volume 6, p. 873.

8) See Cavalli-Sforza, L.L., et al. (1994), p. 145 regarding skin color, and pp. 266-267 regarding hair and eye color. Darker pigmentation than in northern Europe is also found in southern parts of Spain, Italy, and Greece.

9) Also see Lynn & Vanhanen (2002), especially Table 6.1 and Appendix 1.

CHAPTER 45

THE RISE OF SCIENCE

Section 1 – Introduction

The rise of science is the most important feature of the modern era. The first part of that era, 1500-1700 AD, may be called "early modern times." This chapter will discuss the major mathematical and scientific advances made in that period.[1]

Section 2 – Mathematics

A) *Notation*. An important factor in the advance of mathematics was the adoption of improved notations for numbers, and for algebraic and arithmetic operations and relationships. The now-standard *positional notation* for representing integers by a series of digits was invented by Hindu mathematicians during the Middle Ages. Subsequently, positional notation was adopted by Arab mathematicians, and from there it spread to Europe. The use of "Arabic numerals" was described by the Italian mathematician Fibonacci in 1202.

Various other features of our present notation in arithmetic and algebra were also developed in early modern times. These include:

- Using the signs "+" "×" and "=" to indicate addition, multiplication, and equality.
- Using superscripts to indicate exponents.
- Using the letters occurring late in the alphabet (such as x, y, and z) to represent unknown quantities, and the early letters (such as a, b, and c) to represent known constants.

B) *Calculus*. The invention of calculus was the most important mathematical innovation of early modern times. To understand the type of problems that are treated by calculus, consider a quantity to which additions are made continuously during some interval of time. The basic problem dealt with in *integral calculus* is how to determine the total amount accumulated during that interval. Of course, if the additions are made at a constant rate, then simple multiplication will suffice. (Just multiply the rate of increase by the length of the time interval.) In many cases of practical interest, however, the rate of increase is not constant, but varies continuously, and in such cases a more complicated procedure, called *integration*, is required.

Differential calculus deals with a slightly different problem. Consider the case of a quantity that is varying, and where we know the value of the quantity at each instant. Is there some procedure that will enable us to determine the exact rate of change at each instant? Of course, if the rate of change is constant, then we can solve the problem simply by using division. (Simply divide the total change in the quantity during the time interval by the length of that time interval.) However, in those cases where the rate of change is not constant a more complicated procedure, called *differentiation*, is required.

Integration and differentiation are inverse procedures. That is, each one undoes the operation of the other. (If you found this point obvious, you are more perceptive than any mathematician prior to Isaac Newton, who invented calculus in 1665.) In the real, physical world, processes that occur at varying rates are much more common than those that occur at constant rates. The invention of calculus was therefore a breakthrough of the greatest importance to science.

An important preliminary to the development of calculus was the invention of *analytic geometry* — a method of describing each point in space by a set of numbers (its coordinates), and various geometric figures by means of algebraic formulas. Analytic geometry was invented by the French philosopher/scientist/mathematician René Descartes, and was published in 1637 as an appendix to his celebrated philosophical work, the *Discourse on Method*.

Calculus was invented by a British mathematician, Isaac Newton, in 1665-1666. Beginning in 1669, Newton showed manuscripts of his work to various colleagues; however, it was not until after 1700 that he actually published his work. Meanwhile (probably about 1675), the German scholar Leibniz had independently invented calculus. Leibniz published his work in 1684, and it was primarily because of his book that most European mathematicians became acquainted with the techniques of calculus.

C) *Logarithms*. Before there were calculators, the multiplication or division of two numbers was often a time-consuming task. An ingenious method by which that task could be replaced by the mere *addition* of certain related quantities (the *logarithms* of the two numbers) was devised in 1614 by John Napier. Logarithms also provided a rapid method of carrying out other mathematical operations, such as, extracting square roots (or higher roots of a number), or raising a number to a power. They also have various other uses in both pure and applied mathematics. Napier's invention is perhaps the most notable example of a breakthrough in mathematics (or any other field) attributable almost entirely to the work of a single person.

D) *Miscellaneous other advances*. In the mid-17th century, two French mathematicians, Pierre de Fermat and Blaise Pascal, laid the foundations for the theory of probability. The *binomial theorem* was formulated by Isaac Newton around 1665.

Section 3 – Astronomy

   A) *Copernicus, Brahe, and Kepler*. Nicolaus Copernicus was born in 1473 in Poland. His great book, *De Revolutionibus Orbium Coelestium*, in which he proposed the heliocentric hypothesis — the notion that the Earth is not the center of the universe, but that (like the other planets) it revolves about the Sun — was published in 1543, the year he died. It turned out to be the seminal book in the origin of modern science, and it set off a debate that was to last for a century and a half.

   Although many abstract arguments were presented for and against the heliocentric theory, there were some people who understood that the observational evidence would prove crucial. Among these was the Danish nobleman, Tycho Brahe (1546-1601), the first great observational astronomer.

   To conduct his observations, Tycho built an astronomical observatory, and equipped it with the best scientific instruments available at the time. (These did not include any telescopes, since the telescope had not yet been invented.) When those instruments failed to meet his strict requirements for accuracy, Tycho designed increasingly more sophisticated and accurate ones. Using these costly instruments, Tycho diligently carried out an extensive program of astronomical observations, which he conducted with unprecedented accuracy.

   Tycho's ambitious program soon became too costly for him to pay for himself. For a while, he was able to persuade the King of Denmark to finance it, but eventually, the king decided that the project was too expensive. However, Tycho (who by that time was the most famous astronomer in Europe) was able to convince the head of the Holy Roman Empire to give him the title "Imperial Mathematician" and to build Tycho another expensive observatory near Prague in which he could continue his observations.

   Although Tycho assembled a great mass of accurate observational data, he lacked the mathematical skills needed to analyze that data and to determine whether or not it supported the heliocentric theory. In 1599, he therefore hired a poor, but very talented young German mathematician, Johannes Kepler (1571-1630), to be his assistant and to analyze the data. Tycho died unexpectedly in early 1601, and his young assistant was chosen to succeed him as Imperial Mathematician.

   Kepler was convinced that the heliocentric theory was correct, and he attempted to find planetary orbits about the Sun that were consistent with Tycho's meticulous observations. After years of work, Kepler succeeded in doing so. However, to his surprise, the planetary orbits turned out to be ellipses, not epicycles as all astronomers since Ptolemy had believed.[2]

   Kepler summarized his results in three laws ("Kepler's laws of planetary motion"). The first two were included in his magnum opus *Astronomia Nova*, which was published in 1609. The third law was published in 1619. Kepler's three laws completely described the observed motions of the planets; however, Kepler was not able to explain *why* the planets moved in those orbits.

B) _Galileo_. Galileo Galilei (1564-1642) was the complete scientist — brilliant, imaginative, good with his hands, skilled at mathematics, a good speaker and writer, and possessing sharp eyesight. Although he never obtained a college degree, his talent was so obvious that as a young man he was hired as an instructor of mathematics at the University of Pisa. A few years later, he became a professor at the University of Padua, where he stayed for 18 years (1592-1610).

Galileo had long been convinced of the correctness of the Copernican theory. However, since public adherence to that theory was now prohibited by the Church, he kept his astronomical ideas to himself during his years at Padua, and spent his time conducting ingenious experiments in the field of mechanics (the branch of physics that deals with the motions of material objects). He kept careful notes of his experiments, but during his years at Padua he did not publish many of the results, and had he died when he was 44 years old, he would not be remembered today.

The turning point of Galileo's life came in 1608, when an otherwise obscure Dutch lensmaker, Hans Lippershey, constructed the first telescope. News of this device spread rapidly across Europe, and the following year Galileo built an improved version of Lippershey's device. Other people were building telescopes at that time, but most of them were using the "spyglasses" to observe objects situated on the surface of the Earth. Galileo, though, turned his telescope to the skies, and in the course of a single year made the most remarkable set of discoveries in the history of astronomy:

1) The Moon is not perfectly round, but has tall mountains on it (whose heights he calculated from the lengths of their shadows), as well as nearly circular shallow depressions which he called craters.

2) The Earth is not the only planet that has a moon. Using his telescope, he discovered four moons (the "Galilean satellites") revolving about the planet Jupiter.

3) The Milky Way is composed of enormous numbers of faint stars, too faint to be seen separately without a telescope.

4) The Sun has small dark areas on its surface ("sunspots"). Since each of those spots gradually moves from west to east across the surface of the Sun, taking about 28 days to complete a cycle, Galileo concluded that the Sun is rotating on its axis.

Galileo promptly published his discoveries in his first book, _Siderius Nuncius_ (1610). The book soon made him famous. Emboldened, he then started to publicly defend the heliocentric theory. This resulted in a papal decree (issued in 1616) ordering him to desist, and not to espouse the heliocentric theory in public.

Seven years later, though, the pope died, and Galileo — believing that the new pope would be more open-minded on the subject than the former one — decided to write a book summarizing the arguments in favor of the heliocentric theory. That book, the _Dialogue on the Two Chief World Systems_ (1632), was an immediate success, and did much to change scientific opinion on the question. However, Galileo's defiance of the 1616 papal decree resulted in his being arrested, tried, and convicted by the Roman Inquisition (1633). Threatened with torture and death, Galileo publicly recanted his views. However, since everyone understood the circumstances of his recantation, it had little effect on the scientific debate.

The recantation enabled Galileo to avoid the death penalty, but he was sentenced to house arrest for the remainder of his life. He made use of that time to write up the results of the mechanical experiments that he had performed many years earlier at Padua. Those experiments, and the conclusions that Galileo drew from them, were published in his last book, the *Dialogue Concerning Two New Sciences* (1638).

Section 4 – Mechanics

During the Renaissance, European scholars tended to accept Aristotle's ideas concerning mechanics. Unfortunately, in this field his views were far off the mark. Important progress in the field began to be made only when scholars began to disregard Aristotle's ideas and instead carry out their own experiments. The outstanding figure in this shift was Galileo, who is credited with at least three major discoveries in the field of mechanics:

1) *Uniform acceleration under gravity*. Aristotle had said that heavy objects naturally fall more rapidly than lighter ones. By conducting experiments, Galileo demonstrated that — aside from the effects of air resistance, which are usually small — heavy and light objects fall at the same rate. He also showed that a falling object tends to increase its speed in a steady fashion (that is, it undergoes uniform acceleration).

2) *Inertia*. Aristotle had claimed that a moving object will automatically slow down. Galileo suggested that any such slowing is the result of friction; in the absence of friction, a moving object will continue moving indefinitely and with undiminished speed. This hypothesis was later adopted by Isaac Newton and incorporated into his theories as the "first law of motion."

3) *Composition of velocities*. Galileo showed that the velocity of an object could be viewed as the *geometric* addition (in modern terms, the "vector sum") of the various velocities imparted to it. This, too, became central to Newton's theories on mechanics. Most prior scholars had not realized this, and consequently had reached incorrect conclusions on many topics (for example, the effect of the Earth's rotation on projectiles or on falling objects).

Although Galileo was never able to construct a complete theory of mechanics, by sweeping away the erroneous suggestions of Aristotle he prepared the way for Isaac Newton to create a more satisfactory theory.

Section 5 – Isaac Newton

The English scientist Isaac Newton (1642-1727) is generally considered to be the most important scientist who ever lived. After inventing integral calculus (while still in his early twenties!) he went on to make momentous contributions to both physics and astronomy.

Newton used as his starting points the advances in physics made by Galileo and the advances in astronomy made by Copernicus and Kepler. To these, he added several important insights of his own, and he wove them all together to create the first comprehensive and predictive system of mechanics, a system which could be applied both to the motions of the planets and to the motions of objects on Earth.

His greatest achievement in physics was the formulation of his three "laws of motion." These were presented in his most important book, *Philosophia Naturalis Principia Mathematica* ("Mathematical Principles of Natural Philosophy"), published in 1687. (The book is commonly referred to simply as the *Principia*.) The *Principia* also presented Newton's celebrated "law of universal gravitation," an explicit mathematical description of the force that, among other things:

- Causes objects near the surface of the Earth to fall.
- Causes the Earth and planets to revolve about the Sun.
- Causes the Earth to be round.

In the *Principia*, Newton applied his theories to the motions of planets, and he demonstrated that the force of gravitation should cause them to move in elliptical orbits about the Sun. He also calculated how fast they should move, and how long each planet should take to complete its orbit. The orbits predicted by Newton's theory turned out to be exactly the same as the observed orbits of the planets, as described by Kepler. Since Newton's laws also explained the motion of the Moon, as well as an enormous variety of mechanical phenomena on the Earth, it seemed clear that his theories were correct.

Another result of Newton's work was to end the dispute concerning the heliocentric theory. Since Newton's laws not only described the motions of the planets about the Sun, but also *explained* why they moved in exactly those orbits, all serious scientists soon agreed that the heliocentric theory was correct.

Newton's *Principia* thus provided a clear foundation to both mechanics and astronomy. Since then, progress in both fields — and, indeed, in all branches of physics — has been rapid, and applications of those scientific advances have revolutionized the world.

Section 6 – Optics

The phenomena of reflection and refraction had been observed in ancient times — probably, indeed, in prehistoric times. The ancient Greeks had formulated the law of reflection; however, they had not been able to find the correct formula for the phenomenon of refraction (the peculiar bending of light rays as they pass through water or glass). That law is far from obvious, and it was not until the early 17th century that the Dutch mathematician Willibrord Snell managed to formulate it. A much more subtle phenomenon, the *diffraction* of light (i.e., the ability of a wave of light to spread out as it passes around an obstacle) was discovered later in the 17th century by the Italian scientist Francesco Grimaldi.

Isaac Newton was responsible for another major discovery in optics: White light is actually a combination of all the colors of the rainbow. Newton showed how, by using a prism, one could separate white light into its components, and also how the separate colors could be recombined to form white light again. He also used his knowledge of optics to design and build a new type of telescope, the *reflecting telescope*.

Another important invention was the microscope. Simple lenses had been used for magnification since the 15th century. Sometime about 1600, it was realized that a suitable combination of lenses could be used to make a more powerful instrument, the *compound microscope*.

The period also saw serious discussions concerning the nature of light. Newton suggested that light consists of a stream of particles. An alternative theory, that light consists of *waves*, was introduced in the late 17th century by the Dutch scientist Christiaan Huygens (1629-1695). Huygens' wave theory of light was better able to explain the optical phenomena known at the time; however, because of Newton's great reputation, for over a century most scientists accepted the particle theory.

Huygens ("The Dutch Newton") was a remarkable scientist himself. Among his other achievements were:

- The discovery of the rings of Saturn.
- The discovery of Saturn's largest moon, Titan.
- The invention of the pendulum clock.
- The first estimate of the distance to a star (other than the Sun).

Section 7 – Other advances in physics and chemistry

A) *Electricity and Magnetism*. Lodestones had been known to the ancient Greeks, and the mariner's compass had been developed in the Middle Ages and improved by Peregrinus in the 13th century. However, the first careful discussion of the properties of magnets was *De Magnete*, written in 1600 by the English physician William Gilbert. Gilbert not only summarized the earlier knowledge in the field, but also presented the results of his own experiments. He was the first person to realize that the Earth itself is a large magnet. He also briefly discussed electric attractions, and clearly distinguished them from magnetism.

About 1670, Otto von Guericke (a German scientist, and also the mayor of Magdeburg) devised the first electrostatic generator. His device consisted of a ball of sulfur that could be rotated rapidly by means of a crank, while simultaneously being rubbed. The ball soon accumulated a large static charge — so large, indeed, that it gave off big electric sparks. By making it easy to generate sizable electric charges, his invention stimulated research in the study of electricity.

B) *Thermodynamics*. Not much was done in this field during early modern times. However, sometime around 1592, Galileo constructed the first thermometer. An improved version was designed by Guillaume Amontons in the next century. Another early advance was made by Newton when, after a series of experiments, he formulated "Newton's law of cooling."

C) *Chemistry*. Less progress was made in this field than in physics. However, in *The Sceptical Chymist* (1661), the British scientist Robert Boyle made a clear distinction between elementary substances and compounds, and he also distinguished between acids, bases, and neutral substances. Boyle accepted the atomic hypothesis, the notion that material objects were composed of minute particles (or *atoms*), and that in gases those particles were widely separated from each other.

D) *Gas laws*. This view led Boyle to conduct a series of experiments in which he demonstrated that, other factors being equal, the density of a gas is proportional to the pressure. (This is now called *Boyle's law*.) A few years later, Amontons showed that the volume of a gas increases as the temperature goes up, and that the increase is proportional to the increase in temperature. (By combining these two laws, one could obtain the celebrated "ideal gas law," but this was not done until considerably later.)

Section 8 – Biology and Medicine

An important event in the biological sciences was the publication, in 1543, of Vesalius' great book on human anatomy, *De Humani Corporis Fabrica*.

William Harvey, an English physician, is famous for discovering that the blood circulates about the body, and that the circulation is driven by the contractions of the heart. In his book, *De Motu Cordis* (1628), Harvey clearly described both the general circulation and the pulmonary circulation of the blood, and he presented (with abundant diagrams) the experimental evidence from which he had drawn his conclusions. Harvey's discovery was a crucial breakthrough in the field of physiology, and is indispensable to our understanding of how the body functions.

The only objection to Harvey's hypothesis was that neither he nor anyone else had ever seen the minute blood vessels (the *capillaries*) through which, according to Harvey, the blood went from the tiniest arteries into the tiniest veins. These capillaries are too small to be seen by the naked eye; however, in 1661, by making use of a compound microscope, Marcello Malpighi was able to observe them, thus removing the last objection to Harvey's theory.

Two other early microscopists were Jan Swammerdam (who in 1658 discovered the red blood corpuscles) and Robert Hooke (who in 1665 published the first description of plant cells).

However, the greatest of the early microscopists was a Dutch layman, Antony van Leeuwenhoek (1632-1723). Oddly, Leeuwenhoek never used a compound microscope; instead, he utilized "simple microscopes," each consisting of a single tiny lens with a very short focal length. By grinding these lenses with very great precision, he was able to achieve a resolving power greater than that obtained by any compound microscopes of the day. Using these instruments, together with his own sharp eyesight, Leeuwenhoek made a whole series of discoveries. The greatest of these was made in

1674, when he discovered microorganisms — or, as he put it "very tiny animalcules" — in a drop of water. (The type he saw are today called protozoa.) Nine years later, he discovered a much smaller type of microbe, the type now called bacteria. Once Leeuwenhoek described protozoa, and made his discovery public, it was not long before other scientists observed them too. However, since no one else had lenses of his quality, it was over 70 years until anyone else observed bacteria.

Bacteria (and, more generally, microorganisms) perform many important functions, and the study of microbes is indispensable for an understanding of biology. However, the most striking feature of microbes is that they are the cause of most contagious diseases. This important idea — the *germ theory of disease* — had been suggested long before Leeuweehoek. (For example, the Roman scholar Marcus Terentius Varro [116-27 BC] described the notion explicitly in the 1st century BC.) However, by actually observing microorganisms Leeuwenhoek made the germ theory of disease much more plausible (although there is no record that he discussed the theory himself). Despite Leeuwenhoek's discovery, the germ theory of disease did not become generally accepted until the last half of the 19th century.

Section 9 – Summary

The enormous scientific advances made by Europeans between 1540 and 1700 — we might call them collectively "the Scientific Revolution" — dwarf even the noteworthy advances made by the ancient Greeks. Indeed, they are greater than all the scientific advances made throughout the entire world in all prior ages combined. One might truly say that science, as an organized human activity, came into existence in this period. What had previously been a sporadic activity, one occasionally indulged in by isolated persons, became an important, continuing project of a small but important community.

Another aspect of the Scientific Revolution was the formation of scientific societies and scientific journals. The most famous of those societies was the *Royal Society of London for the Promotion of Natural Knowledge*, usually called simply the *Royal Society*. It was founded in 1660, formally chartered by King Charles II in 1662, and began publishing its *Philosophical Transactions* in 1665.

A striking aspect of the Scientific Revolution is how suddenly and unexpectedly it occurred. Table 45-1 lists several of the major books and discoveries that were involved in the rise of mathematical and scientific theory between 1500 and 1700 AD. Note that none of them predates 1540, and only two predate 1600. However, starting in 1600 there was a virtual explosion of growth in those fields.

Today, most people expect that there will be continuing rapid progress in science. However, the Scientific Revolution had *not* been generally anticipated in 1500. Rather than being a simple continuation of prior progress, the Scientific Revolution stands in striking contrast to the almost miniscule rate of scientific progress that had prevailed between 200 and 1500 AD. This begs the question: What triggered the Scientific Revolution in Europe?

Section 10 – What triggered the Scientific Revolution?

The Scientific Revolution was preceded by:

1) The increasing prosperity of Europe during the Late Middle Ages;

2) The rediscovery of the ancient Greek writings (particularly those of Aristotle, Euclid, and Ptolemy) during the Renaissance; and

3) Gutenberg's invention of printing, an invention which (in combination with the art of papermaking) made books available at low cost.

Although these were preconditions for the Scientific Revolution, it seems unlikely that they alone triggered it. Rather, the proximate cause of the rapid growth of science in Europe in early modern times was probably the greatly increased number of intellectual Europeans who chose to devote themselves to the fields of mathematics and pure science.

The period 1300-1540 had been one of great intellectual activity in Europe. However, during those years many more people were devoting their time and energy to the arts and humanities than were engaging in scientific or mathematical studies.

The preference of most intellectuals for the arts and humanities (rather than science and mathematics) was not a peculiarity of the Renaissance. That had been the case in *every* prior society. What needs to be explained, therefore, is why the fraction of intellectuals who chose to engage in math and science, although still a minority, was so much larger in 17th-century Europe than it had been in earlier ages.

A reasonable guess is that it was the introduction of the heliocentric hypothesis by Copernicus that was responsible. That hypothesis engendered within the intellectual classes in Europe an ongoing and emotional controversy. It was that controversy which — after percolating for half a century — sparked the great increase in interest in scientific matters that resulted in the Scientific Revolution.

Why did Copernicus's book — a highly mathematical work on a technical subject — arouse such passionate feelings? After all, prior to 1543 most European intellectuals had shown comparatively little interest in scientific questions. (For example: the debates over the atomic hypothesis and the germ theory of disease did not engender great popular interest, nor was anyone imprisoned for espousing those theories.)

The difference was that the Copernican theory had some implications that were far from technical. The heliocentric theory appeared to radically alter man's place in the universe and — more importantly — his relation to God. The earlier, geocentric theory had placed the Earth at the center of the universe. The Earth and its inhabitants were therefore at the very center of God's creation, and we could therefore make the comforting assumption that human beings were of very great interest to Him.

In the heliocentric theory, however, the Earth is just one of the Sun's planets, and the Sun is merely one of a vast number of stars. If Copernicus was correct, it was therefore reasonable to assume that the universe contains many other objects similar to the

TABLE 45-1

SOME MAJOR SCIENTIFIC BOOKS AND DISCOVERIES BETWEEN 1500 AND 1700

Year	Book	Scientist	Topic
1543	*De Revolutionibus*	Copernicius	heliocentric theory
1543	*De Humani Corporis Fabrica*	Vesalius	human anatomy
1600	*De Magnete*	Gilbert	magnetism; electricity
1609	*Astronomia Nova*	Kepler	laws of planetary motion
1610	*Siderius Nuncius*	Galileo	discoveries with telescope
1614	*Logarithmorum Descriptio*	Napier	logarithms
1628	*De Motu Cordis*	Harvey	circulation of the blood
1632	*Dialogue on the Two Chief World Systems*	Galileo	heliocentric theory
1637	*Discourse on Method*	Descartes	analytic geometry
1638	*Dialogue on Two New Sciences*	Galileo	mechanics
1661	*The Sceptical Chymist*	Boyle	chemistry
1674	---	Leeuwenhoek	discovery of microorganisms
1684	*Nova Methodus pro Maximis et Minimis*	Leibniz	calculus
1687	*Philosophia Naturalis Principia Mathematica*	Newton	laws of motion and gravitation
1690	*Traité de la Lumière*	Huygens	wave theory of light

Earth; and it is reasonable to wonder whether the inhabitants of this one tiny planet are of *special* concern to God. It was this implication that made the question of the truth or falsity of the heliocentric theory of such great interest to so many people. (Note the parallel to the reaction in the 19th and 20th centuries to Darwin's theory of evolution.)

FOOTNOTES – CHAPTER 45

1) Most of the facts presented in this chapter can be found in standard textbooks on the history of science or in individual articles in the *Encyclopaedia Britannica*. Another useful source is *Asimov's Biographical Encyclopedia of Science and Technology* (second revised edition), by Isaac Asimov (1982).

2) Epicycles and ellipses are two very different classes of geometric curves. Although both had been studied by ancient Greek mathematicians, no scientist before Kepler had suggested that ellipses had anything to do with planetary orbits.

CHAPTER 46

CONSTITUTIONAL DEMOCRACY

Section 1 – Introduction

Prior to modern times, most states were monarchies, and republics were rare. In the last few centuries, though, many countries have become constitutional republics (often referred to as *democracies*). In most cases, the change to a republican form of government can be traced back, directly or indirectly, to political developments that occurred in England during the 17th century.

Section 2 – Background to the origin of constitutional democracy in England

The roots of democracy in England were not revolts by the masses against monarchical rule, but rather the efforts of feudal lords to protect themselves from despotic kings. England had been a monarchy during the late middle ages, but one in which the feudal lords had considerable power. In the early 13th century, King John (reigned 1199-1216) made strong efforts to increase his tax revenues, in the process antagonizing many of the English churchmen and feudal lords. Fearing heavier taxation and progressive loss of their powers, many of the English barons rebelled against John, and in 1215 AD they raised an army to oppose him. In order to placate them and retain his throne, John signed a document, the *Magna Carta* (or "Great Charter") in which he agreed that the barons and churchmen had various privileges that he had no right to infringe upon.

An important article in the Magna Carta was paragraph 12, which provided that "No scutage (a type of tax, no longer levied today) shall be imposed in our kingdom unless by common counsel of our kingdom…" In later years, this idea was expanded to the notion that no taxes of any sort could be added or increased without the consent of Parliament. Magna Carta also stated that all English freemen had certain rights: In particular, paragraph 39 stated that "No free man shall be arrested or imprisoned … in any way … except by the lawful judgment of his peers…"

King John died the following year, but his successor, Henry III, reissued the Magna Carta (with slight revisions) in 1216, 1217, and 1225. In the course of time, Englishmen came to consider the Magna Carta the foundation of their liberty.

The powers of the English Parliament developed gradually, starting in the 13th century. The early Parliaments were simply large councils convoked by the king to decide various state questions. Although members of these councils were often prominent nobles or churchmen, their original function was only advisory. The king was not bound by their decisions, but he usually followed them. Gradually, though, Parliament acquired greater powers. In 1340, when King Edward III was in need of extra funds in order to finance a war in France, he persuaded the barons to provide the money by promising that in the future no tax would be levied without Parliamentary approval. This, obviously, was an extension of the promise made in paragraph 12 of the Magna Carta.

By 1500, the practice had developed of Parliament drafting legislation, with the understanding that it would become the law of the land only if signed by the king. Under the great Tudor monarchs of the 16th century (Henry VIII and Elizabeth I), most laws originated in that manner. Although it was still possible to do so, only rarely did either Henry or Elizabeth resort to legislating by royal proclamation without Parliamentary approval.

Section 3 – The struggle against royal supremacy in 17th century England

The successor to Queen Elizabeth was James I, and his son was Charles I (reigned 1625-1649). Charles was autocratic in temperament, and he soon came into serious conflict with Parliament. In 1629, Charles decided to solve these problems by dissolving Parliament and ruling alone. However in 1640, when he was badly in need of additional funds, he summoned another Parliament in the hope that they would authorize additional taxes. The conflict between Charles and Parliament soon resumed, and a civil war broke out in 1642.

For the first two years, the Royalist armies got the better of the fighting. It was not until the emergence of a brilliant military leader named Oliver Cromwell (1599-1658) that the tide turned in favor of the Parliamentary forces. Cromwell played an important role in both the Battle of Marston Moor (1644), which was the turning point of the war, and in the decisive Battle of Naseby (1645). The war ended in 1646, with Charles I a prisoner.

The following year, though, King Charles escaped, setting off a second round of fighting. The King's armies were defeated again in 1648, and the victorious rebels then had Charles tried for treason. At the trial, Charles claimed that "a king cannot be tried by any superior jurisdiction on Earth." Nevertheless he was convicted, sentenced to death, and (in January 1649) executed.

The victorious Parliamentary forces, however, were unable to agree on a suitable constitution. As a result, the next few years were a period of great turmoil, during which Cromwell was, for all practical purposes, a military dictator. Cromwell died in 1658, and was succeeded by his son Richard.

Richard was an ineffective leader, and within a year he was forced to resign. The next year (1660), Parliament invited the eldest son of Charles I to become king, after obtaining his promise that he would not infringe upon the rights of Parliament, and that he would grant a general amnesty. In general. the new king kept his promise, although a few of the leading rebels were executed when Charles II took the throne, and the corpse of Oliver Cromwell was dug up and hung. (Richard Cromwell felt it prudent to leave the country; but he later returned and was not harmed.) Charles II had a long reign (1660-1685), but he was always careful not to make Parliament feel that he was trying to restore royal absolutism.

Charles II died in 1685 and was succeeded by his brother, James II. James was more autocratic than his brother, and he soon came into conflict with Parliament. James dissolved Parliament in 1687, and the following year a rebellion (the "Glorious Revolution") broke out. James's opponents invited William of Orange — a Dutchman, but in the royal line, as he was a grandson of Charles I — to replace James on the throne and rule as a constitutional monarch. William accepted the offer, and landed in England with an army of 14,000. Much of James's army soon deserted, and James fled the country rather than give battle. William and his wife Mary (who was the daughter of James II) were declared joint rulers in 1689. Since then, the supremacy of Parliament has never been seriously challenged.

Section 4 – The spread of constitutional democracy to other regions

Although England is a small country, the English Civil War and the revolution of 1688-89 have affected much of the world, since the establishment of constitutional democracy in many other countries can be clearly traced to the English example.

A) *The United States of America*. From an early date, the English colonies in North America had their own little "Parliaments." The American colonists had always tended to dislike royal interference in their affairs, and consequently most of them sympathized with the Parliamentary side in the English Civil War. Nevertheless, the American colonists did not revolt against the British crown until late in the following century. Two major factors were involved in their eventual decision to do so:

- The feeling that King George III was a despot who was infringing upon their ancient liberties, liberties that in principle all Englishmen possessed.

- The desire of the colonists to rule themselves, and therefore to be independent of the English government, whether or not it was despotic.

Today it seems obvious that, because of the growth of national feeling, the American colonists would sooner or later have demanded independence (as the British colonists in Canada, Australia, and New Zealand did in the following century). However, during the American Revolutionary War (1775-1783) the colonists stressed the first reason (even though it seems clear today that the British monarch, George III, was not much of a despot by historical standards).

Perhaps because of their opposition to the regime of George III, when the American colonists gained their independence they adopted a form of government in which an elected legislature was the dominant power. In general, the constitution that the

Americans drew up in 1787 provided for a much less authoritarian system than the one then prevailing in England. (For example, it provided much more protection for free speech and a free press.)

B) *English colonies elsewhere*. The English colonies in Canada, Australia, and New Zealand were established much later than those in America. Canada did not become a British colony until 1763 (when it was ceded to England by France); Australia, not until 1788; and New Zealand, not until 1840. All those colonies possessed elected legislatures from an early date, and the British settlers all claimed rights similar to those existing in England. In the course of the 19th century, Britain granted independence to each of those colonies, and in each case it was achieved without fighting. Although they nominally recognized the British crown, as a practical matter each of the three countries became constitutional republics, and they have remained so ever since.

India was a special case because — unlike the four countries just mentioned — the number of English settlers remained very small compared with the native population. Nevertheless, in time, English political ideas deeply influenced the Indians themselves. As a result, India became a constitutional republic when English rule ended, and it remains so.

C) *The European continent*. In 1700, most of the important European states were governed by hereditary monarchs, without powerful elected legislatures to constrain them. Furthermore, most Europeans accepted that as the natural system.

In France, during the "Enlightenment" of the 18th-century (see chapter 48), many French thinkers proposed reforms of the existing political system, reforms that would restrict the powers of the monarch, or even eliminate the monarchy entirely. Those scholars were to some extent influenced by the examples of ancient Athens and Rome; however, they were more strongly influenced by the contemporary example of England. (After all, Athens had eventually decayed, and the Romans had abandoned their republican form of government, but England was flourishing.)

A striking example of the influence of England on the French thinkers is provided by Voltaire (1694-1788), probably the most celebrated figure of the French Enlightenment. Voltaire had visited England in 1726 and spent over two years there. After his return, he wrote *Les Lettres Philosophiques* (1734), often called "*Letters on the English*." In that book — the first major book of the Enlightenment — Voltaire drew a generally favorable picture of England, and he presented its political system as a model to his fellow Frenchmen.

The reformist ideas of the French philosophers spread through the French middle classes, and to some extent within the aristocracy as well, and were a major cause of the French Revolution of 1789. Although that revolution led to the autocratic Napoleon, and later (in 1815) to a restoration of the French monarchy, the notion of a constitutional republic did not die in France. The last French monarch (Napoleon III) abdicated in 1870, and since then France has been a constitutional republic.

The ideas of the French Enlightenment — in particular, its condemnation of royal absolutism — spread widely through Western and Central Europe, and eventually into Eastern Europe as well. The growth of those ideas was partly due to the power and prestige of France, but also to the continued example of England. In the course of the 19th and 20th centuries, every European country adopted a republican form of government. (Some of them have retained monarchs, but in all those cases the monarchs have become mere figureheads.)

D) *Other regions*. In the 19th and early 20th centuries, large parts of the world were ruled by European countries. The European settlers in Asia and Africa had not come to those countries in order to bring democracy to the natives; inevitably, though, the settlers brought with them the ideas that were surging through their home countries. Those ideas included the notion that absolute monarchy was a poor form of government, and that giving political power to an elected legislature was a vast improvement. As a result, most of those Asian, African, and South American countries adopted democratic constitutions when they gained their freedom. (However, in many of those countries constitutional rule soon broke down.)

Section 5 – Why did constitutional democracy begin in *England*?
Why, for example did it not originate in France, or Germany, or Italy, or Russia, or China, or Japan? To answer this question, we should consider the conditions that lead to the adoption and continuance of a democratic form of government in a country.

1) *High intelligence*. Constitutional democracy is a difficult form of government to practice, and experience shows that countries where the average IQ is low have rarely been able to practice it successfully, even if helped from the outside. This factor favored the origin of modern constitutional republics in Europe, and particularly in northern Europe. However, it does not explain why neither China, nor Japan, nor Korea developed constitutional republics on their own.

2) *A high rate of literacy*. After Gutenberg invented printing, this factor favored Europe, since the availability of inexpensive books led to increased literacy. Note that the absence of an alphabet hindered the growth of literacy in China in two ways: It made the process of learning to read far more difficult, and it made the printing of books more expensive.

3) *Openness to change*. In a country formerly ruled by a monarch — as almost all countries were prior to 1500 — the establishment of a constitutional democracy represents a drastic change. Such an innovation was more likely to occur in a country in which the culture was already experiencing fairly rapid change, and in which openness to change was therefore more widespread. At least from 1400 on, this factor favored the origin of democracy in European countries, rather than China. From 1500 on, this factor particularly favored the European countries bordering on the Atlantic, since they were most involved in the overseas explorations and settlements that began after 1492.

4) *Rejection of a central religious authority*. During the Middle Ages, most people in Western Europe had accepted the authority of the pope in religious matters

and of their king in secular matters. An important feature of the Reformation was the rejection of papal authority. In the countries where this had occurred, people became more willing to question authority in general, including the authority of their monarchs. As a practical matter, this meant that the Protestant countries, such as England and Holland, were more ready to demand limitations on royal power than the Catholic countries, such as Italy, Spain, and Portugal.

5) *Geographic isolation*. If a country lacks geographic protection from dangerous neighbors, the monarch is likely to maintain a large army. Such an army — even if intended primarily to defend the country against foreign invaders — can be used to crush domestic groups that attempt to limit the monarch's power. Furthermore, in such countries emergencies frequently arise (because of external threats) that call for restricting individual rights in order to preserve the nation. This factor hindered the development and maintenance of democracy in countries such as France, Germany, and Hungary, while favoring it in such countries as England, Iceland, and Japan.

6) *Ethnic homogeneity*. If a country contains two or more large ethnic groups that hate and fear each other, then a given ethnic group is often unwilling to risk letting its vital interests be decided by a vote in which a large part of the electorate is hostile to it. This factor worked against the establishment of democracy in the Ottoman Empire, or in the Habsburg dominions. (It still has that effect in many of the African countries.) Conversely, the absence of ethnic conflicts favored the establishment of democracy in such countries as England, Finland, Sweden, Norway, Denmark, and Iceland.

Note that every one of these six factors favored the establishment and maintenance of constitutional democracy in England, and that England was the *only* large country in which all six factors were positive.

CHAPTER 47

THE INDUSTRIAL REVOLUTION

Section 1 – Introduction

The Industrial Revolution may be defined as the period when production by hand tools (powered primarily by the muscles of human beings or animals) was replaced by production using heavy machinery (often powered by fuels), thereby enormously increasing productivity, and resulting in the change from a largely agrarian economy to one dominated by industrial production. It resulted in an unprecedented increase in human wealth and a radical change in living conditions.

Section 2 – Origin and spread

The Industrial Revolution (hereafter abbreviated *IR*) began in England in the mid-18th century. It spread to the United States and Belgium about 1800, and to France about 1825. It did not commence in Germany until after 1850, roughly a hundred years after it had begun in England.

The *IR* did not begin in Eastern Europe or in Southern Europe until the late 19th century, and in most Asian, African, and South American countries until the 20th century. By now, every country on Earth has been affected.

Section 3 – Some important technological advances in the Industrial Revolution

The early stages of the *IR* in England were marked by advances in the techniques of textile production. Among the early inventions were:

1) The fly-shuttle (by John Kay, in 1733).

2) The "spinning jenny" (by James Hargreaves, in 1764).

3) The water frame (by Richard Arkwright, in 1769).

Far more important was the invention (by James Watt, in 1769) of an improved steam engine. This was the central invention of the *IR*, since it not only increased productivity, but also led to great improvements in transportation.

In the 1770s, Richard Arkwright combined these various inventions, and thereby created the first modern factories. Arkwright's factories were very different from the older workshops in their size, in the amount of machinery they contained, in their use of steam power, and in the way that they were organized. The enormous success of his factories made it inevitable that the factory system would spread.

Meanwhile, other men had realized that steam engines could also be used to power boats. Attempts were made to do so soon after Watt's invention, but it was not until 1807 that Robert Fulton invented the first practical steamboat.

The use of steam engines to power land vehicles posed more difficult problems: Steam engines were so heavy that a steam-powered land vehicle could not be supported on ordinary roads. The solution — a steam-powered train running on steel tracks, with wooden cross-ties to support the weight — was conceptually easy, but difficult and expensive to implement. It was not until 1825 that George Stevenson constructed the first practical railroad, and not until 1830 that he built the first intercity railroad. From 1840 on, the growth of railroads was a major factor in the *IR*.

Section 4 – The "Second Industrial Revolution"
A new series of innovations began about 1870, and they became so important that they are often called the "Second Industrial Revolution." These changes included techniques of mass production (such as the assembly line) as well as the use of electricity.

Since World War II, there has been still another wave of drastic changes in production techniques — this one involving automation, computerized control, and robotics. We are still in the midst of this "Third Industrial Revolution."

Section 5 – Why did the Industrial Revolution originate in *Great Britain*?
Unlike the scientific revolution of the 16th and 17th centuries, the Industrial Revolution originated in a single country. However, the question of why it began in that particular country, and no other, is not addressed in most history books. It appears to me that a combination of factors was involved:

1) To begin with, it seems clear that the *IR* could have originated only in a country where the average intelligence of the inhabitants was very high. That high average intelligence was found only in the countries of Europe, North America, and northern Asia. Within Europe, this factor slightly favored the high-latitude countries.

2) The *IR* was unlikely to originate in a region with a low population even if the average intelligence of the population was high, because such a region was unlikely to have a sufficient number of highly talented persons. This factor made it unlikely that the *IR* would originate in regions such as Iceland, Scandinavia, or the British colonies in North America.

3) The *IR* was more likely to arise in a region where slavery was rare or absent, since an abundance of cheap slave labor decreased the need for labor-saving machinery. This factor favored the European countries.

4) The *IR* was more likely to originate in a region where there was considerable intellectual ferment. In the period following the Renaissance, the Reformation, and the

rise of science, this factor favored such countries as England, Holland, Germany, France, and Italy. On the other hand, the lack of intellectual freedom helps to explain why the *IR* did not originate in Spain or Portugal (where the Inquisition had crushed the expression of heterodox opinions), nor in Russia.

5) In Western Europe, the effects of overseas explorations and conquests, and the growth of colonies had added to the intellectual ferment. This factor favored Spain, Portugal, Britain, and France over regions such as Italy, Germany, and Poland which (since they did not border on the Atlantic) had little to do with those explorations, and had no overseas colonies.

6) The *IR* was less likely to originate in a region that was politically fragmented (such as Germany or Italy) because in such a region the "free trade zone" was small, and the advantages of mass production were less. This factor favored Britain, France, Spain, and Russia. It also favored countries, such as Portugal, that had large overseas colonies which could serve as "captive markets" for goods produced in the homeland.

7) The *IR* was more likely to originate in a country with abundant iron ore and coal, as those particular natural resources were especially important in the *IR*. This factor favored Britain, Germany, and France.

8) Finally, the *IR* was more likely to arise in a country where property rights were secure. This factor would tend to favor a country with a democratic government, or one with a limited monarchy (such as Britain) over countries that had autocratic governments.

Although several of these factors were present in some other countries (such as Spain, France, and Germany), the only place where *all* of them were present was Britain. This does not prove that the Industrial Revolution was inevitably destined to start in 18th-century Britain, but it does seem to make its inception there more likely than in any other place.

CHAPTER 48

THE ENLIGHTENMENT AND THE FRENCH REVOLUTION

Section 1 – Introduction

The Industrial Revolution that commenced in the 18th century has radically altered the material circumstances of human beings. At the same time as that revolution was starting in England, another quite different movement, an *intellectual* revolution was going on in Western Europe, one which was radically altering the way men think, and which would ultimately give rise to a new civilization. That intellectual movement is usually called the *Enlightenment*, and its central idea was the notion that all existing institutions and beliefs should be re-examined by the untrammeled application of human reason.

This basic notion led to new ideas in many different fields of thought, including political theory, economic theory, and legal reform, but most of all in matters concerning religion. In keeping with the central theme of the Enlightenment, most of the philosophers involved were deeply skeptical of all "revealed religions" and their doctrines. Many of those philosophers were deists who believed in "natural religion" (i.e., one knowable from human reason, without any divine revelation); others were atheists or agnostics. Virtually all of them were fiercely anti-clerical.

During the thirteen centuries preceding the Enlightenment, Europe was often called *Christendom*, because the Christian religion was the central feature of European culture. That had not been the case during the earlier period when the classical civilizations of Greece and Rome were at their height, nor is it today. Although Christians still comprise a large part of the population of Europe, their religion no longer dominates the culture of the continent. Indeed, the cultural unit to which Europe and America now belong is usually referred to as "Western Civilization." The transition from classical civilization to Christendom took place in the fourth century AD. The "Enlightenment" of the 18th-century initiated the transition into the comparatively secular age of today.

Section 2 – Characteristic attitudes

Anti-monarchical attitudes were also commonplace among the philosophers of the Enlightenment. Some of them merely wished to replace absolute monarchies with constitutional ones; others wished to eliminate monarchies entirely and replace them with constitutional republics. A famous comment attributed to Denis Diderot (1713-1786) sums up the attitudes of the more radical thinkers: "Mankind will never be free until the last king is strangled with the entrails of the last priest."

Most of the philosophers involved in the Enlightenment were enthusiastic about scientific progress, and virtually all were scornful of superstition. In economic matters, they tended to favor fewer government restrictions on private transactions, and they strongly favored the rights of private property. Most of them supported freedom of speech, press, and religion; and they were opposed to slavery and serfdom.

Section 3 – Scientific developments

One reason for their enthusiastic support of science was the impressive set of discoveries that occurred during the 18th century. The successors of Newton made major advances in the field of mechanics; other scientists produced the first steady electric currents; and the French scientist Lavoisier ("the Newton of chemistry") laid the foundations of that important field. In addition, many mathematical advances were made that have practical applications in science and engineering.

Indeed, advances were made in almost every field of science in the 18th century, including astronomy, biology, geology, and physics. (This was in addition to the series of inventions involved in the Industrial Revolution.)

Section 4 – Some important individual figures

The most famous of the great figures of the Enlightenment was the witty and prolific French writer François Marie Arouet (1694-1778), better know by his pseudonym *Voltaire*. As a young man, Voltaire's anti-establishment comments got him thrown in jail, and for a while he was forced to leave France. The two years he then spent in England were a turning point in his life, and he became convinced of the superiority of the English constitutional system over the authoritarian regime operating in his native land. After returning to France, he wrote his first major philosophical work, *Letters on the English*, a book whose publication in 1734 might be taken as the start of the Enlightenment. Although personally rather anti-Semitic, Voltaire was a passionate opponent of religious persecution, and he inveighed against it constantly. He was also a consistent proponent of freedom of speech. His attitude was, "I disapprove of what you say, but will defend to the death your right to say it," although he never put it in exactly those words.

Some of the other famous philosophers of the Enlightenment are listed in Table 48-1. (Most of them also wrote on other topics as well as the ones listed.)

Rousseau (1712-1778) was a prolific writer. Although one of the most famous figures in the Enlightenment, he was in many ways an anomaly. He tended to trust men's instincts over their reason, and was dubious of the advantages of scientific progress. He might be called a rebel within the rebellion.

TABLE 48-1
SOME MAJOR ENLIGHTENMENT PHILOSOPHERS

Name	Country	Main field of interest
Jean-Jacques Rousseau	Switzerland	Educational theory; political theory.
Adam Smith	Scotland	Economic theory. (*The Wealth of Nations*, 1776.)
David Hume	Scotland	Epistemology; critical analyses of religious beliefs.
Charles-Louis de Montesquieu	France	Political theory. (*The Spirit of Laws*, 1750.)
Cesare Beccaria	Italy	Criminology. (*Crimes and Punishments*, 1764.)
Jeremy Bentham	England	Legal reform.

The most ambitious work of the Enlightenment was the seven-volume *Encyclopédie*, assembled under the direction of Denis Diderot. In this celebrated encyclopedia, topics were presented from the rationalist point of view of the Enlightenment philosophers.

Section 5 – Origins

Among the precursors of the Enlightenment were the Renaissance and the Reformation. The writings of René Descartes (1596-1650) and of the English philosophers Francis Bacon (1561-1626) and John Locke (1632-1704) were also influential. Perhaps even more important was the impact of the rise of science. The intellectual grandeur of the Newtonian system, with its remarkable explanatory power, stimulated the expectation that human reason could solve all problems. In addition, the Church's frequent opposition to free discussion of scientific matters (Galileo's conviction by the Roman Inquisition was a notorious example) was a factor in the anti-clerical attitude of the Enlightenment philosophers.

Section 6 – The American constitutional convention

The nature of the government that the Americans adopted after gaining independence from England was strongly influenced by the ideas of the Enlightenment. Among the signs of this are:

1) The American colonists' Declaration of Independence (1776) prominently mentioned "natural rights," a characteristic idea of the Enlightenment.

2) Many of the American "Founding Fathers" (including both George Washington and Thomas Jefferson) were deists. However, unlike many of the leaders of the French Revolution, they were not hostile to religion but merely wanted to safeguard freedom of conscience, and avoid an established religion.

3) The constitution they adopted provided for a republic, not a monarchy. Furthermore, it gave no rights to any hereditary aristocracy.

4) As suggested by Montesquieu, the American constitution provided for a division of powers between the executive, legislative, and judicial branches of government.

5) The American constitution protected the rights of private property, and it provided for freedom of speech, freedom of the press, and freedom of religion.

Section 7 – The French Revolution

At the beginning of the 18th century, France was a powerful, prosperous country, perhaps the richest in the world. The French king, Louis XIV (the "Sun King"), was a capable and admired monarch. Although the aristocracy consumed an unreasonable share of the national income, there was a sizable middle class, and the peasantry was clearly better off than in most countries. The Capetian dynasty, which had ruled France for over seven centuries, seemed as solid as a rock. Nevertheless, by the end of the century a mighty revolution had occurred, the monarchy had been cast aside, and a sweeping series of changes had been instituted.

The causes of that vast upheaval have been much discussed. It is true that during the 18th century France had fought a series of expensive (and not very successful) wars; but no major war directly preceded the great revolution of 1789. More important, probably, were the endless series of budget deficits. The French monarchy was living beyond its means, and the accumulated debt was causing serious problems.

It seems clear, however, that the key factor leading to the French Revolution was a change in public attitudes toward the monarchy, a change that derived from the Enlightenment. Many Frenchmen had come to believe that the existing system of government was so inefficient, so unreasonable, and so inequitable that it could no longer be defended. The French government, those persons felt, *must* be reformed, and the reforms could wait no longer.

Two external factors enhanced that feeling. One of these was the example of a functioning constitutional monarchy right across the English Channel. The other was the example that the Americans had provided of a people ridding themselves of their monarch and — guided only by their reason and good sense — freely instituting a new form of government.

The immediate event that resulted in the Revolution was the decision of the French king, Louis XVI, to call a meeting of the *Estates-General* — a representative assembly that had evolved in medieval times, but had not met since 1614 — in order to deal with the fiscal crisis facing the government. (One is reminded of the decision of Charles I in England to call Parliament into session for a similar purpose, a decision that eventually led to a successful rebellion against his rule.)

The Estates-General had never possessed the powers of the English Parliament. However, with the example of that Parliament before them, and faced with a feckless monarch, it soon asserted stronger powers than it had previously held. It held its first meeting in May 1789, and by late June one of its components (the *Third Estate*, whose members represented the middle classes) boldly transformed itself into a "National Assembly." The king objected, and when it seemed as if he was about to forcibly dissolve the Assembly, a major riot ensued, a riot that ended in the destruction of the Bastille (a notorious prison that was a symbol of the arbitrary rule of the king).

That autumn, the National Assembly drew up a constitution that greatly limited the powers of the monarch. In 1790, the King accepted that constitution, thereby satisfying the demands of the moderate reformers (led by Count Mirabeau) who had launched the Revolution. By then, however, more radical elements were gaining power, and after Mirabeau's death in March 1791 the drift to the left accelerated.

The monarchy was abolished in 1792, and Louis XVI was executed the following January. By April 1793, the radicals had concentrated governmental power in a small *Committee of Public Safety* led by Danton and Robespierre. The result was the infamous "Reign of Terror." This culminated in March and April of 1794, when Robespierre had several of the other revolutionary leaders executed, including Danton. Less than four months later, however, Robespierre was himself overthrown, and he and his main supporters were sent to the guillotine. In 1795, a new constitution (the third since the start of the Revolution) was instituted, providing for a bicameral legislature, and vesting executive power in a five-man *Directory*.

More significant than the political struggles at the top, however, were the other radical changes that occurred between 1789 and 1794. Among those changes were:

1) The feudal rights and privileges of the aristocracy were stripped away. In addition, much of the land owned by aristocrats was taken over by peasants, and many of the aristocrats fled the country.

2) The privileges of the Catholic Church and its clergy were largely abolished.

3) The old provinces (such as Gascony, Normandy, and Brittany) were abolished. Instead, France was divided into 83 newly-drawn departments, more equal in size than the old provinces had been.

4) The army was reorganized, and a draft instituted.

5) The old calendar was discarded completely. What had been September 22, 1792, became the beginning of the year 1 of the revolutionary calendar. The old months were discarded too, and twelve new ones adopted. (The new calendar was abandoned in 1806.)

6) A law was passed abolishing the worship of God, and establishing the worship of Reason in its place!

Section 8 – Foreign wars

Naturally, most other European governments were shocked at what was going on in France. For a while, they simply watched in horror; but in the spring of 1792, Austrian and Prussian armies invaded France, at least partly in order to suppress the Revolution and restore the French monarchy. At first, the allied armies advanced easily, and many people thought that the disorder in France would lead to the defeat of its armies. But a drawn battle at Valmy, in September 1792, brought a temporary halt to the allies' advance.

In early 1793, England, Holland, and Spain joined the alliance against France. However, by the end of the year, the reorganized French army had beaten back the allies and had overrun Belgium and part of Holland. Prussia withdrew from the war in early 1795, and Spain withdrew a few months later, but fighting continued with Austria and England.

Section 9 – Napoleon

Not surprisingly, the long series of foreign wars eventually resulted in the rise to power of a military man. Napoleon Bonaparte was born in Corsica in 1769, and he graduated from a French military college in 1785. It was not, however, until 1793 (when he was given command of the French artillery involved in the siege of Toulon) that he engaged in any military action. He distinguished himself in the siege, and was promptly promoted.

In 1796, he was given command of the French army in Italy. He achieved a spectacular series of victories there, and in 1797 he returned to Paris, a hero. Two years later, Napoleon seized power in a coup against the Directory and established a new government, the *Consulate*, with Napoleon as "first consul." The new constitution was submitted to a plebiscite and won overwhelming approval. Thereafter, Napoleon was, in effect, the dictator of France.

In his younger days, Napoleon had been a member of the Jacobins (a political club that supported radical ideas), and during his years as head of the French government he always claimed to be supporting the ideals of the Revolution. However, in 1802, he had himself declared "consul for life," with the right to name his successor; and in 1804 he dropped any pretense that France was a republic and had himself declared Emperor. He later installed three of his brothers on the thrones of other European countries.

During his reign, Napoleon had the legal system of France drastically revised and codified. The resulting *Code Napoléon* (which was well organized, and drafted with unusual clarity) included various reforms that had been urged by Enlightenment philosophers. For example, under the Code there were no privileges of birth, and all men were equal under the law. It became the basis for many of the law codes later adopted by other European countries. In addition, Napoleon emancipated the Jews, reformed the French judiciary, and created the University of France.

In 1802, Napoleon concluded a peace treaty with Britain, bringing to an end the series of wars in which France had been embroiled for a decade. However, his ambitions made it impossible for peace to continue for long. Hostilities with England resumed the following year, and for the rest of his reign France was constantly at war, and French troops repeatedly invaded other European states. Napoleon's military genius enabled him to win most of the land battles against England and her allies; but England could not be defeated as long as her navy dominated the seas. Napoleon therefore attempted to build a navy that could rival England's. In 1805, however, the French fleet was totally routed at the Battle of Trafalgar, and thereafter England's control of the seas was not seriously disputed.

In 1812, Napoleon committed a major strategic error by invading Russia. The result was a disastrous defeat, and other European countries saw the opportunity of at last throwing off the French yoke. At the Battle of Leipzig, in 1813, the allied armies inflicted a crushing defeat on Napoleon's forces. Napoleon resigned a few months later, and was banished. He returned to France in 1815, and was restored to power; but 100 days later he suffered a final defeat at the Battle of Waterloo.

The victorious allies restored the French monarchy, with the brother of Louis XVI as king. The new king, Louis XVIII, realized that many of the changes that had occurred during the Revolution could not be reversed, and he did not try to do so. Instead, he ruled as a constitutional monarch. Nominally, the Revolution had been defeated. In practice, though, most of the reforms urged during the Enlightenment (and desired by the moderate leaders of the rebellion, such as Mirabeau) had been implemented; and in the course of a quarter-century of wars the basic ideas of the Enlightenment had been spread far and wide.

In France itself, the public was divided between those who favored a constitutional monarchy and those who desired a republic, and the six decades after 1815 saw a good deal of turmoil. Eventually, though, the monarchists lost out, and since 1870 France has been a republic.

CHAPTER 49

THE NINETEENTH CENTURY

Section 1 – Overview

The dominant feature of this century was the rise of applied science. Although many previous centuries had seen improvements in technology, those improvements were generally not due to advances in basic scientific knowledge. In the 19th century, though, there was both a rapid increase in scientific knowledge and widespread application of it to practical ends. Many of those applications were of major importance, with the result that everyday life in Western Europe and the United States changed considerably in the course of the century.

At the same time, of course, the Industrial Revolution was causing a remarkable increase in human productivity and wealth. As both the increase of wealth and the introduction of new inventions were proceeding most rapidly in Europe and America, these regions kept pulling further and further ahead of the other parts of the world. By the end of the century, European power was at its peak.

Within Europe, the period 1815-1914 saw relatively few wars. However, the rapid changes in technology and social attitudes resulted in great turmoil in many countries.

Section 2 – Scientific advances

The 19th century saw enormous scientific progress, dwarfing even that of the 17th century, with advances in many different fields. Table 49-1 lists some of the more prominent advances.

    A) *Electricity and Magnetism*. Rather little was known about these subjects in the 18th century, and as late as 1780, not a single equation had been formulated in either field. However, in 1785, Coulomb discovered the law ("Coulomb's law") expressing the force between two static electric charges. A few years later he also discovered the law for the force that two magnets exert on each other.

    In 1800, Alessandro Volta succeeded in constructing a battery capable of producing a sizable, steady electric current. Later that year, William Nicholson used a similar device to send an electric current through water and to thereby break the water up into its constituent elements (hydrogen and oxygen). This was the first example of a chem-

TABLE 49-1

SOME 19th-CENTURY SCIENTIFIC DISCOVERIES & THEORIES

Discovery or theory	Principal scientist	Date
A) Physics		
Ultraviolet radiation	Johann Ritter	1801
Electromagnetic induction	Michael Faraday	1831
Conservation of energy	James Joule	1847
Second law of thermodynamics	Rudolf Clausius	1850
Spectroscopy	Gustav Kirchhoff	1859
Basic laws of electricity & magnetism	James Clerk Maxwell	1865
Statistical mechanics	Ludwig Boltzmann	1871
Nature of light, electromagnetic waves	James Clerk Maxwell	1873
X-rays	Wilhelm Röntgen	1895
Radioactivity	Antoine Henri Becquerel	1896
Electrons	J. J. Thomson	1897
Quantum theory (beginnings)	Max Planck	1900
B) Chemistry		
Atomic theory (applied to chemistry)	John Dalton	1808
Notion of chemical equilibrium	Alexander Williamson	1850
Periodic table of elements	Dimitri Mendele'ev	1869
Ions and ionic dissociation	Svante Arrhenius	1884
C) Mathematics		
Non-Euclidean geometry	Nikolai Lobachevski	1829
Transfinite numbers	Georg Cantor	1874
D) Biology		
Theory of evolution	Charles Darwin	1859
Laws of heredity	Gregor Mendel	1866
Germ theory of disease	Louis Pasteur	1870
Viruses	Martinus Beijerink	1898
E) Geology and Anthropology		
Ice ages	Louis Agassiz	1840
Dinosaurs	Richard Owen	1842
Homo erectus	Marie Eugene Dubois	1894

ical reaction initiated by an electric current. In 1807, Humphry Davy built a larger, more powerful version of Volta's battery and employed it to break up potash, thereby isolating a previously unseen element, the metal *potassium*. Within two years, he had discovered five other new elements in the same fashion.

Progress in the fields of electricity and magnetism was rapid during the first half of the 19th century, with the contributions of Michael Faraday (1791-1867) being particularly important. This progress culminated in the 1860's, when James Clerk Maxwell (1831-1879) succeeded in formulating the extremely sophisticated set of four equations ("Maxwell's equations") that describe the complex set of forces that are involved when electrical charges or magnets are moving. What makes Maxwell's equations so important is that they are general laws that hold in *all* cases involving electricity and magnetism.

By a careful analysis of his equations, Maxwell — probably the most brilliant theoretical scientist of the entire century — deduced that it was possible to produce "electromagnetic waves," and that such waves should travel at the speed of light. From this, he concluded that ordinary light *consists* of electromagnetic waves. Furthermore, he predicted, there should be other electromagnetic waves, with wavelengths too long or too short to be seen by the human eye. Maxwell's surprising hypothesis was derived from highly abstract mathematical analysis; but in 1888, Heinrich Hertz produced waves in his laboratory that had exactly the properties predicted by Maxwell.

The waves produced by Hertz (which are today called *microwaves*) are much longer than those of visible light. A few years later, the Italian inventor Guglielmo Marconi used even longer electromagnetic waves (now called *radio waves*) for signaling purposes.

B) *Thermodynamics*. The laws of thermodynamics (the study of heat and temperature) were unknown in 1800. Indeed, the very nature of heat was still in dispute, although a few perceptive persons had already deduced the correct answer. By the end of the century, it was well-established that thermal energy was the energy of the random motions of the molecules within a body or system, and the subject had been analyzed in great detail.

An important insight was gained in 1847, when James Joule published the results of experiments which demonstrated that the kinetic energy of a moving object could be transformed into thermal energy. In such cases, Joule showed, the *sum* of the mechanical and thermal energy of the system remains unchanged. Joule's discovery is often called the *first law of thermodynamics*. That law, when extended to include other forms of energy as well, is known as the *law of conservation of energy*, and is one of the basic laws of physics.

A few years later, William Kelvin and Rudolf Clausius formulated the *second law of thermodynamics*, one of the most subtle, sophisticated, and important of all physical laws. (The gist of that law is that, although the total energy is conserved, the amount of *usable* energy in a closed system decreases. However, a precise statement of the law is far too abstruse to be described here.)

C) *Chemistry*. The great breakthrough here was the introduction, by John Dalton in 1808, of the atomic theory. According to that theory: (a) Each elementary substance (or "chemical element") is composed of identical minute particles called atoms, with each type of atom being characteristic of one specific element; and (b) Each compound substance (or "chemical compound") consists of minute particles called molecules, and each type of molecule consists of a *specific* combination of atoms. Dalton's theory provided a firm basis for understanding chemistry, and subsequent progress in the field was rapid.

For a long time, many chemists believed that the chemistry of living organisms was fundamentally different than that of inorganic matter. However, in the mid-19th century it was established that organic compounds are invariably composed of ordinary atoms, and that they obey exactly the same chemical laws as do inorganic compounds. In principle, any organic compound can be synthesized entirely from inorganic compounds (although in practice the synthesis may be difficult).

D) *Mathematics*. The 19th century produced a host of mathematical innovations. Some of them (such as the advances in number theory, non-Euclidean geometry, and group theory) had no immediate practical applications. Others (such as vector analysis, matrix theory, and Fourier analysis) had numerous practical applications in science and engineering.

E) *Astronomy*. An important breakthrough in this field was the discovery, by Wollaston in 1802, that the spectrum of the Sun includes various thin dark lines. In 1814, Fraunhofer observed almost 600 such lines, and carefully recorded their positions in the spectrum. A few decades later, Kirchhoff showed that the spectral lines were caused by atoms of particular chemical elements that were present in the Sun's atmosphere. In 1868, Janssen and Lockyer used this technique to discover a new chemical element (which they named *helium*) in the Sun's atmosphere — an element that had never been observed on Earth!

Meanwhile, observations had shown that other stars also had dark lines in their spectra, although often very different ones than those in the Sun's spectrum. By the end of the century, it was realized that a careful study of a star's spectral lines could provide a great deal of information about the star, including its chemical composition, its velocity, and its temperature — information that nobody in 1800 had thought we would *ever* be able to discover. As a result, spectroscopy has become the most important observational technique in astronomy.

F) *Biology*. Two ideas of the greatest importance — the germ theory of disease, and the theory of evolution — were presented in the 19th century. The germ theory had been proposed several times in the past, but it was not until the work of Louis Pasteur (1822-1895) that it became generally accepted. The idea that the species we see today have not always been around, but rather have evolved from earlier forms, had also been suggested many times. Darwin's great contribution was to suggest a mechanism (natural selection) by which that evolution occurred.[1]

G) *Geology and Anthropology*. Although bones that we now realize came from dinosaurs had been observed many times, their significance was not realized until the 19th century. In addition, for the first time, remains of extinct "nearly human" species, including the Neanderthals and *Homo erectus*, were discovered.

An unexpected discovery was that there had been periods in the past (the "ice ages") when glaciers covered much of Europe and North America.

Section 3 – Major inventions

Table 49-2 lists some of the noteworthy inventions made in the 19th century.[2] Ten of the most important ones have been placed at the top of the list. It is worth noting that — except for the steam engine — no mechanical invention of the 18th century compares in importance to those ten items (or, arguably, to any item in Table 49-2). The burst of practical inventions that were made in the 19th century was truly unprecedented.

Section 4 – Pre-eminence of Europeans in mathematics, science, and invention

The reader may have noticed that the most of the inventors and scientists whose contributions were described in the last two sections came from just a few countries. This can be seen more clearly by examining Table 49-3, in which 34 of the most prominent 19th-century scientists, mathematicians, inventors, and medical innovators are listed, along with the country that each came from. Table 49-4 provides a breakdown, by country of origin, of the persons listed in Table 49-3.

As can be seen from Table 49-4, all of the important discoveries and inventions of the 19th century were made by Europeans, or by Americans of European descent, and the great majority of them came from those countries in which the Industrial Revolution started earliest, or made the greatest progress in the course of that century. This suggests that the advent of the Industrial Revolution was a major causative factor in the burst of scientific inventions and discoveries made during that period. Consistent with that is the presence on the list of only one person from Italy, and not a single one from Spain, Portugal, or Greece. The Industrial Revolution did not reach those countries until late in the century, and made little progress in them before 1900.

Section 5 – European colonialism and imperialism

The 19th-century expansion of European power and control was most striking in Africa, Australia, and the Indian subcontinent.

TABLE 49-2

SOME NOTABLE 19th-CENTURY INVENTIONS

Invention	Inventor	Date
Railroad	George Stephenson	1825
Camera	Louis Daguerre	1837
Anesthesia	William T. G. Morton	1846
Antiseptic surgery	Joseph Lister	1867
Telephone	Alexander Graham Bell	1876
Light bulb (incandescent)	Thomas Edison	1879
Preventive inoculation	Louis Pasteur	1881
Electric power distribution system	Thomas Edison	1882
Automobile	Karl Benz; Gottlieb Daimler	1885
Radio	Guglielmo Marconi	1894
Steamboat	Robert Fulton	1807
Canning of foods	Nicolas Appert	1811
Electric motor	Michael Faraday	1821
Electric generator	Michael Faraday	1831
Revolver	Samuel Colt	1835
Telegraph	Samuel Morse	1840
Vulcanized rubber	Charles Goodyear	1844
Sewing machine	Elias Howe	1846
Farm machinery (reaper)	Cyrus McCormick	1847
Elevator	Elisha Graves Otis	1852
Machine gun	Richard Gatling	1862
Dynamite	Alfred Nobel	1866
Typewriter	Christopher Sholes	1868
Internal combustion engine (4-stroke)	Nikolaus August Otto	1876
Phonograph	Thomas Edison	1877
Skyscrapers	William Le Baron Jenney	1885
Aluminum (practical smelting process)	Charles Hall; Paul Héroult	1886
Artificial fabric (rayon)	Louis Chardonnet	1889
Motion pictures	Louis & Auguste Lumière	1895
Submarine	John P. Holland	1898

TABLE 49-3

BIRTHPLACES OF SOME NOTABLE 19th-CENTURY SCIENTISTS & INVENTORS

Name	Birthplace	Accomplishment
Charles Darwin	England	Theory of evolution
James Clerk Maxwell	Scotland	Laws of electromagnetism
Louis Pasteur	France	Preventive inoculation
Michael Faraday	England	Electric motors & generators
John Dalton	England	Atomic theory
Thomas Edison	USA	Electric light; phonograph
Alexander Graham Bell	Scotland	Telephone
Guglielmo Marconi	Italy	Radio
William T. G. Morton	USA	Anesthesia
Louis Daguerre	France	Photography
Karl Benz/Gottlieb Daimler	Germany	Automobile
Max Planck	Germany	Quantum theory
Wilhelm Röntgen	Germany	X-rays
Auguste & Louis Lumière	France	Motion pictures
George Stephenson	England	Railroad
Joseph Lister	England	Antiseptic surgery
Ludwig Boltzmann	Germany	Statistical mechanics
Gregor Mendel	Austria	Laws of heredity
Dmitri Mendele'ev	Russia	Periodic table of elements
Louis Chardonnet	France	Artificial fabric (rayon)
Karl Friedrich Gauss	Germany	Mathematics
Gustav Kirchhoff	Germany	Spectroscopy
Nikolai Lobachevski	Russia	Non-Euclidean geometry
Antoine Henri Becquerel	France	Radioactivity
Nikolaus August Otto	Germany	Internal combustion engine
Frederick W. Taylor	USA	Industrial management
Marie Curie	Poland	Radium
Martinus Beijerinck	Netherlands	Viruses
Robert Fulton	USA	Steamboat
Rudolf Clausius	Germany	Laws of thermodynamics
Louis Agassiz	Switzerland	Ice ages
Elias Howe	USA	Sewing machine
Cyrus McCormick	USA	Reaping machine
Georg Cantor	Germany	Mathematics

TABLE 49-4

BREAKDOWN BY COUNTRY OF ORIGIN OF 19th-CENTURY SCIENTISTS, MATHEMATICIANS, & INVENTORS

Country	Scientists	Mathematicians	Inventors*	Total
Germany	5	2	2	9
Great Britain	4	0	3	7
United States	0	0	6	6
France	2	0	3	5
Russia	1	1	0	2
Austria	1	0	0	1
Italy	0	0	1	1
Netherlands	1	0	0	1
Poland	1	0	0	1
Switzerland	1	0	0	1
Total	**16**	**3**	**15**	**34**
Britain + USA	4	0	9	13
Germany + Austria	6	2	2	10
France + Switzerland	3	0	3	6
Other Europe	3	1	1	5
Total	**16**	**3**	**15**	**34**

* Includes two persons whose fields were medicine.

A) <u>Africa</u>. In 1800, most of the interior of SSA (sub-Saharan Africa) was a *terra incognita* that had not been mapped or explored by Europeans. Major exploration of the "secluded zone" (most of eastern, central and southern Africa) started with the expeditions of David Livingstone between 1841 and 1873. Subsequent expeditions by Richard Burton, by John Speke, and by Henry M. Stanley also added greatly to European knowledge of Africa.

French forces had entered Algeria (in North Africa) in 1830, and by 1870 they had conquered the northern and central portions of the country. In time, many French settled there, although they never comprised a majority of the population.

Prior to 1880, however, the only European colonies in the interior of sub-Saharan Africa were in the far south. The Dutch had founded Capetown as early as 1652. By 1795 that colony extended as far north as the Orange River; but in 1806, England gained control of the colony. In 1835, about 12,000 Boers (descendants of the Dutch settlers) migrated northward to escape British rule; and in 1838, at the Battle of Blood River, they won a decisive victory over a much larger Zulu force. This enabled the Boers to establish two independent states in the interior, Transvaal (1852) and Orange Free State (1854). However, most of SSA was still independent of European rule.

Then, in the last quarter of the 19th century (mostly between 1880 and 1890) European countries seized control of almost all of SSA. In addition, France occupied Tunisia (1881) and England occupied Egypt (1882). As a result, at the end of the century England and France possessed the largest African empires, followed by Portugal, Belgium, and Germany. (Italy gained control of Libya in 1911, and the French took over Morocco in 1912.) However, in most of those colonies the numbers of European settlers were very small.

B) Asia. Results were very different in Asia. Many parts of that continent — including China, Japan, Korea, Thailand, Iran, Afghanistan, and the interior of Arabia — never became European colonies. Also, much of the Middle East remained under the control of the Ottoman Empire in 1900, although the English had established protectorates over various emirates on the Arabian coast.

The Indian subcontinent, though, had come under British control. England had already established itself as the dominant European power in the region by 1800; and by 1858, the English controlled all of India, either directly or by treaties with native princes who accepted British sovereignty in return for internal autonomy. The British also took control of Burma (in stages) between 1826 and 1886, and of Ceylon (Sri Lanka) in 1896.

Although India was Britain's most important, profitable, and populous colony, only about 65,000 British soldiers were stationed there.[3] English colonists in India never comprised as much as 0.1% of the total population.

Other parts of Asia that were colonized by Europeans included:

- Vietnam, Laos, and Cambodia, which were all French colonies.
- Most of Central Asia, which was part of the Russian Empire.
- Indonesia, which was ruled by the Dutch.
- Malaya and parts of Borneo, which were ruled by England. The British had also set up several smaller but important colonies, including Hong Kong and Singapore.

C) Australia, Tasmania, and New Zealand. These had been discovered by Europeans in the 17th century, but were not settled until much later. The English settlement of Australia began in 1778, when the British government sent about 700 convicts there. Shipments of English convicts to Australia and Tasmania continued until 1840; however, in time the convicts became greatly outnumbered by voluntary settlers from England. The Australian aborigines were few in number and technologically backward, and in general they were pushed aside by the European settlers and dispossessed of their lands. Today, the aborigines comprise only a tiny fraction of the population.

Before the Europeans arrived, the Tasmanians had been cut off from the rest of the world (including Australia) for about ten thousand years, and the aborigines living there were even more primitive than the Australians. The English settlers treated the native population (which, in 1800, was about 4000) with great brutality, and no full-blooded Tasmanians survived the 19th century.

The aboriginal inhabitants of New Zealand, the Maori, were of Polynesian origin and were not related to the Australians. A Dutch mariner had discovered New Zealand in 1642, but almost no Europeans settled there until the first half of the 19th century. In 1840, English representatives signed a treaty with Maori chieftains by which the Maori agreed to English sovereignty in exchange for promises to respect their rights and land holdings. However, the English settlers (who by 1858 outnumbered the Maori) did not keep those promises. Warfare resulted, which of course was won by the much better-armed Europeans. Unlike the Australian and Tasmanian aborigines, though, the Maoris have remained a substantial element, and now comprise about 10% of the population.

To summarize: By the end of the 19th century, the only large non-European countries to retain their independence were China, Japan, and the Ottoman Empire, although several mid-sized countries (Korea, Thailand, Iran, Afghanistan, and Ethiopia) were also independent. The largest European empire (in population controlled) was that of the British.

Were the 19th-century Europeans unusually greedy or imperialistic? Not really. Throughout history it has been typical for powerful nations or leaders to extend their domains. (Think of the Babylonians, Assyrians, Persians, Macedonians, Romans, Arabs, Chinese, Turks, Mongols, Manchus, Zulus, and Japanese.) The remarkable extent of the 19th-century European empires was not due to any unusual avarice, but merely to the unusual opportunity that their superior technology provided.

Section 6 – Political and social changes within Europe
Since the social and political history of 19th-century Europe is well covered in many history books, I will mention only the main trends here. In the course of the century, several of the attitudes of the Enlightenment spread widely within Europe. Among these attitudes were:

1) Disapproval of the power and privileges of monarchs and aristocrats. (In the course of the century, those privileges were greatly curtailed in most European countries.)

2) Religious skepticism, and disapproval of clerical power and influence.

3) Confidence in science.

In the first half of the 19th century, disapproval of the institution of slavery became widespread within Europe. This led to the abolition of slavery in many European colonies, and the suppression of the slave trade in many other parts of the world. The century also saw an increase in the legal rights accorded to women, although in no country were they accorded full equality. There was a gradual increase in support for social welfare policies and for socialist ideas. Funding of public education increased steadily.

In general, nationalist feelings grew stronger during the century, and increased in strength relative to religious, local, and family loyalties. One result of this was the unification of Germany; another was the unification of Italy. (At the beginning of the century, both regions had consisted of many small, independent states.) However, the nationalist desires of many groups in Eastern Europe, such as the Poles and the Czechs, were thwarted by the large empires that ruled them.

The rapid changes that occurred throughout the century led to a great deal of social and political turmoil, including a fair number of violent rebellions and revolutions. However, in the period 1815-1914 (i.e., from the final defeat of Napoleon at Waterloo until the outbreak of World War I) there were relatively few wars between European countries. In comparison, the interval 1600-1815 had been much bloodier, and the 20th century turned out to be worse still.

Section 7 – Westernization

During the 19th and 20th centuries, many Asian and African countries began adopting Western technology, and also Western social and political attitudes and practices. This occurred even in countries that were not conquered by Europeans. The extent and rapidity of westernization in a given country depended on a variety of factors:

- *The terrain*. Westernization tended to be slow in jungle, mountain, or desert regions.

- *The nature of the economy prior to contact with Europeans*. It also tended to be slow in regions where most aborigines were herdsmen or hunter-gatherers.

- *The duration of European control or contact*. In those regions that the Europeans did not enter until comparatively recently the onset of westernization was delayed and the process was less complete.

- *The average intelligence of the inhabitants of the country or region*. Where that was comparatively low, as in SSA, westernization has been slow and incomplete; where it was high, as in Japan, westernization was relatively rapid.

Westernization has tended to make the differences in wealth and income between the various parts of the Earth smaller than they would otherwise be, since the relatively backward areas of the world have been able to obtain the benefits of modern science and technology without having to make the discoveries and inventions themselves.

It has been repeatedly said that European imperialism often caused great suffering to the inhabitants of non-European countries. That is true; but it should also be noted that, since westernization was to a large extent a consequence of European imperialism, an indirect effect of that imperialism has been a great increase in the wealth and health of non-European countries.

Section 8 – Japan

Europeans had reached Japan in the 16th century, and for a while European traders and missionaries had considerable influence there. But in the 17th century the Japanese government decided to cut off trade and contacts with the West. Foreigners were driven out, Japanese were forbidden to travel abroad, and trade was virtually ended.

This period of isolation lasted for over 200 years. Then in 1853 (and again in 1854) American warships entered Tokyo Bay and insisted that Japan be at least partly opened to foreign trade. Other foreign interventions followed.

Japan was thrown into turmoil, but by 1868 the Japanese had decided on a policy of westernization, which was carried out with remarkable speed. Within five years, a draft was instituted, the western calendar adopted, and the first Japanese railroad line constructed. Within 30 years, a new constitution was promulgated, new law codes were adopted, and the armed forces were reorganized (all based on western models). A few years later, in 1904-05, the Japanese amazed the world by badly defeating the Russians in a war — the first time since 1700 that a third-world country had defeated a European one.

There were several reasons for the extraordinary speed with which Japan was able to adopt Western technology and transform itself into a major world power. Beyond question, though, one of those reasons was the high natural intelligence of the Japanese.

Section 9 – The rise of the United States of America

In 1783, the United States was a young, seemingly unimportant country on the fringes of the Western world. By 1900, it led the entire world in GNP, and it had also produced a thriving literature, including such noteworthy figures as Mark Twain, Edgar Allan Poe, and Walt Whitman. In addition, the country had produced a great number of important inventions, including the steamboat, the telegraph, the telephone, anesthesia, the phonograph, the light bulb, and a system for generating electric power and distributing it to the public — perhaps the most impressive set of inventions ever produced by a single country in one century.

What were the factors behind this extraordinary success? Among the advantages that the United States started the century with were:

1) It had large amounts of arable land, and abundant mineral resources. Indeed, it had a far higher ratio of natural resources to population than any of the European countries did.

2) Because most of the original settlers had come from England, it started with a relatively literate population. It also had a democratic government, which respected property rights and other individual liberties, and which permitted a large degree of economic freedom.

3) The citizenry consisted almost entirely of whites from northern Europe, a group that possessed a much higher average intelligence than the world at large.

4) It was protected from attack by European countries by its location on the other side of a wide ocean.

However, the new nation also started with certain disadvantages. The most important of these was the presence of two large, alien groups in its territory — the Indian aborigines and the black slaves.

Since the new nation was located on land that had been stolen from the aborigines, and since it was busily engaged in stealing the rest of their land, the hostility of the Indian tribes was virtually inevitable. Fortunately for the white citizens, the aborigines were technologically backward and far too few in number to seriously threaten the new country or to prevent the continued seizure of their lands.

The Negroes presented a far more difficult problem for the whites, simply because of their numbers: In 1800, they comprised 19% of the population. Because of the high number of blacks, it was difficult to either deport them or to indefinitely suppress them; nor, given the very real grievances that the blacks had, would it have been easy to assimilate them.

The institution of slavery was the cause of great discord among the white citizens themselves, and it eventually resulted in a bloody and costly civil war. In addition, the low average IQ of the blacks ensured that once freed they would be an economic drag on the country.

The racial problem in the United States has not yet been solved, and is still one of the greatest problems facing the country. However, during the 19th century, the combination of advantages listed above — together with the adoption of a wise constitution, and the unusually high character of the country's first president — proved to be far more important than the country's racial problems.

Section 10 – Developments in Latin America
In 1800, most parts of South and Central America were colonies of either Spain or Portugal. In the early 19th century, though, there were a series of rebellions against foreign rule. As a result, between 1811 and 1825 all the Spanish colonies on the mainland achieved independence, and Brazil became an independent monarchy. (It became a republic in 1889.)

The Spanish colonies all became constitutional republics when they gained their independence. However, those republics were generally unstable, and in subsequent decades there were frequent revolutions and coups, sometimes resulting in constitutional rule, but often leading to rule by autocrats or military juntas. Why were those South American republics so unstable? Several factors may have contributed:

1) Unlike the English colonies in North America, the Spanish colonies in the New World had been given very little experience in self-government during the colonial era.

2) Inequality of wealth was much more pronounced in Latin America than it had been in the British colonies in North America.

3) The Spanish Inquisition had functioned for many years in Spain's American colonies, with the result that freedom of speech and of the press had not become established there, as they had in the United States and Canada.

4) In most Latin American countries, whites made up a much smaller fraction of the population than they did in Anglo-America, and as a result those countries had lower average IQs, which made it more difficult for constitutional republics to function.

Probably because of the lower average intelligence in Latin America (compared with Europe and Anglo-America), the region made almost no contribution to the growth of science and technology in the 19th century.

The fraction of the population that is white varies considerably from one Latin American country to another. As might be expected, the countries in which that fraction is highest also have the highest mean IQs, and the highest per capita incomes. (See Table 49-5.)

TABLE 49-5

COMPARISONS BETWEEN SOME LATIN AMERICAN COUNTRIES

Country	Percent of population that is white (a)	Mean IQ (b)	Per capita GDP 2000 AD (c)
Argentina	85	96	$12,900
Uruguay	88	96	9,300
Colombia	20	89	6,200
Peru	15	90	4,550
Guatemala	negligible	79	3,700

a) *World Almanac* (2003 edition). In all of these countries (with the exception of Peru) the majority of the non-whites were mestizos.

b) Lynn & Vanhanen (2002), Table 6.1.

c) GDP = gross domestic product. Source: *World Almanac* (2003 edition).

FOOTNOTES – CHAPTER 49

1) Alfred Russel Wallace devised the same theory independently at about the same time as Darwin did.

2) Table 49-2 could easily have been made much longer: Omitted, for example, were such innovations as synthetic dyestuffs, large suspension bridges, Pasteurized milk, and the chlorination of public water supplies.

3) *Encyclopaedia Britannica* (15th edition, 1986), article on "India," volume 21, p. 93.

CHAPTER 50
THE JEWS

Section 1 – Introduction

A major theme of this book has been the importance of human intelligence, and the importance in history of differences in the mean intelligence of various ethnic groups. It would therefore be inappropriate not to discuss the Jews, as they appear to be the ethnic group with the highest average IQ. However, to understand the origin of their high average IQ, we must first look at Jewish history.

Section 2 – Jewish history through 70 AD

Much of their early history was discussed in section 27-9. The original Hebrew kingdom, with its capital in Jerusalem, was destroyed by the Babylonians in 586 BC. In the course of the next thousand years many Jews migrated from Asia into Egypt and southern Europe.

A new Jewish state arose in the second century BC, but it was destroyed by the Romans in 70 AD. The victorious Romans also destroyed the temple in Jerusalem, which had previously been the center of Jewish religious ceremonies.

This forced a change in Jewish religious practices, which thereafter placed great emphasis on the study of the Old Testament and the Talmud (a lengthy set of commentaries on the Bible, and on ethical and religious questions). Such studies required an ability to read, so learning to read became a religious requirement for Jews. As a result, at a time when relatively few gentiles could read and write, the large majority of adult male Jews were literate.

Section 3 – The Jewish gene pool

As far as we can tell, the original Hebrew tribesmen were genetically very similar to the other Semitic peoples who lived near them in Southwest Asia.

Throughout ancient and medieval times, male converts to Judaism were very rare, since circumcision was required in order to convert, and very few adult males were willing to submit to that procedure. As a result, even today, the genes on the Y-chromosomes of Jews living in different countries are very similar to each other, and to those in other Middle Eastern groups such as Syrians and Palestinians.[1]

However, until the 4th century AD, it seems to have been fairly common for Jewish males to marry gentile women, with the resulting children reared as Jews. As a result, Jews in most countries tend to physically resemble the non-Jewish inhabitants of the regions they inhabit more than they resemble Jews in distant lands;[2] and a study of neutral genes shows that European Jews are closely related genetically to the European average.[3]

After the 4th century AD, when Christianity became the established religion within the Roman Empire, Jews were forbidden to either proselytize or to marry Christian women. Thereafter, there were very few additions to the Jewish gene pool in Europe. The same thing happened in the Middle East after the Moslem conquest in the 7th century AD.

Section 4 – Ashkenazim and Sephardim

By 1600, most Jews living in Europe, North Africa, or the Western Hemisphere fell into one of two main groups, the *Ashkenazim* and the *Sephardim*. (The descendants of Jews living in Asia at that time form a third group, the Oriental Jews.)

The Ashkenazim (roughly speaking, the Jews of northern Europe), were primarily descended from Jews who had settled in the Rhine Valley between 500 and 1100 AD. For the most part, those settlers were Jews who had migrated from southern Europe after the fall of Rome, although some may have migrated there even earlier. It appears likely that many of the original migrants were long-distance traders.[4]

It has sometimes been suggested that many Ashkenazim are descended from the Khazars (a Turkish tribe that established a large kingdom in the Ukraine in the 6th century AD, and whose ruler converted to Judaism in the 8th century).[5] However, that intriguing hypothesis, which had always been rejected by the majority of scholars, has been disproved by recent DNA studies.[6]

In the late Middle Ages, and in early modern times, the Ashkenazim gradually increased in numbers, and many of them migrated into Eastern Europe, particularly into Poland and Lithuania. By 1800, they made up the large majority of world Jewry. In the late 19th and early 20th centuries, many of them migrated to the Western Hemisphere, particularly to the United States.

The Sephardim are primarily descended from Jews who lived in Spain and Portugal during the late Middle Ages. (Most of those were descended from Jews who had lived within the Roman Empire.) By 1000 AD, the Jewish community in Spain had become large and prosperous. However, starting in the late 1300s there were increasingly severe persecutions of the Spanish Jews, culminating in their expulsion from Spain in 1492 and from Portugal in 1497. Many of the Jewish refugees from Spain and Portugal went to Holland, and some wound up in the New World, but the majority migrated eastward to the Ottoman Empire, or to other parts of southern Europe or North Africa.

In the course of the next five centuries, many of the Sephardim in Western Europe intermarried with Ashkenazi Jews, and many of the Sephardim in the Middle East intermarried with Oriental Jews. As a result, the fraction of living Jews who can be clearly identified as Sephardim is fairly small. (Most of the Israeli Jews who are called Sephardim are in fact either Oriental Jews or of mixed Sephardic-Oriental descent.[7])

Section 5 – Occupational structure of the Ashkenazi Jews

In the late Middle Ages and early modern times, the Ashkenazi Jews had a very unusual distribution of occupations. As the group had originated as emigrants and traders, relatively few of them were farmers (even in those countries where they were permitted to own land). Many other careers were closed to them. They could not be members of the aristocracy (and therefore, they were not large landowners); nor could they be army officers; and, of course, they could not be members of the Christian clergy. In addition, most of the medieval guilds in northern Europe excluded them.[8]

They could, however, be merchants, and many of them were. Furthermore, many rulers, particularly in Poland and Lithuania, welcomed them as bureaucrats and tax collectors. Also, a considerable number of them became moneylenders.[9] (That occupation was closed to Christians, since Church law prohibited the taking of interest; for centuries, therefore, the Jews had a near-monopoly in that field.)

As a result, in late medieval and early modern times a surprisingly high fraction of Ashkenazi Jews became concentrated in a few fields — including trade, moneylending, tax collection, and the bureaucracy — and in each of those fields above-average intellectual ability was very important for success.

Section 6 – Evidence of the high average intelligence of the Jews

It has long been noted that Jews are greatly over-represented in the learned professions and in other intellectual occupations.[10] For example, the fraction of American scientists, college professors, lawyers, physicians, journalists, writers, movie producers, and economists who are Jews is very much higher — by about a factor of ten — than the fraction of Jews in the general population. Also, despite widespread anti-Semitism in the old Soviet Union (including quotas restricting their access to universities), Jews comprised about one-quarter of the Soviet Academy of Science.

It is striking that, although Jews comprise only about ¼ of one percent of the world's population, in the course of the 20th century they were awarded 128 Nobel Prizes, or about 20% of the total number. (The persons who award the Nobel Prizes are not Jews, and the Jewish Nobel laureates were concentrated in fields in which the standards are relatively objective — 22 in chemistry, 31 in physics, and 44 in biology and medicine.)

Nobel Prizes are not awarded for achievements in mathematics. The most prestigious prize in that area is probably the Fields Medal, and Jews dominate the list of its recipients. Jews are also greatly over-represented in the ranks of top chess and bridge players. Additional evidence of high Jewish intelligence is provided by the survival of the state of Israel for over 50 years, despite the enormous advantages that the hostile Arab states have in population, territory, and natural resources.

All of this is consistent with the performance of Jews on standard IQ tests. Some typical results[11] (there are many others) are:

1) A study of 770 Jewish students attending public high schools in Philadelphia found that their average score on the Otis IQ test was 115.

2) A study of over 1200 students attending all-day Hebrew schools in America found that their average IQ was over 118.

3) A study of schoolchildren in London in the late 1920s found that, after discounting for the fathers' occupational backgrounds, Jewish children outscored the others by about 9 points. (Without such discounting, the difference between the two groups would have been even larger.)

4) A large study of a representative sample of children in Scotland found that the average IQ of the Jewish children was 118.

5) A study of 400 children in Israeli *kibbutzim* (collective farms) found that their average IQ was about 117.

A reasonable inference from these studies (all of which involved Ashkenazi Jews) is that the mean IQ of Ashkenazi Jews is in the neighborhood of 115. What little information we have suggests that the average IQ of Oriental Jews is much lower. Convincing data concerning the IQ of Sephardic Jews is lacking; however, their achievements in late medieval and early modern times suggest a high level of intelligence.[12]

Even before any of those studies were made, there was a widespread belief that Jews were very clever. Indeed, the economic success of Jews has often engendered theories that they were conspiring together in some tricky, dishonest way. No evidence of such a conspiracy has been produced, and it seems clear that the economic success of the Jews is easily explained by their high average intelligence, and is no greater than would be expected of a group with a mean IQ of 115.

Section 7 – An attempted environmentalist explanation

In recent decades, the only ideologically acceptable explanation for the high IQ of the Ashkenazim has been the environmental one, which assumes that there is no genetic basis to their high average IQ, but that it is entirely due to the very high emphasis that Jewish culture places on education and learning. Unfortunately for this hypothesis, studies show that an enriched childhood environment has (statistically) rather little effect on adult IQ.

For example, as mentioned in section 3-8, there is almost no correlation between the adult IQs of otherwise unrelated children who were adopted at an early age and reared in the same family.[13] Also, studies show that even carefully-planned and well-financed programs designed to provide especially enriched childhood environments do not succeed in increasing adult IQs by more than about 5 points.[14] (See section 16-2D, and Table 16-3.) Therefore, even if we assumed that every Jewish household — and no gentile one — provided a very intellectually stimulating environment (which is obviously an extreme exaggeration), that would account for less than half of the observed 15-point difference between Jewish and gentile IQs. The proposed environmental explanation is therefore clearly inadequate.

Furthermore, the emphasis that non-Jewish Europeans place on learning and education has increased markedly in the last century; so if that was the main factor involved then the IQ difference between Jews and gentiles should have decreased sharply during that time, whereas in fact it has not.

Section 8 – Some suggested genetic explanations

It has often been suggested that the persecution which European Jews endured during the Middle Ages resulted in a strong selection effect in favor of those with higher native intelligence. Since severe discrimination against Jews continued for roughly fifteen centuries (or sixty generations), the selection effect would not have had to be very great to have produced a marked increase in the average IQ of the group. Superficially, this sounds plausible. However, if being persecuted or strongly discriminated against is enough to cause a large increase in IQ, then the average IQ of the Gypsies — who for centuries have been discriminated against in virtually every country — should also be very high, whereas it is in fact below the European average; and American blacks, who (even after being released from slavery) faced massive discrimination should be smarter still. Furthermore, Oriental Jews in Arab lands were at least as badly discriminated against as the Ashkenazim, but they do not, on average, possess high IQs.

Another hypothesis involves the high esteem in which rabbis were held within the Jewish community. According to that theory, wealthy Jews thought it prestigious to have their daughters marry rabbis; and the rabbis (whose ranks included many of the most intelligent Jews) therefore had large numbers of surviving children.[15] A problem with that suggestion is that rabbis always comprised a very small fraction of the Jewish community, so it is hard to see how the effect could account for the observed 15-point difference between Jewish and Christian IQs. Note also that the opposite custom — priestly celibacy in Catholic countries — does not seem to have created any significant difference between the IQs in Western Europe and those in Eastern Europe (where priests were always free to marry).

However, two other genetic hypotheses appear to have some merit. One of these is that modern Jews are descended from only a small subset of the original Hebrew tribesmen, in particular from the predominantly upper-class (and presumably more intelligent) group who were carried away in exile after the Babylonian conquest in 586 BC.[16]

The other hypothesis is that, since the Ashkenazi community originally derived from long-distance merchants, they were not a random subset of Jews from southern Europe, but rather were derived mostly from the upper end of the IQ distribution.

Section 9 – A recent suggestion

A very interesting hypothesis has recently been introduced by Cochran, Hardy, and Harpending (hereafter referred to as CHH). According to them, the high IQ of modern Ashkenazi Jews is an example of Darwinian evolution, resulting from the fact that for centuries a high proportion of their ancestors occupied an unusual economic niche, a niche which placed great practical value on high intelligence. For centuries, those Jews who succeeded as merchants, tax collectors, and moneylenders became relatively prosperous, and many of their offspring survived. Those who lacked the intellectual ability needed for those occupations remained (or became) poor, and relatively few of their offspring survived.[17]

Note that although the evolutionary process involved was triggered by environmental factors, it resulted in a genetic change (an increased frequency of various alleles that lead to increased intelligence), and it is primarily that genetic change that is responsible for the high IQs found today among Ashkenazim. A combination of several conditions was required for this evolutionary process to occur:

1) An economic niche was available that strongly rewarded persons of high native intelligence, and that could not be filled by gentiles living in the region (because of laws prohibiting Christians from taking interest, and also because of the low literacy rate of the surrounding population).

2) Many other occupations were closed to Jews.

3) The evolutionary effect on the Jewish gene pool was not diluted by external input, since for a long time there was very little intermarriage between Jews and gentiles.

Note that this unusual combination of circumstances had not existed in classical Greek or Roman times. Nor did it exist in the Moslem world, where there were several other groups who had commercial experience and were literate enough to be bureaucrats and tax collectors (Greeks, Armenians, and many Moslems), and where most Jews were either craftsmen or confined to menial occupations. However, the process may have occurred within the Sephardic community as well, since Spanish Jews were also heavily involved in trade, and were employed by monarchs as advisors, bureaucrats, and tax-collectors.[18]

Section 10 – Genetic diseases common among Ashkenazi Jews

The CHH paper identifies some of the alleles involved in the high average IQ of the Ashkenazim. Some of them are responsible for higher levels of glucosylceramide (a compound which has been shown by *in vitro* experiments to promote axonal growth and branching of neurons), or of GM2 ganglioside (which increases dendritogenesis). The paper also discusses other alleles common among Ashkenazi Jews, some of which improve DNA repair.

However, like many other alleles, those that are responsible for the high IQ of the Ashkenazim have various side effects. In particular, although a single copy of one of these alleles has a beneficial effect on an individual's intelligence, having two copies of such an allele normally results in a serious genetic disease. (This is analogous to the case of sickle-cell anemia, which was discussed in section 14-3.)

As a result, Ashkenazi Jews have a much higher incidence of several genetic diseases than their Christian neighbors do. There are at least eight such diseases, the best known of which are Tay-Sachs and Gaucher's disease.[19] It is striking that, in Israel, 15% of those adult Jews who suffer from Gaucher's disease are engineers or scientists, compared with only 1.35% of other working-age Jews.

It had earlier been suggested that the high frequency of those genetic diseases in Ashkenazi Jews is due to other factors, such as genetic drift. However, the CHH paper refutes those suggestions by a careful statistical analysis.

Section 11 – A tentative history of Jewish IQs

As so many hypotheses have been discussed, it seems advisable to present an overall scenario which explains the resulting distribution of Jewish IQs. The calculations which follow are, of course, only very rough estimates; but the assumptions they are based on are reasonable, and the results are consistent with what we know about medieval Jews and their activities.

a) The average IQ of the original Hebrew tribesmen was probably similar to that of the other Semitic tribes then living in the region (i.e., about 87).

b) The Hebrews who were exiled to Babylon after the Babylonians conquered Jerusalem in 586 BC (and from whom most later Jews are descended) were not a random sample, but consisted to a large extent of the upper classes. As a result, the mean IQ of their descendants in Babylon was probably about 7 points higher than that of the original Hebrew population,[20] and it was the descendants of those Jews who eventually spread throughout the Middle East, and into Europe and North Africa.

c) In the course of the next thousand years, there was a substantial degree of intermarriage between male Jews and females from the peoples they lived among. In Europe, in Greek and Roman times, the effect of this intermarriage was to slightly increase the average IQ of the Jewish community, which may have reached about 97 by 300 AD.[21] However, in the Middle East — where typical IQs were a good deal lower than in Europe — the effect of intermarriage was to lower the average IQ of the Jewish community by several points.

d) The Ashkenazi community was derived in large part from long-distance traders who migrated north during the Middle Ages. Such merchants were a small and unrepresentative subset of the Jews who had lived in the Roman Empire during its final centuries, and their average IQ was significantly higher than other Roman Jews. Averaging in those migrants who were not merchants, the mean IQ of the early Ashkenazim was about 9 points higher than that of the Roman Jews,[22] or 106.

e) Particularly in northern Europe (but also to some extent in Spain) a large number of Jews were concentrated in an economic niche that included trade, moneylending, and the bureaucracy. Those who possessed high intelligence flourished in that niche; those who lacked the necessary intellectual talents did not, and they had fewer surviving children. Over the course of centuries, this evolutionary process led to a slow increase in the average intelligence of the European Jews. It probably raised Sephardic IQs to about 110, and the Ashkenazi average to about 115.

Section 12 – Broader significance of the CHH paper

The significance of that paper goes far beyond the question of the IQ of Ashkenazi Jews. Since we know that genetic factors play a part in an individual's intelligence, it has long been clear that there must be some specific alleles that affect IQ. The politically correct position in recent decades has been to assert that *all* such alleles are equally distributed among ethnic groups (for otherwise, ethnic differences in IQ would not be caused entirely by differences in upbringing and environment).

Although that assertion never seemed reasonable, and was not backed by experimental data, until recently its proponents could say that no specific allele had been identified that affected intelligence and that was unequally distributed among ethnic groups. That claim can no longer be made; and the purely environmentalist explanations of racial differences in intelligence is no longer tenable.

FOOTNOTES – CHAPTER 50

1) Hammer, M.F., et al. (2000). See particularly Figure 2 and the discussion on p. 6772.

2) Patai and Wing (1975), *The Myth of the Jewish Race*. See section 4 (pp. 31-39) of chapter 1.

3) See Cochran, G., J. Hardy. & H. Harpending (in press), especially Table 1 and pp. 14-15.

4) See Cochran, G., J. Hardy. & H. Harpending (in press), p. 10 and sources cited therein.

5) An excellent presentation of that hypothesis, along with a history of the Khazar state, can be found in Arthur Koestler's book (1976), *The Thirteenth Tribe*.

6) See Hammer, M.F., et al. (2000).

7) *Encyclopaedia Judaica* (1971), volume 14, article on Sephardim. See particularly pp. 1175-1176.

8) *Encyclopaedia Judaica* (1971), volume 7, article on Guilds. See particularly p. 972.

9) See *Encyclopaedia Judaica* (1971), volume 12, article on Moneylending. See particularly p. 254. Also see Cochran, Hardy, & Harpending (in press), p. 11.

10) Data on the disproportionate number of Jews who have made important contributions in the arts and sciences can be found in many places, for example in Murray, Charles (2003), *Human Accomplishment*, pp. 275-283.

11) For a more detailed description of the examples mentioned here see Storfer, Miles D. (1990), *Intelligence and Giftedness*, pp. 315-319, and sources cited therein.

12) See chapter 6 of Patai, Raphael (1977) *The Jewish Mind*.

13) Jensen, Arthur (1998), p. 178.

14) See Weinberg, Scarr, & Waldman (1992), or Table 12.5 on p. 474 of Jensen (1998).

15) For a more detailed description of this hypothesis, and the arguments in its favor, see chapter 16 of Weyl, Nathaniel (1989), *The Geography of American Achievement*.

16) This hypothesis was proposed by Cyril Darlington (1969) in *The Evolution of Man and Society*. See also Weyl, Nathaniel (1989), pp. 133-136.

17) Cochran, G., J. Hardy. & H. Harpending, (in press).

18) *Encyclopaedia Judaica* (1971), volume 17, article on Spain. See particularly pp. 228-230.

19) Cochran, G., J. Hardy. & H. Harpending (in press), especially Tables 2 and 3 and pp. 16-24.

20) This assumes that about 10% of the population was exiled to Babylonia. Assuming a normal distribution, the top 10% of the population have IQs that are 19 points or more above the mean. Since not all the exiles were in the top 10% of the IQ distribution (and taking into account regression to the mean), the mean IQ of the Babylonian Jews should have exceeded that of the original Hebrew population by somewhere between 1/4 and 1/2 (say, 3/8) of 19 points. Now $3/8 \times 19$ is about 7 points, and $7 + 87 = 94$.

21) This is midway between 94 and the mean IQ of southern Europeans (about 100).

22) The merchants themselves probably came from the top 5% of the population. In a normal distribution, the top 5% have IQs of 24 or more points above the mean. Following the reasoning in footnote 20, the mean IQ of the early Ashkenazi Jews was therefore about $3/8 \times 24$ points (= 9 points) above the mean of the Roman Jews; and $97 + 9$ is 106.

CHAPTER 51

THE TWENTIETH CENTURY

Section 1 – Technological developments

The 20th century saw remarkable advances in science and technology. More than any other century, it deserves to be called "The Age of Science." Some of the noteworthy advances are listed in Tables 51-1 and 51-2.

Many of those discoveries and inventions are of great importance, and some (such as computers and genetic engineering) are truly revolutionary in their impact. Almost all of the scientists and engineers involved in those breakthroughs were European or American whites.

Section 2 – Major wars
A) World War I

For nearly a century after the final defeat of Napoleon in 1815 there was comparatively little fighting between the major European powers. This relatively peaceful period ended in the summer of 1914. The war that began then — the one the combatants called *The Great War*, and we today call *World War I* — lasted four full years, and was the largest and bloodiest war the world had ever seen.

The war originally pitted Germany and Austria-Hungary (the "Central Powers") against England, France, Russia, and Serbia (the "Allies"). However, Turkey and Bulgaria later joined the Central Powers; and Italy, the United States, and many smaller countries eventually joined the Allies.

A striking feature of the war was the dominance of automatic weapons in ground warfare. Attempts to advance against positions defended by machine guns proved extremely costly to attacking infantry. As a result, on some fronts — particularly the Western Front, where German troops were facing British and French forces — the fighting was stalemated, with heavy casualties on both sides but relatively little conquest of territory. Although aircraft and tanks were eventually used in the fighting, they were not yet sufficiently advanced to have a great impact.

TABLE 51-1

SOME 20th-CENTURY ADVANCES IN MATHEMATICS, PURE SCIENCE, & MEDICINE

A) **Discoveries in Physics**

    The theory of special relativity
    The theory of general relativity
    The atomic nucleus
    Quantum mechanics

B) **Discoveries in Biochemistry**

    The structure of proteins
    The structure and functioning of DNA
    The nature of viruses

C) **Advances in Mathematics**

    Statistical theory
    Gödel's "incompleteness theorem"

D) **Discoveries in Astronomy and Geology**

    Cosmic rays
    White dwarfs, neutron stars, and pulsars
    Quasars
    Black holes
    Structure and evolution of the stars
    The expansion of the universe
    Internal structure of the Earth, other planets, and comets
    Continental drift and plate tectonics
    Methods of radioactive dating

E) **Advances in Medicine**

    Broad-spectrum antibiotics (such as penicillin and streptomycin)
    Improved methods of birth control (contraceptive pills; IUDs)
    Improved anesthetics
    Synthetic vitamins
    Anti-depressants
    Laser surgery
    Organ transplants
    CAT scans and MRIs

TABLE 51-2
20th-CENTURY INVENTIONS

A) <u>Some inventions of the 20th century</u>

Air conditioning
Airplanes
Artificial fabrics (polyester, nylon, etc.)
Computers (also PCs and handheld calculators)
Communication satellites
Copying machines
Fax machines
Frozen foods
Genetic engineering (still in its infancy)
Guided missiles
Home appliances (refrigerators, microwave ovens, etc.)
Internet
Lasers and masers
Nuclear weapons
Nuclear power plants
Plastics
Radar
Spacecraft
Television
Weather forecasting

B) <u>19th-century inventions in which major improvements were made</u>

Automobiles
Mass production techniques (automation, industrial robots)
Motion pictures (sound, color)
Photography (Polaroid cameras, digital cameras)
Radio (voice, music, FM)
Telephones (long distance dialing, cell phones)

It has often been mentioned that World War I was a particularly pointless war: There were no major ideological conflicts involved, and the countries and governments that entered the war had relatively little to gain and a great deal to lose. For example:

a) For Russia — which in 1905 had lost a war to Japan (which at the time had been considered a minor power) — to get into an easily avoidable war with Germany (which in 1914 possessed the world's strongest army) strikes one today as the height of folly.

b) Perhaps even more foolish were the decisions of Italy (in May 1915), Bulgaria (in October 1915), and Rumania (in August 1916) to enter the war, after it was already clear that the casualties and costs of the war were far greater than had been anticipated in the summer of 1914.

As the various nations' decisions to go to war appear in hindsight to be so irrational, there has been a great deal of discussion of the "underlying causes of the war." Among the most common suggestions are:

- Intense nationalism in the various European countries.
- A lack of realization of how great the costs of the war would be.
- The existence of a complex set of alliances that dragged into the war various powers that were not involved in the original dispute (between Austria-Hungary and Serbia) that started it.
- The natural proclivity to violence of many human beings (particularly males).

It has also been pointed out that several major powers adopted conspicuously poor tactics and strategy. For example, the original German strategy (the "Schlieffen plan") called for Germany to launch an all-out assault on their western front in the hope of achieving a quick victory over France, and only then attacking Russia. It is plain in hindsight that the reverse strategy — attacking Russia first, while defending on their western front — would have been far superior, and indeed may have given Germany a relatively cheap victory. The most likely reason that the Germans adopted such a flawed plan was that they grossly overestimated the strength of the large, but qualitatively inferior, Russian army. This was a surprising mistake to make, since the past four centuries had provided numerous examples of large armies being defeated by smaller, but technologically superior ones.

An even more striking example was the repeated attempts, by all the major armies, to have infantry units advance against positions that were heavily defended by machine guns, even though the enormous cost of such tactics was demonstrated in the first few months of the war, and repeatedly thereafter. (Indeed, the defensive power of machine guns against infantry had been demonstrated fifty years earlier, during the American Civil War, even though the machine guns used in that war were far inferior to those available in World War I.[1])

As a direct consequence of World War I, the Habsburg, Ottoman, Romanov, and Hohenzollern dynasties (in Austria, Turkey, Russia, and Germany respectively) all came to an abrupt end. The German and Russian empires both lost a fair amount of territory, while the Habsburg and Ottoman empires were completely dismantled. As a result, several new countries (including Finland, Estonia, Latvia, Lithuania, Poland, Hungary, Czechoslovakia, Yugoslavia, Syria, Lebanon, and Iraq) were set up, or regained their independence. In many cases, an attempt was made to have the political boundaries of the new countries follow ethnic and linguistic boundaries.

Another consequence of the enormous loss of life that occurred in World War I was a great increase in pacifist sentiment throughout Europe. This, in turn, made European countries far less willing to resort to force to retain their overseas colonies, or even to defend themselves against aggressors, such as Nazi Germany. A less tangible consequence of World War I was a marked decline within Europe of the public's confidence in their governments and institutions.

B) The rise of Communism

Following the overthrow of the Tsarist government in early 1917, an attempt was made to establish a constitutional republic in Russia. Later that year, however, a rebellion led by V. I. Lenin overthrew that provisional government and established a Communist government in its place. The Communists renamed the Russian Empire the *Union of Soviet Socialist Republics* (or *USSR*, or *Soviet Union*).

The USSR soon became a harsh, totalitarian despotism. During the 70-odd years that the Communists ruled the country, they killed some 30 million people (some by starvation, others by privation in slave labor camps, others by direct execution). They also established a rigidly socialist government, replacing the prior free-market economy with a system of government ownership of the means of production, and widespread central planning.

The Soviet government also adopted a policy of encouraging the formation of Communist governments in other countries. This policy sometimes entailed subverting other governments and fomenting civil wars, which led to great turmoil and bloodshed in many parts of the world.

C) World War II

This war was even larger and bloodier than World War I had been. It eventually included two large coalitions: the "Axis Powers" (which included Germany, Italy, Japan, and a few smaller countries) and the "Allied Powers" (which included France, England, China, the United States, and many smaller countries). However, it began as two separate wars:

    a) A war that started in 1937 between Japan and China; and

    b) A war that started in 1939 between Germany on one side and Poland, England, and France on the other.

The two wars merged together in December 1941 when Japan attacked both the United States and England, and Germany declared war on the United States.

When the war began, the Soviet Union was an ally of Germany; however, in June 1941 Germany attacked the USSR, and thereafter the USSR was a member of the Allied coalition. The war ended in 1945 with the complete triumph of the Allied powers.

No previous war had seen such a profusion of new weapons. Early in the war, in their "blitzkrieg" attacks, the German armies made effective use of tanks and tactical aircraft. Throughout the war, the major powers made strenuous efforts to improve the quality of their weapons and to develop new ones. The Germans developed long-range missiles; and in the final year of the war the United States produced atomic weapons. Two of these were used in August 1945 (against the Japanese cities of Hiroshima and Nagasaki) and their use resulted in a quick end to the war.

In both world wars, Germany fought against England, France, Russia, and the United States. Therefore, as far as the European portion of the war was concerned, World War II may be regarded as a continuation or "second round" of World War I. However, World War II also involved a major ideological clash, not present in the first war.

The German dictator, Adolf Hitler, and the party that he headed (the *National Socialist* or *Nazi* party) claimed that Germans were inherently superior to all other peoples; and that Germany was therefore entitled to rule the world. One of their goals was to permanently subjugate and enslave other peoples whom they deemed inferior, such as Russians, Poles, and other Slavs. Furthermore, the German government embarked upon a program of completely exterminating certain peoples whom they considered undesirable (most notably the Jews, but also the Gypsies). These horrifying policies resulted in millions of additional deaths in excess of those that would have been the normal consequence of such a large war.

Obviously, Hitler's theories were not adopted on the basis of scientific data, but were merely rationalizations to justify his plans for foreign conquest. It is therefore not surprising that they were scientifically incorrect, and often ridiculous. Of course, even had Hitler's racial theories been factually correct, they would not have justified the ghastly policies he pursued, and he is rightly considered to be one of the most evil men who ever lived.

D) Consequences of World War II

The war resulted in the formation of a bipolar world, with two great rival powers — the United States and the Soviet Union — dominating the world militarily. At the end of the war, the United States occupied Japan and the western portion of Germany, while the Soviet Union occupied the eastern part of Germany and most of Eastern Europe. The character of those occupations, however, was very different. In the countries occupied by the USSR, the Russians set up Communist dictatorships that were subservient to the Soviet Union. The Americans ruled West Germany and Japan for only seven years, during which time constitutional republics (which still endure) were established in both countries. Among the other consequences of the war were:

1) In the 20 years following World War II, many countries in Asia and Africa that had been European colonies demanded and obtained their independence.

2) The United Nations was established, primarily in the hope that it would decrease the chance of future wars.

3) The ideology of Hitler and the Nazi party was totally discredited. Indeed, ever since then, a simple way to attack an idea or proposal without discussing it on its merits has been to allege that it is similar to some Nazi policy.

E) The Cold War

At the end of World War II, Germany, Italy, and Japan had been defeated and devastated; Britain and France had been greatly weakened; and China and India were not yet fully industrialized. That left only two great powers, the United States and the Soviet Union.

Most of the world was war-weary. But the Soviet Union was headed by an ambitious (indeed, megalomaniac) dictator, Josef Stalin, who was eager to extend Russian control over other countries. Furthermore, Stalin was supported by many persons living outside the USSR who desired the establishment of Communist governments. The result was the *Cold War*, a long struggle for dominance between the Soviet Union and the United States (and their respective allies), a struggle that continued for over 40 years.

Both sides soon acquired large arsenals of nuclear weapons. As a result, both the USA and the USSR avoided any direct fighting between their own armed forces and those of the other country. However, there were various wars (for example in Korea, in Vietnam, and in Afghanistan) in which one of the great powers used its troops. There were also wars between allies of the two countries (for example, Israel and Egypt), and there were various rebellions and civil wars involving supporters of the two great powers.

The Cold War was a complex struggle, involving not merely warfare and an arms race, but also economic and diplomatic competition, espionage, and propaganda. It was also an extremely costly struggle, more expensive financially than even World War II had been.

In general, the USSR did better than the USA in the propaganda and espionage aspects of the conflict. Indeed, a considerable number of citizens in Western countries were either Communists or supported them. (For example, in the national elections held in France in 1946, the Communists received over 40% of the votes.)

What finally decided the Cold War, though, was the dismal economic performance of the USSR. This resulted in widespread disillusionment with Communism within the Soviet Union itself. Combined with the nationalist aspirations of the various non-Russian peoples in the USSR, this eventually led to the breakup of the Soviet Union.

As a result, socialism as an economic system has been discredited almost everywhere. However, *social welfare* policies — which, unlike socialism, do not require government ownership of most of the means of production — still retain widespread support throughout the world.

Section 3 – Decolonization

A striking feature of the 20th century was the liberation of almost all of the colonies that European countries had previously acquired in Asia and Africa. In general, the European countries were reluctant to relinquish their colonies, and it was not until after World War II that they did so. There were several reasons why they then lost their colonies so quickly.

1) During that conflict, the Allied powers fighting Germany had claimed that the war was a "fight for freedom." Therefore, when Germany was defeated, many Europeans saw the hypocrisy of their continuing to rule Asian and African colonies.

2) The European powers had been weakened by World War II, and their populations were war-weary.

3) Each time an Asian or African colony achieved independence, other colonies were further encouraged to press their demands. At the same time, voters in European countries became convinced of the futility of attempting to hold onto their remaining colonies.

4) During the Cold War, the Soviet Union repeatedly encouraged independence movements in the overseas colonies of America's European allies.

By and large, Britain and America were readier to grant independence to overseas colonies than were most countries. More specifically:

A) *North Africa and the Middle East.*

- Britain had granted independence to Egypt in 1922, and to Iraq in 1932; however, English influence remained strong in both countries. Jordan became independent in 1946, and Israel (a special case) in 1948.
- Italy relinquished control of Libya at the end of World War II.
- The French gave up control of Syria and Lebanon in 1946; but they held on to Morocco until 1956, Tunisia until 1957, and Algeria until 1962. The war of independence in Algeria was particularly bloody.

B) *Asian countries.*

- The Philippines obtained independence from the United States in 1946, without any fighting.
- Britain relinquished control of India in 1947. Due to religious tensions between Hindus and Moslems, two states were set up: India and Pakistan.
- Britain granted full independence to both Burma and Sri Lanka (Ceylon) in 1948.
- The Netherlands attempted to reestablish control of Indonesia at the end of World War II. However the Indonesians rebelled, and after three years of

fighting they obtained full independence in 1949.

- France attempted to reestablish control of Indo-China (Vietnam, Laos, and Cambodia) at the close of World War II. A war of independence ensued, and the French withdrew in 1954.
- England recognized the independence of Malaya and Singapore in 1955.
- The Russian colonies in Central Asia (such as Uzbekistan and Tajikistan) did not obtain independence until 1991.

C) *Sub-Saharan Africa*.

In 1960, almost all of this region was still under European control. Then, in the brief interval 1960-1966, over two dozen countries obtained their independence from France, England, and Belgium. Portugal hung onto Angola and Mozambique until 1975; but by the end of the century, there were no European colonies left in Africa.

Section 4 – The Far East

At the beginning of the century, most non-European countries had not yet industrialized and were much poorer than Europe and America. To a large extent, this was still true in 1945, when World War II ended. During the Cold War, it became common to collectively refer to the poor countries in Asia, Africa, and Latin America as the "third world," with the United States (and its allies) and the Soviet Union (and its allies) as the first two worlds. However, not all those third-world countries have been equally successful in the decades since World War II.

Based on the information presented earlier in this book, one might have predicted in 1945 that the third-world countries whose populations were primarily of Mongolid stock would probably, because of their higher average intelligence, become considerably more prosperous than the others. Let us see how well such expectations have been confirmed by events.

A) *Japan*. This country is not well endowed with either mineral resources or arable land, and before the war was widely thought to be overpopulated. Furthermore, the country had been devastated by American bombing, including nuclear attacks on Hiroshima and Nagasaki. Nevertheless, Japan made remarkable economic advances in the decades following World War II, and by 1980 its gross national product had outstripped every European country and was second only to the USA. In addition, it had become a stable constitutional republic.

B) *South Korea and Taiwan*. Neither of these countries is particularly rich in natural resources, and both countries were threatened by neighbors who wished to annex them (South Korea by North Korea; Taiwan by mainland China). Nevertheless, both countries have become prosperous, and both appear to have developed into stable constitutional republics.

C) *North Korea*. In that country, on the other hand, the Russians installed a Communist regime at the end of World War II, and that regime adopted a centrally-planned socialist economic system. Such systems have failed badly in every country in which they have been tried, and it is not surprising that the economy of North Korea has not performed nearly as well as that of South Korea.

D) *Mainland China*. A Communist regime gained power there in 1949. For several decades thereafter the economy of mainland China performed very badly, despite the country's possession of large amounts of arable land and abundant mineral resources. Starting about 1980, though, the government has gradually replaced its socialist economic policies with free-market policies. Since then, the Chinese economy has been expanding rapidly, and its gross domestic product is now one of the highest in the world.

E) *Hong Kong and Singapore*. These had been British colonies before World War II. Hong Kong remained a British colony until 1997, when it was annexed by mainland China. Singapore was an English colony until 1959; it was then part of Malaysia for a while, but it became fully independent in 1965.

Hong Kong has an area of less than 400 square miles; and Singapore, with less than 250 square miles, is even smaller. Each has a population density of over 10,000 persons per square mile. Although they have excellent harbors, and are well situated for trade, they are lacking in mineral resources, and do not have enough land to feed their populations. In both cases, however, the population consists primarily of ethnic Chinese; and despite their lack of natural resources they have been outstanding economic successes.

F) *Indonesia*. This country is far better endowed with natural resources than the others discussed in this section. Nevertheless, its per capita income is less than one-fifth that of South Korea, and a still smaller fraction of the others (see Table 51-3). The difference in prosperity is readily explained by the difference in the nature of the populations. Indonesia is not populated primarily by Mongolids, but by σ-3s; and the mean IQ in Indonesia is far below that of the other countries just mentioned.

Section 5 – Sub-Saharan Africa

The situation in this region is almost exactly the reverse of the Far East. Since mean IQs in SSA are only about 70, it might reasonably have been predicted in 1945 that (despite the presence of large mineral resources) the economic performance of the countries in this region would be very poor. This has in fact occurred. Most countries in SSA are economic basket cases, and they are heavily dependent on foreign aid. The large majority of them have per capita GDPs of under $2000/year, and in some cases, less than $1000/year.

Aside from the Republic of South Africa, where the economic performance is greatly enhanced by the presence of about six million whites (over 13% of the population), the ten most populous countries in the region are: Nigeria, Ethiopia, Congo-Kinsasha (formerly Zaire), Tanzania, Sudan, Kenya, Uganda, Ghana, Mozambique, and Côte d'Ivoire. As can be seen from Table 51-4, at the end of the century those countries had a combined GDP of about 403 billion dollars — only slightly more than that of tiny Taiwan, which had only 1/20 the population and 1/300 the area of those ten countries.

The region's performance has been equally poor in political matters. Regardless of the constitutions in force when the European colonial powers relinquished control, most of the countries in SSA quickly became corrupt despotisms. In most of them, the statistics concerning crime, education, and matters of health are also bleak.[2]

Section 6 – The Islamic World

As can be seen from Table 51-3, the economic performance of the Islamic countries of North Africa and the Middle East has been intermediate between the two regions just discussed. This might have been anticipated, since the mean IQs in this region are intermediate between those prevailing in sub-Saharan Africa and the Far East. However, two additional factors have been important in the Moslem world: the presence of large reserves of oil in many of those countries, and the religious factor.

Iran, Iraq, Algeria, Libya, and Kuwait all have very large reserves of petroleum, and Saudi Arabia has the largest reserves in the world. On a per capita basis, several of the small countries bordering the Persian Gulf — including Qatar, Bahrain, and the United Arab Emirates — have even richer supplies of oil.

Despite the income from petroleum, the economic performance of those countries has been unimpressive. The per capita GDP of oil-drenched Kuwait is lower than that of such oil-poor countries as South Korea, Japan, Singapore, or Israel. (Note also that the roughly three billion dollars a year that Israel receives from the USA makes up less that 3% of Israel's gross domestic product, and that even without that aid Israel's per capita GDP would well exceed that of Kuwait or Saudi Arabia.)

The Islamic countries have also been hampered in their development by the very conservative nature of the prevailing religion and by the presence of a sizable number of religious extremists. One result has been that very few of those countries have been able to maintain constitutional governments for long. The militaristic nature of the religion (unlike Jesus, Muhammad was not a pacifist, and many of his early followers were conspicuous militarists) has probably been an additional source of some of the region's problems.

Section 7 – Immigration into Western countries

Movement and mixing of peoples have occurred throughout history. However, the extent of such movement and mixing has been much larger in the last five centuries than in any prior epoch.

From 1500 to 1900, the most prominent of such population movements involved the emigration of Caucasoids from Europe into other continents, often taking over large regions from the native inhabitants. Since 1950, though, the direction of the flow of people has been reversed. Many non-Europeans have migrated to Europe, the United States, Canada, and Australia, while relatively few Europeans have migrated to third-world countries. For example:

a) Large numbers of people from India and Pakistan have migrated to Great Britain.

TABLE 51-3

RECENT ECONOMIC PERFORMANCE OF SOME ASIAN AND NORTH AFRICAN COUNTRIES

Country	Population (a)	GDP (b)	Per capita GDP (c)	Average IQ (d)
North Africa				
Egypt	70.7	247	3,500	83
Libya	5.4	45	8,300	
Tunisia	9.8	63	6,400	
Algeria	32.3	171	5,300	
Morocco	31.2	105	3,400	85
Persian Gulf states				
Kuwait	2.1	29	13,800	
United Arab Emirates	2.4	54	22,500	
Qatar	0.8	15	18,800	
Bahrain	0.7	10	14,300	
Other Southwest Asia				
Syria	17.2	51	3,000	
Lebanon	3.7	18	4,900	86
Jordan	5.3	17	3,200	
Saudi Arabia	23.5	232	9,900	
Oman	2.7	20	7,400	
Iran	66.6	413	6,200	84
Turkey	67.3	444	6,600	90
Israel	6.0	110	18,300	(e)
Far East				
Japan	127.0	3,150	24,800	105
South Korea	48.3	765	15,800	106
Taiwan	22.5	386	17,200	104
Singapore	4.5	110	24,400	103
Indonesia	232.1	654	2,800	89

(a) In millions. (Source: *World Almanac*, 2003.)
(b) In billions of US dollars. (Source: *World Almanac*, 2003.)
(c) In US dollars. (Obtained from figures in two previous columns, and rounded.)
(d) Source: Lynn & Vanhanen (2002), Table 6.1.
(e) Lynn gives this as 94. However, that figure is so discordant with other studies of Jewish IQs that it seems likely that the studies on which Lynn's figure is based involved some serious error.

TABLE 51-4

MOST POPULOUS COUNTRIES IN SUB-SAHARAN AFRICA

Country	Population	Area	GDP	Per capital GDP
Nigeria	129.9	351,700	117,000	950
Ethiopia	67.7	432,300	39,200	600
Congo	55.2	875,500	31,000	600
Tanzania	37.2	342,100	25,100	710
Sudan	37.1	917,400	35,700	1,000
Kenya	31.1	219,800	45,600	1,500
Uganda	24.7	77,100	26,200	1,100
Ghana	20.2	88,800	37,400	1,900
Mozambique	19.6	302,700	19,100	1,000
Côte d'Ivoire	16.8	122,800	26,200	1,600
(Combined)	**439.5**	**3,730,200**	**402,500**	**916**

Note: The population figures are in millions. The areas are in square miles. The GDPs (gross domestic products) are in thousands of US dollars. The combined per capita GDP for the 10 countries was derived by dividing the total GDP by the total population. However, the per capita GDPs for the individual countries were taken directly from the source, even though division of the figure in column 4 by that in column 2 usually yielded a somewhat smaller figure.

Source: *World Almanac*, 2003. Most of the data was 1 to 3 years old.

b) Many people from Latin America (in particular, from Mexico) have migrated to the United States.

c) Many Moslems from North Africa and the Middle East have migrated to Western Europe.

d) There has been a substantial migration of people from East Asian countries (such as Vietnam, Korea, and the Philippines) into the United States.

This flow of people from third-world countries into Europe and America has been accomplished not by military force, but by peaceful immigration. Moreover, the recent movement of people has been very one-sided. For example:

a) The number of persons of Indian or Pakistani descent who are living in Great Britain today is much greater than the number of persons of British descent who are living in the Indian subcontinent, or who ever lived there.

b) The number of Arabs living in France today is far higher than the number of Frenchmen who are living in the Arab world, or who ever lived there.

To summarize: The overall movement of third-world peoples into first-world countries in the last half-century is much larger than any movement of people in any other 50-year stretch in history, and it is rapidly altering the demographic map of the world.

FOOTNOTES – CHAPTER 51

1) Tuchman, Barbara (1962), *The Guns of August*.

2) See, for example, the annual *Human Development Report* issued by the United Nations. In the one for the year 2000 (see the *Washington Times*, 7/3/2000) all 24 of the lowest-ranked countries (and none of the top 70) were located in Africa.

CHAPTER 52

SOME BROAD TRENDS IN HISTORY

Section 1 – Conquests

Throughout history, most of the instances of people from one region attacking and conquering substantial portions of another region have involved "northerners" invading more southerly lands. The European conquests of third-world countries in recent centuries are the most obvious examples of this, but the pattern existed long before modern times.

China, for example, has never been attacked by any of the populous countries south of it, but it has been repeatedly attacked from the north. Indeed, on two occasions northern invaders conquered all of China. In both cases (the Mongols in the 13th century; the Manchus in the 17th) the northern invaders had much smaller populations than China. Furthermore, within China itself, it was the northerners (under Shih Huang Ti, and the Han dynasty rulers) who first created a unified country by conquering southern China.

India, despite its large population, has never invaded the countries north of it, but rather has been repeatedly invaded from the north and northwest.

- a) About 6000 BC, Dravidian-speaking tribes entered India from Iran and eventually took over the entire subcontinent.

- b) In the second millennium BC, northern India was invaded and conquered by the Aryans, a group of Indo-European tribes who entered from the northwest. Although the Aryan invaders were greatly outnumbered by the natives, they eventually took over virtually all of northern India.

- c) More recently, during the last 2200 years, India has been invaded by a succession of northern peoples, including the Sakas, the Yüeh-chih, the Ephthalites, the Arabs (via Persia), and various other raiders, such as Mahmud of Ghazni, and Tamerlane.

Note also that the three Indian dynasties which came closest to ruling the entire subcontinent (the Mauryas, the Guptas, and the Mughals) all originated in the north.

The Greeks were not the original inhabitants of Greece, but were invaders who entered from the north about 2000 BC. Although the Greeks later founded many colonies in Sicily and southern Italy, the most notable conquests of the Greek-speaking peoples were those made by Alexander the Great in the 4th century BC. Alexander came from Macedonia, a large kingdom in northern Greece. He made some minor conquests in Thrace (the region north of Macedonia), but the large regions that he conquered — in Greece, Anatolia, the Fertile Crescent, Egypt, Iran, and parts of India — were all south of his kingdom.

The ancestors of the Romans entered Italy from the north, probably in the second millennium BC. Although the Romans conquered substantial regions that were north of Italy (including Gaul, Britain, and parts of Germany), most of the lands they conquered were south of them. Most of Spain, Asia Minor, and Greece lie south of Rome; while Syria, Judea, and North Africa (including Carthage and Egypt) are all far south of Rome. In the end, of course, the Roman Empire was overthrown by Germanic tribes from the north.

The Arab conquests are the only major counter-example to the general rule. Although the Arabs established settlements in regions south of Arabia (most notably along the East African coast), most of the Arab conquests were of regions well north of Mecca.[1] However, Arab control of Southwest Asia only lasted for a few centuries. It ended when the region was invaded by Turkish tribes (from Central Asia) and by the Mongols (from northern Asia), who between them ruled most of Southwest Asia for over nine hundred years.

The most extensive conquests of pre-modern times were those made by the Mongols. Although the Mongols did conquer some territory north of their homeland (for example, central Russia), they left most of Siberia alone; and the great bulk of their conquests (Central Asia, southern Russia, Southwest Asia, Korea, and China) were in regions to the south of them.

The obvious — and, I believe, the correct — explanation for the military superiority of the northerly peoples is the higher average intelligence of those peoples compared with the inhabitants of more tropical regions.

Section 2 – Major intellectual advances
During the Paleolithic, the coldest regions that were inhabited by sizable numbers of *HSS* were in northeast Asia (northern China, and nearby regions) and in Europe; and it was in those regions that groups with the highest average IQ evolved.

The Middle East, although not as cold as Europe and northern Asia, still had much colder winters than did India, Australia, Indonesia, Southeast Asia, and SSA. As a result, the inhabitants of the Middle East evolved higher intelligence than the inhabitants of the more tropical regions.

Therefore, if the main thesis of this book is correct, we should expect that most of the important intellectual advances of the human species were made by Caucasoids or

Mongoloids. Let us see if that expectation is borne out by the facts.

1) Almost all the important scientific advances and inventions of the last two centuries have been made by European Caucasoids (see chapters 49 and 51).

2) The same is true for the scientific discoveries and technological advances that were made between 1500 and 1800 (see chapters 45 and 47).

3) In the period between 600 BC and 1500 AD, several of the most important advances were made by Chinese, and most of the others by Caucasoids. (For the accomplishments of the Greeks, Romans, and Chinese see chapters 29, 30, and 35. For those made by persons living in the Middle East or India see chapters 34 and 36.)

4) The meagerness of contributions from Southeast Asia, Australia, and SSA during the Neolithic Era and pre-modern times is also apparent (see chapters 37, 38, and 41). This was true even in the Late Paleolithic (see chapter 19).

The expectation is therefore strongly confirmed by the historical facts.

Section 3 – Why didn't the northern peoples dominate the tropical ones earlier?

Since the higher average IQ of the northerners originated in prehistoric times, why was it not until recently that they gained control of the more tropical regions? Two factors seem to be involved:

The first factor was that the peoples residing in the Middle East and central China had originated agriculture earlier than the northerners did. This had occurred (see chapter 23) because the milder climate there made the introduction of agriculture easier than in more northern climates; and in addition, the Middle East had a large number of plants and animals that were both useful and easily domesticated. As a result, the Middle East and central China obtained a large head start on the more northern peoples.

The second factor was that in pre-modern times it was hard to move armies over large distances. It was not until fairly recently that the growth of technology enabled the Europeans to project their power far overseas; until then, most of the backward regions of the Earth were protected by geographic barriers, and by the sheer distance between them and the more advanced peoples.

Section 4 – The connection between average intelligence and national income

It is well known that more intelligent people have, on average, higher incomes than less intelligent ones. Of course, not every smart person is rich, nor is every rich person smart, but the statistical correlation between IQ and income is substantial.[2] This is because a high intelligence enables a person to be more productive.

It follows that a country whose citizens have a high average IQ will (other things being equal) be likely to have a higher average income than a nation whose citizens have a lower average IQ. Of course, other things are not always equal. Nevertheless, if one were to look at a large number of countries, one would expect to find a correlation between mean IQ and per capita income.

Richard Lynn & Tatu Vanhanen have researched this question extensively and have published their findings.[3] Their data makes it plain that there is indeed a high correlation between the average IQ of a country and its income. The simplest explanation for this is that the citizens of the countries that have higher mean IQs are, on average, much more productive of useful goods and services than are the citizens of other lands.

FOOTNOTES – CHAPTER 52

1) Their most northerly conquests (in Spain and in Central Asia) were about 1400 miles north of Mecca. The most southerly was at Sofala, about 2800 miles south of Mecca.

2) According to Jensen, the correlation coefficient is 0.40 (see Jensen, Arthur [1998], p. 568). However, the studies cited by Lynn & Vanhanen suggest that $r = 0.34$ is a better estimate (see Lynn, Richard & Tatu Vanhanen [2002], pp. 28-29). In any event, the correlation between IQ and income is substantial.

3) See Chapter 7 of *IQ and the Wealth of Nations* (Lynn & Vanhanen, 2002). The data in their Table 7.1 (pp. 88-89) indicates that since 1987 the correlation between average national IQ and per capita GNP has consistently been greater than $r = 0.60$.

CHAPTER 53

SOME FINAL COMMENTS AND PREDICTIONS

Section 1 – Central hypothesis of this book

The central hypothesis of this book is that genetic differences between human groups (in particular, differences in average native intelligence) have been an important factor in human history. The opposite hypothesis — that genetic differences between human races are insignificant — is at present the conventional hypothesis and the only politically correct one.

Section 2 – Some scientific criteria for acceptance of a hypothesis

Scientists have set certain general criteria that must be met before a hypothesis is accepted. Among these criteria are:

1) The hypothesis must be consistent with the observational data.

2) If two or more different hypotheses are both consistent with the observational data, we should accept the simplest of those hypotheses. The exact meaning of the word "simplest" is usually not defined; however, in general, the "simplest hypothesis" is the one that makes the fewest independent assumptions. This principle is usually referred to as *Occam's razor*.

3) A hypothesis that makes no testable predictions should not be accepted as a scientific theory. A hypothesis that does make testable predictions lays itself open to being disproved, or falsified (which is why this criterion is sometimes termed *falsifiability*). If, however, a hypothesis continues to meet experimental challenges and is not falsified, then our confidence in the hypothesis is increased.

Section 3 – Does the central hypothesis of this book meet the above criteria?

This hypothesis is consistent with the observational data. In contrast, the opposite hypothesis is badly inconsistent with the historical record and also with a great deal of current data. (That is why I have included so much data and so many examples in the preceding chapters.)

Of course, supporters of the conventional view have come up with ad hoc explanations for many of those inconvenient facts. However, Occam's razor should cause us to reject any such set of ad hoc explanations in favor of a simple, unifying principle that has so much explanatory power.

Section 4 – Predictions: Limitations

Many historians offer few, if any, testable predictions to support their hypotheses. This is understandable, since human affairs are so complex, and there are so many different factors at work. I do not pretend that my hypothesis will enable us to foretell who will be elected president of the United States in 2016, nor who will win the World Series in that year. And, alas, I cannot use it to construct a table listing the prices on the New York Stock Exchange ten years from now, or even next week.

However, if my hypothesis made no predictions at all — other than obvious ones that supporters of the reverse hypothesis would also make (for example: "Twenty years from now, people will still be employing electricity to operate many types of equipment") — then it would have no real content, and should not be taken seriously. I will therefore present a few predictions that can be made using my hypothesis.

Section 5 – Predictions concerning future achievements

a) Very few, if any, of the major advances that will be made during the 21st century in the fields of mathematics, computer science, physics, chemistry, astronomy, geology, biology, engineering, or medicine will be made by African Negroes; and disproportionately few will be made persons of predominantly Negro ancestry living on other continents, or by Australian or New Guinean aborigines.

b) Members of those same groups will provide disproportionately few world champions in chess during the coming century. They will also provide disproportionately few of the world's leading duplicate bridge players.

c) Most of the major advances in the fields mentioned above will be made by either whites of European ancestry or by Mongolids of Chinese, Japanese, or Korean ancestry. Furthermore, most of the leading chess and duplicate bridge players will come from those groups.

Section 6 – Predictions concerning results of intelligence testing

a) Little or no IQ data is yet available regarding Eskimos, Lapps, Siberian aborigines, Mongols, or Tibetans. I predict that if and when the intelligence of members of these groups is tested, the results will show that the average intelligence of most of these groups will be fairly high, and will probably fall in the range 85-105.

b) Similarly, little or no IQ data is yet available regarding the Congoid Pygmies, the Andaman Islanders (and other Negrito groups), or many of the Bantu-speaking tribes in SSA. I predict that if and when the intelligence of members of those groups are tested, the results will show that the average IQ of most of those groups is quite low, and will probably fall in the range 60-85.

Section 7 – What if these predictions turn out to be wrong?

If most of these predictions turn out to be wrong, I would have to admit that my hypothesis is incorrect.

APPENDIX 1
CHRONOLOGY

The dates presented here are the author's best estimates. The reader should be warned that virtually all old dates are doubtful, and reputable sources often disagree with each other. A question mark after a date indicates that it is particularly doubtful. Some dates in this table are not directly attested, but have been arrived at by interpolation or inference. For the most part, this chronology ends at 1500 AD, although a few later dates have been included.

Although many dates in this table were derived from carbon-14 dating (see Appendix 2), they have been calibrated and are intended as estimates of actual calendar years. The abbreviation "kya" means "thousands of years ago," and has been used for all dates prior to the invention of writing (3400 BC, or 5.4 kya).

Event or development	**kya**
Australopithecus afarensis.	3800
Earliest known members of genus *Homo*.	2500
Paleolithic Era begins. Earliest stone tools (= Oldowan tools).	2500
Homo erectus originates (in Africa).	1800
Pleistocene Epoch begins.	1700
Control of fire.	1700
Homo erectus spreads out of Africa.	1700
Acheulian tools.	1500
Australopithecines extinct.	1000
Homo erectus present in China.	700
Archaic *Homo sapiens* present in Europe.	350
Archaic *Homo sapiens* present in China.	230
Early Neanderthals in Western Europe.	150
Transitional forms between archaic *Homo sapiens* and *Homo sapiens sapiens* (= *HSS*) at sites in sub-Saharan Africa, such as Omo.	130

Appendix 1: Chronology

	kya
Upper Pleistocene begins.	125
Middle Paleolithic begins.	125
Riss glacial period ends. Eemian interglacial period begins.	125
Mousterian toolkit developed in Europe.	125
HSS present at South African sites (such as Klasies River).	100
Some early *HSS* reach Israel.	92
Start of Würm glacial period.	75
R_0 split off from N_0 in Africa and migrate to Red Sea area.	62
σ-group splits off from R_0 and migrates east. The remaining R_0 (the μ-group) settle in the Middle East and eventually spread out from there.	60
Some Neanderthals settle in Middle East.	60
Some of the σ-group (the σ-1) settle in India.	57
Migrants from India (the σ-2) settle SEA (= Southeast Asia).	55
Some σ-2 enter the Sundaland Peninsula from SEA.	53
First settlements in *Greater Australia*. Settlers are σ-4, an offshoot of the σ-2.	50
Some *HSS* (the μ-2) migrate from Middle East into Central Asia.	50
Some *HSS* (the μ-3, or *Cro-Magnon*) migrate into Eastern Europe.	46
Australian megafauna eliminated.	45
Migrants from SEA (the σ-3) enter southern China. They gradually occupy most of southern and central China.	45
Upper Paleolithic begins.	40
Ancestors of Mongoloids split off from μ-2 in Central Asia. They migrate north, and then east, eventually reaching Mongolia.	40
Cro-Magnon enter Western Europe.	40
Neanderthal groups in Middle East die out.	40
Earliest known human settlements in New Guinea.	40
Early rock paintings in Australia.	40
Region in and around northern Mongolia becomes heartland of the Proto-Mongoloids.	35
Aurignacian tool industry begins in Europe.	34
Earliest cave paintings in Western Europe.	32
Sewing needle invented.	30 ?
Earliest human settlements in northern Russia and Siberia.	30
Pre-Amerindians (= M-2) split off from main Mongoloid group and migrate eastward. Those who remain behind are the *Asian Mongoloids* or *Mongolids*.	30
Negroids split into *Sanids* and *Negrids*.	30 ?
A group of Mongolids migrate from Mongolia to northern China, probably via Manchuria. Those who remain behind are the *Northern Mongolids*.	29
Neanderthals die out.	28

	kya
New Guinea highlands settled.	26
Early rock paintings in Namibia (in southern Africa).	26
"Venus figurines" in Europe.	25
Solutrean tool industry begins in Europe.	21
Start of several waves of Mongolids who migrate northward into Siberia. (These are the *Early Siberians*.)	20
Negrids divide into Negroes and Pygmies.	20 ?
Bow and arrow invented.	20 ?
Coldest period of last ice age. Sea level is at its lowest point. Land bridge (Beringia) connects northeast Asia and Alaska.	18
Some M-2 enter Beringia.	18
M-2 enter northern Alaska. (Southern Alaska was covered by ice.)	17
Magdalenian tool industry begins in Europe.	17
Cave paintings at Lascaux, in southern France.	17
Paleo-Indians migrate south through Canada (through gap between ice sheets) and reach what is now the USA.	16
Early settlement at Meadowcroft Rockshelter, in Pennsylvania.	16
Mexico settled by Paleo-Indians from USA.	15
Paleo-Indian settlement at Monte Verde, in central Chile.	14.5
Fishhooks, harpoons, and spear-throwers being used in Europe.	14
Start of *Clovis* culture in USA.	13.5
Some Northern Mongolids migrate into Korea, and thence into Japan, where the Jomon culture soon arises.	13
Japanese produce world's earliest pottery.	13
Paleo-Indian settlement at Fell's Cave, near southern tip of South America.	12.7
Dogs domesticated in Middle East.	12
Most megafauna in Western Hemisphere killed off by now.	11
Speakers of Proto-Na-Dene enter Canada.	11 ?
Earliest known domesticated crops (at Abu Hureyra, in Syria).	10.6
EA (ancestors of Eskimos and Aleuts) split off from the other Asian Mongoloids and migrate northeast.	10.5
Pleistocene Epoch ends, Holocene begins.	10
End of last glacial period, sea level rises. Australia, New Guinea, and Tasmania separate from each other. Indonesian islands separate from each other. Bering Strait now separates Alaska and Asia.	10
Agriculture (with wheat and barley) is firmly established in parts of the Fertile Crescent, and is spreading into eastern and central Anatolia.	10

Appendix 1: Chronology

	kya
First farm animals (goats) domesticated in Middle East. Sheep domesticated soon thereafter.	10
First sizable town (Jericho, with a population of about 1000).	10
Squash domesticated in Mexico.	10
Agriculture spreads into western Anatolia.	9.5
Agriculture arises independently in Yangtze Valley, in central China. (Main crop was rice.)	9.5
Earliest use of pottery in Middle East.	9
Agriculture (including domesticated sheep and goats) spreads to Greece, brought in by µ-1 farmers from Anatolia.	9
Era of maximum wetness in Sahara. Cattle present then, and for next 3500 years.	9
EA (ancestors of Eskimos and Aleuts) enter Alaska.	9
Domesticated cattle in Middle East.	8.7
First cloth produced (linen, in Middle East).	8.5
µ-1 from Fertile Crescent (speaking Proto-Dravidian) spread agriculture into Iran.	8.5
Agriculture spreads into northern Balkans.	8.5
British Isles separate from continental Europe as sea level rises.	8.5
Agriculture in northern China. (Main crop was millet.)	8.4
Earliest known city (Çatal Hüyük, in Anatolia).	8.2
Copper smelting invented (in Middle East).	8.2
Agriculture spreads to parts of Italy.	8
Domesticated cattle in Europe.	8
Farmers from Middle East (speaking early Afro-Asiatic languages) enter Egypt, eventually take over entire country.	8
µ-1 farmers (speaking early Dravidian languages) enter western Pakistan. They gradually take over India, though with some cross-breeding with σ-1.	8
Saharan rock paintings (including pictures of cattle).	8
Irrigation developed in Middle East.	7.5
Agriculture spreads to Ethiopia (from Southwest Asia, or from Egypt).	7.5
Farmers from Egypt, speaking Afro-Asiatic languages, spread across North Africa. (Their descendants are the Berbers.)	7.5
Agriculture practiced in the Sudan.	7
Agriculture spreads to southern Germany.	7
Plow invented (Middle East).	6.5
Potter's wheel invented (Middle East).	6.5
Agriculture in Ukraine.	6.5

	kya
Eskimos and Aleuts separate from each other. Thereafter, the Eskimos gradually expand into northern Alaska, and from there eastward.	6.5
Horses domesticated (Eurasian Steppes).	6
Kurgan people in steppe region north and northeast of Caspian Sea. They were probably the original Indo-European speakers.	6
Agriculture spreads to England and northern France.	6
Maize domesticated (Mesoamerica).	6
Agriculture arises independently in New Guinea highlands.	6
Earliest production of woolen cloth (Middle East).	6
Donkey domesticated (North Africa).	6
Earliest fermented beverages.	6
Introduction of domestic sheep and goats into SSA (sub-Saharan Africa).	6
σ-3 farmers from southern China, speaking Proto-Austroasiatic, move into Vietnam and Thailand.	6
Bronze invented (Middle East).	5.8
First use of wheeled vehicles.	5.6
Rise of Sumerian civilization; first large city is Uruk.	5.5
Kurgan people (early Indo-Europeans) have spread into the Ukraine, and started to move into Eastern Europe.	5.5
Agriculture spreads to Scotland and Scandinavia.	5.5
Building of megaliths begins along southern and western fringes of Europe.	5.5
Some σ-3 farmers from southern China (speaking Proto-Austronesian) settle Taiwan and gradually occupy entire island.	5.5
Progressive desertification of Sahara begins.	5.5

Note: 5.5 kya = 3500 BC. From here on, dates are given in BC or AD.

	BC
Sumerians invent writing. **START OF RECORDED HISTORY.**	3400
Early hieroglyphic writing in Egypt.	3100
Menes unifies Egypt. Start of 1st Egyptian dynasty.	3100
Sedentary agriculture fully established in Mexico.	3000
Earliest pottery in Western Hemisphere.	3000
Agriculture established in Andean region of South America. Llama and alpaca domesticated there.	3000
Agriculture in tropical West Africa.	3000
Early Bronze Age in parts of Europe.	3000
Some Austronesian farmers (σ-3) migrate from Taiwan to Philippine Islands, gradually displacing σ-2 aborigines, who were hunter-gatherers.	3000

	BC
Indus Valley civilization begins.	2700
"Corded Ware culture" (probably Indo-European) in Germany, Poland, and northern Russia. Other Indo-Europeans in northern Balkans.	2700
Great Pyramid (Pyramid of Cheops) built.	2550
Austronesian farmers from Philippines enter Borneo and Sulawesi, and gradually spread through Indonesia, displacing σ-2 aborigines.	2500
By now, σ-3 occupy most of Southeast Asia, largely displacing σ-2.	2500
Tibet settled (from China).	2500 ?
Several plants cultivated in eastern USA, but inhabitants remain primarily hunter-gatherers.	2500
Manioc cultivated in Amazonia.	2500
Sargon of Akkad conquers Sumeria, sets up first large empire in history.	2340
Eskimos start eastward expansion along north coast of Alaska and Canada.	2300
First large Chinese kingdom (Hsia dynasty, on North China Plain).	2205
Start of Minoan civilization on Crete.	2200
Chinese writing begins. (But no surviving samples until much later.)	2200 ?
Earliest Hittite kingdom in Anatolia.	2000
First wave of Greeks enter Greece from north.	2000 ?
Indus Valley civilization flourishing in northwest India.	2000
Some σ-3 from SEA enter eastern India (origin of Munda-speakers in India).	2000 ?
First wave of Eskimos (the Dorset) reach Labrador and Baffin Island.	2000
Spoked wheels invented (Middle East).	2000
Stonehenge constructed.	2000
Earliest use of bronze in China.	1900
Some Austronesians from Indonesia migrate eastward, enter coastal New Guinea (and, a century later, the Bismarck Islands). Crossbreeding with the σ-4 produce the ancestors of the Polynesians.	1800
Code of Hammurabi.	1770
Hsia dynasty replaced by Shang dynasty kingdom on North China Plain.	1766
Indus Valley civilization declining.	1700
First alphabet (North Semitic).	1600
Hittites rule Anatolia, sack Babylon.	1600
Major volcanic eruption in Aegean. Minoan civilization declines.	1600
Polynesians reach Solomon Islands.	1600
Aryans enter northwest India. End of Indus Valley civilization. (Aryan tribes eventually conquer most of northern and central India.)	1550
Ironworking invented (by Hittites, in Anatolia).	1500
Earliest surviving samples of Chinese writing.	1500

	BC
First use of bow and arrow in Western Hemisphere (in Alaska).	1500
Mycenaean civilization flourishing in central Greece.	1500
End of Minoan civilization.	1450
Egyptian king Ikhnaton establishes first monotheistic religion.	1370
Polynesians settle Fiji.	1300
Earliest Hindu text, the *Rigveda*, composed (but not written down until much later).	1300
Rameses II (presumed Pharaoh of Exodus story) reigns in Egypt.	1250
Hebrew tribes invade Canaan.	1200
Hittite Empire destroyed.	1200
Indo-Europeans enter Italy.	1200
Second wave of Greeks (the Dorians) invade Greece from north.	1200
Olmec civilization begins in southern Mexico, near Gulf coast.	1200
Mycenaean civilization collapses, plunging Greece into a "Dark Age" that lasts for over three centuries.	1150
Shang dynasty falls, replaced by Chou dynasty kingdom in China.	1122
Ironworking spreads to India and Europe.	1000
King David rules in Jerusalem.	1000
Expansion of Bantu-speaking peoples from West Africa begins. Bantus eventually occupy most of central and southern Africa.	1000
Austronesians enter southern Malaya, probably from Sumatra.	1000
Ancestors of Karens enter northern Burma from Tibet.	1000 ?
Proto-Altaic (spoken by Northern Mongolids in and around Mongolia) splits into 3 branches (Turkic, Mongolian, and Manchu/).	1000 ?
Maize introduced into American Southwest from Mexico.	1000
Beginning of Etruscan civilization in northern Italy.	900
Greece emerging from its "Dark Age."	800
Carthage founded (by Phoenicians).	800
Earliest ironworking in sub-Saharan Africa (in present-day Nigeria).	800
Chou dynasty kingdom in China declines. It eventually disintegrates into several warring states.	770
Rome founded.	753
Greeks begin founding colonies in Sicily and southern Italy.	750
Prophet Isaiah preaching in Jerusalem.	740
Homer composes the *Iliad* and the *Odyssey*.	730
Height of Assyrian power in Middle East.	700
First writing in Western Hemisphere (Zapotec hieroglyphic) developed.	700
Zoroaster preaching in Iran, founds new religion.	650
Assyrian Empire destroyed; Babylonia becomes dominant in Mesopotamia.	612

	BC
Thales (first major Greek philosopher).	600
China enters Iron Age.	600
End of Olmec civilization in Mesoamerica.	600
Celts expanding from Germany into France, Iberia, and British Isles.	600
Babylonians conquer Jerusalem. End of ancient Hebrew state.	586
Cyrus the Great of Persia conquers Babylonia, rules most of Southwest Asia.	539
Gautama Buddha teaching in India.	528
Persians conquer Egypt.	525
Rome becomes a republic. (It had previously been a monarchy.)	509
Confucius teaching in China.	500
Burmese enter Burma from Tibet.	500
Start of "Golden Age of Greece."	500
Greeks repulse Persian invasion at Battle of Marathon.	490
Greeks defeat Persian fleet at Battle of Salamis.	480
Ezra compiles the *Torah* ("Five books of Moses"), heart of the *Old Testament*.	450
Sparta triumphs over Athens in Peloponnesian War.	404
Lao Tzu teaching in China.	350 ?
Alexander the Great overthrows Persian Empire, rules Egypt and Southwest Asia. A few years later he invades western India.	330
Chandragupta Maurya founds Mauryan Empire (in India).	321
Seleucid Empire founded. At its peak it ruled most of Middle East.	312
Euclid writes the *Elements* (axiomatic treatment of geometry).	300
Peak of Carthaginian power.	300
Romans gains control of virtually all of central and southern Italy.	270
Start of First Punic War between Rome and Carthage.	264
The Indian emperor Asoka converts to Buddhism, helps spread the religion.	250
Attacks by Hsiung-nu become a major problem in northern China, remain so for several centuries.	250
Shih Huang Ti conquers all of northern China, establishes Chinese Empire. He institutes sweeping reforms, and constructs the Great Wall of China.	221
Han dynasty begins in China.	202
Carthage completely defeated by Rome in Second Punic War.	201
End of Mauryan Empire in India.	185
Rome completes conquest of Macedonia and Greece.	146
Parthians control most of Mesopotamia and Iran.	138
Chinese conquer Vietnam. They rule it for next thousand years.	111
Empire of Han dynasty in China reaches its greatest extent under Han Wu Ti.	100
Introduction of camels into North Africa.	100

	BC
Julius Caesar completes conquest of Gaul.	51
Octavian (= Augustus Caesar) completes conquest of Egypt, defeats his rivals, and becomes the first Roman emperor. Rome rules almost entire Mediterranean world.	30

	AD
Turkish tribes begin migrating into Central Asia.	1
Tungus tribes begin migrating into Siberia, displacing Early Siberians.	1
Maize introduced into eastern USA.	1
Crucifixion of Jesus.	30
Buddhism enters China.	65
First Hinduized state in Southeast Asia (Funan, in Cambodia). Thereafter, there is continuing influence of Indian culture in SEA.	100
Paper invented (in China, by Ts'ai Lun).	105
Peak of Roman power.	117
Buddhism spreads into Burma.	200
Edict of Caracalla grants citizenship to all free men in Roman Empire.	212
End of Han dynasty, Chinese Empire disintegrates.	220
Sassanid (neo-Persian) Empire founded; it soon rules Mesopotamia as well.	224
Start of classic period of Mayan civilization in Yucatán.	300
Invention of stirrups (probably in the Eurasian steppes).	300
Constantine the Great, the first Christian emperor of Rome, issues the Edict of Milan, legalizing Christianity.	313
Gupta Empire founded in India.	320
Buddhism spreads into Java.	350
Huns invade Eastern Europe.	370
Gothic cavalry, using improved saddles and stirrups, crushes large Roman army at Adrianople, and establishes superiority of cavalry over infantry.	378
Paganism suppressed within Roman Empire.	392
Eastern part of Roman Empire becomes a separate state, later called the "Byzantine Empire."	395
Visigoths sack Rome.	410
Huns (under Attila) defeated at Battle of Châlons.	451
Fall of (Western) Roman Empire. Most of Western Europe is conquered by Germanic tribes. Start of the Dark Ages in Western Europe.	476
Hawaiian Islands and Easter Island settled by Polynesians.	500
Madagascar settled by Austronesians, probably from Borneo.	500
Teotihuacán (in Valley of Mexico) at its peak.	500

	AD
End of Gupta dynasty in India.	540
Turkish peoples rule most of Central Asia by now.	550
Buddhism enters Japan.	550
Most of China reunited under Sui Wen Ti.	589
Sui dynasty replaced by T'ang dynasty.	618
Muhammad founds Islam.	622
Buddhism established in Tibet.	650
Arabs complete conquest of Fertile Crescent, Egypt, and Persia. (Eventually, most of the inhabitants convert to Islam.)	651
Umayyad Caliphate founded, with its capital in Damascus.	661
Arabs complete conquest of North Africa.	705
By now, the Arabs have also conquered most of Spain, part of Turkey, and parts of northwest India and Central Asia.	715
Arab siege of Constantinople fails.	718
Moslem invasion of France is repulsed by Franks at the Battle of Tours.	732
T'ang dynasty in China at its peak.	750
Most of SEA is predominantly Buddhist by now.	750
Classical Mayan civilization at its peak.	750
Teotihuacán burned and abandoned.	750
Umayyad Caliphate overthrown, replaced by Abbasid Caliphate.	750
Arabs defeat Chinese army in Central Asia, rule region for next century.	751
Viking raids begin along coasts of Western Europe.	787
Frankish ruler Charlemagne is crowned "Roman Emperor" by Pope.	800
Harun al-Rashid reigns in Baghdad. Caliphate near its zenith.	800
Khmer kingdom in Cambodia.	800
Thais start to migrate into Thailand from southern China.	800
New Zealand settled by Polynesians (from Cook Islands or Society Islands).	800
Burmese rule most of Burma (Pagan kingdom).	850
Chinese produce first printed book, the *Diamond Sutra*.	868
Iceland settled (by Vikings).	874
Magyars enter Hungary.	900
Classic Mayan civilization collapses.	900
T'ang dynasty collapses; partial disintegration of Chinese Empire.	907
Vietnam gains independence from China.	939
Toltecs conquer the Valley of Mexico.	950
By now, Turks have regained control of Central Asia, but have been converted to Islam.	950
Gunpowder invented in China.	950 ?

	AD
Sung dynasty gains control of China.	960
Agriculture (including maize) established in eastern USA.	1000
Turks enter Iran and northern India from Central Asia.	1000
Printing with movable type invented in China (but does not become important there).	1045
Seljuk Turks conquer Baghdad and take over Abbasid Caliphate.	1055
Battle of Hastings. Normans gain control of England.	1066
Seljuks crush Byzantine army at Manzikert, conquer most of Anatolia.	1071
Crusades begin.	1096
Sung dynasty loses control of northern China to Juchen, a Manchu people.	1126
Temple complex completed at Angkor Wat (in Cambodia).	1150
Toltec Empire in Mexico collapses.	1168
Magnetic compass in use in both Europe and China.	1200
Genghis Khan unites Mongol tribes.	1206
Magna Carta signed.	1215
Mongols conquer Central Asia.	1220
Thais rule most of Thailand (Sukhothai kingdom).	1220
Mongols conquer northern China.	1234
Mongols conquer Russia, attack Poland and Hungary the following year.	1240
Peak period of Mesa Verde pueblos in southwestern US.	1250
Mongols overthrow Abbasid Caliphate, rule most of Southwest Asia.	1258
Mongols, under Kubilai Khan, complete conquest of China.	1279
Eyeglasses invented in Italy.	1285
Marco Polo writes about his travels in Asia, particularly China.	1298
Italian Renaissance begins.	1300
Beginning of Ottoman state in Asia Minor.	1300
Islam spreads to Malaya and Indonesia.	1300
Siege artillery being used in Western Europe.	1324
Aztecs found Tenochtitlán (now called Mexico City).	1325
English longbowmen rout French armored knights at Battle of Crécy.	1346
The "Black Death" (bubonic plague) strikes Europe, and in next three years kills one-third of the population. There were comparable losses in Asia and Africa during that century.	1347
Mongols expelled from China; Ming dynasty founded.	1368
Tamerlane ravages Central Asia, India, Persia, Russia, and Turkey.	1370 - 1402
Ottoman Turks conquer Constantinople. End of Byzantine Empire.	1453
Gutenberg invents printing with movable type.	1454

	AD
Incan Empire rises to power in Andean region.	1460
Columbus crosses Atlantic, discovers "New World."	1492
Vasco da Gama reaches India from Europe by sailing around Africa.	1498
Aztecs dominate central Mexico.	1500
Protestant Reformation begins.	1517
Trans-Atlantic slave trade begins.	1520
Cortés overthrows Aztec Empire, conquers Mexico.	1521
Incan Empire in Peru at its zenith.	1525
Mughal Empire founded in northern India.	1526
Pizarro overthrows Incan Empire, conquers Peru.	1533
Copernicus's book, *De Revolutionibus*, published.	1543
Handguns become important in warfare.	1550
Ottoman Empire reaches its zenith under Suleiman the Magnificent.	1560
Beginning of rapid Russian expansion into Siberia.	1581
Telescope invented.	1608
Manchus conquer China.	1644
Isaac Newton's *Principia* published.	1687
James II deposed, ending attempts to establish an absolute monarchy in England.	1689
Beginning of the Enlightenment in France.	1734
Industrial Revolution begins in England.	1750
French Revolution begins.	1789

APPENDIX 2
DETERMINING ANCIENT DATES

Section 1 – Relative dating

Any serious study of history depends critically upon our ability to date the sites, artifacts, events, and cultures that we are studying. Events that occurred within historical times can often be dated by means of written records. Unfortunately, prior to about 5000 years ago there were no written records. In many cases, though, we can still determine the *relative* order of various events and cultures.

In order to do this, archaeologists take careful note of the various layers existing at a given site. The general rule is that the top layers are the most recent, and the lowest layers the most ancient. This is the same general rule that geologists follow. However, far more anomalies occur with human sites than with rock strata, since ancient humans sometimes dug into the ground and left more recent objects in the lower levels of a site.

Just as geologists use the fossils existing in a layer of rock to date it, so archaeologists use human artifacts to date a site. Pottery can be very useful for this purpose, particularly if we can relate it to pottery produced in other locations. However, humans did not make pottery until about 13,000 years ago.

Stone tools and weapons, though, have been used for over two million years. The typical forms of tools produced in various epochs have been much studied, and they often provide a useful method of dating sites. In general, stone tools — and the methods of manufacturing them — became more sophisticated in the course of time. Table A2-1 lists several of the major stone tools industries (based on style, and method of manufacture) and indicates their sequence.

Section 2 – Absolute dating

We would, of course, much prefer to know not merely the *order* in which various events occurred (or epochs began) but also *when* they occurred or began. Fortunately, modern science has provided us with several methods for dating prehistoric materials. Among the more important methods are dendrochronology, carbon-14 dating, potassium-argon dating, thermoluminescence, and varves.[1] Some of the other methods that have been proposed are amino-acid racemization, paleomagnetic dating, and obsidian hydration, but so far those methods have rarely proven useful.

TABLE A2-1

SOME MAJOR PREHISTORIC STONE TOOL INDUSTRIES

Name	Approximate starting date (in kya*)
Oldowan	2,500
Acheulian	1,500
Mousterian	125
Aurignacian	34
Solutrean	21
Magdalenian	17

* kya = thousands of years ago

Section 3 – Dendrochronology

Dendrochronology is a method of dating wooden artifacts that was developed by Andrew E. Douglass in the early 20th century. It is based on the observation that there are certain species of trees for which the width of the annual tree rings varies greatly from year to year, depending on the amount of rain that fell during the year. If two trees that grew in the same region had lifetimes that partly overlapped, then a late section of annual rings for one tree can be matched up with an early section of annual rings for the other tree. By inspecting a series of trees with partly overlapping lifetimes, one can construct a complete sequence of relative dates. If the date of the last ring on the most recent tree can be established (by a written record of when that tree was cut down), then the entire sequence can be converted into exact calendar years.

As it turns out, only a few species of trees are usable for this purpose, and complete sequences have been constructed in only a few regions. These regions include portions of the United States, Great Britain, and continental Europe. In the best cases, sequences obtained using bristlecone pines go back about 8200 years.

No other method gives dates that are more reliable or more precise that those obtained by dendrochronology. Were it not for the fact that the method can only be used in some regions — and even in those regions for only the last few thousand years — it would always be the preferred dating method.

Section 4 – Carbon-14 dating

Carbon atoms are present in all organic material. There are three naturally-occurring isotopes of carbon, two of which are stable, and one of which is radioactive. The two stable isotopes are carbon-12 (which is the most common type) and carbon-13. The radioactive isotope is carbon-14, which is comparatively rare, accounting for less than one carbon atom in a trillion. The three isotopes are often designated ^{12}C, ^{13}C, and ^{14}C (or C^{12}, C^{13}, and C^{14}).

As the half-life of ^{14}C (the time it takes for half the atoms of a given mass of ^{14}C to decay radioactively) is only about 5,730 years, all of the ^{14}C atoms originally present on the Earth have long since decayed. The only reason that we still find ^{14}C atoms on Earth is that nitrogen atoms in the upper atmosphere are sometimes struck by cosmic rays (high-energy particles originating in outer space) and are transformed into ^{14}C atoms. The newly-produced ^{14}C atoms then drift down into the lower atmosphere, where they combine with oxygen to form carbon dioxide molecules. (These have the same chemical properties as carbon dioxide molecules that contain a ^{12}C atom.)

Atmospheric mixing is rapid, and the different types of carbon dioxide become uniformly distributed in the atmosphere within a year or two. At equilibrium (the usual situation) the loss of ^{14}C atoms by radioactive decay is balanced by the production of new ^{14}C atoms by cosmic rays.

Since plants are constantly taking in carbon dioxide from the atmosphere and converting it into organic matter by photosynthesis, living plants contain the same fraction of ^{14}C atoms as the atmosphere does. After a plant dies, though, it immediately stops taking in carbon dioxide; and from then on no new carbon atoms are added to the plant. However, the ^{14}C atoms already in the plant continue to decay at the usual rate. The ratio of ^{14}C to ^{12}C atoms in the plant therefore continually decreases after the plant dies. There is a simple formula that connects the $^{14}C/^{12}C$ ratio to the time interval since the death of the plant. As we are able to measure the amounts of ^{12}C and ^{14}C present in a piece of wood (or other artifact made of organic material), we can calculate the time interval involved.

Although the method is simple in principle, there are several problems which limit the reliability of dates obtained from carbon-14 measurements. In the first place, there are limits as to how accurately we can measure the amount of ^{14}C in the object we are examining. Because the actual amount of ^{14}C in an object decreases with age, the ratio of the uncertainty to the true amount is greater for old objects than for young ones. This renders the method useless for dating objects older than about 50,000 years.

Another problem is that the object we are attempting to date may have become contaminated with carbon from another source. If that has occurred, the method will yield an estimate that is intermediate between the true age of the object itself and the age of the other source. This can result in major errors.

A third problem is that — contrary to our original expectations — the number of cosmic rays reaching the Earth has not been constant throughout the past 50,000 years, but has varied significantly. The reason for this is that cosmic rays are deflected by magnetic fields, and the magnetic field of the Earth has varied significantly during that time. (Variations in the magnetic field of the Sun may also play a part in this.) The result is that the equilibrium amount of ^{14}C in the atmosphere has varied. The concentration of ^{14}C has usually been higher than it is today, thereby causing the carbon-14 dating method to underestimate the age of objects.

This problem was discovered when a sizable number of discrepancies were noticed between ages measured by the carbon-14 method and the ages of the same objects as determined by dendrochronology. Fortunately, this suggested a simple method of solving the problem. The relationship of "radiocarbon ages" to true ages (i.e., ages as established by dendrochronology or by written records) has now been established and published, and it is now standard practice to use this relationship to recalibrate ages obtained by the carbon-14 method.

A major advantage of the carbon-14 dating method is its very wide applicability. It can be employed not merely for wooden objects, but also for virtually any organic remains. (Rope, reeds, and linen are examples of some of the materials that can be dated in this fashion.) As a result, the majority of dates in this book have been obtained by the carbon-14 method.[2]

Section 5 – Potassium-Argon dating

This method is also based on radioactive decay; but rather than using ^{14}C, it is based on the decay of ^{40}K (an isotope of potassium) into ^{40}Ar (an isotope of argon). Since the decay rate of ^{40}K is very low (its half-life is more than a billion years), this method of dating is useful only for specimens that are at least 250,000 years old.

Section 6 – Thermoluminescence

There are certain materials which, when exposed to radiation, are able to absorb some of the energy received and store it. If the object is later heated, it will release the stored energy in the form of light. Thereafter, it can again store energy, and the process can be repeated indefinitely.

If we find such an object — for example, an ancient piece of pottery — we can heat a portion of it under laboratory conditions, and carefully measure the energy of the light released. If in addition, we know, or can estimate, the intensity of the radiation that the object was exposed to — and that is a very big "if" — then we can estimate how long it has been since the last time the object was heated. (In the case of a piece of pottery, that could be when it was originally baked.)

The idea of dating by means of thermoluminescence is ingenious, but the practical difficulties are very large. Consequently, not all dates obtained by this method are considered to be reliable. However, as there are instances where no other method of dating an artifact is available, the method has considerable practical importance.

Section 7 – Varves

There are situations where sediments are laid down over a long stretch of years, but vary in a definite, easily recognizable manner *within* each year. Such sediments contain a succession of thin layers or *varves*, where a varve refers to the entire set of layers formed during a single year. In such cases, by simply counting the varves one can determine the date of each varve and the number of years needed to form the entire sediment.

Of course, if storms have destroyed some of the original varves the dates obtained in this fashion will be incorrect. Generally, though, dating of varved deposits is quite reliable. The main shortcoming of the method is that varved deposits are fairly rare. They are most commonly used to date glacial lakes.

Section 8 – Summary

Every known method of archaeological dating has some drawbacks. Most of the dates used in this book come from carbon-14 dating. The raw ^{14}C dates have usually been calibrated so that they agree with the time-scale provided by dendrochronology. For objects that are no more than 8200 years old, the dates obtained in this manner are probably within about 100 years of the true date. Quoted dates that are earlier than that are progressively less reliable, and the method is useless beyond 50,000 years ago.

Dates obtained directly by dendrochronology or by counting of varves are more reliable, but are less often obtainable. Dates cannot be obtained by the potassium-argon method unless the object involved is at least 250,000 years old. Even then, uncertainties of a few percent are the rule.

Problems in dating are most acute for the interval between 250,000 and 50,000 years ago. For this period we rely heavily on relative dating methods. Attempts can be made to determine absolute ages by means of other methods, such as thermoluminescence; nevertheless, most dates prior to 50,000 years ago are less reliable than we would wish.

FOOTNOTES – APPENDIX 2

1) See chapter 1 of Poirier, Frank & Jeffrey McKee (4th edition, 1999). Also see Fagan, Brian M. (2001), pp. 10-11.

2) Descriptions of the C-14 dating method are included in most leading textbooks of archaeology or anthropology. See, for example: Poirier & McKee (1999), pp. 7-9; or Fagan, Brian M. (2001), p. 101; or Diamond, Jared (1999), pp. 95-97.

APPENDIX 3

DESCRIPTION OF COMPUTER SIMULATION

Section 1 – General description

In this computer simulation, the world was divided into 27 large regions, and the growth of intelligence in each one was tracked at 1000-year intervals. The increase of intelligence within each region during each such interval was assumed to be proportional to the "harshness factor" of that region. This is equivalent to the formula:

$$IQ_{new}(r) = IQ_{prior}(r) + K \times HF(r)$$

where r denotes the individual region, HF is the harshness factor, and the constant K is a free parameter. The assumed harshness factors ranged from zero to 5, with the highest factors occurring in regions in high northern latitudes, and the lowest factors assigned to tropical regions. It was found that the value $K = 0.15$ gives the best fit to the modern data.

The assumed initial conditions were that at 60 kya every existing human group had a mean IQ of 70. This figure was not chosen arbitrarily, but in order to match the measured IQs of blacks living in sub-Saharan Africa today (see Table 15-2).

It was assumed that, whenever humans (i.e., *HSS*) entered a region not previously inhabited by humans, any earlier hominids residing there were eliminated without significant interbreeding. However, if human migrants entered a region already inhabited by *HSS*, it was assumed that the mean IQ of the resulting population was a weighted average of the IQs of the invaders and the indigenous population. This is equivalent to the formula:

$$IQ_{resulting} = (IQ_{migrants} \times f) + (IQ_{indigenous} \times [1 - f])$$

where the factor f (the percentage of the resulting gene pool that comes from the migrants) must be estimated separately for each migration considered.

Some regions were given two harshness factors: a "normal" one applying to the Holocene Epoch (the last 10,000 years), and another one for the long glacial period (the Würm) that was in force during the preceding 50,000 years. However, the period from

TABLE A3-1
REGIONS USED IN COMPUTER SIMULATION

Region	Harshness factors Normal	Harshness factors Glacial	Date first entered (a)	Region from which first entered
Sub-Saharan Africa	0	0	–	–
Middle East	1	2	60	Sub-Saharan Africa
North Africa	1	1	60	Sub-Saharan Africa
India	0	0	57	Middle East
Southeast Asia	0	0	55	India
Indonesia	0	0	53	Southeast Asia
Taiwan/Philippines	0	0	53	Indonesia
Southern China	2	3.5	45	Southeast Asia
Australia	2	2	50	Indonesia
New Guinea	1	1	50	Indonesia
Melanesia	1	1	36	New Guinea
Polynesia	2	2	3	Indonesia (b)
Micronesia	2	2	3	(c)
Southeast Europe	2	3.5	46	Middle East
Southwest Europe	2	3.5	40	Southeast Europe
Russia	4	5	30	Southeast Europe
Northern Europe	3.5	5	30	(d)
Central Asia	2	2	50	Middle East
Mongolia/Southern Siberia	4.5	5	35	Central Asia
Northern China	4	5	29	Mongolia/S. Siberia
Japan/Korea	3	3	30	Mongolia/S. Siberia
Northeast Siberia	5	5	19	Japan/Korea
Arctic North America	5	5	17	Northeast Siberia
Northern USA	4	5	16	Arctic N. America
Southern USA	2	3.5	15	Northern USA
Mesoamerica	0	0	15	Southern USA
South America	0	0	14	Mesoamerica

(a) Expressed in kya (= thousands of years ago)
(b) Through Melanesia, with some interbreeding
(c) 75% from Polynesia; 25% from Taiwan/Philippines
(d) 50% from Southeast Europe; 50% from Southwest Europe

40 kya to 30 kya, during which there was a partial let-up from the severe cold, was assigned an intermediate harshness factor, midway between the two listed. The period from 12 kya to 10 kya was considered a transition period, and was also assigned the intermediate harshness factor.

Section 2 – Regions, and their initial settlement

Table A3-1 lists the 27 regions used in this simulation. The table shows the estimate used for the date that each region was first settled by *HSS*. It was assumed that at 60 kya *HSS* had only recently entered the Middle East and North Africa. For most regions, the table also lists where the original settlers came from.

Section 3 – Later migrations

Each entry in the list of migrations which follows includes:

- The region the migrants came from.
- The region they entered.
- The approximate date of the migration. (It should be understood, of course, that most migrations were spread out over a sizable interval.)
- The fraction, f, of the gene pool of the receiving region that derived from the migrants (evaluated after most migrants had entered).

The effect of the migration on the gene pool of the region from which the migrants came was assumed to be negligible. The migrations included in the simulation fall into several categories.

A) *Pre-Neolithic*.

1) The migration of Northern Mongolids from Mongolia/Southern Siberia into Japan/Korea (assumed date: about 13 kya; f = 0.8).

2) In order to represent the intermingling of aborigines living in Australia and New Guinea during the long period that the two regions formed a single landmass, it was assumed that *each* millennium in that interval saw a migration of people from Australia into New Guinea (with f = 0.01), and a simultaneous migration in the other direction (also with f = 0.01).

B) *Migrations driven by agriculture*. (See chapter 22.)

1) The invasion of India by farmers from the Middle East speaking Proto-Dravidian (date: 8 kya; f = 0.8).

2) The invasion of North Africa by farmers from the Middle East speaking Proto-Afro-Asiatic (date: 8 kya; f = 0.8).

3) The invasion of Southeast Europe by farmers from the Middle East (date: 8 kya; f = 0.75).

4) The subsequent invasions of Southwest Europe and Northern Europe by farmers from Southeast Europe (date: 7 kya; f = 0.75 and 0.667 respectively).

5) The invasion of Taiwan and the Philippines by farmers from Southern China speaking Proto-Austronesian (date: 5 kya; f = 0.85).

6) The subsequent invasion of Indonesia from the Philippines by Austronesian-speaking farmers (date: 4 kya; f = 0.8).

7) The invasion of Southeast Asia by farmers from Southern China (date: 6 kya; f = 0.75).

C) *Indo-European expansions*. (See chapter 26.)

1) Russia into Southeast Europe (date: 4 kya; f = 0.8).

2) Russia into Northern Europe (date: 4 kya; f = 0.8).

3) Northern Europe into Southwest Europe (date: 3 kya; f = 0.8).

4) Russia into Central Asia (date: 5 kya; f = 0.5).

5) Central Asia into India (date: 3 kya; f = 0.2).

D) *Migrations and invasions since 3 kya*.

1) Northern China into Southern China (date: 2 kya; f = 0.333).

2) Northern China into Southern China (date: after 1 kya; f = 0.2).

3) Southern China into Southeast Asia (date: 1 kya; f = 0.333).

4) Arabs from the Middle East into North Africa (date: 1 kya; f = 0.15).

5) Turkish tribes from Mongolia/Siberia into Central Asia (date: 1 kya; f = 0.5).

6) The subsequent migration of Turkish tribes from Central Asia into the Middle East (date: 1 kya; f = 0.2).

7) Germanic tribes from Northern Europe into Southwest Europe (date: 1 kya; f = 0.2).

8) Slavic tribes from Russia into Southeast Europe and Northern Europe (date: 1 kya; f = 0.2).

Section 4 – Omissions

The colonizations and migrations that have occurred since 1492 were not included in this simulation. As a result, the IQs listed for "0 kya" really refer to the situation in 1500 AD. In particular, the IQ figures for the Western Hemisphere and Australia refer to the aboriginal populations only, and the figures for Europe and the United States omit recent migrants from Asia and Africa.

Aside from that, migrations *within* a single region (for example: the invasion of Central and Southern Africa by West African Negroes in the course of the last 2500 years) have been ignored. In addition, the population movements resulting from the establishments of most early empires (such as the Assyrian, Babylonian, Persian, and Roman Empires) have been omitted.

Appendix 3: Description of Computer Simulation

Because of the omission of these (and other) migrations, and because of the numerous other approximations made, this simulation was only intended to be a rough approximation of what actually occurred. That such a simple model can reproduce within a few IQ points the distribution of mean IQs that we observe today suggests that it includes the most important factors bearing on the formation of differences in the mean intelligence of human groups, and that the omitted factors are of secondary importance.

APPENDIX 4

CALCULATIONS CONCERNING THE NEOLITHIC TRANSITION

The computer simulation described in chapter 17 divided the Earth into 27 regions, which are listed in Table A3-1. With regard to their suitability for the invention of agriculture, those regions fall into seven categories:

1) *Regions where the climate was too harsh for agriculture to be invented*. This category includes eight regions: Northern Europe, Russia, Mongolia/Siberia, North China, Japan/Korea, Northeast Siberia, Arctic North America, and Northern USA. In each of those regions the HF (harshness factor) was greater than 2.0, thus making the region unsuitable for the invention of agriculture.

2) *Regions where the average intelligence was far too low for agriculture to be invented*. This category includes five regions: India, Southeast Asia, Indonesia, Taiwan/Philippines, and sub-Saharan Africa. In none of those regions was <IQ> (the average IQ) greater than 71 prior to the immigration of groups that had already mastered agriculture. This is far lower than the threshold IQ for originating agriculture, which even in the most benign climates is about 79 (see section 23-3 and Table 23-1).

3) *Regions with moderate climates, and where the average intelligence was moderately high, but not quite high enough to enable the development of agriculture*. This category includes four regions:

 (a) North Africa (HF = 1; threshold IQ = 79) came very close. The computer simulation described in chapter 17 indicates that
 at 10 kya, <IQ> was 77,
 at 9 kya, <IQ> was 78,
 and at 8 kya, agriculture was introduced into the region from the Middle East.

 (b) Central Asia (HF = 2; threshold IQ = 88) also came close. The computer simulation indicates that
 at 10 kya, <IQ> was 85,
 at 6 kya, <IQ> was 86,
 and at 5 kya agriculture was introduced into the region from the Middle East.

Appendix 4: Calculations Concerning the Neolitic Transistion 441

(c) Melanesia (HF = 1; threshold IQ = 79) also came close. The computer simulation indicates that
> at 10 kya, <IQ> was 77,
> at 5 kya, <IQ> was 78,

and at 4 kya, agriculture was introduced into the region from Indonesia.

(d) In Australia (HF = 2; threshold IQ = 88) the computer simulation indicates that <IQ> never exceeded 84.

4) <u>*Regions with warm climates, adequate IQs, and suitable flora and fauna*</u>. There were two such regions:

(a) In the Middle East, the harshness factor decreased from 2.0 to 1.0 as the last ice age drew to a close, and the threshold IQ decreased from 88 to 79 (see section 23-5 and Table 23-1). Meanwhile, <IQ> was gradually increasing. The computer simulation indicates that
> at 14 kya: HF = 2;   threshold IQ = 88;   <IQ> = 83,
> at 12 kya: HF = 1.5; threshold IQ = 83.5; <IQ> = 84,

suggesting that the Neolithic transition began there about 12 kya.

(b) In Southern China (a region which was defined as including the basin of the Yangtze River), the climate was too severe during the last glacial period to permit the invention of agriculture. However, the HF decreased to 2.0 at the end of the Ice Age, about 10 kya. At that time, according to the computer simulation, <IQ> was 88, as was the threshold IQ, thus permitting the Neolithic transition to begin. The earliest signs of agriculture there date to about 9.5 kya, in close conformity to the theoretical calculation.

5) <u>*Regions where the threshold IQ was met, but there was a scarcity or absence of suitable crops*</u>. There were five regions in this category:

(a) Mesoamerica was settled about 15 kya. From Table 17-1, we see that the original settlers had an average IQ of about 89. This far exceeded the threshold IQ for the region, which was only 79. Until about 11 kya, there was an abundance of large game in the area, making agriculture unnecessary. In this region, the Neolithic transition began about 10 kya (when squash was first domesticated); however, sedentary agriculture was not established until about 5 kya. The main reason for the unusual length of the Neolithic transition in this region was the lack of any easily-domesticated cereal crop (see section 23-7, subsection C).

(b) South America was settled about 14 kya. Table 17-1 shows that the average IQ of the original settlers was about 89, which exceeded the threshold IQ for the region. The first area in which sedentary agriculture became established was the Peruvian section of the Andean region, about 5 kya. The probable reason for the delay was the absence of cereal crops. The wild ancestor of quinoa (the first cereal to be cultivated in Peru) was not indigenous to that country, but to Argentina. There is no sign that wild quinoa reached Peru before 6 kya, and it was domesticated there by 5 kya. The use of corn eventually spread from Mexico to the Andean region, but that did not occur until very much later.

(c) In the Southern USA, the HF did not fall to 2.0 until the end of the last ice age, about 10 kya. At that time, the average IQ in the region was about 91, which was well above the threshold IQ. However, there were no suitable core crops in the region (see section 23-7, subsection E). As a result, sedentary agriculture was not established there for a long time. The introduction (about 2 kya) of the Mexican triad of corn, squash, and beans solved that problem, and by 1 kya sedentary agriculture became established there.

(d) Southeast Europe and Southwest Europe were too cold for agriculture to originate in until the end of the last ice age, about 10 kya. At that point, the harshness factor went down to 2.0, with the result that the threshold IQ was 88. The computer simulation indicates that the average IQ was then 92. Conditions were then ripe for the invention of agriculture, except that there was a paucity of core crops in both regions. We cannot be sure what the result would have been, because a developed agriculture (based on wheat and barley) was brought in from the Middle East at about 9 kya.

6) *Regions where the question of the invention of agriculture never arose because the original settlers already practiced farming when they entered the region.* There were two such regions, Polynesia and Micronesia.

7) *New Guinea.* The harshness factor of New Guinea has been estimated at 1.0, so the threshold IQ was 79. The computer simulation gave:

        at 7 kya: $<IQ> = 78$,
        at 6 kya: $<IQ> = 78$,
        at 5 kya: $<IQ> = 79$.

This suggests that the Neolithic transition should have commenced there about 5 kya; however, the archaeological evidence indicates that it actually started about 6 kya. The most likely cause of this discrepancy is the presence of minor inaccuracies in the computer simulation.

BIBLIOGRAPHY

Adovasio, J.M., et al. (1990). "The Meadowcroft Rockshelter radiocarbon chronology, 1975-1990." American Antiquity, 55 (2), pp. 348-354.

Adovasio, J.M., et al. (1999). "No vestige of a beginning nor prospect of an end: Two decades of debate on Meadowcroft Rockshelter." Pages 416-431 in *Ice Age Peoples of North America* (editors: R. Bonnichsen & K. Turnmire). Corvallis, OR: Oregon State University Press.

Adovasio, J.M. & Jake Page (2002). *The First Americans*. New York: Random House.

Adovasio, J.M. & D.R. Pedler (1997). "Monte Verde and the antiquity of humankind in the Americas." *Antiquity, 71*, pp. 573-580.

Aitken, M.J. & H. Valladas (1993). "Luminescence dating relevant to human origins." Pages 27-39 in *The Origin of Modern Humans and the Impact of Chronometric Dating* (editors: M.J. Aitken, C.B. Stringer, & P.A. Mellars). Princeton: Princeton University Press.

Ama, P.F.M., et al. (1986). "Skeletal muscle characteristics in sedentary black and Caucasian males." *Journal of Applied Physiology, 61*, pp. 1758-1761.

Anderson, Britt (2003). "Brain imaging and *g*." Chapter 2 in *The Scientific Study of General Intelligence* (editor: Helmuth Nyborg). Oxford, UK: Pergamon.

Andrae, Tor (1936). *Mohammed: The Man and his Faith*. (Originally published in German [1932]; English translation by Theophil Menzel.) London: George Allen & Unwin.

Andreasen, N.C., et al. (1993). "Intelligence and brain structure in normal individuals." *American Journal of Psychiatry, 150*, pp.130-134.

Asimov, Isaac (1982). *Asimov's Biographical Encyclopedia of Science & Technology* (Second revised edition). Garden City, NY: Doubleday.

Axelrod, R. & W.D. Hamilton (1981). "The evolution of cooperation." *Science, 211*, pp. 1390-1396.

Baker, John R. (1974). *Race*. Oxford University Press. Reprinted (1981) Athens, GA: Foundation for Human Understanding.

Bar-Yosef, O. (1989). Chapter 30 in *The Human Revolution* (editors: P. Mellars & C. Stringer). Princeton: Princeton University Press.

Bat Ye'or (1985). *The Dhimmi: Jews and Christians under Islam*. (Originally published in French [1980]; English translation by David Maisel & Paul Fenton.) Rutherford, NJ: Fairleigh Dickinson University Press.

Bayley, Nancy (1965). "Comparisons of mental and motor test scores for ages 1-15 months by sex, birth order, race, geographical location, and age of parents." *Child Development, 36*, pp. 379-411.

Bonnichsen, R. & K. Turnmire (1999). "An introduction to the peopling of the Americas." Pages 1-26 in *Ice Age People of North America* (editors: R. Bonnichsen & K. Turnmire). Corvallis, OR: Oregon State University Press.

Bouchard, T.J., Jr., et al. (1990). "Sources of human psychological differences: the Minnesota study of twins reared apart." *Science, 250*, pp. 223-228.

Bouchard, T.J., Jr. & M. McGue (1981). "Familial studies of intelligence: A review." *Science, 212*, pp. 1055-1059.

Bowler, James M., et al. (2003). "New ages for human occupation and climatic change at Lake Mungo, Australia." *Nature, 421*, 837-840.

Bräuer, Günter (1989). "The Evolution of Modern Humans." Chapter 8 in *The Human Revolution* (editors: P. Mellars & C. Stringer). Princeton: Princeton University Press.

Brooks, Alison S. & Bernard Wood (1990). "The Chinese side of the story: Human fossils in China." *Nature, 344*, pp. 288-289.

Brown, Peter (1993). "Recent Human Evolution in East Asia and Australasia." In *The Origin of Modern Humans and the Impact of Chronometric Dating* (editors: M.J. Aitken, C.B. Stringer, & P.A. Mellars). Princeton: Princeton University Press.

Buj, V. (1981). "Average IQ values in various European countries." *Personality and Individual Differences, 2*, pp. 168-169.

Bulmer, M.G. (1970). *The Biology of Twinning in Man.* Oxford: Clarendon Press.

Burt, Cyril (1966). "The genetic determination of differences in intelligence: A study of monozygotic twins reared together and apart." *British Journal of Psychology, 57*, pp. 137-153.

Cann, Rebecca L., Mark Stoneking, & Allan C. Wilson (1987). "Mitochondrial DNA and human evolution." *Nature, 325*, pp. 31-36.

Cavalli-Sforza, L.L. (2000). *Genes, Peoples, and Languages.* New York: North Point Press.

Cavalli-Sforza, L.L. & Cavalli-Sforza, F. (1995). *The Great Human Diasporas.* (Originally published in Italian [1993]; English translation by Sarah Thorne.) New York: Addison-Wesley.

Cavalli-Sforza, L.L., P. Menozzi, & A. Piazza (1994). *The History and Geography of Human Genes* (abridged paperback edition). Princeton: Princeton University Press.

Chappell, J., et al. (1996). *Antiquity, 70*, pp. 543-552.

Chipuer, H.M., M.J. Rovine, & R. Plomin (1990). "LISREL modeling: Genetic and environmental influences on IQ revisited." *Intelligence, 14,* pp. 11-21.

Chomsky, Noam (1975). *Reflections on Language.* New York: Pantheon.

Clark, J. Desmond (1989). "The origins and spread of modern humans: a broad perspective on the African evidence." Chapter 29 in *The Human Revolution* (editors: P.A. Mellars & C. Stringer). Princeton: Princeton University Press.

Clark, J. Desmond (1993). "African and Asian perspectives on the origin of modern humans." In *The Origin of Modern Humans and the Impact of Chronometric Dating* (editors: M.J. Aitken, C.B. Stringer, & P.A. Mellars). Princeton: Princeton University Press.

Cochran, G., J. Hardy, & H. Harpending (in press). "Natural history of Ashkenazi intelligence." *Journal of Biosocial Science, 38*(?). (Published online in 2005; the page numbers in the citations refer to the 35-page online version of the article.)

Coleman, J., et al. (1966). *Equality of Educational Opportunity.* Washington, DC: Government Printing Office.

Collier's Encyclopedia (1963 edition). Crowell-Collier Publishing Company.

Columbia History of the World (1981 edition). (Editors: John A. Garraty & Peter Gay). New York: Harper & Row.

Crocker, J. & B. Major (1989). "Social stigma and self-esteem: The self-protective properties of stigma." *Psychological Review, 96,* pp. 608-630.

Crowley, T. & R.M.W. Dixon (1981). Article on "Tasmanian" in *Handbook of Australian Languages* (editors: R.M.W. Dixon & B.J. Blake).

Darlington, Cyril (1969). *The Evolution of Man and Society.* New York: Simon & Schuster.

Dawkins, Richard (1989). *The Selfish Gene* (2nd edition). Oxford: Oxford University Press.

Dawkins, Richard (2004). *The Ancestor's Tale.* New York: Houghton Mifflin.

Deacon, H.J. (1989). "Late Pleistocene Palaeoecology and Archaeology in the Southern Cape, South Africa." Chapter 28 in *The Human Revolution* (editors: P. Mellars & C. Stringer). Princeton: Princeton University Press.

Detterman, D.K. & M.H. Daniel (1989). "Correlations of mental tests with each other and with cognitive variables are highest for low IQ groups." *Intelligence, 13,* pp. 349-359.

Diamond, Jared (1992). *The Third Chimpanzee.* New York: HarperCollins.

Diamond, Jared (1999). *Guns, Germs, and Steel* (paperback edition). New York: Norton.

Dillehay, Thomas (2000). *First Settlement of America: A New Prehistory.* New York: Basic Books.

Dixon, R.M.W. (1980). *The Languages of Australia.* Cambridge, UK: Cambridge University Press.

DK Atlas of World History (2001 edition). New York: Dorling Kindersley.

Dobzhansky, T. (1970). *Genetics of the Evolutionary Process.* New York: Columbia University Press.

Dupuy, R.E. & Dupuy, T.N. (1993). *The Harper Encyclopedia of Military History* (4th edition). New York: HarperCollins.

Egan, V., et al. (1994). "Size isn't everything: A study of brain volume, intelligence and auditory evoked potentials." *Personality and Individual Differences, 17,* pp. 357-367.

Eggenberger, D. (1967). *A Dictionary of Battles.* New York: Thomas Crowell.

Encyclopaedia Britannica (15th edition, 1986).

Encyclopaedia Judaica (1972). Jerusalem, Israel: Keter Publishing House, Ltd.

Encyclopedia of World History (5th edition, 1972 [editor: William Langer]; 6th edition, 2001 [editor: Peter Stearns]). Boston: Houghton Mifflin.

Entine, Jon (2000). *Taboo: Why Black Athletes Dominate Sports and Why We're Afraid to Talk about it.* New York: Public Affairs.

Eveleth, P.B. & J.M. Tanner (1976). *Worldwide Variation in Human Growth.* Cambridge: Cambridge University Press.

Fagan, Brian M. (2001). *People of the Earth* (10th edition). Upper Saddle River, NJ: Prentice-Hall.

Fiedel, Stuart J. (1992). *Prehistory of the Americas* (2nd edition). Cambridge, UK: Cambridge University Press.

Flynn, James R. (1984). "The mean IQ of Americans: Massive gains 1932 to 1978." *Psychological Bulletin, 95,* pp. 29-51.

Flynn, James R. (1987). "Massive gains in 14 nations: What IQ tests really measure." *Psychological Bulletin, 101,* pp. 171-191.

Flynn, James R. (1994). "IQ gains over time." Pages 617-623 in *Encyclopedia of Human Intelligence* (editor: R.J. Steinberg). New York: Macmillan.

Frearson, W.M. & H.J. Eysenck (1986). "Intelligence, reaction time (RT) and a new 'odd-man-out' RT paradigm." *Personality and Individual Differences, 7,* pp. 808-817.

Freedman, Daniel G. (1979). *Human Sociobiology: A Holistic Approach.* New York: Free Press.

Fullagar, R.D., D. Price, & L. Head (1996). "Early human occupation of northern Australia: Archaeology and thermoluminescence dating of Jinmium rock-shelter." *Antiquity, 70,* pp. 751-753.

Gardner, H. (1983). *Frames of Mind: The Theory of Multiple Intelligences.* New York: Basic Books.

Garn, S.M. (1963). "Human biology and research in body composition." *Annals of the New York Academy of Sciences, 110,* pp. 429-446.

Garner, W. & A. Wigdor (1982). *Ability Testing* (I & II). Washington, DC: National Academy Press.

Geber, M. (1958). "The psycho-motor development of African children in the first year, and the influence of maternal behavior." *Journal of Social Psychology, 47,* pp. 185-195.

Gibbon, Edward (1776-1788). *History of the Decline and Fall of the Roman Empire.*

Gimbutas, Marija (1970). "Proto-Indo-European culture: The Kurgan culture during the fifth, fourth, and third millennia B.C." Pages 155-195 in *Indo-European and Indo-Europeans* (editors: G. Cardona, H.M. Hoenigswald, and A. Senn). Philadelphia: University of Pennsylvania Press.

Gimbutas, Marija (1973). "The beginning of the Bronze Age in Europe and the Indo-Europeans: 3500-2500 B.C." *Journal of Indo-European Studies, 1,* pp. 163-214.

Gimbutas, Marija (1977). "The first wave of Eurasian steppe pastoralists into Copper Age Europe." *Journal of Indo-European Studies, 5,* pp. 277-338.

Gimbutas, Marija (1980). *Journal of Indo-European Studies, 8,* pp. 273-315.

Gottfredson, Linda (in press). "Implications of cognitive differences for schooling within diverse societies." In *Comprehensive Handbook of Multicultural School Psychology* (editors: C.L. Frisby & C.R. Reynolds). New York: Wiley.

Gould, Stephen J. (1981; revised edition, 1996). *The Mismeasure of Man.* New York: Norton.

Grant, Madison (1921). *The Passing of the Great Race* (4th edition, reprinted 2000). North Stratford, NH: Ayer Company Publishers.

Great Books of the Western World (1952); editor: Robert M. Hutchins. Chicago: Encyclopaedia Britannica.

Greenberg, Joseph, C.G. Turner II, & S.L. Zegura (1986). "The settlement of the Americas: A comparison of the linguistic, dental, and genetic evidence." *Current Anthropology, 27 (5),* pp. 477-497.

Groube, L., et al. (1986). "40,000-year-old human occupation site at Huon Peninsula, Papua, New Guinea." *Nature, 324,* pp. 453-455.

Hacker, Andrew (1992). *Two Nations.* New York: Charles Scribner's Sons.

Hamilton, W.D. (1964). "The genetic evolution of social behaviour." *Journal of Theoretical Biology, 7*, pp. 1-52.

Hammer, M.F., et al. (2000). "Jewish and Middle Eastern non-Jewish populations share a common pool of Y-chromosome biallelic haplotypes." *Proceedings of the National Academy of Science, 97*, pp. 6769-6774.

Hanson, Victor Davis (2001). *Carnage and Culture.* New York: Anchor Books.

HarperCollins Atlas of World History (1999 edition). Ann Arbor, MI: Borders Press.

Hart, Michael H. (1992). *The 100: A Ranking of the Most Influential Persons in History* (revised edition). Secaucus, NJ: Citadel Press.

Heaney, R.P. (1995). "Bone mass, the mechanostat, and ethnic differences." *Journal of Clinical Endocrinology and Metabolism, 80,* pp. 2289-2290.

Hedges, Larry V. & Amy Nowell (1998). Chapter 5 in *The Black-White Test Score Gap* (editors: Christopher Jencks & Meredith Phillips). Washington, DC: The Brookings Institution.

Herodotus. *History.* (English translation by George Rawlinson.) Published in Volume 6 of *Great Books of the Western World.* Chicago, IL: Encyclopaedia Britannica (1952).

Herrnstein, Richard J. & Charles Murray (1994). *The Bell Curve.* New York: The Free Press.

Heyerdahl, Thor (1950). *Kon-Tiki.* Chicago: Rand McNally.

Heyerdahl, Thor (1953). *American Indians in the Pacific: The Theory behind the Kon-Tiki Expedition.* Chicago: Rand McNally.

Himes, John H. (1988). "Racial variation in physique and body composition." *Canadian Journal of Sport Science, 13*, pp. 117-126.

Historical Atlas of the Ancient World (2000 edition). (editor: John Haywood). New York: Barnes & Noble.

Holden, C. & R. Mace (1997). "Phylogenetic analysis of the evolution of lactose digestion in adults." *Human Biology, 69*, pp. 605-628.

Horai, S., et al. (1995). "Recent African origin of modern humans revealed by complete sequences of hominoid mitochondrial DNAs." *Proceedings of the National Academy of Sciences, 92*, pp. 532-536.

Howell, R.J., et al. (1958). "A comparison of test scores for the 16-17 year age group of Navajo Indians with standardization norms from the WAIS." *Journal of Social Psychology, 47,* pp. 355-359.

Hume, David (1748). *An Enquiry Concerning Human Understanding.* Reprinted in volume 35 of *Great Books of the Western World* (1952).

Ibn Warraq (1995). *Why I am Not a Muslim.* Amherst, NY: Prometheus Books.

Jencks, Christopher (1998). "Racial bias in testing." Chapter 2 in *The Black-White Test Score Gap* (editors: C. Jencks & M. Phillips). Washington, DC: Brookings.

Jencks, Christopher & Meredith Phillips [editors] (1998). *The Black-White Test Score Gap*. Washington, DC: Brookings.

Jensen, Arthur (1969). "How much can we boost IQ and scholastic achievement?" *Harvard Educational Review, 39*, pp. 1-123.

Jensen, Arthur (1980). *Bias in Mental Testing*. New York: The Free Press.

Jensen, Arthur (1987). "Individual differences in the Hick Paradigm." Pages 101-175 in *Speed of information-processing and intelligence* (editor: P. A. Vernon). Norwood, NJ: Ablex.

Jensen, Arthur (1992). "The importance of intraindividual variability in reaction time." *Personality and Individual Differences, 13*, pp. 869-882.

Jensen, Arthur (1993). "Spearman's hypothesis tested with chronometric information-processing tasks." *Intelligence, 17*, pp. 47-77.

Jensen, Arthur (1998), *The g Factor: The Science of Mental Ability.* Westport, CT: Praeger.

Jensen, Arthur & C.R. Reynolds (1982). "Race, social class, and ability patterns on the WISC-R." *Personality and Individual Differences, 3*, pp. 423-438.

Jensen, Arthur & P.A. Whang (1993). "Reaction time and intelligence: A comparison of Chinese-American and Anglo-American children." *Journal of Biosocial Science, 25,* pp. 397-410.

Jones, Rhys (1989). "East of Wallace's line: Issues and problems in the colonization of the Australian continent." Chapter 35 in *The Human Revolution* (editors: P. Mellars & C. Stringer). Princeton: Princeton University Press.

Jordan, J. (1969). "Physiological and anthropometric comparisons of Negroes and whites." *Journal of Health, Physical Education, and Recreation, 40*, (Nov-Dec 1969), pp. 93-99.

Juel-Nielsen, N. (1965). "Individual and Environment: A psychiatric-psychological investigation of monozygotic twins reared apart." *Acta Psychiatrica Scandinavia, Supplementum 183*.

Kelly, Robert L. (1996). "Ethnographic analogy and migration to the western hemisphere." Chapter 15 in *Prehistoric Mongoloid Dispersals* (editors: T. Akazawa & E.J. Szathmary). Oxford University Press.

Kimura, M. (1983). *The Neutral Theory of Molecular Evolution*. Cambridge, UK: Cambridge University Press.

Klein, Richard G. (1989; 2nd edition, 1999). *The Human Career*. Chicago: University of Chicago Press.

Koestler, Arthur (1976). *The Thirteenth Tribe.* New York: Random House.

Lamb, H.H. (1995). *Climate, History and the Modern World* (2nd edition). London: Routledge.

Latourette, K.S. (1950). *The Chinese: Their History and Culture* (3rd edition, revised). New York: Macmillan.

Levesque, M., et al. (1994). "Muscle fiber type characteristics in black African and white males before and after 12 weeks of sprint training." *Canadian Journal of Applied Physiology, 19, Supplement,* p. 25.

Levin, Michael (1997). *Why Race Matters.* Westport, CT: Praeger.

Lieberman, Philip (1968). "Primate vocalizations and human linguistic ability." *Journal of the Acoustical Society of America, 44*, pp. 1574-1584.

Lieberman, Philip & E.S. Crelin (1971). "On the speech of Neanderthal Man." *Linguistic Inquiry, 2,* pp. 203-222.

Lieberman, Philip, E.S. Crelin, & D.S. Klatt (1972). "Phonetic ability and related anatomy of the newborn, adult human, Neanderthal man and the chimpanzee." *American Anthropologist, 74,* pp. 287-307.

Lings, Martin (1983). *Muhammed: His life based on the earliest sources.* Rochester, VT: Inner Traditions International.

Loeb Classical Library. Boston, MA: Harvard University Press.

Loehlin, J.C., et al. (1975). *Race Differences in Intelligence.* San Francisco: W.H. Freeman.

Loomis, W.F. (1967). "Skin-pigment regulation of vitamin-D biosynthesis in man." *Science, 157*, pp. 501-506.

Lynn, Richard (1991). "Race differences in intelligence: A global perspective." *Mankind Quarterly, Volume XXXI, No. 3,* pp. 255-296.

Lynn, Richard (1992). "Intelligence, Ethnicity and Culture." In *Cultural Diversity and the Schools* (editors: J. Lynch, C. Modgil, & S. Modgil). London: Palmer Press.

Lynn, Richard & S. Hampson (1986a). "Intellectual abilities of Japanese children: An assessment of 2-8 year olds derived from the McCarthy Scales of Children's Abilities." *Intelligence, 10*, pp. 41-58.

Lynn, Richard & S. Hampson (1986b). "The structure of Japanese abilities: An analysis in terms of the hierarchical model of intelligence." *Current Psychological Research and Reviews, 4,* pp. 309-322.

Lynn, Richard & S. Hampson (1987). "Further evidence on the cognitive abilities of the Japanese: Data from the WPPSI." *International Journal of Behavioral Development, 10,* pp. 23-36.

Lynn, Richard & K. Hattori (1990). "The heritability of intelligence in Japan." *Behavior Genetics, 20*, pp. 545-546.

Lynn, Richard & Tatu Vanhanen (2002). *IQ and the Wealth of Nations*. Westport, CT: Praeger.

Malina, Robert M. (1988). "Racial/ethnic variation in the motor development and performance of American children." *Canadian Journal of Sport Science, 13*, pp. 136-143.

Mallory, J.P. (1989). *In Search of the Indo-Europeans*. London: Thames & Hudson.

Martin, Paul S. (1973). "The discovery of America." *Science, 179*, pp. 969-974.

Maynard Smith, J. (1976). "Group selection." *Quarterly Review of Biology, 51*, pp. 277-283.

McDaniel, Michael A. (2005). "Big-brained people are smarter: A meta-analysis of the relationship between in vivo brain volume and intelligence." *Intelligence, 33*, pp. 337-346.

McElwain, D.W. & G.E. Kearney (1973). Chapter 5 in *The Psychology of Aboriginal Australians* (editors: G.E. Kearney, P.R. de Lacey, & G.R. Davidson). Sydney: John Wiley and Sons.

McEvedy, Colin (1980). *The Penguin Atlas of African History*. London: Penguin Books.

McNeill, William H. (1998 edition). *Plagues and Peoples*. Garden City, NY: Anchor Press/Doubleday.

Mellars, P.A. (1993). "Archaeology and the population-dispersal hypothesis of modern human origins in Europe." In *The Origin of Modern Humans and the Impact of Chronometric Dating* (editors: M.J. Aitken, C.B. Stringer, & P.A. Mellars). Princeton: Princeton University Press.

Meltzer, David, et al. (1997). "On the Pleistocene antiquity of Monte Verde, southern Chile." *American Antiquity, 62 (4)*, pp. 659-663.

Metheny, Eleanor (1939). "Some differences in bodily proportions between American Negro and white male college students as related to athletic performance." *Research Quarterly, volume X* (December 1939), pp. 41-53.

Michael, John S. (1988). "A new look at Morton's craniological research." *Current Anthropology, 29*, pp. 349-354.

Miller, Edward M. (1994). "Paternal provisioning versus mate seeking in human populations." *Personality and Individual Differences, 17*, pp. 227-255.

Mingroni, Michael A. (2004). "The secular rise in IQ: giving heterosis a closer look." *Intelligence, 32*, pp. 65-83.

Mischel, W. (1958). "Preference for delayed reinforcement: An experimental study of a cultural observation." *Journal of Abnormal and Social Psychology, 56,* pp. 57-61.

Montagu, Ashley (1972). *Statement on Race* (3rd edition). New York: Oxford University Press.

Montie, J.L. & J.F. Fagan (1988). "Racial differences in IQ: Item analysis of the Stanford-Binet at 3 years." *Intelligence, 12,* pp. 315-332.

Morris, R.D. & W.D. Hopkins (1995). "Amount of information as a determinant of simple reaction time in chimpanzees (*Pan troglodytes*)." Unpublished report, Yerkes Regional Primate Center, Emory University, Atlanta, GA.

Morton, Samuel G. (1849). "Observations on the size of the brain in the various races and families of man." *Proceedings of the National Academy of Science, 4,* pp. 221-224.

Murray, Charles (2003). *Human Accomplishment.* New York: HarperCollins.

New Century Foundation (1999). *The Color of Crime.* Oakton, VA: New Century Foundation.

Newman, H.H., F.N. Freeman, & K.J. Holzinger (1937). *Twins: A Study of Heredity and Environment.* Chicago: University of Chicago Press.

Nisbett, Richard E. (1998). Chapter 3 in *The Black-White Test Score Gap* (editors: C. Jencks & M. Phillips). Washington, DC: Brookings.

Niswander, K.R. & M. Gordon (1972). *The Women and their Pregnancies.* Philadelphia, PA: Saunders.

Nriagu, Jerome (1983). "Saturnine gout among Rome's aristocrats: Did lead poisoning contribute to the fall of the empire?" *New England Journal of Medicine, 308*, pp. 660-663.

Osborne, R.T. & F.C.J. McGurk [editors] (1982). *The Testing of Negro Intelligence* (vol. 2). Athens, GA: Foundation for Human Understanding.

Papiernik, E., et al. (1986). "Ethnic differences in duration of pregnancy." *Annals of Human Biology, 13*, pp. 259-265.

Past Worlds: Atlas of Archaeology (2003 edition). Ann Arbor, MI: Borders Press.

Patai, R. (1977). *The Jewish Mind.* New York: Scribner's. (Paperback edition, 1996, Wayne State University Press.)

Patai, R. & J.P. Wing (1975). *The Myth of the Jewish Race.* New York: Charles Scribner's Sons.

Paul, S.M. (1980). "Sibling resemblance in mental ability: A review." *Behavior Genetics, 10*, pp. 277-290.

Pavlov, P., et al. (2001). "Human presence in the Arctic nearly 40,000 years ago." *Nature, 413*, pp. 64-67.

Pedersen, N.L., et al. (1992). "A quantitative analysis of cognitive abilities during the second half of the life span." *Psychological Science, 2*, pp. 346-353.

Pinker, Steven (1997). *How the Mind Works.* New York: Norton.

Pinker, Steven (2000). *The Language Instinct* (First Perennial Classics edition). New York: HarperCollins. (Original publication by William Morrow, 1994.)

Pinker, Steven (2002). *The Blank Slate.* New York: Viking.

Pitulko, V.V., et al. (2004). "The Yana RHS site: Humans in the Arctic before the latest glacial maximum." *Science, 303*, pp. 52-56.

Plomin, R. (1990). "The role of inheritance in behavior." *Science, 248*, pp. 183-188.

Poirier, Frank E. & Jeffrey K. McKee (1999). *Understanding Human Evolution* (4th edition). Saddle River, NJ: Prentice Hall.

Post, Richard H. (1982). "Population differences in visual acuity." *Social Biology, 29*, pp. 319-343.

Raz, N., et al. (1993). "Neuroanatomical correlates of age-sensitive and age-invariant cognitive abilities: An *in vivo* MRI investigation." *Intelligence, 17*, pp. 407-422.

Reed, T.E. (1969). "Caucasian genes in American Negroes." *Science, 165,* pp. 762-768.

Renfrew, Colin (1987). *Archaeology and Language: The Puzzle of Indo-European Origins.* New York: Cambridge University Press.

Renfrew, Colin (1989). "The Origins of Indo-European Languages." *Scientific American, 261(4)*, pp. 106-114.

Reynolds, C.R., et al. (1987). "Demographic characteristics and IQ among adults: Analysis of the WAIS-R standardization sample as a function of the stratification variables." *Journal of School Psychology, 25*, pp. 323-342.

Ridley, Matt (2000). *Genome.* New York: HarperCollins.

Rightmire, G.P. (1989). "Middle Stone Age Humans from Eastern and Southern Africa." Chapter 7 in *The Human Revolution* (editors: P. Mellars & C. Stringer). Princeton: Princeton University Press.

Roberts, R., et al. (1990). "Thermoluminescence dating of a 50,000-year-old human occupation site in Northern Australia." *Nature, 345*, pp. 153-156.

Roberts, R., et al. (1998). "Optical and radiocarbon dating at Jinmium rock shelter in Northern Australia." *Nature, 393*, pp. 358-362.

Rodinson, Maxime (1971). *Mohammed.* New York: Pantheon Books. (Originally published [1961] in French; English translation by Anne Carter.)

Ross, R., et al. (1986). "Serum testosterone levels in healthy young black and white males." *Journal of the National Cancer Institute, 76,* pp. 45-48.

Rowe, David C. (1994). *The Limits of Family Influence.* New York: Guilford.

Ruhlen, Merritt (1991). *A Guide to the World's Languages (Volume 1: Classification).* (First edition 1987; postscript added in 1991.) Stanford, CA: Stanford University Press.

Rushton, J.P. (1997). *Race, Evolution, and Behavior* (first paperback edition). New Brunswick, NJ: Transaction Publishers.

Rushton, J.P. & C.D. Ankney (1992). "Brain size and cognitive ability: Correlations with age, sex, social class, and race." *Psychonomic Bulletin and Review, 3,* pp. 21-36.

Rushton, J.P. & Arthur Jensen (2005). "Thirty years of research on race differences in cognitive ability." *Psychology, Public Policy, and Law, 11,* pp. 235-294.

Ryan, William & Walter Pitman (1998). *Noah's Flood.* New York: Simon & Schuster.

St. John, J., et al. (1976). "North Western Ontario Indian children and the WISC." *Psychology in the Schools, 13,* pp. 407-411.

Sarich, Vincent & Allan C. Wilson (1967). "Immunological Time Scales for Hominid Evolution." *Science, 158,* pp. 1200-1203.

Sattler, J.M. (2001). *Assessment of Children: Cognitive Applications* (4th edition). San Diego, CA: Jerome M. Sattler, Publisher.

Scarborough, John (1984). "The myth of lead poisoning among the Romans." *Journal of the History of Medicine, 39,* pp. 469-475.

Scarr, Sandra (1981). *Race, Social Class, and Individual Differences in IQ.* Hillsdale, NJ: Erlbaum.

Scarr, Sandra & K. McCartney (1983). "How people make their own environments: A theory of gene-environment effects." *Child Development, 54,* pp. 424-435.

Shields, J. (1962). *Monozygotic Twins Brought Up Apart and Brought Up Together.* London: Oxford University Press.

Shuey, Audrey M. (1966). *The Testing of Negro Intelligence* (2nd edition). New York: Social Science Press.

Smith, Bruce D. (1998). *The Emergence of Agriculture.* New York: Scientific American Library.

Snyderman, Mark & Stanley Rothman (1990). *The IQ Controversy* (paperback edition). New Brunswick, NJ: Transaction Publishers.

Spearman, Charles (1904). "General Intelligence, objectively determined and measured." *American Journal of Psychology, 15,* pp. 201-293.

Stoneking, M., et al. (1993). "New approaches to dating suggest a recent age for the human mtDNA ancestor." In *The Origin of Modern Humans and the Impact of Chronometric Dating* (editors: M. Aitken, C. Stringer, and P. Mellars). Princeton: Princeton University Press.

Storfer, Miles D. (1990). *Intelligence and Giftedness.* San Francisco, CA: Jossey-Bass.

Straus, Lawrence G. (2000). "Solutrean settlement of North America? A review of reality." *American Antiquity, 65 (2),* pp. 219-226.

Stringer, Chris (1989). "The origin of early modern humans: A comparison of the European and non-European evidence." Chapter 14 in *The Human Revolution* (editors: P. Mellars & C. Stringer). Princeton: Princeton University Press.

Stringer, Chris & Robin McKie (1996). *African Exodus.* New York: Henry Holt.

Symons, Donald (1979). *The Evolution of Human Sexuality.* Oxford: Oxford University Press.

Thernstrom, A. & Thernstrom, S. (2003). *No Excuses.* New York: Simon & Schuster.

Thomas, Hugh (1999). *The Slave Trade* (paperback edition). New York: Simon & Schuster.

Thompson, James W. & Edgar N. Johnson (1937). *An Introduction to Medieval Europe: 300-1500.* New York: W.W. Norton.

Thucydides, *The History of the Peloponnesian War* (English translation by Richard Crawley, revised by R. Feetham). Published (1952) in volume 6 of *Great Books of the Western World.* Chicago: Encyclopaedia Britannica.

Trask, R.L. (1996). *Historical Linguistics.* Edward Arnold Publishers, Ltd.

Trivers, R.L. (1971). "The evolution of reciprocal altruism." *Quarterly Review of Biology, 46,* pp. 35-57.

Trivers, R.L. (1972). "Parental investment and sexual selection." Pages 136-179 in *Sexual Selection and the Descent of Man* (editor: B. Campbell). Chicago: Aldine.

Tryon, Darrell T. (1985). "The peopling of the Pacific: a linguistic appraisal." Chapter 9 in *Out of Asia: Peopling the Americas and the Pacific* (editors: R. Kirk & E. Szathmary). Canberra: Journal of Pacific History.

Tuchman, Barbara (1962). *The Guns of August.* New York: Scribner's.

Turner, G.H. & D.J. Penfold (1952). "The scholastic aptitude of the Indian children of the Caradoc reserve." *Canadian Journal of Psychology, 6,* pp. 31-44.

Valladas, H., et al. (1988). "Thermoluminescence dating of Mousterian 'Proto-Cro-Magnon' remains from Israel and the origin of modern man." *Nature, 331,* pp. 614-616.

Villee, Claude A. (1972). *Biology* (6th edition). Philadelphia, PA: Saunders.

Wallace, R.A. (1992). *Biology: The World of Life* (6th edition). New York: HarperCollins.

Weinberg, R.A., S. Scarr, & I.D. Waldman (1992). "The Minnesota Transracial Adoption Study: A follow-up of IQ test performance in adolescence." *Intelligence, 16,* pp. 117-135.

Weyl, Nathaniel (1989). *The Geography of American Achievement.* Washington, DC: Scott-Townsend.

Whitney, Glayde (1999). "On the Races of Man." *Mankind Quarterly* (Vol. XXXIX, No. 3). Reprinted (2002), in *Race, Genetics & Society* (editor: Kevin Lamb), Washinton, DC: Scott-Townsend.

Wickett, J.C., P.A. Vernon, & D.H. Lee (1994). "*In vivo* brain size, head perimeter, and intelligence in a sample of healthy adult females." *Personality and Individual Differences, 16,* pp. 831-838.

Wickett, J.C., P.A. Vernon, & D.H. Lee (1996). "General intelligence and brain volume in a sample of healthy adult male siblings." *International Journal of Psychology, 31,* pp. 238-239 (abstract).

Wickler, S. & M. Spriggs (1988). "Pleistocene human occupation of the Solomon Islands, Melanesia." *Antiquity, 62,* pp. 703-706.

Wilson, Edward O. (1998). *Consilience.* New York: Knopf.

Wilson, Edward O. (2000). *Sociobiology: The New Synthesis* (25th anniversary edition). Cambridge, MA: Harvard University Press.

Wilson, Glenn (1992). *The Great Sex Divide.* Washington, DC: Scott-Townsend.

Wolpoff, M.H. (1989). "Multiregional evolution: The fossil alternative to Eden." Chapter 6 in *The Human Revolution* (editors: P. Mellars & C. Stringer). Princeton: Princeton University Press.

World Almanac and Book of Facts (2003). New York: World Almanac Books.

Wright, Nancy M., et al. (1995). "Greater secretion of growth hormone in black than in white men: Possible factor in greater bone mineral density." *Journal of Clinical Endocrinology and Metabolism, 80,* pp. 2291-2297.

Wurm, S.A. (1972). *Languages of Australia and Tasmania.* The Hague: Mouton.

Zubrow, Ezra (1989). Chapter 13 in *The Human Revolution* (editors: P. Mellars & C. Stringer). Princeton: Princeton University Press.

Zweig, Stefan (1938). *Conqueror of the Seas: The Story of Magellan.* New York: The Literary Guild.

INDEX

Abbasid Caliphate 250-251, 427-428
Abecedarian Project 108
Abelard, Peter 316
Abraham (Hebrew patriarch) 202
Abu Bakr (caliph) 247
Abu Hureyra 139, 142-143, 420
Acheulian tools 29-30, 133, 418, 431
adopted children 24, 108-109, 113, 115, 118, 126, 129-130, 139, 141, 144
adoptive emperors 224
Adrianople, Battle of 239
Aegean Sea 187, 213, 423
Aeschylus 217, 266
Aesop's Fables 217
Afghanistan 183, 187, 194-195, 247, 268, 270, 292, 296, 382-383, 404
Africa (*See* particular countries or regions.)
African blacks 81, 87, 94, 101, 107, 254
"African Eve" 31
Afro-Asiatic languages 54, 151, 153, 184, 186, 249, 421
Agincourt, Battle of 318
agnostics 367
agriculture, origin of 139-143
　in China 141, 167-168, 421, 441
　in Middle East 139-140, 142-143, 420-421, 441
　in New Guinea 141, 168, 171, 442
　in Western Hemisphere 141, 167-171, 421-423, 441-442
　preconditions for 160-167
Ahmes Papyrus 209
AHS *See*: archaic *Homo sapiens*.
Ainu 58, 301
airplanes 400
Akbar (Mughal emperor) 271, 296
Akkad, Akkadian 179, 198-199, 423
Aku-Aku (Thor Heyerdahl) 286

Alaric 231
Alaska 49, 62, 74-75, 124, 163, 290, 292, 300-301, 338, 420-424
Albanian 53, 189
Albertus Magnus 316
alchemy 252, 317
Aleutian Islands, Aleuts 290, 301, 420-422
Alexander the Great 201-202, 208, 215, 226, 270, 413, 424
algebra 209-210, 262, 346
　earliest known text 209
Algeria 54, 151, 236, 247, 295, 299, 381, 405, 408-409
Alhazen 253
Ali (4th caliph) 247
alleles 5-6, 9, 12, 61, 81-82, 150, 158, 394-396
　dominant, recessive 5
　(*Also see*: genes.)
Almagest (Ptolemy) 216-217, 330
Almoravids 312
Altai Mountains 72-73
Altaic languages 55, 290, 292-293, 297, 299, 324, 424
altruism **35-39**
　definition of 35
　reciprocal 36
　(*Also see*: kin selection.)
Amazonia 168, 171, 423
American blacks 16, 82-87, 92-95, 102-105, 107, 110, 113-117, 127
　hybridization among 14, 16
American
　Civil War 401
　constitution 360, 370
　Revolutionary War 360
　literary figures 385
　(*Also see*: USA.)

American Indians 14, 63, 67, 72-75, 82, 87, 95, 100-101, 169, 181, 288-289, 300-303, 305, 336-338 (*Also see*: Amerids; Amerind languages; pre-Amerindians; and specific tribes.)
Amerids 14, 72, 74, 78
Amerind languages 57, 301
Amerindians *See*: American Indians.
Amharic 54, 153
Analects (Confucius) 261
analytic geometry 160, 347, 356
Anasazi 305
Anatolia 139, 142-143, 157, 170, 179, 183-186, 194, 199-200, 215, 220, 226, 243-244, 251, 266, 293, 295, 307, 413, 420-421, 423, 428
Anatolian languages 53, 194-195
anatomy (human) 331, 353, 356
Andaman Islands, Andamanese 58, 71, 417
Andes 168, 171, 303, 306, 335
anesthesia 379-380, 385
Angkor Wat 314, 428
Anglo-Saxon Chronicle 244
Angola 111, 406
animal husbandry 142
  (*Also see* specific animals.)
Anselm (Saint) 316
antibiotics 399
anti-Semitism 368, 391
antiseptic surgery 379-380
ants 35, 41, 126
Apaches 57, 301
Apollonius of Perga 216
applied science (rise of) 374
Aquinas, Thomas 252, 316
Arabian Nights 252
Arabic numerals 252, 317, 346
Arabization 249
Arabs, Arabic, Arabia 3, 54, 69, 110, 153, 181, 184, 197, 201, 205, 240, 242-256, 261, 264-265, 271, 280, 295, 299, 312-313, 316-317, 324, 329, 331, 342-343, 346, 382-383, 393, 408-413, 427, 439
  conquests 247-250
    achievements 251-253
      (*Also see*: Islam; Muhammad; Moslems; dhimmis.)
Aramaic 54

archaeological periods 46-47
archaic *Homo sapiens* 30-32, 67-69, 162, 268, 418
architecture 110, 211, 218, 224, 244, 245, 252, 263, 273, 274, 280, 287, 314, 316
Arctic North America 124, 436, 440-441
Arctic Ocean 74, 290
Argentina 171-172, 335, 387, 441
Aristarchus of Samos 217
Arkwright, Richard 364
Armenian 52-53
Art of War, The (Sun-Tzu) 264
Arthasastra (Kautilya) 273
artificial fabrics 379-380, 400
artificial selection 141
artillery 319, 327, 332, 342, 372, 428
  (*Also see*: cannons.)
Aryans 50, 186, 194-196, 268, 270-273, 412, 423
    invasion of India 268
    and modern Germans 194
Ashkenazim 390-397
Ashurbanipal (library of) 200, 202
Asia (*See* particular countries or regions.)
Asia Minor 157, 189, 194, 224, 244, 293, 413, 428
Asimov, Isaac 119, 357
Asoka 270, 272, 425
Assyria 54, 179, 186-187, 197-198, 200, 203, 207, 252, 383, 425, 439
Astronomia Nova (Kepler) 348, 356
astronomy 177, 210, 216-217, 314, 330, 332, 348-351, 368, 377, 399, 417
  (*Also see*: Aristarchus; Copernicus; Galileo; Kepler; Newton; Ptolemy; Tycho.)
Atahualpa 335
atheists 367
Athens 201, 214-215, 218, 263, 361, 425
atomic nucleus 399
atomic theory of matter 375, 377, 380
atomic weapons 403
Attila the Hun 231, 426
Augustine (Saint) 224
Aurangzeb 271, 296
Aurignacian tools 133-136, 419, 431
aurochs 142-143, 170, 176

Australia 13, 15, 49, 61-71, 78, 87, 101, 124, 165-167, 172-174, 181, 184, 216, 225, 245, 251, 264, 269, 274, 275, **281-288**, 360-361, 378, 382-383, 408, 413-414, 417, 419-420, 436-438, 441
   destruction of megafauna 419
Australian aborigines 173, 269, 283, 284, 287, 382
Australoids 13-14, 63, 65, 150
Australopithecus 28-29, 32, 137-138, 162, 418
Austria 99, 241-242, 322, 372, 380-381, 398, 401
Austria-Hungary 398, 401
Austric language family 277, 279-280
Austroasiatic languages 276-277, 279, 422
Austronesian languages 153, 155-157, 184, 277, 282, 284-287, 422-423, 438
   spread of 153, 156, 285
automobile 379-380
Avars 184, 241-242, 292
Averroës 252
Avicenna 252
axiomatic treatment of geometry 216, 262, 425
Aztecs 167, 180, 304, 306, 334-336, 429-430

Bab el Mandeb 49
Babar (Mughal emperor) 271, 296
Babylonia 2, 54, 147, 179, 187, 197-201, 203, 207, 210, 213, 226, 252, 256, 383, 389, 393, 395, 397, 425, 439
Bach, Johann Sebastian 266
Bacon, Francis 369
Bacon, Roger 316
bacteria 354
Baffin Island 290, 423
Baghdad 251, 256, 293, 427, 428
Bahrain 408-409
Baikal, Lake 62, 73, 344
Balboa, Vasco Núñez de 334
Balearic Islands 223, 316
Balkans 73, 157, 189, 194, 224, 232, 242-244, 251, 295, 321, 323, 421, 423
Balto-Slavic languages 53, 189, 195
Baluchistan 149
bands (primitive) 40-41, 144

Bangladesh 268
Bannockburn, Battle of 322
Bantu languages 156-157, 181, 184, 310-311, 315, 417, 424
   spread of 156-157, 311, 315
   (*Also see*: Niger-Congo languages.)
Banu Qurayza 255
Basque 55, 58, 195
battery (electric) 374, 376
Bayazid (Ottoman emperor) 296
Becquerel, Antoine Henri 375, 380
Bede 244
Beethoven, Ludwig van 266
Behistun 256
Beijing 29, 263, 293, 297
Belgium 99
Bell Curve, The (Herrnstein & Murray) 26, 102
Bell, Alexander Graham 379-380
Bengali 52, 53, 194
Bentham, Jeremy 369
Benz, Karl 379-380
Beowulf 244
Berbers, Berber languages 3, 54, 67, 151, 187, 242, 249, 312, 421
Berelekh 74-75, 290
Bering Sea 49, 344
Bering Strait 74, 290, 420
Beringia 49, 74, 300, 302, 338, 420
Bhagavadgita 273
Bhutan 268
Bias in Mental Testing (Jensen) 26, 102
Binet, Alfred 20
biology 4, 8-9, 14, 210, 217, 331, 353-354, 368, 374, 377, 391, 417
bipedal locomotion 28
birth control 399
Bismarck Islands 78, 155, 285, 423
   (*Also see*: New Britain.)
black athletes (performance of) 84-87
Black Death, the 234, 428
Black Sea 49, 194, 199, 205, 214, 242, 295
Black-White Test Score Gap, The (Jencks & Phillips) 26, 93, 96, 102, 118
Blank Slate, The (Steven Pinker) 9
blitzkrieg 403
block printing 326
Blood River, Battle of 382

blood types 61, 80, 87
Bluefish Cave (Alaska) 62, 75
Boccachio 321
Boers 381-382
Bolivia 304, 335
Boltzmann, Ludwig 375, 380
Book of the Dead 209
boomerang 283
Border Cave (South Africa) 31
Borneo 49, 62, 155, 279, 382, 423, 426
bow and arrow 420, 424
Boyle, Robert 353, 356
Boyle's law 353
Brahe, Tycho 348
Brahmans 272
brain size 2, 20, 23, 25, 28-30, 80, 88, 90, 110, 117
    correlation with intelligence 23, 25, 122
    other species 28-30, 137
    racial differences 88, 110, 117
brains 23, 28-30, 122
  chemistry 23
  are metabolically expensive 28, 122
  microstructure 23
Brazil 50, 301, 338-339, 345, 386
"breed true" 11-12
bridge, duplicate 2, 111, 391, 417
Britain, British 18, 46, 52, 70, 97, 101, 184-185, 187, 194, 242, 271, 322, 347, 353, 360-361, 365-366, 373, 381-383, 386, 398, 404-405, 407-408, 411, 413, 421, 425, 431
    British colonies 271, 360-361, 365, 381-383, 386, 407, 411
    British Isles 194, 242, 425
    inventors and scientists 275-281
    philosophers *See*: Bacon; Locke; Hume.
Broca's area 31
bronze 147-148, 176, 187, 210, 266, 306, 308, 311, 327, 422-423
Bronze Age 266, 306, 327, 422
bubonic plague 234, 428
  (*Also see*: Black Death.)
Buddha, Gautama 272, 425
Buddhism 263, 272, 274, 280, 426-427
Buenos Aires 335, 345
Bulgaria 52-53, 62, 73, 99, 398, 401
Bulgars 292

Burma, Burman, Burmese 54-55, 272, 276, 279-280, 341-342, 382, 405, 424-426, 428
"burning of the books" 259
Bushmen 13, 16, 86, 156, 310
  (*Also see*: Hottentots; Khoisan; Sanids.)
Byzantine Empire 201, 208, 232, 237, 243-244, 247, 249, 251, 253, 293, 295, 316, 319, 321, 427-429
Byzantium 231 (*Also see*: Constantinople.)

Cabral, Pedro 338
Cactus Hill (Virginia) 75
Cahokia 305
Cajamarca, Battle of 335
calculus 346-347, 350, 356
Caligula 227
calligraphy 211, 252, 264
Calvin, John 330
Cambodia 314, 382, 406, 426-428
  (*Also see*: Khmers.)
camels 143, 176, 302-303, 312, 425
camera *See*: photography.
Cameroon 156
Canaan, Canaanites 54, 198, 202, 424
Canada 49, 76, 100, 124, 163, 290, 292, 300-301, 339, 360-361, 387, 408, 420, 423
Canadian Indians 100
Canary Islands 328
Cannae, Battle of 227
cannons 319, 327, 336, 342
  vs. castles 319
  vs. city walls 319
  (*Also see*: artillery; gunpowder.)
Cape Bojador 328
Cape of Good Hope 328-329
Cape Verde 328
Cape Verde Islands 314, 338
Capetown 381
Caracalla (Roman emperor) *See*: Edict of Caracalla.
Caracas 334
carbon-14 dating 157, 301, 418, **430-434**
Carthage 187, 202, 221-223, 225-226, 413, 425-426
Carver, George Washington 113
Caspian Sea 183, 187, 189, 194, 242, 422

caste system (India) 271-273, 275
  connection with race 272
Çatal Hüyük 140, 143, 199, 421
cathedrals 263, 316
Catholic Church, the Church 238, 241,
  320-321, 329-330, 349-350, 363, 369, 371,
  391, 393
    split with Eastern Orthodox 321
    (Also see: Christianity; crusades;
    Inquisition.)
Caucasian languages 57
Caucasoids 10, 14, 16, 63, 65, 70, 72-73, 78,
  84, 88, 114, 129, 148, 150-151, 207, 235,
  268-270, 285, 289, 293, 301-302, 310-311,
  408, 413-414
Caucasus Mountains 190-193, 195
cavalry 237-240, 245, 293, 317, 318, 336,
  342, 426
    vs. infantry 237-240
    (Also see: battles of Adrianople;
    Crécy; Hastings; and Tours.)
cave paintings 134-135, 419-420
Çayönü 142-143
celibacy, priestly 393
Celts, Celtic 2, 52-53, 189, 194-195,
  220-223, 425
    languages 52, 189
Central America 219, 334-335, 386
  (Also see: Mesoamerica.)
Central Asia 29, 30, 63, 72, 73, 78, 87, 124,
  142, 161, 165, 166, 183, 187, 194, 201,
  249, 250, 255, 260, 270, 272, 292, 293,
  295, 297, 344, 382, 406, 413, 415, 419,
  426-429, 436, 438, 440
Ceylon. See: Sri Lanka.
Chaco Canyon 305
Chad, Lake 54, 151
Chadic languages 54, 151
Chaldeans 200
Châlons, Battle of 231, 426
Chan Chan 236
Chandragupta I (India) 270, 271, 273, 425
Chandragupta Maurya 270, 273, 425
Charlemagne 241-242, 244, 322, 427
Charles I (England) 359-360, 371
Charles II (England) 354, 360
Charles Martel 241
Chatham Islands 154

chemical elements, periodic table of 377
chemistry 23, 210, 217, 252, 263, 352-353,
  356, 368, 375, 377, 391, 417
Cheng Ho 264, 266, 324
Cheops 423
chess 2, 111, 391, 417
CHH paper 394-396
chiefdoms 40, 144, 283, 286-287
Chile 74, 301, 303-304, 335, 420
chimpanzees 21, 28, 41, 67, 112, 137
Chimú Empire 236, 304
Ch'in dynasty 258-260
China, Chinese 2-3, 10, 12, 14, 29-31, 62,
  65, 70-75, 78, 88, 95, 110, 124, 128-129,
  141, 144, 146-148, 153, 161, 164, 166-169,
  172-173, 194, 204-205, 219, 254-255,
  257-267, 269-270, 272, 275-277, 279-280,
  287, 289-290, 293, 296-297, 299, 306, 319,
  326-329, 342-344, 362, 382-383, 402, 404,
  406-407, 409, 412-414, 417-419, 421-429,
  436, 438
    agriculture in 2, 141, 144, 161, 164,
      167-169, 172, 257, 421, 440-441
    comparisons with West 265-266,
      316-317, 323-324, 331-333
    conquered by outsiders 3, 293, 296-299,
      412, 429
    early humans in 62, 64, 70, 72-75,
      77-78, 418-419
    exploration by Chinese 263-264
    history 258-261
    Homo erectus in 29-30
    intelligence of 95, 124, 166, 331-332,
      409, 413
    inventions by 146-147, 254, 262, 319,
      326-327, 331, 414, 427-428
    language 54-56, 258
    literary and artistic achievements 260
    northern vs. southern China 257, 266
    practical outlook of 262, 332
    science and mathematics 219, 262-263
    writing 180, 332, 362
    (Also see: Confucius; North China
    Plain; Mongoloids; Southern
    Mongolids.)
Ch'ing dynasty 259, 261
chlorination of water 388
Chou dynasty 258-259, 266-267, 424-425

Christendom 323, 367
Christianity 202, 204, **228-229**, 232,
    236-238, 241-242, 271, 274, 316, 319-321,
    323, 329-330, 344, 367, 390-391, 393-395,
    426
    establishment of 229
    ethical doctrines 228
    theology 229
        (*Also see*: Catholic Church; crusades;
        Jesus; Pope; Protestant Reformation.)
Chukchi peninsula 74
Chukchi-Kamchatkan languages 57
Church, the 238, 241
circulation of the blood 353, 356
circumcision 229, 389
city-states 179, 198, 201, 213, 215, 218
Clovis (Frankish leader) 241
Clovis hypothesis 302-303
Clovis spearpoints 302
coal 317, 366
Cochran, G. 394, 396-397
    (*Also see*: CHH paper.)
Code Napoléon 372
Code of Hammurabi 423
Code of Justinian 243
Cold War 404-406
cold winters (evolutionary effect of) 2,
    121-125, 257, 277, 287
Colombia 334-335, 387
coloni 231 (*Also see*: serfs.)
colonialism 378, 381-383
    (Also see: colonization; European;
    decolonization.)
colonization 214, 290, 328, 334-335, 337,
    339, 341, 343, 345
Color of Crime, The 132
Columbia River 301
Columbus, Christopher 266, 328, 429
Commodus (Roman emperor) 230, 232
Communism 402-404, 406-407
    (*Also see*: USSR.)
compass (magnetic) 254, 262, 317, 331, 342,
    352, 428
complex societies 144
computer simulation of growth of IQ
    123-125, 135, 254, 280, 435-442
    description of 123, 125, 435-439
    results of 124

computers 1, 32, 112, 365, 398, 400, 417
Confucius 259-261, 264, 266, 425
    ethical teachings 261
Congo rainforest 104, 156, 311-312
Congo Republic (= Congo-Brazzaville) 97
Congo-Kinsasha. *See*: Zaire.
conservation of energy, law of 375-376
Constantinople 319, 321, 327, 427-428.
    (*Also see*: Byzantium; Istanbul.)
constitutional democracy **358-363**, 368,
    386-387, 403, 406
    why begin in England 362
contagious diseases 336, 354
    (*Also see* specific diseases such as
    smallpox or malaria.)
Copernicus, Nicolaus 266, 331, 348, 351,
    355, 429
copper 143, 147, 187, 198-199, 210
Corded Ware culture 423
Cordilleran ice sheet 49
core crops 165-170, 442-443
corn 142, 165, 169-170, 174, 303, 441-442
    (*Also see*: maize; teosinte.)
Coronado, Francisco de 335
correlation coefficient (= r) 18, 415
Corsica 223, 316, 372
Cortés, Hernando 334-335, 429
cosmic rays 399, 432
Côte d'Ivoire 407, 410
cotton 146-148, 306
Coulomb's law 374
cowpox 338
Crécy, Battle of 318, 428
Crete 180, 185, 187, 213, 423
crime rates 132
Crimea 293, 295
criminology 369
Croesus (Lydian king) 200
Cro-Magnons 66, 73, 78, 419
Cromwell, Oliver 359-360
crossbow 318
Crusades 316, 319-320, 428
Cuba 334, 345
cultural diffusion 149, 156-158
cuneiform writing 179-180, 186, 256
Curie, Marie 380
Cuzco 335
Czechs 52-53, 99, 384, 402

Daguerre, Louis 379-380
Daic languages 277
Daimler, Gottlieb 379-380
Dalton, John 375, 377, 380
Damascus 247, 427
Dante Alighieri 321
Danton, Georges 371
Darius the Great (= Darius I, Persia) 201, 214
Dark Ages 237-238, 242-245, 253, 260, 316-317, 321, 426
Darwin, Charles 1, 7, 9, 15, 37, 141, 357, 375, 378, 380, 388
dating methods *See*: determining ancient dates.
David (Hebrew king) 198, 202, 424
Davy, Humphry 376
De Humani Corporis Fabrica (Vesalius) 331, 353, 356
De Magnete (Gilbert) 352, 356
De Motu Cordis (Harvey) 353, 356
De Revolutionibus Orbium Coelestium (Copernicus) 331, 348, 356, 429
Declaration of Independence 370
Decline and Fall of the Roman Empire, The (Gibbon) 236
decolonization 405
deists 367, 370
demic expansion 149, 156-157, 184, 187
Democritus 217
dendrochronology 430-431, 433-434
Denmark, Danes, Danish 242, 322, 348, 363
Descartes, René 347, 356, 369
Descent of Man, The (Darwin) 9, 15
determining ancient dates **430-434**
devsirme system 295
dhimmis 249, 255
Dialogue Concerning Two New Sciences (Galileo) 350
Dialogue on the Two Chief World Systems (Galileo) 349
Diamond Sutra, The 326, 427
Dias, Bartolomeu 328
Diderot, Denis 368-369
Diet of Worms 330
diffraction of light 351
digit span 21-22, 111
dilution effect 343

dinosaurs 375, 378
Diocletian (Roman emperor) 230-232
  wage and price controls 230
Discourse on Method (Descartes) 347, 356
Diu, Battle of 341
divorce rates 127, 132
dizygotic twins (frequency of) 80, 130
DNA 5-6, 13, 31, 60-61, 63, 112, 187, 287, 310-311, 390, 394, 399
  junk DNA 6
  mitochondrial DNA 31
  (*Also see*: genes.)
dogs 11-12, 15, 32, 35, 126, 143, 171, 420
  breeds of 11
  domestication of 143
domesticated crops (earliest) 420
donkeys 143, 422
Dorians 214, 424
Dorset Eskimos 423
Douglass, Frederick 113
Dr. Dunkenstein 86
Dravidian languages 56, 149-150, 157, 184, 186-187, 268-270, 273, 412, 421, 437
Drew, Charles 113
dual code of morality **40-42**, 65
Dürer, Albrecht 321
Dutch 52-53, 341-342, 344, 351-353, 381-383 (*Also see*: Holland; Netherlands.)
dynamite 379

EA See: Eskimo-Aleut.
early human sites (*HSS*)
  in Africa 31
  outside Africa 62
early modern times 71, 142, 282-283, 296, 325, 340, 346, 352, 355, 390-392
East Africa 28-29, 54, 76, 151, 181, 310, 312-313
East African Negroes 157, 310, 312, 315
East Indies 341-342 (*Also see*: Sumatra; Java; Borneo; Sulawesi)
Easter Island 111, 153, 155, 162, 181, 285-287, 314, 426
Eastern Europe 30, 231, 321-323, 362, 364, 384, 390, 393, 403, 419, 422, 426
eclipses 306
Ecuador 304, 335

Edict of Caracalla 233, 426
Edict of Milan 229, 426
Edison, Thomas Alva 379-380
Edward III (England) 359
Egypt 2, 54, 73, 76, 101, 139, 141, 144,
    147-148, 151, 168, 180-182, 187, 197-198,
    200-202, 204, **206-212**, 213, 215, 219-220,
    223-224, 226, 232, 243, 247-252, 266, 295,
    307, 311, 341, 382, 389, 404-405, 409,
    413, 421-422, 424-427
   Egyptian hieroglyphics 182
   "the gift of the Nile" 206
   Upper & Lower Egypt 207
   importance of ancient Egypt 209-212
   why usually overrated 211
Eightfold Path 272
Elamites 150, 153, 179, 187, 199
electricity 352, 356, 365, 368, 374-376, 379-
    380, 417
   electric generators and motors 379
   electric power distribution 379
electromagnetic waves 375-376
Elements (Euclid) 215-216, 265, 330, 371,
    374-377, 380, 425
Elizabeth I (England) 359
ellipses 216, 348, 357
emancipation of women 254
embryology 217
encephalization 28, 129
Encyclopédie 369
England, English 52-53, 55, 157, 160, 220,
    224, 226-227, 231, 237, 242-245, 255,
    317-318, 322, 330, 339-340, 342-343, 345,
    350-353, 358-373, 380-386, 398, 402-407,
    422, 428-429
   and constitutional democracy 358-363
   and Industrial Revolution 364-366
   Norman Conquest 243
   kings and queens (*See* individual rulers.)
      (*Also see*: Britain; British Empire;
      English Civil War; United Kingdom.)
English Civil War 359-360
Enlightenment, the 361-362, **367-373**, 383,
    429
Ephthalites 271, 412
epicycles 348, 357
epidemics 233-234, 236, 340
epistemology 369

Equatorial Guinea 97
Eratosthenes 216
Erech *See*: Uruk.
Eskimo-Aleut 57, 290, 291
Eskimos 67, 290, 292, 301, 417, 420-423
Estates-General 370-371
Estonia 402
Ethiopia 54, 97, 139, 141, 151, 153, 168,
    176, 181, 206, 311, 313, 383, 407, 410, 421
Etruscans 58, 182, 185-187, 211, 221-222,
    424
Euclid 214, 216, 265-266, 320, 332, 255,
    425 (*Also see*: axiomatic treatment;
    Elements.)
Euphrates River 140, 197
Eurasia 2, 142, 174, 176, 314
Euripides 214, 217, 266
Europe 1-3, 10, 29-31, 46, 61, 63, 65
   comparison with China 265-266,
      316-317, 323-324, 331-333
   comparison with other regions 324, 331
      (*Also see* particular regions, such as
      Western Europe.)
Evenki 292
evolution, theory of **4-9**
exogamy 40
eyeglasses *See*: spectacles.
Ezra (Jewish religious leader) 425

factories 364-365
Fagan, Brian M 33, 42, 62, 138, 145, 159,
    172, 299, 309, 434
falsifiability 416
Faraday, Michael 375-376, 379-380
Fell's Cave (Patagonia) 300, 420
Ferdinand II (Aragon) 321, 329
Fermat, Pierre de 347
fermented beverages 146, 422
Fertile Crescent 139, 141, 144, 149-151,
    153, 157, 161, 164, 170, 197-198, 200-201,
    210, 215, 226, 249, 270, 293, 295, 307,
    311, 413, 420-421, 427
feudal system 240-241, 243
Fibonacci 346
Fiedel, Stuart J. 299, 309
Fiji 154-155, 281, 285, 424
Finland, Finns 57, 99, 195, 363, 402

fire (mastery of) 29, 418
firearms 32, 318, 332, 336, 340, 342, 344
fishhooks 134, 136, 284, 420
Five Books of Moses 203, 425
"five good emperors" (= adoptive emperors) 224, 230
flax 146, 148
Flynn effect 94-95, 97-99, 101, 116, 120
Flynn, James R. 116, 120
Four Noble Truths 272
France, French 29-30, 51, 53, 55-56, 58, 62, 99, 134, 157, 184-185, 194-195, 206, 214, 224-226, 231, 237-238, 241-243, 249, 318, 320, 322, 330, 339, 341, 344, 347, 359, 361-364, 366-373, 380-382, 398, 401-406, 411, 420, 422, 425, 427, 429
   (*Also see*: Franks; French Revolution; Gaul; Enlightenment; Napoleon; and individual monarchs.)
Franks 237, 239, 241, 249, 427
freedom of
   religion 370
   speech 368
   the press 370
   (*Also see*: Voltaire.)
French and Indian War 339
French Enlightenment 361-362
French Revolution 361, 367, 369-373, 429
   Reign of Terror 371
   (*Also see*: Louis XVI; Mirabeau; Napoleon; Robespierre.)
fruits (cultivation of) 142, 146

g factor 18-19, 26, 98, 111
g factor, The (Arthur Jensen) 26, 120
Gabon 111
Galapagos Islands 281
Galen 224
Galileo 254, 266, 349-352, 356, 369
gamma rays 5
Ganj Dareh 142-143
Gao 312
Gardner, Howard 17, 26
Gatling, Richard 379
Gaucher's disease 395
Gaul, Gauls 53, 194, 222, 224, 231, 234, 241, 413, 426

Gautama. *See*: Buddha.
genes 5-9, 11, 24, 35-38, 41-45, 60-62, 65, 83, 110, 112, 121, 130-131, 151, 157-158, 220, 286, 337, 389-390
   dominant, recessive 5
   (*Also see*: alleles; DNA.)
Genesis 205
genetic drift 6-9, 11, 79, 395
genetic engineering 398, 400
Geneva 330
Genghis Khan 251, 260, 271, 292-293, 296, 322, 428
Genome (Ridley) 6, 119
geologic epochs 47
geology 368, 375, 378, 399, 417
geometry 160, 209-210, 216, 262, 347, 356, 375, 377, 380, 425
   axiomatic treatment of 216, 262, 425
   non-Euclidean 375
   (*Also see*: Euclid; *Elements*.)
George III (England) 360
germ theory of disease 354-355, 375, 377
Germany, Germans 2, 46, 52-53, 55, 99, 157, 184, 186-187, 189, 194-195, 206, 231, 233, 237-238, 241-243, 316, 322, 326, 330, 343, 347-348, 352, 362-364, 366, 380-382, 384, 398, 401-405, 413, 421, 423, 425
   Germanic languages 52-53, 56, 242
   Germanic tribes 2, 231, 233, 237-238, 241-242, 413, 427, 439
   unification of 384
   (*Also see*: Charlemagne; Franks; Holy Roman Empire.)
gestation period 80, 130
Ghana 97, 312, 407, 410
Gibbon, Edward 236
Gilbert, William 352
Gimbutas, Marija 183, 195
Giza 208
glacial periods *See*: ice ages.
glass 204, 306, 316, 336, 351
Goa 341
Gobi Desert 74
Gödel, Kurt 399
Golden Horde, Khanate of the 295-296, 323
Gothic architecture 245, 316
Gottfredson, Linda 96

grammar 32, 51, 194, 273
  (*Also see*: syntactic language.)
Granada 316, 322
Grand Canal (China) 263
gravitation, law of 351, 356
Great Books of the Western World 205, 212, 229
Great Britain 46, 322, 365, 381, 408, 411, 431 (*Also see*: Britain; England; United Kingdom.)
Great Flood, the 205
Great Pyramid (= pyramid of Cheops) 208, 423
Great Wall of China 259, 263, 425
Great Zimbabwe 313
Greater Australia 49, 68-70, 78, 282, 419
Greece, Greeks 2-3, 52-53, 56, 65, 99, 157, 164, 179, 181, 184-186, 188-189, 191-193, 201-202, 208, 211, **213-220**, 221-226, 231-232, 234, 239, 244-245, 249-250, 252, 263, 274, 280, 285, 295, 317, 320-321, 324, 330, 332, 345, 351-352, 354-355, 357, 394-395, 413-414, 423-426
  alphabet 202
  arts and literature 217-218
  Dorian Greeks 214, 424
  history of 213-215
  math and science 216-217
  mythology 217
  philosophy 218
  why did they achieve so much? 218-220
    (*Also see*: Alexander the Great; Athens.)
Greenberg, Joseph 284, 288, 309
Greenland 124, 243, 290, 292
Gregory I (Pope) 244
Grotte Chauvet (France) 134
group selection 36, 38, 41
Guatamala 304
Guericke, Otto von 352
guided missiles 400
guilds (medieval) 391, 396
Guinea 97
guinea pigs 306
gunpowder 254, 262, 265, 317-319, 327, 331-332, 342, 427
  (*Also see*: cannons; firearms.)

Guns, Germs, and Steel (Jared Diamond) 71, 116, 173, 177, 314, 345
Gupta Empire (India) 270-271, 427
Gutenberg, Johannes 266, 326-327, 355, 362, 428
Gutenberg Bible 327
Gypsies 53, 393, 403

Habsburg dynasty 322-323, 401-402
Hadrian (Roman emperor) 224
Hagia Sophia 244, 263
hair color 80-81
Haiti 339, 345
half-life 432-433
Hammurabi 199, 423
Han dynasty 259-260, 412, 426
Han Fei Tzu 258
handguns 319, 325, 327, 332, 336, 429
Hanson, Victor Davis 205, 220, 239
Harappa 269
Hardy, Jason 394, 396-397
  (*Also see*: CHH paper.)
Harpending, Henry 394, 396-397
  (*Also see*: CHH paper.)
harpoons 420
harshness factor 123, 163-164, 167, 435-437, 440-442
Harun al-Rashid 251, 427
Harvey, William 353, 356
Hastings, Battle of 240, 245, 318, 428
Hatti 186 (*Also see*: Hittites.)
Hausa 56
Hawaii 155, 281-282, 285, 287, 426
Head Start programs 108, 170, 219, 414
Hebrews 3, 54, 56, 198, 202-203, 209, 389, 392-393, 395, 397, 424-425 (*Also see*: Jews; Judea; Israel.)
Hegira 246
heliocentric theory 217, 331, 348-349, 351, 355-357 (*Also see*: Copernicus; Kepler; Galileo; Newton.)
helium 377
Henry II (England) 322
Henry III (England) 358
Henry VIII (England) 359
Henry the Navigator 266, 328
Heraclius 243-244

hereditary aristocracy 237, 239, 370
heritability 24-26, 104, 126
   defined 26
Hero of Alexandria 224
Hertz, Heinrich 376
heterosis 15, 120
   (*Also see*: hybrid vigor.)
Heyerdahl, Thor 285-286, 288, 301-302
HF *See*: harshness factor.
HGHG See: *History and Geography of Human Genes.*
hieroglyphics 181-182, 198, 209
Hindi 52-53, 56, 194
Hinduism, Hindus 265, 271-274, 295, 405
Hipparchus 216-217, 265
Hippocrates 214, 217, 236
hippopotamus 236
hips, width of 80, 83-86, 122
Hiroshima 403, 406
Hispanics 101
Hispaniola 334, 339, 345
historical determinism 225
History (Herodotus) 205, 212, 218
History and Geography of Human Genes (Cavalli-Sforza) 60-63
History of the Peloponnesian War (Thucydides) 218, 220
Hitler, Adolf 403, 404
Hittites 53, 153, 179, 185-186, 194, 199-200, 210, 220, 423-424
Hmong 57, 276
Holland 186, 237, 363, 366, 372, 379, 390
   (*Also see*: Dutch; Netherlands.)
Holocaust, the 403
Holocene Epoch 46-47, 420, 435
Holy Roman Empire 241, 322, 348
hominids 28-30, 32-33, 41, 65, 69-70, 73-74, 123, 138, 268, 435
Homo erectus 68-69, 76, 133, 137-138, 162, 268-269, 375, 378, 418
Homo sapiens 2, 8, 28-33, 60, 67-69, 76, 79, 162, 268, 418 (*Also see*: Neanderthals; archaic *Homo sapiens*.)
Homo sapiens neanderthalensis 30
   (*Also see*: Neanderthals.)
Homo sapiens sapiens 2, 8, 28-33, 60-61, 63, 65, 67-69, 73, 79, 121, 123, 137, 268-269, 277, 413, 418-419, 435, 437

linguistic skills 31
   expansion out of Africa **60-67**
Hong Kong 95, 382, 407
Hooke, Robert 353
hoplites 239
Hottentot apron 310
Hottentots 13, 16, 156, 310 (*Also see*: Bushmen; Khoikhoi; Khoisan; Sanids.)
Hsia dynasty 258-259, 423
Hsiung-nu 425
HSS See: *Homo sapiens sapiens*.
Hulagu (Mongol leader) 251
human genome 6
human races 2, 10, 11, 12, 13, 14, 15, 79, 128, 129, 416
human sacrifices 304
humanism 320
Hume, David 229, 369
Hungary, Hungarians. 57, 323
   (*Also see*: Magyars.)
Huns 184, 231, 242, 271, 289, 292, 426
hunter-gatherers 40, 149, 150-151, 153, 155-156, 161, 170, 273, 277, 283, 312, 344, 384, 422-423
Huntington's chorea 112, 119
Huon Peninsula 62, 70
Hus, Jan 330
Huygens, Christiaan 352, 356
hybrids 12, 14, 65, 71, 114, 120, 150, 156, 158, 310-311, 343
   hybrid vigor 12, 20
   (*Also see*: heterosis.)
Hyksos 207

Iberian Peninsula 316, 321
Iberians 185, 187
Ibn Batuta 252, 255, 317
Ibn Khaldun 252
Ibn Warraq 255-256
ice ages **46-50**, 68, 74, 123, 163-164, 167, 277, 283, 300, 302, 311, 375, 378, 380, 420, 441-442
   chronology of 47
   sea level change 49-50
   map 48
   (*Also see*: Riss; Würm.)
ice caps 49, 74, 300

Iceland 52, 76, 243, 322, 363, 365, 427
ideal gas law 353
Ikhnaton 202, 209, 424
Il milione 317
Iliad (Homer) 217, 313, 424
illegitimate births 127, 132
Illyria 189, 224, 234
immigration into Western countries 408, 411
Incas, Incan Empire 59, 181, 304, 306, 335, 429 (*Also see*: Machu Picchu; Quechua.)
incestuous mating 12
incompleteness theorem 399
India 2, 12, 31, 49-50, 52, 58, 65, 68-70, 72, 76-78, 87, 101, 110, 124, 139, 141, 147-150, 161, 163, 165-168, 181, 183, 186, 194-195, 215, 255, 263-264, **268-275**, 277, 279-280, 292-293, 295-297, 307, 317, 324, 328-329, 331, 341-342, 361, 382, 388, 404-405, 408, 412-414, 419, 421, 423-429, 436-438, 440
    arts and literature 273
    caste system 271-272, 275
    climate and its effects 268, 275
    history 268-271
    mathematics and science 274
    religions 271-273
    settlement (three waves of) 268-270
    tribal peoples 273
        (*Also see*: Dravidian languages; Hinduism; Indic languages; Indus Valley civilization; Mehrgarh; Munda languages.)
Indian Ocean 49, 58, 68-69, 264, 268, 279, 313-314, 329, 341-342
Indian subcontinent 149, 268, 271, 274, 378, 382, 411
Indic languages 52-53, 194-195
Indo-European, Indo-Europeans 2-3, 52-56, **183-196**, 198, 201, 208, 222, 226, 242, 249, 422-424
Indo-Iranian 53
Indonesia 2, 49, 56, 62, 65, 68, 70-71, 78, 101, 124-125, 141, 153, 155-156, 163, 165-166, 168, 171, 219, 255, 264, 275-276, 279-282, 284-285, 287, 314, 328, 341-342, 382, 405, 407, 409, 413, 420, 423, 428, 436, 438, 440-441

Indo-Pacific languages 57, 284, 288
    (*Also see*: Papuan; New Guinea.)
Indus Valley civilization 269-271, 423
    (*Also see*: Harappa; Mohenjo-Daro.)
industrial management 380
Industrial Revolution **364-366**, 367-368, 374, 378, 429
    steam engine 364
    why did it begin in England? 365
infantry 238-240, 245, 317, 318, 327, 398, 401, 426
    vs. calvary *See*: cavalry.
influenza 336-337
inoculation 379-380
Inquisition 91, 254, 350, 366, 369, 387
    Roman 350, 369
    Spanish 254, 366, 387
insect-borne diseases 338
    (*Also see*: malaria; yellow fever.)
Institutes of the Christian Religion (John Calvin) 330
"institutional racism" 114
intelligence 1-4, **17-29**, 38, 86, 90-99, 101, 104, 107, 110-117, 121-125, 128, 135-138, 148, 150, 156-158, 162-167, 169-171, 173, 187, 204, 219-220, 226, 234-235, 254, 257-258, 269-270, 275, 277, 280, 287, 289, 299, 307, 311, 314-315, 332, 343, 362, 365, 384-385, 387, 389, 391-396, 406, 413-414, 416-417, 437, 439-440
    described 17-18
    general, and g factor 18-19
    group differences in **91-102**
    heritability of 23-25
    importance of 22-23
    increase in past 100,000 years 121-125
    testing of 20-21
    variation with age 19
        (*Also see*: IQ; *g* factor; Jensen; racial differences; nature or nurture.)
internal combustion engine 379-380
internet 400
Inuit 292 (*Also see*: Eskimos.)
invaders 412
inventions 1, 23, 32, 111, 135-136, 143, 146-148, 160, 162-163, 171, 174, 178-181, 199, 254, 262, 265, 274-275, 315, 318, 324-327, 331-332, 346-347, 352, 355,

ABOUT THE AUTHOR

Michael H. Hart was born in New York City in 1932. He received a bachelor's degree from Cornell University, where he majored in mathematics. He later received a Ph.D. in astronomy from Princeton University. He also has an M.S. in physics, an M.S. in computer science, and a law degree.

Dr. Hart was for many years a college professor, teaching courses in astronomy, in physics, and in the history of science. He also worked at NASA Goddard Space Flight Center (Greenbelt, MD), at Computer Science Corporation (Falls Church, VA), and at the National Center for Atmospheric Research (Boulder, CO).

He is the author of *The 100: A Ranking of the Most Influential Persons in History* (1978, Hart Publishing Company; revised edition 1992, Citadel Press), and also of *A View from the Year 3000* (1999, Poseidon Press). In addition, he has published a variety of technical articles in scientific journals.

Zambia 97
Zapotek (hieroglyphic writing) 180, 305, 424
zebras 176
Zheng He *See*: Cheng Ho.
Zhoukoudian (cave, China) 29, 62
Zimbabwe 97, 111, 313
Zoroaster 424
Zulus 382-383
Zwingli, Huldreich 330

μ-group 63-65, 72-75
μ-1 64, 66, 73, 76-78
μ-2 64, 66, 73, 77-78
μ-3 64, 66, 73, 77-78

σ-group 63-65, 68-71
σ-1 64, 66, 69, 71, 77
σ-2 64, 66, 69-71, 77
σ-3 64, 66, 70-71, 77, 257, 282, 285-287
σ-4 64, 66, 70-71, 77, 282, 286-287

Vikings 242-243, 285, 317, 327, 427
viruses 375, 380, 399
Visigoths 231, 237, 242, 426
Visual arts 218, 252, 320, 321
vitamin D 81
Volta, Alessandro 374, 376
Voltaire 361, 368
vulgar Latin 238

wage and price controls 230
Waldo, Peter 330
Wales 53, 318, 322
Wallace, Alfred Russel 388
war chariots 238
Waterloo, Battle of 373, 384
Watt, James 364-365
wave theory of light 352, 356
Wealth of Nations, The (Adam Smith) 369
Wernicke's area 31
West Africa 141, 145, 156, 168, 255, 310-315, 328, 337, 340, 422, 424
West Indies 161, 337-340
Western Civilization 367
Western Europe 30, 46, 73, 148, 231-245, 249, 252-253, 302, 304, 316-324, 327, 362, 366-367, 374, 390, 393, 411, 418-419, 426-428
Western Hemisphere 2, 61, 67, 74, 78, 82, 141, 143, 146, 148, 167-169, 172-177, 180, 216, 251, **300-309**, 326-328, 334-340, 342, 390, 420, 422, 424, 438
   agriculture 303
   collapse of civilizations 305
   destruction of megafauna 302-303
   writing 305-306
   how far behind Old World? 307-308
     (*Also see*: American Indians; Mesoamerica; New World.)
Westernization 384-385
Westminster Abbey 316
wheels, spoked 423
White Huns 271
white light, composite nature of 352
William of Orange 360
William the Conqueror 243, 322
wolves 11, 32
women, emancipation of 254, 383

wool 266, 306
World War I 59, 92, 104, 295, 384, 398, 401-403
World War II 115, 251, 365, 402-406
writing 9, 46, 54, 147-148, 177-182, 185-186, 197-199, 204, 209-210, 213-214, 220, 225, 262, 265, 273, 283-284, 286, 303, 305-306, 308, 312-315, 326, 332, 336, 418, 422-423, 424
   alphabetic 179
   China 180
   cuneiform 179
   earliest 179, 422
   Egyptian hierglyphics 180
   logosyllabic 178
   syllabic 178
   sumeria 179
   western Hemisphere 180, 303
     (Also see: alphabet; Zapotek.)
Würm (glacial period) 46-47, 162, 419, 435
Wycliffe, John 330

xenophobia (among other animals) 41
Xenophon 218
Xerxes 201, 214
X-rays 5, 375, 380

Yakuts 292
yams 142, 146, 165, 168, 171, 176, 288, 311
Yana River 75
Yangtze River 141, 257, 441
Yarmuk, Battle of the 247-248
Y-chromosomes 389
yellow fever 336-338
Yellow River 263
Yenisei River 58, 344
Yüan dynasty 259, 261
Yucatán 110, 176, 304, 334, 426
Yüeh-chih 271, 412
Yugoslavia 402
Yukaghir 58

Zagros Mountains 197
Zainab 255
Zaire (= Congo-Kinsasha) 97, 407

transition to modern times **325-333**
  why was Europe the site? 331-333
Transvaal 382
Treaty of Tordesillas 338
"tribe that conquered a continent" 183
trigonometry 216
tropical West Africa 141, 156, 168, 311, 422
Ts'ai Lun 262, 426
Tuamotu Islands 281, 285
Tuareg 54, 312
tuberculosis 338
Tuchman, Barbara 411
Tungus, Tungusic 260, 292, 296, 426
Tunisia 202, 247, 382, 405, 409
Turkey, Turks 101, 139, 143, 197, 199, 201, 213, 242-244, 251, 255, 271, 289, 293, 295-297, 299, 319, 398, 401, 409, 427-429
  (*Also see*: Anatolia; Ottoman Empire.)
turkeys 306
Turkic languages 56, 292
"turn the other cheek" 228
twentieth Century **398-411**
  Asian and African countries 406-410
  Cold War 404
  decolonization 405-406
  World Wars, I and II 398, 402-404
  scientific advances 398-399
  technological developments 398, 400
twins 24, 80-83, 84, 126, 130
  frequency of 83-84, 130
  identical twins reared separately 24, 126
Tycho Brahe 348
typewriter 379
typhus fever 336

Uganda 97, 111, 407, 410
Ukraine 53, 157-158, 187, 323, 390, 421-422
ultraviolet radiation 5, 81, 375
Umar ibn al-Khattab (caliph) 247
Umayyad Caliphate 247, 249-250
uncertainty principle 227
United Arab Emirates 408-409
United Kingdom 99
  (*Also see*: Britain; British Empire; England; Great Britain.)
United Nations 404, 411
United States of America *See*: USA.

Upanishads 273
Ur (Sumerian city) 198, 205
Ural Mountains 344
Uralic languages 58, 186, 195, 323
Urban II (Pope) 319-320
Urdu 53
Ur-Nammu (Sumeian ruler) 205
Uruguay 335, 387
Uruk (= Erech) (Sumerian city) 198, 422
USA (= United States of America) 2, 14-15, 20, 49, 62, 74, 76, 82-84, 86-87, 92-93, 96, 100-101, 114, 124, 131-132, 141, 160-161, 163-164, 166, 168, 170-172, 174, 300-303, 305, 333-334, 340, 360, 364, 374, 380-381, 385-387, 390, 398, 402-406, 408, 411, 417, 420, 423, 426, 428, 432, 436, 439, 441-442
  Civil War 386, 401
  constitution 370, 386
  inventions 385
  literary figures 385
  racial problems 386
  Revolutionary War 360
    (*Also see*: American; American Indians.)
USSR (= Soviet Union) 402-406
  despotic nature of 402
  economic performance 404
  (*Also see*: Cold War; Communism.)
Uzbekistan 30, 295-296, 406

Valley of Mexico 304, 426, 427
Valley of the Kings 209
Valmy, Battle of 372
Vandals 231, 237, 243
Vanhanen, Tatu *See*: Lynn & Vanhanen.
Varro, Marcus Terentius 354
varves 430, 433-434
Vasco da Gama 328-329, 341, 429
Vedas 273
Venezuela 334-335
Venus figurines 420
Vera Cruz 303-304
vertical leap 86, 90
Vesalius, Andreas 331, 353, 356
Vienna 322
Vietnam 276, 279, 382, 404, 406, 411, 422, 425, 427

Suleiman the Magnificent (Ottoman ruler) 429
Sultanate of Delhi 271, 293, 296
Sumatra 49, 155, 279, 342, 424
Sumeria 58, 147-148, 179-180, 186, 197-199, 252, 422-423
Sun 91, 209, 217, 330-331, 348-349, 351-352, 355, 370, 377, 432
    rotation of 349
    sunspots 349
    (*Also see*: heliocentric theory.)
Sundaland Peninsula 49-50, 68-70, 78, 419
Sung dynasty 259-260, 428
Sungir 62
Sunnis 247
Sun-Tzu 264
Swahili 56, 181
Sweden, Swedish 52-53, 99, 242, 322, 363
sweet potatoes 142, 146, 165, 176, 303, 306
swine flu 337, 338
Switzerland 99, 187, 322, 330, 369, 380-381
swords 306, 317, 336
syllabic writing system 178, 180, 213-214
Synoptic Gospels 228
syphilis 87, 338
Syria 139, 142-143, 199, 201, 203, 207, 223-224, 243, 247, 251, 389, 402, 405, 409, 413, 420
Syriac 54, 249
Syrian War 223

T'ang dynasty 259-260, 427
Taiwan 95, 125, 153, 168, 263, 279, 297, 406-407, 409, 422, 436, 438, 440
Taj Mahal 275, 296
Tajikistan 406
Talmud 389
Tamerlane 271, 295-296, 323, 412, 428
Tanzania 29, 97, 407, 410
Tao Te Ching (Lao Tzu) 264
Tasmania 49, 58, 68, 70, 78, 282, 284, 288, 382-383, 420
Tassili-n-Ajjer (Algeria) 236
Taylor, Frederick W. 380
Tay-Sachs disease 395
teff 174
telegraph 379, 385

telephone 379-380, 385
telescope 348-349, 352, 356, 429
television 400
temperature 7, 18-19, 110, 353, 376-377
"Ten Lost Tribes" 203
Tenochtitlán 304, 306, 314, 428
teosinte 142, 169-170, 174, 303
    (*Also see*: corn; maize.)
Teotihuacán 111, 304, 306, 314, 426-427
testosterone 127-128, 131
Thailand 62, 101, 272, 276, 279, 341-342, 382-383, 422, 427-428
thalassemias 80, 82
Thales of Miletus 425
Theodosius I (Roman emperor) 229, 232
thermodynamics 352, 375-377, 380
    first law of 376
    second law of 375-377
thermoluminescence 430, 433-434
Third Estate 371
Third Industrial Revolution 365
third-world countries 111, 385, 406, 408, 411-412
threshold IQ 163-164, 166-167, 169-171, 440-442
Thucydides 218, 220
Tiahuanaco 304
Tibet 54-55, 272, 276, 279, 293, 297, 417, 423-425
    (*Also see*: Sino-Tibetan.)
Tibeto-Burman languages 54-55
Tierra del Fuego 74
tigers 32, 302
Tigris River 140, 197
tilted axes 174-176
Timbuktu 312
time preferences 127
Titicaca, Lake 304
Tocharian 53
Toktamish 295
Toltecs 304, 427
tomatoes 176
Torah, the 203, 425
Torres Strait 283
Toulon, siege of 372
Tours, Battle of 239-241, 245, 249, 427
Trafalgar, Battle of 373
transfinite numbers 375

Slavic languages 52-53
Slavic tribes, expansion into Europe 322
smallpox 80, 82, 236, 252, 336-338, 342
    effect in New World 336-337
Smith, Adam 369
Smith, Bruce D. 145, 159, 172
Snell, Willibrord 351
Snyderman & Rothman 112
social welfare policies 45, 384, 404
socialism 404 (*Also see*: Communism.)
societal structures 144
socioeconomic status 108
"sociologist's fallacy" 108, 118
Socotra 341
Solomon (Hebrew king) 203
Solomon Islands 70, 78, 155, 281, 423
Solutrean tools 420, 431
Somalia 54, 174, 311, 313
Songhai 312, 340
sorghum 142, 146, 165, 168, 174, 311
South Africa 97, 310, 312, 407
    Republic of 97, 407
South America 58, 61, 68, 124, 141, 143, 146, 161, 164, 166-167, 170, 184, 219, 245, 268, 281, 285, 300, 302-304, 306, 314, 334, 338, 342, 420, 422, 436, 441
South Korea 95, 406-409
Southeast Asia 62, 65, 68-72, 78, 124, 141, 165-166, 168, 181, 242, 257, 263-264, 272, **276-280**, 287, 293, 295, 302, 341, 413-414, 419-423, 426-427, 436, 438, 440
    migrations into 277-280
southern Africa 10, 13, 31, 76, 156, 310, 311, 313, 381, 420, 424, 438
Southern Mongolids 74, 289-290
Southwest Asia 30, 63, 73, 78, 142, 151, 153, 161-162, 197, 207, 210, 251, 266, 280, 293, 311, 389, 409, 413, 421, 425, 428
    (*Also see*: Middle East.)
Soviet Union 402-406
    (*Also see*: USSR; Russia.)
soybeans 142, 146, 167
Spain, Spanish 51, 53, 55, 58-59, 62, 99, 157, 164, 167, 185, 194-195, 223-226, 231, 237-238, 241-243, 249-250, 254-255, 304, 306, 312, 317, 321-322, 328-329, 334-340, 342-345, 363, 366, 372, 378, 386-387, 390, 394-395, 397, 413, 415, 427

Sparta 215, 425
spears 239, 306, 336
spear-throwers 420
species 32, 33
spectacles 254, 317, 428
spectroscopy 375, 377, 380
speech (human) 31-33, 238, 254, 272, 319-320, 361, 368, 370, 387
    syntactic language
Speke, John 381
Sphinx 209
Spice Islands 328
Spirit of Laws, The (Montesquieu) 369
squash 169-170, 176, 306, 421, 441-442
Sri Lanka. (= Ceylon) 255
SSA *See*: sub-Saharan Africa.
Ssu-ma Ch'ien 262, 266
Stalin, Josef 404
Stanley, Henry M. 381
Step Pyramid 208
steppe, the Steppes 72, 183, 187, 189, 194, 422, 426
stirrups 239, 426
stone tool industries, prehistoric 430-431
    (*Also see* particular industries, such as Acheuelian, Aurignacian, etc.)
Stonehenge 423
stotting 35-36, 39
Strait of Gibraltar 50, 210
strong environmentalism 103-104, 115
strong hereditarianism 103-104, 115, 120
submarine 379
sub-Saharan Africa 2, 13, 30, 50, 60-61, 63-67, 76, 82, 94, 110-111, 116-117, 119, 121-124, 130-131, 146, 156, 163, 165-166, 173-177, 181, 245, 251, 269, 274, 286, 307, **310-315**, 340, 381-382, 384, 406-408, 410, 413-414, 417-418, 422, 424, 435-436, 440
    (*Also see*: secluded zone.)
subspecies 11, 30, 31, 32, 79, 126, 127, 128
Sudan 97, 410
Sudan, the 311
sugar 87, 146, 339
Sui dynasty 259-260, 263, 427
Sui Wen Ti 427
Sukhotai kingdom 279
Sulawesi (= Celebedes) 155, 423

Sahara Desert 54, 151, 176, 236, 311-312, 421-422
   desertifiction of 311
   period of maximum wetness 311, 421
Sahulland 68, 70
St. Anselm 316
St. Augustine 224
Sakas 270, 412
Salamis, Battle of 201, 205, 214, 425
saltpeter 318
Samarkand 295-296
Samoa 155, 281, 285
Sanids 13-14, 76, 156, 310, 419
   (*Also see*: Bushmen; Hottentots; Khoikhoi; Khoisan.)
Sanskrit 52-53, 185, 194, 270, 273
Sardinia 52, 221, 223, 242, 316
Sargent test 90
Sassanid dynasty 243, 247
   (*Also see*: Iran; Persia.)
SAT (tests) 20, 107-108, 113, 115, 119
Saxons 231, 237, 241
Scandinavia 46, 157, 187, 238, 242, 322, 343, 365, 422
Sceptical Chymist, The (Robert Boyle) 353, 356
Schlieffen plan 401
science (*See* individual fields such as: astronomy; biology; chemistry; geology; mechanics; optics; physics.)
science, rise of 326, 330, **346-357**, 366, 369
Scientific Revolution 354-355, 365
Scotland 157, 221, 322, 369, 380, 392, 422
sculpture 218, 252, 256, 264, 273-274, 280, 287
Scythians 53, 194
SEA *See*: Southeast Asia.
sea level, changes in 49, 74, 420-421
secluded zone of SSA 2, 110, 286, 313-314, 381
   backwardness described 313-314
Second Industrial Revolution 365
second law of thermodynamics 375-376
Seleucid Empire 203, 223, 425
self-esteem (supposed lack of among blacks) 113, 117
Selfish Gene, The (Richard Dawkins) 7, 39
Selim II (Ottoman emperor) 295

Seljuk Turks 244, 251, 293, 428
Semang 71, 277, 279-280
Semitic languages 54, 56, 151, 153, 179, 181, 186, 198-199, 201, 219
Senegal 176, 328, 341
Sephardic Jews, Sephardim 390-392, 394, 396
Septimius Severus 230
Serbia 398, 401
serfs 231, 237, 240-241, 368
SES (= socioeconomic status) 108, 110
sewing needle 419
sexual behavior and attitudes **43-45**
sexual selection 5, 9, 131, 310
Shah Jehan 271, 296
Shaker Heights (Ohio) 113
Shakespeare, William 254
Shang dynasty 258-259, 423-424
Shang Yang 258
Shari'a 253
Shi Huangdi *See*: Shih Huang Ti.
Shih Huang Ti (Chinese emperor) 258-260, 412, 425
Shih-chi 262
Shiites 247
Siberia 46, 49, 58, 62, 72-74, 78, 121-122, 124-125, 130-131, 135, 163, 264, 289-290, 292, 297, 300-302, 338, 344, 413, 417, 419-420, 426, 429, 436-438, 440
   Russian expansion into 429
   Siberian aborigines 290, 344, 417
Sicily 214, 221-223, 242, 316, 413, 424
   early inhabitants of 222
sickle-cell anemia 79-81, 395
Siderius Nuncius (Galileo) 349, 356
Sierra Leone 97, 328
silk 266
Singapore 95, 382, 406-409
Sinitic languages 54
Sino-Tibetan languages 54-56
Sirius, heliacal rising of 207, 209-210
Skhul (cave, Israel) 61, 63
skin color 10, 60, 80-81, 114, 119, 345
skyscrapers 379
slavery 107, 254-255, 314, 365, 368, 383, 386, 393
   abolition of 254, 365, 383
   trans-Atlantic slave trade 429

nature or nurture **103-120**
when and why they arose **121-125**
radio waves 376
radioactive dating 399
radioactivity 375, 380, 432-433
radiocarbon ages, recalibration of 431
(*Also see*: carbon-14 dating.)
radium 380
railroad 365, 379-380, 385
Ramayana 273
Rameses II (Egypt) 424
Raphael 321, 396
rayon 379-380
reaction time experiments 20-21, 26
(Also see: "odd-man-out".)
reaping machine 380
reciprocal altruism 36-38
Reconquista 321
Red Sea 49, 63, 151, 153, 210, 295, 310, 341, 419
reflection, law of 351
Reformation *See*: Protestant Reformation.
refraction of light 253, 351
Reign of Terror 371
reincarnation 272
relativity, theory of 399
religious skepticism 383
religious tolerance 254
remnant factor 105-107
Renaissance 234, 241, 320-321, 323, 325, 350, 355, 365, 369, 428
literary and artistic figures 321
Renfrew, Colin 184-187, 195-196
replication 7
reproductive strategies 43, 45, 129
republics 358, 361, 362, 368, 386, 387, 402, 403, 406
Revolutionary War *See*: American.
Rhazes 252
Rhine 224, 241, 390
Rhine-Danube line 224
Ricci, Matteo 263
rifle 327
Rigveda 186, 271, 273, 424
Rio de la Plata region 335
rise of applied science 374
Riss glacial period 47, 419
r-K 128, 129, 130

Robespierre, Maximilien 371
rock paintings
Australian 419
Namibian 420
Saharan 236, 421
Roman Empire 51, 201, 203, 221-243, 260, 263, 321-322, 348, 390, 395, 413, 426-427
formation of 222-224
decline and fall **230-236**
Eastern Roman Empire 232, 237
Western Roman Empire 213-232, 237, 240, 243, 321
climate change 234-235
social decay 221, 232-235
(*Also see*: Byzantine Empire; Italy; Roman; and individual names such as Augustus; Constantine; Diocletian.)
Romance languages 52
Romanesque architecture 245, 316
Romany *See*: Gypsies.
Rome, Romans 3, 51, 184-185, 194, 201, **221-227**, 228-239, 241, 243-245, 253, 320-321, 328-330, 361, 367, 389-390, 413-414, 425-427
history 222-224
achievements 224-225
(*Also see*: Italy; Roman Empire.)
Rongorongo 181-182
Röntgen, Wilhelm 375, 380
Rousseau, Jean-Jacques 368-369
royal absolutism 360, 362
Royal Society of London 354
r-Strategist 129
Ruhlen, Merritt 59, 280, 288, 299
Rumania 52-53, 99, 221, 238, 295, 401
Rushton, J.P. (= J. Phillip) 89-90, 95, 102, 104, 120, 125, 129, 132
Russia 46, 52-53, 62, 72-73, 99, 124, 134-136, 143, 147-148, 158, 161, 183, 186-187, 189, 194, 242, 255, 293, 295, 321-323, 344, 362, 366, 373, 380-382, 385, 398, 401-404, 406, 413, 419, 423, 428-429, 436, 438, 440
Russo-Japanese War 385
rye 141-142, 303

Planck, Max 375, 380
Pleistocene 46, 47, 163, 418, 419, 420
Pliocene Epoch 46-47
plow 265, 273, 306, 421
poetry 204, 217
   epic poetry 244, 252-253, 264, 273-274, 313, 329, 333
   lyric poetry 252, 264, 273
Poitiers 241, 242, 245, 318
Poland 46, 52-53, 59, 99, 114, 186, 189, 194, 293, 322-323, 343, 348, 366, 380-381, 384, 390-391, 402-403, 423, 428
Poland-Lithuania 322
"Polish jokes" 114
Polybius 225
Polynesia 76, 78, 124, 155-156, 281-282, 285-287, 301-302, 314, 383, 423-424, 426-427, 436, 442
Ponce de Leon 334
pongids 28
Pope 238
   Gregory I 244
   Urban II 319-320
     (*Also see*: Papacy; Catholic Church; Christianity.)
Portugal, Portuguese 51, 53, 55-56, 99, 238, 251, 313, 317, 321, 324, 327-329, 338-345, 363, 366, 378, 382, 386, 390, 406
positional notation 252, 274, 306, 317, 320
   (*Also see*: Arabic numerals.)
potatoes 142, 146, 165, 168, 171, 176, 303, 306
Potosí (Bolivia) 335
potter's wheel 313, 421
pottery 134-136, 146-147, 176, 198, 210, 283, 285, 290, 306, 308, 420-422, 430, 433
poverty (as an explanation for IQ differences) 103, 105, 107-108, 113
Powell, Colin 113
Prague 348
Praxiteles 218
pre-Amerindians 73, 289, 419
pre-Columbian civilizations 303-305
priestly celibacy 393
Prince, The (Machiavelli) 273
Principia (= *Philosophia Naturalis Principia Mathematica*) 351, 356, 429
promiscuity (of males) 43, 45

property rights 366, 385
Prophets (Hebrew) 203-204, 206
Protestant Reformation 326, 329-330, 363, 365, 369, 429
Proto-Altaic 292, 424
Proto-Austric 277, 279
Proto-Austroasiatic 277
Proto-Bantu 156
Proto-Dravidian 150
Proto-Germanic 52, 189
Proto-Indo-European 3, 52, 183, 187
Proto-Slavic 52
Prussia 59, 372
Ptolemaic dynasty 208
public education 384
Pueblo Indians 305
Puerto Rico 334
Punic wars 223, 233
Punjabi 194
Pygmies 13-14, 76, 83, 86, 104, 156, 277, 310, 417, 420
   Mbuti 83
pyramid, pyramids
   Egyptian 208-209, 211, 423
   New World 306
   of skulls 296
Pyrenees 195
Pyu Kingdom (Burma) 279

Qadisiya, Battle of 247
Qafzeh (cave, Israel) 61, 63
Qatar 408, 409
quantum theory 22, 375, 380
Quebec 339
Quechua 57
quick-twitch muscle 80
quinoa 165, 168, 171, 441

R_0 group 63, 69, 419
rabbis 393
Race, Evolution, and Behavior (Rushton) 129-130 (*Also see*: Rushton, J.P.)
racial differences 79, 82-84, 86, 88
   behavioral **126-132**
   intellectual **91-102**
   physical **79-90**

Old Testament 198, 200, 203-204, 229, 389, 425
Oldowan tools 29, 133-134, 418, 431
Olduvai gorge 29, 133
Olmecs 302-303, 424-425
Omayyad *See*: Umayyad.
Omo (Ethiopia) 31, 418
Omotic languages 54
"one drop rule" 14
optics 252-253, 351-352, 376
   wave theory of light 352, 376
   white light, nature of 352
      (*Also see*: Newton; Huygens; reflection; refraction; diffraction.)
Orange Free State 382
Origin of Species, The (Darwin) 7, 9, 141
Ostrogoths 231, 237, 243
Otto, Nikolaus August 379-380
Ottoman Empire 251, 295, 322, 363, 382-383, 390, 402, 429
"out of Africa" model 30-31, 60-66

Pacific Islands 184, 281-283, 285, 287
Pacific Ocean 299, 329, 334, 344
pagans, paganism 229, 238, 242, 426
   outlawed 229
Pakistan 149-150, 180, 268-269, 405, 408, 421
Palatine Chapel 245
Paleo-Indians 143, 169, 176, 301-303, 420
Paleolithic Era 22, 42, 44, 46, 47, 131, 133, 143, 144, 161, 162, 163, 418
Palestine, Palestinians 143, 202, 320, 389
Panama 334-335
Panini 273
Panipat, Battle of 296, 342
Papacy 238, 329 (*Also see*: Pope.)
Papua, Papuan 57, 284-285 (*Also see*: Indo-Pacific languages; New Guinea.)
Paraguay 335
parental investment theory 43, 131
Parliament 358-360, 371
Parthenon 218, 263
Parthian Empire 183, 201
Pascal, Blaise 347
Pasteur, Louis 375, 377, 379-380
Pasteurized milk 388

paternal investment theory 128, 130-131
Patriarch of Constantinople 321
Pax Romana 224
Pearl Harbor 113
peer pressure on black students 114, 117
Pelasgians 185, 187, 214
penicillin 160, 399
Pennsylvania 62, 75, 300, 340, 420
Peregrinus 352
Periodic table of elements 375, 380
Persia 49, 53, 110, 198, 200-203, 214-215, 218, 223, 226-227, 239, 243, 247, 249, 251, 255-256, 264-265, 296, 383, 408-409, 412, 425-428, 438
   (*Also see*: Iran; Sassanid Empire.)
Persian Gulf 49, 197-198, 264, 408-409
Peru 100, 110, 161, 171, 236, 285-286, 301, 302, 304, 335, 338, 344, 387, 429, 441
phalanx 239
Philip II (Macedonia) 215
Philippines 71, 78, 125, 141, 153, 155, 168, 219, 264, 276, 279, 281, 287, 343, 405, 411, 423, 436, 438, 440
Philistines 202
Phillips, Meredith 93, 96, 102, 118 (*Also see: The Black-White Test Score Gap.*)
Philosophia Naturalis Principia Mathematica See: *Principia*.
philosophy, philosophers 211, 214, 217-218, 244, 252, 258-261, 264-265, 280, 316-317, 320-321, 347, 351, 361, 367-369, 372, 425
Phoenician alphabet 179, 202
Phoenicians 3, 54, 179, 187, 201-202, 210, 219, 222, 285, 424
photography 379, 380, 400
Phrygians 189, 200
physics 111, 210, 216, 217, 227, 253, 263, 349-353, 368, 375-376, 391, 399, 417
   (*Also see*: electricity; gravitation; laws of motion; magnetism; mechanics; optics.)
Pi Sheng 262, 266, 326
pictograms 178, 180
Picts 185
PIE See: Proto-Indo-European.
Pinker, Steven 9, 34, 39, 42, 45, 119, 132
Pithecanthropus erectus 29
Pizarro, Francisco 335, 429

Negroes 1, 10, 13-14, 54, 76, 79, 81, 88, 92, 129, 151, 156-157, 310-312, 315, 386, 417, 420, 438
   East African 156, 310, 312, 315
   West African 156, 310, 312, 315, 439
   (*Also see*: African blacks; American blacks; Negrids; Negroids.)
Negroids 13-14, 63, 76, 84, 88, 129, 135, 310, 419
Nehavend, Battle of 247-248
Nenana River Valley 300
Neolithic Era 46, 133, 144, 147, 148, 163, 165, 219, 325, 414
Neolithic Revolution
   description **139-145**
   explanations **160-172**
Neolithic transition 167, 169-170, 440-442
   calculations **440-442**
Nepal 53, 268
Nes, Nesili 186. (*Also see*: Hittites.)
Netherlands 99, 380, 381, 405
   (*Also see*: Dutch; Holland.)
New Britain 70
New Guinea 49, 58, 62, 65, 68, 70-71, 78, 124, 141, 155, 161, 164-166, 168, 171, 173, 181, 264, **281-288**, 419-420, 422, 436, 437, 442
   aborigines 284, 417
   agriculture in 284, 442
   highlands 71, 141, 171, 173, 284, 420, 422
   languages 57, 284-285
   (*Also see*: Papua.)
New Mexico 302, 305
New Orleans 339
New Spain 335
New Stone Age 46, 147
New Testament 228
New World 74, 82, 110, 141, 143, 147, 167, 174, 180, 219, **300-309**, 327, 334, 336-339, 342, 386, 390, 429 (*Also see*: Western Hemisphere.)
New Zealand 68, 76, 155, 281-282, 285, 360-363, 427 (*Also see*: Maoris.)
Newfoundland 243
Newton, Isaac 117, 160, 254, 266, 347, 350-353, 356, 368, 429
Niah Cave (Borneo) 62

Niger-Congo languages 56, 156, 311
Nigeria 97, 156, 311, 407, 410, 424
Nile 151, 206-209
Nilo-Saharan languages 57, 157
nineteenth century **374-388**
   inventions 378-381
   scientific discoveries 374-378
   political and social changes 383-384
   (*Also see*: colonialism; rise of applied science; Westernization.)
Ninety-five Theses (Martin Luther) 330
Nineveh 197, 200
NM See: Northern Mongolids.
Nobel Prizes 379, 391
nomadism 144
non-Euclidean geometry 375, 377, 380
Normandy 243, 322, 371
Norsemen. *See:* Vikings.
North Africa 2, 63, 73, 76, 124, 134, 142, 151, 153, 165-166, 176, 183-184, 224, 231, 235, 237, 242-243, 247, 249, 255, 295, 381, 390, 395, 405, 408-409, 411, 413, 421-422, 425, 427, 436-438, 440
North China Plain 14, 74, 257-258, 423
North Korea 406-407
North Semitic alphabet 179, 181, 423
Northern Asia 2, 63
Northern Mongolids 74, 289-293, 419-420, 424, 437
   expansions of 290-293
Norway, Norwegian 52-53, 99, 242, 322, 363
Notre Dame de Paris (cathedral) 316
Nova Scotia 339
Nubians 210
nuclear weapons 400, 404
nucleotides 5-6, 61
Nurhachi (Manchu leader) 297

Oaxaca 180, 303, 305
Occam's razor 116-117, 416
"odd-man-out" experiments 21
   (*Also see*: reaction time experiments.)
Odyssey (Homer) 217, 424
Ogadai Khan 293
Okhotsk, Sea of 344
Old Stone Age 46

miracles, reason to doubt 228
Mismeasure of Man, The (Stephen Gould) 88, 90
Mississippi Valley 339
Mississippian culture 305
Mohacs, Battle of 323
Mohenjo-Daro 140, 269
moneylending 391, 394-396
Mongolia, Mongols 72-74, 124, 163, 240, 251, 259-261, 279, 289, 292-297, 322-323, 344, 383, 412-413, 417, 419, 424, 428, 436-438, 440 (*Also see*: Genghis Khan; Kubilai Khan; Khanate of.)
Mongolids 14, 72-74, 81, 95, 101, 131, 135, 156, 289-290, 292, 406-407, 417, 419-420, 424, 437 (*Also see*: Northern Mongolids; Southern Mongolids.)
Mongoloids 10, 14, 63, 65, 70, 72-74, 82, 84, 87-88, 95, 129, 148, 204, 257, 302, 414, 419-420
Monk's Mound 305 (*Also see*: Cahokia.)
monotheism 199, 202, 209, 246, 424
monozygotic apart 24
Monte Alban 303
Monte Verde (Chile) 62, 74, 301, 303, 420
Montesquieu, Charles-Louis de 369-370
Montezuma 335
Morocco 54, 101, 151, 221, 247, 250, 328, 340, 382, 405, 409
Morton, Samuel 88, 90
Morton, William T.G. 379-380
Moscow 294
Moses (Hebrew leader) 202-203
(*Also see*: *Five Books of Moses*.)
Moslem world 244, 246-255, 264, 313, 394, 408
  cultural achievements 251-254
  explanation for backwardness 254-255
  (*Also see*: Arabs; dhimmis; Islam; Muhammad.)
Moslems 208, 239-244, 246-255, 264, 271-273, 295-296, 312-313, 319-322, 390, 394, 405, 408, 411, 427 (*Also see*: Islam; Muhammad; Moslem world.)
motion pictures 379-380, 400
Mousterian tools 30, 133-134, 419, 431
movable type 262, 325-326, 332, 428
Mozambique 251, 406-407, 410

Mozart, Wolfgang Amadeus 266
Mu'awiya (caliph) 247
Mughal Empire 271, 275, 296-297, 429
Muhammad, the Prophet 243, 246-247, 249, 251, 255, 261, 408, 427
  biography of 246
  character 246, 255
  massacre of prisoners of war 255
  (*Also see*: Islam; Moslems; Koran.)
mulattos 343
multiregional model 30-31
Munda languages 279, 423
Murray, Charles 26, 102, 104, 118-119, 396
music 244, 253, 273-274, 280, 400
  (*Also see*: individual composers.)
musket 327
mutagenic chemicals 5
mutations 4-5, 7, 61, 338
myopia 88
MZA *See*: twins, identical.

N_0 group 63, 76, 419
Na-Dene languages 301, 420
Nagasaki 344, 403, 406
Namibia 312, 420
Napier, John 347, 356
Napoleon Bonaparte 361, 372-373, 384, 398
Napoleon III 361
Naseby, Battle of 359
nationalism 401
natural rights 370
natural selection 2, 4, 6-9, 11, 23, 35-38, 43, 79, 82, 121, 130, 158, 173, 378
  (*Also see*: artificial selection; Darwin; evolution; genetic drift.)
nature or nurture 101, **103-120**
  possible hypotheses 103
Navajo 100, 301, 305
Nazca 304
Nazis 91, 402-404
Neanderthals 13, 30, 62-63, 65, 73, 76, 378, 418-419
  replacement or hybridization 65
Negrids 13-14, 76, 310, 419-420
Negritos 71, 153, 277, 417

Mary II (England) 360
mass production 325-326, 365-366, 400
Massagetae 201
mate selection 40, 43-44, 115
　by females 44
　by males 44-45
　human eggs are a scarce resource 43
mathematics 2, 12, 18, 111, 115, 177, 202, 210-211, 214, 216, 219, 224, 244, 250, 252, 254, 262-263, 265, 274-275, 280, 306, 313-314, 317, 324, 332, 346-347, 349, 355, 375, 377-378, 380, 391, 399, 417
　　irrational numbers 216
　　logarithms 347
　　prime numbers 216
　　non-Euclidean geometry 375, 377, 380
　　　(*Also see*: algebra; calculus; geometry; positional notation; trigonometry; Euclid; Newton.)
Mauretania 312
Mauryan Empire 270-271, 425
Maxwell, James Clerk 375-376, 380
Mayas 177, 180, 304-306, 314, 336, 426-427
Mayflower, the 339
Mbuti. *See*: Pygmies.
McCormick, Cyrus 379-380
ME *See*: Middle East.
Meadowcroft Rockshelter 62, 75, 300, 420
measles 236, 252, 336-338
Mecca 246, 251, 295, 312, 413, 415
mechanics 22, 83, 217, 331, 349, 350-351, 356, 368, 375, 380, 399
　　Newtonian 351
　　quantum 2, 375, 380
　　statistical 375
Medes 200
medicine 211, 217, 252, 254, 317, 353, 381, 391, 399, 417
Medina 246
Mediterranean Sea 49-50, 146, 201-202, 205, 208, 210, 213, 222-223, 242, 247, 295, 312, 426
megafauna 49, 419-420
megaliths 422 (*Also see*: Stonehenge.)
Mehmed II (Ottoman emperor) 295
Mehrgarh 149-150
Melanesia 76, 78, 124, 155-156, 165-166, 281-282, 284-287, 436, 441

menarche, age at 80, 83, 130
Mendel, Gregor 375, 380
Mendele'ev, Dimitri 375
Mesa Verde (Chile) 305, 428
Mesoamerica 2, 116, 124, 141, 146, 161, 162, 164, 166-170, 174, 176-177, 180, 300, 302-306, 314-315, 336, 422, 425, 436, 441
Mesopotamia 58, 179, 197, 199-200, 203, 211, 247, 424-426
Messapians 222
mestizos 94, 101, 343, 387
metalworking 32, 204, 210, 265-266, 311
　(*Also see*: bronze; ironworking.)
Mexican immigrants 100-101
Mexico 100, 111, 164, 169-170, 176, 181, 219, 301-305, 314, 334-335, 338, 344, 411, 420-422, 424-425, 427-430, 442
　Valley of Mexico 304, 427-428
Mexico City 301, 304, 428
Miao-Yao languages 57, 276-277
Michelangelo Buonarroti 266, 321
Micronesia 76, 78, 101, 124, 155-156, 281-282, 287, 436, 442
microorganisms 354, 356
microscope 352, 353
　(*Also see*: Leeuwenhoek.)
Middle Ages 237-245, 316-324, 346, 352, 355, 358, 362, 390-391, 393, 395
　early **237-245**
　late **316-324**
Middle East 2, 29-30, 54, 63, 68-69, 72-73, 76, 124, 139, 142, 146-151, 153, 156-158, 161, 164-170, 174, 176, 180, 183-184, **197-205**, 213, 219, 221, 226, 251, 265-266, 268-269, 307-308, 315, 317, 382, 390, 395, 405, 408, 411, 413-414, 419-425, 436-438, 440-442
　dessication of 204
　(*Also see*: Southwest Asia.)
migrations driven by agriculture **149-159**, 437
Miller, Edward M 131-132
Milwaukee Project 108
Ming dynasty 259, 261, 264, 297, 428
Minnesota Transracial Adoption Study 109, 115
Minoan civilization 180, 189, 213, 423-424
Mirabeau, Count Honoré 371, 373

Legalist school 258
Leibniz, Gottfried Wilhelm 160, 347, 356
Leipzig, Battle of 373
Lenin 402
Leonardo da Vinci 266, 321
Letters on the English (Voltaire) 361, 368
Libya 223, 247, 382, 405, 408-409
Lieberman, Philip 34
life expectancy 81, 325
light *See*: optics.
Linear A 180, 182, 185, 213-214
Linear B 185, 214
linen 266, 421, 433
lions 32, 302
Lippershey, Hans 349
lips, everted 10, 81, 302
literature 24, 110, 184, 204, 209-211, 214, 217-218, 224, 241, 251-252, 264, 265, 267, 273-274, 280, 306, 313, 320-321, 324, 345, 385
Lithuania 53, 322-323, 390-391, 402
Liujang (China) 62
Livingstone, David 381
llama 143, 171, 303, 422
Locke, John 369
Loeb Classical Library 220, 227
logarithms 347, 356
logosyllabic writing 178-180, 182, 213, 306
Lombards 237, 241
London (England) 316, 354, 392
Long Rongrien Cave 62
longbow 318-319, 428
Louis XIV (France) 370
Louis XVI (France) 370-371, 373
Louis XVIII (France) 373
"love your enemy" 261
Lumière, August & Louis 356, 379-380
Luther, Martin 330
Lydian 53, 200
Lynn & Vanhanen 94-95, 97-102, 345, 387, 409, 415
Lynn, Richard 104, 125, 345, 387, 409, 415
  (*Also see*: Lynn & Vanhanen.)

M-1 73-74, 78, 257, 289
M-2 73-74, 78, 289, 419-420
Macao 344

Maccabean revolt 203
Macedonia 201, 213, 215, 223, 225-226, 239, 383, 413, 425
  (*Also see*: Alexander the Great.)
Machiavelli, Niccolò 273
machine guns 379, 398, 401
Machu Picchu 110, 306, 314
Madagascar 50, 71, 76, 153, 155, 314, 426
Magdalenian tools 133-134, 136, 420, 431
Magellan, Ferdinand 266, 329, 333
Magellan, Straits of 329
Magna Carta 358-359, 428
magnetism 352, 356, 374-376
Magnus, Albertus 316
Magyars 184, 242, 323, 427
  (*Also see*: Hungary.)
Mahabharata 273
Mahmud of Ghazni 292, 412
maize 141, 146, 165, 168, 303, 306, 422, 424-426, 428 (Also see: corn; teosinte.)
Malacca 341
malaria 80-82, 215, 336-338, 342
  (*Also see*: sickle-cell anemia.)
Malays, Malaya, Malay Peninsula 49, 71, 155, 276-277, 279, 341, 406, 424, 429
Malaysia 71, 407
Mali 312
Mallory, J.P. 183, 195-196, 227
Malpighi, Marcello 353
Malthusian equilibrium 161
Mamelukes 341
Mamun the Great (caliph) 251
Manchus, Manchuria 74, 259-261, 292, 296-297, 383, 412, 419, 424, 428, 430
  assimilation of 297
Mandarin Chinese 54
Manila 343
manioc 142, 303, 423
Mansu Musa 312
Manzikert, Battle of 244, 293, 428
Maoris 383
Marathon, Battle of 201, 214, 239, 425
Marco Polo 264, 317, 331, 428
Mariana Islands (Pacific) 154, 281
Mark Antony 224
Marshall, Thurgood 113
Marston Moor, Battle of 359
Martin, Paul S. 309

genetic diseases of 394-395
moneylending 394-396
    (*Also see*: anti-Semitism; Hebrews; Israel; Judea.)
"Jim Crow" 104
Jinmium rockshelter 62
jizya 249
Jomon culture (Japan) 420
Jordan 405, 409
Joule, James 375-376
Juchen 260, 296, 297, 428
Judea 203 (*Also see*: Jews; Israel)
Julius Caesar 224, 426
Justinian I (Eastern Roman emperor) 243-244
    Code of Justinian 243

K'ang-hsi 297
Kalidasa 273
Kalmar, Union of 322
Kamchatka 74, 292
Karakorum 293
Karens 276, 279, 424
karma 271
Karnak, temples at 209
Kashmir 58
Kautilya 273
Kennewick Man 301, 309
Kenya 54, 97, 407, 410
Kepler, Johannes 253, 266, 348, 351, 356-357 (*Also see*: laws of planetary motion.)
Khanate of
    Chagatai 295
    the Crimea 293
    the Golden Horde 295-296
Khanbaligh (= Beijing) 293
Khazars 292, 390
Khmers 276, 428
Khoikhoi (=Hottentots) 16, 310
    (*Also see*: Bushmen; Khoisan; Sanids.)
Khoisan 13, 14, 310
    (*Also see*: Bushmen, Hottentots; Sanids.)
kibbutzim 392
kin selection 37-39, 41
King Philip's War 345
King, Martin Luther 113

Kirchhoff, Gustav 375, 377, 380
Klasies River 31, 419
knights 239-240, 245, 317-319, 428
Koestler, Arthur 396
Kon-Tiki (Thor Heyerdahl) 285, 288, 302
Koran 247, 249, 252, 255
Korea 55, 58, 74, 78, 95, 124, 179, 272, 290, 293, 297, 362, 382-383, 404, 406-409, 411, 413, 420, 436-437, 440
Kose Dagh, Battle of 293
K-strategists 129
Kubilai Khan 261, 293, 297, 317, 428
Kurgan people 183, 187, 422
Kuwait 221, 408-409
kya (defined) 30

Labrador 243, 290, 423
lactose intolerance 80
Lake Baikal 62, 73, 344
Lake Chad 54, 151
Lake Titicaca 304
land reform 223
language families 52-57, 277
    table of 56-57
language isolates 55, 58
Lao Tzu 264, 425
Laos 276, 382, 406
Lapita (pottery) 285
Lapps 67, 81, 417
Lascaux (cave, France) 420
Late Middle Ages **316-324**, 355, 358, 390-391
Latin 51, 52, 53, 181, 185, 194, 202, 221, 222, 227, 238, 242, 244, 252, 253, 321, 386, 387, 406, 411
Latin alphabet 181, 202
Latin America 386-387, 406, 411
latitude and longitude 216
Latvia 53, 102
Laurentian ice sheet 49
Lavoisier, Antoine Laurent 368
laws of heredity 375, 380
laws of motion 350-351, 356
laws of planetary motion 348, 356
lead-poisoning hypothesis 234-235
Lebanon 201, 207, 243, 402, 405, 409
Leeuwenhoek, Antony van 353-354, 356

364-365, 368, 374, 378-379, 384-385, 398, 400, 414, 418, 426, 440-442
   19th-century 378-381
   20th-century 399-400
   Chinese *See*: China.
   (*Also see* specific inventions, such as steam engine.)

IQ 2, 19-25, 92-119, 121-123, 125, 128, 136, 150, 157, 162-167, 169-171, 173, 177, 220, 235, 254, 257-258, 269-270, 275, 280, 287, 311, 314, 331, 342, 362, 386-387, 389, 392-397, 407-409, 413-415, 437, 439-442
   definition of 19-20
   black-white differences 92-94
   hypothetical scores from computer models 124
   mean IQs of various groups 94-101
   tests 20-21
   (*Also see*: Flynn effect; *g* factor; intelligence.)

IQ and the Wealth of Nations (Lynn & Vanhanen) 415

IR (*See*: Industrial Revolution.)

Iran 53, 69, 73, 101, 139, 142-143, 150, 179, 183, 194-195, 197, 199-201, 215, 225-226, 249, 251, 256, 268, 270, 292-293, 295, 382-383, 408-409, 412-413, 421, 428
   (*Also see*: Persia.)

Iraq 58, 101, 179, 205, 251, 255, 402, 405, 408

Ireland 70, 99, 242

ironworking 156, 176, 204, 266, 311, 423-425

irrigation 265, 306, 421

Isabella I (Castile) 321

Isaiah (Hebrew prophet) 424

Isfahan 296

Islam 2, 204, **246-247**, 249, 251, 253-256, 271-272, 274, 280, 312, 427-428
   conversion from 249
   (*Also see*: Arabs; dhimmis; Moslems; Muhammad.)

isolated languages *See*: language isolates.

Israel 61, 67, 201-203, 207, 391, 395, 404-405, 408-409, 419
   (*Also see*: Canaan; Jews; Judea; Palestine.)

Israeli-Arab conflict 391

Istanbul 236 (*Also see*: Constantinople.)

Italian Renaissance 234, 320, 428

Italic languages 51-53, 188, 193-195

Italy, Italians 58, 99, 157, 164, 184-185, 194, 210, 214, 220-223, 225-226, 317-318, 320, 322, 327-329, 331, 341, 345-346, 251, 362-363, 366, 369, 372, 376, 378, 380-382, 384, 398, 401-402, 404-405, 413, 421, 424-425, 428
   early inhabitants of 221-222
   unification of 388
   (*Also see*: Rome; Roman Empire.)

Ivan the Great (= Ivan III) 323

Jacob (Hebrew patriarch) 202

Jakarta 342

Jamaica 334

James I (England) 359

James II (England) 360, 429

Janissaries 295

Japan 49, 58, 74, 78, 110, 124, 134, 136, 146-147, 264, 272, 281, 290, 302, 343-344, 362-363, 382-385, 401-404, 406, 408-409, 420, 427, 436-438, 440
   ban of contact with West 344
   attempt to ban Christianity 344
   (*Also see*: Jomon culture.)

Japanese-Americans 113-114

Java 29, 49, 155, 426

"Java Man" (= *Pithecanthropus erectus*) 29

Jefferson, Thomas 370

Jencks, Christopher 26, 93, 96, 102, 118
   (*Also see*: *Black-White Test Score Gap*.)

Jensen, Arthur 26-27, 90, 96, 102, 104, 106, 118-120, 397, 415

Jericho 143, 148, 421

Jerusalem 198, 202-203, 320, 389, 395, 424-425

Jesus 199, 228-229, 238, 246, 261, 266, 408, 426 (*Also see*: Christianity.)

Jews 88, 114, 202-203, 228, 238, 244, 246, 255, 372, **389-397**, 403, 409
   Asheknazim & Sephardim 380-381
   history 202-204, 389, 395-396
   evidence of high intelligence 391-392
   explanations for high intelligence 392-396